Introduction to
CATALOGING
and
CLASSIFICATION

Books Written by Bohdan S. Wynar

Technical Processes in Libraries (1961)

Ukrainian Industry: A Case Study (1964)

Ukrainian Economic Studies Abroad: Historical Materials and Sources (1965)

Introduction to Bibliography and Reference Work: A Guide to Materials and Sources (1967, 1966, 1963)

Library Acquisitions (1971, 1968)

Research Methods in Library Science (1971)

Economic Thought in Kievan Rus' (1974)

Reference Books in Paperback: An Annotated Guide (1976, 1972)

Works Edited by Bohdan S. Wynar

Encyclopedia of Ukraine (1955-)

Studies in Librarianship, University of Denver, Graduate School of Librarianship (1961-66)

American Reference Books Annual (1970-)

Research Studies in Library Science (1970-)

Best Reference Books (1976)

Dictionary of American Library Biography (1978)

Colorado Bibliography (1980)

Bohdan S. Wynar, *Bohdan S.*

Introduction to

CATALOGING
and
CLASSIFICATION

6th Edition

with the assistance of
Arlene Taylor Dowell
and
Jeanne Osborn

1980
Libraries Unlimited, Inc. • Littleton, Colorado

657p.

LIBRARIES UNLIMITED, INC.
P.O. Box 263
Littleton, Colorado 80160

Library of Congress Cataloging in Publication Data

Wynar, Bohdan S
    Introduction to cataloging and classification.

    Bibliography: p. 641
    Includes indexes.
    1. Cataloging. 2. Classification--Books.
I. Dowell, Arlene Taylor, 1941-   joint author.
II. Osborn, Jeanne, joint author. III. Title.
Z693.W94 1980   025.3   80-16462
ISBN 0-87287-220-3
ISBN 0-87287-221-1 (pbk.)

Libraries Unlimited books are bound with Type II nonwoven material that meets and exceeds National Association of State Textbook Administrators' Type II nonwoven material specifications Class A through E.

To the memory of

Dr. John Phillip Immroth,

my former student, colleague, and friend.

PREFACE TO THE SIXTH EDITION

Since the publication of the first edition in 1964, this textbook has become widely known in the library profession in this country and abroad. It is both an introductory text for the beginning student in library science and a handy companion volume for practicing catalogers. Subsequent editions were published at frequent intervals, with the fifth edition appearing in 1976. That edition was prepared with the assistance of the late John Phillip Immroth, my former student at the Graduate School of Librarianship and Information Management, University of Denver, who later worked with me as administrative assistant to the dean at the Graduate School of Library and Information Science at SUNY, Geneseo. To his memory I wish to dedicate this new edition.

In the preface to the fifth edition it was indicated that this text was designed to meet the needs of beginning courses in cataloging and classification. A major portion of the text was devoted to interpreting the *Anglo-American Cataloging Rules*, published in 1967 (*AACR 1*), incorporating all major additions and changes up to the end of 1975. The chapters on classification and subject headings were also revised and enlarged to include additional examples pertaining to number building, use of area tables, detailed explanations of Dewey Decimal Classification and LC tables and LC notations, etc. A complete new chapter on comparative classification was also added.

In this preface I will discuss only the most important changes in this completely revised edition, since it is hoped that most libraries and library schools will keep the previous edition at hand (the fifth edition remains in print and is available from the publisher). The chapters on classification and subject headings have been substantially revised and updated and contain much new material. In this new edition the nineteenth edition of the *Dewey Decimal Classification* is discussed as are additions and changes in the Library of Congress classification schedules. Also somewhat expanded are the brief surveys of Cutter's Expansive Classification, Brown's Subject Classification, Bliss's Bibliographic Classification (in its incipient second edition), the Universal Decimal Classification, and Ranganathan's Colon Classification. The *Sears List of Subject Headings*, now in its eleventh edition, is also discussed, as are new changes and additions to the Library of Congress subject headings list (*LCSH 8*).

This edition also contains a new chapter on recent developments in document indexing and other types of verbal analysis for subject retrieval. It includes an introduction to the PRECIS indexing technique and identifies the

Broad System of Ordering (BSO) as a major current attempt to construct an umbrella classification or switching language for mediating concept interpretation and subject access among several more precise, locally developed indexing modes. A complete new chapter identifies filing assumptions and dilemmas, giving a review of the *ALA Rules for Filing Catalog Cards*, second edition, as well as a short discussion of shelflist filing. A major portion of the chapter on centralized processing deals with bibliographic networking, looking particularly at OCLC, Inc., RLIN, WLN, and UTLAS, with a short summary of future prospects for online bibliographic searching and cataloging. The final chapter, on cataloging records and routines, addresses the current interest in authority files, as well as the problems and prospects of closing existing card catalogs for conversion to book, COM, or machine-readable catalog formats.

Dr. Jeanne Osborn, Professor of Library Science at the University of Iowa, was responsible for revisions of the above mentioned chapters, and I am greatly indebted for her able assistance in this difficult task. As Sayers once said, we cannot reason, even in the simplest manner, unless we possess in a greater or lesser degree the power of classifying; or, to put it in simpler terms, we must first see things together before we can tell them apart. Thus, the knowledge of classification systems is a prerequisite for the retrieval process, a fact well known to information scientists and reference librarians. Hopefully, these chapters will help readers better to understand the basic principles of classification theory and its applications, as well as some aspects of cataloging routines or practices in many libraries in the United States and abroad. Other aspects—purely theoretical, highly technical, or of an administrative nature—are outside the scope of this text and should be reserved for advanced courses in classification theory, management, bibliographic control, and information dissemination and retrieval.

Finally, at the end of 1978, after several years of preparation, a second edition of the *Anglo-American Cataloguing Rules* (*AACR 2*) was published. The underlying theory pertinent to this edition is discussed in a number of articles, and a brief evaluation of *AACR 1* and *AACR 2* is provided on pages 30-43 of this text, with references to pertinent literature. Probably the most important articles were written by Michael Gorman,[1] Wesley Simonton,[2] and Phyllis A. Richmond,[3] who provide concise insight into fundamental principles of the second edition, addressing some basic changes as well as some specifications of the options adopted by the Library of Congress and other cataloging agencies. It is sufficient to say here that, in contrast to the structure of *AACR 1* (the division of the rules into three parts that were not mutually exclusive), the rules in the second edition are divided into two parts: the first covers bibliographic description, the second discusses the choice and form of access points (headings).

The controversy that has arisen about *AACR 2* has centered upon choice of access points and form of heading for those access points chosen. The

---

[1]Michael Gorman, "The Anglo-American Cataloguing Rules, Second Edition," *Library Resources & Technical Services* 22 (Summer 1978):209-226.

[2]Wesley Simonton, "An Introduction to *AACR 2*," *Library Resources & Technical Services* 23 (Summer 1979):321-39.

[3]Phyllis A. Richmond, "AACR 2—A Review Article," *Journal of Academic Librarianship* vol. 6, no. 1 (March 1980):30-37.

major objection stems not from a disagreement with the philosophy of *AACR 2* (although map librarians have protested dropping the concept of corporate authorship), but from the effect that new forms of heading will have on existing catalogs. This is a legitimate concern, although impact studies generally are showing that the problems will not be as great as feared. Part I of *AACR 2*, Description, has generally been ignored in all the discussion — yet this is one of the major contributions of this new code. It gives us a single standard for cataloging all types of materials and patterns of publication. The resulting differences from past practice are greater for some materials than for others. Specialists in cataloging serials or sound recordings, for example, may at first be somewhat frustrated. But it seems that, for the first time, it is now possible to learn one set of principles of description and then move with ease from one type of material or pattern of publication to the next. Optimistically, it can even be said that at last we have a theory of descriptive cataloging.

It should also be noted that in the process of reconciling the North American and British texts, it was decided to use British spelling, if the British spelling appears as an alternative in *Webster's New International Dictionary*. In cases where terminology differs, British usages have been chosen in some cases (e.g., "full stop" instead of "period"), while American usages appear in other cases (e.g., "parentheses" instead of the British, "brackets"). In this text, it was decided to use American spelling and terminology, except when specific *AACR 2* rules are directly quoted.

Inevitably, *AACR 2*, presenting a rather significant departure from the previous standards, introduces a number of difficulties and even some factual errors. Only a few of these are discussed in this text, because it might be premature to make a final evaluation of *AACR 2*, especially concerning its impact on prevailing cataloging practices in our libraries. For example, one of the problems faced in constructing uniform titles is the choice of a title when titles of a book appear in more than one form. This problem is discussed in chapter 25 of *AACR 2* and in this text in chapter 20. The examples in *AACR 2* "are illustrative and not prescriptive" (Rule 0.14), but unfortunately, there are several errors in these "examples." For instance, examples in chapter 23 showing "(Germany)" as an addition are simply not correct, because of the political division of the country into two areas that need to be distinguished. The Library of Congress has decided that the additions should be "Germany (West)" for the Federal Republic of Germany, and "Germany (East)" for the German Democratic Republic. Similar *AACR 2* errors in fact and interpretation are rather confusing to the uninitiated.

As an approach to such difficulties, each chapter in Part II of this text includes one or more complete bibliographic entries illustrating the application of the rules from the corresponding chapter of *AACR 2*. These sample entries are constructed progressively — that is, rule-by-rule — through the course of the chapter. Future implementation decisions by the Library of Congress may well affect these examples, but every available LC decision has been employed in constructing them. Because of the increasing use of machine-readable cataloging, a format was chosen for these examples that is not dependent on the format of typed cards. Every effort has been made to present the most complete entries possible, while at the same time omitting those portions that may divert attention from the entry element being illustrated in a particular figure.

Each of these omissions has been indicated by a heading that identifies the essential element that follows the omission.

Throughout *AACR 2* there are "optional" rules that allow for adding or deleting information in certain instances, or that allow alternative methods of handling certain situations. Each cataloging agency must decide whether and how to apply these options. Because so many libraries rely on the Library of Congress for cataloging data, this text includes a discussion of LC's decision about application of each option as it occurs in the rule sequence. Obviously, the Library of Congress will make many more decisions in this important matter by the time it adopts *AACR 2* and closes its card catalog in January 1981.

This text incorporates a selection of basic rules from *AACR 2* with appropriate explorations and examples of their application. This difficult task was admirably accomplished by Arlene Taylor Dowell, the author of the well-received book, *Cataloging with Copy* (Libraries Unlimited, 1976), who wrote chapters 3-6 and 8-21, and also revised the initial two chapters on principles of cataloging and the development of cataloging codes. Chapter 7, "Description of Published Music," was prepared by Associate Professor Elaine Svenonius, Graduate School of Librarianship and Information Management, University of Denver. Several chapters, especially chapter 14, "Description of Serials," were read by Dr. Neal Edgar, Research Librarian, Kent State University. Helpful suggestions were also received from Mary Larsgaard, Map Librarian, Colorado School of Mines, pertaining to the description of cartographic materials (chapter 5).

Ms. Dowell received many helpful suggestions and recommendations from a number of experts and it is only appropriate to acknowledge her indebtedness to the following individuals: Don Daidone, Map Librarian, Carol M. Newman Library, Virginia Polytechnic Institute and State University, Blacksburg; Sue A. Dodd, Data Librarian, Institute for Research in Social Science, University of North Carolina at Chapel Hill; William R. Erwin, Jr., Assistant Curator, Manuscript Department, William R. Perkins Library, Duke University, Durham, NC; Marilyn Norstedt, Serials Automation Coordinator, Carol M. Newman Library, Virginia Polytechnic Institute and State University, Blacksburg.

She would like to thank the following people who work at the Library of Congress for their substantial help and assistance: Laura Brank, Senior Cataloger, Romance Languages Section, Descriptive Cataloging Division; Judith P. Cannan, Head of English Language Cataloging Section, Serials Division; Gerald Gibson, Head, Curatorial Services, Motion Picture, Broadcasting, and Recorded Sound Division; David Remington, Chief of Cataloging, Distribution Service Division; Vivian Schrader, Former Head, Audiovisual Section of Descriptive Cataloging Division; and especially Paul W. Winkler, joint editor of *AACR 2*, and Senior Descriptive Cataloging Specialist, Office for Descriptive Cataloging Policy.

She would like also to thank her husband, David R. Dowell, Assistant University Librarian for Administrative Services, William R. Perkins Library, Duke University, for his help and patience throughout a very concentrated project.

In closing, I can repeat what was said in the preface to the fifth edition: "It must be kept in mind that the principles, and even basic concepts, of cataloging and classification are constantly changing. To keep pace with these developments, it is our intention to continue the periodic revision of this text, and it is hoped that, as in previous editions, it will provide the instructor of cataloging courses with a necessary, basic foundation, and from this foundation, the individual instructor can build and elaborate as he or she desires." The additional references to other texts included in this new edition may be of some assistance in this task.

And again, I would like to say that the interpretive art of cataloging should continue in its own right as a separate discipline of library science. Some cataloging courses may need to be revised to emphasize this interpretive function, but I do not believe that they should be merged with information retrieval courses or courses in bibliography and reference. Hybrid courses can destroy or weaken the knowledge of each of the separate fields. Although automation and centralized processing may lead to a decrease in the number of professional catalogers in larger libraries, there should be an increase in the number of librarians who know how to interpret the catalog and its theoretical structure.

The constantly increasing publication rate of material in all fields places a greater demand on the library profession. It provides an entirely new set of objectives for library service in terms of transmitting this large volume of information to its potential users. In this new context the role of the traditional cataloger needs to be carefully re-examined. The paramount need is to continue the search for more efficient codes and classification schemes for organizing the available information, since, if they are used and modified in accordance with users' needs, cataloging codes and classification schemes can provide much needed guidance. This search should be undertaken not only by catalogers but also by reference librarians and information specialists, because these are the groups that are actively participating in designing an information system to meet the new requirements of our expanding universe.

It would be difficult to acknowledge all the resources that have contributed to the preparation of the new edition and all the fellow librarians who were kind enough to send their suggestions to this new edition. Not all of them can be incorporated, primarily because of the necessary economy to keep this text in one volume.

I should like to acknowledge my indebtedness to the following colleagues: Jerry Cao, Assistant Professor, School of Library Science, University of Southern California; Elizabeth Chambers, Assistant Professor, Department of Library Science, Northern Illinois University, DeKalb; John P. Comaromi, Chief, Decimal Classification Center, Processing Services, Library of Congress; Mildred H. Downing, Assistant Professor, School of Library Science, University of North Carolina, Chapel Hill; Neal L. Edgar, Research Librarian, Kent State University; Roy W. Evans, Associate Professor, School of Library and Informational Science, University of Missouri—Columbia; Josephine Riss Fang, Professor, School of Library Science, Simmons College; Oliver T. Field, Associate Professor, Graduate School of Librarianship and Information Management, University of Denver; Maurice J. Freedman, Associate Professor, School of Library Service, Columbia University;

Benjamin Guise, Assistant Professor, School of Librarianship, Western Michigan University, Kalamazoo; Vera G. Guthrie, Head, Department of Library Science and Instructional Media, Western Kentucky University, Bowling Green; Joe A. Hewitt, Associate University Librarian for Technical Services, University of North Carolina, Chapel Hill, who assisted in the preparation of chapter 30, "Centralized Processing and Networking"; Clara O. Jackson, Associate Professor, School of Library Science, Kent State University; Merle E. Lamson, Associate Professor, School of Library and Information Sciences, Brigham Young University; Mary Larsgaard, Map Librarian, Colorado School of Mines, Golden; Tanja Lorković, Head, Cataloging Department, University of Iowa, Iowa City; Margaret Maxwell, Associate Professor, Graduate Library School, University of Arizona, Tucson; Francis Miksa, Associate Professor, Graduate School of Library Science, Louisiana State University, Baton Rouge; Harry S. Otterson, Lecturer, School of Information and Library Studies, State University of New York at Buffalo; Barbara Perrins, Assistant Professor, Division of Library Science and Instructional Technology, Southern Connecticut State College, New Haven; Edith Phillips, Associate Professor, Division of Library Science, Wayne State University, Detroit; Phyllis A. Richmond, Professor, School of Library Science, Case Western Reserve University, Cleveland; Theodore Samore, Professor, School of Library Science, University of Wisconsin—Milwaukee; E. Ruth Schneider, Assistant Professor, Department of Library Science, Murray State University; Wesley Simonton, Director, Library School, University of Minnesota, Minneapolis; Mary Ellen Soper, Assistant Professor, School of Librarianship, University of Washington, Seattle; Elaine Svenonius, Associate Professor, Graduate School of Librarianship and Information Management, University of Denver; Frank L. Turner, Associate Director, School of Library Science, Texas Woman's University, Denton; D. Kathryn Weintraub, Associate Professor, Graduate Library School, University of Chicago; Francis J. Witty, Professor, Graduate Department of Library and Information Science, Catholic University of America, Washington, D.C.

I am especially grateful to the editorial staff of Libraries Unlimited, for their careful and exacting readings of the revisions and many valuable additions. An overall editorial supervision was provided by the managing editor, Christine Gehrt Wynar, who also prepared an analytical index to this edition. Fred W. Ramey's copyediting of this edition has been invaluable. And finally, I want to point out that this edition's improved appearance is due entirely to Judy Caraghar's meticulous work in graphics. In this task she was ably assisted by Stephanie Van Bogart. Any errors of omission or commission are, of course, entirely my own. I would appreciate suggestions as to how this book can be improved to meet the needs of library science classes and practicing catalogers.

March 1980   Bohdan S. Wynar

TABLE OF CONTENTS

Part III – Subject Analysis

1 PRINCIPLES OF CATALOGING

The purposes of this chapter are to introduce the basic concepts of cataloging and to provide a preliminary discussion of descriptive cataloging. The first section of the basic concepts part of this chapter defines the terms "catalog," "cataloging," "entry," and "bibliographic record." The next section, "Characteristics of a Catalog," describes the differences between library catalogs and bibliographies and/or indexes. The physical formats and characteristic qualities of various types of catalogs are compared. This is followed by an examination of the concept of the unit record, with examples. The discussion of basic concepts of cataloging continues with a discussion of three ways to arrange entries in a catalog. These three methods of arrangement are represented by the dictionary catalog, the divided catalog, and the classified catalog. Finally, there is a discussion of the purposes of a catalog.

The second part of this chapter serves as a basic introduction to descriptive cataloging. After a definition of descriptive cataloging and an explanation of its purpose, there is a section on how to examine the parts of an item that are essential to a catalog description—that is, how to read "technically" the item to be cataloged. The chief source of information and its component parts—the title proper and its various forms, the statement of responsibility, the edition, and the publication and distribution information—are all defined and described. This is an extremely important section, because it contains many technical definitions that are needed for an understanding of descriptive cataloging rules. The next section discusses the form of the catalog record and its eight separate parts: heading, body of the entry, physical description, series, notes, standard number, tracing, and call number. The last section of this first chapter is a preliminary introduction to the formats to be followed in typing catalog cards (indentions, spacing, punctuation, capitalization, abbreviations, and numerals).

BASIC CONCEPTS

DEFINITIONS

In order to provide access to the holdings of a library, an index or list of the materials in the collection must be maintained. In libraries the principal index or list of available materials is called the catalog. A catalog is a list—arranged by alphabet, by number, or by subject—of books, maps, coins, stamps, sound recordings, or materials in any other medium that constitute a collection. Its prime purpose is to record, describe, and index the holdings of a specific collection. The collection may be private or it may represent the resources of a museum or of a library. Cataloging is the process of preparing a catalog, or of preparing bibliographic records that will become entries in a catalog.

Why prepare catalogs? Catalogs are necessary whenever a collection grows too large to be remembered item for item. A small private library or a classroom library will have little need for a formal catalog; the user can recall each book by author, title, or subject. When such a collection becomes a little larger, an informal arrangement, such as grouping the books by subject categories, provides access to them. But when a collection becomes too large for such a simple approach, a formal record is necessary.

The use of a collection of any sort large enough to be cataloged depends upon the system by which each item is primarily identified in the catalog. In an art museum exhibition catalog the artist's name and the number assigned to each painting are of utmost importance. A catalog of musical phonograph records will be itemized by composer and often by performer. Ordinarily, a collection of books will be listed by author; if the author is unknown, listing will be by title, or by any other information that provides positive identification. Such information is called an entry.

In a library, each entry in the catalog is the representation of a bibliographic record at a particular point in the catalog. A bibliographic record is a transcription of the complete cataloging information for any item. The purpose of a bibliographic record is 1) to provide all the information necessary to describe an item accurately both physically and intellectually in order to distinguish it from every other item, and 2) to provide its location in the collection. When such a record is entered in the catalog at each of several access points (e.g., author, title, subject), these entries then become an index to the collection. Thus, in the catalog the patron can find two important pieces of information: whether the library has the item wanted, and, if so, where it is located in the collection.

CHARACTERISTICS OF A CATALOG

Certain characteristics and functions of library catalogs distinguish them from other different but closely related forms of library tools — bibliographies and indexes. A bibliography, in simple terms, lists the literature on one subject — not only books but sometimes also pamphlets, articles in periodicals, documents, or other material not revealed in the ordinary library catalog. It may list the works of a certain author, describing all editions of those works. In contrast, a library catalog lists, arranges, and describes the holdings of a specific library or collection. The main functions of a library catalog are to enable a patron to determine

1) whether the library contains a certain item,
2) which works by a particular author are in the collection,
3) which editions of a particular work the library has, and
4) what materials the library has on a particular subject.

The rules for making catalog entries are, in general, standard rules that have national and, to a large extent, international acceptance. The current standard is the *Anglo-American Cataloguing Rules*, 2nd ed., referred to hereafter as *AACR 2*.[1] On the other hand, descriptive bibliographical practice follows a variety of codes for recording authors' names, for capitalization and punctuation, etc.; this is because the bibliographer's concern is not so much with choice and form of entry as with a critical appraisal of the history of the edition and the format of the work.

A library catalog frequently is described as an "index." It may be more exact to say that a catalog leads the reader to a particular item in the collection, showing the user the location of the item, its physical description, and its subject content. (More detailed discussion of the problem of revealing the intellectual content of an item will be found in the chapter on subject headings.) An index exhibits the analyzed contents of a single item, of the items in a certain class or collection, or of one or more periodicals, reports, or documents. The purpose of an index is to show in what particular book, periodical, document, etc., and at what specific place the information on a certain topic or subject can be found.

TYPES OF CATALOG ACCORDING TO FORMAT

Presently, the library catalog exists in one of several physical formats: book catalog, card catalog, microform catalog, or online computer catalog. The printed book or book catalog is the oldest type known in the United States; it was used by many American libraries as the most common form of catalog until the late 1800s. For example, the report of the Bureau of Education in 1876 gives a list of 1,010 printed book catalogs, 382 of them published from 1870 to 1876. Because the book catalogs were rather expensive to produce and quickly became outdated, they were gradually replaced by card catalogs. In a survey of 58 typical American libraries undertaken in 1893, 43 libraries had complete card catalogs and 13 had printed book catalogs with card supplements.[2] Thus, for many years book catalogs were out of favor in American libraries. It was only with more modern, cheaper methods of printing and with the advent of automation for quicker cumulation that book catalogs again became popular with certain types of libraries. An example of a book catalog produced by more modern production techniques is the Library of Congress *Catalog of Books Represented by Library of Congress Printed Cards*, known since 1956 as the *National Union Catalog*. This catalog is published monthly, with quarterly, semiannual, annual, and quinquennial cumulations. The *National Union Catalog* is produced by photographic reduction of pre-existing catalog cards; hence, it is a by-product of a card catalog. A similar technique is used by a number of commercial publishers (e.g., G. K. Hall), who reproduce card catalogs of certain libraries in a book catalog format.

Beginning in the 1950s, a new type of book catalog appeared, based on the use of computers. These computer-produced catalogs, which use machine-readable cataloging records, vary widely in format, typography, extent of bibliographical detail, and pattern of updating. Their main drawback is still their cost; at this point only a few libraries can afford them. One of the best examples of a computer-produced book catalog is the *Current Catalog* of the National Library of Medicine, started in 1966. It is published biweekly, with quarterly, semiannual, and annual cumulations. The Library of Congress also publishes part of its book catalog series via computer. *Films and Other Materials for Projection* is an example. Other examples are the New York Public Library Catalogs and several county system catalogs.

The card catalog is the library catalog most often found in the United States. Each entry is prepared on a standard 7.5x12.5 cm. card (roughly 3x5-inches); these cards are then filed, usually in alphabetical order, in trays. Entries on cards in the past were most often prepared by photo-reproduction of a printed or typed original. However, they are increasingly being computer-produced from machine-readable catalog records.

Microform catalogs have become much more popular with the development of computer-output microform (COM). COM catalogs are produced in either microfilm [i.e., "a length of film bearing a number of microimages in linear array" (*AACR 2*, p. 567)] or microfiche [i.e., "a sheet of film bearing a number of microimages in a two-dimensional array" (*AACR 2*, p. 567)]. It is feasible with this form of catalog to provide a completely integrated new catalog every three months or so, rather than providing supplements to be used with a main catalog. COM catalogs are possible even for small libraries, through commercial vendors to whom the library may send its new bibliographic records. The vendor processes the new bibliographic records, integrates them with the particular library's existing catalog and sends new COM catalogs at specified intervals. Many libraries now have COM catalogs, and there is a voluminous amount of literature on the subject.[3]

The online computer catalog is still in the experimental stages. Bibliographic records stored in the computer memory are printed on a video screen (Cathode Ray Tube, commonly referred to as a CRT) in response to a request from a user. Entries may comprise the full bibliographic record or only parts of it, depending on the system and/or the desires of the user. Such systems are still costly, and none is yet fully operational as a "catalog," although several are working well as "finding lists" for acquisitions of recent years. An example of this is the Library Control System (LCS) of the Ohio State University Library. A more detailed discussion of developments in computer cataloging is given in this text in the chapters on end processes and on networks.

QUALITIES OF CATALOG FORMAT

An effective catalog in any format should possess certain qualities that will allow it to be easily consulted and maintained. If it is too difficult, too cumbersome, or too expensive, it is virtually useless. Hence the following comparative criteria exist for judging a catalog:

1) A catalog should be flexible and up-to-date. A library's collection is constantly changing. Since the catalog is a record of what is available in that library, entries should be added or removed as books are added to or discarded from the collection. The card catalog is totally flexible. Cards can be easily added to or removed from the trays whenever necessary. Changes can be made on cards and they can be refiled. However, especially in large libraries, filing backlogs often accumulate, resulting in long delays in entering current or changed records into the catalog. Book and COM catalogs are inflexible in that once they have been printed, they cannot admit additions or deletions except in supplements or new editions of the catalog. On the other hand, because they are computer-produced, they can provide much more flexibility in making changes in existing entries. One instruction can be made to change

many entries, while with a card catalog, each change must be made by hand. In addition, computer-produced catalogs can be more current in situations where large filing backlogs have existed. The online computer catalog is potentially the most flexible and current. Additions, deletions, and changes can be made at any time, and the results are instantly available to the user.

2) A catalog should be constructed so that all entries can be quickly and easily found. This is a matter of labeling, filing, and, in the case of online catalogs, simple and clear access codes. So far as the card catalog is concerned, the contents of each tray must be identified to the extent that a patron who wants to locate, for example, the works of Charles Dickens can find the Dickens entries easily. Labeling of each tray is essential; the patron must know exactly what part of the alphabet is contained in each one. Within the trays themselves, arrangement of entries must be such that items are not overlooked because the filing is not alphabetical, and guide cards should be sufficiently plentiful to identify coverage. Book catalogs are usually labeled on the spine, like encyclopedias. Often they have guides at the top of each page, indicating what entries are covered there. Microfilm catalogs typically are stored in readers that are equipped with alphabetic index strips designed to get the user to the desired part of the alphabet. Microfiche catalogs have at the top of each sheet of fiche eye-readable labels that indicate the part of the alphabet covered. Typically, each sheet of fiche has a microimage index in one corner that tells in which cross section of the fiche particular parts of the alphabet are found. Filing arrangement in computer-produced catalogs is not the same as in traditionally-filed card catalogs because of the difficulty of programming computers to arrange according to traditional library filing rules. As a result, traditional rules are being re-evaluated.

Entries are located in online catalogs by means of access codes. The computer must be told, for example, whether an author, title, or subject search is desired, and then it must be told enough about the desired heading to search for it. Combinations of letters and/or words used to communicate such information to the computer are called "search keys." Ease of constructing the search keys will be a major factor in the success of online catalogs.

3) A catalog should be economically prepared and maintained. The catalog that can be prepared most inexpensively and with greatest attention to currency has obvious advantages.

4) A catalog should be compact. It should not only take up the least possible amount of space, but it should also be easily removable for consultation and prolonged study if possible. The catalog most closely fitting this description is the microfiche catalog, although its use requires a reader. With the development of small, portable microfiche readers, such catalogs could conceivably be taken to individual homes or offices. Microfilm catalogs take up little space, but readers are not portable. Because only one person at a time can use a microfilm catalog, multiple copies (including multiple readers) are usually required. Book catalogs are compact and can be removed for private study, but again, multiple copies may be required in a single location. An online catalog is as compact as the terminal used to gain access to it and can be accessible from any location having terminal access to the memory bank containing the catalog. The card catalog is the least compact, and it cannot be removed for private consultation.

In summary, the following observations can be made about the major types of catalog:

Cards for the card catalog are easy to prepare and relatively inexpensive. The chief virtue of the card catalog is its flexibility. Though it is not compact and trays cannot ordinarily be removed for long intensive study, it should be remembered that many people can use it at the same time, as long as they do not need the same drawer.

The book catalog is expensive to prepare unless numerous copies of the catalog are required; library systems that need multiple copies will find the book catalog less costly than the card catalog. Entries can be found quickly in the book catalog, and it is compact, easy to store, and easy to handle. However, it lacks flexibility.

The microform catalog is much less expensive than the book catalog, and there is evidence that its maintenance is less expensive than the card catalog, although the initial investment in catalog conversion to machine-readable form is high. It is compact and easy to store. It can be flexible if the library can afford to run new cumulations often.

The online computer catalog is the most flexible and current. It is also compact. However, it is quite expensive, a drawback that may be overcome with continued development.

THE UNIT RECORD

The Library of Congress did not begin to sell its standard printed catalog cards to libraries until 1901. Before that, individual libraries had to devise their own sets of cards to identify and describe the contents of each book. Duplicating machines were comparatively rudimentary and very expensive; therefore, the cataloger usually typed the card information or wrote it out in longhand. Obviously, under these conditions, it was costly to duplicate every necessary detail on each card in the set. For the sake of economy, only one card (the main entry card) was likely to carry complete bibliographic information. All other cards (secondary entry cards) were highly abbreviated.

When the Library of Congress decided to print cards and to sell them, it discovered that the most economical method was to print all cards of one set exactly alike. In this way it was not necessary to have one set for main entry and other sets for each other entry. This was the genesis of the unit card system of cataloging; encouraged by the development of duplicating machines, this system became almost universal in American libraries. With the recent advent of book, COM, and online catalogs, however, the economical advantage of having a unit record reproduced at each entry point has been reversed. It is more economical to print only abbreviated entries at all but one entry point.

In a card catalog, the unit card system of providing multiple entries for an item is one in which a basic card, complete with all cataloging information, is used as a unit for identical duplication of all other necessary cards. After the reproduction of the unit card, all that is needed is the addition of appropriate added entries at the top of each card. This system has an important advantage for the patron: no matter what card is consulted—author, title, or subject—complete descriptive and bibliographical information for the item will be found. In most computer-produced catalogs, as already mentioned, abbreviated records are printed at all but one entry point. In printed catalogs, the fullest record is usually the main entry; in online catalogs, the user usually must ask for the full bibliographic record from whatever entry is found. In either case, finding complete information often requires two searches.

The main entry is the basic catalog entry; it is usually the author entry, and it ordinarily gives all the information that identifies the work. Generally, it carries a record of all secondary entries under which the work is entered in the catalog. This record is called the tracing, and it is an essential part of the system. The set of entries may have to be changed after it has been entered into the catalog or it may be necessary to remove it altogether. The set cannot be changed or removed unless all the entries of the set can be located. The tracing, usually found at the bottom of the main entry record (or sometimes on the reverse if in card format), gives this information.

Secondary entries, or added entries, are any entries other than the main entry. They may reflect joint authors, editors, illustrators, translators, performers, etc.; titles; subjects; or any other information that is sufficiently important or memorable that the patron might use it for searching. Obviously, the number of added entries will vary from item to item. There are usually at least four entries for every item: a main entry (author), a shelflist (for the library records), a title (added) entry, and a subject (added) entry. Often, however, added title entries are not made for such titles as *Works*, or *Selected Works*, because these are not distinctive enough to warrant a separate entry. Also, some items do not receive subject added entries (e.g., fiction, in many libraries). The topic of subject added entries is discussed under subject headings in the chapter on Verbal Subject Analysis. In addition to the usual four entries for each item, added entries for subject, joint authors, etc., are made as needed. Some items may require seven or eight added entries; some may need just one or none at all.

There are three basic types of library catalog entries: main entry and added entry (both of which are prepared by descriptive cataloging rules), and subject added entry (prepared by subject cataloging procedures). In most cases the main entry is the author entry. For example, a copy of *Computers in Business Management: An Introduction*, by James A. O'Brien (see Figs. 1.2−1.4) will have as its main entry O'Brien, James A., 1936- . The title, *Computers in Business Management: An Introduction*, is an added entry. It describes the book by providing further identification apart from the author, whose name may not always be recalled. "Business--Data Processing" is a subject added entry for this book; it describes the intellectual content of the book. When this subject entry is filed with similar ones, it indicates one of many possible items on a single topic. It must be remembered that a patron may not know the author or title of a book or other type of material on a certain subject. In such a case the only approach is to seek out information by subject.

The following are transcriptions of the title page of a book and the label of a sound disc. Complete sets of entries are shown for each.

Fig. 1.1 Transcription of title page of a book.

COMPUTERS IN BUSINESS MANAGEMENT
An Introduction

James A. O'Brien

Professor of Finance and Management Information Systems
School of Business and Administration
Eastern Washington State College

Revised Edition

1979

Richard D. Irwin, Inc.
Homewood, Illinois 60430

Irwin-Dorsey Limited
Georgetown, Ontario L7G 4B3

An added entry for the series that includes this title is allowable but has not been included below. Provisions for use of added entry for series are discussed under Rule 21.30L on pages 295-96 of this text.

Fig. 1.2. The unit record—serves as the main entry record.

658.054	O'Brien, James A., 1936-
O13c	Computers in business management : an intro-
1979	duction / James A. O'Brien. – Rev. ed. –
	Homewood, Ill. : R.D. Irwin, 1979.

xiv, 497 p. : ill. ; 25 cm. – (The Irwin series in information and decision sciences)

Bibliography: p. 488-489.
Includes index.
ISBN 0-256-02121-X

1. Business–Data processing. I. Title.

Fig. 1.3. Subject heading added to unit record.

⟶ BUSINESS--DATA PROCESSING

658.054	O'Brien, James A., 1936-
O13c	Computers in business management : an intro-
1979	duction / James A. O'Brien. -- Rev. ed. --
	Homewood, Ill. : R.D. Irwin, 1979.

xiv, 497 p. : ill. ; 25 cm. – (The Irwin series in information and decision sciences)

Bibliography: p. 488-489.
Includes index.
ISBN 0-256-02121-X

1. Business--Data processing. I. Title.

Fig. 1.4. Unit record with added entry for title.

→ Computers in business management

658.054   O'Brien, James A., 1936-
O13c   Computers in business management : an intro-
1979   duction / James A. O'Brien. -- Rev. ed. --
         Homewood, Ill. : R.D. Irwin, 1979.
           xiv, 497 p. : ill. ; 25 cm. -- (The Irwin series in
         information and decision sciences)

         Bibliography: p. 488-489.
         Includes index.
         ISBN 0-256-02121-X

         1. Business–Data processing.   I. Title.

On the shelflist used for the inventory record, librarians make notations on the record (depending on individual practice) indicating number of copies, price, accession number (if used), date when a copy was noted missing from the shelves, etc.

Fig. 1.5. Unit record used as shelflist.

658.054   O'Brien, James A., 1936-
O13c   Computers in business management : an intro-
1979   duction / James A. O'Brien. -- Rev. ed. --
         Homewood, Ill. : R.D. Irwin, 1979.
           xiv, 497 p. : ill. ; 25 cm. -- (The Irwin series in
         information and decision sciences)

cop 1   Bibliography: p. 488-489.
cop 2   Includes index.
         ISBN 0-256-02121-X

         1. Business–Data processing.   I. Title.

Fig. 1.6. Transcription of the label of a sound disc.

® "Columbia." ℞ Marcas Reg.

NEIL DIAMOND
Jonathan Livingston Seagull

AL 32550

Prologue 3:19
Be 6:28
Flight of The Gull 2:23
Dear Father 5:12
Skybird 1:12
Lonely Looking Sky 3:12

Produced by TOM CATALANO

℗ 1973 CBS. Inc.
SIDE 1
KS 32550
STEREO

COLUMBIA

Fig. 1.7. The unit record (main entry).

M
1527
D52

Diamond, Neil.
    Jonathan Livingston Seagull [sound recording] / [words and music by] Neil Diamond. – New York : Columbia Records, c1973.
    1 sound disc (52 min.) : 33 1/3 rpm, stereo ; 12 in. + 1 pamphlet ([10] p. : col. ill. ; 31 cm.)

    Produced by Tom Catalano.
    Original motion picture sound track.
    Columbia: KS 32550.

    1. Moving-picture music--Excerpts. I. Catalano, Tom. II. Title.

Fig. 1.8. Unit record with added entry for producer.

Catalano, Tom

M
1527
D52

Diamond, Neil.
Jonathan Livingston Seagull [sound recording] / [words and music by] Neil Diamond. – New York : Columbia Records, c1973.
1 sound disc (52 min.) : 33 1/3 rpm, stereo ; 12 in. + 1 pamphlet ([10] p. : col. ill. ; 31 cm.)

Produced by Tom Catalano.
Original motion picture sound track.
Columbia: KS 32550.

1. Moving-picture music--Excerpts. I. Catalano, Tom. II. Title.

Fig. 1.9. Subject heading added to unit record.

MOVING-PICTURE MUSIC--EXCERPTS

M
1527
D52

Diamond, Neil.
Jonathan Livingston Seagull [sound recording] / [words and music by] Neil Diamond. – New York : Columbia Records, c1973.
1 sound disc (52 min.) : 33 1/3 rpm, stereo ; 12 in. + 1 pamphlet ([10] p. : col. ill. ; 31 cm.)

Produced by Tom Catalano.
Original motion picture sound track.
Columbia: KS 32550.

1. Moving-picture music--Excerpts. I. Catalano, Tom. II. Title.

Fig. 1.10. Unit record with added entry for title.

Jonathan Livingston Seagull [sound recording]

M
1527
D52

Diamond, Neil.
Jonathan Livingston Seagull [sound recording] / [words and music by] Neil Diamond. – New York : Columbia Records, c1973.
1 sound disc (52 min.) : 33 1/3 rpm, stereo ; 12 in. + 1 pamphlet ([10] p. : col. ill. ; 31 cm.)

Produced by Tom Catalano.
Original motion picture sound track.
Columbia: KS 32550.

1. Moving-picture music--Excerpts.   I. Catalano, Tom.   II. Title.

Fig. 1.11. Unit record used as shelflist.

M
1527
D52

Diamond, Neil.
Jonathan Livingston Seagull [sound recording] / [words and music by] Neil Diamond. – New York : Columbia Records, c1973.
1 sound disc (52 min.) : 33 1/3 rpm, stereo ; 12 in. + 1 pamphlet ([10] p. : col. ill. ; 31 cm.)

cop 1

Produced by Tom Catalano.
Original motion picture sound track.
Columbia: KS 32550.

1. Moving-picture music--Excerpts.   I. Catalano, Tom.   II. Title.

ARRANGEMENT OF ENTRIES IN A CATALOG

A catalog must be arranged according to some definite plan. Depending on the subject and scope of the collection, many arrangements are possible. But no matter which one is used, it should cover the contents of the collection and guide the person who consults it to these contents.

Catalogs are ordinarily arranged according to one of three systems: dictionary, divided, or classified. The differences between them lie in the arrangement and filing of the entries.

Dictionary Catalogs

In the dictionary arrangement of entries, widely used in American libraries, all the entries — main, added, and subject — are combined, word by word, into one alphabetical file. This arrangement is said to be simple; undoubtedly it is, in the sense that only one file need be consulted. As the library grows, however, the dictionary arrangement becomes cumbersome and complex because all entries are interfiled. The problem becomes partly one of filing (are books by Charles Dickens, for example, filed before those about him?) and partly one of dispersion. The subject of "industrial relations" has many aspects. How can all these aspects be located if they are entered under headings from "A" for "arbitration" to "W" for "wages"? Two primary justifications are offered in favor of the dictionary arrangement: most patrons seek material on one aspect of a subject rather than upon the broad subject itself, and patrons are provided with ample *see* and *see also* references, which direct them to other aspects of their subjects.

Divided Catalogs

In the 1930s the realization that dictionary catalogs were becoming more and more complex led to a modification of the dictionary arrangement. The result was the divided catalog, which, in its most common form, is in reality two catalogs: one for main and added entries other than subject; the other for subject entries only. The divided catalog permits a simpler filing scheme than does the dictionary catalog. Thus it is easier to consult, although the problem of scattered subjects still exists. There is a further complication implicit in this arrangement. The patron must determine whether an author or title entry or a subject entry is wanted before knowing which part of the catalog must be checked. When this divided approach is used, books about Dickens and books by Dickens are not filed together in the catalog. Patrons will need some guidance and education in this matter.

There are a few libraries that use other types of divided catalogs, such as the three-way divided catalog consisting of separate sections for author, title, and subject entries. Although this system may simplify the filing of cards, it can be even more confusing for a patron than the two-way divided catalog. In this arrangement, entries for books by Dickens will be filed under Dickens' name in the author catalog, the titles of his individual novels will be filed in the title catalog, and books about Dickens will be filed in the subject catalog.

Another type of two-way divided catalog is a name/title catalog and a topical subject catalog. In such a divided catalog names and titles that are used even as subject headings are filed in the name/title section. This type of divided catalog allows all the material by and about an author or a title to be filed together. Thus, to continue our previous example, books by and books about Dickens would be filed together in the same catalog. This system is potentially less confusing to the patron than any other form of divided catalog.

Classified Catalogs

The classified catalog has the longest history of all. Many American libraries used this form before they changed to the more popular dictionary form. It, too, is based upon some special system of classification. For example, the shelflist, a record of the holdings of a library arranged by classification number, is a classified catalog of a kind. But in a true classified catalog, a bibliographic record may be entered under as many classification numbers as apply to its contents, not under just one number as in a shelflist. In addition, the shelflist lacks an alphabetical subject index. The major advantage of a classified catalog is that because it uses symbols or numbers it can keep up with changing terminology and thus be up to date. For efficient use it must have an alphabetical subject index. Perhaps its greatest disadvantage is that it is constructed on a particular classification scheme (even though this was an advantage as noted above). Since many patrons are not familiar with classification numbers, they would need special assistance when consulting the classified catalog. However, some fields—particularly the sciences—can make good use of such a catalog, inasmuch as science changes so rapidly. Since the classified catalog is flexible and can be easily updated, several large science and technology libraries provide this kind of index to their resources. A good example of a classified catalog is at the John Crerar Library in Chicago. This type of catalog arrangement will be discussed in greater detail in the chapter on Subject Headings.

Classified catalogs are also of value in locations where the patrons may speak one of two or more languages. In such a case, an alphabetical subject index may be made in each language. In Quebec, for example, where both English and French are spoken, there would be one major classified catalog with French and English indexes.

Classified catalogs are actually only the subject part of a divided catalog. They must be accompanied by an author/title catalog.

PURPOSES OF A CATALOG

The multiple-entry dictionary catalog, the standard form used in American libraries, records the holdings of a library in such a way as to offer the user a variety of approaches to the information sought. The objectives of this type of catalog as stated by Charles A. Cutter in his *Rules for a Dictionary Catalog* are still valid today, although modern practice indicates that they are incomplete. These objectives, first formulated in 1904, are as follows:

Objects

1) To enable a person to find a book when one of the following is known:
   a)The author
   b) The title
   c) The subject

2) To show what the library has
d) By a given author
e) On a given subject
f) In a given kind of literature

3) To assist in the choice of a book
g) As to the edition (bibliographically)
h) As to its character (literary or topical).

Means

1) Author entry with the necessary references (for a and d)
2) Title entry or title reference (for b).
3) Subject entry, cross references, and classed subject table (for c and e)
4) Form entry and language entry (for f)
5) Edition and imprint, with notes when necessary (for g)
6) Notes (for h)[4]

Amplification of Cutter's Objects and Means

To conform to modern practice, the first objective needs to be rephrased as follows: To enable a person to find any intellectual creation whether issued in a print or non-print format. Cutter's first object is inadequate even for printed materials inasmuch as "book" does not unambiguously encompass "periodical," "serial," or "pamphlet." In addition, as stated, the objective makes no provision for audiovisual materials (e.g., "filmstrip," "tape recording").

Cutter's object "e" is too simplistic. Rephrased, it should read "on given and related subjects." It is clearly a prime function of a dictionary catalog to guide the user in the system of subject headings that any particular library may have adopted. Cutter's apparent assumption that the user always has a clearly formulated "given" subject in mind is contrary to all observation of catalog users.

Cutter's objectives remained the primary statement of catalog principles until 1961, when the International Federation of Library Associations (IFLA) at the Paris Conference approved a statement about the purpose of an author/title catalog. It stated that the catalog should be an efficient instrument for ascertaining:

1) whether the library contains a particular book specified by:
a) its author and title, *or*
b) if no author is named in the book, its title alone, *or*
c) if author and title are inappropriate or insufficient for identification, a suitable substitute for the title,

and 2) a) which works by a particular author *and*
b) which editions of a particular work are in the library.[5]

These descriptions point out the dual functions that exist within the modern catalog causing it to be a finding list (see 1.a-c) for some purposes and a collocating device (see 2.a-b) for others. The catalog is a finding list in that it can provide the user with the necessary access to an individual item, whether the user approaches the item by author, title, or subject. In this sense the catalog is a finding list made up of specific individual pieces of information. A simple type of finding list would be a list of the titles of all the books in a collection. In fact, the white pages of the telephone directory may be considered as a typical finding list. In 1936, Julia Pettee pointed out the meaning of the finding list theory:

> The identification of the literary unit and the attribution of authorship in establishing the form of entry is so thoroughly ingrained in our catalogers [that] it may be a surprise to many to be told that these principles, in the long history of cataloging, are something very new and that they have not yet attained universal acceptance. The older working principle upon which all European rules have developed is that the catalog is a ready finding list for the particular book wanted, irrespective of its relation to any other book.[6]

A catalog constructed on this principle is efficient in showing whether or not a particular work by a certain author is in the collection. The deficiency is its failure to relate a particular work to other materials — that is, it does not fulfill functions 2.a-b stated above. The collocating (assembling) function provides means for bringing together in one place in a catalog all entries for like and closely related materials — e.g., for displaying together all the works of an author in the library collection. In 1977, Sally Hart McCallum discussed the meaning of the collocating function:

> Collocation is the arranging of elements in certain positions, particularly side by side. . . . It is usually found in the catalog in two forms: in the collocation of works of a single author, and in the collocation of editions of a work. The structure which this arrangement gives to the catalog helps to distinguish it from a simple list of items and extends the instrument's control over the documents in its domain.[7]

To achieve collocation, the main entry for a work must be in one "correct" form. Cataloging strictly from title pages, which is sufficient for a finding list, would result in scattering rather than collocating related works. For example, the works of an author writing under more than one name or using various forms of a name would not have the same main entry and would be filed in several different places in the catalog. The library dictionary catalog represents an attempt to combine both the finding list and collocating device principles in construction and arrangement of entries. The advantage of utilizing both features in one catalog is obvious; at the same time, however, it results in a complex instrument, difficult to construct and often frustrating to use. The function of the main entry, the choosing of this entry and the form to follow must be viewed in this relationship to basic properties of the catalog.

Several solutions are used to deal with this problem. Main entries may be arranged according to the form of the author's name as it appears on the title page, in which case the collocating of all works of the same author is achieved by using cross-references. The same approach may be used for titles. In this case, main entries are arranged according to the titles of the particular works; collocation of the various editions, translations, or literary forms of the same work is accomplished by using added entries.

The other method is to establish one "correct" form for an author's name, so that all publications by this author are automatically collocated in one place. Again, cross references are required to provide access to the form of name actually on the title page, or to variant forms widely known, for which some readers may search. In a similar manner, the title form is chosen according to the original, best known, or some other accepted uniform title; the result of this is that all editions, translations, etc., of the same work are automatically collocated in one place. In this case, references or added entries are provided for titles of the work that vary from the chosen heading.

Thus, a basic decision to be made, one of cataloging policy for the library, is whether uniform headings are to be adopted or headings are to follow the form of name and title as these appear on the title page of each work. *AACR 2* provides guidance in this matter; as can be seen from a study of rules for form of entry, *AACR 2* encourages use of the author's name as commonly known, and of more uniform headings for certain entries. In either case, added entries and references of various types are essential if the objectives of the catalog are to be fulfilled. *AACR 2* consistently stresses that catalogers must consider added entries and references whenever a choice between two possible entries or forms of entry is necessary. The decision of how extensively to follow this practice is, of course, left to each individual library.

DESCRIPTION OF MATERIAL TO BE CATALOGED

DEFINITION AND PURPOSE OF DESCRIPTIVE CATALOGING

Descriptive cataloging is that phase of the cataloging process which is concerned with the identification and description of an item, the recording of this information in the form of a cataloging record, and the selection and formatting of access points—with the exception of subject access points. The term refers to the physical make-up of the item and to the responsibility for intellectual contents, without reference to its classification by subject or to the assignment of subject headings, both of which are the province of subject cataloging.

Identification and description are closely interrelated processes in descriptive cataloging. Identification consists of the choice of conventional elements, formulated by a set of rules that catalogers use to describe an item. When the cataloger has properly identified these conventions, they are described in a catalog record in such a fashion that the description is unique and can be applied to no other item in the collection.

What are the conventional elements that a cataloger tries to identify for the convenience of the patron? The majority of patrons will search for a specific item either by person(s) responsible for the contents or by title. This is universal. All catalogers, therefore, will ordinarily try to identify the person(s) responsible for the contents of an item and its title.

Many readers also wish to identify a particular edition of a work when there has been more than one; therefore, additional information must be added to the statements of title and responsibility. A particular edition may be identified by the number of the edition (e.g., 5th edition), the name of the edition (e.g., Student Edition), the name of the editor, the reviser, the illustrator, the translator, the performer, the producer, the publisher, the date of publication as well as the copyright date, or even the series of which the edition is a part. Even the size, the type or number of illustrations, or the extent of the item (e.g., number of pages of a book or number of frames of a microfiche) may be helpful information for a reader seeking a specific edition of a work.

TECHNICAL READING OF AN ITEM TO BE CATALOGED

In order to identify conventional elements of an item so that they can be described on a catalog record, it is necessary to know not only what to look for, but also how to look. Technical reading in this manner is scarcely the same as reading for information or for entertainment, when the entire item may be read, seen, or heard. Obviously, the cataloger will have no time for "reading" of this sort, and, therefore, must learn to read technically. Reading technically involves recognizing quickly certain devices peculiar to the particular type of item being cataloged. In this way, the cataloger can quickly determine what the item is about and how it can be described uniquely in such a way that this information can be passed on to the readers. The following discussion contains definitions useful to the cataloger in both descriptive cataloging and subject cataloging.

The first part of an item that the cataloger examines in detail is the chief source of information. This source varies according to the type of material. In books, manuscripts, printed music, and printed serials, it is the title page. In microforms and films it is the title frame. For sound recordings, it is the label and sometimes a container that is affixed to the item (e.g., cassette of a tape cassette). For cartographic and graphic materials and for three-dimensional artifacts and realia, the chief source of information is the object itself, including permanently affixed labels or unifying containers. If machine-readable data files have internal user labels, these are used as the chief source; otherwise accompanying printed documentation is used. In all these cases, the chief source of information may be absent for some reason, in which case cataloging rules prescribe alternate sources. But usually the chief source of information provides the most complete bibliographic information about the item: the author or other person responsible for the intellectual contents, the fullest form of the title, the name and/or number of the edition, the name of the publisher, distributor, etc., and the place and date of publication, distribution, etc.

The first element that the cataloger ordinarily notices is the title. The title from the chief source of information, which is generally the item's official title, is called the title proper; as such, it is used in all library records, in trade catalogs, and in bibliographies. It may or may not adequately describe the contents of the item. The book title, *A Short History of the United States*, is self-evident, but the title of the serial, *Toward Freedom*, needs an explanation. A glance through an issue will reveal that the serial discusses the development of new nations; this will be indicated as a subject heading on the catalog record.

In addition to the major part of the title, some items have secondary parts. The alternative title is introduced by "or" and was widely used in books published before the twentieth century. As in Gilbert and Sullivan's *Patience, or, Bunthorne's Bride*, it amplifies the title by telling the reader that "Patience," in this case, is a woman's name rather than the name of a specific virtue. The parallel title is the title proper written in another language or in another script. For instance, a bilingual book on snowmobiles in the Province of Quebec has its title proper in French, *La motoneige au Québec*, and its parallel title in English, *Snowmobiling in Quebec*. Other title information is often used to qualify the title proper. Such qualifications are often called subtitles. For example, the complete title of a tape cassette is *Behavior Control: The Psychologist as Manipulator*. "The Psychologist as Manipulator" is the subtitle. It explains the aspect of behavior control covered in the tape. There is also other title information that is not "subtitle" but does give further explanatory information. In the title, *Barbara Morgan Photography: Trisolini Gallery of Ohio University, Athens, Ohio, January 9-February 3, 1979*, the "other title" information tells where and when the show was held.

The title proper and other titles in the chief source of information, however, are not the only possible ones. Other titles exist, and the cataloger must note those that vary significantly from the title proper. When such titles are noted, the patron who knows a work only by a variant title can be directed to it. For example, Haydn's *Symphony 94 in G Major* is also known as the "Surprise Symphony"; many patrons would look for this popular form of the title instead of the title proper. Books may carry a cover title (i.e., title printed on the cover), binder's title (i.e., title lettered on the original spine of the book), or running title (i.e., title repeated at the top of each page or each alternate page of the book) that differs from the title proper. Sound recordings, motion pictures, or graphic materials may have titles on their containers that differ. Serials may have title variations on the cover or on an added title page.

The series title, however, is not a title variation, but indicates the series, if any, to which the item belongs. A series may be the work of one author, as in Will Durant's *The Story of Civilization*, which consists of several uniform volumes. This is called an author's series. A series may also be issued by a publisher who commissions several authors to write one or more volumes on a specified subject. Such is the case with the Rinehart *Rivers of America* series of many volumes. Or perhaps an author is not commissioned but submits a work that happens to fit into a category established by the publisher. Such is the case with Dodd, Mead's *Red Badge* series of mystery novels. Such series are called publishers' series.

The monographic series is a series that is usually issued with some regularity; each title in a monographic series is given a number, usually in chronological order. For many patrons, the name of the series and the number of a title in it are the important identifying elements. Patrons often do not remember individual authors and titles but look for these under the series name. Thus, though author and title of an individual item are major identifying elements, the series title in a monographic series assumes a significant role.

The second element to be identified by the cataloger is the statement of responsibility. This is also found in the chief source of information and is usually the author, whose name is usually the main entry. According to *AACR 2*, an author is "the person chiefly responsible for the creation of the intellectual or artistic content of a work" (p. 568). In addition to writers of books and composers of music, this includes cartographers, artists, photographers, performers, etc. It may be necessary to locate some information about an unfamiliar author. For example, if the work is imaginative in nature, the author's nationality must be known since most classification schemes use the device of nationality to classify novels, drama, and poetry. This is discussed in the chapters on classification in this text. Information about an author may sometimes be found in the chief source of information, in an introduction, or in material accompanying the item, such as the dust jacket of a book or the container of a disc.

However, an author is not the only possibility for inclusion in a statement of responsibility. Any person or persons responsible for intellectual or artistic content or for performance, or any corporate body from which the content is issued may need to be included in the catalog record.

The edition of the item, if named, is usually found in the chief source of information, but may also be found in other places. In a book, a piece of printed music, or a serial it may appear in the preliminaries [i.e., title page, verso (or back) of the title page, any pages preceding the title page, and the cover], in the preface to the work, or in a colophon (i.e., a statement at the end of the work). In cartographic or graphic material, sound recordings, motion pictures and videorecordings, machine-readable data files, and three-dimensional artifacts, the edition may appear in accompanying printed material. For those items with a container, the edition may be found there.

The edition is distinguished from a printing or issue in that a new edition indicates that certain specific changes—additions, deletions, modifications—have been made from earlier versions of the item. On the other hand, a new printing (or reprinting) or issue, means that more copies of the work were manufactured in order to keep up with demand. In the case of books and book-like materials, printings may have minor corrections or revisions, usually incorporated into the original type image. For other materials, a new issue may have slight variations from the original.

Editions may be named (e.g., "revised and enlarged," "abridged," "expurgated") or numbered (e.g., "5th edition"). Any of these edition statements indicates to the cataloger and the patron that some change in content or in form has been made. This information is very important to a scholar. To study the development of a poet, the literary scholar must have early and late editions of the poet's work. A physicist might want only the latest edition of a book on thermodynamics. More information concerning the verification of publication dates and of editions will be found in the chapters on descriptive cataloging.

Because the name of the publisher or distributor, etc., might indicate the type or quality of a work, this information might be important to the patron who must choose one item from several on a specific subject. If the publisher or distributor, etc., is noted for excellence in a certain area (e.g., Skira in art; McGraw-Hill in technology), publisher/distributor information has some value to the patron. This information, including place and date, is usually found in the chief source of information, but may also be found in the same other locations as the edition statement. If the item is copyrighted, the copyright date and the holders of the copyright must be listed in or on the item. This information is important when the publication date and the copyright date differ. In such a case, both dates are given in the catalog record.

The cataloger must learn to assess quickly the details of physical description. These include the extent of the item (e.g., number of pages or volumes, number of pieces, length of playing time), dimensions (e.g., height), and physical data other than extent or dimensions (e.g., presence of illustrations, playing speed, material of which made).

The cataloger must also be quick to identify other important and useful pieces of information about an item. Such information as variant titles of the same work (e.g., original title of a translation), language, edition history, accompanying materials, intended audience, contents of multi-volume items, and presence of bibliographies should often be noted in the catalog record. The standard number [e.g., International Standard Book Number (ISBN) and International Standard Serial Number (ISSN)] is becoming increasingly important as a means of unique international identification. It is often given in the catalog record.

If there is a preface, the cataloger should read it as an aid to determination of the author's plan or objective. This provides a key to the subject matter of the item. Similar aids are introductions, forewords, accompanying printed materials, and containers. The table of contents, with its listing of topics, is a valuable indication of the scope of a work. An index is also a good source for determining subject content and special emphases. Bibliographies may also serve as an aid by indicating an author's point of view.

FORM OF THE CATALOG RECORD

Uniformity is necessary in the form of the catalog record. If certain standards are followed throughout, patrons will universally recognize all the elements that make up the record. They will know, for example, that the publisher information will always follow the rest of the body of the entry and that the physical description area consists of certain items arranged in a specific order. This information then becomes readily identifiable.

Although various arrangements are possible, most libraries follow the Library of Congress classification system, simply because LC printed cards have been so extensively used. When pre-existent records are not available, the cataloger devises a record very similar in form to that used by the Library of Congress. Doing this makes all the records as uniform as possible and therefore easy to consult.

Not all specific elements are present in every item to be cataloged, but all elements present should be recorded. Contemporary cataloging practice assumes that patrons are best served if these elements are recorded in the same order on all entries. This order is achieved in a manual system by recording elements in a specified order, ordinarily formatted in paragraph form. In a computer system, the elements must be tagged to give the system information about the element and its place in the record. The computer will format a properly tagged record in the order desired when printing it as entries on cards, in book or COM catalogs, or on a CRT. The order and usual paragraph formatting of a printed catalog entry are outlined below, followed by an example record shown in printed card format and in Machine-Readable Cataloging (MARC) format.

I. HEADING
   A. Author or other person or corporate body chosen as main entry, *or*
   B. Title, if (A) cannot be ascribed.

II. BODY OF THE ENTRY (first paragraph)
   A. Title and statement of responsibility area
     1. Title proper (including alternative title, if any)
     2. General material designation (GMD)
     3. Parallel title(s), other title information, if any
     4. Statement(s) of responsibility
   B. Edition area
     1. Edition statement (named, numbered, or a combination of the two)
     2. Statements of responsibility relating to the edition, but not to all editions
   C. Material (or type of publication) specific details area
     1. For cartographic materials, statements of scale and projection
     2. For serial publications, numeric and/or alphabetic designation (e.g., No. 1-) and/or chronological designation (e.g., 1967-)
   D. Publication, distribution, etc., area
     1. Place of publication, distribution, etc.
     2. Name of publisher, distributor, etc.
     3. Statement of function of publisher, distributor, etc. (e.g., production company) when necessary for clarity
     4. Date of publication, distribution, etc., including copyright date, if necessary
     5. Place of manufacture, name of manufacturer, date of manufacture, if name of publisher is unknown

III. PHYSICAL DESCRIPTION AREA (second paragraph)
   A. Extent of item (e.g., number of pages, volumes, discs, frames, etc.
   B. Other physical details (e.g., illustrative material, playing speed, material of which made)
   C. Dimensions (e.g., height, diameter)
   D. Accompanying material (e.g., teacher's guide, separate maps)

IV. SERIES AREA, if any (following physical description area as continuation of second paragraph)
   A. Title proper of series, parallel title(s), other title information
   B. Statement(s) of responsibility relating to series
   C. ISSN of series
   D. Numbering within series
   E. Subseries
   F. Second and following series, each in its own set of parentheses

V. NOTE AREA (each note is separate paragraph). Necessary data that cannot be incorporated in above parts of the record.

VI. STANDARD NUMBER AND TERMS OF AVAILABILITY AREA (paragraph following last note)
   A. Standard number (e.g., ISBN, ISSN)
   B. Key-title of a serial
   C. Terms of availability (e.g., price, or for whom available)

VII. TRACING (separate paragraph)
   A. Subject heading(s)
   B. Added entries for joint authors, editors, etc.
   C. Title added entry or entries
   D. Series added entry or entries

VIII. CALL NUMBER (formatted in upper left corner of entry or on line following tracing)
   A. Classification number
   B. Cutter number and work mark, if any

Fig. 1.12. Identification of information included in a catalog card.

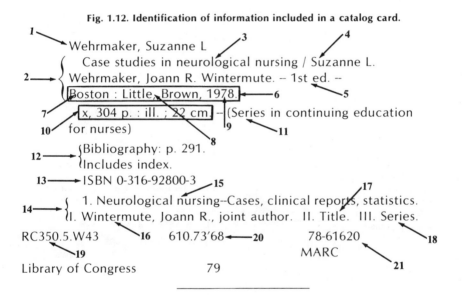

Key for figure 1.12.

1.	Heading: author's name	11.	Series statement
2.	Body of the entry	12.	Notes
3.	Title proper	13.	Standard number (ISBN)
4.	Statement of responsibility	14.	Tracing
5.	Edition statement	15.	Subject heading
6.	Publication, distribution, etc. area	16.	Added entry for personal name
7.	Place of publication	17.	Title added entry
8.	Publisher	18.	Series added entry
9.	Date of publication	19.	Library of Congress call number
10.	Physical description area	20.	Dewey classification number
		21.	Library of Congress card number

Fig. 1.13. Identification of information in a MARC record.

```
OCLC: 4617812      Rec stat: c Entrd: 790329        Used: 800123
Type: a Bib lvl: m Govt pub:   Lang: eng Source:   Illus: a
Repr:     Enc lvl:   Conf pub: 0 Ctry:  mau Dat tp: s M/F/B: 10
Indx: 1 Mod rec:   Festschr: 0 Cont: b
Desc: i Int lvl:    Dates: 1978,
  1 010       78-61620
  2 040       DLC ‡c DLC ‡d MQM
  3 020       0316928003 ◄─── 13
  4 050  0    RC350.5 ‡b .W43 ◄─── 18
  5 060       WY 160.3 W414c 1978
  6 082       610.73/68 ◄─── 19
  7 090       ‡b
  8 049       OCLC                        1
 17 ─ 9 100  10  Wehrmaker, Suzanne L.           3            4
 10 245 00    Case studies in neurological nursing / ‡c Suzanne L. Wehrmaker,     2
Joann R. Wintermute.            5
 11 250        1st ed. ◄─── 7        8          9
 12 260  0    (Boston : ‡b Little, Brown, ‡c 1978.) ◄─── 6
 13 300       (x, 304 p. : ‡b ill. ; ‡c 22 cm.) ◄─── 10
 14 440  0    (Series in continuing education for nurses) ◄─── 11
 15 504       (Bibliography: p. 291.) ◄─── 12
 16 500       (Includes index.             15
 17 650  0    (Neurological nursing ‡x Cases, clinical reports, statistics.)
 18 650  2    (Nervous System Diseases ‡x nursing ‡x examination questions )  ◄─── 14
 19 650  2    (Neurology ‡x nursing texts )
 20 (700) 10  (Wintermute, Joann R., ‡e joint author.)
 20                            16          21
```

Key for figure 1.13.

1. Heading: author's name
2. Body of the entry
3. Title proper
4. Statement of responsibility
5. Edition statement
6. Publication, distribution, etc., area
7. Place of publication
8. Publisher
9. Date of publication
10. Physical description area
11. Series statement
12. Notes
13. Standard number (ISBN)
14. Tracing
15. Subject heading
16. Added entry for personal name
17. MARC indicator that tells computer that title will be added entry
18. Library of Congress call number
19. Dewey classification number
20. MARC tag
21. MARC subfield code

TYPED CARDS

There are still many libraries that find it necessary to type at least some catalog cards locally. For these libraries, the following instructions illustrate a simple and generally effective method for doing so. The sections on punctuation, spacing, capitalization, abbreviations, and numerals are useful in creating original bibliographic records, whether they are input online in MARC format or are to be hand-typed.

The following formalized rules may seem arbitrary, but they are essential for uniformity. Practice will make a typist proficient within a short time. Indention rules are given first. These are followed by detailed explanations of the typing rules (spacing, punctuation, capitalization, etc.) using ISBD format.

Indentions

Most standard printed cards have the great advantage of more than one style and size of type to help differentiate between distinct items on the card. Lacking this advantage, typewritten cards must rely upon a standardized system (as follows) of spacing and punctuation for clarity.

The main entry heading begins nine spaces from the left margin of the card. This segment of nine spaces is called the first indention.

Second indention begins four typewriter spaces to the right of the main entry—or 13 spaces from the left margin. Second indention is used to align title, collation, notes, and tracing. Any of this information that is too long to be recorded on one line is brought back to first indention in standard paragraph form. All added entries at the top of the card begin at the second indention.

Occasionally there is need of a third indention (16 spaces from the left margin or seven spaces to the right of the beginning of the main entry). This will occur in three instances:

1) When the author entry is too long to be contained on one line, the overflow is carried to third indention. (To use second indention in this case would be confusing because the title begins at second indention.)

2) When an added entry is too long for one line, the second line will carry over to third indention.

3) In the cataloging of one volume or piece of a set that is in progress, the succeeding volumes or pieces must be allowed for. In this case the typist will space to third indention in the collation and type the specific material designation [e.g., "cassettes," "reels," or "v." (for "volumes")]. When the set is complete, it then becomes a simple matter to type the completed number of pieces directly to the left of the designation.

Card Format

The main entry heading begins on the fourth line from the top of the card. A typewritten catalog card is single-spaced throughout, with the following exceptions:

1) Double-space before the beginning of the first note.

2) Begin the tracing at the bottom of the card, but above the hole.

Fig. 1.14 is a sample form showing the location of information on a catalog card, indentions, spacing after punctuation, and vertical spacing between parts of the card. The small numbers "1" and "2" have been inserted to clarify the exact number of spaces to be used in each instance. Fig. 1.15 illustrates the format for the second card, which is to be used when there is too much information to fit onto one card. Detailed instructions for spacing, punctuation, and capitalization (ISBD) are given in the following sections.

Fig. 1.14. Sample form for typed card.

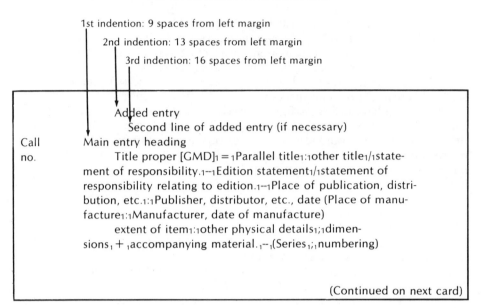

1st indention: 9 spaces from left margin

2nd indention: 13 spaces from left margin

3rd indention: 16 spaces from left margin

Added entry
Second line of added entry (if necessary)
Call   Main entry heading
no.   Title proper [GMD]₁ =₁Parallel title₁:₁other title₁/₁state-
ment of responsibility.₁--₁Edition statement₁/₁statement of
responsibility relating to edition.₁--₁Place of publication, distribution, etc.₁:₁Publisher, distributor, etc., date (Place of manu-
facture₁:₁Manufacturer, date of manufacture)
extent of item₁:₁other physical details₁;₁dimen-
sions₁+₁accompanying material.₁--₁(Series₁;₁numbering)

(Continued on next card)

Fig. 1.15. Sample for supplementary typed card.

Added entry
Second line of added entry (if necessary)
Call   Main entry heading
no.   Title proper [GMD]₁...₁date of publication, etc.₂(Card 2)

Notes.
ISBN

1.₁Subject heading--Subheading.₂ 2.₁Subject heading--
Subheading.₂ I.₁Added entry.₂ II.₁Title.₂ III.₁Series.

The Library of Congress carries the tracing for the card set in paragraph form at the bottom of the card just above the hole (see example on page 27). For typed cards the tracings, instead of being placed on the front, may be typed on the back of the main entry card. This is particularly true when the tracings are long. In any case, the form, once established, should not vary. The subject headings are typed first in order of importance. If they are equally important, the order does not matter, except that biographical headings, or others in which the person is the subject, always come first. Each subject heading is preceded by an arabic numeral. Here again uniformity must be maintained, depending on the kind of heading established.

Those entries that bring out descriptive elements of a book rather than its subject are preceded by roman numerals and come after all subject entries. As part of the tracing, they follow a specific order: joint author, editor, translator, or any other individual person who has helped to create the work; corporate entries or sponsoring agencies such as societies, university departments, bureaus and the like; title; series.

Detailed rules and examples pertaining to the elements that make up the catalog card and the specifications for personal names will follow in succeeding chapters on descriptive cataloging and rules for personal names.

Works entered under title are typed in the form called the hanging indention. The title begins at first indention and is continued at second indention. Physical description and notes are indented as for all other cards. See sample below.

Fig. 1.16. Typed form for hanging indention.

¹Title entry
1st indention

²2nd indention

```
1 ──────► An illustrated dictionary of geography / edited
2 ──────► by R. Ogilvie Buchanan. -- London : Heine-
         mann Educational, 1974.
         242 p. : ill. (some col.), col. maps ; 22 cm.
         ISBN 0-435-34390-4
         1. Physical geography--Dictionaries.  2. Geog-
         raphy--Dictionaries.  I. Buchanan, R. Ogilvie
         (Robert Ogilvie), 1894-
```

Spacing

1) The main entry heading begins on the fourth line from the top of the card.

2) Single space the lines, with the exceptions of double spaces before the first note and before the tracing.

3) The call number begins on the fourth line from the top of the card. Indent the call number one space from the left edge of the card.

4) Leave one space before and one space after

   a) Equals signs
      used to indicate parallel titles:
         La motoneige au Québec = Snowmobiling in Quebec
      used to separate alternative numbering systems in serials:
         Vol. 4, no. 1-   = No. 13-
      used to separate ISSN from key title:
         ISSN 0040-9898 = Toward freedom

   b) Colons
      used before other title information:
         On the contrary : articles of belief, 1946-1961.
      used between place of publication, etc., and publisher, etc.:
         New York : Macmillan

(Item b continues on page 28)

b)   Colons (cont'd)

used between the extent of item and other physical details in in the physical description area:
> 1 disc (45 min.) : 33 1/3 rpm, stereo

used between standard number and terms of availability:
> ISBN 0-87287-153-3 : $15.00

used between different parts of additions to corporate names:
> Alessandria (Italy : Province)

c)   Diagonal slashes used to indicate a statement of responsibility:
> Instrument pilot's guide / by L. W. Reithmaier

d)   Dashes used following the periods (full stops) that precede the edition area, the material specific details area, the publication, distribution, etc., area, and the series area:
> by L. W. Reithmaier. -- 2nd ed. -- Fallbrook, Calif.
> 26 cm. -- (Oxford in Asia university readings)

e)   Semicolons
used to indicate different functions of subsidiary responsibility:
> by W. W. Hellon ; photography, Woodward C. Helton and James McKinney ; illustrator, Pete Dykes

used to precede dimensions in the physical description area:
> 219 p. : ill. ; 24 cm.
> 1 score (8 p.) ; 31 cm.

used in the publication, etc., area to separate two places or two places and publishers, etc.:
> Toronto ; New York
> London : Oxford University Press ; Berkeley : University of California Press

used to precede numbering of a series or subseries:
> Studies in Nigerian languages ; no. 1

used to separate projection from statement of scale in cartographic materials:
> Scale 1:50,000 ; Transverse Mercator proj.

used to separate a new sequence of numbering from an old sequence of numbering in serials:
> No. 1 (Winter 1970)-no. 20 (Fall 1974) ; Vol. 1, no. 1 (Jan. 1975)-

f)   The plus sign used to separate accompanying materials from the dimensions in the physical description area:
> 30 cm. + 1 atlas

g)   The mark of omission (. . .) used to show omission of part of an element:
> by Jack P. Segal . . . [et al.]

5) Leave one space after

   a) all commas, closing parentheses, and closing square brackets

   b) periods (full stops) that end each area of the description or that are used after abbreviations

   c) colons that follow the introductory wording in notes:
      Title on spine: Eighteenth century Franklin County deeds

6) Leave two spaces after

   a) the period (full stop) separating the titles and statements of responsibility of works in an item lacking a collective title:
      Henry Esmond : a novel / by Thackery. Bleak house : a novel / by Dickens

   b) each item in the tracing:
      I. Title. II. Series.

7) Omit the space before all commas, periods (full stops), hyphens, closing parentheses, and closing square brackets.

8) Omit the space after all hyphens, opening parentheses, and opening square brackets.

NOTE: The peculiarities of ISBD spacing result from the dual use of punctuation marks: they can be used either as marks of punctuation or as marks of separation. The function of a mark in a particular instance determines the spacing around it. The ISBD rules for punctuation and spacing were designed for international standardization of bibliographic format so that records could be exchanged between countries, and would have clearly identifiable parts regardless of language differences or differences in meaning of punctuation marks. The ISBD rules also simplify the conversion of bibliographic records to machine-readable form.

Punctuation

1) Use commas

   a) in the statement of responsibility between names of persons or bodies performing the same function but which are not connected with a conjunction in the chief source of information:
      by Martin L. Bowers, Jon R. Carr, William Knight

   b) between the name of the publisher, etc., and the date of publication, etc., or between name of manufacturer and date of manufacture in the publication, distribution, etc., area:
      American Library Association, 1978

   c) between variations in dates in the publication, etc., area:
      1979, c1977

d)   between different pagination sections of a printed work:
        xxi, 259, 27 p., 15 leaves of plates

e)   between the series or subseries and its ISSN:
        Studies in biology, ISSN 0537-9024

f)   to separate a surname and a forename

g)   following personal names, when additions are made:
        Smith, Paul, 1941-
        John Paul II, Pope

h)   to separate a smaller place from its larger jurisdiction when both are used as an addition to a name:
        Hope Valley (Durham, N. C.)

i)   wherever required by grammar and there is no punctuation prescribed in the rules

2)   Use semicolons

a)   to indicate different functions of subsidiary responsibility:
        by John Hinterberger ; illustrated by Jacques Rupp

b)   preceding dimensions in the physical description area:
        ill. (some col.) ; 30 cm.
        1 score (28 p.) ; 28 cm.

c)   preceding the numbering of a series or subseries:
        (Studies in Nigerian languages ; no. 1)
        (Studies in biology, ISSN 0537-9024 ; no. 102)

d)   between a series of titles by the same author from a work lacking a collective title:
        Romeo and Juliet ; King Lear ; Macbeth / by
        William Shakespeare. --

e)   between two places of publication, etc., in the publication, etc., area:
        London ; New York :

f)   between two separate places of publication, etc., and publishers, etc.:
        London : Oxford University Press ; Berkeley : University of California Press

g)   between two sequences of numbering, dates, etc.:
        1941-1943 ; 1944-1947
        Vol. 10, no. 3 (Mar. 1973)-vol. 12, no. 12 (Dec.
        1975) ; no. 1 (Jan. 1976)-

h)   between statement of scale and projection in cartographic materials:
        Scale 1:50,000 ; Transverse Mercator proj.

3)   Use periods (full stops)

a)   at the end of the publication, distribution, etc., area unless the final mark of punctuation is a square bracket:
        Oxford University Press, 1979.
        Aero Publishers, 1979 [c1976]

b)   at the end of each note:
> Includes index.
> Title from container.

c)   at the end of each entry in the tracing:
> 1. Sociology.
> I. Title. II. Series.

d)   between a series of separate titles and statements of responsibility from a work lacking a collective title:
> The sorcerer's apprentice / Dukas. Night on bald mountain / Mussorgsky.

e)   preceding the title of a supplement or section:
> Journal of chemical engineering. Supplement

f)   between the title of a series and the title of a subseries:
> Pacific linguistics. Series C

g)   after abbreviations as indicated by the current usage of the language concerned:
> ill.
> min.

h)   before subheadings of a corporate body heading:
> United States. Antarctic Projects Office

4)   Use parentheses

a)   to enclose the place and name of the manufacturer:
> (London : Wiggs)

b)   to enclose the series area:
> (Books that matter)

c)   to specify the number of components as part of the extent of an item:
> 1 microfiche (140 fr.)
> 1 tape (1 hr. 15 min.)
> 3 v. (xix, 1269 p.)

d)   in the physical description area to indicate some of the illustrative matter is in color:
> ill. (some col.)

e)   for the physical details of accompanying material in the physical description area:
> 2 v. ; 32 cm. + 1 atlas (159 leaves of plates : 25 col. maps ; 43 cm.)

f)   to enclose statements of coordinates and equinox in cartographic materials:
> (W 126° -- W 64° / N 49° -- N 23°)

g)   to enclose a date following a numeric and/or alphabetic designation:
> No. 1 (Jan. 1978)

h)   for designation of theses:
> Thesis (M.A.)--University of Denver, 1978.

i)   to enclose qualifications to the standard number or terms of availability:

ISBN 0-87287-161-4 (pbk.)

$10.00 ($8.00 to students)

j)   to enclose date, number, place, or other designation added to a corporate or geographic name:

Franklin County Legal Journal (Corporation)

5)   Use colons

a)   before other title information:

Human action : a treatise on economics

French rooster : [poem]

b)   between place of publication, etc., or manufacture and the name of the publisher, etc., or manufacturer:

New York : Macmillan

c)   between the extent of item and other physical details in the physical description area:

1 globe : col., plastic, mounted on metal stand

d)   between standard number and terms of availability:

ISBN 0-87287-153-3 : $15.00

e)   between different additions to corporate names:

WUNC (Radio station : Chapel Hill, N. C.)

Symposium on Computer Applications in Medical Care (2nd : 1978 : Washington, D. C.)

f)   between the introductory wording and the main content of notes:

Bibliography: p. 190-191.

Summary: A poetical journey into the unconscious of a woman in search of personal power

First ed. published with title: Technical topics for the radio amateur.

Credits: Script, Al DeZutter.

g)   in the scale ratio in cartographic materials:

Scale 1:250,000

Note that in f) there is no space before the colon, and in g) there is no space before or after the colon. In these cases, the colon is used as a mark of punctuation rather than a mark of separation.

6)   Use period (full stop) and dash

a)   preceding the edition area, the material specific details area, the publication, distribution, etc., area, and the series area:

/ drawn by Robert Morgan. -- Rev. ed. -- Scale 1:500,000. -- London :

; 78 x 80 cm. -- (World climatology series)

In the cases in a) the format is period-space-hyphen-hyphen-space. The dash is represented by two hyphens on the typewriter.

b)   for sequence in a contents note:
   Contents: The ethic of the group / L. C.
   Eisley.--Science and human values / G.
   Seldes.--Law and the limits / W. Hurst.

In this case, the format is period-hyphen-hyphen. There is no space before or after the dash. NOTE: This punctuation is not prescribed in *AACR 2* but is given here for the instruction of the typist.

7)   Dashes are used in theses notes:
   Thesis (Ph.D.)--Yale, 1979.

Note that there is no space before or after the dash.

8)   Diagonal slashes are used before the statement of responsibility in the title and statement of responsibility area, the edition area, the series area, and the contents note:
   Introduction to sociology / Paul Sites
   (Reports / British Library, Research & Development ; no. 5416)

9)   Use equals signs

a)   before parallel titles:
   La nuit : Etüde für Klavier = Night : piano study

b)   before alternative numbering systems in serials:
   Vol. 4, no. 1-   = No. 13-

c)   before a key title in the standard number area:
   ISSN 0190-1427 = AJS update

10)   Plus signs are used to separate accompanying materials from the dimensions in the physical description area:
   30 cm. + 1 disc

11)   Question marks are used to denote

a)   conjectural additions:
   [Pittsburg? Calif.]
   Pittsburg [Calif.?]

b)   uncertain dates:
   [1892?]
   [189-?]
   [18--?]

12)   Use hyphens

a)   to follow the numeric and/or alphabetic designation and/or the date of first issue of a serial:
   No. 1 (Jan. 1978)-

13) Use square brackets

    a)   to show that the information enclosed has been supplied from a source other than the prescribed source of information according to *AACR 2.*

        Cristiana [Oslo]
        3^e [ed.]
        French rooster : [poem]

(The prescribed sources of information vary according to the specified area of the record and the type of material being cataloged. These are discussed in general in chapter 3 of this textbook, and more specifically in chapters 4-14.)

    b)   to enclose the general material designation (GMD):

        The curious campaign of the comma king [filmstrip]

It should be noted that adjacent elements in one area that require square brackets, should be enclosed in the same set, except for the GMD which is always enclosed in its own square brackets:

        -- [S.1. : s.n., 1974?]

Elements in different areas that require brackets are each enclosed in their own set of brackets:

        / [Compiler, Dencho Vlaev]. -- [Sofia] :

14) Omissions of parts of elements, such as an unimportant part of a long title, or all but the first responsible party when more than three are named, are indicated by three dots, called "the mark of omission":

        The Dickens concordance, being a compendium of names and characters and principal places in all the works of Charles Dickens . . .

        / [edited by] Henry P. David . . . [et al.]

It should be noted that omissions of *entire* elements or areas are not indicated by the mark of omission.

Capitalization

The rules for capitalization, in general, follow standard style for the language involved. Rules for capitalization are given extensive coverage in *AACR 2,* Appendix A, first covering rules in general and then giving specific rules by language. An important exception to normal usage is that a title is written like an ordinary sentence; the first word is capitalized, e.g.,

    The will to live
    Act one.

If, however, the main entry of a work is its title proper, and if the first word of such a title is an article, the next word is also capitalized, e.g.,

The Will to live.
An Introduction to the physical sciences.

The capitalization of other words in the title is governed by ordinary rules for capitalization; e.g.,

Across five Aprils.
The Spirit of St. Louis.

The first word of every title, alternative title, or parallel title is capitalized, e.g.,

Letters from the West, or, A caution to emigrants.
El gato = The cat.

Abbreviations

Abbreviations are used except in the recording of titles and statements of responsibility wherever they fall in the description and in quoted notes. Acceptable abbreviations are those listed in *AACR 2*, Appendix B. Some abbreviations may be used only for the heading (*see* B.2), and single letter abbreviations are not used to begin a note. When in doubt, the cataloger should *not* abbreviate.

Numerals

Rules for numerals are given in *AACR 2*, Appendix C. There are rules prescribing when to substitute arabic for roman numerals; when to spell out numerals; when to substitute Western-style numerals for Oriental numerals; and how to record inclusive numbers, alternative dates, and ordinal numerals.

PRE-ISBD CATALOGING FORMAT

Before the introduction of ISBD in the United States in 1974, the cataloging differed from present cataloging in some ways. Less information was recorded, but what was given appeared in basically the same order as that information does now. The punctuation and spacing was simpler, in one sense, because punctuation was used only for punctuating, not also for separating areas and elements of description. In another sense, however, there was more difficulty in judging, for example, whether to use a comma, semicolon, or colon before a subtitle. And because "double punctuation" was strictly avoided, new catalogers often had difficulty learning, for example, not to precede or follow a square bracket with the comma or period called for by rules of grammar (e.g., the correct form was [New York] Macmillan [1961] *not* [New York], Macmillan, [1961].) A side-by-side comparison of ISBD punctuation and pre-ISBD punctuation may be found in *Cataloging with Copy*, Appendix F,[8] and many examples of pre-ISBD copy appear throughout the book.

CONCLUSION

This chapter has presented an overview of the entire cataloging process. Greater detail about the content of description is discussed in chapters 3-15. Choice and form of headings is covered in chapters 16-20. Subject analysis is given thorough treatment in Part III, with chapters 22-25 devoted to classification, and chapters 26-28 devoted to subject headings. The final Part deals in more detail with networking, computer cataloging, and with cataloging routines and end processes.

FOOTNOTES

[1] *Anglo-American Cataloguing Rules*, 2nd ed. (Chicago, American Library Association, 1978).

[2] A good discussion of the historical development of cataloging practices is presented in an article written by Charles Martel, "Cataloging: 1876-1926," reprinted in *The Catalog and Cataloging*, edited by A. R. Rowland (Hamden, CT, Shoe String Press, 1969), pp. 40-50.

[3] A listing of libraries with COM catalogs and a bibliography may be found in *Commercial COM Catalogs: How to Choose, When to Buy*, compiled by the Catalog Use Committee, Reference and Adult Services Division, American Library Association for use at a workshop held during the 1978 ALA Annual Conference.

[4] Charles A. Cutter, *Rules for a Dictionary Catalog*, 4th ed. (Washington, GPO, 1904), p. 12.

[5] International Conference on Cataloguing Principles. Paris, 9th-18th October, 1961, *Report* (London, International Federation of Library Associations, 1963), p. 26.

[6] Julia Pettee, "Development of Authorship Entry and the Formulation of Authorship Rules as Found in the Anglo-American Code," *Library Quarterly* 6 (July 1936): 271.

[7] Sally Hart McCallum, "Some Implications of Desuperimposition," *Library Quarterly* 47 (April 1977): 114.

[8] Arlene Taylor Dowell, *Cataloging with Copy* (Littleton, CO, Libraries Unlimited, 1976), pp. 258-66.

2 DEVELOPMENT OF CATALOGING CODES

The *Anglo-American Cataloguing Rules*, second edition (*AACR 2*), is the result of a progression of ideas about how to approach the cataloging process in order to prepare catalogs that provide the best possible access to library collections. *AACR 2* represents the current agreements that have been reached in order to standardize cataloging practice and thereby facilitate cooperation among libraries. It expands on the agreements presented in earlier codes and forms the basis for further agreements that will be added to future codes.

The first cataloging rules were prepared by individuals. Panizzi's British Museum *Rules for the Compiling of the Catalogue* (1841) was the first major modern statement of principles underlying cataloging rules; as such, it has exerted an influence on every Western world code that has been published since its publication. Cutter's *Rules for a Dictionary Catalog*, in its fourth edition at his death in 1903, presented the first complete set of rules for a dictionary catalog. From the beginning of the twentieth century codes have been drawn up by committees, but the influence of those early farsighted individuals continued through LC *Rules on Printed Cards* (1903 through the 1930s), LC *Rules for Descriptive Cataloging* (1949), ALA *Rules* (1908, 1941, 1949), *AACR 1* (published in 1967), and the present *AACR 2*.

The ALA *Rules* of 1908 were the result of a seven-year study by a committee of ALA and the (British) Library Association. In 1901 the Library of Congress began its printed card service, with the result that libraries became interested in ways to use LC cards with their own cards. One of the important responsibilities of the committee was to formulate rules to encourage incorporation of LC printed cards into catalogs of other libraries. The committee attempted to reconcile the cataloging practices of LC with those of other research and scholarly libraries. The use of LC cards increased dramatically between 1908 and 1941; standardization of library catalogs progressed. However, the ALA *Rules* were not expanded during this 33-year period, drastically curtailing attempts of cataloging practice to stay in touch with cataloging done at the Library of Congress. In 1930 a subcommittee was appointed by ALA to begin work on a revision of cataloging rules, and the problems were outlined. Dissatisfaction with the 1908 code was expressed on the grounds of "omissions"; the basic rules were not in question. Expansion was required to meet the needs of large scholarly libraries or specialized collections:

> The preliminary edition, published in 1941, expanded the rules of 1908 to make more provision for special classes of material: serial publications, government documents, publications of religious bodies, anonymous classics, music and maps; to amplify existing rules to cover specific cases of frequent occurrence.[1]

The revised edition of 1949 states that,

> the chief changes from the preliminary edition are a rearrangement
> of the material to emphasize the basic rules and subordinate their
> amplifications, and to make the sequence of rules logical as far as
> possible; reduction of the number of alternate rules; omission of
> rules for description; rewording to avoid repetition or to make the
> meaning clearer; and revision, where possible, of rules inconsistent
> with the general principles.[2]

The 1941 and 1949 rules were sharply criticized for being too elaborate
and often arbitrary; emphasis had shifted from clearly defined principles to a
collection of rules developed to fit specific cases rather than the conditions that
the cases illustrated. Lubetzky commented that any logical approach to
cataloging problems was blocked by the maze of arbitrary and repetitious rules
and exceptions to rules.[3]

ANGLO-AMERICAN CATALOGING RULES, 1967 (AACR 1)

The Catalog Code Revision Committee that prepared the 1967 *Anglo-
American Cataloging Rules* realized that revision must be a complete re-
examination of the principles and objectives of cataloging, not merely a
revision of specific rules. First, the objectives of the catalog were agreed upon;
it was further decided that certain general principles should be the basis for
rules of entry and heading. These general principles of the new code were
based on the "Statement of Principles" approved by 53 countries at the International Conference on Cataloguing Principles in Paris, October 1961. This
was an important step toward international bibliographical standardization.

AACR 1 was oriented toward large research libraries, although in a few
instances of obvious conflict, alternate rules were provided for use by non-
research libraries. Unlike the 1949 ALA code which was only for entry and
heading, *AACR 1* incorporated rules for entry and heading, description, and
cataloging of non-book material. An important shift occurred in the
philosophy underlying the rules for entry: "The entry for a work is normally
based on the statements that appear on the title page or any part of the work
that is used as its substitute."[4] This meant that information appearing only in
the preface, introduction, or text was not to be considered unless title page
information was vague or incomplete. Another basic shift in point of view was
to that of cataloging by types of authorship rather than by types of works, and
by classes of names rather than classes of people.

Unlike earlier codes, *AACR 1* emphasized that choice of entry was a completely separate activity from construction of the heading used for the entry
chosen. General principles became the basis for the rules for choice of entry:

1) Entry should be under author or principal author when one can be
   determined.

2) Entry should be under title in the case of works whose authorship is
   diffuse, indeterminate, or unknown.

Application of rules based on these principles continued the practice of choosing a main entry, with other names and/or titles becoming added entries. However, the choice was no longer a result of first determining the type of work involved and then finding the specific rule for that type.

The construction of the headings for names that were to be main or added entries centered on two problems: choice of a particular name, and the form in which that name is presented in the heading. Rules for form of name became based on a general principle of using the form of name used by a person or corporate body rather than the full name or official name as the 1949 ALA *Rules* directed. Thus a person could be entered under an assumed name, nickname, changed name, etc. However, a person who used both his or her real name and an assumed name was still entered under the real name, and a person who used a full form of a forename, even though rarely, was entered under the fullest form ever used. Another change was to use a firmly-established English form of name rather than the vernacular form for many well-known names (e.g., Horace, not Horatius Flaccus, Quintus).

Another very important area of change was in the form of entry for corporate bodies. The general rule followed the principle of using the form of name the body itself uses. Entry was usually under that form of name except when the rules provided for entry under a higher body or under the name of the government. However, the North American text gave exceptions exempting specified bodies of an institutional nature from the principle of entry under name; these were to be entered under place as in the old rules. These exceptions were contrary to the Paris Principles and to the British text of *AACR 1*, but they had been requested by the Association of Research Libraries, whose member libraries feared being overburdened with the necessity for changing thousands of entries already in catalogs.

The fear of the research libraries was also eased by the Library of Congress' January 1967 announcement of the policy of superimposition:

> This means that the rules for choice of entry will be applied only to works that are new to the Library and that the rules for headings will be applied only to persons and corporate bodies that are being established for the first time. New editions, etc., of works previously cataloged will be entered in the same way as the earlier editions (except for revised editions in which change of authorship is indicated). New works by previously established authors will appear under the same headings.[5]

This policy has continued throughout the duration of the application of *AACR 1*. As a result, thousands of headings have been made in a form created under the 1949 ALA *Rules* or earlier rules on bibliographic records that are otherwise *AACR 1* records. The abandonment of the policy of superimposition with the implementation of *AACR 2* is a major step toward ultimate user-convenience in finding entries and will improve international cooperation; but for many large libraries, thousands of entries in pre-*AACR* form already in catalogs will have to be dealt with.

In 1974 the rule in *AACR 1* for corporate body entry under place was dropped. But because of superimposition, only new corporate bodies were established and entered under their own names. Besides this change, some forty other rules were changed, and three chapters were totally revised in the years following publication of *AACR 1*. Perhaps the most significant change was the application of standards of bibliographic description, based on International Standard Bibliographic Description (ISBD), to descriptive cataloging of monographs, audiovisual media, and special instructional materials. ISBD facilitates the international exchange of bibliographic information by standardizing the elements to be used in the bibliographic description, assigning an order to these elements in the entry, and specifying a system of symbols to be used in punctuating these elements. (These symbols were discussed and illustrated in chapter 1 of this text.) In addition:

> ISBD requires that a publication be totally identified by the description. It is independent of the provisions for headings, main or added, and of the provisions for the use of uniform titles; these were internationally standardized by the Paris Principles.[6]

ANGLO-AMERICAN CATALOGUING RULES, SECOND EDITION (AACR 2)

The numerous changes to rules in *AACR 1* and the progress toward an international standard for description not only of monographs, but of serials and all media, were two of the reasons for the meeting in 1974 of representatives of the national library associations and national libraries of Canada, the United Kingdom, and the United States to plan for the preparation of *AACR 2*. Two other reasons were a proliferation of other rules for non-book materials that reflected dissatisfaction with *AACR 1* treatment of these materials and LC's announcement of intention to abandon the policy of superimposition.[7] The objectives established at that meeting were:

1) To reconcile in a single text the North American and British texts of 1967

2) To incorporate in the single text all amendments and changes already agreed and implemented under the previous mechanisms

3) To consider for inclusion in AACR all proposals for amendment currently under discussion between the American Library Association, the Library Association, the Library of Congress, and the Canadian Library Association; any new proposals put forward by these bodies and the British Library; and any proposals of national committees of other countries in which AACR is in use

4) To provide for international interest in AACR by facilitating its use in countries other than the United States, Canada, and the United Kingdom.[8]

The representatives at the 1974 meeting also agreed to establish a Joint Steering Committee for Revision of *AACR* (JSC) made up of one voting and one non-voting representative of each author organization. The JSC was to appoint an editor from each side of the Atlantic and was generally to oversee the process of revision through to publication.

The result of the revision process was what the preface to *AACR 2* calls a continuation of the first edition: "for, in spite of the changes in presentation and content which it introduces, these are still the *Anglo-American Cataloguing Rules*, having the same principles and underlying objectives as the first edition, and being firmly based on the achievement of those who created the work, first published in 1967."[9] However, *AACR 2*, published in late 1978 but not to be implemented by the major national libraries until January 1981, has some significant differences that are worth noting here.

In the process of reconciling the North American and British texts, it was decided to use British spelling of words if the British spelling appears as an alternative in *Webster's New International Dictionary*. In cases where terminology differs, British usages have been chosen in some cases (e.g., "full stop" instead of "period"), while American usages appear in other cases (e.g., "parentheses" instead of the British "brackets").

One significant change is in the presentation of rules for description: one general chapter presents broad provisions that can be applied in many different situations. This chapter is followed by specific chapters for different types of materials and for different conditions and patterns of publication. The rules for description are deliberately less specific in legislating ways to handle certain phenomena. The cataloger is thereby encouraged to exercise judgment in interpreting the rules in light of the needs of the user being served. One possibility for such interpretation is that *AACR 2* provides three "levels" of description with increasing amounts of detail at each level. The cataloger may choose the level that provides the amount of detail relevant to the particular library's users, and, at the same time, meet the standards called for in a set of international cataloging rules.

In the rules for choice of access points, it is significant that less emphasis has been placed on "main" entry, although the concept is still present. However, many people believe that when multiple access points are readily available, and when the bibliographic description is complete by itself, there is no need to designate one of the access points as the "main" one. This concept, then, may disappear in future codes. A significant change in choice of main entry is that a corporate body is no longer considered to be an "author." Instead, there are now specified categories of works that are entered under corporate body. This concept greatly reduces the number of corporate main entries made.

Another important change in choice of access points is the abandonment of "form subheadings" (e.g., "Laws, statutes, etc.," "Treaties, etc.," "Liturgy and ritual") for legal and religious works. In some of these cases, the function of the form subheadings is now performed by uniform titles.

Rules for form of headings for personal names now emphasize using the form of name most often used by an author (e.g., Benjamin Disraeli instead of Earl of Beaconsfield; Bernard Shaw instead of George Bernard Shaw). If an author uses more than one name and is not known predominantly by one of them, multiple headings are made for that author. For persons who are not known as authors, emphasis is on using the name that is best known.

For corporate names, too, there is more emphasis on using the name as it is used by the body, removing provisions for inverting, amplifying, etc., that appeared in *AACR 1* (e.g., W. K. Kellogg Arabian Horse Center instead of

Kellogg (W. K.) Arabian Horse Center). Geographic names are treated more internationally (e.g., states of Australia and counties of England are treated like states of the United States).

A detailed list of the changes in *AACR 2* may be found in the article "AACR 2: Background and Summary" cited in footnote 7. This article also points out some general advantages of *AACR 2*. First, *AACR 2* lays the groundwork for much more international and national cooperative cataloging, which is expected to improve greatly library service of a bibliographic nature and to result in considerable cost savings. Second, by providing the framework for standard description of all library materials, it makes possible an integrated, multimedia catalog. Third, it is expected to reduce user search time by providing headings that conform more often to the forms found in works and citations. Fourth, personal name headings are expected to be more stable than formerly, thus reducing catalog maintenance costs.[10]

Rule interpretations made by LC in their process of applying *AACR 2* are published regularly in *Cataloging Service Bulletin*. Official changes made to the rules are also published there. In an attempt to reduce costs of implementing *AACR 2*, LC has chosen to allow certain already established names to continue to be used in pre-*AACR 2* form when the change would be relatively insignificant and does not affect the first entry element of any name and in some cases, later elements of a famous name. A list of these "compatible" headings has also been published.[11] Other libraries must decide whether to follow LC's lead in this implementation. For those that use LC copy, however, the cost of not following LC may be prohibitive. Even following LC, however, the administrative problems of applying new rules within a catalog based on several earlier sets of rules require full and intense study. Some libraries have felt that they must close existing catalogs and start new ones with the new rules.[12] Others have decided that if LC's projection is correct—that 11 percent of all headings are different according to the LC implementation of *AACR 1*—the solution should be to absorb the 11 percent into the existing catalog by interfiling, providing *See also* cross references, or changing old headings to the new form.[13]

It is hoped that chapters 3 through 21 of this text will prove helpful in illustrating the basic rules. The complete *AACR 2* should be consulted for additional rules covering aspects of problems too detailed for inclusion in this text, and for further explanations, definitions, and references.

FOOTNOTES

[1]*A.L.A. Cataloging Rules for Author and Title Entries* (Chicago, American Library Association, 1949), p. viii.

[2]*A.L.A. Cataloging Rules*, p. ix.

[3]Seymour Lubetzky, *Cataloging Rules and Principles: A Critique of the ALA Rules for Entry and a Proposed Design for Their Revision* (Washington, Processing Department, Library of Congress, 1953); also, by the same author, *Code of Cataloging Rules, Author, and Title; an Unfinished Draft . . . with an Explanatory Commentary by Paul Dunkin* (Washington, American Library Association, 1960).

[4]*Anglo-American Cataloging Rules, North American Text* (Chicago, American Library Association, 1967), p. 9. (*AACR 1* was issued in two editions: the North American text and the British text.)

[5]Library of Congress, Processing Department, *Cataloging Service*, bulletin 79 (Jan. 1967): 1.

[6]"International Standard Bibliographic Description," *Cataloging Service*, bulletin 105 (Nov. 1972):2.

[7]"AACR 2: Background and Summary," *Library of Congress Information Bulletin* 37 (Oct. 20, 1978):640.

[8]*Anglo-American Cataloguing Rules*, 2nd ed. (Chicago, American Library Association, 1978), pp. vi-vii.

[9]*AACR 2*, p. v.

[10]"AACR 2: Background and Summary," p. 652.

[11]"Implementation of AACR 2 at the Library of Congress," *Cataloging Service Bulletin*, no. 6 (Fall 1979):5-8.

[12]Richard M. Dougherty, "Closing the Card Catalog: A Survey on the Status of Planning in ARL Libraries," in: *Freezing Card Catalogs* (Washington, Association of Research Libraries, 1978); S. Michael Malinconico and Paul J. Fasana, *The Future of the Catalog: The Library's Choices* (White Plains, NY, Knowledge Industry Publications, 1979); Joseph Rosenthal, "Planning for the Catalogs: A Managerial Perspective," in: Association of Research Libraries, *Minutes of the Ninety-Second Meeting*, May 4-5, 1978, Nashville, TN, pp. 33-39, also in *Freezing Card Catalogs* (Washington, Association of Research Libraries, 1978). *See also* the discussion in chapter 32 of this text.

[13]Arlene Taylor Dowell, "Staying Open in 1981," *HCL Cataloging Bulletin*, no. 39 (March/April 1979):11-15; Joe A. Hewitt and David E. Gleim, "Adopting AACR 2: The Case for Not Closing the Catalog," *American Libraries* 10 (March 1979):118-21.

3 GENERAL RULES FOR DESCRIPTION

INTRODUCTION

This chapter covers in some detail the rules for descriptive cataloging. (A basic introduction to description and basic definitions are given in the first chapter of this text.) Only the more general rules are covered here, however. The reader should carefully examine *AACR 2*, chapter 1, for more complex problems.

The first chapter of *AACR 2* covers description in general and is applicable to all types of materials (e.g., print, sound recordings, etc.) in all conditions (e.g., microform), and patterns (e.g., serial) of publication. Chapters 2 through 12 of *AACR 2* cover in detail various types of material and conditions and patterns of publication. These chapters often refer back to chapter 1 for rules that are generally applicable, but they also give specific guidance for situations that are peculiar to the type of material or condition of publication under discussion. Chapters 2 through 12 cover:

2	Books, Pamphlets, and Printed Sheets
3	Cartographic Materials
4	Manuscripts (including Manuscript Collections) ˙
5	Music
6	Sound Recordings
7	Motion Pictures and Videorecordings
8	Graphic Materials
9	Machine-Readable Data Files
10	Three-Dimensional Artifacts and Realia
11	Microforms
12	Serials

Chapter 13, rather than dealing with a type of material or condition of publication, covers a special problem in cataloging: analysis. These *AACR 2* chapters are covered in chapters 4 through 15 of this text. There are purposely no chapters numbered 14 through 20 in *AACR 2*. These numbers were left vacant for later construction of rules for new types of material (e.g., holograms) as it becomes necessary to develop rules for cataloging them.

An important concept in using chapters 1 through 12 of *AACR 2* is that the rule numbers are mnemonic. In ISBD there are eight "areas" of description as follows:

1	Title and statement of responsibility area
2	Edition area
3	Material (or type of publication) specific details area
4	Publication, distribution, etc., area

5   Physical description area
6   Series area
7   Note area
8   Standard number and terms of availability area

Not all areas are used in describing all library materials, but in chapters 1 to 12 of *AACR 2*, all are mentioned, if only to say that the area in question is not used to describe the particular material (e.g., Rule 2.3, Material (or Type of Publication) Specific Details Area: "This area is not used for printed monographs."). The rules are numbered in such a way that the number preceding the period is the chapter number and the number following the period is the rule number. Rules 1 through 8 in each chapter represent the eight "areas" named above. Thus, Rule 1.2 deals with the edition area in general, while Rule 5.2 covers the edition area for music, and Rule 8.2 covers the edition area for graphic materials. Further, the rule numbers are subdivided by letters sometimes followed by numerals which are also mnemonic. In the general chapter, Rule 1.1D is the rule for parallel titles; for books, the comparable rule is 2.1D, and for serials it is 12.1D. In addition to the rules for "areas," all the chapters have general rules assigned the numeral "0." Chapters 1-2 and 5-12 also have rules 9 "Supplementary items," and 10 "Items made up of several types of materials." These rules do not all have exactly the same heading, but address the same concept (e.g., Rule 10 for serials is entitled, "Sections of Serials"). Chapters 1-3, 5, and 8 have a Rule 11 "Facsimiles, Photocopies, and Other Reproductions." However, Rule 11 for sound recordings is somewhat different, being entitled, "Nonprocessed Sound Recordings" and deals with unique recordings rather than reproductions. Chapter 2 has, in addition, Rules 12 through 18 that deal specifically with early printed monographs.

Throughout *AACR 2* there are "optional" rules that allow for adding or deleting information in certain instances, or that allow alternative methods of handling certain situations. Each cataloging agency must decide whether and how these options will be applied. Because so many libraries rely on the Library of Congress for cataloging data, this text includes, in this chapter and the ones on *AACR 2* that follow, a discussion of LC's decision about application of each option as it occurs in the rule sequence.

RULE 1.0.   GENERAL RULES

1.0A.   Sources of information

1.0A1.   "Each chapter in Part I contains a specification of the chief source of information for each material or type of publication covered by that chapter. . . . Prefer information found in that chief source to information found elsewhere. . . . Enclose in square brackets information taken from outside the prescribed source or sources."

1.0A2.   "Items lacking a chief source of information." This may be a problem with such items as locally produced sound recordings. If the item cannot be used as a basis for description, take the information from any available source and give a note explaining the source of the supplied data.

1.0C.   Punctuation

Punctuation is covered in detail in the first chapter of this text and so is not discussed here or at the beginning of each "area" of the description. Most areas in most chapters have a rule numbered "A1" (1.1A1, 1.2A1, 1.4A1, etc.) in which detailed guidance for punctuation of specific areas of the description is given.

1.0D.   Levels of detail in the description

"The elements of description provided in the rules in this and in following chapters constitute a maximum set of information. This rule sets out three recommended levels of description containing those elements that must be given as a minimum. . . ." Figs. 3.1 and 3.2 illustrate the first and second levels for the same item. The third level includes every possible element set out in the rules and is likely to be used only in cataloging such things as rare items.

Fig. 3.1. Rule 1.0D1. First level of description.

Facing zero population growth. -- Duke University Press, 1978.
xiv, 288 p.

Bibliography: p. [241]-277.
Includes indexes.
ISBN 0-8223-0412-0

Note: Cataloging to the first level of description requires use of only Rules 1.1B, 1.1F, 1.2B, 1.3, 1.4D, 1.4F, 1.5B, 1.7, and 1.8B.

Fig. 3.2. Rule 1.0D2. Second level of description.

Facing zero population growth : reactions and interpretations, past and present / Joseph J. Spengler. – Durham, N.C. : Duke University Press, 1978.

xiv, 288 p. ; 25 cm. – (Studies in social and economic demography ; 1)

Bibliography: p. [241]-277.
Includes indexes.
ISBN 0-8223-0412-0 : $18.75

1.0E.   Language and script of the description

In general, information given in the title and statement of responsibility, edition, publication, and series areas is transcribed in the language as given in the item. Elements in other areas are given in the language of the cataloging agency.

1.0F.   Inaccuracies

"Transcribe an inaccuracy or a misspelled word as it appears in the item. Follow such an inaccuracy either by *[sic]* or by the abbreviation *i.e.* and the correction within square brackets. Supply a missing letter or letters in square brackets." *See* Figs. 3.3 and 3.4.

Fig. 3.3. Rule 1.0F. Correction of inaccuracies.

Obvious error
indicated by
[sic]

The Lekwa family/= Familien Lekva / written and published by Verl L. Lekwa from material gathered by he [sic] and Barbara Jean Lekwa Sansgaard and James Ernest Sansgaard. -- Columbus Junction, Iowa : V. L. Lekwa, 1973.

129 p. : ill. ; 23 cm.

Fig. 3.4. Rule 1.0F. Correction of inaccuracies.

Abbreviation,
"i.e." with cor-
rection in square
brackets

The 1866 census records of Jackson and Kannebec [i.e. Kanabec] Counties, Minnesota / Sherman Lee Pompey. -- Independence, Calif. : Historical and Genealogical Pub. Co., c1965.

[6] leaves ; 28 cm.

Cover title.

1.0H.   Items with several chief sources of information

Single part items. An item that has more than one chief source of information should generally be described from the first one, with a few major exceptions outlined in this rule. For example, in cataloging sound recordings, two or more chief sources of information (e.g., labels on both sides of a disc) should be treated as a single source. Also, the chief source with the latest date of publication, distribution, etc., should be preferred. In addition, *AACR 2* prescribes preferences to follow by language, if there are different languages in the chief source (*See AACR 2*, pp. 16-17).

Multipart items. The chief source of information for the first part of a multipart item should be used for the basic description, with variations in later parts shown in notes. If the first part is missing, use the first part that is available. If there is no "first" part, use the part that gives the most information or the unifying container.

RULE 1.1.   TITLE AND STATEMENT OF RESPONSIBILITY AREA

1.1A.   Preliminary Rule

1.1A2.   Sources of information

"Take information recorded in this area from the chief source of information for the material. . . .

"Record the elements of data in the prescribed order, even if this means transposing data, unless case endings are affected, or the grammatical construction of the data would be disturbed, or one element is inseparably linked to another. In the latter cases, transcribe the data as found."

1.1B.   **Title proper**

1.1B1.   "Transcribe the title proper exactly as to wording, order, and spelling, but not necessarily as to punctuation and capitalization." *See* Fig. 3.5.

**Fig. 3.5. Rule 1.1B1. Transcription of title using exact words,
but inserting commas and changing capitalization.**

Chief source of information: Feeling Mad
                             Feeling Sad
                             Feeling Bad
                             Feeling Glad

Transcription: Feeling mad, feeling sad, feeling bad, feeling glad.

"An alternative title is part of the title proper (see Glossary, Appendix D). Follow the first part of the title and the word *or* (or equivalent) with commas and capitalize the first word of the alternative title." *See* Fig. 3.6.

Fig. 3.6. Rule 1.1B1. Transcription of alternative title as part of title proper.

Alternative   Maria, or, The wrongs of woman / by Mary
title   Wollstonecraft ; with an introduction by Moira
                Ferguson. -- New York : Norton, [1975]

1.1B2.   "If the title proper includes a statement of responsibility or the name of a publisher, distributor, etc., and the statement or name is an integral part of the title proper (i.e., connected by a case ending or other grammatical construction), transcribe it as such." *See* Fig. 3.7.

Fig. 3.7. Rule 1.1B2. Transcription of title proper including author's name.

Bill Collins' Book of movies. -- Stanmore, N.S.W. : Cassell Australia, 1977.

236 p. : ill. ; 30 cm.

ISBN 0-7269-1376-6(bound). -- ISBN 0-7269-1369-3(pbk.)

1.1B4. "Abridge a long title proper only if this can be done without loss of essential information. Never omit the first five words of the title proper (excluding the alternative title). Indicate omissions by the mark of omission [. . .]." *See* Fig. 3.8.

Fig. 3.8. Rule 1.1B4. Abridgement of long title proper.

Hearings before the Subcommittee on the Rules and Organization of the House of the Committee on Rules, House of Representatives, Ninety-fifth Congress, second session . . . – Washington, D.C. : G.P.O., 1979.

1.1B7. "Supply a title proper for an item lacking the prescribed chief source of information or its substitute from the rest of the item, or a reference source, or elsewhere. If no title can be found in any source, devise a brief descriptive title. Enclose such a supplied or devised title in square brackets." *See* Fig. 3.9.

Fig. 3.9. Rule 1.1B7. Devised title proper enclosed in square brackets.

[Map of Kerr Lake Recreation Area, North Carolina]

1.1C. *Optional addition.* **General material designation**

1.1C1. "Choose one of the lists of general material designations given below.

"The following general material designations are recommended for British and North American use. If general material designations are to be used in cataloguing, British agencies should use terms from list 1 and North American agencies, terms from list 2."

Note: This is one time that *AACR 2* prescribes different practices for British and American catalogers.

LIST 1	LIST 2
cartographic material	{ map { globe
graphic	{ art original (chart { filmstrip { flash card { picture { slide (technical drawing 'transparency

(List continues on page 50)

machine-readable data file	machine-readable data file
manuscript	manuscript
microform	microform
motion picture	motion picture
multimedia	kit
music	music
	$\left\{\begin{array}{l}\text{diorama} \\ \text{game} \\ \text{microscope slide} \\ \text{model} \\ \text{realia}\end{array}\right.$
object	
sound recording	sound recording
text	text
videorecording	videorecording

"Use the terms from the list chosen in all descriptions for which general material designations are desired."

The Library of Congress plans to follow this option in its machine-readable records by indicating the general material designation [GMD] for each item cataloged. However, in eye-readable forms of the records LC will continue to display GMDs to the same extent as under *AACR 1*, with the addition of microforms.[1]

It should be noted that by making the North American list more detailed, *AACR 2* may cause a problem for North American catalogers. Because terms are very specific, there may be no term for some items. For example, a toy is not really a "game" or a "model" nor do any other terms fit. Yet the British term "object" would fit nicely.

1.1C2. "If an item consists of material falling within one category in the list chosen, add the appropriate designation immediately following the title proper." For example:

Fig. 3.9a. Rule 1.1C2. GMD following the title proper.

Scared straight! [motion picture]

Basic concepts of humanistic psychology [sound recording]

Great musicals of the American theatre [text]

1.1C3. "If the item is a reproduction in one material of a work originally presented in another material (e.g., a text as microform; a map on a slide), give the general material designation appropriate to the material being described. . . ." For example, this videorecording, although originally issued as a 16mm motion picture, would be entered as:

The Americans, 1776 [videorecording]

This set of 105 slides which was originally issued as a filmstrip would be entered as:

Blood pressure [slide]

1.1C4. "If an item contains parts belonging to materials falling into two or more categories in the list chosen and if none of these is the predominant constituent of the item, give the designation *multimedia* or *kit* (see 1.1C1 and 1.10)." For example, the following item contains one book, one sound cassette, one poster, two puppets and an activity guide, but would be entered as:

Why mosquitoes buzz in people's ears [kit]

1.1D.   **Parallel titles**

1.1D1.   "Record parallel titles in the order indicated by their sequence on, or by the layout of, the chief source of information." See Fig. 3.10.

Fig. 3.10. Rule 1.1D1. Transcription of parallel title.

¹Sign for parallel title

1

La motoneige au Québec = Snowmobiling in Quebec. – Québec : Direction générale du tourisme, [1972]

₂

²Parallel title

70 p. ; 18 cm.

Cover title.
French and English.
Includes index.

1.1D2.   "In preparing a second-level description (see 1.0D2), give the first parallel title. Give any subsequent parallel title that is in English. . . ." See Fig. 3.11.

Fig. 3.11. Rule 1.1D2. Transcription of a second parallel title that is in English.

Divertimento a flauto traverso con fagotto = Divertimento für Querflöte und Fagott = Divertimento for flute and fagott.

"In preparing a third-level description (see 1.0D3), transcribe all parallel titles appearing in the chief source of information. . . ."

1.1D4.   "Record parallel titles appearing outside the chief source of information in a note (see 1.7B5)."

1.1E.   Other title information

1.1E1.   "Transcribe all other title information appearing in the chief source of information according to the instructions in 1.1B." *See* Figs. 3.12, 3.13, and 3.14.

Fig. 3.12. Rule 1.1E1. Transcription of other title information.

Subtitle

The midnight patrol : the story of a Salvation Army lass who patrolled the dark streets of London's west end on a midnight mission of mercy / by Phyllis Thompson. -- London : Hodder and Stoughton, 1974.

155 p. ; 21 cm.

Bibliography: p. 157.
ISBN 0-340-17896-5 : £2.10

Fig. 3.13. Rule 1.1E1. Transcription of two kinds of other title information.

[1]Subtitle

[2]Other title information

The American view : art from 1770 to 1978 : Kennedy Galleries, December 6, 1978 to January 6, 1979. -- New York : The Galleries, [c1978]

[88] p. : ill. (some col.) ; 28 cm.

Includes index.

Fig. 3.14. Rule 1.1E1. Transcription of other title information following GMD.

[1]GMD

[2]Other title information

The Scales of justice [filmstrip] : our court system / Center for Humanities, Inc. -- White Plains, N.Y. : Guidance Associates, 1979.

1.1E3.   Lengthy other title information
"If the other title information is lengthy, either give it in a note (see 1.7B5) or abridge it." *See* Fig. 3.15.

Fig. 3.15. Rule 1.1E3. Abridgement of lengthy other title information.

Amtrak authorization : hearings before the Subcommittee on Transportation and Commerce of the Committee on Interstate and Foreign Commerce, House of Representatives, Ninety-fifth Congress, second session, on H.R. 11493 ... H.R. 11089 ... March 20, 21, and April 5, 1978. – Washington, D.C. : G.P.O., 1978.

Abridged other title information

v, 221 p. ; 24 cm.

"Serial no. 95-125."

1.1E5.   "Transcribe other title information following the title proper or parallel title to which it pertains." *See* Fig. 3.16.

Fig. 3.16. Rule 1.1E5. Transcription of other title information following title proper or parallel title to which it is appropriate.

La nuit : Etüde für Klavier = Night : piano study : op. 31, Nr. 3 / Alexander Glasunow. – Frankfurt : M. P. Belaieff, [1975]

7 p. ; 31 cm.

"M. P. Belaieff, Nr. 111."

1.1E6.   "If the title proper needs explanation, make a brief addition as other title information, in the language of the title proper." *See* Fig. 3.17. Such additions are preceded by a colon so as to distinguish them from GMDs.

Fig. 3.17. Rule 1.1E6. Addition of explanatory term as other title information.

Addition to title

Beginnings : [poems] / by Carol Lynn Pearson ; illustrated by Trevor Southey. – Garden City, N.Y. : Doubleday, 1975, c1967.

63 p. : ill. ; 24 cm.

ISBN 0-385-07711-4 : $3.95

1.1F.   **Statements of responsibility**

1.1F1.   "Record statements of responsibility appearing prominently in the item in the form in which they appear there. If a statement of responsibility is taken from a source other than the chief source of information, enclose it in square brackets." *See* Figs. 3.18-3.19.

Fig. 3.18. Rule 1.1F1. Statements of responsibility recorded as they appear in chief sources of information.

And then there's always the possibility of disappearing altogether [motion picture] / Pegarty Long. -- Malibu, Calif. : Long, 1978.

Fig. 3.18a.

Dear Dr. Stopes : sex in the 1920s / edited by Ruth Hall. -- London : Deutsch, 1978.

218 p. ; 24 cm.

ISBN 0-233-97027-4 : £6.50

Fig. 3.19. Rule 1.1F1. Statement of responsibility taken from outside chief source of information.

Statement of
authorship

Ben Oliel and Seeley / [Dorothy Wood Ewers]. -- [Crete? Ill.] : D. W. Ewers, [1966]

ca. 200 p. : 30 cm.

1.1F2. "If no statement of responsibility appears prominently in the item, neither construct one nor extract one from the content of the item." *See* Fig. 3.20.

Fig. 3.20. Rule 1.1F2. Item bearing no prominent statement of responsibility.

Blood pressure [slide]. -- Garden Grove, Calif. : Trainex Corp., [1979?]

105 slides : col. + 1 sound cassette (29 min. ; mono.), instructor's guide, and vis-u-test.

It should be noted that serials and other items often have identical titles proper (e.g., Bulletin). When no statement of responsibility is given, nondistinctive titles become a problem when the title is the main entry and when it is necessary to make an added entry for that title on the record for another work. It has been proposed that this problem should be solved with uniform titles. (*See* discussion in chapter 20.)

1.1F5. "When a single statement of responsibility names more than three persons or corporate bodies performing the same function, or with the same degree of responsibility, omit all but the first of each group of such persons or bodies. Indicate the omission by the mark of omission (...) and add *et al.* (or its equivalent in non-roman scripts) in square brackets." *See* Fig. 3.21.

Fig. 3.21. Rule 1.1F5. Transcription of statement of responsibility with more than three persons performing the same function.

[1] First named author of a group of more than three subsidiary authors

Studies in modality / Nicholas Rescher ; with the collaboration of Ruth Manor ... [et al.]. – Oxford : Blackwell, 1974.

xi, 156 p. : 22 cm. – (American philosophical quarterly monograph series ; no. 8)

[2] Mark of omission and [et al.]

Includes bibliographical references and indexes.

ISBN 0-631-11520-X : £2.30

1.1F6. "If there is more than one statement of responsibility, record them in the order indicated by their sequence on, or by the layout of, the chief source of information. . . . [In case of doubt, use] the order that makes the most sense." *See* Fig. 3.22.

Fig. 3.22. Rule 1.1F6. Transcription of more than one statement of responsibility.

Subsidiary authors

Looking backwards / Colette ; translated from the French by David Le Vay ; with an introd. by Maurice Goudeket. -- Bloomington : Indiana University Press, 1975.

214 p. ; 24 cm.

Translation of: Journal a rebours and De ma fenetre.
ISBN 0-253-14900-2

1.1F7. "Include titles and abbreviations of titles of nobility, address, honour, and distinction, initials of societies, qualifications, etc., with the names of persons in statements of responsibility if:

a)   such a title is necessary grammatically ...

b)   the omission would leave only the person's given name or surname ...

c)   the title is necessary to identify the person ...

d)   the title is a title of nobility or is a British title of honour (Sir, Dame, Lord, or Lady).

"Omit all other titles, etc., from the names of persons in statements of responsibility. Do not use the mark of omission." *See* Fig. 3.23.

**Fig. 3.23. Rule 1.1F7. Transcription of a title of address in a
statement of responsibility.**

**Title "Mrs."
necessary to
identify author**

Suppression of Mutiny, 1857-1858 / Mrs. Henry
Duberly. – New Delhi : Sirjana Press ; Ludhiana :
distributors, Book Center, 1974.

168 p. : maps ; 23 cm.

Originally published as: Campaigning experiences in Rajpootana and Central India during the suppression of the Mutiny, 1857-58. 1859.
  "First edition: India - August, 1974."
  Rs35.00

1.1F8. "Add an explanatory word or short phrase to the statement of responsibility if the relationship between the title and the person(s) or body (bodies) named in the statement is not clear." *See* Figs. 3.24 and 3.25.

**Fig. 3.24. Rule 1.1F8. Explanatory phrase added to statement of
responsibility for clarity.**

**Necessary
addition**

Modern literary manuscripts, acquired with
the aid of the Arts Council of Great Britain : an
exhibition held in the King's Library in the British
Museum, 2 July-29 September 1974 / [catalogue
compiled] by W. H. Kelliher. -- London : British
Museum for the British Library Board, 1974.

20 p. : ill., facsims. ; 25 cm.

Includes index.
ISBN 0-7131-0489-2 : £0.30

**Fig. 3.25. Rule 1.1F8. Omission of explanatory words in statement
of responsibility.**

**[1] [by] not
added**
**[2] [and] not
added**

Potters of Southern Africa / G. Clark, L. Wagner. – 1st ed. – Cape Town : C. Struik, 1974.
200 p. : ill. (some col.) ; 29 cm.

Includes index.
ISBN 0-86977-046-2

Note: In cataloging prior to 1974, both "[by]" and "[and]" would have been added to this example.

1.1F12. "Treat a noun phrase occurring in conjunction with a statement of responsibility as other title information if it is indicative of the nature of the work. . . .

"If the noun or noun phrase is indicative of the role of the person(s) or body (bodies) named in the statement of responsibility rather than of the nature of the work, treat it as a part of the statement of responsibility. . . .

"In case of doubt, treat the noun or noun phrase as part of the statement of responsibility." *See* Figs. 3.26 and 3.27.

Fig. 3.26. Rule 1.1F12. Noun phrase transcribed as other title information.

Noun phrase indicative of nature of the work

Walt Whitman's poetry : a study & a selection / by Edmond Holmes. -- Philadelphia : R. West, 1978.

132 p. ; 23 cm.

"Selections from Leaves of grass": p. [77]-132.
Originally published: London : J. Lane, 1902.
ISBN 0-8492-5220-2(bound) : $12.50

Fig. 3.27. Rule 1.1F12. Noun phrase transcribed as part of statement of responsibility.

Noun phrase indicating role of corporate body

Copyright, working within the revision law : proceedings of the Spring Copyright Conference, Seven Springs Resort, Champion, Pa., May 27-28, 1977 / conference sponsored by Pennsylvania Learning Resources Association ... [et al.]. -- [S.l.] : The Association, 1977.

168 p. ; 29 cm.

Bibliography: p. 165.
Includes index.

1.1F13. "When a name associated with responsibility for the item is transcribed as part of the title proper (see 1.1B2) or other title information (see 1.1E4), do not make any further statement relating to that name unless such a statement is required for clarity, or unless a separate statement of responsibility including or consisting of that name appears in the chief source of information." *See* Figs. 3.28 and 3.29.

Fig. 3.28. Rule 1.1F13. Person responsible is transcribed as part of the title proper and thus is not repeated as a statement of responsibility.

Horowitz in concert [sound recording] : recorded at his 1966 Carnegie Hall recitals. -- [New York] : Columbia Master works, 196-.

2 sound discs (81 min.) : 33 1/3 rpm, stereo ; 12 in.

[1]Author's name as part of the title	McGuffey's New third eclectic reader for young learners / by Wm. H. McGuffey. – New York : Gordon Press, 1974.
[2]Separate author statement	242 p. : ill. ; 24 cm.
	Originally published: New York : American Book Co., 1885. (Eclectic educational series) ISBN 0-87968-142-X

1.1G. Items without a collective title

1.1G1. "If, in an item lacking a collective title, one work is the predominant part of the item, treat the title of that part as the title proper and name the other parts in a note (see 1.7B18)."

1.1G2. "If, in an item lacking a collective title, no one part predominates, record the titles of the individually titled parts in the order in which they are named in the chief source of information, or in the order in which they appear in the item if there is no single chief source of information. Separate the titles of the parts by semicolons if the parts are all by the same person(s) or body (bodies), even if the titles are linked by a connecting word or phrase." *See* Figs. 3.30 and 3.30a.

Fig. 3.30. Rule 1.1G2. Transcription of titles of two sides of a recording
by the same person. Each title is taken from a separate label, and there is
no linking word.

African politics ; More songs from Kenya [sound recording] / David Nzomo.

Fig. 3.30a. Rule 1.1G2. Transcription of titles of two works that are published
in the same book. The title page gives the linking word "and."

Fantazias ; and, In nomines / by Henry Purcell ; edited with a foreword by Anthony Ford.

"If the individual parts are by different persons or bodies, or in case of doubt, follow the title of each part by its parallel titles, other title information, and statements of responsibility and a full stop followed by two spaces." *See* Fig. 3.31.

Fig. 3.31. Rule 1.1G2. Transcription of separate titles and statements of responsibility for work that lacks a collective title.

¹Separate title and statement of responsibility

The suicide meet / Mary Humphrey Baldridge. Pickle / by Sheila Junor-Moore. The saga of the elk / by Jim Taylor. What it means to me to be a Canadian / compiled from Calgary School children, grades 6 and 7. -- Toronto : Playwrights Co-op, 1977.

²Name-title added entries for separate titles

34 p. ; 28 cm.

ISBN 0-88754-067-8 : $3.00

2⟶ I. Junor-Moore, Sheila. Pickle. 1977. II. Taylor, Jim, 1937-   The saga of the elk. 1977. III. What it means to me to be a Canadian. IV. Title.

RULE 1.2.   EDITION AREA

1.2B.   Edition statement

1.2B1.   "Transcribe the edition statement as found on the item. Use standard abbreviations (see Appendix B) and numerals in place of words (see Appendix C)." *See* Figs. 3.32 and 3.33.

Fig. 3.32. Rule 1.2B1. Transcription of edition statement.

Export/import traffic management and forwarding / by Alfred Murr. -- 3rd ed., rev. and enl. / Cambridge, Md. : Cornell Maritime Press, 1974.

Edition with abbreviations

ix, 603 p. : forms ; 24 cm.

Bibliography: p. 594-595.
Includes index.
ISBN 0-87033-023-3 : $14.00

Fig. 3.33. Rule 1.2B1. Transcription of edition statement.

Edition with foreign abbreviations

Heidegger / Pierre Trotignon. -- 2ᵉ éd. revue et corr. -- [Paris] : Presses universitaires de France, 1974, c1965.

128 p. ; 18 cm. -- (Collection SUP. Philosophes)

Bibliography: p. [124]-126.

1.2B4. *"Optional addition.* If an item lacks an edition statement but is known to contain significant changes from previous editions, supply a suitable brief statement in the language and script of the title proper and enclose it in square brackets."

The Library of Congress is not applying this option because "there would be too much danger of bibliographic 'ghosts.' The notes area seems a better place for information of this type that the cataloger feels should be supplied."[2]

1.2C.   Statements of responsibility relating to the edition

1.2C1. "Record a statement of responsibility relating to one or more editions, but not to all editions, of a given work following the edition statement if there is one. Follow the instructions in 1.1F for the transcription and punctuation of such statements." *See* Fig. 3.34.

Fig. 3.34. Rule 1.2C1. Transcription of statement of responsibility relating to this edition but not to all editions.

Statement
of authorship
in edition
area

The Oxford school dictionary / compiled by Dorothy C. Mackenzie. – 3rd ed. / rev. by Joan Pusey. -- Oxford [England] : Clarendon Press, 1974.

xii, 371 p. ; 21 cm.

ISBN 0-19-910208-2 : £0.75

1.2C2. "In case of doubt about whether a statement of responsibility applies to all editions or only to some, or if there is no edition statement, give such a statement in the title and statement of responsibility area. When describing the first edition, give all statements of responsibility in the title and statement of responsibility area (see 1.1F)."

RULE 1.3.   MATERIAL (OR TYPE OF PUBLICATION) SPECIFIC DETAILS AREA

This area, so far, has been used only for cartographic materials and for serials. Therefore, the content of this area is discusssed in the chapters specifically devoted to the description of these materials.

RULE 1.4.   PUBLICATION, DISTRIBUTION, ETC., AREA

1.4B.   General rules

1.4B1. "This area is used to record all information about the place, name, and date of all types of publishing, distributing, releasing, and issuing activities."

1.4B6. "If the original publication details are covered by a label containing publication details relating to a reproduction, give the publication details of the reproduction in this area. Give the publication details of the original in a note if they can be easily ascertained." *See* Fig. 3.35.

Fig. 3.35. Rule 1.4B6. Publication details from label transcribed in publication, distribution, etc., area with original publication details in a note.

[1] **Publisher information relating to reproduction**

Human potentialities [sound recording] / Herbert A. Otto. – New York : J. Norton Publishers, [1974?]   [1]

1 tape reel (27 min.) : 3 3/4 ips, mono. ; 5 in.

[2] **Publication details of original**   [2]

Publisher information under label reads:
New York : McGraw-Hill, 1968

1.4B8. This rule is intended to aid in the choice of which places and names to record when there is more than one of either. The rule applies to single items or to multipart items that have more than one place and/or name involved. The names may or may not be those of agencies performing the same function in relation to the item being cataloged. The form in which to record the chosen places and names is prescribed in Rules 1.4C and 1.4D.

"If an item has two or more places of publication, distribution, etc., and/or names of publishers, distributors, etc., named in it, describe it in terms of the first named place of publication, distribution, etc., and the corresponding publisher, distributor, etc. Always add the place and name of a publisher if the first named place refers to a distributor, releasing agency, etc. If any subsequent place or name is distinguished by the layout of the source of information as being that of the principal publisher, etc., add that place and name."

A secondarily named place in the country of the cataloging agency is added (with its corresponding publisher, etc., if it has one). *See* Figs.3.36-3.38.

Fig. 3.36. Rule 1.4B8. Transcription of names of both producer and distributor.

The Plow that broke the Plains [videorecording] / United States Resettlement Administration. – Washington, D.C. : National Archives and Records Service : distributed by National Audiovisual Center, 1978.

Fig. 3.37. Rule 1.4B8. Transcription by a U.S. cataloging agency of U.S. city following foreign city.

[1] **Foreign city**

[2] **U.S. city**

Educational theory : an introduction / [by] T. W. Moore. – London ; Boston : Routledge and K. Paul, 1974.   [1]   [2]

**Fig. 3.38. Rule 1.4B8. Transcription by a U.S. cataloging agency of U.S. city
and publisher following foreign city and publisher.**

[1]**Foreign city
and publisher**

[2]**U.S. city and
publisher**

Genetics of forest ecosystems / Klaus Stern,
Laurence Roche. – London : Chapman and Hall ;
New York : Springer-Verlag, 1974.

1.4C.   **Place of publication, distribution, etc.**

1.4C1.   "Record the place of publication, etc., in the form and grammatical case in which it appears."

1.4C3.   "Add the name of the country, state, province, etc., to the name
of the place if it is considered necessary for identification, or if it is considered
necessary to distinguish the place from others of the same name. Use the
English form of name if there is one (see 23.2A). Use abbreviations appearing
in Appendix B." *See* Figs. 3.39-3.41.

**Fig. 3.39. Rule 1.4C3. Addition of country in brackets where city alone
appeared in prescribed source of information.**

**Name of Coun-
try added**

Vanished fleets : sea stories from old Van Die-
man's land / by Alan Villiers. – Cambridge [Eng-
land] : P. Stephens, 1974.

It should be noted here that in *AACR 2*, chapter 23, on geographic names, it is
prescribed that for cities in the British Isles, the county or region is added instead of the name of the country. It is not clear whether those additions are
meant to be applied under Rule 1.4C3, as well. The reader should watch for
further rule interpretations concerning this matter. If the principles in chapter
23 apply here, the addition in the above example would be "[Cambridgeshire]"
rather than "[England]."

**Fig. 3.40. Rule 1.4C3. Addition of state to name of city. Name of state
appeared in prescribed source of information and was judged necessary for
identification of the city.**

**Name of
State added**

Hans in luck [motion picture]. -- Santa Monica,
Calif. : Bosustow Productions, 1978.

**Fig. 3.41. Rule 1.4C3. Name of state not added to city even though
it appeared in prescribed source of information, because it was not considered
necessary to identify the city.**

**Name of
State not
added**

Troll tales of Tumble Town [filmstrip] / Don
Arthur Torgersen. – Chicago : Coronet Instructional Media, 1978.

1.4C6. "If the place of publication, distribution, etc., is uncertain, give the probable place in the language of the chief source of information, with a question mark." *See* Fig. 3.42.

Fig. 3.42. Rule 1.4C6. Transcription of probable place of publication with question mark.

Place uncertain

A century in Singapore : 1877-1977 / Hongkong and Shanghai Banking Corporation. – [Singapore? : Hongkong and Shanghai Banking Corp., 1977?]

"If no probable place can be given, give the name of the country, state, province, etc. If, in such a case, the country, state, province, etc., is not certain, give it with a question mark." *See* Fig. 3.43. Note: Interpretation of this new rule may cause some difficulty to catalogers. Since "Washington" can be used to refer to the state as a probable place of publication, the city of the same name must now be given as "Washington, D.C." LC intends to use Washington, D.C. whenever it appears on the source of information. No decision is available at this time concerning New York as a state versus New York as a city. Catalogers should watch for LC decisions concerning this problem.

Fig. 3.43. Rule 1.4C6. Transcription of country in lieu of city for place of publication, etc.

Name of Country

Out of the writers' workshop / edited by Kwabena Asiedu. – [Ghana] : National Association of Writers, c1974.

79 p. ; 21 cm.

Selections from 2 workshops organized by the National Association of Writers held at Wesley College, Kumasi, Ghana, May 16-19, and at Girl Guides Training Centre, Accra, June 4-8, 1974.

"If no place or probable place can be given, give the abbreviation *s.l.* (sine loco), or its equivalent in nonroman scripts." *See* Fig. 3.44.

Fig. 3.44. Rule 1.4C6. Transcription of abbreviation "s.l." when no place or probable place is known.

Place unknown

Precious cargo / by Ralph Byrne. – [S.l. : R. Byrne], c1978.

Note: Upper case "S.l." results from its beginning an area of the description.

1.4C7. *"Optionally*, add the full address of a publisher, distributor, etc., to the name of the place. Enclose such an addition in parentheses. Do not add the full address for major trade publishers."

LC is applying this option when the information is readily available: "Acquisition and reference librarians have made a strong case for the inclusion of this information, particularly when the bibliographic record shows no ISBN."[3] *See* Fig. 3.45.

Fig. 3.45. Rule 1.4C7. Addition of full address of publisher to the place of publication, etc.

Journey into small groups / William Bangham. -- Memphis (1548 Poplar Avenue, Memphis, Tenn. 38104) : Lay Renewal, c1974.

1.4D. **Name of publisher, distributor, etc.**

1.4D1. "Give the name of the publisher, distributor, etc., following the place(s) to which it relates."

1.4D2. "Give the name of a publisher, distributor, etc., in the shortest form in which it can be understood and identified internationally." *See* Fig. 3.46.

Fig. 3.46. Rule 1.4D2. Transcription of name of publisher in shortest identifiable form.

Publisher's
name abbre-
viated

The Basic book of antiques / by George Michael. -- New York : Arco Pub. Co., [1974]

It is important to note the term "internationally." Because there is now more emphasis on creating bibliographic records for an international audience, the publisher, distributor, etc., area may need fuller information than has been adequate in the past.

1.4D3. "Do not omit from the phrase naming a publisher, distributor, etc.:

a) words or phrases indicating the function (other than solely publishing) performed by the person or body." *See* Figs. 3.47 and 3.48.

Fig. 3.47. Rule 1.4D3a. Transcriptions of name of publisher, distributor, etc., including words and phrases indicating functions performed.

Published
for ...
by ...

At the edge of megalopolis : a history of Salem, N. H., 1900-1974 / [Noyes, Turner]. -- Canaan, N. H. : Published for the Town of Salem, N. H., by Phoenix Pub., c1974.

Fig. 3.48.

Distributor
indicated

The National labor relations act : a guidebook
for health care facility administrators / Dennis D.
Pointer and Norman Metzger. – New York : Spectrum Publications : distributed by Halsted Press,
[1975]

"b) parts of the name required to differentiate between publishers,
distributors, etc." For example:

Encyclopaedia Britannica Educational Corp.
Encyclopaedia Britannica, Inc.

(These are separate bodies and cannot be identified simply as:
Encyclopaedia Britannica).

1.4D4. "If the name of the publisher, distributor, etc., appears in a
recognizable form in the title and statement of responsibility area, give it in the
publication, distribution, etc., area in a shortened form. If, in such a case, the
publisher, distributor, etc., is a person rather than a corporate body, give the
initials and the surname of the person." *See* Fig. 3.49.

**Fig. 3.49. Rule 1.4D4. Transcription of shortened form of name that appears in
full form in the title and statement of responsibility area.**

Shortened
name

The Dexter Avenue Baptist Church, 1877-1977 /
edited by Zelia S. Evans, with J. T. Alexander.
– 1st ed. -- [Montgomery, Ala.] : The Church,
c1978.

Brackets are not required for this shortened form unless the name is in
brackets in the title and statement of responsibility area. *See* Fig. 3.50.

**Fig. 3.50. Rule 1.4D4. Transcription in brackets of abbreviated form of name that
appears in brackets in the statement of responsibility.**

Statement of
responsibility

Federal funds in Maine : a second look / [pre-
pared for the Governor by the Dept. of Finance
and Administration, Bureau of the Budget]. -- Au-

Shortened
name placed
in brackets

gusta : [The Bureau], 1974.

1.4D6.   "If the name of the publisher, distributor, etc., is unknown, give the abbreviation *s.n.* (sine nomine) or its equivalent in nonroman scripts." *See* Fig. 3.51.

Fig. 3.51. Rule 1.4D6. Transcription of "s.n." to indicate that the name of the publisher is unknown.

Publisher
unknown

The story of Lanark / prepared and written by Elizabeth L. Jamieson. -- [S.l. : s.n.], c1974.

1.4D7.   "In case of doubt about whether a named agency is a publisher or a manufacturer, treat it as a publisher."

1.4E.   *Optional addition.* **Statement of function of publisher, distributor, etc.**

1.4E1.   "Add to the name of a publisher, distributor, etc., one of the terms below:

distributor
publisher
producer
     (*used for a producing entity other than a production company*)
production company

unless:

a)   the phrase naming the publisher, distributor, etc., includes words that indicate the function performed by the person(s) or body (bodies) named

or b)   the function of the publishing, distributing, etc., agency is clear from the context."

See Figs. 3.48 (page 65) and 3.52 below.

Fig. 3.52. Rule 1.4E1. Transcription in brackets of function performed following name of agency.

Term show-
ing function

Live or die [motion picture] / E. C. Brown Founda-tion. – [Illinois?] : Wexler Film Productions, Inc. ; Highland Park, Ill. : Perennial Education [distributor], 1978.

LC is applying this option, but is leaving the judgment for its need in each case up to the individual cataloger. It has warned that there will be no great effort to achieve uniformity.[4]

1.4F.   Date of publication, distribution, etc.

1.4F1.   "Give the date of publication, distribution, etc., of the edition named in the edition area. If there is no edition statement, give the date of the first edition. . . ."

1.4F2.   "Give the date as found in the item even if it is known to be incorrect. If a date is known to be incorrect, add the correct date. . . . If necessary, explain any discrepancy in a note." *See* Fig. 3.53.

Fig. 3.53. Rule 1.4F2. Transcription of a date known to be incorrect, followed by the correct date in brackets.

[1]Imprint date on title page

[2]Corrected imprint date

New Industrial polymers : a symposium sponsored by the Division of Organic Coatings and Plastics Chemistry at the 167th meeting of the American Chemical Society, Los Angeles, Calif., April 1-2, 1974 / Rudolph D. Deanin, editor. -- Washington, D.C. : American Chemical Society, 1972 [i.e., 1974]

1.4F3.   "Give the date of a particular reissue of an edition as the date of publication only if the reissue is specified in the edition area (see 1.2D). In this case, give only the date of the reissue." *See* Figs. 3.54 and 3.55.

Fig. 3.54. Rule 1.4F3. Transcription of original date. No mention is made of the fact that the item in hand is a 1974 reissue of the 1959 work.

Original date

The rebellion of 1914-15 : a bibliography / compiled by Gerald Dennis Quinn. -- [Cape Town] : University of Cape Town Libraries, 1959.

1.4F4.   If publication and distribution dates differ, the distribution date is added only if thought to be significant. When both dates are given, each is given after the name to which it applies. If the dates are the same, the date is given after the publisher or distributor named last. *See* Fig. 3.52.

1.4F5.   "*Optional addition.* Add the latest date of copyright following the publication, distribution, etc., date if it is different." *See* Fig. 3.55. NOTE: The copyright date is always preceded by a "c."

**Fig. 3.55. Rule 1.4F5. Transcription of copyright date that varies
from publication date.**

[1]Date of
reissue specified
in edition
area
[2]Copyright date

A pocket guide to chess endgames / David
Hooper. – 1st ed. reprinted. – London : G. Bell,
1973, c1970.

1   2

LC is following this option because it believes that the copyright date is of
great importance in bibliographic identification.[5]

1.4F6. "If the dates of publication, distribution, etc., are unknown, give
the copyright date or, in its absence, the date of manufacture (indicated as
such) in its place." *See* Fig. 3.56.

Fig. 3.56. Rule 1.4F6. Use of copyright date when publication date is unknown.

Copyright
date

How to deal with a horse / Patricia Stillwagon.
– South Brunswick : A. S. Barnes, c1974.◄——

1.4F7. "If no date of publication, distribution, etc., copyright date, or
date of manufacture can be assigned to an item, give an approximate date of
publication." *See* Figs. 3.57 and 3.58. *See also* examples in *AACR 2*, chapter 1,
page 36.

Fig. 3.57. Rule 1.4F7. Transcriptions of approximate dates of publication.

Believed to
be 1974

A genealogy of the Beeson family / compiled
by Margaret Ailene Beeson. -- Greensboro, N. C. :
M. A. Beeson, [1974?]

Fig. 3.58.

Uncertain
date

This is Hungary / by Zoltán Halász. -- [Rome :
Hungarian Press Office, between 1970 and 1974]

1.4F8. "If two or more dates are found on the various parts of a
multipart item (e.g., if such an item is published in parts over a number of
years), give the earliest and latest dates." Give only the earliest date and a
hyphen followed by four spaces when a multipart item is incomplete. Many
libraries then add the latest date when the item is complete. *See* Fig. 3.59.

Fig. 3.59. Rule 1.4F8. Transcription of earliest and latest dates of a
multipart item.

¹Inclusive
dates

The German colonies in South Russia 1804 to
1904 / by P. Conrad Keller ; translation A. Becker. -- [Saskatoon : Western Producer], c1968-1973. ◄——1

²Two vol-
ume work

2 ——►2 v. : ill., maps ; 22 cm.

1.4G. Place of manufacture, name of manufacturer, date of manufacture

1.4G1. "If the name of the publisher is unknown, give the place and
name of the manufacturer if they are found in the item." *See* Fig. 3.60.

Fig. 3.60. Rule 1.4G1. Transcription of place and name of manufacturer
following date when publisher is unknown.

¹Place of publi-
cation unknown

²Name of pub-
lisher unknown

³Manufactur-
er's imprint

      1   2
Holtz/Lou./
     The offensive side of Lou Holtz / by Lou Holtz.
– [S.l. : s.n.], c1978 (Little Rock, Ark. : Parkin
Printing Co.) ◄——3

1.4G4. *"Optional addition.* Give the place, name of manufacturer,
and/or date of manufacture if they differ from the place, name of publisher,
distributor, etc., and date of publication, distribution, etc., and are found in
the item and are considered important by the cataloguing agency."

LC is applying this option with emphasis on the last phrase. In some cases
information about a printer, for example, can be valuable. However, LC
believes "that a high degree of uniformity need not be attempted when
deciding in precisely which cases such data 'are considered important by the
cataloguing agency' "[6]

RULE 1.5. PHYSICAL DESCRIPTION AREA

1.5A3. "If an item is available in different formats (e.g., as text and
microfilm; as sound disc and sound tape reel), give the physical description of
the format in hand. *Optionally*, make a note describing other formats in which
it is available (see 1.7B16)."

The part of this rule that calls for describing text on microfilm as
microfilm is causing controversy in the library community. It is believed by
many librarians that the importance of text on microfilm is as a version of the
text. The fact that the version is in microform rather than regular print is, to
these persons, less important than the description of the original in terms of
number of pages of text. On the other side, there are those who say that the
purpose of bibliographic description is to describe the item in hand. If it is two

sheets of microfiche, it is not the same as a 350-page bound volume. This debate is likely to continue for some time.

The option of making a note describing other formats is being applied by LC. They believe it helpful to library users to be able to see information about other existing forms of the same item.[7] *See* Fig. 3.61.

Fig. 3.61. Rule 1.5A3 and 1.5B1. Transcription of extent of item in hand with note of other physical formats in which the work is available.

[1]Number of physical units
[2]Note of other existing forms of same item

Benjamin and the miracle of Hanukah [videorecording] / Benjamin & Associates. – Wilmette, Ill. : Films Inc., 1978.

1 — 1 videocassette (30 min.) : sd., col. ; 3/4 in.

U standard.

2 — Also issued as Betamax or VHS cassette and as motion picture.

1.5B. **Extent of item (including specific material designation)**

1.5B1. "Record the number of physical units of the item being described by giving the number of parts in arabic numerals and the specific material designation as detailed in the following chapters." *See* Fig. 3.61 above.

How to record the extent of item for different types of materials is covered in detail in each chapter on a type of material. Where appropriate, additions in parentheses are made following the number of physical units (e.g., number of frames on a filmstrip, playing time), and these are explained fully in the following chapters.

1.5B5. "In describing a multipart item that is not yet complete, give the specific material designation alone preceded by three spaces. . . . *Optionally*, when the item is complete, add the number of physical units." *See* Fig. 3.62.

Fig. 3.62. Rule 1.5B5. Transcription of designation preceded by three spaces for incomplete item.

Designation for incomplete multipart item

Deaths, marriages, and much miscellaneous from Rhinebeck, New York newspapers, 1846-1899 / [compiled by Arthur C. M. Kelly]. – Rhinebeck, N.Y. : Kelly, 1978-

⟶ v. ; 30 cm.

Includes index.
Contents: v. 1. Deaths.

The Library of Congress is applying the option; so if the work in Fig. 3.62 becomes complete in, say, 3 volumes, the physical description area will read: 3 v. ; 30 cm.

1.5C.   Other physical details

1.5C1.   "Give physical data (other than extent or dimensions) about an item as instructed in the following chapters." *See* Fig. 3.63.

Fig. 3.63. Rule 1.5C1. Transcription of other physical details following extent of item.

Physical data about presence of illustrations	Reactive intermediates. -- Vol. 1 (1978)- New York : John Wiley & Sons, c1978- v. : ill. ; 24 cm.

1.5D.   Dimensions

The dimensions of an item serve as an aid in finding it on the library shelves. Dimensions are especially valuable for libraries with separate storage areas for oversized items. They also serve the user who wishes to borrow an item through interlibrary loan.

1.5D1.   "Give the dimensions of an item as instructed in the following chapters." *See* Fig. 3.64.

Fig. 3.64. Rule 1.5D1. Transcription of dimensions following extent of item, there being no "other" physical details.

Height in centimeters	Repartee : for orchestra / Eric Wild. – Toronto : Clark & Cruickshank, c1974. 1 score (21 p.) ; 28 cm.

1.5E.   Accompanying material

Accompanying material includes answer books, teacher's manuals, atlases, portfolios of plates, slides, phonodiscs, booklets explaining audiovisual materials, and other such items. These materials often are placed in pockets inside the cover of the work being cataloged, or they may be loose inside the container. Their description may make up the fourth element of the physical description area.

1.5E1.   "There are four ways of recording information about accompanying material:

a) record the details of the accompanying material in a separate entry

or b) record the details of the accompanying material in a multilevel description (see chapter 13 [*AACR 2*])

or c) record the details of the accompanying material in a note (see 1.7B11) ...

or d) record the name of accompanying material at the end of the physical description."

See Fig. 3.65.

Fig. 3.65. Rule 1.5E1d. Transcription of the name of accompanying material as the last element of the physical description area.

Accompany-
ing material

The reading process : the teacher and the learner / Miles V. Zintz. – 2nd ed. – Dubuque, Iowa : W. C. Brown Co., [1975]

xi, 575 p. : ill. ; 24 cm. + instructor's manual.

"*Optional addition.* If method *d* is applicable and further physical description is desired, add a statement of the extent, other physical details, and dimensions of the accompanying material as appropriate. . . ." *See* Fig. 3.66.

Fig. 3.66. Rule 1.5E1d, optional addition. Transcription of physical description for accompanying material.

Accompany-
ing material
with its
physical
description

There is no such phenomenon / Rita Arditi Volk. – San Francisco : Sedarsky-Besse Associates, 1974.

158 p. : ill. ; 29 cm. + 1 sound disc (5 min. : 33⅓ rpm : 7 in.)

LC is applying this option on a case-by-case basis to items that are substantial in extent or are significant for some reason (e.g., non-print items accompanying text).[8]

RULE 1.6. SERIES AREA

The first definition of "series" as it appears in the *AACR 2* Glossary is: "A group of separate items related to one another by the fact that each item bears, in addition to its own title proper, a collective title applying to the group as a whole."

1.6B. Title proper of series

1.6B1. "If an item is one of a series, record the title proper of the series as instructed in 1.1B (see also 12.1B2)." *See* Fig. 3.67.

Fig. 3.67. Rule 1.6B1. Transcription of series title proper in parentheses.

Series
title

Peaches : for flute and piano / André Previn.
–New York : Edition W. Hansen/Chester Music,
[c1978]

1 score (8 p.) + 1 part ; 30 cm. – (The Chester
woodwind series)

Other title information is seldom recorded for series. It is recorded only if valuable for identifying the series. When other title information or parallel titles for series are recorded, they are transcribed according to the same rules used for the title and statement of responsibility area.

1.6B2. This rule gives a hierarchy for choice among variant series titles that may appear in an item. A title in the chief source of information is preferred. If variants appear in the chief source, the one that identifies most adequately and succinctly is used. The same criterion is applied to variant titles, none of which is in the chief source of information.

1.6E. **Statements of responsibility relating to series**

1.6E1. "Give statements of responsibility appearing in conjunction with the series title if they are considered to be necessary for identification of the series. Follow the instructions in 1.1F when recording a statement of responsibility relating to a series." *See* Fig. 3.68.

**Fig. 3.68. Rule 1.6E1. Transcription of series statement of
responsibility following series title.**

[1]Generic
title

The Cooper River environmental study / by Frank
P. Nelson, editor. -- Cayce : South Carolina
Water Resources Commission, 1974.

[2]Statement
of responsi-
bility

164 p. : ill. ; 28 cm. – (Report / South Carolina
Water Resources Commission ; no. 117)

1.6F. **ISSN of series**

The ISSN is the International Standard Serial Number, assigned to a serial as an internationally agreed-upon unique identifier. It is useful for identification and ordering purposes.

1.6F1. "Record the International Standard Serial Number (ISSN) of a series if it appears in the item being described (see also 1.6H4). Record the ISSN in the standard manner, i.e., ISSN followed by a space and two groups of four digits separated by a hyphen." *See* Fig. 3.69.

Fig. 3.69. Rule 1.6F1. Transcription of ISSN following series title.

¹**Series title**
²**ISSN**
³**Series
number**

Report on social security for Canada / Leonard
Marsh ; with a new introduction by the author ;
and a preface by Michael Bliss. – Toronto ; Buffalo : University of Toronto Press, [1975] ₁

    xxxi, 330 p. ; 23 cm. – (The Social history of
Canada, ISSN 0085-6207 ; 24) ←——3

    2

1.6G.   Numbering within series

1.6G1.   "Record the numbering of the item within the series in the terms
given in the item. Use standard abbreviations (see Appendix B) and substitute
arabic numerals for other numerals or spelled out numbers (see Appendix C)."
See Fig. 3.70.

**Fig. 3.70. Rule 1.6G1. Transcription of series numbering as given
in the item.**

¹**Series
title**
²**Series
number**

Administrative process : a guide to practice
before administrative agencies. -- [Harrisburg] :
Pennsylvania Bar Institute, c1978. ₁ ₂

    vi, 161 p. ; 28 cm. – (PBI publication ; no. 95)

1.6H.   Subseries

    AACR 2 defines subseries: "A series within a series; that is, a series which
always appears in conjunction with another, usually more comprehensive,
series of which it forms a section. Its title may or may not be dependent on the
title of the main series."

1.6H1.   "If an item is one of a subseries (a series within a series, whether
or not it has a dependent title) and both the series and the subseries are named
in the item, give the details of the main series (see 1.6A-1.6G) first and follow
them with the name of the subseries and the details of that subseries." Parallel
titles, other title information, statements of responsibility, ISSN, and numbering are transcribed for subseries in the same way as for series. *See* Fig. 3.71.

Fig. 3.71. Rule 1.6H1. Transcription of subseries information following series title.

[1] Series title
[2] Subseries title
[3] ISSN for subseries
[4] Numbering for subseries

> Children's language at four and six : a longitu-
> dinal and multivariable study of language abili-
> ties among children / Barbro Eneskär. – Lund :
> LiberLäromedel/Gleerup, 1978. ➤1
>
> 69 p. : tables ; 25 cm. – (Studia psychologica et
> paedagogica. Series altera, ISSN 0346-5926 ; 42)
> 2 ———————————— ➤3 ➤4

1.6J.   More than one series statement

1.6J1.   "The information relating to one series or series and subseries constitutes collectively one series statement. If an item belongs to two or more series and/or series and subseries, make separate series statements and enclose each statement in parentheses. . . . If the criterion applies, give the more specific series first." *See* Fig. 3.72.

Fig. 3.72. Rule 1.6J1. Transcription of two series statements, each in its own set of parentheses.

[1] First series
[2] Second series

> History of the western Gangas / B. Sheik Ali.
> –1st ed. – Mysore : Prasaranga, University of My-
> sore, 1976. ➤1
>
> xiii, 416 p., [31] leaves of plates : ill., maps ; 26
> cm. – (Comprehensive history of Karnataka ; v. 1)
> (Other publications / University of Mysore ; 61)
> ———————————— ➤2

RULE 1.7.   NOTE AREA

Many works require description beyond that presented formally in the title and statement of responsibility area through the series area. Notes qualify or amplify the formal description. Some notes contribute to identification of a work (e.g., a note giving the original title of a translated work). Some contribute to the intelligibility of the record (e.g., a note explaining the relationship to the work of a person who has been given an added entry). Other notes aid the reader who does not have in hand an exact citation (e.g., a summary or contents note). Still other notes characterize an item (e.g., a thesis note), or give its bibliographic history (e.g., notes giving previous titles).

1.7A.   Preliminary rule

1.7A3.   Form of notes

This rule gives general guidelines for the formulation of notes.

Order of information. In any one note, data that correspond to data found in descriptive areas preceding the notes area are transcribed in the same order in the note. The prescribed punctuation is used with the exception that a period (full stop), space, dash, space is replaced simply by a period (full stop). *See* Fig. 3.73.

Fig. 3.73. Rule 1.7A3. Transcription of information in the note in the same order it would be transcribed above, but without any period, space, dash, space separating areas.

Priceless pearls : [poems] / by A. S. H. Hossain. -- Calcutta : M.S.S. Hossain, 1890.

iv, ix, 147 p. ; 18 cm.

With: The lament of Islam / A. S. H. Hossain. Calcutta: [s.n.], 1894.

Quotations. "Give quotations from the item or from other sources in quotation marks. Follow the quotation by an indication of its source, unless that source is the chief source of information. Do not use prescribed punctuation in quotations."

Formal notes. "Use formal notes employing an invariable introductory word or phrase or a standard form of words when uniformity of presentation assists in the recognition of the type of information being presented or when their use gives economy of space without loss of clarity."

Informal notes. "When making informal notes, use statements that present the information as briefly as clarity, understandability, and good grammar permit."

1.7B. Notes
    A general outline of notes is given here followed by some examples (*see* Figs. 3.74-3.79 on pages 77-79). More specific applications are discussed in the following chapters where notes applicable to the various types of material are discussed in detail.
    Notes are to be given in the order listed here. Upon examination, one can determine the logic of the order. First come notes concerning the nature and language of the item. Then come notes that relate to the areas of description from title through series in the order in which they appear in the body of the entry. These are followed by notes that characterize and summarize the item.

1.7B1. Nature, scope, or artistic form of the item

1.7B2. Language of the item and/or translation or adaptation

1.7B3. Source of title proper

1.7B4. Variations in title

1.7B5.   **Parallel titles and other title information**

1.7B6.   **Statements of responsibility**

1.7B7.   **Edition and history**

1.7B8.   **Material specific details**

1.7B9.   **Publication, distribution, etc.**

1.7B10.   **Physical description**

1.7B11.   **Accompanying materials and supplements**

1.7B12.   **Series**

1.7B13.   **Dissertations**

1.7B14.   **Audience**

1.7B15.   **Reference to published descriptions**

1.7B16.   **Other formats available**

1.7B17.   **Summary**

1.7B18.   **Contents**

1.7B19.   **Numbers borne by the item (other than those covered in 1.8)**

1.7B20.   **Copy being described and library's holdings**

1.7B21.   **"With" notes**

Fig. 3.74. Rule 1.7B. Transcriptions of notes.

Title varia-   American dainties and how to prepare them / by
tion (1.7B4)   an American lady. – London : R. Jackson,
         [190-?]

         iv, 92 p. ; 19 cm.

         Cover title: American fancy groceries and
recipes by an American lady for 170 dainty
dishes.

Fig. 3.75. Rule 1.7B. Transcriptions of notes.

[1] **Statement of responsibility (1.7B6)**

[2] **Physical description (1.7B10)**

[3] **Audience (1.7B14)**

[4] **Other formats available (1.7B16)**

[5] **Contents (1.7B18)**

Troll tales of Tumble Town [filmstrip] / Don Arthur Torgersen. – Chicago : Coronet Instructional Media, 1978.

6 filmstrips : col. ; 35 mm. + 6 sound cassettes (102 min.) and program guide.

1 — Illustrations, Tom Dunnington.

2 — Sound accompaniment compatible for manual and automatic operation.

3 — For elementary grades.

4 — Also issued with sound accompaniment on disc.

5 — Contents: 1. Muddlepuddle, the troll who lived in the lake (51 fr.).--2. Rumplegrumple, the trickiest troll (49 fr.).--3. Tamtammy MacTroll and the scariest night in Troll Forest (51 fr.).--4. Terrabulous Troll goes to school (52 fr.).--5. Ravencraven, the wicked witch of Troll Cave (47 fr.).--6. Frozenose and Snozenose, the angry giants of Troll Mountain (48 fr.).

Fig. 3.76. Rule 1.7B. Transcriptions of notes.

[1] **Quoted note on history (1.7B7)**

[2] **Edition and history note (1.7B7)**

[3] **Contents (1.7B18)**

Annals of Athens, Georgia, 1801-1901 / by Augustus Longstreet Hull ; with an introductory sketch by Henry Hull. -- Danielsville, Ga. : Heritage Papers, c1978.

xiv, 568 p., [6] leaves of plates : ill. ; 23 cm.

1 — "These sketches ... were for the most part first published in the Southern watchman in 1879."

2 — Reprint with additions and corrections. Originally published: Athens, Ga. : Banner Job Office, 1906.

3 — Includes index.

Fig. 3.77. Rule 1.7B. Transcriptions of notes.

[1]History
note (1.7B7)

[2]Summary
(1.7B17)

Arson : fire for hire [motion picture] / ABC News.
– New York : McGraw-Hill Films, 1978.

1 film reel (27 min.) : sd., col. ; 16 mm. +
teacher's guide.

1 ——►Originally broadcast on the ABC television
program Close-up.

2 ——► Summary: Explains that arson is the fastest
growing crime in America, and that in many
places it has become a big and profitable
business. Points out that one of the reasons for
the increase in arson is the lack of effective law
enforcement and prosecution.

Fig. 3.78. Rule 1.7B. Transcriptions of notes.

[1]Physical
description
(1.7B10)

[2]Contents
(1.7B18)

[3]Contents
(1.7B18)

Air law / Shawcross and Beaumont. – 4th ed. /
Peter Martin ... [et al.]. – London : Butterworths,
1977-

v. : ill., forms ; 26 cm.

1 ——►Loose-leaf (v. 2) for updating.
2 ——►Includes bibliographical references and index.
3 ——►Contents: v. 1. General text.–v. 2. Noter-up,
treaties, and legislation.

Fig. 3.79. Rule 1.7B. Transcriptions of notes.

[1]Thesis note
for doctoral
work (1.7B13)

[2]Institution
granting degree
(1.7B13)

[3]Contents
(1.7B18)

Robert Harley as secretary of state, 1704-1708
/ by John Henry Davis. – Chicago : [s.n.], 1932.

xiv, 218 leaves ; 32 cm. [2]

1 ——►Thesis (Ph.D.)–University of Chicago.
3 ——►Bibliography: leaves 198-218.

RULE 1.8. STANDARD NUMBER AND TERMS OF AVAILABILITY AREA

1.8B. Standard number

1.8B1. "Give the International Standard Book Number (ISBN), or International Standard Serial Number (ISSN), or any other internationally agreed standard number for the item being described." *See* Fig. 3.80.

Fig. 3.80. Rule 1.8B1. Transcription of standard number for the item being described.

Standard
number

    Angel makers / by Penny Kemp. – 1st ed. – Tor-
onto : Playwrights Co-op, 1978.

    41 p. ; 28 cm.

——►ISBN 0-88754-089-9

1.8B2. "If an item bears two or more such numbers, record the one which applies to the whole item, or applies to the item being described.

"*Optionally*, record more than one number and add a qualification as prescribed in 1.8E. Give a number for a complete set before the number(s) for the part(s). Give numbers for parts in the order of the parts."

LC will apply the option because of the continuing growth in importance of standard numbers.[9] *See* Fig. 3.81.

Fig. 3.81. Rule 1.8B2, option. Transcription of more than one standard number on a record.

[1]Standard
number for hard
back edition   1
[2]Standard
number for
paperback edition

    Bean Street : poems / by John S. Morris. -- Fay-
etteville, Ark. : Lost Roads Pub. Co., 1977.

    32 p. ; 22 cm. – (Lost roads ; no. 4)

    ISBN 0-918786-06-1(bound). – ISBN 0-918786-
07-X(pbk.)   ◄2

1.8C.   **Key-title**

1.8C1.   "Add the key-title of a serial, if it is found on the item or is otherwise readily available, after the ... ISSN. Give the key-title even if it is identical with the title proper. If no ISSN is given, do not record the key-title." *See* Fig. 3.82.

Fig. 3.82. Rule 1.8C1. Transcription of key-title of a serial following ISSN.

Italian-American identity. – Vol. 1 (Jan. 1977)-
   . – [New York : Identity Enterprises for the Ameri-
can-Italian, 1977-   ]

   v. : ill. ; 28 cm.

Monthly.
Running title, Jan. 1977-   : Identity.
ISSN 0163-0423 = Italian-American identity

1.8D.   *Optional addition.* **Terms of availability**

1.8D1.   "Give the terms on which the item is available. These terms consist of the price (given in numerals with standard abbreviations) if the item is for sale, or a brief statement of other terms if the item is not for sale."
LC is applying this option as a continuation of past practice. They believe that experience has proven the usefulness of this information.[10] *See* Fig. 3.83.

Fig. 3.83. Rule 1.8D1. Transcription of terms of availability following standard number.

[1]Standard number

[2]Price

Plot counter-plot / Anna Clarke. -- London : Collins [for] the Crime Club, 1974.

192 p. ; 21 cm. -- (Crime club)

1⟶ ISBN 0-00-231637-4 : £2.00 ⟵2

1.8E.   **Qualification**

1.8E1.   "Add after the standard number or terms of availability, as appropriate, a brief qualification when an item bears two or more standard numbers ... [*See* Fig. 3.81] and *optionally* when the terms of availability (see 1.8D) need qualification." LC is applying the option.[11]

RULE 1.9.   SUPPLEMENTARY ITEMS

1.9A.   "Describe supplementary items which are to be catalogued separately (see 21.28) as separate items. For instructions on the recording of the title proper of supplementary items, the titles proper of which consist of two or more parts, see 1.1B9."

1.9B.   "Choose one of the following methods of describing supplementary items described dependently:

1)   record the supplementary item as accompanying material (see 1.5E)." *See* Figs. 3.65 and 3.66 on page 72.

"or 2)   record minor supplementary items in the note area (see 1.7B11)

or 3)   use the multilevel description (see 13.6)."

RULE 1.10.   ITEMS MADE UP OF SEVERAL TYPES OF MATERIALS

1.10A.   "This rule applies to items that are made up of two or more components, two or more of which belong to distinct material types (e.g., a sound recording and a printed text)."

1.10B. "If an item has one predominant component, describe it in terms of that component and give details of the subsidiary component(s) as accompanying material following the physical description (see 1.5E) or in a note (see 1.7B11)." *See* Fig. 3.84.

Fig. 3.84. Rule 1.10B. Description of item made up of two components, one of which is predominant.

[1]Predominant component

Alcohol and your body [filmstrip]. -- Kansas City, Mo. : McIntyre Productions, 1978.

[2]Subsidiary component

1 filmstrip (96 fr.) : col. ; 35 mm. + 1 sound cassette (27 min.). -- (Health)

Writer, Al DeZutter.
Sound accompaniment compatible for manual and automatic operation.
Summary: Deals with the increasing problem of teenage alcoholism, helping students understand the nature of alcohol and its physical effects on the body.

1.10C. "If an item has no predominant component, follow the rules below in addition to the rules in this chapter and the rules in the appropriate following chapters."

1.10C1. General material designation
The instructions in 1.1C4 are followed except when an item has no collective title. Then the appropriate GMD is given after each individual title.

1.10C2. Physical description
"Apply whichever of the following three methods is appropriate to the item being described:

a) Give the extent of each part or group of parts belonging to each distinct class of material as the first element of the physical description (do this if no further physical description of each item is desired), ending this element with *in container*, if there is one, and following it with the dimensions of the container." *See* Fig. 3.85.

Fig. 3.85. Rule 1.10C2a. Transcription of parts of a kit as a listing of extent of item of each part.

Sharks [kit] / National Geographic Society. – Washington, D. C. : The Society, c1978.

3 study prints, 1 filmstrip (4 fr.), 1 sound cassette (15 min.), 30 narration scripts, 1 teacher's guide, 2 duplicating masters, 2 worksheets; in container, 34 x 30 x 5 cm. – (Learning shelf kit)

"*or* b)   Give separate physical descriptions for each part or group of parts belonging to each distinct class of material (do this if a further physical description of each item is desired). Give each physical description on a separate line." *See* Fig. 3.86.

The Bingo Long Traveling All-Stars & Motor Kings [kit]. – New Rochelle, N.Y. : Spoken Arts, 1978.

4 filmstrips : col. ; 35 mm.
4 sound cassettes (44 min.) : 2 track, mono.
1 teacher's guide (28 p.) ; 24 cm.
8 duplicating masters ; 28 x 22 cm. – (Black culture against the odds)

"*or* c)   For items with a large number of heterogeneous materials, give a general term as the extent (see also 1.5B). Give the number of such pieces unless it cannot be ascertained." *See* Fig. 3.87.

Safety begins with you [kit]. – New York : Children's Media Productions, c1979.

24 various pieces. – (School craft kits)

1.10C3.   Notes

"Give notes on particular parts of the item all together following the series area or following the physical description(s) if no series area is present."

RULE 1.11.   FACSIMILES, PHOTOCOPIES, AND OTHER REPRODUCTIONS

Facsimiles, photocopies, or other reproductions of printed texts, maps, manuscripts, printed music, and graphic items are described in such a way that the details of the facsimile, etc., are given in all areas except the note area. If the title of the facsimile, etc., is different, the title of the facsimile, etc., is given as title proper. The same is true for edition, publication details, or series. In these cases, the details of the original are given in a single note in the notes area. The details of the original are given in the same order as they would appear in the main part of the description.

If the facsimile, etc., is in a different form of material than the original, the chapter relating to the form of the facsimile, etc., is used. For a manuscript reproduced as a book, the chapter on description of books would be used. For maps reproduced on microfilm, the chapter on description of microforms would be used. *See* Fig. 3.88.

Fig. 3.88. Rule 1.11. Description of a photoreproduction as a reproduction with details of the original given in a note.

The Expert gardener. – Amsterdam : Theatrum Orbis Terrarum ; Norwood, N.J. : W. J. Johnson, 1974.

54 p., [2] leaves of plates : ill. ; 21 cm. – (The English experience, its records in early printed books published in facsimile ; no. 659)

Photoreprint of: The Expert gardener, or, A treatise containing certaine necessary, secret, and ordinary knowledges in grafting and gardening ... faithfully collected out of sundry Dutch and French authors. London : Printed by Richard Herne, 1640.

FOOTNOTES

[1]"Display of General Material Designations," *Cataloging Service Bulletin* no. 5 (Summer 1979):4. One of the GMDs affected by this decision is [text]; few catalogers will use this GMD, and it will not appear in the eye-readable forms of the Library's records.

[2]"AACR 2 Options to be Followed by the Library of Congress, Chapters 1-2, 12, 21-26," *Library of Congress Information Bulletin* 37 (July 21, 1978):423.

[3]"AACR 2 Options," p. 423.

[4]"AACR 2 Options," p. 423.

[5]"AACR 2 Options," p. 423.

[6]"AACR 2 Options," p. 423.

[7]"AACR 2 Options," p. 423.

[8]"AACR 2 Options," p. 424.

[9]"AACR 2 Options," p. 424.

[10]"AACR 2 Options," p. 424.

[11]"AACR 2 Options," p. 424.

4 DESCRIPTION OF BOOKS, PAMPHLETS, AND PRINTED SHEETS

INTRODUCTION

This chapter and the ten following ones each discuss application of the general rules for description to a different type of material, or a pattern or condition of publication. Emphasis in each chapter is upon those areas where the description of a type of material must be unique to that type: chief and prescribed sources of information, material specific details, physical description, and notes. For each type of material one or more items has been chosen as an example to demonstrate the building of a bibliographic record from the title through the standard number and terms of availability. For each item, the chief source of information is illustrated. Then, as each rule is delineated, the element of description covered by that rule is added to the record as it would be in the cataloging process. Because no one item can demonstrate every eventuality, other examples of particular instances are also given throughout each chapter.

RULE 2.0. GENERAL RULES

2.0A. Scope
"The rules in this chapter cover the description of separately published monographic printed items of all kinds (referred to hereafter in this chapter as *printed monographs*). These items comprise books, pamphlets, and single sheets. For microform reproductions of printed texts, see chapter 11 [chapter 13 of this text]. For serial printed texts, see chapter 12 [chapter 14 of this text]."

2.0B. Sources of information

2.0B1. Chief source of information
"The chief source of information for printed monographs is the title page. . . ." If there is no title page, then the part of the item that gives the most complete information is used as a substitute for the title page. In this case, the part used as a substitute is specified in a note, and the information from the substitute is treated as if it were from a title page. That is, brackets are not used for information from a substitute title page. If the item has no part that can substitute, information may be taken from any available source.

If information that would ordinarily appear on a title page is given on facing pages, both pages are treated as "the title page."

2.0B2.   **Prescribed sources of information**

"The prescribed source(s) of information for each area of the description of printed monographs is set out below. Enclose information taken from outside the prescribed source(s) in square brackets.

AREA	PRESCRIBED SOURCES OF INFORMATION
Title and statement of responsibility	Title page
Edition	Title page, other preliminaries, and colophon
Publication, distribution, etc.	Title page, other preliminaries, and colophon
Physical description	The whole publication
Series	The whole publication
Note	Any source
Standard number and terms of availability	Any source"

Figures 4.1-4.3 illustrate the title page and "other preliminaries" for the book that is used in this chapter to illustrate building a description. "Preliminaries" is defined in *AACR 2* as "the title page or title pages of an item, together with the verso of each title page, any pages preceding the title page(s), and the cover." "Colophon" is defined as "a statement at the end of an item giving information about one or more of the following: the title, author(s), publisher, printer, date of publication or printing. . . ." The book used here has a plain front cover, with the information on the spine duplicating that on the title page. It has no colophon. Colophons are not common in English language books but are found more often in books in other languages.

Fig. 4.1. Title page.

Handbook of
Data Processing for Libraries

Second Edition

SPONSORED BY THE COUNCIL
ON LIBRARY RESOURCES

Robert M. Hayes
University of California, Los Angeles

Joseph Becker
Becker and Hayes, Inc.
Los Angeles, California

A WILEY-BECKER & HAYES SERIES BOOK

MELVILLE PUBLISHING COMPANY
Los Angeles, California

Fig. 4.2. Verso of title page.

Copyright © 1970, 1974, by John Wiley & Sons, Inc.
Published by **Melville Publishing Company**,
a Division of John Wiley & Sons, Inc.
All rights reserved. Published simultaneously in Canada.

Library of Congress Cataloging in Publication Data:

Hayes, Robert Mayo, 1926-
    Handbook of data processing for libraries.
    (Information sciences series)
    "A Wiley-Becker & Hayes series book."
    Includes bibliographies.
    1. Libraries--Automation. 2. Electronic data processing--Library science.
I. Becker, Joseph, joint author. II. Title.
Z678.9.H36   1974   025'.02'02854   74-9690
ISBN 0-471-36483-5

Printed in the United States of America
10 9 8 7 6 5 4 3 2 1

Fig. 4.3. Recto and verso of leaf preceding title page.

Information Sciences Series

Editors
ROBERT M. HAYES
University of California
Los Angeles, California

JOSEPH BECKER
President
Becker and Hayes, Inc.

Consultant
CHARLES P. BOURNE
University of California
Berkeley, California

Joseph Becker and Robert M. Hayes:
INFORMATION STORAGE AND RETRIEVAL

Charles P. Bourne:
METHODS OF INFC

Harold Borko:
AUTOMATED LAN(

Russell D. Archibald
NETWORK-BASED

Launor F. Carter:
NATIONAL DOCUN
AND TECHNOLOG'

Perry E. Rosove:
DEVELOPING COM

F. W. Lancaster:
INFORMATION RE⁻

Ralph L. Bisco:
DATA BASES, CON

Charles T. Meadow:
MAN-MACHINE CC

Gerald Jahoda:
INFORMATION ST(

Robert S. Taylor:
THE MAKING OF A LIBRARY

Herman M. Weisman:
INFORMATION SYSTEMS, SERVICES, AND CENTERS

Jesse H. Shera:
THE FOUNDATIONS OF EDUCATION FOR LIBRARIANSHIP

Charles T. Meadow:
THE ANALYSIS OF INFORMATION SYSTEMS, Second Edition

Stanley J. Swihart and Beryl F. Hefley:
COMPUTER SYSTEMS IN THE LIBRARY

F. W. Lancaster and E. G. Fayen:
INFORMATION RETRIEVAL ON-LINE

Richard A. Kaimann:
STRUCTURED INFORMATION FILES

Thelma Freides:
LITERATURE AND BIBLIOGRAPHY OF THE SOCIAL SCIENCES

Manfred Kochen:
PRINCIPLES OF INFORMATION RETRIEVAL

Robert M. Hayes and Joseph Becker:
HANDBOOK OF DATA PROCESSING FOR LIBRARIES, Second Edition

2.0D.-2.0H.

Levels of description, language and script, inaccuracies, accents and other diacritical marks, and items with several title pages are treated as discussed in the general chapter on description.

RULE 2.1.   TITLE AND STATEMENT OF RESPONSIBILITY AREA

2.1B.   **Title proper**

2.1B1.   "Record the title proper as instructed in 1.1B." *See* Fig. 4.4.

Fig. 4.4. Rule 2.1B. Transcription of title proper.

Handbook of data processing for libraries

2.1C.   *Optional addition.* **General material designation**

As discussed in the general chapter, the GMD "[text]" that is appropriate to the material of this chapter is to be included in machine-readable records by the Library of Congress, but is not to be displayed in eye-readable forms of those records. Its use is not illustrated in this chapter. *See* footnote 1, page 84.

2.1D.-2.1E.

Parallel titles and other title information are transcribed as instructed in 1.1D.-1.1E.

2.1F.   **Statements of responsibility**

2.1F1.   "Record statements of responsibility relating to persons or bodies as instructed in 1.1F." *See* Fig. 4.5.

Fig. 4.5. Rule 2.1F. Addition of statements of responsibility.

Handbook of data processing for libraries / Robert M.
Hayes, Joseph Becker ; sponsored by the Council on Library
Resources

2.1G.   If an item lacks a collective title, titles of parts are transcribed as instructed in 1.1G.

RULE 2.2. EDITION AREA

2.2B. Edition statement

2.2B1. "Transcribe a statement relating to an edition of a work that contains differences from other editions of that work, or that is a named reissue of that work, as instructed in 1.2B." *See* Fig. 4.6.

Fig. 4.6. Rule 2.2B. Addition of edition statement.

Handbook of data processing for libraries / Robert M. Hayes, Joseph Becker ; sponsored by the Council on Library Resources. – 2nd ed.

2.2C. Statements of responsibility relating to the edition

2.2C1. "Record a statement of responsibility relating to one or more editions, but not to all editions, of a work as instructed in 1.2C." An example of this is Fig. 3.34 in the preceding chapter of this text (page 60).

RULE 2.3. MATERIAL (OR TYPE OF PUBLICATION) SPECIFIC DETAILS AREA

"This area is not used for printed monographs."

RULE 2.4. PUBLICATION, DISTRIBUTION, ETC., AREA

2.4B. General rule
"For items with mulitple or fictitious places and name of publishers, distributors, etc., follow the instructions in 1.4B."

2.4C. Place of publication, distribution, etc.

2.4C1. "Record the place of publication, distribution, etc., as instructed in 1.4D." *See* Fig. 4.7.

2.4D. Name of publisher, distributor, etc.

2.4D1. "Record the name of the publisher, distributor, etc., as instructed in 1.4D." *See* Fig. 4.7.

2.4E. *Optional addition.* Statement of function of distributor
"Add to the name of a distributor a statement of function as instructed in 1.4E."

As mentioned in the discussion of 1.4E, LC is applying this option. Example:

− [Leicester] : Leicester University Press ; Atlantic High-
lands, N.J. : Humanities Press [distributor], 1977.

2.4F.   Date of publication, distribution, etc.
"Record the date of publication, distribution, etc., as instructed in 1.4F."
See Fig. 4.7.

Fig. 4.7. Rule 2.4F. Addition of publication details.

Handbook of data processing for libraries / Robert M.
Hayes, Joseph Becker ; sponsored by the Council on Library
Resources. − 2nd ed. − Los Angeles : Melville Pub. Co.,
c1974.

_____

Note that there are two copyright dates on the verso of the title page (Fig. 4.2).
The date that corresponds to the edition statement is the one chosen for
transcription.

2.4G.   Place of printing, name of printer, date of printing
If the publisher is unknown, the place and name of the printer are given.
Optionally, the place and name of the printer are given in addition to the
publisher if they are found in the item and are considered to be important. As
discussed with 1.4G2, LC is applying the option with little effort to define
"important" consistently. An example of the transcription of place and name
of printer is Fig. 3.60 in the preceding chapter.

RULE 2.5.   PHYSICAL DESCRIPTION AREA

2.5B.   Number of volumes and/or pagination

Single volumes

2.5B1.   "Record the number of pages or leaves in a publication in
accordance with the terminology suggested by the volume." The following
terms are used:

Term used	Situation
pages (abbreviated "p.")	[volume with leaves printed on both sides]
leaves	[volume with leaves printed on only one side]
columns	[volume with more than one column to a page and numbered in columns]

(List continues on page 92)

Term used (cont'd)	**Situation (cont'd)**
leaves, pages, and/or columns (in sequence)	[volume that contains sequences of leaves, pages, and/or columns]
broadside	[broadside]
sheet	[folder and other single sheets]
case	[case]
portfolio	[portfolio]

"For the treatment of unnumbered leaves of plates, see 2.5B10."

2.5B2. "Record the number of pages, leaves, or columns in terms of the numbered or lettered sequences in the volume. Record the last numbered page, leaf, or column in each sequence and follow it with the appropriate term or abbreviation." Examples:

92 p.	[46 leaves printed on both sides]
62 leaves	[62 leaves printed only on one side]
ix, 289 p.	[last numbered page in roman numerals sequence and in arabic numerals sequence]
iv leaves, 224 p.	[last numbered leaf and last numbered page]

See Fig. 4.8 (page 97).

2.5B3. "Disregard unnumbered sequences, unless such a sequence constitutes the whole (see 2.5B7) or a substantial part (see also 2.5B8) of the publication, or unless an unnumbered sequence includes page(s), etc., that are referred to in a note. When recording the number of unnumbered pages, etc., either give the estimated number preceded by *ca.*, without square brackets, or enclose the exact number in square brackets." Examples:

79, [1], 64 p.	[unnumbered page referred to in note]
Bibliography: p. [80]	[note requiring use of unnumbered page]

2.5B5. "If the numbering within a sequence changes (e.g., from roman to arabic numerals), ignore the numbering of the first part of the sequence." Example:

252 leaves	[item numbered i-vii followed by leaves 8-252, for a total of 252 leaves — not 7 leaves followed by 252 leaves as would be indicated by: vii, 252 leaves]

2.5B7. "If the volume is printed without pagination or foliation, ascertain the total number of pages, etc., and give the number in square brackets. For larger items, estimate the number of pages and give the estimated number preceded by *ca.*, without square brackets." Examples:

[12] p.   [unnumbered pages counted]

ca. 200 p.   [unnumbered pages approximated]

2.5B8. "If the volume has complicated or irregular paging, record the pagination using one of the following methods, depending upon the nature or extent of the complications:

a) Record the total number of pages or leaves (excluding those which are blank or contain advertising or other inessential matter) followed by the words *in various pagings* or *in various foliations.* . . .

b) Record the number of pages or leaves in the main sequences of the pagination and add the total number, in square brackets, of the remaining variously paged sequences. . . .

c) Describe the volume simply as *1 v. (various pagings), 1 case,* or *1 portfolio*, as appropriate. . . ."

Examples:

86 p. in various pagings   [total number of pages]

273 leaves in various foliations   [total number of leaves]

128, ix, [48] p.   [two main sequences followed by number of pages in several smaller sequences]

1 v. (various pagings)   [indication of many sequences — perhaps some are numbered, some are not, some may be lettered — too complicated for use of alternatives "a" or "b"]

2.5B10.   Leaves or pages of plates

"Record the number of leaves or pages of plates at the end of the sequence(s) of pagination, whether the plates are found together or distributed throughout the publication, or even if there is only one plate." If such plates are unnumbered, follow 2.5B7. If paging is complex, follow 2.5B8. If there are both leaves and plates, use the term that is predominant. Examples:

vi, 224, [9] p., 26 leaves of plates   [numbered leaves of plates]

176, p., [16] p. of plates   [unnumbered pages of plates]

74 leaves, [33] leaves of plates   [unnumbered leaves of plates]

398, [1] p., [1] leaf of plates

Bibliography: p. [399]

[unnumbered page with bibliography note referring to it and an unnumbered plate]

Publications in more than one volume

2.5B17.-2.5B18.

A printed monograph in more than one physical part is described with the number of whichever of the following terms is appropriate:

volumes — each bibliographic unit in its own binding

parts — bibliographic units bound several to a volume

pamphlets — collections of pamphlets bound together or assembled in a portfolio

pieces — items of varying character, assembled for cataloging as a collection

case(s) — box(es) containing bound or unbound material

portfolio(s) — container(s), usually consisting of two covers joined at the back and tied at the front, top, and/or bottom, holding loose papers, illustrative materials, etc.

Examples:

5 v.   [each of five bibliographic units bound separately]

25 pts.   [each part issued separately but specified by the publisher that they should be bound several to a volume when complete]

2 cases   [unbound material held together as a bibliographic unit in two boxes]

2.5B19.   "If the number of bibliographic volumes differs from the number of physical volumes, record the fact in the form *[bibliographic] v. in [physical]*." Example:

3 v. in 1

2.5B20.　　　"If a set of volumes is continuously paged, give the pagination in parentheses after the number of volumes. Ignore separately paged sequences of preliminary matter in volumes other than the first." Example:

>　　2 v. (ix, 1438 p., 32 leaves of plates)

2.5B21.　　　*"Optional addition.* If the volumes in a multivolume set are individually paged, give the pagination of each volume in parentheses after the number of volumes." Example:

>　　3 v. (vi, 49; 62; 58 p.)

　　The Library of Congress is applying this option only when the information is especially significant as, for example, in the case of early printed books.[1]

2.5B23.　　　**Braille or other raised types**
　　If appropriate, add to the number of volumes or leaves one of the following phrases:

>　　of braille
>　　of Moon type
>　　of jumbo braille
>　　of microbraille
>　　of press braille
>　　of print/braille [eye-readable print and braille]
>　　of print/press braille

Examples:

>　　3 v. of jumbo braille
>
>　　484 leaves of braille

2.5C.　　　**Illustrative matter**

2.5C1.　　　"Describe an illustrated printed monograph as *ill.* unless the illustrations are all of one or more of the particular types mentioned in the next paragraph. If only some of the illustrations belong to these types, give the abbreviation *ill.* first. Tables are not illustrations. Disregard illustrated title pages and minor illustrations (decorations, vignettes, etc.)." *See* Fig. 4.8 (page 97).

2.5C2.　　　"If the illustrations are of one or more of the following types, and are considered to be important, designate them by the appropriate term or abbreviation (in this order):"

TERM	ABBREVIATION (IF ALLOWED)
charts	
coats of arms	
facsimiles	facsim., facsims.
forms	
genealogical tables	geneal. table(s)
maps	
music	
plans	
portraits (use for both single and group portraits)	port., ports.
samples	

"Designate all other types as *ill.*" Examples:

47 p. : ill., ports.	[contains illustrations, some of which are portraits]
280 p. : facsims.	[the only illustrations are facsimiles]
176 p., [24] p. of plates : ill., coats of arms, maps, plans	[illustrations include three of the specific types in rule 2.5C2, in addition to other illustrations]

2.5C3. "Describe coloured illustrations (i.e., those in two or more colours) as such." Examples:

48 p. : ill. (some col.)	[some illustrations in color]
216 p. : ill., maps (some col.), col. ports.	[some maps in color, all portraits in color]
xiv, 182 p. : col. ill.	[all illustrations in color]

2.5C4.-2.5C8.

Treatment of special cases (e.g., number of illustrations known, special locations of illustrations, works consisting of all or nearly all illustrations) is delineated in these rules in *AACR 2* which should be consulted when such special cases arise.

2.5D.   **Size**

2.5D1.   "Give the height of the volume(s) in centimetres, to the next whole centimetre up (e.g., if a volume measures 17.2 centimetres, record it as 18 cm.). Measure the height of the binding if the volume is bound. Otherwise, measure the height of the item itself. If the volume measures less than 10 centimetres, give the height in millimetres." *See* Fig. 4.8.

Fig. 4.8. Rule 2.5D1. Addition of physical description.

Handbook of data processing for libraries / Robert M. Hayes, Joseph Becker ; sponsored by the Council on Library Resources. – 2nd ed. -- Los Angeles : Melville Pub. Co., c1974.

xvi, 688 p. : ill. ; 24 cm.

Note: Book actually measures 23.4 centimeters but is recorded as 24.

2.5D2.   "If the width of the volume is either less than half the height or greater than the height, give the width following the height preceded by a multiplication sign." Examples:

ca. 150 p. : ill. ; 34 x 16 cm.   [width less than half the height]

ii, 97 p. : ill., ports. ; 18 x 21 cm.   [width greater than the height]

2.5D3.-2.5D5.

These rules in *AACR 2* cover unusual cases and should be consulted when one is cataloging sets with items of varying sizes, or single sheets.

2.5E.   **Accompanying material**

2.5E1.   "Record the name, and *optionally* the physical description, of any material that is issued with the item and is intended to be used in conjunction with it, as instructed in 1.5E." Example:

142 p. : ill., maps ; 39 cm. + 1 overlay grid

The Library of Congress is applying this option on a case-by-case basis to items that are substantial in extent or that are significant for some reason.[2]

2.5E2.   "If the accompanying material is issued in a pocket inside the cover of the publication, specify its location in a note (see 2.7B11)." Example of note:

Overlay grid in pocket inside back cover.

RULE 2.6.   SERIES AREA

2.6B.   **Series statements**

2.6B1.   "Record each series statement as instructed in 1.6." *See* Fig. 4.9.

Fig. 4.9. Rule 2.6B. Addition of series statements.

Handbook of data processing for libraries / Robert M.
Hayes, Joseph Becker ; sponsored by the Council on Library
Resources. – 2nd ed. – Los Angeles : Melville Pub. Co.,
c1974.
   xvi, 688 p. : ill. ; 24 cm. – (Information science series) (A
Wiley-Becker & Hayes series book)

Note: It will be noticed that in the CIP (i.e., Cataloging in Publication) on the
verso of the title page (Fig. 4.2, page 87), "A Wiley-Becker & Hayes series
book" is given as a quoted note rather than as a series. The interpretation by
LC is that it is a characterization of books of that publisher, rather than a
series. This was an interpretation in *AACR 1* that has been omitted from
AACR 2. "A Wiley-Becker & Hayes series book" fits the *AACR 2* definition of
"series."

RULE 2.7.   NOTE AREA

2.7B.   Notes

   "Make notes as set out in the following subrules and in the order given
there." As noted in the preceding chapter, notes for all materials are given in
the same order. The ones particularly applicable to printed monographs are
illustrated here.

2.7B1.   Nature, scope, or artistic form

   "Make notes on these matters unless they are apparent from the rest of the
description." *See* Fig. 4.10.

**Fig. 4.10. Rule 2.7B1. Addition of note about
nature of publication.**

George Robert Bonfield, Philadelphia marine painter,
1805-1898. -- [Philadelphia] : Philadelphia Maritime Museum, c1978.
   78 p. : ill. (some col.) ; 22 x 29 cm.

——► Catalog of an exhibition.
Bibliography: p. 76-77.

2.7B2.   Language of item and/or translation or adaptation

   "Make notes on the language of the item, or on the fact that it is a translation or adaptation, unless this is apparent from the rest of the description." *See*
Figs. 4.11 and 4.12.

**Fig. 4.11. Rule 2.7B2. Addition of note about
language of publication.**

Pastoral : mediaeval into Renaissance / Helen Cooper. –
Ipswich : Brewer ; Totowa, N.J. : Rowman & Littlefield,
1977.

257 p., [2] leaves of plates : ill. ; 24 cm.

─────► Verse passages in Latin and medieval French.
Bibliography: p. [235]-248.
Includes index.
ISBN 0-87471-906-2 (Rowman & Littlefield) : £8.50

Fig. 4.12. Rule 2.7B2. Addition of note about translation.

Weather and climate : in colour / Svante Bodin ; ill. by
Studio Frank. – Poole [Eng.] : Blanford Press, 1978.

272 p. : col. ill. ; 19 cm. – (Blanford colour series)

─────► Translation of: Vader och vind.
Includes index.
ISBN 0-7137-0858-1 : £4.95

2.7B3.   Source of title proper

"Make notes on the source of the title proper if it is other than the chief
source of information." *See* Fig. 4.13.

**Fig. 4.13. Rule 2.7B3. Addition of note on source
of title proper.**

Unbranched dorsal-fin rays and subfamily classification
in the fish family Cyprinidae / by William A. Gosline. -- Ann
Arbor : University of Michigan, 1978.

21 p. ; 23 cm. – (Occasional papers of the Museum of
Zoology, University of Michigan ; no. 684)

─────► Caption title.
Bibliography: p. 19-21.

2.7B4.   Variations in title

"Make notes on titles borne by the item other than the title proper." *See*
Fig. 4.14.

Fig. 4.14. Rule 2.7B4. Addition of note on variant title.

Starring pelicans, cats, and frogs : from the award winning ABC television children's series / a creation of ABC
News ; written by Lester Cooper ; edited by Julie Duffy ;
illustrated by Ed Cage and Novle Rogers ; photography by
H. Michael Stewart. -- 1st ed. -- Dallas : Handel, 1978.

63, [1] p. : col. ill. ; 29 cm. -- (Animals, animals, animals /
Lester Cooper ; no. 1)

———►Cover title: ABC TV's award winning animals, animals,
animals.
Bibliography: p. [64]
Summary: Text and illustrations introduce pelicans,
cats, frogs, and toads. Based on the television series "Animals, animals, animals."
ISBN 0-917080-03-3

2.7B5. Parallel titles and other title information

"Give parallel titles and other title information not recorded in the title
and statement of responsibility area if they are considered to be important."
See Fig. 4.15.

**Fig. 4.15. Rule 2.7B5. Addition of note on other title information
not recorded above.**

Travels of a latter-day Benjamin of Tudela / Yehuda
Amichai ; [translated from the Hebrew by Ruth Nevo]. --
Webster Groves, Mo. : Webster review ; Berkeley, Calif. :
distributed by Serendipity Books Distribution, 1977.

64 p. ; 22 cm. -- (Webster review ; v. 3, no. 3)

———►At head of title: A special issue.
ISBN 0-917146-10-7 : $1.25

2.7B6. Statements of responsibility

". . . Give statements of responsibility not recorded in the title and statement of responsibility area. Make notes on persons or bodies connected with a
work, or significant persons or bodies connected with previous editions, not
already named in the description." *See* Fig. 4.16.

Fig. 4.16. Rule 2.7B6. Addition of note on responsible bodies, combined with note on nature of work.

Statewide coordination and governance of postsecondary education : quality, costs, and accountability : the major issues of the '80s / [editors, Robert Berdahl, Martha Levin, John Ziegenhagen]. -- Wayzata, Minn. : Spring Hill Center, c1978.

46 p. ; 28 cm.

⟶ Papers from a conference held Dec. 11-13, 1977, at Spring Hill Center, and sponsored by the center and the Education Commission of the States.
Includes bibliographical references.
ISBN 0-932676-05-7

Note: The statement of responsibility incorporated in the note above did not appear in the chief source of information but was composed by the cataloger from information that appeared elsewhere. Had it appeared in the chief source of information it would have been transcribed in the statement of responsibility area (*see* Fig. 4.5, page 89).

2.7B7.   Edition and history

"Make notes relating to the edition being described or to the bibliographic history of the work." *See* Figs. 4.17 and 4.18.

Fig. 4.17. Rule 2.7B7. Addition of note on original of edition being described.

The English Lake District as interpreted in the poems of Wordsworth / by William Knight. – Norwood, Pa. : Norwood Editions, 1978.

viii, xvi, 270 p. : port. ; 23 cm.

⟶ Reprint of: 2nd ed. Edinburgh : D. Douglas, 1891.
Includes bibliographical references.
ISBN 0-8482-1426-9 : $30.00

Fig. 4.18. Rule 2.7B7. Addition of note about previous closely related work.

"Steam and petticoats" : the early railway era in southwestern Ontario / by Wayne Paddon. -- [S.l. : s.n.], c1977 (London : M. Kelly)

304 p. : ill. ; 24 cm.

⟶ Continues: Story of the Talbot settlement.
Includes bibliographical references and index.

2.7B9. Publication, distribution, etc.

"Make notes on publication, distribution, etc., details that are not included in the publication, distribution, etc., area and that are considered to be important." *See* Fig. 4.19.

**Fig. 4.19. Rule 2.7B9. Addition of note on printing
and distribution.**

Proteus / Morris West ; illustrated by Robert Heindel. – Limited 1st ed. -- Franklin Center, Pa. : Franklin Library, 1979.

305 p. : ill. ; 24 cm.

⟶ Printed for members of the First Edition Society.

2.7B10. Physical description

"Make notes on important physical details that are not already included in the physical description area." *See* Fig. 4.20.

**Fig. 4.20. Rule 2.7B10. Addition of note giving
further physical details.**

Lessons & complaints / James Purdy. – New York : Nadja Editions, [1978]

[5] p. ; 25 cm.

⟶ "Limited to 174 numbered copies and 26 lettered." No. 103.

Note: Some notes in this category are "copy-specific." "No. 103" in Fig. 4.20 is such a note. See the discussion of this problem under Rule 2.7B20.

2.7B11. Accompanying material

"Make notes on the location of accompanying material if appropriate." *See* example under 2.5E2.

2.7B12. Series

"Make notes on series data that cannot be given in the series area." Example:

Originally issued in series : Research studies in library science.

2.7B13. Dissertations

"If the item being described is a dissertation or thesis presented in partial fulfillment of the requirements for an academic degree, give the designation of the thesis (using the English word *thesis*) followed by a brief statement of the degree for which the author was a candidate (e.g., M.A. or Ph.D., or, for theses to which such abbreviations do not apply, *doctoral* or *master's*), the name of the institution or faculty to which the thesis was presented, and the year in which the degree was granted." *See* Fig. 4.21.

Fig. 4.21. Rule 2.7B13. Addition of notes to description of a master's thesis.

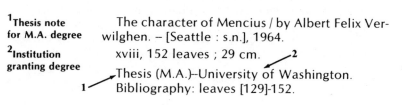

[1]Thesis note
for M.A. degree

[2]Institution
granting degree

The character of Mencius / by Albert Felix Ver-
wilghen. – [Seattle : s.n.], 1964.

xviii, 152 leaves ; 29 cm. —[2]

[1]—Thesis (M.A.)–University of Washington.
Bibliography: leaves [129]-152.

"If the publication is a revision or abridgement of a thesis, state this." *See* Fig. 4.22.

Fig. 4.22. Rule 2.7B13. Addition of note to description of a revised Ph.D. thesis.

Television fraud : the history and implications of the quiz show scandals / Kent Anderson. -- Westport, Conn. : Greenwood Press, 1978.

xii, 226 p. ; 22 cm. – (Contributions in American studies, ISSN 0084-9227 ; no. 39)

——►Based on the author's thesis (Ph.D.)–University of Washington.
Bibliography: p. [209]-215.
Includes index.
ISBN 0-313-20321-0 : $18.95

2.7B14.   Audience
"Make a brief note of the intended audience for, or intellectual level of, an item if this information is stated in the item." Example:

For adults learning to read.

2.7B17.   Summary
"Give a brief objective summary of the content of an item unless another part of the description gives enough information." *See* Fig. 4.23.

Fig. 4.23. Rule 2.7B14. Addition of summary note.

Angels and me / written by Carolyn Nystrom ; illustrated , by Dwight Walles. – Carol Stream, Ill. : Creation House, c1978.

32 p. : ill. (some col.) ; 26 cm. – (The Mustard seed library)

——►Summary: Text and suggested Biblical verses discuss the importance of God's angels.
ISBN 0-88419-128-1 : $4.95

2.7B18.   Contents

"Make a note of the contents of an item, either selectively or fully, if it is considered necessary to show the presence of material not implied by the rest of the description, or to stress items of particular importance, or to list the contents of a collection. When recording titles formally, take them from the head of the part to which they refer rather than from contents lists, etc." *See* Figs. 4.24-4.30.

Fig. 4.24. Rule 2.7B18. Addition of selective contents notes.

Creative quilting / by Elsa Brown. – New York : Watson-Guptill Publications, 1975.

1
[1]Bibliography note
144 p. : ill. ; 27 cm.
Bibliography: p. 141-142.
2 Includes index.
[2]Index note
ISBN 0-8230-1105-4

Fig. 4.25.

Human sexuality in health and illness / Nancy Fugate Woods ; with a chapter by James S. Woods. – Saint Louis : Mosby, 1975.

x, 232 p. ; 23 cm.

Includes bibliographies and index.
ISBN 0-8016-5620-6

Bibliography and index notes combined

Fig. 4.26.

Political dynamics : impact on nurses and nursing / Grace L. Deloughery, Kristine M. Gebbie. – Saint Louis : Mosby, 1975.

ix, 236 p. ; 27 cm.

Includes bibliographical references and index.
ISBN 0-8016-1245-4

Fig. 4.27. Rule 2.7B18. Addition of contents note for collection of works of one author.

At peace : stories / by Ann Copeland. -- [Ottawa] : Oberon Press, c1978.

164 p. ; 23 cm.

Contents: Siblings.--The Lord's supper.--Higher learning.--The golden thread.--Cloister.--Jubilee.--At peace.
ISBN 0-88750-270-9.   – ISBN 0-88750-271-7(pbk.)

Fig. 4.28. Rule 2.7B18. Addition of contents note for collection of works by different authors.

Classics of organization theory / edited by Jay M. Shafritz, Philip H. Whitbeck. -- 1st ed. -- Oak Park, Ill. : Moore Pub. Co., c1978.

xi, 323 p. : ill. ; 23 cm.

Includes bibliographical references.
——► Contents: Of the division of labour / Adam Smith.--The principles of scientific management / Frederick Winslow Taylor.--General principles of management / Henri Fayol.--Bureaucracy / Max Weber.--The giving of orders / Mary Parker Follett.--Notes on the theory of organization / Luther Gulick.--The scalar principle / James D. Mooney.

Fig. 4.29. Rule 2.7B18. Addition of contents note for multi-volume work.

The collected works of Sir Winston Churchill. -- Centenary limited ed. -- London : Library of Imperial History, 1973-

v. : ill. ; 24 cm.

——► Contents: v. 1. My early life. My African journey.--v. 2. The story of the Malakand field force.
ISBN 0-903988-01-1 (v. 1)

Fig. 4.30. Rule 2.7B18. Addition of partial contents note.

Voices of the Black theatre / by Loften Mitchell. -- Clifton, N.J. : J. T. White, [1975]

ix, 238 p. : ill. ; 24 cm.

Contains taped individual recollections of Black theatrical figures with introductory essays and comments by L. Mitchell.
Includes index.
——► Partial contents: The words of Eddie Hunter.--The words of Regina M. Andrews.--The words of Dick Campbell.--The words of Abram Hill.--Interlude: Paul Robeson.--The words of Frederick O'Neal.--The words of Vinette Carroll.--The words of Ruby Dee.
ISBN 0-88371-006-4

Note: *AACR 2* does not prescribe punctuation for contents notes. The above examples are punctuated according to the pre-*AACR 2* Library of Congress practice, although the examples in *AACR 2* omit the periods before the dashes.

2.7B19.   Numbers borne by the item

"Make notes of important numbers borne by the item other than ISBNs (see 2.8B)." *See* Fig. 4.31.

Fig. 4.31. Rule 2.7B19. Addition of note giving number of the item.

Uranium mill tailings control : hearings before the Subcommittee on Energy and the Environment of the Committee on Interior and Insular Affairs, House of Representatives, Ninety-fifth Congress, second session ... held in Washington, D.C. ... – Washington, D.C. : G.P.O., 1978.

v, 716 p. : graphs ; 24 cm.

——▸ "Serial no. 95-30."

2.7B20.   Copy being described and library's holdings

"Make notes on any peculiarities or imperfections of the copy being described that are considered to be important. If the library does not hold a complete set of a multipart item, give details of the library's holdings." Note: These notes are "copy-specific." That is, a note made under this rule will be applicable only to the copy held by the cataloger who is creating the description. This is fine in an individual library. However, if the library belongs to a network and creates online original cataloging that other libraries eventually use as a basis for their cataloging, this type of note can be a source of difficulty, as is known by libraries that have had to change LC's copy-specific notes to reflect local cataloging. Examples:

Library's copy autographed by the author.

Library lacks v. 3.

2.7B21.   "With" notes

"If the description is of a separately titled part of an item lacking a collective title, make a note beginning *With:* listing the other separately titled parts of the item in the order in which they appear there." *See* Fig. 3.73 (page 76) in the preceding chapter.

The only notes required by the book whose title page and other preliminaries are shown in Figs. 4.1-4.3 are bibliography and index notes. It can be noted in the CIP in Fig. 4.2 that there was to be a note "Includes bibliographies." However, this note is intended to be used when the citations are listed in some logical order (e.g., alphabetical or chronological). In this case, the listings are in the order to which they are referred in each chapter. In addition, there is an index. Therefore, the note should be constructed as in Fig. 4.32.

RULE 2.8.   STANDARD NUMBER AND TERMS OF AVAILABILITY AREA

2.8B.   International Standard Book Number (ISBN)

2.8B1.   "Record ISBNs as instructed in 1.8B."

2.8C. *Optional addition.* **Terms of availability**

"Record the price or other terms on which the item is available." *See* Fig. .32.

Fig. 4.32. Rule 2.8C. Addition of note, ISBN, and price.

Handbook of data processing for libraries / Robert M. Hayes, Joseph Becker ; sponsored by the Council on Library Resources. – 2nd ed. – Los Angeles ; Melville Pub. Co., c1974.

xvi, 688 p. : ill. ; 24 cm. – (Information science series) (A Wiley-Becker & Hayes series book)

Includes bibliographical references and index. ISBN 0-471-36483-5 : $30.00

RULES 2.9-2.11.

Supplementary items, items made up of several types of material, facsimiles, photocopies, and other reproductions are described as instructed in the general chapter under Rules 1.9-1.11.

EARLY PRINTED MONOGRAPHS

RULES 2.12-2.18

These rules give instructions for describing early printed monographs. In general, description follows the general rules, but necessary additions, modifications, and differences are given in these rules. The ISBD(A) – the International Standard Bibliographic Description for Ancient Books – had not been completed before publication of *AACR 2*, and rules have been found to be inadequate by rare book catalogers. LC is compiling rules for the bibliographic description of early printed books and later books that need special treatment. The compilation is based primarily on *AACR 2*, but includes provisions from the ISBD(A) and a few rules appearing in neither place. LC plans to publish these rules and to adopt them at the same time it adopts *AACR 2*.

FOOTNOTES

[1]"AACR 2 Options to be Followed by the Library of Congress, Chapters 1-2, 12, 21-26," *Library of Congress Information Bulletin* 37 (July 21, 1978): 424.

[2]"AACR 2 Options," p. 424.

5 DESCRIPTION OF CARTOGRAPHIC MATERIALS

INTRODUCTION

This chapter is the first of several that cover the description of materials that have been variously called "nonbook," "non-print," "audio-visual," or "media"—the last term often including monographic materials, as in "School Media Center." Often these special materials are not handled in the same way as monographs are handled. An administrative decision within each library determines whether to catalog and/or classify each of these special materials; because of the dimensions many cannot be shelved with corresponding monographic materials. This is true of cartographic materials, with the exception of atlases. But even atlases may present shelving problems, because they are often quite large. The dimensions of maps, also, are of significance in their description because this will directly influence the location of particular maps in a given collection, a consideration that often makes classification relatively insignificant and description of greater importance. If the librarian cannot easily remember the contents of the collection, then cataloging control is needed. If the library has only six maps, for instance, there is little need to catalog them. Sixty maps, however, or even sixteen, may well need to be cataloged. The disadvantage of failing to catalog descriptively any special materials is that the patron must look somewhere other than in the main catalog for the record of the material. It is strongly recommended that as many special materials as possible be cataloged descriptively and thus recorded in the main catalog. Past problems in doing this have been greatly eased by the publication of *AACR 2* with its integrated approach to the description of special materials. In *AACR 2* all materials are described according to the same set of principles.

RULE 3.0. GENERAL RULES

3.0A. Scope
"The rules in this chapter cover the description of cartographic materials of all kinds. Cartographic materials include all materials that represent, in whole or in part, the earth or any celestial body. These include two- and three-dimensional maps and plans (including maps of imaginary places); aeronautical, navigational, and celestial charts; atlases; globes; block diagrams; sections; aerial photographs with a cartographic purpose; bird's eye views (map views); etc. . . ."

3.0B. Sources of information

3.0B1. Atlases have the same chief source and prescribed sources of information as books. *See* 2.0B in the preceding chapter.

3.0B2.   **Chief source of information**

"The chief source of information (in order of preference) is:

a)   the cartographic item itself; when an item is in a number of physical parts, treat all the parts (including a title sheet) as the cartographic item itself

b)   container (portfolio, cover, envelope, etc.) or case, the cradle and stand of a globe, etc.

"If information is not available from the chief source, take it from any accompanying printed material (pamphlets, brochures, etc.)."

3.0B3.   **Prescribed sources of information**

"The prescribed source(s) of information for each area of the description of cartographic materials is set out below.

AREA	PRESCRIBED SOURCES OF INFORMATION
Title and statement of responsibility	Chief source of information
Edition	Chief source of information, accompanying printed material
Mathematical data	[same as for edition area]
Publication, distribution, etc.	[same as for edition area]
Physical description	Any source
Series	[same as for edition area]
Note	Any source
Standard number and terms of availability	Any source"

Figures 5.1-5.5 show the chief sources of information for two maps that are used in this chapter to demonstrate the building of descriptions for cartographic materials.

**Fig. 5.1. Chief source of information from
map number 1.**

WEST INDIES

AND CENTRAL AMERICA

Compiled and Drawn in the Cartographic Division of the
National Geographic Society

MELVIN M. PAYNE, PRESIDENT

for THE NATIONAL GEOGRAPHIC MAGAZINE

MELVILLE BELL GROSVENOR, EDITOR-IN-CHIEF
FREDERICK G. VOSBURGH, EDITOR
WELLMAN CHAMBERLIN, CHIEF CARTOGRAPHER
ATHOS D. GRAZZINI, ASSOCIATE CHIEF CARTOGRAPHER

Oblique Mercator Projection

SCALE 1 : 4,815,360 OR 76 MILES TO THE INCH

0	50	100	150	200	250	300

STATUTE MILES

0	50	100	150	200	250	300

KILOMETERS

Highways: ★ *Places with Scheduled Air Service*   *Prevailing Winds*

═══ *Superhighways*   ⸳⸳⸳ *Canals*   *Warm Currents*

≡ ≡ ≡ *Under Construction*   ⚑ *Oil Fields*   *Swamps*

─── *Other Roads*   ─── *Oil Pipe Lines*   *Elevations in Feet*

─── *Railroads*   ∴ *Ruins*   *Depth Curves and Soundings in Fathoms*

③ *Red circled numbers are reference keys to the larger scale inset maps*

WASHINGTON : JANUARY 1970

Fig. 5.2. Upper right corner of map number 2.

BATH ALUM QUADRANGLE
VIRGINIA – BATH CO.
7.5 MINUTE SERIES (TOPOGRAPHIC)
SW/4 WILLIAMSVILLE 15' QUADRANGLE

Fig. 5.3. Lower right corner of map number 2.

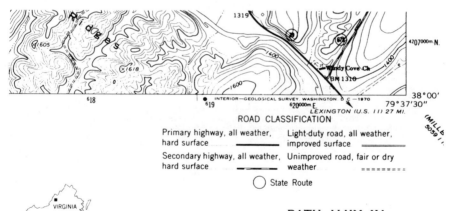

ROAD CLASSIFICATION

Primary highway, all weather, hard surface	Light-duty road, all weather, improved surface
Secondary highway, all weather, hard surface	Unimproved road, fair or dry weather

◯ State Route

QUADRANGLE LOCATION

BATH ALUM, VA.
SW/4 WILLIAMSVILLE 15' QUADRANGLE
N3800—W7937.5/7.5

1968

AMS 5060 II SW—SERIES V834

Fig. 5.4. Lower left corner of map number 2.

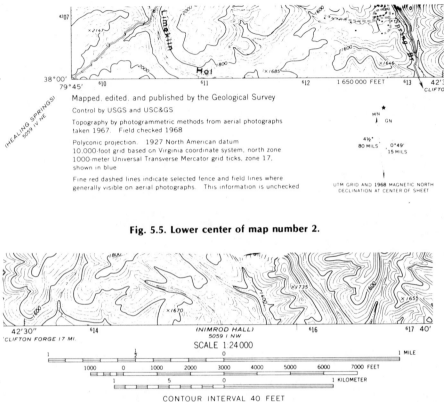

Fig. 5.5. Lower center of map number 2.

3.0D.-3.0H.

Levels of description, language and script, inaccuracies, accents and other diacritical marks, and items with several title pages are treated as discussed in the general chapter on description.

3.0J.   Description of whole or part

"In describing a collection of maps, describe the collection as a whole [*see* Fig. 5.6] *or* describe each map (giving the name of the collection as the series) [*see* Fig. 5.18, page 123], according to the needs of the cataloguing agency. If the collection is catalogued as a whole, but descriptions of the individual parts are considered desirable, see chapter 13 [chapter 15 of this text]." *See* examples in *AACR 2*, pages 86-87. The use of *series* in this rule may be misleading because a map series differs from a book series (*see* glossary).

Fig. 5.6. Rule 3.0J. Description of a map collection as a whole.

Louisiana 1:25,000 : A.M.S. V885 / U.S. Army Map
    Service. -- Scale 1:25,000 ; Transverse Mercator
    proj. -- Washington, D.C. : The Service, 1948-

    maps : col. ; 56 x 50 cm. or smaller.

Issued in 7 1/2 minute quadrangles.
"Contour Interval 5 feet."
Includes location index and index to boundaries.
Accompanied by : index to series.

RULE 3.1.   TITLE AND STATEMENT OF RESPONSIBILITY AREA

3.1B.   Title proper

3.1B1.   "Record the title proper as instructed in 1.1B." *See* Fig. 5.7.

Fig. 5.7. Rule 3.1B1. Transcription of title proper for map number 1.

West Indies and Central America

3.1B2.   "If the title proper includes a statement of the scale, include it in the transcription." For example:

Arabian peninsula 1:500,000 / prepared by . . .

3.1B3. "If the chief source of information bears more than one title, choose the title proper as instructed in 1.1B8. If both or all of the titles are in the same language and script, choose the title proper on the basis of the sequence or layout of the titles. If these are insufficient to enable the choice to be made or are ambiguous, choose the most comprehensive title." *See* Fig. 5.8.

Fig. 5.8. Rule 3.1B3. Transcription of the most comprehensive title from map number 2.

Bath Alum quadrangle, Virginia — Bath Co.

3.1B4. "If the item lacks a title, supply one as instructed in 1.1B7. Always include the name of the area covered in the supplied title."

3.1C. *Optional addition.* **General material designation**

The GMDs appropriate to materials in this chapter are [map], [globe], or [text] (for atlases). However, the Library of Congress is not using GMDs for cartographic materials, and their use is not illustrated in this text.[1]

3.1D. **Parallel titles**

3.1D1. "Record parallel titles as instructed in 1.1D."

3.1E. **Other title information**

3.1E1. "Record other title information as instructed in 1.1E." For example:

France : industrial centers

State of California : south half

3.1E2. "If neither the title proper nor the other title information includes an indication of the geographic area covered by the item, or if there is no other title information, add, as other title information, a word or brief phrase indicating the area covered." For example:

Land use and industry : [in East Germany]

3.1F. **Statements of responsibility**

3.1F1. "Record statements of responsibility as instructed in 1.1F." *See* Figs. 5.9 and 5.10.

Fig. 5.9. Rule 3.1F. Addition of statements of responsibility to the descriptions for maps number 1 and 2.

West Indies and Central America / compiled and drawn in the Cartographic Division of the National Geographic Society, for The National geographic magazine

Fig. 5.10.

Bath Alum quadrangle, Virginia — Bath Co. / mapped, edited, and published by the Geological Survey

---

3.1G. Items without a collective title

3.1G1. "If a cartographic item lacks a collective title, *either* describe the item as a unit . . . [as instructed in 1.1G], *or* make a separate description for each separately titled part . . . , *or* (in certain circumstances) supply a collective title (see 3.1G5)."

3.1G5. "If a cartographic item lacking a collective title consists of a large number of physically separate parts, supply a collective title as instructed in 3.1B4." For example:

[Maps of the United States]

RULE 3.2. EDITION AREA

3.2B. Edition statement

3.2B1. "Transcribe a statement relating to an edition of a work that contains differences from other editions, or that is a named revision of that work, as instructed in 1.2B." For example:

World atlas / Rand McNally. -- Imperial ed.

RULE 3.3. MATHEMATICAL DATA AREA

3.3B. Statement of scale

3.3B1. "Give the scale of a cartographic item as a representative fraction expressed as a ratio (1:   ). Precede the ratio by the word *scale*. Give the scale even if it is already recorded as part of the title proper or other title information." *See* Figs. 5.11 and 5.12 (pages 116-17).

"If a verbal scale statement is found on the item, record it as a representative fraction in square brackets. . . .

"If a representative fraction or a verbal scale statement is found in a source other than the chief source of information, the scale is given in square brackets in the form of a representative fraction. . . .

"If no statement of scale is found on the item, its container or case, or accompanying material, compute a representative fraction from a bar graph, a grid or by comparison with a map of known scale. Give the scale preceded by *ca.* . . . ." Usually, map librarians will determine the scale of an item by using a measuring device known as a "natural scale indicator" before resorting to a bar graph or grid.

"If the scale cannot be determined by any of the above means, give the statement *Scale indeterminable.*"

3.3B2. *Optional addition.* "Give additional scale information that is found on the item (such as a statement of comparative measures or limitation of the scale to particular parts of the item). Use standard abbreviations and numerals in place of words. Precede such additional information by a full stop."

The Library of Congress is applying this option.[2] *See* Fig. 5.11.

3.3B3.-3.3B8.

Detailed instructions for recording more than one scale value, and for handling other problems, are given in these rules, which should be consulted when one is doing in-depth map cataloging.

3.3C.   Statement of projection

3.3C1. "Give the statement of projection if it is found on the item, its container or case, or accompanying printed material. Use standard abbreviations (see Appendix B) and numerals in place of words (see Appendix C)." *See* Figs. 5.11 and 5.12.

3.3C2. *Optional addition.* "Add associated phrases connected with the projection statement if they are found on the item, its container or case, or accompanying printed material. Such associated phrases concern for example, meridians, parallels, and/or ellipsoid." For example:

> Lambert conformed conic proj. based on standard parallels
> 33° and 45°

The Library of Congress is applying this option.[3]

3.3D.   *Optional addition.* Statements of coordinates and equinox

These rules for adding coordinates and equinox to the description will be applied by LC when the information is readily available although they are not illustrated here. An optional statement, recorded in 3.3D1, giving meridians, other than the Greenwich prime meridian, in the note area is also being applied by LC.[4]

Fig. 5.11. Rule 3.3. Addition of mathematical data to the descriptions for maps number 1 and 2.

West Indies and Central America / compiled and drawn in the Cartographic Division of the National Geographic Society, for The National geographic magazine. – Scale 1:4,815,360. 1 in. to 76 miles ; Oblique Mercator proj.

Fig. 5.12.

Bath Alum quadrangle, Virginia--Bath Co. / mapped,
  edited, and published by the Geological Survey. -- Scale
  1:24,000 ; Polyconic proj.

RULE 3.4.   PUBLICATION, DISTRIBUTION, ETC., AREA

The details in this area are recorded in the same manner as discussed in the
general chapter under Rule 1.4. The options also are being applied by LC in
the same manner as discussed there. *See* Figs. 5.13 and 5.14.

**Fig. 5.13. Rule 3.4. Addition of publication details to the descriptions
of maps number 1 and 2.**

West Indies and Central America / compiled and drawn in
  the Cartographic Division of the National Geographic
  Society, for The National geographic magazine. -- Scale
  1:4,815,360. 1 in. to 76 miles ; Oblique Mercator proj. --
  Washington, [D.C.] : The Society, 1970.

Fig. 5.14.

Bath Alum quadrangle, Virginia--Bath Co. / mapped,
  edited, and published by the Geological Survey. -- Scale
  1:24,000 ; Polyconic proj. -- Washington, D.C. : For sale by
  U.S. Geological Survey, 1968.

RULE 3.5.   PHYSICAL DESCRIPTION AREA

3.5B.   Extent of item (including specific material designation)

3.5B1.   "Record the number of physical units of a cartographic item by
giving the number of units in arabic numerals and one of the following terms,
as appropriate. If the item is in manuscript, add *ms.* to the term used.

(List appears on page 118)

aerial chart	map section
aerial remote sensing image	orthophoto
anamorphic map	photo mosaic
atlas	(controlled)
bird's-eye view *or* map view	photo mosaic
block diagram	(uncontrolled)
celestial chart	photomap
celestial globe	plan
chart	relief model
globe	remote-sensing image
(for globes other than celestial	space remote-sensing
globes)	image
hydrographic chart	terrestrial remote-sensing
imaginative map	image
map	topographic drawing
map profile	topographic print

"If the parts of the item are very numerous and the exact number cannot be readily ascertained, give an approximate number." Generally, map librarians find it more practical either to count the items or to leave the number open. *See* Figs. 5.15 and 5.16 (page 120).

3.5B2. "If there is more than one map, plan, etc., on a sheet, specify the number of maps, etc." For example:

8 maps on 2 sheets

"If maps, plans, etc., are printed in two or more sections but so designed that they could be fitted together to form a single map, plan, etc., or more than one map, plan, etc., give the number of complete maps, plans, etc., followed by the number of sections." For example:

1 aerial chart in 6 sections

3.5B3. "Add, to the statement of extent for an atlas, the pagination or number of volumes as instructed in 2.5B." For example:

1 atlas (20 leaves)

3.5C. **Other physical details**

3.5C1. "Give the following details, as appropriate, in the order set out here:

number of maps in an atlas

colour

material

mounting"

3.5C2. "Specify the number of maps in an atlas as instructed in 2.5C."
For example:

1 atlas (5 v.) : 250 col. maps

3.5C3. Colour

"If the item is coloured or partly coloured, indicate this. Disregard coloured matter outside a map, etc., border." *See* Figs. 5.15 and 5.16.

3.5C4. Material

"Record the material of which the item is made if it is considered to be significant (e.g., if a map is printed on a substance other than paper)." For example:

1 relief model : col., plastic

3.5C5. Mounting

"If the item is mounted or has been mounted subsequent to its publication, indicate this." For example:

1 globe : col., plastic, mounted on wooden stand

1 map : col., mounted on linen

3.5D. Dimensions

This rule is divided into four subparts that tell how to give dimensions for the different kinds of cartographic material: two-dimensional items, atlases, relief models, and globes. An optional fifth subpart covers dimensions of containers.

3.5D1. Maps, plans, etc.

"For two-dimensional cartographic items, give the height x width in centimetres, to the next whole centimetre up. . . . Give the measurements of the face of the map, etc., measured between the neat lines." The diameter of a circular map is given, and if measuring the map itself is difficult (e.g., there are no neat lines, or the shape is irregular), the dimensions of the sheet are given. The neat line marks the point at which the mapping detail ends. *See* Fig. 5.16.

AACR 2 gives detailed rules for describing maps in sections, folded maps, maps with substantial text, maps printed on both sides, and collections of maps of different sizes. *See* Fig. 5.15. The cataloger doing detailed map cataloging should consult this rule in *AACR 2* and the manual by the Anglo-American Cataloguing Committee on Cartographic Materials which is scheduled to be published early in 1981.

3.5D2. Atlases

"For atlases, give the dimensions as instructed in 2.5D."

3.5D3.   **Relief models**

"For relief models, give the height x width in centimetres as instructed in 3.5D1, and *optionally* add the depth."

The Library of Congress is applying this option.[5]

3.5D4.   **Globes**

"For globes, give the diameter, specified as such."

3.5D5.   *Optional addition.* **Containers**

"Add the dimensions of a container, specified as such, to the dimensions of the item." For example:

> 1 relief model : col., wood ; 50 x 35 x 4 cm. in box,
> 26 x 19 x 9 cm.

LC is applying this option.[6]

3.5E.   **Accompanying material**

3.5E1.   Material issued with the item is treated, by both *AACR 2* and LC, as described in the general chapter under 1.5E1.

Fig. 5.15. Rule 3.5. Addition of physical details to description of map number 1.

West Indies and Central America / compiled and drawn in
 the Cartographic Division of the National Geographic
 Society, for The National geographic magazine. -- Scale
 1:4,815,360. 1 in. to 76 miles ; Oblique Mercator proj. --
 Washington, [D.C.] : The Society, 1970.
 1 map : col. ; 67 x 97 cm. folded to 15 x 22 cm.

Fig. 5.16. Rule 3.5. Addition of physical details and series to the description of map number 2.

Bath Alum quadrangle, Virginia–Bath Co. / mapped,
 edited, and published by the Geological Survey. -- Scale
 1:24,000 ; Polyconic proj. – Washington, D.C. : For sale by
 U.S. Geological Survey, 1968.
 1 map section : col. ; 58 x 43 cm. – (7.5 minute series :
 topographic)

RULE 3.6.   SERIES AREA

3.6B.   **Series Statements**

3.6B1.   "Record each series statement as instructed in 1.6." *See* Fig. 5.16 and the discussion of 3.0J.

RULE 3.7.   NOTE AREA

3.7B.   Notes

"Make notes as set out in the following subrules and in the order given there." Following are some typical notes used for cartographic items. For further details consult *AACR 2*, pages 103-108. Notes for atlases also use Rule 2.7 for books.

3.7B1.   Nature and scope of the item
Example:

Shows locations of important historical events.

3.7B2.   Language
Example:

Place names in Arabic and English.

3.7B4.   Variations in title
Example:

Title in lower right corner: Bath Alum, Va.

3.7B6.   Statements of responsibility
Example:

Grid and marginal information added by the Army Map Service.

3.7B7.   Edition and history
Example:

First published under title: Geographic map of the . . . Kingdom of Saudi Arabia.

3.7B8.   Mathematical and other cartographic data
Examples:

"Contour interval 50 feet."

Relief shown by hachures, shading, spot heights, etc.

3.7B10.   Physical description
Example:

Maps issued in envelopes bearing copies of inset maps of cities.

3.7B11.   Accompanying material
Example:

> Accompanied by: Index to maps of Arabia / issued by
> Army Map Service. 1 sheet ; 25 x 36 cm.

3.7B18.   Contents
Examples:

> Each sheet includes: "Index to adjoining sheets,"
> glossary, and "Sources of base compilation."

> Inset: Area west of Apalachicola River.

> Parts: 1. Evanston, Ill., 1963.--2. Chicago Loop, Ill.,
> 1965.--3. Blue Island, Ill.-Ind., 1965.

> Includes stratigraphic section, col. cross section, and
> quadrangle location map.

3.7B19.   Numbers (other than Standard Numbers)
Examples:

> Supt. of Docs. no.: I 19.2:V88/4.

> Publisher's no.: AMS 5060 II SW-Series V834.

See also Figs. 5.17 and 5.18.

**Fig. 5.17. Rule 3.7B. Addition of notes to description of
map number 1.**

West Indies and Central America / compiled and drawn in
  the Cartographic Division of the National Geographic
  Society, for The National geographic magazine. – Scale
  1:4,815,360. 1 in. to 76 miles ; Oblique Mercator proj. –
  Washington, [D.C.] : The Society, 1970.
  1 map : col. ; 67 x 97 cm. folded to 15 x 22 cm.

  Shows locations of important historical events.
  Supplement to: National geographic magazine, vol. 137,
no. 1 (Jan. 1970).
  Includes 38 insets.

Fig. 5.18. Rule 3.7B. Addition of notes to description of map number 2.

Bath Alum quadrangle, Virginia–Bath Co. / mapped, edited, and published by the Geological Survey. -- Scale 1:24,000 ; Polyconic proj. -- Washington, D.C. : For sale by U.S. Geological Survey, 1968.

1 map section : col. ; 58 x 43 cm. – (7.5 minute series : topographic)

Title in lower right corner: Bath Alum, Va.
"Topography by photogrammetric methods from aerial photographs."
Publisher's no.: AMS 5060 II SW-Series V834.

RULE 3.8.   STANDARD NUMBER AND TERMS OF AVAILABILITY AREA

The details and options in this area are treated as discussed in the general chapter under Rule 1.8. Atlases will often have ISBNs. Some maps that are issued serially may have been assigned ISSNs. However, most cartographic items at this time do not bear international standard numbers.

FOOTNOTES

[1]"AACR 2 Options Proposed by the Library of Congress, Chapters 2-11," *Library of Congress Information Bulletin* 38 (Aug. 10, 1979): 307-308.

[2]"AACR 2 Options," p. 308.

[3]"AACR 2 Options," p. 308.

[4]"AACR 2 Options," p. 308.

[5]"AACR 2 Options," p. 309.

[6]"AACR 2 Options," p. 309.

6 DESCRIPTION OF MANUSCRIPTS AND MANUSCRIPT COLLECTIONS

INTRODUCTION

The challenge of cataloging manuscripts is that each is unique. The manuscript or the manuscript collection does not exist in another library, except perhaps in reproduction. It is not the kind of material for which catalogers can find cataloging copy already in existence. In addition, such materials often do not have any clearly defined chief source of information, and, indeed, they often do not have clearly defined titles. There may be difficulty even reading the handwriting in which a manuscript is written. It may be difficult to know whether one is dealing with an original or with a handwritten copy, and if a copy, the date it was copied and by whom. The manuscript cataloger is often dealing with events and names of persons not recorded elsewhere. These problems and others are addressed in chapter 4 of *AACR 2*. The most important of these rules are discussed below.

RULE 4.0.   GENERAL RULES

4.0A.   Scope
"The rules in this chapter cover the description of manuscript (including typescript) texts of all kinds, including manuscript books, dissertations, letters, speeches, etc., legal papers (including forms completed in manuscript), and collections of such manuscript texts. For reproductions of manuscript texts published in multiple copies, see chapter 2 [chapter 4 of this text] or chapter 11 [chapter 13 of this text], as appropriate. For manuscript cartographic items, see also chapter 3 [chapter 5 of this text]. For manuscript music, see also chapter 5 [chapter 7 of this text]."

4.0B.   Sources of information

4.0B1.   Chief source of information
"The chief source of information for a manuscript text is the manuscript itself." The manuscript itself, however, may have scattered or incomplete information. Therefore an order of preference is set up in this rule: a title page if there is one, then colophon, caption, heading, and the text itself. A source that was originally part of the manuscript, however, is preferred to a title page, etc., that may have been added later. If information cannot be taken from the manuscript itself, the following sources, in this order, may be used:

"another manuscript copy of the item

a published edition of the item

reference sources

other sources"

The whole collection is treated as the chief source of information for a manuscript collection.

4.0B2.   Prescribed sources of information

"The prescribed source(s) of information for each area of the description of manuscript texts is set out below. . . .

AREA	PRESCRIBED SOURCES OF INFORMATION
Title and statement of responsibility	Chief source of information and manuscript or published copies
Date	[same as above]
Physical description	Any source
Note	Any source"

The major parts of the sources of information for an individual manuscript are shown as Figs. 6.1-6.3. These will be used to demonstrate the building of a description for a single manuscript. The description of a manuscript collection will be illustrated by describing the collection of papers of William Alexander Smith, who operated business enterprises in Anson County, North Carolina, and invested in a number and variety of businesses in other states in the late nineteenth and early twentieth centuries. The collection includes correspondence, legal papers, volumes, clippings, genealogy, pictures, bills, receipts, promissory notes, etc.

Fig. 6.1. Outside of letter shown in Fig. 6.2.

Windsor 3: Feb. 1793.

Note from the King

Fig. 6.2. Letter from George III to Henry Dundas.
[Reproduced by permission of the Manuscript Department,
William R. Perkins Library, Duke University.]

Fig. 6.3. Transcription of letter shown in Fig. 6.2.

[*Windsor, 3 Feb. 1793, 9:10 a.m.*] Mr. Secretary Dundas is to summon the Privy Council at the Queen's House for tomorrow at three o'Clock. I am glad to find the French are taking steps that must cut off the correspondence between the two Nations, and consequently puts an end to Lord Auckland's desire now before Me of intriguing with Du Mourier.

GR.

P.S. As the enclosed Warrants are all the Same and as many more will be necessary it might be a great saving of time in the Secretary's office if they were Printed and only the blanks filled up when meant to be issued I should equally as now Sign them.

RULE 4.1. TITLE AND STATEMENT OF RESPONSIBILITY AREA

4.1B. **Title proper**

4.1B1. "Record the title proper as instructed in 1.1B." Example:

Tract's critticall and historicall

4.1B2. "If a manuscript text or manuscript collection lacks a title or lacks some of the data prescribed for the material below, supply one as instructed below.

"**Manuscript volumes and similar material.** This section applies to literary manuscripts, diaries, journals, memorandum books, account books, etc. Supply a brief title indicating the nature of the material. For manuscripts of subsequently published works, supply the title by which the work is known." For example:

[A Collection of 17th century English poetry]

Note: This volume contains copies of English poetry of the 17th century. Some of the poems are attributed to authors.

"**Ancient, medieval, and Renaissance manuscripts.** *AACR 2* gives here only general guidance that for these and Oriental manuscripts without title pages, either the cataloger should follow the rules for early printed monographs, or a title should be supplied as instructed for manuscript volumes in the paragraph above.

"**Letters, etc.** This section applies to single letters, postcards, telegrams, radiograms, etc. Supply a title consisting of the word *Letter* (or *Postcard*, *Telegram*, etc.), the date of writing (expressed as year, month, day), the place of writing, the name of the addressee, and place to which addressed. Enclose any details not taken from the letter, etc., its envelope, or enclosures, in square brackets." *See* Fig. 6.4.

Fig. 6.4. Rule 4.1B2. Supplied title for the manuscript in
Fig. 6.2. [Place to which addressed is unknown.]

[Letter] 1793 Feb. 3, Windsor [to Henry] Dundas

"**Speeches, sermons, etc.** Supply a title for a speech, sermon, etc., consisting of an appropriate word (*Speech, Address*, etc.) followed by the place and/or the occasion of the delivery." For example:

[Sermon, written after the fall of Fort Sumter]

"**Legal documents.** This section applies to legal documents such as wills, deeds, mortgages, leases, warrants, commissions, etc. Supply a title for a legal document consisting of a word or brief phrase characterizing the document, the date of signing (expressed as year, month, day)[,] the name(s) of persons concerned other than those responsible for the document, and the occasion for the document if it can be expressed concisely. Enclose any details not taken from the document in square brackets." For example:

> [Commission] 1864 June 6, [commissioning] James Wall Scully as Colonel in the 10th Regiment, Infantry, Tennessee Volunteers.

"**Collections of manuscripts.** This section applies to collections of manuscript materials formed by or around a person, family, corporate body, or subject. The materials may be in their original form or reproductions, and may include photographs and printed materials. Supply a title by which the collection is known, or a title indicating the nature of the collection. Unless more specific terms are used, use *Letters* for letters by an individual, *Correspondence* for letters between persons or to a person or persons, *Papers* for miscellaneous personal or family material, and *Records* for materials relating to a corporate body." For example, the supplied title for the collection of papers of William Alexander Smith, described on page 125 would be:

> [Papers]

"**Miscellaneous single manuscripts.** For manuscript texts not covered by the above sections, supply a title by which the manuscript is known, or supply a title indicating the nature of the material."

"Indicate the source of a supplied title in the note area (see 4.7B3)."

4.1C. *Optional addition.* General material designation

The appropriate GMD for the material covered by this chapter is "[manuscript]." However, LC is not applying the GMD option to manuscripts, and its use is not illustrated in this text.

4.1D.-4.1E.

Parallel titles and other title information are recorded as instructed in the general chapter under 1.1D-1.1E with one addition:

4.1E2.

"If a letter, etc., speech, sermon, etc., or legal document has a title lacking the information specified for supplied titles for those documents (see 4.1B2), add the information as other title information." For example:

> The duty of communicating in the Lord's Supper enforced : [sermon]

4.1F.   **Statements of responsibility**

4.1F1.   "Record statements of responsibility appearing on the manuscript as instructed in 1.1F." Examples:

> Tract's critticall and historicall / compiled by Sir
> James Turner, Kny't

> [Sermon, written after the fall of Fort Sumter] / Thomas
> Smyth

See also Fig. 6.5.

Fig. 6.5. Rule 4.1F1. Addition of statement of responsibility to description of manuscript collection.

[Papers] / William Alexander Smith

4.1F2.   *"Optional addition.* If the name appended to, or the signature on, a manuscript is incomplete, add to it the name of the person concerned." The Library of Congress is following this option, because "truncated names are apt to appear often on manuscripts, particularly letters." If the option is applied, better identification is provided.[1] *See* Fig. 6.6.

Fig. 6.6. Rule 4.1F2. Addition of name to incomplete statement of responsibility for single manuscript.

[Letter] 1793 Feb. 3, Windsor [to Henry]
Dundas / GR [George III]

4.1F3.   "If a manuscript lacks a signature or statement of responsibility, supply the name(s) of the person(s) responsible for it, if known."

RULE 4.2.   EDITION AREA

"This area is not used for manuscript texts."

RULE 4.3.   MATERIAL (OR TYPE OF PUBLICATION) SPECIFIC DETAILS AREA

"This area is not used for manuscript texts."

RULE 4.4.   DATE AREA

This area, it will be noted, is in the place of the "Publication, distribution, etc., area." It omits details of place and name of publisher (this being unpublished material) and includes only date, and then only if it is not already in the title. The date of a single manuscript is given as a year, optionally followed by the month and day. LC will follow the option when the information is readily available.

For a manuscript collection, inclusive years are given. *See* Fig. 6.7.

Fig. 6.7. Rule 4.4. Addition of date to description of manuscript collection.

[Papers] / William Alexander Smith. -- 1765-1949.

RULE 4.5.   PHYSICAL DESCRIPTION AREA

4.5B.   Statement of extent

4.5B1.   Single manuscripts

"Record sequences of leaves or pages, whether numbered or not, as instructed in 2.5B." *See* Fig. 6.8 (page 131).

"If the manuscript has been bound, add *bound* at the end of the pagination." Example:

128 leaves, bound

There is an option to add the number of leaves if this is different from the number of pages. LC is not applying this option.[2]

4.5B2.   Collection of manuscripts

"If a collection occupies one linear foot or less of shelf space, record the extent in terms of the number, or approximate number of items (the number of bound and unbound items separately expressed), or the number of containers or volumes. *Optionally,* if the number of volumes or containers is recorded, add the number or approximate number of items." LC is applying this option.[3] Examples:

1 v. (208 items)

2 boxes (110 items), 2 v. (68 items)

ca. 600 items

"If the collection occupies more than one linear foot of shelf space, record the extent in terms of the number of linear feet occupied. *Optionally,* add the number or approximate number of items or containers or volumes." LC is applying the option.[4]

This provision, although easy enough to apply, yields information that may be essentially meaningless to the user. For example, the William Alexander Smith collection of papers that is being used as an example in this chapter has 11,573 items in 51 boxes that measure 44 x 30 x 9 centimeters. It also has 101 volumes. The number of feet of shelf space taken up depends on whether the boxes are stored vertically (not usual in manuscript collections) or horizontally with the long side out or the short side out. There is also a question of how many boxes are stacked on top of one another. Therefore, we have chosen to illustrate the extent of this item in terms of containers and volumes. *See* Fig. 6.9

4.5C.   Other physical details

Illustrated matter is described as instructed in 2.5C or 8.5C. In addition, if a single manuscript is made of material other than paper, the type of material is recorded. Example:

42 leaves : parchment, col. ill.

4.5D.   Dimensions

4.5D1.   Single manuscripts

"Give the height of single unbound manuscripts in centimetres to the next whole centimetre up. Add the width if it is less than half the height or greater than the height. If the manuscript is kept folded, add the dimensions when folded." *See* Fig. 6.8.

"Give the dimensions of a bound volume or case as instructed in 2.5D."

4.5D2.   Collections of manuscripts

"If the size of the items, containers, or volumes (depending on the terms of the first statement of extent) is uniform, give that size in centimetres. *Optionally,* if the size is not uniform, give the size of the largest followed by *or smaller.*" LC is not applying the option.[5] *See* Fig. 6.9.

Fig. 6.8. Rule 4.5. Addition of physical description to description of single manuscript.

[Letter] 1793 Feb. 3, Windsor [to Henry] Dundas / G.R. [George III]
1 leaf ; 38 x 46 cm. folded to 23 x 19 cm.

Fig. 6.9. Rule 4.5. Addition of physical description to description of manuscript collection.

[Papers] / William Alexander Smith. -- 1765-1949.
51 boxes (11,573 items), 101 v. ; 44 x 30 x 9 cm.

RULE 4.6.   SERIES AREA

"This area is not used for manuscript texts."

RULE 4.7.   NOTE AREA

4.7B.   Notes

"Make notes as set out in the following subrules and in the order given there." Following are some examples of notes used for manuscripts. For further details consult *AACR 2*, pages 119-24.

4.7B1.   Nature, scope, or form of manuscript(s)

One of the following terms is used:

holograph(s) - manuscript(s) handwritten by the author

ms. - any other handwritten manuscript

mss. - all other collections of handwritten manuscripts

typescript(s)

Copies are noted by adding one of the following:

(carbon copy)

(photocopy)   or the plural,

(transcript, handwritten)   if appropriate

(transcript, typewritten)

The word "signed" is added if appropriate. Examples:

Typescript signed

Mss. (photocopies)

Ms. signed (carbon copy)

Holograph (photocopy)

"In describing a collection of manuscripts, name the types of papers, etc., constituting the collection and mention any other features that characterize it. If the collection is of personal papers, give enough data to identify the person. . . ." *See* Fig. 6.14 (page 134).

4.7B2.   Language(s)

See Fig. 6.10.

**Fig. 6.10. Rule 4.7B2. The language note in this example is
necessary because the places involved and the names of the
correspondents do not lead one to suspect the language would be French.**

[Letter] 1852 Aug. 2, Dublin [to] Lucy [Butler Massy]
London / Anne Butler.
3 p. ; 22 cm.

Holograph signed.
In French.

4.7B6. Statements of responsibility

" . . . Make notes on persons or bodies connected with a work not already
named in the description." *See* Fig. 6.11.

**Fig. 6.11. Rule 4.7B6. Addition of note about a person who has
added to the work of another.**

[Letter] 1776 Jan. 17, Hayes, England [to] Edward
Wilson / James Pitt.
[2] p. ; 20 cm.

Holograph signed.
Holograph signed note by William Pitt appended to
letter.

4.7B7. Donor, source, etc., and previous owner(s)
Example:

Gift of the estate of Mrs. Theodora Cabot, 1955.

See also Figs. 6.13 and 6.14 (page 134).

4.7B9. Published versions

A published transcription of a manuscript can be of great value to the
researcher. This chapter's sample manuscript was transcribed and annotated in
"Some Letters of George III," by W. B. Hamilton, in *The South Atlantic
Quarterly*, Vol. 68, No. 3 (Summer 1969), page 416. Reference to this article
would appear as a note. *See* Fig. 6.13.

4.7B10. Physical description
See Fig. 6.12.

**Fig. 6.12. Rule 4.7B10. The date in the watermark explains the
knowledge that the letter is a copy and not the original.**

[Letter] 1804 Aug. 25, Putney Common [to William]
Pitt / W[illiam] Wilberforce.
[2] p. ; 23 cm.

Ms. (transcript, handwritten).
Paper watermarked: 1834.

4.7B14.   Access and literary rights
Example:

Information on literary rights available in the
repository.

4.7B15.   Reference to published descriptions
Example:

Described in: Manuscripts for research / report of the
director, 1961-1974, North Country Historical Research Center, Feinberg Library, State University College, Plattsburgh,
New York. 1975. p. 31-32.

**Fig. 6.13. Rule 4.7. Addition of notes to the descriptions of
single manuscript and manuscript collection.**

[Letter] 1793 Feb. 3, Windsor [to Henry]
Dundas / G.R. [George III].
1 leaf ; 38 x 46 cm. folded to 23 x 19 cm.

Holograph signed.
Purchase, 1961.
Published in: Some letters of George III / W.B.
Hamilton. p. 416. In The South Atlantic quarterly. Vol. 68,
no. 3 (Summer 1969).

Fig. 6.14.

[Papers] / William Alexander Smith. -- 1765-1949.
51 boxes (11,573 items), 101 v. ; 44 x 30 x 9 cm.

Mss.
Capitalist and businessman operating mainly in North
Carolina from ca. 1866 to 1934. Includes correspondence,
reports, financial statements, writings, legal papers,
volumes, clippings, genealogy, pictures, bills, receipts, and
promissory notes.
Purchase, 1957-1966.

FOOTNOTES

[1]"AACR 2 Options Proposed by the Library of Congress: Chapters 2-11," *Library of Congress Information Bulletin* 38 (Aug. 10, 1979): 309.

[2]"AACR 2 Options," p. 310.

[3]"AACR 2 Options," p. 310.

[4]"AACR 2 Options," p. 310.

[5]"AACR 2 Options," p. 310.

7 DESCRIPTION OF PUBLISHED MUSIC

INTRODUCTION

This chapter deals with musical compositions that are 1) in written (but not micro-) form and 2) published. Music that is unpublished can be described to a limited extent by using the rules in this chapter in conjunction with the rules for manuscripts (*See AACR 2*, chapter 4). Music that is in recorded form is described using *AACR 2*, chapter 6, and music in microform is described using chapter 11.

A musical composition in written form normally appears as a series of staves upon which notes are printed, but occasionally other systems of notation are used. The description of music written for a solo instrument, such as the piano, is relatively straightforward. The description of music written for several instrumental or vocal parts (i.e., scores) presents some special problems, especially in the title and statement of responsibility area, in the physical description area and in the notes area.

RULE 5.0.   GENERAL RULES

5.0A.   Scope

"The rules in this chapter cover the description of published music. They do not cover manuscript or other unpublished music in detail, though the use of an additional term in the physical description (see 5.5B) and the use of the specific provisions of chapter 4 will furnish a sufficiently detailed description for the general library catalogue. For the description of recorded music, see chapter 6. For microform reproductions of music, see chapter 11."

5.0B.   Sources of information

5.0B1.   Chief source of information

"If the title page consists of a list of titles including the title of the item being catalogued, use as the chief source of information whichever of the 'list' title page, the cover, or the caption furnishes the fullest information. In all other cases use the title page (see 2.0B1) as the chief source of information."

Title pages of published music sometimes are relatively uninformative. For instance, if the item being cataloged is one of several items collected into a volume, its title may be only briefly listed, along with others, on what is called the "list" title page of the volume; this same title may be given in a fuller form on the cover of the volume or as a caption title above the opening bars of the music itself. Thus, in the description of published music, provision is made for alternative chief sources of information, depending on where the fullest bibliographic information can be found. These sources of information, in order of preference, are caption, cover, colophon, other preliminary matter, and other materials.

5.0B2.   Prescribed sources of information

"The prescribed source(s) of information for each area of the description of published music is set out below. . . .

AREA	PRESCRIBED SOURCES OF INFORMATION
Title and statement of responsibility	Chief source of information
Edition	Chief source of information, caption, cover, colophon, other preliminaries
Publication, distribution, etc.	Chief source of information, caption, cover, colophon, other preliminaries, first page of music
Physical description	Any source
Series	[same as edition area]
Note	Any source
Standard number, etc.	Any source"

Three items are used in this chapter to illustrate the building of descriptive information for published music: a concerto for cembalo and strings by Christoph Schaffrath, three sonatas for four hands by Johann Christian Bach and a quartet for woodwinds by Richard Donovan. Their chief and other sources of information are shown in Figs. 7.1-7.5 and the complete records for these items are shown in Figs. 7.17-7.19 (see page 151).

Fig. 7.1. Chief source of information for a score.

COLLEGIUM MUSICUM: YALE UNIVERSITY · SECOND SERIES · VOLUME VII

Christoph Schaffrath

CONCERTO IN B-FLAT
FOR CEMBALO AND STRINGS

Edited by Karyl Louwenaar

A-R EDITIONS, INC. · MADISON

**Fig. 7.2. Series and availability information found
in a preliminary.**

Collegium Musicum, a series of publications of the Department of Music, Yale University, was initiated by the late Leo Schrade in 1955. The continuing aim of the series, as set forth by Professor Schrade in the first volume, is to "present compositions which, through neglect or lack of knowledge, have been ungraciously forgotten or overlooked, despite their artistic value and historical importance." The series is prepared under the general editorship of Leon Plantinga; materials for publication are chosen and editorial policy is established by a committee of the Yale music faculty.

Subscribers to this series, as well as patrons of subscribing institutions, are invited to apply for information about the "Copyright-Sharing Policy" of A-R Editions, Inc., under which the contents of this volume may be reproduced free of charge for performance use.

Correspondence should be addressed to:

A-R Editions, Inc.
315 West Gorham Street
Madison, Wisconsin 53703

Fig. 7.3. Chief source of information for a score and parts.

THE VALLEY
MUSIC PRESS

RICHARD DONOVAN

QUARTET FOR WOODWINDS

FLUTE, OBOE, CLARINET and BASSOON

Mount Holyoke College
South Hadley, Mass.

Smith College
Northampton, Mass.

Fig. 7.4. Chief source of information for music for one part of the
score and parts shown in Fig. 7.3.

THE VALLEY
MUSIC PRESS

RICHARD DONOVAN

QUARTET FOR WOODWINDS
CLARINET B♭

Mount Holyoke College
South Hadley, Mass.

Smith College
Northampton, Mass.

Fig. 7.5. Chief source of information for music for a solo instrument.

JOHANN CHRISTIAN BACH

DREI SONATEN

FÜR KLAVIER ZU VIER HÄNDEN

HERAUSGEGEBEN VON WILHELM WEISMANN

C. F. PETERS · LEIPZIG

11525

RULE 5.1. TITLE AND STATEMENT OF RESPONSIBILITY AREA

5.1B.   **Title proper**

5.1B1.   "Record the title proper as instructed in 1.1B."

5.1B2.   "If the title, exclusive of the medium of performance,[1] the key, or the opus numbering of the work, consists of a generic term (e.g., trio, symphony, string quartet), treat the statements of medium of performance, the key, and/or the opus numbering as part of the title proper. . . . Otherwise, treat such a statement as other title information (see 5.1E). . . . In case of doubt, treat such a statement as part of the title proper."[2] Note that in the examples given (Figs. 7.1, 7.3, and 7.5) the titles exclusive of key and/or medium of performance consist of a generic term: *concerto, sonaten,* and *quartet.* In the first example the title is rendered distinctive by the addition of a key and a medium of performance (*see* Fig. 7.1, page 138); in the other two examples by the additions of mediums of performance. Examples:

> Concerto in B-flat for cembalo and strings
>
> Quartet for woodwinds
>
> Drei Sonaten für Klavier zu vier Händen

5.1B3. "If a title proper has to be devised by the cataloguer (see 1.1B7), give all the elements prescribed for uniform titles for music (see 25.25-25.36) in the order prescribed there." A title proper is devised only when no title can be found in any source. The elements prescribed for uniform titles for music include, among others, title indicating type of composition, medium of performance, serial numbers, opus numbers, and key. They are discussed in chapter 20 of this text.

5.1C. *Optional addition.* **General material designation**

5.1C1. "Add, immediately following the title proper, the appropriate general material designation as instructed in 1.1C." In most cases the general material designation for published music would be [music]; however, it is important to note here that the adding of a general material designation to published music is an option the Library of Congress does not intend to apply.[3] The point is a moot one. Its stance is that the use of a specific material designation in the physical description area is a better way to indicate the nature of the item.

5.1D. **Parallel titles**

5.1D1. "Record parallel titles as instructed in 1.1D." Examples:

Zwei- und dreistimmige Inventionen = Two and three part inventions

Così fan tutte = Women are like that

5.1E. **Other title information**

5.1E1. "Record other title information as instructed in 1.1E." Other title information includes phrases indicative of the character of the item being described. The instruments for which a piece of music is written are indicative of its character and are recorded as other title information if 1) they appear on the chief source of information and 2) they are not already used to make a generic title distinctive (*see* 5.1B2). Examples:

Quartet for woodwinds : flute, oboe, clarinet and bassoon

The Bells : choral symphony for solo soprano, tenor and baritone

If the medium of performance is not given on the chief source of information, it should be mentioned in a note (*see* 5.7B1).

5.1F. **Statements of responsibility**

5.1F1. "Record statements of responsibility as instructed in 1.1F."

5.1F2. "Add a word or short phrase to the statement of responsibility if the relationship between the title of the work and the person(s) or body (bodies) named in the statement is not clear." *See* Figs. 7.6-7.8.

Fig. 7.6. Rule 5.1F1. Transcription of statement of responsibility for a score.

Concerto in B-flat for cembalo and strings / Christoph Schaffrath ; edited by Karyl Louwenaar.

Fig. 7.7. Rule 5.1F1. Transcription of statements of responsibility for music for solo instrument.

Drei Sonaten für Klavier zu vier Händen / Johann Christian Bach ; herausgegeben von Wilhelm Weismann.

Fig. 7.8. Rule 5.1F1. Transcription of statement of responsibility for a score and parts.

Quartet for woodwinds : flute, oboe, clarinet and bassoon / Richard Donovan.

5.1G.   Items without a collective title

Items without a collective title may take various forms. Several independent works or parts of works may be published together and have a common chief source of information, yet lack a collective title. In this case, Rule 5.1G1 is applied. This rule calls for the listing of each individual title in the title and responsibility area. Works that are published together may, in addition to lacking a collective title, also lack a chief source of information; then 5.1B3, which allows for the devising of a title proper, is applied. It may happen that several independent works or parts thereof are not published together but locally are bound together into one volume; in this case each bibliographically distinct item warrants a separate description and the various descriptions are linked by "With" notes.

5.1G1.   "If an item lacks a collective title, record the titles of the individual works as instructed in 1.1G." The use of 1.1G requires that a decision be made as to whether or not one work predominates in the item: if one work predominates, its title is taken as the title proper and the other works are named in a contents note; if no one work predominates, then the title information and statements of responsibility for each of the works is given. Example:

> Come, let us sing, or, The 95th Psalm ; Lord, how long wilt thou forget me, or Psalm XIII ; As the hart pants, or, The 42nd Psalm : in vocal score / Felix Mendelssohn Bartholdy

RULE 5.2. EDITION AREA

5.2B1.   "Transcribe a statement relating to an edition of a work that contains differences from other editions or that is a named reissue of that work as instructed in 1.2B"; that is, the edition statement is transcribed as it appears on the item, making use of standard abbreviations. *See* Fig. 7.9.

**Fig. 7.9. Rule 5.2. Addition of edition statement to
description of music for solo instrument.**

Drei Sonaten für Klavier zu vier Händen / Johann Christian
Bach ; herausgegeben von Wilhelm Weismann. -- Ed. Peters.

RULE 5.3. MATERIAL (OR TYPE OF PUBLICATION) SPECIFIC
DETAILS AREA

"This area is not used for music."

RULE 5.4. PUBLICATION, DISTRIBUTION, ETC., AREA

Few special features distinguish the "publication, distribution, etc., area" for published music. Other than an instruction not to enclose in brackets a copyright date found only on the first page of a published piece of music and an observation that publishers' numbers and plate numbers should be recorded in the note area, no special provisions are made.

5.4C.   **Place of publication, distribution, etc.**

5.4C1.   "Record the place of publication, distribution, etc., as instructed in 1.4C." *See* Figs. 7.10 and 7.11.

**Fig. 7.10. Rule 5.4C1. Addition of place of publication to
description of a score.**

Concerto in B-flat for cembalo and strings / Christoph
Schaffrath ; edited by Karyl Louwenaar. -- Madison (315 West
Gorham Street, Madison, Wis., 53703)

Note: *See* the discussion of Rule 1.4C7 in chapter 3 of this text for a treatment of the option to include the full address of the publisher, distributor, etc.

**Fig. 7.11. Rule 5.4C1. Addition of place of publication to
description of a score and parts.**

Quartet for woodwinds : flute, oboe, clarinet and bassoon /
Richard Donovan. -- South Hadley, Mass.

5.4D.   Name of publisher, distributor, etc.

5.4D1.   "Record the name of the publisher, etc., and *optionally* the distributor, as instructed in 1.4D." The Library of Congress will apply this option.[4] *See* Fig. 7.12.

5.4D2.   Plate numbers and publishers' numbers

"Record plate numbers and publishers' numbers in the note area (see 5.7B19)."

5.4E.   *Optional addition.* Statement of function of publisher, distributor, etc.

5.4E1.   "Add to the name of a publisher, distributor, etc., a statement of function as instructed in 1.4E." This option will be applied by the Library of Congress selectively when it is deemed necessary for clarification.[5]

5.4F.   Date of publication, distribution, etc.

5.4F1.   "Record the date of publication, distribution, etc., as instructed in 1.4F. If the copyright date is found only on the first page of the music, do not enclose it in square brackets." *See* Fig. 7.13.

5.4G.   Place of printing, name of printer, date of printing

5.4G1.   "If the name of the publisher is unknown, give the place and name of the printer if they are found in the item as instructed in 1.4G."

5.4G2.   "*Optional addition.* Give the place, name of printer, and/or date of printing if they differ from the place, name of publisher, distributor, etc. and date of publication, distribution, etc., and are found in the item and are considered important by the cataloguing agency." This option will be applied by the Library of Congress selectively when it is desired to preserve valuable information about a printer.[6]

RULE 5.5.   PHYSICAL DESCRIPTION AREA

5.5B.   Extent of item (including specific material designation)

The physical description area for published music introduces some special features. One of these is a peculiar use of the specific material designation. Normally, specific material designations are given to different classes of materials that represent different kinds of physical objects. In the case of published music, specific material designations vary under different circumstances, one of them being whether the music is written for a solo instrument or for several instruments. The physical extent of a piece of music written for a solo instrument is described, as for any monograph, in terms of leaves, pages, or volumes. If the option of using the GMD [music], is not applied, then the term *music* is incorporated in the extent of item statement (*see* Fig. 7.18.). Example:

>   36 p. of music.

A specific material designation using the terms *score(s)* and/or *part(s)* is to be given to a piece of music written for several instrumental or vocal parts. The type of score it is—miniature, piano, vocal, etc.—as well as its pagination and the number of copies of it issued by the publisher are to be recorded. (Definitions of different types of scores are given in *AACR 2*, Appendix D.) If the score is accompanied by parts, the number of these issued by the publisher is to be recorded.[7]

5.5B1.   "Record the number of physical units of an item by giving the number of scores or parts in arabic numerals and one of the following terms as appropriate:

>   score
>
>   condensed score
>
>   close score
>
>   miniature score
>
>   piano [violin, etc.] conductor part
>
>   vocal score
>
>   piano score
>
>   chorus score
>
>   part

"For special types of music, use an appropriate specific term (e.g., choir book, table book).

"If none of the terms above is appropriate, use *v. of music*, or *p. of music*, or *leaves of music* unless a general material designation appears in the description, in which case use *v.*, or *p.*, or *leaves. See* Fig. 7.18.

"If the item is a manuscript, add *ms.* to the appropriate term. Give the number of scores and/or parts issued by the publisher. Record differences in the library's holdings and the number of copies of each score or part held by the library in the note area (see 5.7B20)." *See* Fig. 7.14.

5.5B2. "If the item consists of different types of scores, or a score and parts, or different types of score and parts, record the details of each in the order of the list in 5.5B1, separated from each other by a space, plus sign, space." *See* Fig. 7.14.

Fig. 7.14. Rule 5.5B. Addition of extent of item to description of a score and parts.

Quartet for woodwinds : flute, oboe, clarinet and bassoon / Richard Donovan. -- South Hadley, Mass. : Valley Music Press, c1959.
   1 score (35 p.) + 4 parts

5.5B3. "Add, to the statement of extent of an item, the pagination or number of volumes as instructed in 2.5B." *See* Fig. 7.14.

Note: In *AACR 1* the textual matter that precedes the actual staves upon which music is written was not considered part of the score; thus, the extent of an item would appear as "23 p., score (133 p.)," when 23 separately numbered pages of text precede the music. In *AACR 2*, it appears from the examples that separately paged text preceding printed music is to be included in parentheses following the word "score," as in Fig. 7.15. The inference to be drawn is that in *AACR 1* "score" refered only to the printed music, but in *AACR 2* it is being used to refer to the physical item in which the music is contained. This somewhat subtle change is perhaps a consequence of the attempt to classify materials into general and specific types.

5.5C.   **Illustrations**

5.5C1. "Record the details of illustrations as instructed in 2.5C." *See* Fig. 7.15.

Fig. 7.15. Rule 5.5C1. Addition of details of illustrations to description of a score.

Concerto in B-flat for cembalo and strings / Christoph Schaffrath ; edited by Karyl Louwenaar. -- Madison (315 West Gorham Street, Madison, Wis., 53703) : A-R Editions, c1977.
   1 score (x, 77 p., [1] leaf of plates) : facsim.

5.5D.   **Dimensions**

5.5D1. "Record the dimensions of the item as instructed in 2.5D. If the item consists of score(s) and parts, give the dimensions after all the details of the score(s) and parts. If the dimensions of the score(s) and parts differ, give the dimensions of each after the details to which they apply." Examples:

1 score (x, 77 p., [1] leaf of plates) : facsim. ; 28 cm.

47 p. of music ; 23 x 30 cm.

1 score (35 p.) + 4 parts ; 28 cm.

5.5E.   **Accompanying material**

5.5E1.   "Record the name, and *optionally* the physical description, of any material that is issued with the item and is intended to be used in conjunction with it, as instructed in 1.5E." The Library of Congress will apply this option on a case by case basis, when the accompanying material is significant by its extent or for another reason.[8]

RULE 5.6.   SERIES AREA

5.6B.   **Series statements**

5.6B1.   "Record each series statement as instructed in 1.6." *See* Fig. 7.16.

**Fig. 7.16. Rule 5.6B1. Addition of series statement
to description of a score.**

Concerto in B-flat for cembalo and strings / Christoph Schaffrath ; edited by Karyl Louwenaar. -- Madison (315 West Gorham Street, Madison, Wis., 53703) : A-R Editions, c1977.

1 score (x, 77 p., [1] leaf of plates) : facsim. ; 28 cm. – (Collegium Musicum / Yale University, ISSN 0147-0108. Second series ; v.7)

RULE 5.7.   NOTE AREA

5.7B.   **Notes**

"Make notes as set out in the following subrules and in the order given there." Some typical notes used for published music follow.

5.7B1.   **Form of composition and medium of performance**

"If the musical form of a work is not apparent from the rest of the description, give such a form in a word or brief phrase." Examples of forms of composition are carol, opera, concerto and symphony.

"Name the medium of performance for which a musical work is intended unless it has already been named in the rest of the description in English or in foreign language terms that can be readily understood. Name voices before instruments. Name the voices and instruments in the order of the item being described. Name the voice and instruments in English unless there is no satisfactory English term.

"If the work is for solo instruments, name them all if not more than eleven must be named. If the work is for an orchestra, band, etc., do not list the instruments involved. In describing ensemble vocal music, add to the appropriate term a parenthetical statement of the component voice parts, using the abbreviations *S* (soprano), *Mz* (mezzo-soprano), *A* (alto), *T* (tenor), *Bar* (baritone), and *B* (bass). Repeat the abbreviations, if necessary, to indicate the number of parts." Example:

> For cembalo, 2 violins, viola and violoncello.

5.7B2. Text
"Give the language or languages of the textual content of the work unless they are apparent from the rest of the description. Indicate vocal texts published with part of the music." Examples:

> German and English words.
>
> Words in Yiddish (romanized).

5.7B6. Statements of responsibility
"Make notes on variant names of persons or bodies named in statements of responsibility if these are considered to be important for identification. Give statements of responsibility not recorded in the title and statement of responsibility area. Make notes on persons or bodies connected with a work, or significant persons or bodies connected with previous editions, not already named in the description." Examples:

> Text founded on the drama of the same name by Pushkin.
>
> Version by Rev. J. Troutbeck.

5.7B7. Edition and history
"Make notes relating to the edition being described or to the bibliographic history of the work." Examples:

> Reprint of the 1947 Peters ed.
>
> Edited from ms. sources in the National Library of
> Turin.

5.7B8. Notation
"Give the notation used in an item if it is not the notation normally found in that type of item." The usual kind of music notation is staff notation. Other kinds of notation are plainsong notation, tonic sol-fa notation, shape-note notation, and tablature notation.

5.7B10. Duration of performance and physical description
"Give the duration of performance if it is stated in the item being described. Give the duration in English and in abbreviated form. *See* Fig. 7.19 on page 151.

5.7B18. Contents
"Give a list of the separately titled works contained in an item. Add to the titles opus numbers (if they are necessary to identify the works named) and statements of responsibility not already included in the title and statement of responsibility area. If the works in a collection are all in the same musical form

and that form is named in the title proper of the item, do not repeat the musical form in the titles in the contents note." *See* Fig. 7.18 on page 151. "Make notes on additional or partial contents when appropriate." *See* Fig. 7.18.

5.7B19.   Plate numbers and publishers' numbers

"Record the plate number(s) if they are given on the item. Record publishers' numbers only if the plate number is not given. Designate them as *Pl. no.* or *Publisher's no.* as appropriate.

"In describing an item in several volumes, give inclusive numbers if the numbering is consecutive, otherwise give individual numbers or, if there are more than three of these, the first number and the last number separated by a diagonal slash." Example:

Pl. no. B.S.I. no. 31.

See Fig. 7.18.

5.7B20.   Copy being described and library's holdings

"Give details of peculiarities or imperfections of the copies held. Give details of the number of copies held by the library. Always give the holdings if they affect the use of the item in performance. If the library does not hold a complete set of a multipart item, give this information. Make a temporary note if the library hopes to complete the set." *See* Fig. 7.19.

5.7B21.   "With" notes

"If the description is of a separately titled part of an item lacking a collective title, make a note beginning *With:* listing the other separately titled parts of the item in the order in which they appear there." Example:

With: La plus que lente / Claude Debussy.

**RULE 5.8.   STANDARD NUMBER AND TERMS OF
                     AVAILABILITY AREA**

5.8B.   Standard number

5.8B1.   "Give the International Standard Book Number (ISBN) or International Standard Serial Number (ISSN) assigned to an item. Record these numbers as instructed in 1.8B." *See* Fig. 7.17.

5.8D.   *Optional addition.* Terms of availability

5.8D1.   "Give the terms on which the item is available as instructed in 1.8D." *See* Fig. 7.17. The Library of Congress will apply this option with few exceptions, one of which is the omission of a price from noncurrent items.[9]

Fig. 7.17. Description of a score.

Concerto in B-flat for cembalo and strings / Christoph
Schaffrath ; edited by Karyl Louwenaar. -- Madison (315 West
Gorham Street, Madison, Wis., 53703) : A-R Editions, c1977.

1 score (x, 77 p., [1] leaf of plates) : facsim. ; 28 cm. --
(Collegium musicum / Yale University, ISSN 0147-0108. Second
series ; v.7)

For cembalo, 2 violins, viola and violoncello.

ISBN 0-89579-100-5 : May be reproduced free of charge
for performance use by applying to A-R Editions, Inc.

Fig. 7.18. Description of music for a solo instrument.

Drei Sonaten für Klavier zu vier Händen / Johann Christian
Bach : herausgegeben von Wilhelm Weismann. -- Ed. Peters. --
Leipzig : Peters, [1943?]

47 p. of music : 23 x 30 cm.

Contents: Sonate C dur, op. 15, Nr. 15.--Sonate A dur, op.
18, Nr. 5.--Sonate F dur, op. 18, Nr. 6.

"Zur revision des Notentextes": p. [48]

Publisher's no. 4516.

Fig. 7.19. Description of a score and parts.

Quartet for woodwinds : flute, oboe, clarinet and bassoon /
Richard Donovan. -- South Hadley, Mass. : Valley Music
Press c1959.

1 score (35 p.) + 4 parts ; 28 cm.

Duration: 13 min., 20 sec.

Library has 1 copy of the score and 1 copy of each part.

FOOTNOTES

[1]Mediums of performance consist of the musical instruments, including the
voice, for which music is written.

[2]After introduction of the revised chapter 6 of *AACR 1*, the Library of Congress began recording statements of medium of performance, key and/or opus
numbering as other title information in all cases. Thus, this rule represents a
change from previous practice. One should be alert for interpretations of this
rule. First, it is not entirely clear how much additional information about
medium of performance etc. is needed to supplement a title proper that

consists of a generic term. Second, it seems likely the rule will conflict with the rule governing other title information in the ISBD for Printed Music soon to be published. In the draft ISBD (PM), statements about the medium of performance, the key etc. are regarded as other title information when they are not linguistically and/or typographically an integral part of the title proper. It remains to be seen how this potential conflict will be resolved.

[3]"AACR 2 Options Proposed by the Library of Congress, Chapters 2-11," *Library of Congress Information Bulletin* 38 (Aug. 10, 1979):310.

[4]"AACR 2 Options," p. 310.

[5]"AACR 2 Options," p. 310.

[6]"AACR 2 Options," p. 310.

[7]In previous Library of Congress practice this was not done, on the assumption that individual libraries may count parts differently or have different numbers of parts. A blank space was left on the Library of Congress printed cards before the word *parts*. In *AACR 2* there is provision in the notes area (*see* 5.7B20) for local variations in holdings.

[8]"AACR 2 Options," p. 311.

[9]"AACR 2 Options," p. 311.

8 DESCRIPTION OF SOUND RECORDINGS

INTRODUCTION

The term "sound recording" is used to describe aural media as described under "Scope" below. Most of the rule excerpts and examples in this chapter are for disc or tape recording, the forms most commonly found in libraries. Rules applying to other types of recordings should be consulted in chapter 6 of *AACR 2*.

While the description of sound recordings is now standardized and very closely resembles description of other library materials, classification and/or shelf order varies widely from library to library. There is no generally accepted classification scheme for sound recordings. The simplest methods of organization are those without classification by subject matter: shelving by catalog entry, size or physical form, or by accession number. Others are based on existing classification systems, particularly Dewey with cutter numbers, or use methods devised by individual libraries. The system of organization adopted by any library should be based on the size and type of the record collection, the needs of the patrons, and the requirements of internal control.

Both classification and description of sound recordings are affected by the fact that extremely disparate materials often appear on a single physical item. This problem is addressed for description in *AACR 2*, Rule 6.1G, described below.

RULE 6.0. GENERAL RULES

6.0A. Scope

"The rules in this chapter cover the description of sound recordings in all media, i.e., discs, tapes (open reel-to-reel, cartridges, cassettes), piano rolls (and other rolls), and sound recordings on film (other than those intended to accompany visual images, for which see chapter 7 [chapter 9 of this text]). They do not cover specifically recordings in other forms (wires, cylinders, etc.) or in various experimental media, though the use of appropriate specifications in the physical description (see 6.5) and special notes will furnish a sufficiently detailed description of such items."

The phrase "sound recordings on film" is a problem in this chapter. The term is used by some experts to mean film into which sound has been cut in grooves like grooves in a sound disc, a technique used during World War II for portable field recording. Sound accompanying motion pictures is recorded on film either magnetically or optically and is called "sound track film." In an "original" motion picture the visual images are on one film and the sound track on another; but when copied for distribution, the two are placed on one film. Only depository libraries for original motion pictures, therefore, would be cataloging sound track film. In the physical description area in *AACR 2* chapter 6, the only term used is "sound track film"; Rule 6.0A refers the user to *AACR 2* chapter 7 for "sound recordings on film . . . intended to accompany visual images." There are no provisions in the physical description area for description of recordings where sound grooves have been cut into film. In this text, the *AACR 2* rules for sound track film have been excluded. The reader should be aware of the apparent discrepancy and should watch for new interpretations from the ALA Committee on Cataloging: Description and Access and/or LC.

6.0B.   Sources of information

6.0B1.   Chief source of information
"The chief source of information for each major type of sound recording is set out here.

TYPE	CHIEF SOURCE
Disc	Label
Tape (open reel-to-reel)	Reel and label
Tape cassette	Cassette and label
Tape cartridge	Cartridge and label
Roll	Label
Sound recording on film	Container and label

"If there are two or more chief sources of information as defined above (e.g., two labels on a disc) treat these as a single chief source."

If textual material or a container has a collective title while the chief sources above do not, then the source of the collective title may be treated as chief source. Information not available from the chief source may be taken from accompanying textual material, a container, or other sources, in that order. Prefer printed data to sound data.

6.0B2.   Prescribed sources of information
"The prescribed source(s) of information for each area of the description of sound recordings is set out below. . . .

AREA	PRESCRIBED SOURCES OF INFORMATION
Title and statement of responsibility	Chief source of information
Edition	Chief source of information, accompanying textual material, container
Publication, distribution, etc.	[same as edition area]
Physical description	Any source
Series	[same as edition area]
Note	Any source
Standard number and terms of availability	Any source"

Two items are used in this chapter to illustrate the building of descriptive information for sound recordings: a disc and a tape cassette. Their chief sources of information and accompanying sources are shown in Figs. 8.1-8.4.

Fig. 8.1. Chief source of information from disc.
Both labels are treated as a single chief source.

"SATURDAY NIGHT FIEDLER"

ARTHUR FIEDLER
AND THE BOSTON POPS

MSI-011
(MSI 011-A)
STEREO
SIDE ONE

MIDSONG TM **1. SATURDAY** NIGHT FEVER MEDLEY 18:47
INTERNATIONAL   **a. STAYIN'** ALIVE

b. NIGHT FEVER

c. MANHATTAN SKYLINE

d. NIGHT ON DISCO MOUNTAIN

e. DISCO INFERNO
ALL SELECTIONS BMI

PRODUCED AND ARRANGED BY JOHN DAVIS
EXECUTIVE PRODUCER: TONY D'AMATO
RECORDED   JUNE 7, 1979

℗1979 Midsong
International Records, Inc.

"SATURDAY NIGHT FIEDLER"

ARTHUR FIEDLER
AND THE BOSTON POPS

MSI-011
(MSI 011-B)
STEREO
SIDE TWO

MIDSONG TM
INTERNATIONAL

1. BACHAMANIA 11:32
(Based on Toccata and Fugue in "D" minor and
air for the "G" string)
JOHN DAVIS
(Midsong Music/Monsterous Music) (ASCAP)

PRODUCED AND ARRANGED BY JOHN DAVIS
EXECUTIVE PRODUCER: TONY D'AMATO
RECORDED   JUNE 9, 1979

℗1979 Midsong
International Records, Inc.

© 1978 Midsong International Records, Inc., 1650 Broadway, New York, N.Y. 10019

Fig. 8.2. Information from container of disc.

℗ & © 1979 Midsong International Records, Inc.,
Unauthorized Duplication is a Violation of Applicable Laws.

Fig. 8.3. Chief source of information from tape cassette.
Labels from Tape 2 are identical to these, with the exception
of being labeled "Tape 2." All four labels are treated as a
single chief source.

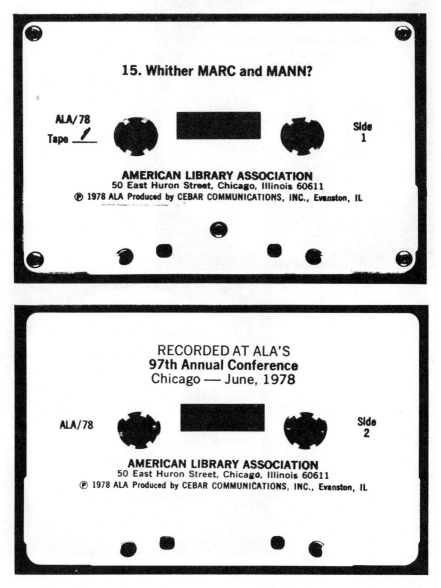

Fig. 8.4. Information about contents of tape from the 1978 American Library Association annual conference program.

Monday, June 26
8:00 a.m.-12:00 noon
Pick Congress Hotel, Great Hall

RTSD CATALOGING AND CLASSIFICATION SECTION

Cosponsored by Resources and Technical Services Division; Reference and Adult Services Division; RASD Catalog Use Committee; and Public Library Association

Chairperson: Elizabeth L. Tate, Rockville, MD

WHITHER MARC AND MANN?

Presiding: Elizabeth L. Tate

Coffee—8:00-8:30 a.m.

"The Essentials or Desiderata of the Bibliographic Record as seen by Public Service Librarians"—William DeJohn, Pacific Northwest Bibliographic Center, Seattle, WA

"The Essentials or Desiderata of the Bibliographic Record as Discovered by Research"—D. Kathryn Weintraub, Graduate Library School, University of Chicago, Chicago, IL

"The Effects of Modern Methods of Bibliographic Control in terms of responsiveness to user needs"—Ruth L. Tighe, National Commission on Library and Information Science, Washington, DC

"Choices for the Future"—Michael Gorman, University of Illinois Library, Urbana, IL

RULE 6.1.   TITLE AND STATEMENT OF RESPONSIBILITY AREA

6.1B.   Title proper

6.1B1.   "Record the title proper as instructed in 1.1B. For data to be included in titles proper for musical items, see 5.1B2." *See* Figs. 8.5 and 8.6.

Fig. 8.5. Rule 6.1B1. Transcription of titles proper of disc and tape.

"Saturday night Fiedler"

Fig. 8.6.

Whither MARC and Mann?

6.1B2.   "If a title proper for a musical work has to be devised by the cataloguer (see 1.1B7), give all the elements prescribed for uniform titles for music (see 25.25-25.36) in the order prescribed there." The elements referred to here are discussed in chapter 20 of this text. Briefly, they include: title indicating type of composition, medium of performance, serial numbers, opus numbers, key, and other identifying elements such as year or place of composition.

6.1C.   *Optional addition.* **General material designation**

6.1C1.   The appropriate GMD for the materials covered by this chapter is "sound recording." It is added following the title proper as instructed in 1.1C. *See* Figs. 8.7 and 8.8.

Fig. 8.7. Rule 6.1C1. Addition of GMD to the descriptions of disc and tape.

"Saturday night Fiedler" [sound recording]

Fig. 8.8.

Whither MARC and Mann? [sound recording]

6.1D.   **Parallel titles**

6.1D1.   "Record parallel titles as instructed in 1.1D."

6.1E.   **Other title information**

6.1E1.   "Record other title information as instructed in 1.1E." Example:

> Teatro del mondo [sound recording] : symphon-
> ic rotations in four scenes for large orchestra

6.1F.   **Statements of responsibility**

6.1F1.   "Record statements of responsibility relating to writers of spoken words, composers of performed music, and collectors of field material for sound recordings as instructed in 1.1F. If the participation of the person(s) or body (bodies) named in a statement found in the chief source of information goes beyond that of performance, execution, or interpretation of a work (as is commonly the case with 'popular,' rock, and jazz music), record such a statement as a statement of responsibility. If, however, the participation is confined to performance, execution, or interpretation (as commonly the case with 'serious' or classical music and recorded speech), give the statement in the note area (see 6.7B6)."

This rule is likely to cause difficulties of interpretation for the cataloger. Statements that would, without question, be statements of responsibility for textual matter are not clearly included here. For example, the cosponsor statement for the program on tape, shown in Fig. 8.4, would be a statement of responsibility for textual matter. But because the cosponsors appear to be neither writers of spoken words nor collectors of field material, the statement seems to be excluded. Likewise, the statement on the disc's chief source of information (Fig. 8.1), "Arthur Fiedler and the Boston Pops" must be relegated to note position because participation seems to be "confined to performance, execution, or interpretation." This is despite the fact that according to Rule 21.23C (*see* chapter 16 of this text), Fiedler would be chosen as main entry for this item. This seems inconsistent with the function of the statement of responsibility for other types of materials. An example of a situation where a statement of responsibility would be recorded according to this rule is the following:

> Individual differences in susceptibility to hypnosis [sound recording] / E. R. Hilgard.
> [This is a lecture given by its author.]

6.1F2.   "If the members of a group, ensemble, company, etc., are named in the chief source of information as well as the name of the group, etc., give them in the note area (see 6.7B6) if they are considered important. Otherwise omit them."

6.1F3.   "Add a word or short phrase to the statement of responsibility if the relationship between the title of the item and the person(s) or body (bodies) named in the statement is not clear." For example:

> The new moon [sound recording] / Sigmund Romberg ; [lyrics by] Oscar Hammerstein

6.1G.   Items without a collective title

6.1G1.   "If a sound recording lacks a collective title, *either* describe the item as a unit (see 6.1G2 . . .) *or* make a separate description for each separately titled work (see 6.1G4)."

This rule is slightly different from 1.1G, which allows for describing the item as a unit, or for treating the title of a predominant part as the title proper with other parts named in a note, but *not* for making a separate description for each separately titled work.

6.1G2. "In describing as a unit a sound recording lacking a collective title, record the titles of the individual works as instructed in 1.1G." For example:

> Rhapsody in blue ; An American in Paris
> [sound recording] / Gershwin

6.1G4. "If desired, make a separate description for each separately titled work on a sound recording. For the description of the extent in each of these descriptions, see 6.5B3. Link the separate descriptions with a note (see 6.7B21)."

RULE 6.2.   EDITION AREA

Elements of the edition area are transcribed for sound recordings in the same manner as instructed in the general chapter under Rule 1.2. Example:

> Brigadoon [sound recording] / book & lyrics by
> Alan Jay Lerner ; music by Frederick Loewe. --
> Collector's ed.

RULE 6.3.   MATERIAL (OR TYPE OF PUBLICATION) SPECIFIC DETAILS AREA

"This area is not used for sound recordings."

RULE 6.4.   PUBLICATION, DISTRIBUTION, ETC., AREA

6.4C.   **Place of publication, distribution, etc.**

6.4C1.   "Record the place of publication, distribution, etc., as instructed in 1.4C." *See* Figs. 8.9 and 8.10.

6.4D2.   "If a sound recording bears both the name of the publishing company and the name of a subdivision of that company or a trade name or brand name used by that company, record the name of the subdivision or the trade name or brand name as the name of the publisher." Example:

> Label on disc reads:
>   SUNSET, a product of Liberty Records
>   A division of Liberty Records, Inc., Los Angeles,
>   California
> Description should read:
>   Los Angeles : Sunset

6.4D3.   "If, however, a trade name appears to be the name of a series rather than of a publishing subdivision, record it as a series (see 6.6). In case of doubt, treat the name as a series."

6.4E.   *Optional addition.* **Statement of function of publisher, distributor, etc.**

6.4E1.   "Add to the name of a publisher, distributor, etc., a statement of function as instructed in 1.4E." LC is applying this option as discussed in the general chapter under 1.4E.

6.4F.   **Date of publication, distribution, etc.**

6.4F1.   "Record the date of publication, distribution, etc., as instructed in 1.4F." *See* Figs. 8.9 and 8.10.

Deciding upon a publication date for sound recordings is somewhat of a problem. There are often no dates at all on sound recordings. In other cases there may be several dates. On more recent recordings there are likely to be at least two dates, one preceded by ℗ and another by ©. The ℗ date is the copyright of the particular performance, while the © date is the copyright of the printed information on the container and/or on accompanying material. The date of actual publication of the item is usually not given. *AACR 2* does not mention the ℗ date. The reader should watch for rule interpretations on this matter.

Fig. 8.9. Rule 6.4. Addition of publication information to the description of a disc.

"Saturday night Fiedler" [sound recording]. – New York : Midsong International Records, 1979.

Note: In Fig. 8.1 the ℗ date is 1979 while the © date is 1978. However, in Fig. 8.2 the date, 1979, is preceded by "℗ & ©." Considering that the performance was recorded in 1979, the 1978 date seems to be an error and is ignored in the catalog record.

Fig. 8.10. Rule 6.4. Addition of publication information to the description of a tape.

Whither MARC and Mann? [sound recording]. – Chicago : American Library Association, 1978 (Evanston, Ill. : Produced by Cebar Communications, Inc.)

6.4F2.   "Give a date of recording appearing on the item in a note (6.7B7)."

6.4G.   **Place of manufacture, name of manufacturer, date of manufacture**

Information is given here as instructed under 1.4G in the general chapter. *See* Fig. 8.10.

RULE 6.5.   PHYSICAL DESCRIPTION AREA

6.5B.   Extent of item (including specific material designation)

6.5B1.   "Record the number of physical units of a sound recording by giving the number of parts in arabic numerals and one of the following terms as appropriate:

sound cartridge	sound tape reel
sound cassette	sound track film [see discussion on
sound disc	p. 153-154]

"Use the terms *piano roll, organ roll*, etc., as appropriate for rolls. . . ."

"*Optionally*, if general material designations are used and the general material designation includes the word *sound*, drop the word *sound* from all of the above terms except the last."

The option is not being applied by LC. Their reasoning is that because the display of GMDs will vary from agency to agency, the physical description should always be complete.[1] *See* Figs. 8.11 and 8.12 (page 165).

6.5B2.   "Add to the designation the stated total playing time of the sound recording in minutes (to the next minute up) unless the duration is less than 5 minutes, in which case give the time in minutes and seconds." *See* Fig. 8.11.

"If no indication of duration appears on the item, its container, or its accompanying textual material, give an approximate time if it can be readily established." *See* Fig. 8.12.

6.5B3.   "If the description is of a separately titled part of a sound recording lacking a collective title (see 6.1G4), express the fractional extent. . . ." Example:

on side 3 of 2 sound cassettes (25 min.)

6.5C.   Other physical details

6.5C1.   "Give the following details, as appropriate, in the order set out here:

type of recording (sound track films)

playing speed

groove characteristics (discs)

track configuration (sound track films)

number of tracks (tape cartridges, cassettes, and reels)

number of sound channels

recording and reproduction characteristics (tapes)

6.5C2.   Type of recording

In *AACR 2* this rule relates only to sound track film and suggests two types: optical or magnetic. As mentioned earlier, a third type (i.e., grooves cut in film) is not mentioned in this chapter. At the present time, technology is such that the other forms of sound recording (i.e., cartridge, cassette, disc, and tape reel) each are recorded in only one way (i.e., grooves for disc, magnetic for the others). It is conceivable, however, that new technology could produce other types of recording, in which case this rule would be expanded to allow for description of type of recording for cartridges, cassettes, etc.

6.5C3.   Playing speed

"Give the playing speed of a disc in revolutions per minute (rpm)." *See* Fig. 8.11.

"Give the playing speed of a tape in inches per second (ips)." *See* Fig. 8.12.

6.5C4.   Groove characteristic

"Give the groove characteristic of a disc if it is not standard for the type of disc." Example:

78 rpm, microgroove

6.5C6.   Number of tracks

"For tape cartridges, cassettes, and reels, give the number of tracks, unless the number of tracks is standard for that item." *AACR 2* notes that 8 tracks is standard for a cartridge and 4 for a cassette.

6.5C7.   Number of sound channels

"Give one of the following terms as appropriate:

    mono.

    stereo.

    quad."

See Figs. 8.11 and 8.12.

6.5C8.   *Optional addition.* Recording and reproduction
**   characteristics**

"For sound recordings, give the recording and reproduction characteristics (e.g., *Dolby processed, NAB standard*).

LC is applying this option when such information is needed in order to select playback equipment.[2]

6.5D.   Dimensions

6.5D1.   "Give the dimensions of a sound recording as set out in the following rules."

6.5D2.   Sound discs
"Give the diameter of the disc in inches." *See* Fig. 8.11.

6.5D4.   Sound cartridges
"Give the dimensions of the cartridge if they are other than the standard dimensions (5 1/4 x 7 3/8 in.) in inches, and the width of the tape if other than the standard width (1/4 in.) in fractions of an inch."

6.5D5.   Sound cassettes
The rule is the same as for cartridges except that the standard dimensions are 3 7/8 x 2 1/2 in., and the standard tape width is 1/8 in.

6.5D6.   Sound tape reels
"Give the diameter of the reel in inches, and the width of the tape if other than the standard width (1/4 in.) in fractions of an inch." Example:

> 2 sound tape reels (ca. 80 min.) : 3 3/4 ips,
> mono. ; 6 in.

6.5D7.   Rolls
"Do not give any dimensions."

6.5E.   Accompanying material
Accompanying material is treated as discussed under 1.5E in the general chapter. Example:

> on 1 side of 1 sound disc (ca. 22 min.) : 33 1/3
> rpm, stereo. ; 12 in. + program notes ([8]p. : ill. ;
> 23 cm.)

Fig. 8.11. Rule 6.5. Addition of physical description to descriptions for disc and tape.

"Saturday night Fiedler" [sound recording]. – New York : Midsong International Records, 1979.

1 sound disc (31 min.) : 33 1/3 rpm, stereo. ; 12 in.

Fig. 8.12.

Whither MARC and Mann? [sound recording]. – Chicago : American Library Association, 1978 (Evanston, Ill. : Produced by Cebar Communications, Inc.)

2 sound cassettes (ca. 150 min.) : 1 7/8 ips, mono.

RULE 6.6. SERIES AREA

6.6B. Series statements

6.6B1. "Record each series statement as instructed in 1.6." Example:

> 2 sound discs (84 min.) : 33 1/3 rpm, stereo. ; 12 in. -- (RCA classique)

RULE 6.7. NOTE AREA

6.7B. Notes
"Make notes as set out in the following subrules and in the order given there." Following are some typical notes used for sound recordings. For further details consult *AACR 2*, pages 158-62.

6.7B1. Nature or artistic form and medium of performance
"Make notes on the form of a literary work or the type of musical work or other description of a recording unless it is apparent from the rest of the description." Example:

> Organ music to demonstrate the instrument; various organists and organs.

6.7B2. Language
"Give the language or languages of the spoken or sung content of the recording. . . ." Example:

> Sung in Latin.

6.7B3.   Source of title proper
Example:

Title from publisher's catalog.

6.7B4.   Variations in title
Example:

Title on container: The last sixteen piano trios.
[Label reads: The last sixteen trios.]

6.7B6.   Statements of responsibility
"Give the names of performers and the medium in which they perform if
they have not already been named in the statements of responsibility and if
they are judged necessary for the bibliographic description. Give also
statements relating to any other persons or bodies connected with a work that
are not named in the statements of responsibility if they are considered important." Examples:

Hollywood Bowl Pops Orchestra ; Carmen
Dragon, arranger-conductor.

Violoncello: Raphael Wallfisch ; piano:
Richard Markham.

Barbara Rondelli, soprano ; Nürnberger Sym-
phoniker, Ljubomir Romansky, conductor.

6.7B7.   Edition and history
"Make notes relating to the edition being described or to the history of the
recording." Examples:

Recorded in San Francisco in 1971.

Originally issued: New York : McGraw-Hill,
1968. (Sound seminars)
Reissue of: Capitol SW-1804.

Side 2: "Based on Toccata and Fugue in 'D'
minor and air for the 'G' string [by J. S. Bach]."

6.7B10.   Physical description
"Indicate important physical details that are not already included in the
physical description area. Do not give any physical details that are standard to
the item being described (e.g., assume that all discs are electrically recorded,
laterally cut, and designed for playing from the outside inward)." Examples:

Impressed on pliable surface with rectangular
edge attached to hard paper cover for support.

6.7B11.   Accompanying material

"Make notes on the location of accompanying material if appropriate."
Examples:

> Program notes in English, French, and German
> on container.

> Program notes by Anthony Hodgson on
> container.

> Program notes: "Dictionnaire de l'orgue," by
> Henri Jarrié (23 p. : ill. ; 25 cm.), inserted in
> container.

6.7B12.   Series

Example:

> Originally issued in series: Musica viva
> Bohemica.

6.7B16.   Other formats available

> Also issued on reel (60 min. : 3 3/4 ips, mono.
> or stereo. ; 5 in.)

6.7B17.   Summary

Give a brief objective summary of the content of a sound recording (other
than one that consists entirely or predominantly of music) unless another part
of the description provides enough information." Example:

> Summary: The author presents an overview and
> introduction to the area of human potentialities
> and its implications for mankind.

6.7B18.   Contents

"Give a list of the titles of individual works contained on a sound recording. Add to the titles statements of responsibility not included in the title and
statement of responsibility area and of the duration of individual pieces if
known." Example:

> Contents: Credo.--Agonia.--Requiem.--Corale.

> Contents: Manon Lescaut : Wo lebte wohl ein
> Wesen (Peter Anders, tenor).--La Boheme : Wie
> eiskalt ist dies Händchen (Helge Rosvaenge,
> tenor).--Madame Butterfly : Eines Tages seh'n wir
> (Maria Cebotari, soprano).

6.7B19.   Notes on publishers' numbers

"Give the publisher's alphabetic and/or numeric symbol as found on the item. Precede the number(s) by the label name and a colon." Examples:

Big Sur Recordings: 7110

Angel: S 37309

6.7B21.   "With" notes

"If the description is of a separately titled part of a sound recording lacking a collective title, make a note beginning *With:* and listing the other separately titled parts of the item in the order in which they appear there." Example:

With: Suite italienne / Igor Stravinskii.
--Vocalise, op. 34, no. 14 / Sergei Rachmaninoff.

Note: A problem in the "With" note has been noted by music librarians. Because the rules for notes call for referring to another bibliographic item by its title proper and statement of responsibility, musical works that are entered under a uniform title may be "lost" to a user of the "With" note. Such musical works seldom have added entries for title proper, and the filing arrangement under the main entry is by uniform title, not title proper. The reader should watch for possible rule interpretations on this matter.

See Figs. 8.13 and 8.14.

Fig. 8.13. Rules 6.7-6.8. Addition of notes and terms of availability to the descriptions of disc and tape.

"Saturday night Fiedler" [sound recording]. --
New York : Midsong International Records, 1979.
  1 sound disc (31 min.) : 33 1/3 rpm, stereo. ;
12 in.

  "Arthur Fiedler and the Boston Pops."
  Produced and arranged by John Davis.
  Side 2: "Based on Toccata and Fugue in 'D' minor and air for the 'G' string [by J. S. Bach]."
  Recorded June 9, 1979.
  Contents: Saturday night fever medley (19 min.).--Bachamania (12 min.).
  Midsong International: MSI-011
  $7.98

Fig. 8.14.

Whither MARC and Mann? [sound recording].
-- Chicago : American Library Association, 1978
(Evanston, Ill. : Produced by Cebar Communications, Inc.)
  2 sound cassettes (ca. 150 min.) : 1 7/8 ips,
mono.

  "Cosponsored by Resources and Technical
Services Division...[et al.]"--1978 ALA confer-
ence program.
  Recorded at ALA's 97th annual conference,
Chicago, June 1978.
  Contents: Introduction / Elizabeth L. Tate.--
The essentials or desiderata of the bibliographic
record as seen by public service librarians /
William DeJohn.--The essentials or desiderata of
the bibliographic record as discovered by
research / D. Kathryn Weintraub.--The effects
of modern methods of bibliographic control in
terms of responsiveness to user needs / Ruth L.
Tighe.--Choices for the future / Michael Gorman.
  ALA/78: 15
  $10.95

RULE 6.8.   STANDARD NUMBER AND TERMS OF AVAILABILITY AREA

This area is treated as described under 1.8 in the general chapter. Sound recordings seldom have international standard numbers, although a few recordings issued serially have ISSNs. Generally the price (availability) is given without being preceded by a standard number. *See* Figs. 8.13 and 8.14.

RULE 6.11.   NONPROCESSED SOUND RECORDINGS

This rule is needed for the cataloging of such locally produced sound recordings as oral history interviews, addresses recorded in local auditoriums, lectures by local professors, or recordings of concerts or plays. The rules for processed sound recordings should be followed as much as possible. However, such recordings may have no title proper and will need to have one formu- lated. No information is given in the publication, etc., area. The date of recording is given in a note. Notes should also give participants and details of the event recorded as well as other notes prescribed in Rule 6.7. *See* Fig. 8.15.

Fig. 8.15. Rule 6.11. Description of a nonprocessed sound recording.

[Interview with Hattie McDonald on her 100th birthday] / interviewed by Susan Hall.
1 sound cassette (50 min.) : 1 7/8 ips, mono.

Recorded in Durham, N.C., July 29, 1979.
Summary: A discussion of life's impressions on the daughter of parents who had been born slaves.

FOOTNOTES

[1]"AACR 2 Options Proposed by the Library of Congress: Chapters 2-11," *Library of Congress Information Bulletin* 38 (Aug. 10, 1979): 312.

[2]"AACR 2 Options," p. 312.

9 DESCRIPTION OF MOTION PICTURES AND VIDEORECORDINGS

INTRODUCTION

This chapter covers all types of motion pictures and videorecordings as described under "Scope" below. As for sound recordings discussed in the preceding chapter, the description of motion pictures and videorecordings is now standardized and closely resembles description of other library materials. Again, however, classification and shelf arrangement is not standardized, and practice varies as much as for sound recordings.

Two of the complications encountered in describing motion pictures and video recordings involve the source of information and the large numbers of people responsible for them. Titles and other information, as they appear in the item itself, in accompanying materials or on containers, often vary considerably. The large number of people involved presents problems for deciding how many "credits" will provide useful description of an item. These and other problems are addressed in the rules that follow, but ultimately the cataloger must use some judgment based upon general principles.[1]

RULE 7.0. GENERAL RULES

7.0A. Scope

"The rules in this chapter cover the description of motion pictures and videorecordings of all kinds, including complete films and programmes, compilations, trailers, newscasts and newsfilms, stock shots, and unedited material."

7.0B. Sources of information

7.0B1. Chief source of information

"The chief source of information . . . is the film itself (e.g., the title frames) and its container (and its label) if the container is an integral part of the piece (e.g., a cassette)."

Information not in the chief source may be taken from accompanying textual material, a container that is not an integral part of the piece, or other sources, in that order.

7.0B2. Prescribed sources of information

"The prescribed source(s) of information for each area of the description of motion pictures and videorecordings is set out below. . . .

AREA	PRESCRIBED SOURCES OF INFORMATION
Title and statement of responsibility	Chief source of information
Edition	Chief source of information and accompanying material
Publication, distribution, etc.	[same as edition area]
Physical description	Any source
Series	[same as edition area]
Note	Any source
Standard number and terms of availability	Any source"

A videocassette is used in this chapter to illustrate the building of descriptive information for motion pictures and videorecordings. Its chief sources of information are shown in Figs. 9.1-9.3.

Fig. 9.1. Transcription of title frames at beginning of videotape.

Automated Check-in

— — —

Locating check-in records

— — —

Using check-in records

Fig. 9.2. Transcription of credit frames at end of videotape.

by
Anne Marie Allison
and
Harry Kamens

— — —

Prepared under the auspices
of Hyman W. Kritzer
Asst. Provost and Director
of Libraries
Kent State University

— — —

directed by
John Dannley

— — —

Produced by
Television Services
Kent State University

Fig. 9.3. Photocopy of cassette label.

AMPEX VIDEOCASSETTE

OCLC #6

Automated Check-in

Time - 14:45

MONO · STEREO
COLOR · BLACK & WHITE
AMPEX CORPORATION · REDWOOD CITY, CA 94063   PLAY LENGTH_____

RULE 7.1.   TITLE AND STATEMENT OF RESPONSIBILITY AREA

7.1B.   Title proper

7.1B1.   "Record the title proper as instructed in 1.1B." *See* Fig. 9.4.

**Fig. 9.4. Rule 7.1B1. Transcription of title proper
of videorecording.**

Automated check-in

_____

7.1B2.   In addition to the general rule for supplying a title where needed, the following specific instructions are given:

"**Commercials.** Supply a title for a short advertising film consisting of the name of the product, service, or other interest advertised, and the word *advertisement*." Example:

[Public library advertisement]

"**Unedited material and newsfilm.** Include in a supplied title for unedited material, stock shots, and newsfilm all the major elements present in the picture in order of their occurrence (e.g., place, date of event, date of shooting (if different), personalities, and subjects)." Example:

[Landing of first Boeing 747 jet at Raleigh-Durham
(N.C.) Airport, Sept. 25, 1979]

"*Optionally*, give a description of the action and length of each shot in a note (see 7.7B18)." LC is applying the option when the material warrants fuller detail.[2]

7.1C.   *Optional addition.* **General material designation**

One of two GMDs is appropriate for material covered by this chapter: "[motion picture]" or "[videorecording]." One of these is added following the title proper as instructed in 1.1C.

It should be noted that a sound track that is integrated or synchronized with an item is not treated separately. The GMD appropriate to the motion picture or videorecording is given alone. *See* Fig. 9.5.

Fig. 9.5. Rule 7.1C. Addition of GMD following the title proper.

Automated check-in [videorecording]

7.1D.-7.1E.   "Parallel titles and other title information are treated as instructed in the general chapter, with one addition:

7.1E2.   "If the item is a trailer containing extracts from a larger film, add [*trailer*] as other title information." Example:

Breaking away [motion picture] : [trailer]

7.1F.   **Statements of responsibility**

7.1F1.   "Record statements of responsibility relating to those persons or bodies credited in the chief source of information with participation in the production of a film (e.g., as producer, director, animator) who are considered to be of major importance to the film and the interests of the cataloguing agency. Give all other statements of responsibility in notes." *See* Fig. 9.6.

**Fig. 9.6. Rule 7.1F1. Addition of statements of responsibility
to the description of the videorecording.**

Automated check-in [videorecording] / by Anne
Marie Allison and Harry Kamens ; directed by John
Dannley

7.1F2.   "Add a word or short phrase to the statement of responsibility if the relationship between the title of the work and the person(s) or body (bodies) named in the statement is not clear." Example:

American movie [motion picture] / [written and produced by] Jan Peterson

7.1F3. "If a statement of responsibility names both the agency responsible for the production . . . and the agency for which it is produced, give the statement as found." Example:

> Iowa's ancient hunters [motion picture] / made by
> University of Iowa Motion Picture Unit for the Office
> of the Iowa State Archaeologist

7.1G. Items without a collective title

7.1G1. "If a motion picture or videorecording lacks a collective title, *either* describe the item as a unit . . . *or* make a separate description for each separately titled work. . . ."

This rule treats these materials in the same manner as sound recordings, rather than as in the general chapter. *See* discussion under 6.1G in the preceding chapter.

RULE 7.2. EDITION AREA

7.2B. Edition statement

"Transcribe a statement relating to an edition of a motion picture or videorecording that contains differences from other editions of that film, or that is a named reissue of that film, as instructed in 1.2B." Example:

> The Braniff Concorde [motion picture] / Braniff Air-
> ways, Inc. -- Spanish ed.

RULE 7.3. MATERIAL (OR TYPE OF PUBLICATION) SPECIFIC DETAILS AREA

"This area is not used for motion pictures and videorecordings."

RULE 7.4. PUBLICATION, DISTRIBUTION, ETC., AREA

7.4C. Place of publication, distribution, etc.

7.4C1. "Record the place of publication, distribution, etc., as instructed in 1.4C." *See* Fig. 9.7 (page 176).

7.4D. Name of publisher, distributor, etc.

7.4D1. "Record the name of the publisher, distributor, releasing agency, etc., and of a production agency or producer not named in the statements of responsibility (see 7.1F) as instructed in 1.4D." Note the addition to this rule specifically calling for production agency in addition to publisher, distributor, and/or releasing agency. *See* Fig. 9.7.

7.4E. ***Optional addition.*** **Statement of function of publisher, distributor, etc.**

"Add to the name of the publisher, distributor, releasing agency, etc., or production agency or producer a statement of function as instructed in 1.4E."

This information is treated in the same manner as in the general chapter, and is being applied on a case-by-case basis by LC.

7.4F. **Date of publication, distribution, etc.**

7.4F1. "Record the date of publication, distribution, release, etc., as instructed in 1.4F." *See* Fig. 9.7.

7.4F2. *Optionally*, give a date of original production differing from the date of publication, distribution, etc., in the note area (see 7.7B9)." Example:

> Washington, [D.C.] : Division of Audiovisual Arts :
> distributed by National Audiovisual Center, 1979.

The record on which the above imprint appears would have the following note:

> Made in 1975.

LC is applying this option.[3]

7.4G. **Place of manufacture, name of manufacturer, date of manufacture**

The rule as stated here is the same as in the general chapter: the details of manufacture are given if the details of publication are unknown. The option also is the same: details of manufacture that are found in the item and are considered important may be given in addition to details of publication. However, LC is not applying the option here, although the comparable option in the general chapter is being applied. The reasoning for this is as follows: "Since production companies (film 'manufacturers') really belong in other areas (7.4D1 and 7.1F1), do not apply the option in 7.4G2."[4]

Fig. 9.7. Rule 7.4. Addition of details of publication, etc., to the description of the videorecording.

> Automated check-in [videorecording] / by Anne
> Marie Allison and Harry Kamens ; directed by John
> Dannley. – [Kent, Ohio] : Produced by Television
> Services, Kent State University, [1977]

Note: The date of publication was taken from advertising matter.

RULE 7.5. PHYSICAL DESCRIPTION AREA

7.5B. **Extent of item (including specific material designation)**

7.5B1. "Record the number of physical units of a motion picture or videorecording by giving the number of parts in arabic numerals and one of the following terms as appropriate:

film cartridge	videocartridge
film cassette	videocassette
film loop	videodisc
film reel	videoreel"

See Fig. 9.8 (page 178).

The option in this rule for dropping "film" or "video" from the above terms when a GMD is used has not been commented on by LC. However, because they are not applying the comparable option for sound recordings, it would be logical to apply the same reasoning here. (*See* the discussion under 6.5B1 in the preceding chapter.)

"Add a trade name or other technical specification to the term for a videorecording if the use of the item is conditional upon this information and if it is only available in that particular form. Otherwise, give the data in the note area (see 7.7B16)." Example:

1 videodisc (MCA DiscoVision)

7.5B2. Playing time in minutes (minutes and seconds if duration is less than five minutes) is added after the number of physical units. This time should be approximated if it is not stated on any of the sources of information. Example:

1 videodisc (MCA DiscoVision) (ca. 35 min.)

See also Fig. 9.8.

7.5C. **Other physical details**

7.5C1. "Give the following details, as appropriate, in the order set out here:

aspect ratio and special projection characteristics (motion pictures)

sound characteristics

colour

projection speed (motion pictures)

playing speed (videodiscs)"

7.5C2. **Aspect ratio and special projection characteristics**

"If a film has special projection requirements, record them as succinctly as possible. . . ." Example:

2 film reels (25 min.) : multiprojector, multiscreen

7.5C3. **Sound characteristics**

"Indicate the presence or absence of a sound track by the abbreviations *sd.* (sound) or *si.* (silent)." *See* Fig. 9.8.

7.5C4.   Colour
"Indicate whether an item is in colour or black and white (using the abbreviations *col.* or *b&w*)." *See* Fig. 9.8.

7.5C5.   Projection speed
"For a film give the projection in frames per second (fps) if this information is considered important."

7.5C6.   Playing speed
"Give the playing speed of a videodisc in revolutions per minute (rpm)." Example:

> 1 videodisc (MCA DiscoVision) (ca. 35 min.) : sd.,
> b&w, 1800 rpm

7.5D.   Dimensions

7.5D2.   "Give the gauge (width) of a motion picture in millimetres. If 8 mm., state whether single, standard, super, or Maurer." Examples:

> 1 film cartridge (4 min.) : si., col. ; super 8 mm.

> 1 film reel (12 min.) : sd., col. with b&w sequences ;
> 16 mm.

7.5D3.   "Give the gauge (width) of a videotape in inches." *See* Fig. 9.8.

7.5D4.   "Give the diameter of a videodisc in inches." Example:

> 1 videodisc (MCA DiscoVision) (ca. 35 min.) : sd.,
> b&w, 1800 rpm ; 12 in.

7.5E.   Accompanying material

7.5E1.   "Record the name, and *optionally* the physical description, of any accompanying material as instructed in 1.5E." Example:

> 1 videocassette (50 min.) : sd., col. ; ½ in. + 1
> script booklet

LC is applying the option on a case-by-case basis.[5]

Fig. 9.8. Rule 7.5. Addition of physical description to the description of the videorecording.

Automated check-in [videorecording] / by Anne Marie Allison and Harry Kamens ; directed by John Dannley. -- [Kent, Ohio] : Produced by Television Services, Kent State University, [1977]

> 1 videocassette (15 min.) : sd., col. ; 3/4 in.

RULE 7.6.   SERIES AREA

7.6B.   Series statements

7.6B1.   "Record each series statement as instructed in 1.6." *See* Fig. 9.9.

**Fig. 9.9. Rule 7.6. Addition of series statement to the description
of the videorecording.**

Automated check-in [videorecording] / by Anne
Marie Allison and Harry Kamens ; directed by John
Dannley. -- [Kent, Ohio] : Produced by Television
Services, Kent State University, [1977]

1 videocassette (15 min.) : sd., col. ; 3/4 in. --
(OCLC ; no. 6)

RULE 7.7.   NOTE AREA

7.7B.   Notes

"Make notes as set out in the following subrules and in the order given there." Following are some typical notes used for motion pictures and videorecordings. For further details consult *AACR 2*, pages 177-80.

7.7B1.   Nature or form
Examples:

Newsreel.

Documentary.

7.7B2.   Language
Example:

In English; also issued in Portuguese and Spanish.

7.7B4.   Variations in title
Example:

Title on container: Alcohol--facts and myths
[Title proper reads: Alcohol--facts, myths, and decisions.]

7.7B6.   Statements of responsibility

"**Cast.** List featured players, performers, narrators, or presenters." Example:

Cast: John Howard Davies, Alec Guinness, Robert
Newton.

"**Credits.** List persons (other than the cast) who have contributed to the artistic and technical production of a motion picture or videorecording and who are not named in the statements of responsibility (see 7.1F). Do not include assistants, associates, etc., or any other persons making only a minor contribution. Preface each name or group of names with a statement of function." Example:

> Credits: Producers, Nick Bosustow, C.B. Wismar ; director, Sam Weiss ; voices, Hans Conreid, June Foray ; music, Larry Wolff ; editor, Lars Floden.

7.7B7.   Edition and history
Example:

> Revised version of the motion picture issued in 1960 under the same title.

7.7B9.   Publication, distribution, etc., and date
Example:

> Issued in 1969 as 16 mm. motion picture.
> [This note is on a videocassette issued in 1978.]

7.7B10.   Physical description
More in-depth physical description than that given in the physical description area can be given if desired. Some possibilities include sound characteristics (e.g., optical or magnetic), length of film or tape, process or color recording system (e.g., Technicolor), form of print (e.g., negative, positive), film base (e.g., nitrate, acetate, polyester), videorecording system, generation of copy, and special projection requirements. Example:

> U standard.

7.7B11.   Accompanying material
Example:

> With teacher's guide and supplementary material.

7.7B12.   Series
Example:

> Part 1 in a series.

7.7B14.   Audience
Example:

> For dental personnel.

7.7B16.   Other formats available
Example:

> Available as cartridge or disc.

7.7B17.   **Summary**

Example:

> Summary: A sports documentary covering three snowmobile races.

7.7B18.   **Contents**

Example:

> Contents: The black league (20 min.)--Doing your own thing (22 min.)--Teamwork against the odds (18 min.)--A new era (15 min.)

See also Fig. 9.10.

Fig. 9.10. Rules 7.7 and 7.8. Addition of notes and terms of availability to the description of the videocassette.

> Automated check-in [videorecording] / by Anne Marie Allison and Harry Kamens ; directed by John Dannley. -- [Kent, Ohio] : Produced by Television Services, Kent State University, [1977]
>
> 1 videocassette (15 min.) : sd., col. ; 3/4 in. -- (OCLC ; no. 6)
>
> "Presented under the auspices of Hyman W. Kritzer, Asst. Provost and Director of Libraries, Kent State University."
> Summary: Presents an introduction to use of the serials check-in subsystem of the OCLC system.
> Contents: Locating check-in records.--Using check-in records.
> $55.00

RULE 7.8.   STANDARD NUMBER AND TERMS OF AVAILABILITY AREA

This area is treated as described under 1.8 in the general chapter. Motion pictures and videorecordings rarely have International Standard numbers. Generally, the price or other statement of availability (such as a statement about rental) is given without being preceded by a standard number. *See* Fig. 9.10.

FOOTNOTES

[1]A discussion of these problems in relation to *AACR 2* may be found in: Michael Gorman, "Cataloging and Classification of Film Study Material," in Nancy Allen, *Film Study Collections* (New York, F. Ungar Publishing, 1979), pp. 113-23.

[2]"AACR 2 Options Proposed by the Library of Congress: Chapters 2-11," *Library of Congress Information Bulletin* 38 (Aug. 10, 1979): 312.

[3]"AACR 2 Options," p. 313.

[4]"AACR 2 Options," p. 313.

[5]"AACR 2 Options," p. 313.

10 DESCRIPTION OF GRAPHIC MATERIALS

INTRODUCTION

Materials covered by this chapter include: art originals, art prints, art reproductions, filmstrips and filmslips, flash cards, flip charts, photographs, pictures, postcards, posters, radiographs, slides, stereographs, study prints, technical drawings, transparencies, and wall charts. Many of these materials are not cataloged and/or classified in many libraries. An administrative decision within each library determines whether to catalog and/or classify these materials. Because most of them cannot be physically shelved with corresponding monographic materials, a book classification system often is not used. Rather, use is made of a simple accession or serial number to keep them in order. On the other hand, catalog records of the materials can easily be interfiled in the catalog with records for monographic or serial material, because, in *AACR 2*, all materials are described according to the same standard — i.e., ISBD(G). Some libraries provide some identification, such as color coding of catalog records that represent the materials listed above when they are interfiled in the main catalog. Other libraries provide separate catalogs for special materials.

This chapter illustrates application of *AACR 2* to a few of the above-named materials that are most often acquired in libraries. The principles may be applied to any of the materials.

RULE 8.0. GENERAL RULES

8.0A. Scope
"The rules in this chapter cover the description of graphic materials of all kinds, . . . and collections of such graphic materials. For visual material recorded on film and intended to be projected so as to create the illusion of movement, see chapter 7 [chapter 9 of this text]. For microforms, see chapter 11 [chapter 13 of this text]. For maps, etc., see chapter 3 [chapter 5 of this text]. For microscope slides, see chapter 10 [chapter 12 of this text]."

8.0B. Sources of information

8.0B1. Chief source of information
"The chief source of information for graphic materials is the item itself including any labels, etc., that are permanently affixed to the item and a container that is an integral part of the item. If the item being described consists of two or more separate physical parts (slide set, etc.), treat a container that is the unifying element as the chief source of information if it furnishes a collective title and the items themselves and their labels do not. If the information is not

available from the chief source, take it from the following sources (in this order of preference):

> container (box, frame, etc.)

> accompanying textual material (manuals, leaflets, etc.)

> other sources

"In describing a collection of graphic materials as a unit, treat the whole collection as the chief source."

8.0B2. Prescribed sources of information

"The prescribed source(s) of information for each area of the description of graphic materials is set out below. . . .

AREA	PRESCRIBED SOURCES OF INFORMATION
Title and statement of responsibility	Chief source of information
Edition	Chief source of information, container, and accompanying material
Publication, distribution, etc.	[same as edition area]
Physical description	Any source
Series	[same as edition area]
Note	Any source
Standard number and terms of availability.	Any source."

A set of stereograph reels is being used in this chapter to illustrate the building of the description for graphic materials. The prescribed sources of information are shown in Figs. 10.1-10.3. At the end of the chapter, given as Figs. 10.10-10.13, are complete examples of cataloging for filmstrips, flash cards, study prints, and slides.

Fig. 10.1. Chief source of information for set of
stereograph reels.

Fig. 10.2. Unifying container for stereograph reel set.

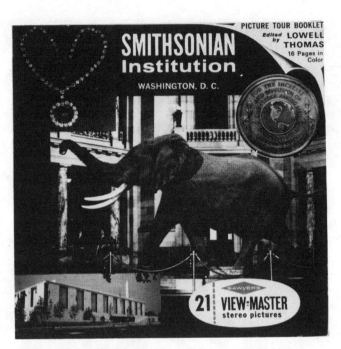

Fig. 10.3. First page of accompanying booklet.

RULE 8.1. TITLE AND STATEMENT OF RESPONSIBILITY AREA

8.1B.   Title proper
"Record the title proper as instructed in 1.1B." *See* Fig. 10.4.

**Fig. 10.4. Rule 8.1B. Transcription of title proper
of stereograph set.**

Smithsonian Institution, Washington,
D.C.

8.1C.   *Optional addition.* General material designation
"Add immediately following the title proper the appropriate general material designation as instructed in 1.1C."

The terms from the North American list under 1.1C that apply to materials in this chapter are: art original, chart, filmstrip, flash card, picture, slide, technical drawing, and transparency. Of these, the Library of Congress is using "filmstrip," "slide," and "transparency." It would use "chart" and "flash card" if it were to start cataloging such material. If it were to start cataloging art originals, pictures, and technical drawings, it would decide then whether or not to display the GMD.[1]

Four special rules appear in a footnote to the North American list in 1.1C, and three of them apply to the material covered by this chapter: "(2) for material treated in chapter 8, use *picture* for any item not subsumed under one of the other terms in list 2; (3) use *technical drawing* for items fitting the definition of this term in the Glossary, appendix D; for architectural renderings, however, use *art original* or *picture*, not *technical drawing*; (4) use *kit* for any item containing more than one type of material if the relative predominance of components is not easily determinable and for the single-medium packages sometimes called 'lab kits.' "

Application of the rules in the footnote would mean that the stereograph set being cataloged as an example in this chapter must have "picture" as its GMD. This seems a strange outcome because a stereograph picture cannot be viewed with the naked eye as is implied by the term "picture." Perhaps "slide" would be closer. In any case, this illustrates the difficulty, mentioned in the general chapter under 1.1C, raised by the specificity of the North American list. The British term "graphic" would be a more accurate description for a stereographic reel than "picture." *See* Fig. 10.5. *See also* Figs. 10.10-10.13 at the end of this chapter.

**Fig. 10.5. Rule 8.1C. Addition of GMD to the description of the
stereograph reel.**

Smithsonian Institution, Washington,
D.C. [picture]

8.1D.-8.1E.

Parallel titles and other title information are given as instructed in the general chapter. Example:

> American women artists [slide] : the twentieth
> century

8.1F.   Statements of responsibility

"Record statements of responsibility as instructed in 1.1F." Example:

> American women artists [slide] : the twentieth
> century / by Mary Stofflet

8.1G.   Items without a collective title

Graphic items, unlike sound recordings and motion pictures (discussed in the two preceding chapters), are treated in this rule as instructed in the general chapter: the titles of the individual parts are recorded in one bibliographic record. The allowance for making a separate description for each separately titled work is not made here.

RULE 8.2.   EDITION AREA

Elements of the edition area are transcribed for graphic materials in the same manner as instructed in the general chapter under Rule 1.2.

RULE 8.3.   MATERIAL (OR TYPE OF PUBLICATION) SPECIFIC DETAILS AREA

"This area is not used for graphic materials."

RULE 8.4.   PUBLICATION, DISTRIBUTION, ETC., AREA

8.4A2.   Art originals, unpublished photographs, etc.

"For art originals and unpublished photographs and other unpublished graphic materials, give only the date in this area. . . ." Example:

> [Polar bears] [art original] / Dorothy S. Taylor. -- 1975.

8.4A3.   Collections of graphic materials

"For collections of graphic materials, give only the inclusive dates of the materials in this area. . . ." Example:

> [Photographs of blue ribbon pigs, Iowa State Fair]
> [picture]. -- 1927-1947.

With the exceptions noted in 8.4A2 and 8.4A3 above, the elements of the publication, distribution, etc., area are recorded as instructed in the general chapter under Rule 1.4. *See* Fig. 10.6.

Fig. 10.6. Rule 8.4. Addition of publication details to the description of the stereograph reel.

Smithsonian Institution, Washington, D.C. [picture]. -- Portland, Ore. : Sawyer's, Inc., [196-?]

Note: The date is presumed to be in the 1960s because reference is made in the booklet to a new building projected for completion in 1969.

RULE 8.5.   PHYSICAL DESCRIPTION AREA

8.5B.   Extent of item (including specific material designation)

8.5B1.   "Record the number of physical units of a graphic item by giving the number of parts in arabic numerals and one of the following terms as appropriate:

art original	postcard
art print	poster
art reproduction	radiograph
chart	slide
filmslip	stereograph
filmstrip	study print
flash card	technical drawing
flip chart	transparency
photograph	wall chart
[abbreviated "photo." or "photos."]	
picture	

"Add to filmstrip and stereograph the words *cartridge* or *reel* when appropriate.

"Add the trade name or other technical specification to the term for a stereograph." *See* Fig. 10.7 (page 192) and Figs. 10.10-10.13 at the end of this chapter.

"If the parts of the item are very numerous and the exact number cannot be easily ascertained, give an approximate number." Example:

ca. 1,200 postcards

"*Optionally*, substitute or add a term more specific than those listed above." LC is applying this option upon the assumption that terms other than those listed are needed.[2]

8.5B2.   "Add to the designation for a filmslip, filmstrip, or stereograph the number of frames or double frames, the latter designated *double frames*." *See* Fig. 10.7.

"If the frames are unnumbered and are too numerous to count, give an approximate figure. . . .

"If the title frames are separately numbered, give separate totals of title frames and other frames." Example:

> 1 filmstrip (58 fr., 5 title fr.)

8.5B3.-8.5B5.

Designations for the number of sheets of a flip chart or the number of overlays for a transparency are added in parentheses to the designation. If multipart items have the same or approximately the same number of components, the addition in parentheses should take the form "(12 sheets each)." If the number of components are not the same in each part, give the total number, if consecutively numbered, or if not numbered, omit the number of components. Examples:

> 1 transparency (3 overlays)
>
> 3 flip charts (10 sheets each)
>
> 4 filmstrips (ca. 40 fr. each)
>
> 5 filmstrips

8.5C.   **Other physical details**

The other physical details required in the description depend upon the kind of graphic material being cataloged. Some require only an indication of color (e.g., col., b&w, sepia). These are:

flash cards	stereographs
pictures	study prints
postcards	transparencies
posters	wall charts

Others require some description of a characteristic in addition to color. These are:

> art prints—process in general terms (e.g., engraving, lithograph) or specific terms (e.g., copper engraving) and color
>
> art reproductions—method of reproduction (e.g., photogravure, collotype) and color
>
> filmstrips and filmslips—indication of sound if it is integral (if sound is not integral, it is described as accompanying material) and color

flip charts—indication of double-sided sheets (if applicable) and color

photographs—indication if photograph is a transparency not designed for projection or if it is a negative print and color. Optionally, the process used may be given. LC will apply this option on a case-by-case basis.

slides—treat sound as it is for filmstrips, and in addition, add the name of the system if the sound is integral. Also indicate color.

Two kinds of items require description of a characteristic, but no indication of color. These are:

art originals—"Give the medium (chalk, oil, pastel, etc.) and the base (board, canvas, fabric, etc.)."

technical drawings—"Give the method of reproduction if any (blueprint, photocopy, etc.)."

One kind of graphic item requires no description for other physical details:

radiograph

See Fig. 10.7 and Figs. 10.10-10.13 for examples of other physical details.

8.5D.   Dimensions

8.5D1.   "Give for all graphic materials except filmstrips, filmslips, and stereographs the height and the width in centimetres to the next whole centimetre up. For additional instructions on the dimensions of art works, slides, technical drawings, transparencies, and wall charts, see 8.5D4.-8.5D6." *See* Figs. 10.10 and 10.11.

8.5D2.   Filmstrips and filmslips
"Give the gauge (width) of the film in millimetres." *See* Fig. 10.12.

8.5D3.   Stereographs
"Do not give any dimensions." *See* Fig. 10.7.

8.5D4.   Art originals, art prints, art reproductions, transparencies
"Give the height and the width of the item, excluding any frame or mount. (See also 8.7B10.)"

8.5D5.   Slides
"Give the height and the width only if the dimensions are other than 5 x 5 cm. (2 x 2 in.)." *See* Fig. 10.13.

8.5D6.   **Technical drawings and wall charts**

"Give the height and the width when extended and (when appropriate) folded."

8.5E.   **Accompanying material**

The description of materials that accompany graphic materials is treated as described in the general chapter under 1.5E. Because of their nature, graphic materials are more likely to have accompanying materials — especially textual instructions of some kind. *See* Fig. 10.7, and Figs. 10.12-10.13.

Fig. 10.7. Rule 8.5. Addition of physical description to the description of the stereograph reel.

Smithsonian Institution, Washington,
D.C. [picture]. -- Portland, Ore. : Sawyer's, Inc.,
[196-?]

    3 stereograph reels (View-master) (7 double fr. each) :
col. + 1 booklet (16 p. : col. ill. ; 11 cm.)

RULE 8.6.   SERIES AREA

8.6B1.   "Record each series statement as instructed in 1.6." *See* Fig. 10.8 and Figs. 10.10-10.11.

Fig. 10.8. Rule 8.6. Addition of series statement to the description of the stereograph reel.

Smithsonian Institution, Washington,
D.C. [picture]. -- Portland, Ore. : Sawyer's, Inc.,
[196-?]

    3 stereograph reels (View-master) (7 double fr. each) :
col. + 1 booklet (16 p. : col. ill. ; 11 cm.). -- (View-master guided picture tour)

RULE 8.7.   NOTE AREA

8.7B.   **Notes**

"Make notes as set out in the following subrules and in the order given there." Following are some typical notes used for graphic materials. For further details, consult *AACR 2*, pages 196-99.

8.7B3.   **Source of title proper**

Example:

    Title from later reproductions.

8.7B4.   **Variations in title**
Example:

Title on container: Saint Pierre of the Cluniac Abbey of
Moissac.

Note: Title proper reads: Moissac, the Romanesque abbey church and its
sculpture.

8.7B6.   **Statements of responsibility**
Example:

Producer, Steven Williamson; art direction, Barbara
Flynn.

See also Fig. 10.9.

8.7B7.   **Edition and history**
Example:

Edited from the motion picture issued in 1977 under the
same title.

See also Fig. 10.12.

8.7B8.   **Characteristics of original of art reproduction, poster,**
         postcard, etc.
"Give the location (if known) of, and other information about, the
original of a reproduced art work." Example:

Original in National Gallery of Art.

8.7B9.   **Publication, distribution, etc.**
Example:

Issued in 3 parts.

See also Fig. 10.13.

8.7B10.   **Physical description**
Example:

For flannel board.

See also Figs. 10.10, 10.12, and 10.13.

8.7B11.   **Accompanying material**
Example:

With teacher's guide and supplementary material.

8.7B14.   **Audience**
See Figs. 10.10, 10.11, and 10.13.

8.7B16.   **Other formats available**
Example:

    Also issued as filmstrip.

See also Figs. 10.12 and 10.13.

8.7B17.   **Summary**
See Figs. 10.9-10.13.

8.7B18.   **Contents**
See Figs. 10.9 and 10.12.

8.7B19.   **Numbers**
"Give important numbers borne by the item other than ISBNs or ISSNs."
See Fig. 10.9.

RULE 8.8.   STANDARD NUMBER AND TERMS OF AVAILABILITY AREA

Details of this area are recorded as instructed in the general chapter under 1.8. Currently, graphic items seldom have standard numbers, leaving the terms of availability to stand alone. *See* Fig. 10.9.

Fig. 10.9. Rule 8.7. Addition of notes and terms of availability to the description of the stereograph reel.

Smithsonian Institution, Washington, D.C. [picture]. -- Portland, Ore. : Sawyer's, Inc., [196-?]
    3 stereograph reels (View-master) (7 double fr. each) : col. + 1 booklet (16 p. : col. ill. ; 11 cm.). -- (View-master guided picture tour)

    Booklet edited by Lowell Thomas.
    Summary: Shows and describes some of the major exhibits housed in three of the buildings of the Smithsonian.
    Contents: Reel 1. Air and space exhibits.--Reel 2. Natural history exhibits.--Reel 3. History & technology exhibits.
    Packet no. A 792.
    $2.25

Fig. 10.10. Example of description of a study print.

Spring and summer holidays [picture]. -- Chicago: Society for Visual Education, c1967.

8 study prints : col. ; 34 x 46 cm. – (Seasons and holidays series)

Text on versos of prints.
For elementary grades.
Summary: Presents ideas for various activities for holidays typical of the spring and summer.

Fig. 10.11. Example of description of a flash card.

Number cards [flash card] : development of number readiness. – Springfield, Mass. : Milton Bradley, c1970.

30 flash cards : col. ; 37 x 30 cm. -- (Early childhood enrichment series)

For primary grades.
Summary: Aids young children in developing number and money concepts.

Fig. 10.12. Example of description of a filmstrip.

The water planet, set I [filmstrip] / Cousteau Society. – Burbank, Calif. : Walt Disney Educational Media Co., 1978.

5 filmstrips : col. ; 35 mm. + 5 sound cassettes (60 min. : 1 7/8 ips, 2 track, mono.) and 1 teacher's guide (25 p. ; 23 cm.)

Adapted from episodes of the television program entitled The undersea world of Jacques Cousteau.
Sound accompaniment compatible for manual and automatic operation.
Also issued with sound accompaniment on disc.
Summary: Jacques and Philippe Cousteau explore the world of the ocean in an effort to foster understanding about the interrelationship of animals, the land, and the sea.
Contents: Return to the sea (130 fr.).–To save a living sea (153 fr.).–The liquid sky (120 fr.).–A sea of motion (133 fr.).–Invisible multitudes (147 fr.).

Fig. 10.13. Example of description of a slide.

Occupied bed making [slide]. -- Garden Grove, Calif. : Trainex Corp., [1979?]

99 slides : col. + 1 sound cassette (15 min. : 1 7/8 ips, mono.), instructor's guide (4 p. ; 18 cm.), and vis-u-test.

Issued in 1974 as filmstrip.
Sound accompaniment for automatic operation only.
For nurses' training.
Also issued with sound accompaniment in Spanish.
Summary: Demonstrates the complete procedure for occupied bed making, from planning a linen stack to checking on the patient's comfort and safety. Explains the steps in making square and mitered corners, as well as techniques for infection control.

RULE 8.9. SUPPLEMENTARY ITEMS

"Describe supplementary items as instructed in 1.9."

RULE 8.10. ITEMS MADE UP OF SEVERAL TYPES OF MATERIAL

Graphic materials fall into this category perhaps more often than any other type. Therefore, a special note should be made here of the possible ways for describing "kits" given in the general chapter (chapter 3 of this text) under Rule 1.10. *See* the examples given there.

RULE 8.11. FACSIMILES, PHOTOCOPIES, AND OTHER REPRODUCTIONS

"Describe facsimiles, photocopies, and other reproductions as instructed in 1.11."

FOOTNOTES

[1]"Display of General Material Designations under AACR 2," *Cataloging Service Bulletin*, no. 6 (Fall 1979):4-5.

[2]"AACR 2 Options Proposed by the Library of Congress, Chapters 2-11," *Library of Congress Information Bulletin* 38 (Aug. 10, 1979):314.

11 DESCRIPTION OF MACHINE-READABLE DATA FILES

INTRODUCTION

The cataloging of machine-readable data files (MRDF) is a very recent addition to the cataloging field. The need for standards for cataloging these materials was recognized in 1970 when ALA's Cataloging and Classification Section established a subcommittee to develop rules for cataloging MRDFs. Since then, steady progress has been made, but the form in which bibliographic information for MRDFs can be found varies so greatly, that cataloging them is somewhat more of a challenge than for most other materials. The state of the art of production of MRDFs is comparable to that of books in the early days of printing. No one source of data comparable to a title page exists. There is no copyright, so "copies" and "editions" can be made freely. These and other problems are addressed in this chapter. Definitions are provided at the chapter's end.

RULE 9.0. GENERAL RULES

9.0A. Scope
"The rules in this chapter cover the description of machine-readable data files of all types and their accompanying documentation. A machine-readable data file is defined as a body of information coded by methods that require the use of a machine (typically a computer) for processing. Examples are files stored on magnetic tape, punched cards (with or without a magnetic tape strip), aperture cards, punched paper tapes, disk packs, mark sensed cards, and optical character recognition font documents. The term *machine-readable data file* embraces both the data stored in machine-readable form and the programs used to process that data."

9.0B. Sources of information

9.0B1. Chief source of information
The chief source of information, according to *AACR 2* is to be an "internal user label," if the MRDF has one. At the present time, such labels have not been implemented by MRDF producers; however, their implementation is being strongly encouraged by persons interested in providing bibliographic access to MRDFs. Such a label would be "file specific" — a title page equivalent that would be part of the file itself that could not be lost or separated from the file it is describing. Upon receiving a data file or program stored on magnetic tape, the user would have a printout of the tape's internal user label (also called a "user header label," or UHL) made, thus revealing the file's bibliographic identity. An example of how such a printout might look is shown as Fig. 11.1.

Fig. 11.1. Example of a User Header Label (UHL) printout for a machine-readable data file.

```
UHL1 GENERAL SURVEYS, 1972-1978 : CUMULATIVE DATA (MACHINE-READABLE
UHL2 DATA FILE) / PRINCIPAL INVESTIGATOR, JAMES A DAVIS ; CONDUCTED FOR
UHL3 THE NATIONAL DATA PROGRAM FOR THE SOCIAL SCIENCES AT THE NATIONAL
UHL4 OPINION RESEARCH CENTER. --CHICAGO : NATIONAL OPINION RESEARCH
UHL5 CENTER (PRODUCER), 1978. --NEW HAVEN, CONN : ROPER OPINION
UHL6 RESEARCH CENTER, YALE UNIVERSITY (DISTRIBUTOR).
```

Note: This example was provided by Shirley Gilbert and Judith Rowe of Princeton University, 1978.

Until such labels become available, the cataloger must use the alternative chief source of information. The rule says that when an internal label is lacking, the chief source is to be the documentation issued by the agency or person(s) responsible for creating, compiling, editing, or producing the file. "Documentation" is a generic term for descriptive information accompanying a MRDF, without which a MRDF cannot be used. There are many different types and styles of such descriptive information (e.g., user's guide, programmer's manual, codebook, questionnaire, data dictionary, tape layout). Such documentation may have a title page (as in Fig. 11.2); it may have none; or information about the file may be presented in a sequential-item format (as in Fig. 11.3). If there is a title page, it may be confusing to the cataloger, because it must serve a dual purpose. It must serve as the title page for the printed documentation, and it must also carry information about the origins of the MRDF being documented. Documentation can be functionally independent, unlike the MRDF it is describing. The Library of Congress catalogs documentation, but not MRDFs. An LC card number that may appear on documentation is for cataloging of the documentation, not of the file (*see* Fig. 11.5, page 202).

If required information is not available from the documentation, it is to be taken from "the following sources (in this order of preference):

other published descriptions of the file

other sources (including the container of the file and its labels)"

Other "published descriptions" that the cataloger may have to search include data abstracts, data directories, inventories, technical reports, monographs based on the analysis or review of the data file or program, and flyers announcing the availability of a MRDF to the public.

Fig. 11.2. Sample title page from MRDF documentation.

JUVENILE DETENTION AND CORRECTIONAL FACILITY CENSUS OF 1971: USER'S GUIDE FOR THE MACHINE READABLE DATA FILE

Produced by
U.S. Bureau of the Census
Washington, D.C.

for

National Criminal Justice Information and Statistics Service
Law Enforcement Assistance Administration
U.S. Department of Justice
Washington, D.C. 20537
1971

LEAA rev. 1975 ed.
Revised by LEAA Data Archive and Research Support Center
Center for Advanced Computation
University of Illinois
Urbana, Il. 61801
(217) 333-3234

User's Guide Prepared by
LEAA Data Archive and Research Support Center
(Under LEAA Grant 77-SS-99-6003)
December 1978

LEAA User's Guide 4th ed.

(Fig. 11.3 appears on page 200)

Fig. 11.3. Sample first page from MRDF documentation that presents information about the file in a sequential-item format.

```
CODEBOOK FOR **IDLRS*300700002    CENSUS DATA ON ECONOMIC DEVELOPMENT PAGE 001

CARD   COLUMNS  MARGINAL                    QUESTIONS AND CODE
 ID     USED     COUNT
                           INTERNATIONAL DATA LIBRARY AND REFERENCE SERVICE
                                      SURVEY RESEARCH CENTER
                                 UNIVERSITY OF CALIFORNIA, BERKELEY

                           300700002 STUDY DESCRIPTION

                    1.  TITLE OF STUDY
                        THE SOCIAL STRUCTURE OF ARGENTINA
                        CENSUS DATA ON ECONOMIC DEVELOPMENT

                    2.  PROJECT DIRECTOR
                        TORCUATO S. DI TELLA

                    3.  ORGANIZATIONS WHICH COLLECTED AND/OR PROCESSED DATA
                        SOCIOLOGICAL INSTITUTE OF THE FACULTAD DE PHILOSOFIA Y
                        LETRAS, BUENOS AIRES
                        INSTITUTO TORCUATO DI TELLA, CENTER OF ECONOMIC
                        INVESTIGATION, BUENOS AIRES

                    4.  DATE OF DATA COLLECTION
                        1965

                    5.  LOCATION OF SAMPLE
                        NATIONAL

                    6.  SAMPLING CRITERIA
                        THE PROVINCES AND THEIR COUNTIES OF ARGENTINA

                    7.  PERSONS INQUIRED ABOUT
                        NA

                    8.  METHOD OF SAMPLING
                        SYSTEMATIC SAMPLE
```

"Other sources" include the data "inventory form" that is often completed by the person or agency that generated a file when such person or agency turns the file over to a data library. The "container of the file and its labels" referred to in the rule are, unfortunately, usually not of much value. A typical label is abbreviated and does not usually bear bibliographic details (*see* Fig. 11.4).

Fig. 11.4. Typical MRDF container label.

```
                    DISK & TAPE LIBRARY
              DONALDSON, LUFKIN & JENRETTE, INC.
              140 BROADWAY, N.Y., N.Y. 10005
```

REEL # OR PACK #	VOL. SER.	PROGRAMMER'S INIT.	UNIT NO.

FILE IDENTIFIER HARRIS	NO. OF REELS	G CREATION DATE J 6/13/75

LABEL DESCRIPTION 2354-TAPE

G EXPIR. DATE J	PROG. NO. REC.0800	FILE DESTINATION 1614	OP.#

9.0B2.   Prescribed sources of information

"The prescribed source(s) of information for each area of the description of machine-readable data files is set out below. . . .

AREA	PRESCRIBED SOURCES OF INFORMATION
Title and statement of responsibility	Chief source of information and documentation issued by the creator, etc., of the file
Edition	[same as above, and] any other published description of the file
Publication, production, distribution, etc.	[same as edition area]
File description	Any source
Series	[same as edition area]
Note	Any source
Standard number and terms of availability	Any source"

The MRDF used in this chapter to illustrate the building of a catalog record is a file of data collected in a national election study. One piece of accompanying documentation is a codebook that incorporates the study description, user's information, question and code level information, and other information. The title page, and two pages of the study description are shown in Figs. 11.5-11.7.

Fig. 11.5. Title page of codebook that accompanies the MRDF used in this chapter to illustrate building a description.

THE CPS 1974 AMERICAN NATIONAL ELECTION STUDY
(CPS STUDY 495441 — ICPR STUDY 7355)

PRINCIPAL INVESTIGATORS
WARREN E. MILLER
ARTHUR H. MILLER
F. GERALD KLINE

THE CENTER FOR POLITICAL STUDIES
THE UNIVERSITY OF MICHIGAN

POST-ELECTION WAVE
NOV.-DEC., 1974; JAN., 1975

ICPR EDITION
FIRST PRINTING, 1975

INTER-UNIVERSITY CONSORTIUM FOR POLITICAL RESEARCH
P.O. BOX 1248
ANN ARBOR, MICHIGAN 48106

LIBRARY OF CONGRESS CATALOG CARD NUMBER 75-12906
ISBN 0-89138-111-2

(Text continues on page 205)

Fig. 11.6. First page of codebook's description of study.

[Underlined portions provide information necessary to the bibliographic record.]

STUDY DESCRIPTION

THE CPS 1974 AMERICAN NATIONAL ELECTION STUDY (CPS # 495441) WAS CONDUCTED BY THE CENTER FOR POLITICAL STUDIES OF THE INSTITUTE FOR SOCIAL RESEARCH, THE UNIVERSITY OF MICHIGAN UNDER THE DIRECTION OF WARREN MILLER, ARTHUR MILLER AND GERALD KLINE. IT WAS THE THIRTEENTH IN A SERIES OF STUDIES OF NATIONAL ELECTIONS PRODUCED BY THE POLITICAL BEHAVIOR PROGRAM OF THE SURVEY RESEARCH CENTER AND THE CENTER FOR POLITICAL STUDIES. THE STUDY WAS SUPPORTED BY GRANTS FROM THE NATIONAL SCIENCE FOUNDATION (SOC 75-02704), THE JOHN AND MARY R. MARKLE FOUNDATION AND THE CARNEGIE CORPORATION.

THE BASIC DESIGN OF THE 1974 STUDY INCLUDES A SUBSET OF THE RESPONDENTS WHO HAD PREVIOUSLY BEEN INTERVIEWED IN THE 1972 POST-ELECTION SURVEY. THIS SET OF PANEL RESPONDENTS WAS THEN AUGMENTED WITH A SET OF NEW INTERVIEWS SELECTED SO AS TO PROVIDE A REPRESENTATIVE CROSS-SECTION OF U.S. CITIZENS WHEN COMBINED WITH THE NON-MOVING PANEL RESPONDENTS. NEW RESPONDENTS WERE NOT, HOWEVER, SELECTED AT THE SAME SAMPLING RATE AS 1972 RESPONDENTS; THUS WEIGHTING IS NECESSARY TO FORM A REPRESENTATIVE CROSS-SECTION FROM THE TWO TYPES OF RESPONDENT. THE 1974 AMERICAN NATIONAL ELECTION STUDY INCLUDES ONLY THE CROSS-SECTION SAMPLES, THAT IS, NON-MOVING PANEL RESPONDENTS AND THE RESPONDENTS WHO WERE ADDED IN 1974. THE STUDY INCLUDES 1575 RESPONDENTS, 14 CARDS OF DATA PER RESPONDENT, AND 564 VARIABLES. RESPONDENTS WERE INTERVIEWED FROM NOVEMBER 5, 1974 THROUGH JANUARY 31, 1975, FOLLOWING THE CONGRESSIONAL ELECTIONS.

THE CPS AMERICAN NATIONAL ELECTION STUDY EXPLORED POLITICAL ATTITUDES AND BEHAVIOR IN THE CONTEXT OF THE WATERGATE EVENTS AND THE 1974 CONGRESSIONAL ELECTIONS. THE PARTY IDENTIFICATION OF THE RESPONDENTS, THEIR VOTING HISTORY, AND INFORMATION ABOUT FACETS OF EARLY POLITICAL SOCIALIZATION WERE OBTAINED. THE RESPONDENTS' SENSE OF POLITICAL EFFICACY AND CIVIC DUTY, THE DEGREE OF THEIR TRUST IN GOVERNMENT, AND THEIR EVALUATIONS OF GOVERNMENTAL RESPONSIVENESS WERE THE SUBJECTS OF QUESTIONS DESIGNED TO MEASURE DIMENSIONS OF THE RESPONDENTS' PERCEPTIONS OF THE RELATIONSHIP OF THE GOVERNMENT TO ITS CITIZENS.

CONSIDERABLE ATTENTION WAS ALSO FOCUSED ON WATERGATE EVENTS. FEELING THERMOMETERS WERE USED TO TAP REACTIONS TO THE PRINCIPAL FIGURES IN THESE EVENTS. ANOTHER SERIES OF QUESTIONS TAPPED ATTITUDES TOWARDS THE JUDICIARY COMMITTEE'S IMPEACHMENT HEARINGS AND THE DECISION TO IMPEACH, NIXON'S RESIGNATION, AND FORD'S PARDON OF NIXON. RESPONDENTS WERE ALSO ASKED TO EVALUATE MEDIA OBJECTIVITY IN COVERAGE OF THE INVOLVEMENT OF THE NIXON ADMINISTRATION IN THE WATERGATE AFFAIR.

Fig. 11.7. Last page of codebook's description of study.

[Underlined portions provide information necessary to the bibliographic record.]

WEIGHTING INFORMATION

THE CPS 1974 AMERICAN NATIONAL ELECTION STUDY SAMPLE CONSISTED OF PANEL AND CROSS-SECTION COMPONENTS. THE RE-CONTACTED RESPONDENTS FORMING THE PANEL WERE FIRST INTER-VIEWED IN THE PRE- AND POST-ELECTION PHASES OF THE 1972 CPS AMERICAN NATIONAL ELECTION STUDY. OF THESE PANEL RESPON-DENTS 1101 WERE FOUND TO REMAIN AT THEIR 1972 ADDRESSES AND WERE INCORPORATED INTO THE 1974 CROSS-SECTION SAMPLE. THESE RESPONDENTS WERE GIVEN A WEIGHT OF 1. TO FORM A REPRESENTATIVE CROSS-SECTION SAMPLE OF ADULTS 16 YEARS AND OVER, 474 NON-PANEL RESPONDENTS WERE SELECTED BY SUB-SAMPLING THE 1972 SAMPLE OF HOUSING UNITS. SINCE THE CROSS-SECTION (NON-PANEL) RESPONDENTS WERE SELECTED WITH A ONE-THIRD FRACTION OUT OF THE AVAILABLE ADDRESSES, THEY WERE GIVEN A WEIGHT OF 3.

NOTE: FOR PURPOSES OF THIS DATASET, PERSONS UNDER THE AGE OF 18 ON NOVEMBER 5, 1974 WERE DROPPED FROM THE SAMPLE.

V2003, WEIGHTING VARIABLE, SHOULD BE USED IN CONJUNCTION WITH ANY ANALYSIS OF THIS DATA. THE WEIGHTED N IS 2523.

FILE STRUCTURE

THE DATA ARE AVAILABLE FROM ICPR IN TWO FORMATS: A CARD IMAGE FILE AND AN OSIRIS DATASET. THE CARD IMAGE FILE CONTAINS 14 DECKS PER RESPONDENT IN A FORMAT BASED ON 80 COLUMN PUNCHED CARDS. THE DATA ARE SORTED BY RESPONDENT WITH ALL DECKS FOR EACH CASE TOGETHER IN ASCENDING ORDER. THERE ARE TWO COMPONENTS TO THE OSIRIS DATASET. THE OSIRIS DICTIONARY CONTAINS ALL TECHNICAL INFORMATION FOR EACH VARIABLE IN THE OSIRIS DATA FILE. THE DICTIONARY OR DICTIONARY-CODEBOOK FILE IS USED IN CONJUNCTION WITH THE OSIRIS SOFTWARE PACKAGE. THE OSIRIS DATA FILE IS CONSTRUCT-ED WITH A SINGLE LOGICAL RECORD OF 923 BYTES FOR EACH RESPONDENT. THERE ARE 564 VARIABLES.

THE OSIRIS DATA FILE CAN BE ACCESSED DIRECTLY BY SOFT-WARE PACKAGES WHICH DO NOT USE THE OSIRIS DICTIONARY BY SPECIFYING THE TAPE LOCATIONS OF THE DESIRED VARIABLES. TAPE LOCATIONS ARE PROVIDED IN THIS CODEBOOK.

THERE IS ONE WEIGHT VARIABLE IN THE CPS 1974 AMERICAN NATIONAL ELECTION STUDY. (SEE V2003; THIS SHOULD BE USED IN CONJUNCTION WITH DATA ANALYSIS PROGRAMS.)

RULE 9.1. TITLE AND STATEMENT OF RESPONSIBILITY AREA

9.1B. Title proper

9.1B1. "Record the title proper as instructed in 1.1B. Record the source of the title proper if taken from outside the file itself in the note area (see 9.7B3)." *See* Fig. 11.8. As explained earlier, the title proper will, of necessity, come from outside the file. *See* Fig. 11.15 (page 213) for the note to this effect.

Fig. 11.8. Rule 9.1B1. Transcription of title proper of the
machine-readable data file.

The CPS 1974 American national election study

9.1B2. "Do not treat a locally assigned data set name as a title proper, unless the creator, etc., of the file has assigned a data set name that is also the title of the file." Because construction of a data set name is subject to a large number of restrictions, varying according to the system (e.g., restrictions on number of characters, or requirements to start the name with certain combinations of letters and numbers), this name is not likely to be able to convey the concept necessary for a file title. This name may, however, be given in a note, if desired (*see* 9.7B4).

9.1B3. "If neither the internal user label nor the documentation supplied by the creator, etc., of the file contains a title for the file, supply a brief descriptive title (see 1.1B7) and enclose it in square brackets. Indicate in a note that the title has been supplied (see 9.7B3)." Example:

[Harris 1967 public opinion survey, no. 1702]

9.1C. *Optional addition.* General material designation

The GMD appropriate to the material in this chapter is "machine-readable data file." The Library of Congress has said that if it ever catalogs MRDFs, it will decide then whether to display the GMD.[1]

Because the GMD is the most direct way to distinguish between the cataloging for the file itself and the cataloging for the documentation, it seems to be a highly desirable addition. It will be illustrated in this chapter. *See* Fig. 11.9.

Fig. 11.9. Rule 9.1C. Addition of GMD to the description
of the MRDF.

The CPS 1974 American national election study
[machine-readable data file]

9.1D.-9.1E.　　　　Parallel titles and other title information are transcribed as instructed in 1.1D.-1.1E.

9.1F.　　　　**Statements of responsibility**

Statements that give the persons or bodies responsible for the *content* of the MRDF are recorded as instructed in 1.1F. However, persons or bodies responsible for preparation of the file in machine-readable form are recorded in the note area. *See* Fig. 11.10.

Fig. 11.10. Rule 9.1F. Addition of statements of responsibility to the description of the MRDF.

The CPS 1974 American national election study [machine-readable data file] / principal investigators, Warren E. Miller, Arthur H. Miller, F. Gerald Kline ; The Center for Political Studies, The University of Michigan.

RULE 9.2.　　EDITION AREA

The rules direct that an edition statement for an MRDF is to be transcribed as instructed in 1.2B; and minor corrections of things such as misspellings or incorrectly transcribed data should not be treated as new editions. A problem is that the definition of "edition" in *AACR 2* cannot be applied to MRDFs as easily as to most other materials. Many changes can be made to an MRDF very quickly and easily. For example, format can be changed from punched card to tape to disc; data can be added or changed or deleted; "translations" can be made of program statements from one program language to another; data elements can be reformatted. As mentioned earlier, there are not yet standards for "publication" in this field. When changes are made, there is no standard internal label to carry a record of the changes. Documentation may or may not be revised when changes are made to the file.

These problems are being addressed by various organizations, including subcommittees of ALA. The reader should watch for new interpretations. In the meantime, the cataloger must use documentation with the edition statements that appear there. *See* Fig. 11.11.

Fig. 11.11. Rule 9.2. Addition of edition statement to the description of the MRDF.

The CPS 1974 American national election study [machine-readable data file] / principal investigators, Warren E. Miller, Arthur H. Miller, F. Gerald Kline ; The Center for Political Studies, The University of Michigan. -- ICPR ed.

RULE 9.3.　　MATERIAL (OR TYPE OF PUBLICATION) SPECIFIC DETAILS AREA

"This area is not used for machine-readable data files."

All of the types of material chapters in *AACR 2* use the above statement for this area. The implication is that use of this area is not permitted for the type of material in question. In the chapter on microforms, however, there is instruction in this area to follow the instructions in Rule 3.3 for microforms of cartographic materials and Rule 12.3 for serial microforms. For most types of material, need for this area is rare; but MRDFs are often produced serially, and occasionally the content of a MRDF is cartographic. The scope note for the chapter on description of serials says that the rules in that chapter are to be used for serial publications of all kinds in all media. Clearly, then, it is permissible, and certainly desirable, to use area 3 when describing a MRDF. All bibliographic data bases, such as the MARC data base, that are available on a subscription basis so that new records are added regularly require serial cataloging. For example:

> Specialized textile information service [machine-readable data file] / compiled in collaboration with British Launderer's Research Association . . . [et al.]. -- 1970-

RULE 9.4. PUBLICATION, PRODUCTION, DISTRIBUTION, ETC., AREA

The details of this area are recorded as instructed in the general chapter under 1.4. Dates other than the date of publication, production, distribution, etc., are to be given in the note area. Such a date might be the date of collection of the data. The cataloger of a MRDF may have some difficulty distinguishing a publisher of documentation from a producer or distributor of the data file. In addition, the roles of producers and distributors in the data community are not always clearly differentiated, nor are they exactly comparable to "publishers." In the case of the MRDF used to build the sample record in this chapter, the Inter-University Consortium for Political Research is the producer of the edition in hand (the "ICPR Edition"). But the edition has been reformatted from the original, which was produced by the Center for Political Studies of the University of Michigan. The glossary at the end of this chapter provides definitions of these terms. *See* Fig 11.12.

Fig. 11.12. Rule 9.4. Addition of details of producer and date to the description of the MRDF.

The CPS 1974 American national election study [machine-readable data file] / principal investigators, Warren E. Miller, Arthur H. Miller, F. Gerald Kline ; The Center for Political Studies, The University of Michigan. -- ICPR ed. -- Ann Arbor, Mich. : Inter-University Consortium for Political Research, 1975.

RULE 9.5. FILE DESCRIPTION AREA

9.5B. Extent of file (including specific material designation)

9.5B1. "Record the number of files making up a machine-readable data file by giving the number of parts in arabic numerals and one of the following terms as appropriate:

> data file
>
> program file
>
> object program"

See Fig. 11.13 (page 209). Note that "program file" and "object program" are used exclusively for computer software programs.

A MRDF may consist of more than one part (or sample); the extent of the file includes the number of parts (or samples). There may also be a case where a MRDF contains a combination of data files and program files. In this case the major file is described first, and the other(s) are added as accompanying material (*see* 9.5D1 below).

9.5B2. "Add in parentheses to the designation for a data file the number of logical records. Add in parentheses to the designation for a program file the number of statements and the name of the programming language." Example:

> 1 program file (633 statements, PL/1)

"Do not add the number of statements to the designation of an object program." "Logical record" is defined in the glossary of *AACR 2* as "a group of words, characters, or bytes identified as a unit on the basis of content function and use." For certain types of social science MRDFs, the phrase "number of logical records" may be equated with "sample size" or the number of respondents in a survey; it may also be equated with the "number of cases," the "number of observations," the "number of units," etc. In the example being cataloged in this chapter, one must read the study description to find in the second paragraph that the study had 1,575 respondents. *See* Fig. 11.13.

Data files that have been converted into so-called "system files" (e.g., SPSS, SAS, OSIRIS) do not translate into logical records. However, the extent of a "system file" may be designated in terms of variables. This information, however, is given in a note, not in the file description area (*see* 9.7B10).

9.5B3. "Add to the designation for a multipart file the number of logical records or statements in each file." Example:

> 2 data files (1,500, 800 logical records)

9.5B4. "Add to the designation for an object program the name, number, etc., of the machine on which it runs." Examples:

> 1 object program (CDC 6600)
>
> 1 object program (UNIVAC 1100/81)

9.5B5. "If the number of logical records or statements in a large file is unknown, give the approximate number of records or statements, or if this cannot be done, omit such data and give a note (see 9.7B10)." Example:

> 5 data files (ca. 7,500 logical records)

9.5C.　　Other file details

"Give other characteristics of the file in the note area (see 9.7B10)." Note that there is no equivalent of dimensions given for an MRDF.

9.5D.　　Accompanying material

9.5D1.　　"Record the designation for a program accompanying a data file or for a file accompanying a program as accompanying material (see 1.5E). *Optionally*, add to the designation the number of statements or logical records in such accompanying programs or files." LC is applying the option when the information is readily available or easy to ascertain.[2] Example:

> 1 program file (400 statements, FORTRAN IV) + 2 data files (300, 700 logical records)

9.5D2.　　"Record the name, and *optionally* the physical description of any other accompanying material (e.g., codebooks, manuals) as instructed in 1.5E." The option is treated by LC as in 9.5D1. *See* Fig. 11.13.

9.5D3.　　"If a file is accompanied by both an eye-readable and a machine-readable codebook, give details of both." Example:

> 1 data file (900 logical records) + 1 machine-readable code-book (4,200 logical records) + 1 codebook (364 p. ; 25 cm.)

9.5D4.　　When the documentation accompanying a file consists of a number of parts, the addition to this area is "+ associated documentation."

Fig. 11.13. Rule 9.5. Addition of file description and accompanying material to the description of the MRDF.

The CPS 1974 American national election study [machine-readable data file] / principal investigators, Warren E. Miller, Arthur H. Miller, F. Gerald Kline ; The Center for Political Studies, The University of Michigan. -- ICPR ed. -- Ann Arbor, Mich. : Inter-University Consortium for Political Research, 1975.

1 data file (1,575 logical records) + 1 codebook (675 p.; 24 cm.)

RULE 9.6.　SERIES AREA

Series statements are recorded as instructed in the general chapter under 1.6. *See* Fig. 11.14.

One must be careful here to record only true series and not the name of the distributor with an identification or "study" number. Two of the examples in *AACR 2* are actually the latter case. "Zentralarchiv" and "ICPR" are distributors (i.e., archives), and the numbers are sequential ID numbers assigned by those distributors. Series statements for MRDFs have not yet been implemented on a large scale.

The CPS 1974 American national election study [machine-readable data file] / principal investigators, Warren E. Miller, Arthur H. Miller, F. Gerald Kline ; The Center for Political Studies, The University of Michigan. -- ICPR ed. -- Ann Arbor, Mich. : Inter-University Consortium for Political Research, 1975.

1 data file (1,575 logical records) + 1 codebook (675 p.; 24 cm) -- (SRC/CPS American national election series; no. 13)

RULE 9.7.   NOTE AREA

9.7B.   Notes

"Make notes as set out in the following subrules and in the order given there." Following are some typical notes used for MRDFs. For further details, consult *AACR 2*, pages 212-15.

9.7B1.   Nature and scope

Example:

> Records cover the science and technology of textiles, plus all relevant patent literature in the United Kingdom and United States dating from 1970 to the present.

9.7B3.   Source of title proper

"Make notes on the source of the title proper if it has been taken from anywhere other than the data file itself." For the near future, this note must always be given, because as explained earlier, there is not yet a standard for including the title in the file itself. *See* Fig. 11.15 (page 213).

9.7B4.   Variations in title

See Fig. 11.15.

9.7B6.   Statements of responsibility

"Give statements relating to collaborators, sponsors, commissioning agents, programmers, systems analysts, etc., and persons or bodies responsible for the preparation of the file in machine-readable form if they are not named elsewhere in the description and are judged necessary for the bibliographic description." *See* Fig. 11.15.

9.7B7.   Edition and history

"Make notes relating to the edition being described or to the history of an item." *See* Fig. 11.15.

"Give the following dates if they are considered to be relevant to the content, use, or condition of the file:

a) the date when data were copied from an outside source . . .

b) the date(s) covered by the data content of a file . . .

c) the date(s) when data were collected . . . [*see* Fig. 11.15]

d) the date(s) of supplementary files if these are not described separately. . . ."

9.7B8. Program
"Give the program version and/or level." Example:

OSIRIS version.

9.7B10. File description and physical description
"If the number of records or statements in a file has not been verified, indicate this.

Size of file not verified

"If the file consists of exemplars retained for their physical characteristics, give a concise physical description of the file.

75 plastic credit cards with magnetic strip on back

"If the number of records or statements in a file cannot be ascertained (even approximately), give a concise description of the file as received.

Received as 2,000 reels of magnetic tape, 800 bpi"
Note: "bpi" stands for "bytes per inch."

This is also the place for notes about the number of variables (e.g., Number of variables: 564) or weighted sample sizes (*see* Fig. 11.15).
The rule also suggests the possibility of including here a physical description of the medium in which the file has been received: number of physical entities, name of the physical medium, and other details such as quantitative properties, trade name, dimensions, etc. However, as discussed under the edition area above, MRDFs can be so easily and quickly changed to a different physical medium that such physical description could quickly become outdated and could be misleading. Therefore, such description is not recommended.

9.7B11. Accompanying material
"Give details of accompanying material not mentioned in the file description area (see 9.5D). If a codebook has an ISBN, give it here." *See* Fig. 11.15.

9.7B12. Series
See Fig. 11.15.

9.7B14.   Audience and restrictions on access
Examples:

> Intended audience: Textile and related industries.

> Variables dealing with the Supreme Court are temporarily restricted.

> Restrictions: available by lease arrangement. Also available through commercial on-line vendors.

9.7B15.   Mode of use
"If the file cannot be used on all facilities available to the user of the catalogue or other list, specify its mode of use."

9.7B16.   Other formats
See Fig. 11.15.

9.7B17.   Summary
See Fig. 11.15.

9.7B18.   Contents
"Make a list of the titles of the individually named parts of a file. Add to the titles the number of logical records or statements in each part." Example:

> Contents: file 1. Faculty (285 logical records).--file 2. Graduate students (580 logical records).--file 3. Undergraduate students (1,080 logical records)

9.7B19.   Numbers borne by the item [other than ISBNs or ISSNs]
Many MRDFs will have *two* study numbers associated with the file: an original number assigned by the producer and an archival identification number applied by a distributor for in-house identification. Such numbers are important to a user for facilitating location or purchase of a copy of the file. These numbers are usually included in the file's documentation. *See* Fig. 11.15.

**RULE 9.8.   STANDARD NUMBER AND TERMS OF
            AVAILABILITY AREA**

The details of this area are given as instructed in the general chapter. However, ISBNs and ISSNs are not yet being assigned to MRDFs. ISBNs and ISSNs assigned to documentation are given in the note area (*see* 9.7B11).

RULE 9.9.   SUPPLEMENTARY ITEMS

"Describe supplementary items as instructed in 1.9."

Fig. 11.15.

The CPS 1974 American national election study [machine-readable data file] / principal investigators, Warren E. Miller, Arthur H. Miller, F. Gerald Kline ; The Center for Political Studies, The University of Michigan. -- ICPR ed. -- Ann Arbor, Mich. : Inter-University Consortium for Political Research, 1975.

1 data file (1,575 logical records) + 1 codebook (675 p.; 24 cm.) -- (SRC/CPS American national election series ; no. 13)

1 ──────▶Title from title page of codebook.
2 ──────▶Also known as: 1974 American national election study.
3 ──────▶Supported by grants from the National Science Foundation (SOC 75-02704), the John and Mary R. Markle Foundation, and the Carnegie Corporation.
4 ──────▶Contains a subset of the respondents previously interviewed in the 1972 post-election survey.
5 ──────▶Data collected Nov., Dec. 1974, and Jan. 1975.
6 ──────▶Weighted sample size is 2523.
7 ──────▶Codebook numbered: ISBN 0-89138-111-2
8 ──────▶Series statement supplied by producer.
9 ──────▶Also available in an OSIRIS system file.
10 ──────▶ Summary: Exploration of political attitudes and behavior in the context of Watergate events and the 1974 congressional elections. Respondents were questioned on many topics including Watergate, mass media, major political issues and problems facing the country, confidence in government, national and personal finances, and quality of life in the U.S.
11 ──────▶ Original study number: CPS study 495441.
11 ──────▶ Archival study number: ICPR study 7355.

[1]Source of title

[2]Variation in title

[3]Additional statement of responsibility

[4]History

[5]History

[6]File description

[7]Accompanying material details

[8]Additional series data

[9]Other formats

[10]Summary

[11]Numbers borne by the item

RULE 9.10. ITEMS MADE UP OF SEVERAL TYPES OF MATERIAL

"Describe items made up of several types of material as instructed in 1.10."

DEFINITIONS

Distribution date. A MRDF distribution date is interpreted as the year the file became available for distribution to the public, usually through an established agency.

Distributor. A MRDF distributor is defined as that organization or person that has been designated by the author or producer to generate copies of a particular file or program. If a distributor is not cited, then it is assumed that the author or producer is fulfilling this function.

Documentation. Documentation is described as descriptive information required to initiate, develop, operate, and maintain machine-readable files and systems. Data-file documentation describes the condition of the data, the creation of the file, and the location and size of the data elements contained in the records. System documentation usually is quite technical and defines the relationship among the various hardware components or software elements. Program documentation explains the purpose and procedures of a given set of software instructions.

Edition. A MRDF edition occurs when one of the following criteria is met: 1) any additions or deletions of the original machine-readable text; 2) any additions or deletions of data elements or variables; 3) any recoding or reformatting of the file; 4) any changes in the number of observations or logical records; and 5) any changes in the programming statements or language.

Internal user label. An internal user label is a machine-readable identifier containing alphabetic and/or numeric characters providing information about the file.

Producer. A MRDF producer is defined as that person or organization with the financial or administrative responsibility for producing a computerized edition of a file or program. Such responsibility may include the various tasks associated with collecting the data or information and converting the information into a computerized format. These tasks may be contracted out or performed by more than one party.

Production date. An MRDF production date is interpreted as the date the file became operational in a computerized form and available for analysis, processing, and possible release to the general public. It may or may not coincide with the date of copyright or the date the work was released to the public. In those cases where the production date has to be approximated, the date of data collection may be used as a point of reference.

FOOTNOTES

[1]"Display of General Material Designations under AACR 2," *Cataloging Service Bulletin*, no. 6 (Fall 1979):4-5.

[2]"AACR 2 Options Proposed by the Library of Congress, Chapters 2-11," *Library of Congress Information Bulletin* 38 (Aug. 10, 1979):314-15.

12 DESCRIPTION OF THREE-DIMENSIONAL ARTIFACTS AND REALIA

INTRODUCTION

Like many graphic materials, discussed in chapter 10, the materials covered by this chapter are not or have not been cataloged or classified in most libraries. With the possibility now of a method of description consistent with that of describing other materials, according to ISBD(G), however, we may soon see much more cataloging of these materials—especially in media centers where emphasis is no longer on the "book" as the principle means of transmitting knowledge.

This chapter illustrates application of *AACR 2* to a few items identified as three-dimensional artifacts and realia. The principles, however, may be applied to any such materials.

RULE 10.0. GENERAL RULES

10.0A.   Scope
"The rules in this chapter cover the description of three-dimensional artefacts of all kinds (other than those covered in previous chapters), including models, dioramas, games (including puzzles and simulations), sculptures and other three-dimensional art works, exhibits, machines, and clothing. They also cover the description of naturally occurring objects, including microscope specimens (or representations of them) and other specimens mounted for viewing. For the description of three-dimensional cartographic materials (relief models, globes, etc.), see chapter 3 [chapter 5 of this text]."

10.0B.   Sources of information

10.0B1.   Chief source of information
"The chief source of information for the materials covered in this chapter is the object itself together with any accompanying textual material and container issued by the 'publisher' or manufacturer of the item. Prefer information found on the object itself (including any permanently affixed labels) to information found in accompanying textual material or on a container."

10.0B2.   Prescribed sources of information
"The prescribed source of information for each area of the description of these materials is set out below. . . ."

AREA	PRESCRIBED SOURCES OF INFORMATION
Title and statement of responsibility	Chief source of information
Edition	Chief source of information
Publication, distribution, etc.	Chief source of information
Physical description	Any source
Series	Chief source of information
Note	Any source
Standard number and terms of availability	Any source"

The item used in this chapter to illustrate the building of a description is a game. Its prescribed sources of information are shown as Figs. 12.1-12.3. In addition, the cataloging for two dioramas and a puzzle are given as Figs. 12.10-12.12 (pages 223-24) to illustrate the application of the principles to other materials.

Fig. 12.1. Top of container of game.

Instructo ® ACTIVITY KIT

The
Classification
Game

Fig. 12.2. End panel of game's container.

Instructo® ACTIVITY KIT

The Classification Game

REORDER NO.

1014

Fig. 12.3. Top and bottom of page of accompanying
textual material.

INSTRUCTO TEACHING GUIDE

Instructo educational materials undergo careful testing and evaluation under actual and varying classroom teaching conditions.

No. 1014 THE CLASSIFICATION GAME

RULE 10.1. TITLE AND STATEMENT OF RESPONSIBILITY AREA

10.1B.   **Title proper**

10.1B1.   "Record the title proper as instructed in 1.1B." *See* Fig. 12.4.

Fig. 12.4. Rule 10.1B. Transcription of title proper of the game
being cataloged.

The classification game

10.1C.   *Optional addition.* **General material designation**
The North American GMDs appropriate to the materials of this chapter
are: diorama, game, microscope slide, model, realia. The Library of Congress
does not now catalog these materials. It has said that for all these types, it
would use the GMD if it does start cataloging the material.[1] The British GMD
for all items covered by this chapter is "object." British catalogers are thus
saved having to decide into which category to place such items as toys (including dolls intended for instruction as well as play), quilts, puppets, etc. *See* Fig.
12.5.

Fig. 12.5. Rule 10.1C. Addition of GMD to description
of the game.

The classification game [game]

10.1D.-10.1E.

Parallel titles and other title information are recorded as instructed in the general chapter under 1.1D.-1.1E.

10.1F.   Statements of responsibility

10.1F1.   "Record statements relating to persons or bodies responsible for the creation of the item, or for its display or selection, as instructed in 1.1F." Example:

> Family portrait [game] / by Sandy Miller

See also Fig. 12.11 (page 223).

RULE 10.2. EDITION AREA

The elements of this area are recorded as instructed in the general chapter under 1.2.

RULE 10.3. MATERIAL (OR TYPE OF PUBLICATION) SPECIFIC DETAILS AREA

"This area is not used for three-dimensional artefacts and realia."

RULE 10.4. PUBLICATION, DISTRIBUTION, ETC., AREA

For most items falling within the scope of this chapter, the details of publication, distribution, etc., are recorded as instructed in the general chapter under 1.4 (*see* Fig. 12.6). However, for "naturally occurring objects" that are not mounted for viewing or packaged for presentation, place, publisher, and date are not recorded. For "artefacts not intended primarily for communication" (e.g., clothing, money, furniture), no place or publisher is recorded. For these items the date of manufacture is given as the first element of this area. Example:

> [White treadle sewing machine] [realia]. – 1890.

If the person or body that has manufactured an object is named in the statement of responsibility (as is the case with hand-made items such as hand-woven tapestries or hand-made pottery), the place and name are not repeated in this area. In such a case, the place, if known, may be part of the cataloger-constructed title proper. *See* Fig. 12.11.

Fig. 12.6. Rule 10.4. Addition of publication details to the description of the game.

> The classification game [game]. -- Paoli, Pa. : Instructo Corp., c1969.

RULE 10.5. PHYSICAL DESCRIPTION AREA

10.5B.   **Extent of item (including specific material designation)**

10.5B1.   "Record the number of physical units of a three-dimensional artefact or object by giving the number of parts in arabic numerals and one of the terms listed below, as appropriate. If none of these terms is appropriate, give the specific name of the item or the names of the parts of the item as concisely as possible.

diorama	microscope slide
exhibit	mock-up
game	model"

Some other possibilities include:

jigsaw puzzle	statue
simulation	sculpture
hand puppet	bowl (or cup, jar, candle
quilt	holder, etc.)
tapestry	dress (or coat, belt, suit, etc.)

The possibilities are nearly endless. *See* Fig. 12.7 and Figs. 12.10-12.12.

"*Optionally*, if general material designations are used and the general material designation consists of one of the above listed terms, drop that term and give the number of pieces alone (see 10.5B2)." LC is not applying this option so that the physical description will be complete whether or not a cataloging agency has chosen to use GMDs.[2]

10.5B2.   "Add to the designation, when appropriate, the number and the name(s) of the pieces." *See* Fig. 12.12.

"If the pieces cannot be named concisely or cannot be ascertained, add the term *various pieces*, and *optionally* give the details of the pieces in a note (see 10.7B10)." LC is applying this option on a case-by-case basis.[3] *See* Fig. 12.7 and Figs. 12.10-12.11.

10.5C.   **Other physical details**

10.5C1.   "**Material.** When appropriate, give the material(s) of which the object is made. If the material(s) cannot be stated concisely, either omit them or give them in a note. Give the material of which a microscope slide is made if it is other than glass." *See* Fig. 12.7 and Figs. 12.10-12.12.

10.5C2.   "**Colour.** When appropriate, give the abbreviation *col.* for multicoloured objects, or name the colour(s) of the object if it is in one or two colours, or give the abbreviation *b&w*. If a microscope slide is stained, state this." Examples:

1 jar : clay, brown and red

1 statue : stone, grey

See also Fig. 12.7 and Figs. 12.10-12.12.

10.5D.   Dimensions

10.5D1.   "Give the dimensions of the object, when appropriate, in centi-metres, to the next whole centimetre up. If necessary, add a word to indicate which dimension is being given. If multiple dimensions are given, record them as height x width x depth (for microscope slides, length x width)." Examples:

1 jar : clay, brown and red ; 32 cm. high

1 paperweight : glass, col. ; 8 cm. diameter

See also Fig. 12.11.

10.5D2.   "If the object is in a container, name the container and give its dimensions either after the dimensions of the object or as the only dimensions." Example:

1 jigsaw puzzle (ca. 60 pieces) ; cardboard, col. ; 18 cm.
diameter in box, 11 cm. diameter x 4 cm.

See also Figs. 12.7, 12.10, and 12.12.

10.5E.   Accompanying material

Accompanying material is recorded as instructed in the general chapter under 1.5. *See* Fig. 12.7.

Fig. 12.7. Rule 10.5. Addition of physical description to description of the game.

The classification game [game]. – Paoli, Pa. : Instructo Corp., c1969.
1 game (various pieces) : cardboard, col. ; in box,
24 x 28 x 8 cm. + 1 teacher's guide (2 p. ; 28 cm.)

RULE 10.6. SERIES AREA

Series statements are recorded as instructed in the general chapter under 1.6. *See* Fig. 12.8.

**Fig. 12.8. Rule 10.6. Addition of series statement to
description of the game.**

The classification game [game]. -- Paoli, Pa. : Instructo
Corp., c1969.
   1 game (various pieces) : cardboard, col. ; in box,
24 x 28 x 8 cm. + 1 teacher's guide (2 p. ; 28 cm.). -- (Instructo activity kit)

RULE 10.7. NOTE AREA

10.7B.   Notes
   "Make notes as set out in the following subrules and in the order given
there." Some typical notes used for three-dimensional artifacts and realia may
be found in Figs. 12.9-12.12 (see pages 223-24). For further details, consult
AACR 2, pages 228-30.

RULE 10.8. STANDARD NUMBER AND TERMS OF
AVAILABILITY AREA

   Details of this area are recorded as instructed in the general chapter under
1.8. Three-dimensional artifacts and realia currently are not given international standard numbers, leaving the terms of availability to stand alone.
See Fig. 12.9.

RULE 10.9. SUPPLEMENTARY ITEMS

   "Describe supplementary items as instructed in 1.9."

RULE 10.10. ITEMS MADE UP OF SEVERAL TYPES OF MATERIAL

   Three-dimensional artifacts may often be found in "kits" made up of
these and other types of material, such as various kinds of graphic materials.
The reader should take note of the possible ways for describing kits given in
the general chapter (chapter 3 of this text) under Rule 1.10. See the examples
given there.

**Fig. 12.9. Rule 10.7. Addition of notes and terms of availability
to description of the game.**

The classification game [game.]. -- Paoli, Pa. : Instructo
Corp., c1969.
1 game (various pieces) : cardboard, col. ; in box,
24 x 28 x 8 cm. + 1 teacher's guide (2 p. ; 28 cm.). -- (Instructo activity kit)

Contains 4 store interiors (3 interlocking pieces each), 4
store floors, and 48 picture cards.
For primary grades.
Summary: Helps students improve organizing and classifying skills by learning to place the appropriate items in
each of four stores: clothing store, food store, pet store, and
toy store.
"No. 1014."
$4.95.

**Fig. 12.10. Example of description of a
published diorama.**

Seasons [diorama] : spring and summer. -- Philadelphia :
Instructo Products Co., c1966.
1 diorama (various pieces) : cardboard, col. ; in box,
30 x 26 x 10 cm.

Contains 4 background scenes and 72 figures of animals,
people, and plants.
Summary: Helps children grasp the concept of change as
it appears in spring and summer.

**Fig. 12.11. Example of description of a
locally produced diorama.**

The sixteenth century printer [diorama] / John Phillips. --
[1976].
1 diorama (various pieces) : plastic, col. ; 75 x 125 x 50 cm.

Title from label.
Contains 1 interior printshop background, 4 figures of
printers, and 3 figures of hand printing equipment.

**Fig. 12.12. Example of description of a
jigsaw puzzle.**

Lord Howe on the Quarter Deck of the Queen Charlotte,
June 1st, 1794 [game]. -- Leeds : J. Waddington, c1970.

1 jigsaw puzzle (ca. 500 pieces) : cardboard, col. ; 38 x 55
cm. in box, 32 x 26 x 5 cm.

Based on a painting by Mather Brown.
Vertical sides in straight lines; horizontal sides form wavy
lines.
Summary: The picture shows a battle scene on the deck
of a British war ship during the Revolutionary War. The officers are in full dress uniforms for 1787-1795 period.

FOOTNOTES

[1]"Display of General Material Designations under AACR 2," *Cataloging Service Bulletin*, no. 6 (Fall 1979):4-5.

[2]"AACR 2 Options Proposed by the Library of Congress, Chapters 2-11," *Library of Congress Information Bulletin* 38 (Aug. 10, 1979):315.

[3]"AACR 2 Options," p. 316.

13 DESCRIPTION OF MICROFORMS

INTRODUCTION

The cataloging of microforms requires knowledge of a number of different types of material. Books, manuscripts, maps, music, and graphic materials all can be reproduced in microform. In addition, microform can be the original means for publication of some kinds of content – especially data stored in a computer. According to *AACR 2*, all microforms whether original publications or reproductions, are described in terms of the microform format with details of the original, when applicable, given in a note. As mentioned on pages 69-70 of this text, this is a controversial method for handling microforms. Those who oppose it say that the user is misled by being given a modern date in the publication, distribution, etc., area when the intellectual content of the item is much older. They are also concerned about short-entry catalogs in which the notes are not printed. Publishers that specialize in reproducing older printed material in microform say that the purpose of the reproduction is to make older materials available for scholarly study and research, not to create a new edition of it as a printed reprint of the text would do. Earlier rules called for description of the original in the major part of the record with microform details in a note. Americans have tended to prefer this method, but Europeans have espoused describing the original in a note. In January, 1980 a subcommittee of ALA's Committee on Cataloging: Description and Access was appointed to examine this question again and put forth a recommendation; the reader should watch for further developments. However, this text will illustrate the method used in *AACR 2,* that the cataloger describes the item in hand, not what it is a reproduction of.

RULE 11.0. GENERAL RULES

11.0A.   Scope
"The rules in this chapter cover the description of all kinds of material in microform. Microforms include microfilms, microfiches, microopaques, and aperture cards. Microforms may be reproductions of existing textual or graphic materials or they may be original publications."

11.0B.   Sources of information

11.0B1.   Chief source of information
The following are the chief sources of information for the different types of microform:

TYPE	CHIEF SOURCE
microfilm	title frame, usually at the beginning of the item giving full title and publication details
aperture cards: set of cards single card	 title card card itself
microfiches and microopaques	title frame, or, if there is none, the eye-readable data at the top of the fiche or opaque

Information that is usually presented on one title frame or card may be presented on successive frames or cards. In this case, treat the successive frames or cards as one chief source.

"If information is not available from the chief source, take it from the following sources (in this order of preference):

> the rest of the item (including a container that is an integral part of the item)

> container

> accompanying eye-readable material

> any other source"

11.0B2. Prescribed sources of information

"The prescribed source(s) of information for each area of the description of microforms is set out below. . . .

AREA	PRESCRIBED SOURCES OF INFORMATION
Title and statement of responsibility	Chief source of information
Edition	Chief source of information, the rest of the item, the container
Special data for cartographic materials and serials	[same as edition area]
Publication, distribution, etc.	[same as edition area]
Physical decription	Any source
Series	[same as edition area]
Note	Any source
Standard number and terms of availability	Any source"

Two items, one in microfilm format and the other in microfiche format are used in this chapter to illustrate the building of description for microforms. Their chief and other sources of information are given as Figs. 13.1-13.5.

Fig. 13.1. Transcription of the first five frames of a microfilm.

Frame 1

WOMEN AND/IN HEALTH

filmed by the
WOMEN'S HISTORY RESEARCH CENTER
JULY 1974

Frame 2

WOMEN'S HISTORY RESEARCH CENTER

2325 Oak Street
Berkeley, California 94707

Frame 3

© Women's History Research Center, Inc. 1974

Reproduction of the material contained herein may not be reproduced in any form except by express permission from Women's History Research Center, Inc. and the Publisher(s).

Frame 4

THIS FILM WAS MADE POSSIBLE BY A REVENUE SHARING GRANT FROM THE ALMEDA COUNTY BOARD OF SUPERVISORS.

Frame 5

Filmed at a reduction ratio of 15:1

Fig. 13.2. Transcription of label on container of first reel of microfilm.

WOMEN AND HEALTH/MENTAL HEALTH
Reel No. 1   Positive
Section I
Women's History Research Center

Fig. 13.3. Transcription of title frame of microfiche.

77-28,548

HANSON, John Frederick, 1949-
THE TRIAL OF LIEUTENANT GENERAL
MASAHARU HOMMA.

Mississippi State University, Ph.D., 1977
History, United States

Xerox University Microfilms, Ann Arbor, Michigan 48106

© 1977
JOHN FREDERICK HANSON

ALL RIGHTS RESERVED

Fig. 13.4. Transcription of eye-readable data at top of fiche.

77-28548   HANSON, John F   THE TRIAL OF LIEUTENANT   1 of 3
                                               GENERAL MASAHARU HOMMA
                Ann Arbor, MI. : University Microfilms International 1978

**Fig. 13.5. Copy of title page of original dissertation
(second frame of microfiche).**

THE TRIAL OF LIEUTENANT GENERAL MASAHARU HOMMA

by
JOHN F. HANSON

A Dissertation
Submitted to the Faculty of
Mississippi State University
in Partial Fulfillment of the Requirements
for the Degree of Doctor of Philosophy
in the Department of History

Mississippi State, Mississippi
August 1977

RULE 11.1. TITLE AND STATEMENT OF RESPONSIBILITY AREA

11.1B.   **Title proper**

11.1B1.   "Record the title proper as instructed in 1.1B." *See* Figs. 13.6 and 13.7.

Fig. 13.6. Rule 11.1B. Transcription of the title proper of the microfilm.

Women and/in health

Fig. 13.7. Rule 11.1B. Transcription of the title proper of the microfiche.

The trial of Lieutenant General Masaharu Homma

11.1C.   *Option addition.* **General material designation**
The GMD for the material covered in this chapter is "microform." LC has decided to add the GMD for microform materials under *AACR 2*, although it was not added in the past.[1] *See* Figs. 13.8 and 13.9.

Fig. 13.8. Rule 11.1C. Addition of GMD to the transcription of title proper.

Women and/in health [microform]

Fig. 13.9.

The trial of Lieutenant General Masaharu Homma [microform]

11.1D.-11.1E.   Parallel titles and other title information are transcribed as instructed in 1.1D and 1.1E.

11.1F.   **Statements of responsibility**

11.1F1.   "Record statements of responsibility as instructed in 1.1F." *See* Figs. 13.10 and 13.11.

Fig. 13.10. Rule 11.1F. Addition of statements of responsibility to the descriptions of microfilm and microfiche.

Women and/in health [microform] / filmed by the Women's History Research Center.

Fig. 13.11.

The trial of Lieutenant General Masaharu Homma [microform] / John Frederick Hanson

11.1G. Items without a collective title

11.1G1. "If a microform lacks a collective title, *either* describe the item as a unit . . . *or* make a separate description for each separately titled work. . . ."

This rule treats these materials in the same manner as sound recordings and motion pictures, rather than as in the general chapter. *See* discussion under 6.1G in chapter 8 of this text. It is common to find several different serial titles on the same roll of microfilm. These are given separate descriptions in most libraries.

RULE 11.2. EDITION AREA

11.2B. Edition statement

11.2B1. "Transcribe a statement relating to an edition of a microform that contains differences from other editions, or that is a named reissue of that microform, as instructed in 1.2B." *See* Fig. 13.12.

Fig. 13.12. Rule 11.2B1. Transcription of a statement relating to the edition of a microform.

Die Kataloge der Frankfurter und Leipziger Buchmessen 1759-1800 [microform] / hrsg. von Bernhard Fabian. -- Microfiche-Ed.

The point to be remembered here is that the edition statement should relate to the edition of the *microform*. The edition statement of the original, if applicable, is recorded in a note.

The remainder of the edition area is treated as instructed in the general chapter.

RULE 11.3. SPECIAL DATA FOR CARTOGRAPHIC MATERIALS AND SERIALS

11.3A.   Cartographic materials

"Record the mathematical data of a cartographic item as instructed in 3.3."

11.3B.   Serials

"Record the numeric and/or chronological or other designation of a serial microform or a serial reproduced in microform as instructed in 12.3." Examples:

> Bulletin of the American Economic Association [microform]. -- 4th ser., no. 1 (Mar. 1911)-no. 6 (Dec. 1911)

> Viewpoint [microform]. -- Vol. 1 (1976)-

RULE 11.4. PUBLICATION, DISTRIBUTION, ETC., AREA

The details of this area are recorded as instructed in the general chapter. Again, it should be remembered that the details recorded here are those of the publication of the *microform*, not those of an original being reproduced. *See* Figs. 13.13 and 13.14.

Fig. 13.13. Rule 11.4. Addition of publication details to descriptions of microfilm and microfiche.

> Women and/in health [microform] / filmed by the Women's History Research Center. -- Berkeley, Calif. : The Center, 1974.

Fig. 13.14.

> The trial of Lieutenant General Masaharu Homma [microform] / John Frederick Hanson. -- Ann Arbor, Mich. : Xerox University Microfilms, 1978, c1977.

It will be noted that the name of the publisher for the microfiche is given differently in the title frame (chief source, Fig. 13.3, page 228) and in the eye-readable data (Fig. 13.4, page 228). Therefore, the name in the chief source is given in Fig. 13.14. However, the date given in the eye-readable data appears to be the publication date, while the date in the title frame is the copyright date; so both are given.

RULE 11.5. PHYSICAL DESCRIPTION AREA

11.5B.   Extent of item (including specific material designation)

11.5B1.   "Record the number of physical units of a microform item by giving the number of parts in arabic numerals and one of the following terms as appropriate:

aperture card   microfilm

microfiche   microopaque

"*Optionally*, if the general material designation *microform* is used, drop the prefix *micro* from these terms." LC is not following this option in order to make the bibliographic description complete so that libraries using LC's records will not be obligated to use the GMD.[2]

"Add to *microfilm* one of the terms *cartridge, cassette,* or *reel*, as appropriate. Add to *microfiche* the term *cassette* if appropriate." *See* Fig. 13.15 (page 233).

"Add the number of frames of a microfiche if it can be easily ascertained. Make the addition in parentheses." *See* Fig. 13.16 (page 233).

11.5C.   Other physical details

11.5C1.   "If a microform is negative, indicate this." Example:

    15 microfiches : negative

11.5C2.   "If a microform contains, or consists of, illustrations, indicate this as instructed in 1.5C." *See* Fig. 13.16.

If "negative" is indicated, the statement of illustrations follows "negative" and a comma. Example:

    15 microfiches : negative, ill.

11.5C3.   "If a microform is wholly or partly coloured, indicate this by using *col.* (for a coloured microform without illustrations), or *col. & ill.* (for a coloured microform with illustrations), or *col. ill.*, etc. (for a microform on which only the illustrations are coloured)."

11.5D.   Dimensions

The dimensions of a microfiche, a microopaque, and an aperture card mount are given as height x width in centimeters to the next whole centimeter up. *See* Fig. 13.16.

The diameter of a microfilm reel is given in inches, to the next whole inch up, if the diameter is other than three inches. In addition, the width of a microfilm is given in millimeters. *See* Fig. 13.15.

11.5E.   Accompanying material

11.5E1.   "Record the name, and *optionally* the physical description, of any accompanying material as instructed in 1.5E." The option is being applied by LC as discussed in the general chapter under 1.5E. Example:

    10 microfilm reels ; 35 mm. + 1 guide (v, 14 p. ;
    23 cm.)

Fig. 13.15. Rule 11.5. Addition of physical description to
description of microfilm.

Women and/in health [microform] / filmed by the
Women's History Research Center. -- Berkeley, Calif. : The
Center, 1974.
    13 microfilm reels on 14 ; 35 mm.

Note: The 14 physical reels are numbered consecutively except that number
"3A" falls between "3" and "4." Therefore the extent of item is given with the
number of bibliographic entities preceding the number of physical ones.

Fig. 13.16. Rule 11.5. Addition of physical description to
description of microfiche.

The trial of Lieutenant General Masaharu Homma
[microform] / John Frederick Hanson. -- Ann Arbor, Mich. :
Xerox University Microfilms, 1978, c1977.
    3 microfiches (231 fr.) : maps ; 11 x 15 cm.

RULE 11.6. SERIES AREA

11.6B.   Series statements

11.6B1.   "Record each series statement relating to a microform as
instructed in 1.6. If the original was published in a series, record it in a note
(see 11.7B12)." Examples:

        116 microfilm reels ; 35 mm. -- (British publishers' archives
    on microfilm)

        7 microfiches ; 11 x 15 cm. -- (Columbia University oral
    history collection ; pt. 2, no. 24)

RULE 11.7. NOTE AREA

11.7B.   Notes
    "In describing an original reproduced in microform, give the notes set out
in the following subrules, and then the notes relating to the original. (For
exceptions, see 11.7B12 below and chapter 12 [chapter 14 of this text].) Combine the notes relating to the original in one note, giving the details in the order
of the areas to which they relate." Example:

        Original: New York : Teachers College, Columbia Univer-
    sity, 1927. xix, 166 p. : ill. ; 24 cm. Bibliography:
    p. 157.

See also Fig. 13.18 (page 236).

Following are some typical notes used for microforms. For further details consult *AACR 2*, pages 243-45.

11.7B1.   Nature, scope or artistic or other form of an item
"Make notes on these matters if they are not already apparent from the rest of the description." Example:

> Extensive collection of feminist serial literature published 1956 through June, 1974.

11.7B4.   Variations in title
See Fig. 13.17 (page 236).

11.7B6.   Statements of responsibility
" . . . Give statements of responsibility not recorded in the title and statement of responsibility area. Make notes on persons or bodies connected with a work . . . not already named in the description." Example:

> Collected by the Women's History Research Center, 1968-1974; transferred to the Special Collections Dept., Northwestern University Library, 1974.

11.7B7.   Edition and history
Example:

> Filmed from the H. G. Wells collection in the Bromley Public Libraries.

11.7B10.   Physical description
Reduction ratio. "Give the reduction ratio if it is outside the 16X-30X range. Use one of the following terms:

Low reduction	*For less than 16X*
High reduction	*For 31X-60X*
Very high reduction	*For 61X-90X*
Ultra high reduction	*For over 90X; for ultra high reduction give also the specific ratio, e.g.,* Ultra high reduction, 150X

Reduction ratio varies"
See Fig. 13.17.

Reader. "Give the name of the reader on which a cassette or cartridge microfilm is to be used if it affects the use of the item."

11.7B11.   Accompanying material
Example:

> With printed index: Index to the archives of Richard Bentley & Son, 1829-1898 / compiled by Alison Ingram. 1977. 128 p. ; 26 cm.

See also Fig. 13.17.

11.7B12.   Series
"Make notes on series data that cannot be given in the series area.

> Original issued in series:
> (*For a reproduction in microform*)

> Originally issued in series:
> (*For a microform previously issued as such in a series*)"

Example:

> Original issued in series: School administration series.

11.7B13.   Dissertations
See Fig. 13.18.

11.7B16.   Other formats available
Example:

> Library also has volumes in printed form and on microfilm.

11.7B17.   Summary
Example:

> Summary: Pamphlets relating to conditions in South Carolina, 1866-1892.

11.7B18.   Contents
See Figs. 13.17 and 13.18.

**Fig. 13.17. Rule 11.7. Addition of notes to the
description of a microfilm.**

Women and/in health [microform] / filmed by
the Women's History Research Center. -- Berkeley, Calif. : The Center, 1974.

13 microfilm reels on 14 ; 35 mm.

1 ——→ Title on reel containers: Women and health/
mental health.

2 ——→ Low reduction. ⟋ 3

¹Variant title

²Reduction
ratio

³Accompanying
material

⁴Contents

Guide issued under title: Guide to the microform edition of the women and health collection. ⟋ 4

Contents: Section 1. Physical and mental
health of women.--Section 2. Physical and mental illness of women.--Section 3. Biology, women
and the life cycle.--Section 4. Birth control/popu-
lation control.--Section 5. Sex and sexuality.--
Section 6. Black and third world women--health.
--Section 7. Special issues of mass periodicals.

**Fig. 13.18. Rule 11.7. Addition of notes to the
description of a microfiche.**

The trial of Lieutenant General Masaharu
Homma [microform] / John Frederick Hanson. --
Ann Arbor, Mich. : Xerox University Microfilms,
1978, c1977.

3 microfiches (231 fr.) : maps ; 11 x 15 cm.

¹Dissertation

²Contents

³Details of the
original

Thesis (Ph.D.)--Mississippi State University,
1977.

Includes bibliography.

Original: vii, 223 leaves ; 28 cm. Typescript.

Bibliography: leaves [220]-223.

RULE 11.8. STANDARD NUMBER AND TERMS OF
AVAILABILITY AREA

This area is treated as described under 1.8 in the general chapter. It should
be remembered that only a standard number assigned to the *microform* is
placed here. A standard number of the original should be included in the note
on details of the original.

RULE 11.9. SUPPLEMENTARY ITEMS
"Describe supplementary items as instructed in 1.9."

RULE 11.10. ITEMS MADE UP OF SEVERAL TYPES OF MATERIAL
"Describe items made up of several types of material as instructed in 1.10."

[RULE 11.11. NONPROCESSED MICROFORMS]
There is no Rule 11.11 in *AACR 2*, but it has come to the attention of ALA's Committee on Cataloging: Description and Access that there is a need for an interpretation to cover cataloging the many microforms that are created (usually by libraries or archives) for the purpose of preservation rather than for commercial purposes. These are comparable to nonprocessed sound recordings covered in Rule 6.11 (*see* pp. 169-70). Both nonprocessed microforms and nonprocessed sound recordings bear the same relationship to commercial products that manuscripts bear to books. The principles found in the manuscripts chapter and in Rule 6.11 should be applied to nonprocessed microforms.

FOOTNOTES

[1]"Display of General Material Designations under AACR 2," *Cataloging Service Bulletin*, no. 6 (Fall 1979):4-5.

[2]"AACR 2 Options Proposed by the Library of Congress: Chapters 2-11," *Library of Congress Information Bulletin* 38 (Aug. 10, 1979):316.

14 DESCRIPTION OF SERIALS

INTRODUCTION

A serial is a publication in any medium issued in successive parts at regular or irregular intervals and intended to continue indefinitely. Serials include both periodicals and non-periodicals. A periodical may be defined as a serial that has a distinctive title and that is issued more frequently than once a year and at regular intervals, with each issue containing articles by several contributors. Non-periodicals are all other forms of serials, such as yearbooks, annuals, memoirs, transactions and proceedings of societies, and any series cataloged together instead of separately.

A clear distinction should be made between serials and monographs. A monograph represents a complete bibliographic unit; it may be issued in successive parts at regular or irregular intervals, but it is *not* intended to continue indefinitely. In most cases, of course, a monographic publication is completed in one volume. However, there are certain types of monographs that are often treated as serials by libraries because they are not complete in one volume. These include continuations of sets, provisional serials, and pseudo-serials. A continuation of a set is a non-serial—i.e., monographic—set in process of publication. The *Oxford History of English Literature* and the *Encyclopedia of Library and Information Science* are examples of continuations of sets. Neither publication is presently complete although many individual volumes have been issued. Such publications require a special order record—i.e., a standing order—for follow-up purposes; if such works are cataloged as sets, this creates problems of accurate records in the library's holdings record for the set. Provisional serials are those publications which are treated as serials while in the process of publication and as non-serials when complete. The justification for such treatment is often a particularly lengthy period of publication and/or a complicated numbering of individual issues. Either of the two previous examples of continuations of sets could be treated by individual libraries as provisional serials. A pseudo-serial is a frequently reissued and revised publication that is generally treated as a monographic work at first publication but that is often treated as a serial after numerous successive editions have appeared. Serial numbering may be taken from the edition number or from the date of publication. Examples of pseudo-serials are Sir John Bernard Burke's *Genealogical and Heraldic History of the Peerage* (commonly called Burke's *Peerage*) or the *Guide to Reference Books* edited successively by Alice Bertha Kroeger, Isadore Mudge, Constance Winchell, and Eugene P. Sheehy. Monographic treatment of a pseudo-serial requires individual descriptive cataloging for each new edition as well as additional added entries for previous editors or compilers. If a pseudo-serial is treated as a serial, the main entry is made under the title instead of the author and will require only one set of catalog entries.

The principles for cataloging serials are generally the same as those for cataloging monographic publications. On the other hand, certain physical characteristics of serial publications (e.g., numerous changes in bibliographic descriptions, including changes of titles) necessitate some special rules. The aim of these special rules is to prepare an entry that will stand the longest time and will allow necessary changes to be made with a minimum of modification. If the serial is still being published or if the library has only part of the set and hopes to complete it, an open entry is prepared according to the rules that are presented in this chapter.

The descriptive cataloging of serials is generally more complex than that of monographs because of their greatly varied and possibly intricate bibliographic structure. On the other hand, classification and subject headings are likely to be somewhat more general, therefore simpler. Indeed, in many libraries, periodicals are not classified at all but are shelved alphabetically by main entry. The detail with which serials are described may vary widely from library to library. Some consider a highly analytic description essential, while others reduce serials cataloging to the title and statement of responsibility area and a holdings note, a method most suitable for computer-produced catalogs.

The serials cataloger is likely to be faced with the problem of describing a full set completely although all that may be at hand are a few volumes or current issues. The most important sources of additional information are the *Union List of Serials, New Serial Titles, British Union Catalogue of Periodicals*, and *Ulrich's International Periodicals Directory*, with its companion publication, *Irregular Serials and Annuals: An International Directory*.[1] Other important sources are the Library of Congress catalogs and national and trade bibliographies, as well as publishers' catalogs. *Titles in Series* is useful for its lists of titles in monographic series, especially those published by university presses, and Bowker's *Books in Series in the United States 1966-1975* lists monographs distributed in popular, scholarly, and professional series.[2] In addition, a Library of Congress publication, *Monographic Series*, lists all monographs cataloged by the Library of Congress that appear as parts of series since 1974 as well as all revised records, regardless of the date of publication. This is a quarterly publication with annual cumulations.[3] OCLC and other data bases would prove sources of additional information, as would published state union lists of serials.

RULE 12.0. GENERAL RULES

12.0A. Scope

"The rules in this chapter cover the description of serial publications of all kinds and in all media."

12.0B. Sources of information

12.0B1. Sources of information. Printed serials

Chief source of information. "The chief source of information for a printed serial is the title page (whether published with the issues or published later) or the title page substitute of the first issue of the serial. Failing this, the chief source of information is the first issue that is available. The title page substitute for an item lacking a title page is (in this order of preference) the cover, caption, masthead, editorial pages, colophon, other pages. If information traditionally given on the title page is given on facing pages, with or without repetition, treat the two pages as the title page."

Prescribed sources of information. "The prescribed source(s) of information for each area of the description of printed serials is set out below. Enclose information taken from outside the prescribed source(s) in square brackets.

AREA	PRESCRIBED SOURCE OF INFORMATION
Title and statement of responsibility	Chief source of information
Edition	Chief source of information, other preliminaries, colophon
Numeric and/or alphabetic, chronological, or other designation	[same as edition area]
Publication, distribution, etc.	[same as edition area]
Physical description	The serial itself
Series	Anywhere in the serial
Note	Any source
Standard number and terms of availability	Any source"

12.0B2.   Sources of information. Nonprinted serials
"Follow the instructions given at the beginning of the relevant chapter in Part I (e.g., for sources of information for a serial sound recording, see chapter 6 [chapter 8 of this text])."

The example to be used in this chapter to illustrate the building of the description of a serial is a journal whose title has changed. The chief source of information and preliminaries are given for each of the two titles as Figs. 14.1-14.4.

Fig. 14.1. Title page of first issue of serial.

THE LIBRARY OF CONGRESS

Quarterly Journal

OF CURRENT ACQUISITIONS

Contents

PUBLISHED AS A SUPPLEMENT TO THE ANNUAL
REPORT OF THE LIBRARIAN OF CONGRESS

July + August + September

1943

Fig. 14.2. Title page of first issue with changed title.

The
Quarterly Journal
OF THE LIBRARY OF CONGRESS

Volume 21	JANUARY 1964	Number 1

CONTENTS

ARTICLE   PAGE

Sarah L. Wallace, *Editor*   Janice B. Harrington, *Assistant Editor*

Published as a Supplement to the Annual Report of the Librarian of Congress

**Fig. 14.3. From page facing title page of
Volume 21, Number 1.**

Cover design: *The Miraculous Image of Our Lady of the Pine Tree.* Anonymous Mexican wood-cut, probably from the late 18th century. (The Prints and Photographs Division)

For sale by the Superintendent of Documents, United States Government Printing Office, Washington, D.C., 20402. Price $2.00 per year, including the *Annual Report of the Librarian of Congress,* domestic; 50 cents additional for foreign mailing; single copies vary in price. This issue is priced at 50 cents.

**Fig. 14.4. Editor's note about title change from
Volume 21, Number 1.**

EDITOR'S NOTE

Maxims to guide him who would make a change are many and conflicting. To Confucius, credited with so many epigrams, is attributed the saying: "Only the very wisest and the very stupidest never change." A German proverb observes that "Man changes often, but gets better seldom." There are other cautions to make one pause: that change never answers the end, that it is seldom made for the better, and that it "doth unknit the tranquil state of men."

Nevertheless, despite these warnings, with this issue the editors have changed the cover, the title, the format, and the date of *The Quarterly Journal of Current Acquisitions.* The change in the first is obvious, even to the casual reader. The second is neither startling nor radical, for which we hope the catalogers in the Nation's many libraries will thank us. The name *The Quarterly Journal of Current Acquisitions* has been exchanged for the one it has always used in popular parlance, *The Quarterly Journal of the Library of Congress.* The format has been altered slightly and will continue on a flexible basis, layouts changing to meet the spirit of the subject and the demands of the materials described.

As to dates, this issue is number one of volume 21. Normally, it would appear in December 1963. Under the new plan, volumes will coincide with calendar years. Therefore, all four issues of volume 21 will appear in 1964, the January 1965 issue beginning volume 22.

To return to the maxims, while change may be sweet, there is also a certain virtue in constancy. The *Journal* continues to be a supplement to the *Annual Report of the Librarian of Congress* describing acquisitions more fully than is possible within the confines of that yearly document. The new title, however, allows authors of these supplemental reports a wider scope. As an example, acquisitions no longer current can be related to new additions and the collections discussed as a whole. Opportunity will be offered to report the use of the collections, the tangible values gained from them through study and research. A miser only counts his gold and stories it away, but a foundation uses its fortune to further mankind. In like manner, the *Quarterly Journal* will report on how the Nation uses the gold in its treasurehouse of knowledge.

Disraeli also had a word on change. He said it is constant. The editors expect to continue the change and growth of this periodical within its basic outlines. Comments from the readers will be welcome.

SLW

RULE 12.1. TITLE AND STATEMENT OF RESPONSIBILITY AREA

12.1B. **Title proper**

12.1B1. "Record the title proper as instructed in 1.1B." *See* Figs. 14.5
and 14.6.

**Fig. 14.5. Rule 12.1B. Transcription of title proper of the
original title of the serial.**

Quarterly journal of current acquisitions

Fig. 14.6. Rule 12.1B. Transcription of title proper of the later title of the serial.

The Quarterly journal of the Library of Congress

12.1B2. "In case of doubt about whether a corporate body's name or an abbreviation of that name is part of the title proper, treat the name as such only if it is consistently so presented in various locations in the serial (cover, caption, masthead, editorial pages, etc.). . . ."

On the title page shown in Fig. 14.1, there could be a question as to whether the title ought to be "The Library of Congress quarterly journal of current acquisitions." However, it is elsewhere referred to in that first issue as "Quarterly journal of current acquisitions."

12.1B3. "If a serial is a separately published section of, or supplement to, another serial and its title proper as presented in the chief source of information consists of (a) the title common to all sections (or the title of the main serial) and (b) the title of the section or supplement, and if these two parts are grammatically independent of each other, record the common title first, and then the section or supplement title preceded by a full stop." For example:

Solar energy. Cummulative index

Major studies of the Congressional Research Service.
Supplement

12.1B5. "If the title of a section or supplement is presented in the chief source of information without the title that is common to all sections, give the title of the section or supplement as the title proper. In the case of a section, give the title that is common to all sections as the title proper of the series (see 12.6B). In the case of a supplement, give the title of the main serial in a note (see 12.7B7k)." For example:

Bibliography of Utah geology
[Note reads:]
Supplement to: Utah geology.

12.1B6. "If the title proper includes a date or numbering that varies from issue to issue, omit this date or numbering and replace it by the mark of omission, unless it occurs at the beginning of the title proper, in which case do not include the mark of omission." For example:

Proceedings of the . . . annual meeting

12.1C. *Optional addition.* **General material designation**

The GMDs appropriate to serials are governed by the type of material being cataloged. As discussed in the general chapter under 1.1C, LC will display only some GMDs in its printed records. The reader should consult the discussion in this text of the GMD rule for the medium in which a serial is produced. For example, the discussion of Rule 2.1C indicates that "[text]" is not used for printed serials, and the application of Rule 9.1C indicates that "[machine-readable data file]" should be used for cataloging serial MRDFs.

12.1D.   **Parallel titles**

12.1D1.   "Record parallel titles as instructed in 1.1D." For example:

> Canadian journal of psychiatry =
> Revue canadienne de psychiatrie

12.1E.   **Other title information**

12.1E1.   "Record other title information as instructed in 1.1E. Treat the full form of an acronym or initialism that is, or is part of, the title proper as other title information if it is given in the chief source of information." For example:

> DNR : daily news record
>
> Pesticide residues in food : report
>
> Index to Title 40 of the Code of federal regulations : protection of environment

12.1F.   **Statements of responsibility**

12.1F1.   "Record statements of responsibility relating to persons or bodies as instructed in 1.1F." *See* Fig. 14.7 which treats the original journal title.

Fig. 14.7. Rule 12.1F1. Addition of statement of responsibility after the title proper.

> Quarterly journal of current acquisitions / The Library of Congress
>
> _____

12.1F2.   "If a statement of responsibility has appeared, in full or abbreviated form, as part of the title . . . , do not give a further statement of responsibility unless such a statement appears separately in the chief source of information." *See* Fig. 14.8 for entry of the journal under its new title.

Fig. 14.8. Rule 12.1F2. Title includes responsible body; therefore no "statement of responsibility" preceded by a slash is given.

> The Quarterly journal of the Library of Congress. --
>
> _____

RULE 12.2. EDITION AREA

12.2B. Edition statement

12.2B1. "Record an edition statement as instructed in 1.2B if it belongs to one of the following types:

a)   local edition statements . . .

b)   special interest edition statements . . .

c)   special format or physical presentation statements . . .

d)   language edition statements . . .

e)   reprint or reissue statements indicating a reissue or revision of a serial as a whole. . . ."

For example:

Taft Foundation reporter. -- Regional ed.

Taft Foundation reporter. -- National ed.

Sea. -- Eastern ed.

See also examples in *AACR 2*. Edition statements are relatively rare in the cataloging of serials.

RULE 12.3. NUMERIC AND/OR ALPHABETIC, CHRONOLOGICAL, OR OTHER DESIGNATION AREA

12.3B. Numeric and/or alphabetic designation

12.3B1. "Give the numeric and/or alphabetic designation of the first issue of a serial as given in that issue. Use standard abbreviations (see Appendix B) and numerals in place of words (see Appendix C). In describing a facsimile or other reprint, give the numeric and/or alphabetic designation of the original. Follow the hyphen with four spaces (see also 12.3F)."

Rules 12.3B1-12.3B3 provide for transcription of a numeric and/or alphabetic designation when there is no date. Rules 12.3C1-12.3C3 treat the transcription of a chronological designation when there is no numeric or alphabetic designation. Rule 12.3C4 covers transcription of both numeric and/or alphabetic designation *and* chronological designation. It would have been clearer if this rule had been accorded a bold face rule heading. The situation covered by Rules 12.3B1-12.3B3 is not the usual one; however, it is relatively common for serials of the "advances in" and "progress in" type to be dated only with an imprint date (*see* Fig. 14.9). Such a date is recorded as part of the publication area rather than part of the numeric, alphabetic, chronological area (*see* Fig. 14.10).

Fig. 14.9. Title page of serial showing date
in imprint only.

ADVANCES IN
CHEMICAL PHYSICS

Edited by I. PRIGOGINE
University of Brussels, Brussels, Belgium

With a Preface by P. DEBYE
Cornell University, Ithaca, New York

VOLUME I

INTERSCIENCE PUBLISHERS, INC., NEW YORK

INTERSCIENCE PUBLISHERS LTD., LONDON   1958

Fig. 14.10. Rule 12.3B1. Transcription of numeric designation
of the first issue of a serial.

Advances in chemical physics. -- Vol. 1 -   . -- New York :
    Interscience Publishers, 1958-

12.3B3.   "If a serial has changed its title but has continued the sequence of numbering, etc., used under the previous title, record the numbering, etc., of the first issue under the new title." *See* examples under 12.3C4.

12.3C.   **Chronological designation**

12.3C1.   "If the first issue of a serial is identified by a chronological designation, record it in the terms used in the item. Use standard abbreviations (see Appendix B) and numerals in place of words (see Appendix C)." For example:

Index to Title 40 of the Code of federal regulations : protection of environment. -- 1978-

HRA, HSA, CDC, OASH, & ADAMHA public advisory committees : authority, structure, functions, members. -- Mar. 1978-

12.3C4. "If the first issue of a serial is identified both by numbering, etc., and a chronological designation, give the numbering, etc., before the chronological designation." For example:

Developmental medicine and child neurology. – Vol. 4 (1962)-

Gas turbine electric plant construction cost and annual production expenses. Annual supplement / Office of Energy Data and Interpretation, Energy Information Administration, U.S. Dept. of Energy. – 2nd (1974)-

See also Figs. 14.11 and 14.13.

Fig. 14.11. Rule 12.3C4. Addition of both numbering and chronological designation to the description of the original title.

Quarterly journal of current acquisitions / The Library of Congress. -- [Vol. 1, no. 1] (July, Aug., Sept. 1943)-

---

Note: It could be argued that because the first issue in this example (Fig. 14.11) does not bear the numbering, "Vol. 1, no. 1," it should not be added to the example. Rule 12.3D, if taken literally, applies only when there is neither numbering nor date on an issue. This could lead to including only the date in Fig. 14.11. However, because the second issue is clearly marked "Volume 1, number 2" (*see* Fig. 14.12), the intended numbering of the first issue seems obvious. Therefore, combining logic with Rule 12.3D yields the solution of the bracketed number.

A difficulty with this rule is that it does not present or refer to a solution for the potential confusion caused by a situation in which the numbering sequence is repeated every year so that there is no overall numbering, but only the dates to distinguish issues (e.g., issues published in 1978 are numbered 1 through 4, issues for 1979 are also numbered 1 through 4, etc.). If the numbering is given first, as is called for in the rules, the implication is that the numbering is continuous and a completed serial could appear to have published only a few numbers over a span of many years [e.g., No. 1 (Winter 1940)-no. 4 (Fall 1979)]. However, a note (suggested under 12.7B8) reading, "Numbering begins each year with no. 1" would explain the situation. The reader should watch for rule interpretations on this matter.

**Fig. 14.12. Title page of second issue, showing
numerical designation.**

THE LIBRARY OF CONGRESS

Quarterly Journal

OF CURRENT ACQUISITIONS

Contents

PUBLISHED AS A SUPPLEMENT TO THE ANNUAL

REPORT OF THE LIBRARIAN OF CONGRESS

October + November + December
1943
Volume 1 + Number 2
Washington

1944

Fig. 14.13. Rule 12.3C4. Addition of both numbering and chronological designation to the designation of the later title.

The Quarterly journal of the Library of Congress. – Vol. 21, no. 1 (Jan. 1964)-

---

12.3D.   No designation on first issue

"If the first issue of a serial lacks a numeric, alphabetic, chronological, or other designation, record *[No. 1]-* or its equivalent in the language of the title proper. If, however, subsequent issues adopt a numbering, follow that."

As mentioned earlier, it should be noted that this rule applies when there is neither numerical nor chronological designation. If an item lacks a numerical designation, but has a date, 12.3C1 should be applied.

12.3E.   More than one system of designation

"If a serial has more than one separate system of designation, record the systems in the order in which they are presented in the chief source of information. Precede the alternative numbering by an equals sign." For example:

The Durham research review / The Institute of Education,
University of Durham. -- [Vol. 1] (July 1950) - v. 8
(Spring 1977) = No. 1-38

Opinions latinoamericanas. – Vol. 1 (July 1978)-   = No.
1-

Note: The rule does not say by word or example whether the chronological designation is repeated following the alternative numbering [e.g., Vol. 1 (July 1978)-   = No. 1 (July 1978)-   ]. Again, the reader is advised to watch for rule interpretations.

12.3F.   Completed serials

"In describing a completed serial, give the designation of the first issue followed by the designation of the last issue." *See* Fig. 14.14.

Fig. 14.14. Rule 12.3F. Addition of designation of last issue to the description of the original title.

Quarterly journal of current acquisitions / The Library of Congress. – [Vol. 1, no. 1] (July, Aug., Sept. 1943)-v. 20, no. 4 (Sept. 1963)

12.3G.   Successive designations

"If a serial starts a new designation system without changing its title proper, give the designation of the first and last issues under the old system, followed by the designation of the first issue under the new system. . . .

"Distinguish between a serial with a common title and a section title (see 12.1B3) and a serial with a new designation system indicated by *new series* or similar wording." For example:

International rehabilitation review. -- Vol. 1 (1962)-v. 26
(1975) ; 1976-

Triquarterly. -- Vol. 1 (Fall 1958)-v. 6 (Spring 1964) ;
No. 1 (Fall 1964)-

American journal of digestive diseases. -- Vol. 5 (1938)-v. 22
(1955) ; New ser., v. 1 (1956)-v. 23 (1978)

RULE 12.4. PUBLICATION, DISTRIBUTION, ETC., AREA

12.4C.   Place of publication, distribution, etc.

12.4C1.   "Record the place of publication, distribution, etc., as
instructed in 1.4C." *See* Figs. 14.15 and 14.16.

12.4D.   Name of publisher, distributor, etc.

12.4D1.   "Record the name of the publisher, distributor, etc. as
instructed in 1.4D." *See* Figs. 14.15 and 14.16.

12.4F.   Date of publication, distribution, etc.
The date of publication is recorded as instructed in 1.4F even if it
coincides with the date given as the chronological designation in the preceding
area. The date of first issue is followed by a hyphen and, if the serial is completed, the date of publication of the last issue. *See* Figs. 14.15 and 14.16.

**12.4G.   Place of manufacture, name of manufacturer, date
    of manufacture**
This information is recorded as discussed in 1.4G.

**Fig. 14.15. Rule 12.4. Addition of publication, distribution, etc.,
information to the description of the original title.**

Quarterly journal of current acquisitions / The Library of
    Congress. -- [Vol. 1, no. 1] (July, Aug., Sept. 1943)-v. 20,
    no. 4 (Sept. 1963). -- Washington, D.C. : The Library,
    1943-1963.

**Fig. 14.16. Rule 12.4. Addition of publication, distribution, etc.,
information to the description of the later title.**

The Quarterly journal of the Library of Congress. -- Vol. 21,
    no. 1 (Jan. 1964)-   . -- Washington, D.C. : For sale by
    the Supt. of Docs., G.P.O., 1964-

Note: Fig. 14.15 treats the original journal title; Fig. 14.16 treats the journal
under its new title.

RULE 12.5. PHYSICAL DESCRIPTION AREA

12.5B.   Extent of item (including specific material designation)

12.5B1.   "For a serial that is still in progress, give the relevant specific material designation (taken from rule 5B in the chapter dealing with the type of material to which the serial belongs, e.g., 11.5B for microform serials) preceded by three spaces. In the case of printed serials, the specific material designation is *v.*" For example:

> Alternative catalog newsletter [microform]. -- No. 2 (June
> 1978)-   . -- Baltimore, Md. : Milton S.
> Eisenhower Library, Johns Hopkins University, 1978-
> microfiches ; 11 x 15 cm.

See also Fig. 14.18 (page 253).

12.5B2.   "For a completed serial, precede the appropriate specific material designation by the number of parts in arabic numerals." For example:

> The Christian's magazine [microform]. -- Vol. 1 (1806)-v. 4
> (1811). -- Ann Arbor, Mich. : University Microfilms,
> 1946-1949.
> 2 microfilm reels ; 35 mm.

See also Fig. 14.17 below.

12.5C.   Other physical details

"Give the other physical details appropriate to the item being described as instructed in rule 5C in the chapter dealing with the type of material to which the serial belongs (e.g., 2.5C for printed serials)."

The term most often used here for printed serials is "ill." The first issue may not be totally representative of details that may be found later, but one cannot expect to keep returning to the record with more details. It is better to be more general with this area of a serial. *See* Figs. 14.17 and 14.18.

12.5D.   Dimensions

12.5D1.   "Give the dimensions of the serial as instructed in rule 5D in the chapter dealing with the type of material to which the serial belongs (e.g., 2.5D for printed serials)." *See* Figs. 14.17 and 14.18.

Fig. 14.17. Rule 12.5. Addition of physical description to the description of the original title.

> Quarterly journal of current acquisitions / The Library of
> Congress. -- [Vol. 1, no. 1] (July, Aug., Sept. 1943)-v. 20,
> no. 4 (Sept. 1963). -- Washington, D.C. : The Library,
> 1943-1963.
> 20 v. : ill. ; 24 cm.

Fig. 14.18. Rule 12.5. Addition of physical description to the
description of the new title.

The Quarterly journal of the Library of Congress. -- Vol. 21,
no. 1 (Jan. 1964)-   . – Washington, D.C. : For sale by
the Supt. of Docs., G.P.O., 1964-
v. : ill. ; 27 cm.

Note: Fig. 14.17 treats the original journal title; Fig. 14.18 treats the journal
under its new title.

12.5E.   Accompanying material

Accompanying material is described only if it is intended to be issued
regularly and used with the serial. Its frequency is given in a note. If issued
only once or irregularly, such material could be described in a note, ignored,
or cataloged separately if it is important enough.

RULE 12.6. SERIES AREA

12.6B.   Series statements

12.6B1.   "Record each series statement as instructed in 1.6. Do not give
series numberings if each issue is separately numbered within the series." For
example:

Wage chronology : Ford Motor Company / U.S. Bureau of
Labor Statistics. . . .
v. ; 28 cm. – (Bulletin / Bureau of Labor Statistics)

RULE 12.7. NOTE AREA

12.7B.   Notes

"Make notes as set out in the following subrules and in the order given
there. In referring to another serial, use the title or heading-title under which
that serial is entered in the catalogue. Otherwise, i.e. (1) if the serial is not in
the catalogue *or* (2) if main entry is not used, use the title proper and statement
of responsibility of the serial."

Following are some typical notes used for serials. For further details consult *AACR 2*, pages 262-68.

12.7B1.   Frequency

Examples:

Eight issues yearly.

Bimonthly.

Semiannual.

12.7B2.   Languages
Examples:

Text and summaries in English or French.

Text in Afrikaans and English.

Summaries in English, 1977-Mar./Apr. 1978; summaries in English
and Spanish, May/June 1978-

12.7B4.   Variations in title
Examples:

Running title: Chemical engineering catalog census.
[Title proper is: CEC census of buyers in the chemical
process industries.]

Each issue has a distinctive title.

12.7B5.   Parallel titles and other title information
Example:

"An international journal of palaeobotany, palynology and allied
sciences."

12.7B6.   Statements of responsibility
Examples:

Official journal of: the American Academy for Cerebral Palsy and
Developmental Medicine.

Issued by graduate students in the Dept. of French at the Pennsylvania State University.

Editor: A. C. Strasburger.

12.7B7.   Relationships with other serials

Continuation. "If a serial continues a previously published serial, whether
the numbering continues or is different, give the name of the preceding serial."
For example:

Continues: Cerebral palsy bulletin.

Continued by. "If a serial is continued by a subsequently published serial,
whether the numbering continues or is different, give the name of the succeeding serial, and, *optionally*, the date of the change." For example:

Continued by: Industrial vegetation, turf and pest
management.

Note: The Library of Congress is applying the options for adding dates under "continued by" and "absorption" when the information is readily available without having to search.[4]

Merger. "If a serial is the result of the merger of two or more other serials, give the names of the serials that were merged." For example:

> Merger of: Mariah; and, Outside.

"If a serial is merged with one or more other serials to form a serial with a new title, give the title of the serial and the title(s)of the serial(s) with which it has merged." For example:

> Merged with: Outside, to become: Mariah/Outside.

Split. "If a serial is the result of the split of a previous serial into two or more parts, give the name of the serial that has been split, and *optionally* the name(s) of the other serial(s) resulting from the split." For example:

> Continues in part: Transportation research.

Note: LC is not applying the option.[5]
"If a serial splits into two or more parts, give the names of the serials resulting from the split." For example:

> Split into: Transportation research. Part A, General; and, Transportation research. Part B, Methodological.

Absorption. "If [a] serial absorbs another serial, give the name of the serial absorbed, and *optionally* the date of absorption." (*See* note on option under "Continued by.") For example:

> Absorbed: American Association of Stratigraphic Palynologists. Proceedings of the annual meeting.

"If a serial is absorbed by another serial, give the name of the absorbing serial, and *optionally* the date of absorption." For example:

> Absorbed by: Palynology.

Reproduction. Example:

> Reprint. Originally published: Washington, D.C. : International Monetary Fund.

Supplements. Examples:

> Supplement to: International financial statistics, 1958-1963; Direction of Trade, 1964-

> Supplements, including laws, ordinances, bills, etc., accompany some numbers.

12.7B8.   Numbering and chronological designation
Examples:

Report year ends Mar. 31.

Numbering begins each year with no. 1.

12.7B9.   Publication, distribution, etc.
Example:

Published: Midland, Mich. : Agricultural Products Dept., Dow
Chemical U.S.A., 1977-1978. [Publisher area reads: Midland, Mich.
: Ag-Organics Dept., Dow Chemical U.S.A., 1969-1978.]

12.7B17.   Indexes
Example:

Indexes: Vols. 4 (1962)-8 (1966) published separately.

12.7B19.   Numbers [other than ISSNs]
Example:

Catalogue 34-217.

12.7B21.   "With" notes
Example:

Filmed with: BYU studies.   Vol. 11, no. 1-v. 13.

See also Figs. 14.19 and 14.20.

**RULE 12.8. STANDARD NUMBER AND TERMS OF
            AVAILABILITY AREA**

The ISSN and key-title are recorded as instructed in 1.8. *See* Fig. 3.82
under that rule in chapter 3 of this text; *see also* Figs. 14.19 and 14.20.

RULE 12.9. SUPPLEMENTS

"Describe supplements as instructed in 1.9."

RULE 12.10. SECTIONS OF SERIALS

"Do not use the 'multilevel' structure, described in chapter 13, for the
description of sections of a serial. Record these as separate serials (see
12.1B3-12.1B5)."

**Fig. 14.19. Rules 12.7 and 12.8. Addition of notes, standard number and key-title
to the description of the original title.**

Quarterly journal of current acquisitions / The Library of
 Congress. -- [Vol. 1, no. 1] (July, Aug., Sept. 1943)-v. 20,
 no. 4 (Sept. 1963). -- Washington, D.C. : The Library,
 1943-1963.

   20 v. : ill. ; 24 cm.

   Quarterly.
   Continued by: The Quarterly journal of the Library of
Congress.
   Supplement to: Annual report of the Librarian of
Congress.
   Vol. 3, no. 2 (Oct. 1945)-v. 20, no. 4 (Sept. 1963) for sale by
the Supt. of Docs., G.P.O.
   ISSN 0090-0095 = Quarterly journal of current
acquisitions

**Fig. 14.20. Rules 12.7 and 12.8. Addition of notes, standard number and key-title
to the description of the later title.**

The Quarterly journal of the Library of Congress. – Vol. 21,
 no. 1 (Jan. 1964)-   . -- Washington, D.C. : For sale by
 the Supt. of Docs., G.P.O., 1964-

   v. : ill. ; 27 cm.

   Quarterly.
   Continues: Quarterly journal of current acquisitions.
   Supplement to: Annual report of the Librarian of
Congress.
   ISSN 0041-7939 = Quarterly journal of the Library of
Congress.

FOOTNOTES

[1]*Union List of Serials in Libraries of the United States and Canada,* 3rd ed.
(New York, H. W. Wilson, 1965); coverage through 1949. *New Serial Titles: A
Union List of Serials Commencing Publication after December 31, 1949*
(Washington, Library of Congress, 1953-). *Ulrich's International Periodicals
Directory 1969-70,* 13th ed. (New York, Bowker, 1969; suppls.). *Irregular
Serials and Annuals: An International Directory* (New York, Bowker, 1967).
British Union Catalogue of Periodicals (London, Butterworths, 1955-58; 4v.).
British Union Catalogue of Periodicals. New Periodical Titles (London, But-
terworths, 1964- ; quarterly).

²*Titles in Series: A Handbook for Librarians and Students* (Metuchen, N.J., Scarecrow Press, 1953-). *Books in Series in the United States 1966-1975: Original, Reprinted, In-Print, and Out-of-Print Books Published or Distributed in the U.S. in Popular, Scholarly, and Professional Series* (New York, Bowker, 1977; suppl.).

³Library of Congress, *Library of Congress Catalogs: Monographic Series* (Washington, 1974-).

⁴"AACR 2 Options to be Followed by the Library of Congress, Chapters 1-2, 12, 21-26," *Library of Congress Information Bulletin* 37 (July 21, 1978):424.

⁵"AACR 2 Options," p. 424.

15 ANALYSIS

INTRODUCTION

Whether or not to describe parts of a work is an ever-present problem in cataloging. When does a part of a larger work deserve description of its own? When such description is warranted, how is it accomplished in relation to the larger work? These are questions addressed by *AACR 2* chapter 13 on "Analysis."

In the Glossary of *AACR 2*, "analytical entry" is defined as "an entry for a part of an item for which a comprehensive entry has been made." "Analytical note" is defined as "the statement in an analytical entry relating the part being analyzed to the comprehensive work of which it is a part." Analytical entries vary from complete bibliographic descriptions to simple added entries for parts mentioned in the description of the larger work. Obviously, preparing additional entries requires time. Usually, the decision in this matter depends on the administrative policy of an individual library and the local needs. In deciding whether analytical entries are needed, certain general principles may be taken into consideration:

1) The availability of printed indexes, bibliographies, and abstracting services that will locate the material to be analyzed.

2) The availability of LC analytics.

3) The quantity and quality of material on the given subject already in the catalog.

4) The quantity of material by the same authors already in the catalog. The best example in this category is provided by the library's policy regarding books in sets that usually represent various types of collections or compilations of one or more authors—e.g., Harvard Classics or Harvard Shelf of Fiction. If the library has little material by an author, the need for analytics may be greater.

5) The parts to be analyzed have a special significance for a given library (e.g., parts written by local noted authors, etc.).

6) The parts occupy the major portion of a given work.

In addition, the rules in *AACR 2* give some guidance in deciding when and how analysis should be accomplished.

However, a basic descriptive question that must be answered before making the decision to analyze a multipart item, and one for which there is no guidance in *AACR 2*, is: What is to be considered a multipart item rather than two or more separate bibliographical entities for cataloging purposes?

A publication issued in two or more volumes may be defined as a set. Usually, monographs in collected sets represent various types of collections or compilations by one or more authors. Many reference books are examples of monographs in collected sets. The number of physical volumes making up such a set may cause problems in cataloging and classification. If the works of a single author are collected in several volumes, the cataloger may be tempted to class each volume separately. On the other hand, the cataloger may only have one volume of a multi-volume set to catalog, and may consider classing it as if the library had the entire set. Although both of these approaches are arguable, the fact remains that neither is really right or wrong. There are no established codes for cataloging and classifying monographs in sets. The principles presented below are provided merely for the consideration of the cataloger; they are not meant to be followed slavishly.

One usually catalogs and classes a set of monographs together if,

1) they are issued in a uniform format,
2) the individual volumes are numbered in consecutive order, and
3) there is a general index to the entire set.

Two additional criteria are,

1) if patrons are likely to expect to find the monographs together as a set, and
2) if there is a possibility that supplements and/or additional volumes will appear at a later date.

However, one usually catalogs and classes a set of monographs separately if,

1) not all the volumes of the set are in the library, nor are likely to be added to the library's collection, and
2) each volume has a separate title, especially in the case of literary works.

Obviously, these two sets of principles are somewhat contradictory and demand individual application in actual practice. The following examples are designed to clarify these problems. First, it should be quite obvious that a set of books comprising an encyclopedia should be cataloged and classed together. An encyclopedia is uniform in format; the individual volumes are consecutively numbered; there is usually a general index to the entire encyclopedia; patrons do expect to find these books together as a set; and supplements and/or yearbooks often appear at a later date. Second, it similarly follows that a set of monographs that is a collection of great works (such as the *Harvard Classics* or the *Great Books of the Western World*) should be both cataloged and classed together. In both of these examples, however, individual volumes have one or more separate titles. Should individual volumes in either of these two sets (both of which, for example, include the plays of William Shakespeare) be classed with other collections of Shakespeare's plays or not? Should the non-literary material in either of these two sets be classed separately in its appropriate location? Either choice will create some problems. It is unwise in either case to try to avoid a record in the catalog for each separate bibliographical unit. The catalog may be the only key the patron uses for discovering the library's holdings. Analysis is one method of solving this particular problem. The use of analytical entries in Figs. 15.7 through 15.10 (see pages 265-66) allows these sets of monographs to be cataloged and classed together while also providing separate entries for individual bibliographical units.

The collected or complete works of one author present another problem of monographs in sets. This is particularly apparent if the author writes in more than one discipline. For example, Will Durant's *Story of Civilization* may be cataloged together or separately. If this work is cataloged together as a set, the individual parts or volumes are listed in a contents note, and the set receives general subject added entries and a general subject classification number. *See* Fig. 15.1. On the other hand, if each of the parts of this work is cataloged separately, the relationship of each part to the main work is shown by a series note. This latter approach allows for a complete publication area, including the date for each part, and for separate specific subject added entries. *See* Fig. 15.2 (page 262). Cataloging each part separately allows the cataloger to choose whether to classify each part separately or in the more general number. There are many advantages to the separate cataloging of parts — advantages in both descriptive and subject cataloging — but it must be remembered that this approach requires the production of more bibliographic records and catalog entries.

Fig. 15.1. Durant's *Story of Civilization* **cataloged as a set using a contents note for the individual bibliographical units.**

Durant, Will, 1885-

Title of entire set ———→The story of civilization / by Will Durant. --
New York : Simon and Schuster, 1935-
v. : ill., maps, ports. ; 28 cm.

Includes bibliographies and indexes.
Contents: pt. 1. Our oriental heritage.--pt. 2.
The life of Greece.--pt. 3. Caesar and Christ.--pt.
4. The age of faith.--pt. 5. The Renaissance.--pt. 6.
The Reformation.

General subject added entries ———→1. Civilization. 2. World history. I. Title.

Fig. 15.2. One part of Durant's work cataloged as a separate bibliographical unit using a series note to relate to the collected set.

¹Title of individual volume

Durant, Will, 1885-

1──▶Caesar and Christ : a history of Roman civilization and of Christianity from their beginnings to A.D. 325 / by Will Durant. -- New York : Simon and Schuster. 1944.

   751 p. : ill., maps, ports. ; 28 cm. – (The

²Title of set

2 ──▶ story of civilization / by Will Durant ; pt. 3)

    3 ──▶ 1. Rome--History. 2. Rome--Antiquities. 3. Christianity. 4. Church history. I. Title. II. Series: Durant, Will, 1885-   The story of civilization.

³Specific subject added entries

An advantage of the second example (Fig. 15.2) is that this method provides separate subject headings for each individual volume. The classification problems will be dealt with on pages 403-404 of this textbook.

RULE 13.1. SCOPE

"Analysis is the process of preparing a bibliographic record that describes a part or parts of a larger item. The rules in this chapter offer various ways of achieving analysis. Some of these methods of analysis are related to provisions found in other chapters, but all the methods are collected here with general guidelines to assist in the selection of one of the means of analysis. . . ."

RULE 13.2. ANALYTICS OF MONOGRAPHIC SERIES AND MULTIPART MONOGRAPHS

"If the item is a part of a monographic series or a multipart monograph and has a title not dependent on that of the comprehensive item, prepare an analytical entry in terms of a complete bibliographic description of the part. Give details of the comprehensive item in the series area (see 1.6)." *See* Fig. 15.3.

Fig. 15.3. Rule 13.2. Complete independent description of a monographic series with the title of the comprehensive series given in the series area.

Chateaubriand : composition, imagination, and poetry / Charles A. Porter. -- Saratoga, Calif. : Anma Libri, 1978.

   145 p. ; 24 cm. – (Stanford French and Italian studies ; v. 9)

   Bibliography: p. 141-145.
   ISBN 0-915838-37-0

RULE 13.3. NOTE AREA

"If a comprehensive entry for a larger work is made, this entry may contain a display of parts in the note area (normally in a contents note). . . ." *See* Fig. 15.4.

Fig. 15.4. Rule 13.3. Display of individual parts of a work in the description for the comprehensive work.

Early development and conceptualization of the field of marketing / edited by Henry Assael. -- New York : Arno Press, 1978.

161 p. in various pagings : ill. ; 24 cm. – (A Century of marketing)

A collection of selections reprinted from various sources published 1901-1960.
Contents: Appraisal of contributions to marketing thought by late nineteenth-century liberal economists / F. G. Coolsen.–Report of the Industrial Commission on the distribution of Farm products / U.S. Industrial Commission.–The elements of marketing / P. T. Cherington.–Modern distribution / J. F. Johnson.–Some problems in market distribution / A. W. Shaw.
ISBN 0-405-11188-6 : $15.00

RULE 13.4. ANALYTICAL ADDED ENTRIES

"If a comprehensive entry for a larger work is made that shows the part either in the title and statement of responsibility area or in the note area, an added entry for the part may also be made. . . . This method is appropriate when direct access to the part is wanted without creating an additional bibliographic record for the part." Such an added entry is composed of the main entry heading and title, if title is not main entry. The title used is the uniform title if there is one, otherwise it is the title proper. *See* Figs. 15.5 and 15.6 (page 264).

RULE 13.5. "IN" ANALYTICS

"If more bibliographic description is needed for the part than can be obtained by displaying it in the note area, the 'In' analytic entry may be considered."

13.5A.   "The descriptive part of an 'In' analytic entry consists of a description of the part analyzed followed by a short citation of the whole item in which the part occurs."
The description of the part contains all the elements of the eight areas of description that apply to the part, with the exception that in the publication,

**Fig. 15.5. Rule 13.4. Unit record for a comprehensive work with
analytical added entries made for the parts.**

Memories of old Dorking / edited by Margaret K. Kohler. --
Dorking : Kohler and Coombes, 1977.

252 p. in various pagings, [8] p. of plates : ill., facsims. ; 23
cm.

Rose's work 1st published in the West Surrey times during 1876 and 1877; Attlee's article 1st published in Dorking
advertiser, 1912; Dinnage's articles 1st published in Dorking
advertiser, 1963.

[1] Parts listed in the note area

Includes index.

[1] → Contents: Recollections of old Dorking / Charles
Rose.--Reminiscences of old Dorking / John Attlee.--Recol-
lections of old Dorking / William Henry Dinnage.

[2] Analytical added entries for the parts

ISBN 0-903967-08-1 : £3.90

1. Dorking, England--Description. I. Kohler, Margaret K. II.
[2] → Rose, Charles, 1818-1879. Recollections of old Dorking.
1977. III. Attlee, John, 1828-1913. Reminiscences of old
Dorking. 1977. IV. Dinnage, William Henry, 1870-1963.
Recollections of old Dorking. 1977.

**Fig. 15.6. Rule 13.4. Unit record to be filed under
analytical added entry for one of the parts.**

Analytical added entry →

Atlee, John, 1828-1913. Reminiscences of old Dorking. 1977.

Memories of old Dorking / edited by Margaret K. Kohler. --
Dorking : Kohler and Coombes, 1977.

252 p. in various pagings, [8] p. of plates : ill., facsims. ; 23
cm.

Rose's work 1st published in the West Surrey times during 1876 and 1877; Attlee's article 1st published in Dorking
advertiser, 1912; Dinnage's articles 1st published in Dorking
advertiser, 1963.

Includes index.

Contents: Recollections of old Dorking / Charles
Rose.--Reminiscences of old Dorking / John Attlee.--Recol-
lections of old Dorking / William Henry Dinnage.

ISBN 0-903967-08-1 : £3.90

1. Dorking, England--Description. I. Kohler, Margaret K. II.
Rose, Charles, 1818-1879. Recollections of old Dorking.
1977. III. Attlee, John, 1828-1913. Reminiscences of old
Dorking. 1977. IV. Dinnage, William Henry, 1870-1963.
Recollections of old Dorking. 1977.

---

distribution, etc., area, only those elements that differ from the whole item are given.

The description of the whole item begins with the word "In," emphasized in some manner (e.g., underlining) followed by: the main entry heading; uniform title (if appropriate); title proper; edition statement; and numeric or other designation (if a serial), or publication details (if a monographic item). *See* Figs. 15.7 and 15.8.

Fig. 15.7. Rule 13.5A. "In" analytic where the part is contained in a monographic item.

Ethelinda : an English novel / done from the Italian of Flaminiani. -- p. [79]-124 ; 17 cm.
————In Croxall, S. A select collection of novels and histories. --2nd ed. -- London : [J. Watts], 1729. -- Vol. 5.

Fig. 15.8. Rule 13.5A. "In" analytic where the part is contained in a serial item.

Library administration in its current development / L. Quincy Mumford and Rutherford D. Rogers. -- p. 357-367 ; 23 cm. -- Includes bibliographical references.
———— In Library trends. -- Vol. 7 (1958-59)

13.5B. Parts of "In" analytics

"If an 'In' analytic entry is made for a part of an item that is itself catalogued by means of an 'In' analytic entry, the 'In' analytic note contains information about the whole item and about the part containing the part being analyzed. Give information about the smaller item first, and then information about the comprehensive item in the form of a series statement." *See* Fig. 15.9.

Fig. 15.9. Rule 13.5B. "In" analytic where the part is contained in a work that is itself part of a larger work.

The school for scandal / Richard Brinsley Sheridan. -- p. [107]-197 ; 22 cm.
———— In Modern English drama. -- New York : Collier, 1961, c1937. -- (The Harvard classics ; v. 18)

RULE 13.6. MULTILEVEL DESCRIPTION

"Multilevel description is normally used by national bibliographies and those cataloguing agencies that prepare entries needing complete identification of both part and comprehensive whole in a single record that shows as its primary element the description of the whole. It may sometimes be used as an alternative to 'In' analytic entries."

The first level of descriptive information shows the description of the whole item. The second level contains description (not repeating information given at the first level) of an individual part or group of parts. If the second level describes a group of parts, then a third level may describe an individual part. *See* Fig. 15.10.

Fig. 15.10. Rule 13.6. Multilevel description showing three levels from most to least comprehensive.

The Harvard classics / [edited by Charles W. Eliot] -- Registered ed. -- New York : Collier, 1961, c1937-1938. -- 50 v. : ill., ports. ; 23 cm. -- "The five-foot shelf of books."

Vol. 18 : Modern English drama / Dryden. . .[et al.]. -- 450 p., [1] leaf of plates.

The school for scandal / Richard Brinsley Sheridan. -- p.[107]-197.

16 CHOICE OF ACCESS POINTS

INTRODUCTION

The rules in *AACR 2*, chapter 21, deal with the choice of access points and not the form of entry. "Choice of access points" means choosing all names and titles under which the description of an item may be sought by a user. For any one item, one of the access points is chosen as a main entry, and the others become added entries. This chapter covers basic choice of main entry under personal author, corporate body, and title (Rule 21.1). More specific guidance is then given for choice of entry for 1) works where there have been changes in title proper (Rule 21.2) or in persons or bodies responsible for the work (Rule 21.3), 2) works of single responsibility (Rules 21.4-21.5), 3) works of shared responsibility (Rule 21.6), 4) collections and works produced under editorial responsibility (Rule 21.7), 5) works of mixed responsibility (Rules 21.8-21.27), and 6) works that are related to other works (Rule 21.28). General rules for added entries are given (Rules 21.29-21.30), followed by special rules for certain legal and religious publications (Rules 21.31-21.39).

The rules covered in this text deal only with basic or general instances; for more complex problems and special cases, the student should consult *AACR 2*, chapter 21. Examples in this text allow the student to see not only the choice of main entry, but also the form of entry and the added entries. The following chapters deal with the rules for these specific forms.

RULE 21.0. INTRODUCTORY RULES

21.0B. Sources for determining access points
Access points for the item being cataloged are determined from the chief source of information or its substitute (*See* Rule 1.0A). Other statements appearing formally in one of the prescribed sources of information should be taken into account, but the emphasis is to be on the chief source of information, making it unnecessary for the cataloger to search in the contents or outside the item for potential access points.

21.0D. *Optional additions.* Designations of function
This option allows for abbreviated designations of function, such as "ed." for "editor" and "tr." for "translator," to be added to a heading for a person. The Library of Congress has decided not to apply this option, at least until completion of international work that is in progress concerning such "relators" between a heading and its use in a particular bibliographic record.

RULE 21.1. BASIC RULE

21.1A. Works of personal authorship
"Personal author" is defined as "the person chiefly responsible for the creation of the intellectual or artistic content of a work." This can include

composers, cartographers, photographers, performers, and others, as well as writers. The general rule is to enter works by one or more persons under the heading for the personal author according to the specific instructions given in Rules 21.4A, 21.5B, 21.6, and 21.8-21.17, and to make added entries as instructed in 21.29-21.30. For example, the sound recording entitled "Where the Blue of the Night Meets the Gold of the Day," which includes songs from the original sound track of Bing Crosby's early films, would be entered under the heading:

Crosby, Bing, 1904-1977.

There would be an added entry for the title.

21.1B.   Entry under corporate body

A corporate body is defined as "an organization or a group of persons that is identified by a particular name and that acts, or may act, as an entity." Guidelines dictate that a corporate body should be considered to have a name: if the words referring to it are a specific appelation, not just a description; if the initial letters of important words are capitalized; and/or if the words are associated with a definite article. Corporate bodies include, for example, associations, institutions, business firms, governments, conferences, ad hoc events (e.g., exhibitions, festivals), and vessels (e.g., spacecraft).

21.1B2.   The general rule is to "enter a work emanating from one or more corporate bodies under the heading for the appropriate corporate body if it falls into one or more of the following categories:

"a)   those of an administrative nature dealing with the corporate body itself

   or its internal policies, procedures and/or operations

   or its finances

   or its officers and/or staff

   or its resources (e.g., catalogues, inventories, membership directories)

b)   some legal and governmental works of the following types:

   laws (see 21.31)

   decrees of the chief executive that have the force of law (see 21.31)

   administrative regulations (see 21.32)

   treaties, etc. (see 21.35)

   court decisions (see 21.36)

   legislative hearings

c)   those that record the collective thought of the body (e.g., reports of commissions, committees, etc.; official statements of position on external policies)

d) those that report the collective activity of a conference (proceedings, collected papers, etc.), of an expedition (results of exploration, investigation, etc.), or of an event (an exhibition, fair, festival, etc.) falling within the definition of a corporate body . . . , provided that the conference, expedition, or event is prominently named in the item being catalogued.

e) sound recordings, films, and videorecordings resulting from the collective activity of a performing group as a whole where the responsibility of the group goes beyond that of a mere performance, execution, etc."

See Figs. 16.4-16.6 on pages 272-73.

21.1B3. If a work falls outside the above categories, the main entry is chosen as if no corporate body were involved, but added entries may be made. Thus, the report of an exhibition entitled "130 Years of Ohio Photography" sponsored by and held in the Columbus Museum of Art would be entered under the heading "Columbus Museum of Art," and an added entry would be made under the title. However, a monograph entitled "Benue through Pictures" that has been put together in the Information Division of Benue, Nigeria, does not fall under one of the five categories of 21.1B2; therefore, the main entry would be under the title, with an added entry under the heading: Benue (Nigeria). Information Division.

21.1B4. If a subordinate unit of a corporate body is involved for a work that falls in a category in 21.1B2, the heading for the subordinate unit is used if the responsibility of that unit is stated prominently. Otherwise, the heading for the parent body is used. For example, the staff directory of the Women's Bureau of the Ministry of Labour in Ontario would be entered under the heading for the Women's Bureau, not that for the Ministry of Labour.

A result of the application of the rules in 21.1B is that cartographic materials are seldom entered under corporate body. Specialists in map cataloging have noted many difficulties with the resulting majority of title main entries: 1) Many such titles are non-distinctive, e.g., Map of . . . , Plan of . . . , etc. 2) Most of the MARC map records currently entered under corporate body (78 percent) would have title main entry under *AACR 2*, thus increasing the number of nondistinctive titles and making access difficult in single entry files, such as union lists. 3) Consistency would be difficult to attain, because many maps have multiple titles, all occurring in the chief source of information. 4) Overprinting of information on base maps often results in composite titles made up of the original title and some new thematic information. 5) "Author" cutters in call numbers would become quite complex because of the increase in generic titles upon which such cutters would be based.[1]

The Library of Congress Geography and Map Division, as well as many individual librarians, have petitioned LC to continue using corporate main entry for much cartographic material. This position has been formally supported by the Anglo-American Cataloguing Committee for Cartographic Material.[2] LC and the National Library of Canada have agreed to support the request.[3] The reader should watch for further developments.

21.1C. **Entry under title**

Entry under title is prescribed in the following cases:

"1)   the personal authorship is unknown (see 21.5), diffuse (see 21.6C2), or cannot be determined, and the work does not emanate from a corporate body

or 2)   it is a collection or a work produced under editorial direction (see 21.7)

or 3)   it emanates from a corporate body but does not fall into one or more of the categories in 21.1B2 and is not of personal authorship

or 4)   it is accepted as sacred scripture by a religious group (see 21.37)."

RULE 21.2. CHANGES IN TITLES PROPER

This rule and the next one fill a need for guidance about when separate main entries should be chosen for different parts of a multipart monograph or of a serial. The cataloger is instructed to choose separate main entries (and thus make separate records) for each edition when the title proper of a monograph changes between editions. However, if the title proper of a multipart monograph changes between *parts*, one title proper (the one that predominates) is to be used for the whole monograph. If the title proper of a serial changes, a separate main entry is chosen for each title, and separate records are made.

21.2A.   The three cases in which a title proper is considered to have changed occur when:

"1)   any change occurs in the first five words (other than an initial article in the nominative case)"

e.g., the change of *Federal Education Program Guide* to *Federal Education Grants Directory* constitutes a change in title proper.

"2)   any important words (nouns, proper names or initials standing for proper names, adjectives, etc.) are added, deleted, or changed (including changes in spelling)"

e.g., *Cataloging Service* changed to *Cataloging Service Bulletin.*

"3)   there is a change in the order of words"

e.g., *Census of Public Water Supplies in Missouri* changed to *Census of Missouri Public Water Supplies.*

According to this definition, change of *Report of the Department of Community Affairs, Division of Veterans Affairs to the Governor* to *Report of the Department of Community Affairs of the Division of Veterans Affairs to the Governor* would not qualify as a change in title proper; the change is not in the first five words, the added words "of the" are not important words, and there is no change in the order of words.

RULE 21.3. CHANGES OF PERSONS OR BODIES RESPONSIBLE FOR A WORK

Monographs that have been modified by a person or body different from the one responsible for the original edition are to be treated according to Rules 21.9-21.23. This means that in some cases, when the nature and/or content has been changed, the main entry will be different from the original; while in other cases, when the modification abridges, rearranges, or updates, for example, the main entry of the original will be used. An example of the first case is shown in Fig. 16.1.

Fig. 16.1. Rule 21.3. Entry of a work whose nature has been changed from that of the original.

Bambi's fragrant forest : based on the original story by Felix Salten / Walt Disney Productions.
Make added entries for persons or bodies responsible for the original and the modification:
1. Salten, Felix, 1869-1945. Bambi. II. Walt Disney Productions.

An example of the second case is shown in Fig. 16.2.

Fig. 16.2. Rule 21.3. Entry of an abridged work.

Salten, Felix, 1869-1945.
Bambi [sound recording] / abridged by Marianne Mantell. Read by Glynis Johns.
Make added entries for persons or bodies responsible for the modification:
I. Mantell, Marianne. II. Johns, Glynis. III. Title.

If responsibility in a multipart monograph changes between parts, the heading appropriate to the first part is used unless a later one predominates, just as with a change of title proper. However, if more than three persons or bodies are finally responsible for a multipart monograph, with none predominant, main entry is changed to title.

There are two conditions under which changes in persons or bodies could require a new entry for a serial:

"1) if the name of a person or corporate body under which a serial is entered changes (see 22.2B or 24.1B)

or 2) if the main entry for a serial is under a personal or corporate heading and the person or corporate body responsible for the serial changes."

The first case is where the serial has a person or body as the main entry and the name of that person or body is later changed to a new form. An example of this is the *Financial Report* of the Board of Trustees of the Firemen's Pension Fund, formerly the Firemen's Pension and Relief Fund. The second case is where the serial has a person or body as the main entry and later a different person or body takes over responsibility for the publication.

RULE 21.4. WORKS FOR WHICH A SINGLE PERSON OR CORPORATE BODY IS RESPONSIBLE

21.4A.   Works of single personal authorship

"Enter a work, a collection of works, or selections from a work or works by one personal author (or any reprint, reissue, etc., of such a work) under the heading for that person whether named in the work or not." For example, this title page is from a work of single personal authorship. The choice of main entry should be the single author, Pamela Bennetts (*see* Figs. 16.3 and 16.3a).

Fig. 16.3. Title page.

Title   ⟶ MY DEAR LOVER ENGLAND

Single author   ⟶ Pamela Bennetts

New York

St. Martin's Press

1975

Fig. 16.3a. Rule 21.4A. A work of single personal authorship.

Personal   ⟶ Bennetts, Pamela.
author main   My dear lover England / Pamela Bennetts.
entry
Make added entry for title:
                  I. Title.

21.4B.   Works emanating from a single corporate body

"Enter a work, a collection of works, or selections from a work or works emanating from one corporate body (or any reprint, reissue, etc., of such a work) under the heading for the body if the work or collection falls into one or more of the categories given in 21.1B2." *See* Figs. 16.4, 16.5, and 16.6.

Fig. 16.4. Rule 21.4B. A work of single corporate responsibility.

Corporate   ⟶ Al-Anon Family Group Headquarters.
body main   World directory of Al-Anon Family Groups
entry (21.1B2,   and Ala-teens.
type a)
Make added entry for title:
                  I. Title.

Fig. 16.5. Rule 21.4B. A work of single corporate responsibility.

Corporate   ⟶ United States. Congress. Senate. Select Com-
body main   mittee on Indian Affairs.
entry (21.1B2,   Consolidating Alaska natives governing bod-
type c)   ies : hearings before the United States Senate,
       Select Committee on Indian Affairs, Ninety-fifth
       Congress, first session, on S. 1920 ... S. 2046. ...

Make added entry for title:
       I. Title.

Fig. 16.6. Rule 21.4B. A work of single corporate responsibility.

Corporate   ⟶ AIAA Communications Satellite Systems Confer-
body main   ence (7th : 1978 : San Diego, Calif.)
entry (21.1B2,   A collection of technical papers : AIAA 7th
type d)   Communications Satellite Systems Conference,
       San Diego, California, April 24-27, 1978.

Make added entry for title:
       I. Title.

21.4C.   Works erroneously or fictitiously attributed to a person or corporate body

When a publication erroneously or fictitiously attributes responsibility to a person or body, enter it under the heading for the actual person or body responsible if possible and appropriate, or else under the title. Make an added entry under the heading for the person or body attributed responsibility if such person or body is real. *See* Fig. 16.7.

Fig. 16.7. Rule 21.4C. Entry under the real author rather than
the attributed author.

Actual   ⟶ Farmer, Philip Jose.
author as   The adventure of the peerless peer / by John
main entry   H. Watson : edited by Philip Jose Farmer.

Note explaining statement of responsibility:
       Written by P. J. Farmer in imitation of A. C.
       Doyle.

Make added entry for title:
       I. Title.

Note: No added entry is made for the attributed author, John H. Watson, since he is a fictional character created by A. C. Doyle in his series of detective stories about Sherlock Holmes and Dr. Watson.

21.4D. Works by heads of state, other high government officials, popes, and other high ecclesiastical officials

21.4D1. Official communications

Two categories of official works are entered under the corporate heading (*see* 24.20 and 24.27B) for the official:

> "a) official communications from heads of state, heads of government, and heads of international bodies (e.g., messages to legislatures, proclamations, and executive orders other than those covered by 21.31)
>
> b) official communications from popes, patriarchs, bishops, etc. (e.g., orders; decrees; pastoral letters; official messages to councils, synods, etc.; bulls; encyclicals; and constitutions)."

An added entry is made under the personal heading for the person. *See* Fig. 16.8.

Fig. 16.8. Rule 21.4D1. Official communication entered under corporate heading.

Main entry ⟶ Maine. Governor (1975-1979 : Longley)
under corpor-   Budget message address of James B. Longley,
ate heading   Governor of Maine, to the One hundred and
         seventh Legislature, State of Maine, February 6,
         1975.
Make added entries:
         I. Maine. Legislature. II. Longley, James B. ⟵
Added entry   III. Title: Budget message address of James B.
under personal   Longley, Governor of Maine ...
heading

21.4D2. Other works

"Enter all other works of such a person under the personal heading. Make an explanatory reference from the corporate heading to the personal heading (see 26.3C1)." *See* Fig. 16.9. For examples of explanatory references see chapter 21 of this text.

Fig. 16.9. Rule 21.4D2. Other works entered under personal heading.

Main entry
under per- ⟶ Jefferson, Thomas, 1743-1826.
sonal heading   The portable Thomas Jefferson / edited and
         with an introduction by Merrill D. Peterson.

Make added entry for person responsible for this edition of the work:
         I. Peterson, Merrill D.

21.4D3.   Collections of official communications and other works
     A collection of official communications *and other works* by *one* person is entered under the personal heading, with an added entry under the corporate heading. A collection of official communications and other works by *more than one* person is entered as a collection (see 21.7), with an added entry for the heading for the office held, if all the persons held the same office.
     A collection of official communications *only* of *more than one* holder of *one* of the offices listed in 21.4D1 is entered under the heading for the office, with an added entry for an openly named compiler.
     There is no rule here for a collection of official communications *only* of more than one holder of *more than one* of the offices listed. Such a work should be treated as a collection and entered as instructed in Rule 21.7.

RULE 21.5. WORKS OF UNKNOWN OR UNCERTAIN AUTHORSHIP OR BY UNNAMED GROUPS

21.5A.   Enter under the title a work of unknown or uncertain responsibility or one that emanates from a body that lacks a name. *See* Fig. 16.10.

Fig. 16.10. Rule 21.5A. Work of unknown authorship entered under title.

Main entry ⟶ Davis, Noble, and Kinder reunions, 1945-1975,
under title   and family trees. – 6th ed. – [S.l. : s.n.], c1978
                 (Baltimore : P. M. Harrod Co.)

Note providing bibliographic history:
                 Edition for 1941 published under title: Davis,
                 Kinder, and Noble reunions, 1930-1935-1940, and
                 family trees.

Make added entry for earlier title:
                 I. Davis, Kinder, and Noble reunions, 1930-
                 1935-1940, and family trees.

21.5C.   "If the name of a personal author is unknown and the only indication of authorship is the appearance in the chief source of information of a characterizing word or phrase or of a phrase naming another work by the person, enter under the word or phrase in the form given in 22.11D. Make an added entry under title." For example, the following title page is from a work with an unknown author, but provides a "characterizing phrase." It would be entered in the form given in Fig. 16.11a.

Fig. 16.11. Title page.

Title	⟶ THE MANUAL OF FRENCH COOKERY
Subtitle	⟶ Dedicated to the Housekeepers and Cooks of England who Wish to Study the ART simplified for the benefit of the most unlearned by
Unknown author	⟶ One who has tested the receipts
Place	⟶ London
Publisher	⟶ Chapman and Hall

Fig. 16.11a. Rule 21.5C. A work of unknown authorship entered under characterizing phrase.

Entry under characterizing phrase

⟶ One who has tested the receipts.
　　The Manual of French cookery : dedicated to the housekeepers and cooks of England who wish to study the art : simplified for the benefit of the most unlearned / by one who has tested the receipts.

Make added entry for title:
　　I. Title.

RULE 21.6. WORKS OF SHARED RESPONSIBILITY

21.6A.　　Scope

"Apply this rule to:

1) works produced by the collaboration of two or more persons

2) works for which different persons have prepared separate contributions

3) works consisting of an exchange between two or more persons (e.g., correspondence, debates)

4) works falling into one or more of the categories given in 21.1B2 that emanate from two or more corporate bodies

5) works listed in 1-3 above that also contain contributions emanating from one or more corporate bodies

6) works resulting from a collaboration or exchange between a person and a corporate body."

Special types of collaboration are covered by rules on mixed responsibility (Rules 21.8-21.27), but when those rules prescribe main entry under the heading for an adapter, for example, and when there is shared responsibility among two or more adapters, then this rule of shared responsibility is applied. This rule does not apply to works produced under editorial direction or to works that are collections of previously existing works.

21.6B. Principal responsibility indicated

21.6B1. Enter a work of shared responsibility under the heading for the principal person or body if one is indicated by wording or typography. Make added entries under the headings for other persons or bodies involved, if there are not more than two. Always make an added entry under the heading for the person or body, other than the principal one, whose name appears first on the title page. *See* Figs. 16.12 and 16.12a.

Fig. 16.12. Title page.

Title	⟶ SPEED, STRENGTH, AND STAMINA
Subtitle	⟶ Conditioning for Tennis
	by
Principal author	⟶ Connie Haynes
	with
Subsidiary authors	⟶ Eve Kraft and John Conroy
	illustrated by
Illustrator	⟶ George Janes

1st edition
Doubleday
Garden City, New York
1975

Since the principal author, Connie Haynes, is indicated on the title page of this work by the wording of the subsidiary authorship statement, the choice of main entry is the principal author.

Fig. 16.12a. Rule 21.6B1. Principal author indicated.

Main entry under principal author ⟶ Haynes, Connie.
   Speed, strength, and stamina : conditioning for tennis / by Connie Haynes, with Eve Kraft and John Conroy ; illustrated by George Janes.

Make added entries for subsidiary authors:
   I. Kraft, Eve. II. Conroy, John, 1908-   . III. Title.

21.6B2. "If principal responsibility is attributed to two or three persons or bodies, enter under the heading for the first named of these." Added entries are made under headings for the other principal author(s), and of a collaborator if there are two principal authors and one collaborator (i.e., there may be no more than two added entries).

21.6C. Principal responsibility not indicated

21.6C1. If principal responsibility is not indicated and if there are not more than three names, enter under the one that is named first and make added entries under the others. *See* Figs. 16.13 and 16.13a.

Fig. 16.13. Title page.

Title ————————→ **MODERN DANCE**

Shared ————————→ Gay Cheney
author

Shared ————————→ Janet Strader
author

second edition

Boston

Allyn and Bacon

In this case of shared authorship, the principal author is not indicated; further, there are not more than three authors listed (i.e., two in this example), so the choice of main entry is the first named author (*see* Fig. 16.13a). If there had been more than three authors on the title page, the choice of entry would have been the title (*see* Fig. 16.14).

Fig. 16.13a. Rule 21.6C1. Principal author not indicated, and not more than three authors.

Main entry ————→ Cheney, Gay.
under first
named author   Modern dance / Gay Cheney, Janet Strader.

Make added entry for second named author:
            I. Strader, Janet.

21.6C2. If principal responsibility is not indicated and there are more than three persons or bodies, enter the work under the title and make an added entry under the heading for the person or body named first in the chief source of information. *See* Fig. 16.14.

Note: If the work is produced under the direction of an editor named in the chief source of information, apply Rule 21.7.

Fig. 16.14. Rule 21.6C2. Principal author not indicated.

Title main ————→ Europe reborn : the story of Renaissance civiliza-
entry   tion / contributors, Julian Mates ... [et al.].

Make added entry for first named author:
            I. Mates, Julian, 1927-

21.6D.   Shared pseudonyms
    If two or more persons collaborate and use a single pseudonym, use the pseudonym as the heading for the works produced by their collaboration." References are made from the real names to the pseudonym and, if the persons are also established singly, from the pseudonym to the real name(s) (*see* 26.2D1). *See* Figs. 16.15 and 16.15a.

Fig. 16.15. Rule 21.6D. Shared pseudonyms.

Main entry ⟶ Ashe, Penelope
under shared   Naked came the stranger / Penelope Ashe
pseudonym

It should be noted that Penelope Ashe is the shared pseudonym of 25 writers who wrote the book in collaboration. Because a number of unnamed persons were involved, explanatory references cannot be made. Such a reference might be made for Lillie Young, one of the contributors, who posed as Penelope Ashe, and who has since published a work under her own name.

Fig. 16.15a. Rule 21.6D. Shared pseudonyms.

Coles, Manning.
A toast to tomorrow / Manning Coles

In this case, the name is the shared pseudonym of Adelaide Frances Oke Manning and Cyril Henry Coles. References would be made from these names to the pseudonym.

RULE 21.7. COLLECTIONS AND WORKS PRODUCED UNDER EDITORIAL DIRECTION

21.7A.   Scope

"Apply this rule to:

1)   collections of independent works by different persons or bodies

2)   collections consisting of extracts from independent works by different persons or bodies

3)   works consisting of contributions by different persons or bodies, produced under editorial direction

4)   works consisting partly of independent works by different persons or bodies and partly of contributions produced under editorial direction."

Do not apply this rule to works that emanate from a corporate body and fall in the scope of 21.1B2 (including papers or proceedings of named conferences).

21.7B.   With collective title

"Enter a work falling into one of the categories given in 21.7A under its title if it has a collective title." Added entries are made under the headings for prominently named editors or compilers if there are not more than three, or for the principal one or the one named first if there are more than three. *See* Figs. 16.16 and 16.17.

Fig. 16.16. Rule 21.7B. Collections and works produced under editorial direction with collective titles. Added entries are made for the first-named editors.

Title main ⎯⎯→ Altruism, morality, and economic theory / edited
entry by Edmund S. Phelps.

Note expanding upon statement of responsibility:
Based on the proceedings of a conference held March 3-4, 1972, sponsored by the Russell Sage Foundation.

Make added entries for persons or bodies responsible for the item:
I. Phelps, Edmund S. II. Russell Sage Foundation, New York.

Fig. 16.17.

Title main ⎯⎯→ The New Cassell's French dictionary : French-
entry English, English-French. – Completely rev. / by Denis Girard ; with the assistance of Gaston Dulong, Oliver Van Oss and Charles Guinness.

Make added entry for editor:
I. Girard, Denis. II. Title: Cassell's French dictionary.

"If such a work includes two or three contributions or independent works, make name-title added entries for each of them." A name-title added entry is composed of the name of a person or corporate body followed by the title of an item for which the person or body is responsible. *See* Fig. 16.18 (page 281) for an example of name-title added entries.

"If there are more than three contributions or independent works but only two or three contributors, make an added entry (or name-title added entry when appropriate) under the heading for each contributor."

"If there are more than three contributors and they are named in the chief source of information, make an added entry under the first-named contributor."

21.7C. Without collective title

"If a work falling into one of the categories given in 21.7A lacks a collective title, enter it under the heading appropriate to the first work or contribution named in the chief source of information." If a chief source is lacking, the first work in the item is used. Added entries are made as instructed in 21.7B. *See* Fig. 16.18.

Fig. 16.18. Rule 21.7C. Collections without a collective title.

Main entry ⟶ Ellsworth, Ralph E., 1907-
under first   Buildings / by Ralph E. Ellsworth. Shelving / by
named author   Louis Kaplan. Storage warehouses / by Jerrold
                  Orne.

Make name-title added entries:
                  I. Kaplan, Louis, 1909-   Shelving. II. Orne,
                  Jerrold, 1921-   Storage warehouses. III. Title.
                  IV. Title: Shelving. V. Title: Storage ware-
                  houses.

WORKS OF MIXED RESPONSIBILITY

21.8A.   Scope

In many works the responsibility is divided. This occurs when different persons or bodies have contributed to the intellectual or artistic content performing different kinds of functions, e.g., writing, adapting, illustrating, translating, etc. Determination of main entry depends to a large extent on the relative importance of such contributions.

The rules in this section are divided into two basic categories of mixed responsibility:

"a)   a previously existing work that has been modified (e.g., a transla-
      tion, a musical arrangement, an adaptation)

b)   a new work to which different persons or bodies have made dif-
      ferent kinds of contributions (e.g., a collaborative work by a writer
      and an artist (see 21.24), a work that reports an interview (see
      21.25))"

WORKS THAT ARE MODIFICATIONS OF OTHER WORKS

RULE 21.9. GENERAL RULE

Works that are modifications of other works may be entered under the heading appropriate to the new work or that appropriate to the original, depending upon the nature of the modification. If the modification has changed the nature or content of the original in a substantial way, or if the medium of expression is different, the new heading is chosen. However, if the modification is an updating, rearrangement, abridgment, or revision where the original person or body is still represented as being responsible, the original heading is chosen. Rules 21.10-21.23 give specific guidance in applying this general rule.

Modifications of Texts (Rules 21.10-21.15)

RULE 21.10. ADAPTIONS OF TEXTS

"Enter a paraphrase, rewriting, adaptation for children, or version in a different literary form (e.g., novelization, dramatization) under the heading for the adapter. If the name of the adapter is unknown, enter under title. Make a name-title added entry for the original work. In case of doubt about whether a work is an adaptation, enter under the heading for the original work." *See* Fig. 16.19.

Fig. 16.19. Rule 21.10. Entry under adapter.

Adapter as   ⟶ Taylor, Helen L.
main entry   Little Pilgrim's progress / by Helen L. Taylor.

Note expanding upon statement of responsibility:
           Adaptation for children of: The Pilgrim's progress / John Bunyan.

Make name-title added entry for original author:
           I. Bunyan, John. The Pilgrim's progress. II. Title.

RULE 21.11. ILLUSTRATED TEXTS

21.11A.   General rule

"Enter a work that consists of a text for which an artist has provided illustrations under the heading appropriate to the text." *See* Fig. 16.20. An added entry for the illustrator may be made if appropriate (*see* 21.30K2). Works of collaboration between an artist and a writer are treated in 21.24.

Fig. 16.20. Rule 21.11. Illustrated text entered under author.

Main entry   ⟶ Day, Jenifer W.
under author   What is a bird? / by Jenifer W. Day ; illustrated by / Tony Chen.

Make added entry for artist:
           I. Chen, Tony. II. Title.

RULE 21.12. REVISIONS OF TEXTS

21.12A.   "Enter an edition that has been revised, enlarged, updated, abridged, condensed, etc., under the heading for the original if the person or body responsible for the original is named in a statement of responsibility or in the title, or if the wording of the chief source of information indicates that that person or body is still considered to be responsible for the work. Make an added entry under the heading for the reviser, abridger, etc." *See* Fig. 16.21.

Fig. 16.21. Rule 21.12A. Revised work entered under original author.

Main entry ⟶ Darwin, Charles, 1809-1882.
under original   The origin of species / Charles Darwin ;
author   abridged and introduced by Philip Appleman.

Make added entry for reviser:
              I. Appleman, Philip, 1926-   II. Title.

21.12B.   "If the wording of the chief source of information indicates that the person or body responsible for the original is no longer considered to be responsible for the work, enter under the reviser, etc. Make a name-title added entry under the heading for the original." *See* Fig. 16.22.

Fig. 16.22. Rule 21.12B. Revised work entered under reviser.

Main entry ⟶ Bedingfeld, A. L.
under reviser   Oxburgh Hall, Norfolk : a property of the Na-
              tional Trust / by A. L. Bedingfeld. – 2nd ed.

Note expanding upon statement of responsibility:
              "First edition, 1953, by Professor F. de
              Zulueta."

Make name-title added entry for original author:
              I. Zulueta, Francis de. Oxburgh Hall, Norfolk.
              II. Title.

RULE 21.13.   TEXTS PUBLISHED WITH COMMENTARY

This rule applies to items comprising a text or texts by one person or body and a commentary or interpretation by another person or body. In essence, the rule calls for entry under the heading appropriate to the commentary if the chief source of information presents the work as a commentary, and entry under the heading for the original work if the chief source of information presents the work as an edition of the original. If the chief source is ambiguous, entry is determined by (in order of preference) emphasis in the preface, the typographic presentation of the text and commentary, or the relative extent of text and commentary. If there is still doubt, the work is treated as an edition with an added entry appropriate to the commentary. *See* Fig. 16.23.

Fig. 16.23. Rule 21.13. Text with commentary entered under commentator.

Main entry ⟶ Fischer, John L.
under named   Annotations to the Book of Luelen / translated
commentator   and edited by John L. Fischer, Saul H. Riesenberg
      and Marjorie G. Whiting.

Note explaining the statement of responsibility:
      Annotations by J. L. Fischer, S. H. Riesenberg,
      and M. G. Whiting.

Make added entries appropriate to the text:
      I. Riesenberg, Saul H. II. Whiting, Marjorie G.
      III. Bernart, Luelen. The book of Luelen.

RULE 21.14. TRANSLATIONS

A single translation is entered under the heading appropriate to the original. An added entry for the translator may be made in accordance with 21.30K1. *See* Fig. 16.24.

Fig. 16.24. Rule 21.14. Translation entered under original author.

Main entry ⟶ Flohr, Salo, 1908-
under origi-   Twelfth chess tournament of nations / Salo
nal author   Flohr ; [translated from the Russian by W.
      Perelman].

A collection of translations of works by different authors is treated as a collection (*see* 21.7).

RULE 21.15. TEXTS PUBLISHED WITH BIOGRAPHICAL/ CRITICAL MATERIAL

21.15A. "If a work consisting of a work or works by a writer accompanied by (or interwoven with) biographical or critical material by another person is presented in the chief source of information as a biographical/critical work, enter it as such (see 21.1-21.7). Make an added entry under the heading appropriate to the work or works included." *See* Fig. 16.25.

Fig. 16.25. Rule 21.15A. Biographical work entered under biographer.

Main entry ⟶ Morse, John T. (John Torrey), 1840-1937.
under   Life and letters of Oliver Wendell Holmes / by
biographer   John T. Morse.

Make added entries for author as subject of the biography and as personal author:
      1. Holmes, Oliver Wendell, 1809-1894.
      I. Holmes, Oliver Wendell, 1809-1894. II. Title.

21.15B. "If the biographer/critic is represented as editor, compiler, etc., enter under the heading appropriate to the work or works included. Make an added entry under the heading for the biographer/critic." *See* Fig. 16.26.

Fig. 16.26. Rule 21.15B. Edited biographical work.

Main entry ⟶ Dover, Thomas, 1660-1742.
under author   Thomas Dover's life and Legacy / edited and
                    introduced by Kenneth Dewhurst

Make added entry for editor:
                    I. Dewhurst, Kenneth, ed. II. Title.

Art Works (Rules 21.16-21.17)

RULE 21.16. ADAPTATIONS OF ART WORKS

AACR 2 defines "Art works" as "paintings, engravings, photographs, drawings, sculptures, etc., and any other creative work that can be represented pictorially (e.g., ceramic designs, tapestries, fabrics)."

21.16A. "Enter an adaptation from one medium of the graphic arts to another under the heading for the person responsible for the adaptation. If the name of the adapter is not known, enter under title. Make a name-title added entry for the original work." *See* Fig. 16.27.

**Fig. 16.27. Rule 21.6A. Adaptation entered under heading
for title because adapter is unknown.**

[1]Main entry   [Mona Lisa [picture] / computer representation
under title   of the original by Leonardo da Vinci, pro-
(adapter   duced via program written at IBM]
unknown)
                    Copies distributed at demonstrations of IBM
[2]Name-title   equipment.
added entry for
original work   I. Leonardo, da Vinci, 1452-1519. Mona Lisa.
[3]Added entry for II. IBM.
responsible
corporate body

21.16B. "Enter a reproduction of an art work (e.g., a photograph, a photomechanical reproduction, or a reproduction of sculpture) under the heading for the original work. Make an added entry under the heading for the person or body responsible for the reproduction." *See* Fig. 16.28.

Fig. 16.28. Rule 21.16B. Reproduction of art work entered under heading for the artist.

Main entry ——→ Hobbema, Meindert, 1638-1709.
under artist   View on a high road [picture] / Hobbema ; National Gallery of Art.

Make added entry for body responsible for reproduction:
      I. National Gallery of Art (U.S.).
      II. Title.

RULE 21.17.   REPRODUCTIONS OF TWO OR MORE ART WORKS

21.17A.   Without text

"Enter a work consisting of reproductions of the works of an artist without accompanying text under the heading for the artist."

21.17B.   With text

When text accompanies reproductions of an artist's works, entry is under the personal heading for the author of the text if that person is represented as author in the chief source of information; an added entry is made under the heading for the artist. Otherwise, or in case of doubt, entry is made under the heading for the artist with an added entry for the person mentioned in the chief source of information as having written the text. *See* Figs. 16.29 and 16.30.

Fig. 16.29. Rule 21.17B. Art reproductions with text entered under author of text.

Main entry ——→ Cassou, Jean, 1897-
under author   Rembrandt / par Jean Cassou
of text

Make added entry for artist:
      I. Rembrandt Harmenszoon van Rijn, 1606-1669.

Fig. 16.30. Rule 21.17B. Art reproductions with text entered under artist.

Main entry ——→ Rembrandt Harmenszoon van Rijn, 1606-1669.
under artist   More drawings of Rembrandt / introduction by Stephen Longstreet.

Make added entry for author of text:
      I. Longstreet, Stephen, 1907-   II. Title.

Musical Works (Rules 21.18-21.22)

RULE 21.18.   GENERAL RULE

21.18A.   Scope

"Apply this rule to:

1)   arrangements, transcriptions, versions, settings, etc., in which music for one medium of performance has been rewritten for another

2)   simplified versions

3)   arrangements described as 'freely transcribed,' 'based on . . . ,' etc., and other arrangements incorporating new material

4)   arrangements in which the harmony or musical style of the original has been changed."

21.18B.   A musical arrangement is defined as a "musical work, or a portion thereof, rewritten for a medium of performance different from that for which the work was originally intended." (*AACR 2*, p. 563). A "simplified version of a work for the same medium of performance" is also regarded as an arrangement. The general rule for a musical arrangement is to enter it under the heading for the original composer whenever possible. An added entry is made for the name of the arranger. *See* Fig. 16.31.

21.18C.   A musical work that is an adaptation represents a more serious departure from the original work than does an arrangement. Thus, generally, the main entry is made under the heading for the adapter, with an added entry given to the author of the original work. Three types of adaptations of music are specified for entry under adapter:

"1)   a distinct alteration of another work (e.g., a free transcription)

2)   a paraphrase of various works or of the general style of another composer

3)   a work merely based on other music (e.g., variations on a theme)."

In case of doubt about whether a work is an adaptation, it is to be treated as an arrangement, transcription, etc. *See* Fig. 16.32.

Fig. 16.31. Rule 21.18. Arrangement of musical work entered under original composer.

Main entry ⟶ Mozart, Wolfgang Amadeus, 1756-1791.
under composer   Eighth quintet, k. 614, fourth movement / W. A. Mozart ; arranged for 2 B♭ trumpets, horn, trombone & tuba by Ralph Lockwood.

Make added entry for arranger:
                I. Lockwood, Ralph.

Fig. 16.32. Rule 21.18. Adaptation of musical work entered under adapter.

Main entry   ⟶ Brahms, Johannes, 1833-1897.
under   Variations and fugue on a theme by Handel,
adapter   op. 24 / Johannes Brahms.

Note explaining the scope of the item:
           The theme is that of the Aria con variazioni
from Handel's Suite for harpsichord, 2nd collection, no. 1.

Make name-title added entry for original work:
           I. Handel, George Frideric, 1685-1759. Suite,
harpsichord, 2nd collection, no. 1, B♭ major. Aria
con variazioni.

RULE 21.19.   MUSICAL WORKS THAT INCLUDE WORDS

21.19A.   General rule

"Enter a musical work that includes words (a song, opera, musical comedy) under the heading for the composer. For librettos, see 21.18. Make added
entries under the headings for the writers of the words if their work is fully
represented in the item being catalogued (e.g., a full score, a vocal score). If
the words are based on another text, make a name-title added entry under the
heading for the original." *See* Fig. 16.33.

Fig. 16.33. Rule 21.19A. Musical comedy entered under composer.

Main entry   ⟶ Adler, Richard
under composer   The pajama game : a musical comedy / music
and lyrics by Richard Adler and Jerry Ross ; book
by George Abbott.

Note expanding statement of responsibility:
           "Based on the novel '7½ cents' by Richard
Bissell."

Make added entries for shared composer and for writer, and an added name-title entry for
original text:
           I. Ross, Jerry. II. Abbot, George. III. Bissell,
Richard. 7½ cents. IV. Title.

21.19C.   Writer's works set by several composers

If the work or works of one writer are set in a collection of songs, etc., by
two or more composers, entry is made according to the rule for collections,
21.7. *See* Fig. 16.34.

Fig. 16.34. Rule 21.19C. Collection of songs with words by one writer and music by several composers; entered as a collection under title.

Title main   ──────▸ A Shakespeare song book / edited by H. A.
entry   Chambers.

Make added entry for writer of words and for editor:
             I. Shakespeare, William, 1564-1616. II. Chambers, H. A.

RULE 21.20. MUSICAL SETTINGS FOR BALLETS, ETC.

"Enter a musical setting for a ballet, pantomime, etc., under the heading for the composer. Make added entries under the headings for choreographers and writers of scenarios, librettos, etc., whose names appear in the chief source of information." *See* Fig. 16.35.

Fig. 16.35. Rule 21.20. Music for a ballet entered under composer.

Main entry   ──────▸ Nabokov, Nicolas.
for composer   Don Quichotte : ballet en 3 actes / Nicolas
             Nabokov ; libretto par Nicolas Nabokov et
             Georges Balanchine.

Make added entry for shared author of libretto:
             I. Balanchine, Georges. II. Title.

RULE 21.21. ADDED ACCOMPANIMENTS, ETC.

"Enter a musical work to which an instrumental accompaniment or additional parts have been added under the heading for the original work. Make an added entry under the heading for the composer of the accompaniment or the additional parts."

RULE 21.22. LITURGICAL MUSIC

"Enter music that is officially prescribed as part of a liturgy as instructed in 21.39."

Sound Recordings (Rule 21.23)

RULE 21.23. ENTRY OF SOUND RECORDINGS

It should be noted that this rule applies only to sound recordings that are modifications of other works. This includes readings of texts and performances of musical works. There is no rule specifically for sound recordings considered to constitute new works, such as recordings of improvisations and lectures. These items would be entered according to the principles of responsibility found in the basic rules. Such works as interviews made as oral history could be entered according to the principles in 21.25.

It should be noted also that this rule must be used in conjunction with Rule 6.1G. If under 6.1G it is decided that a sound recording lacking a collective title should be described as a unit, then one of Rules 21.23B-21.23D will be applied. If, however, it is decided to make a separate description for each separately titled work, Rule 21.23A will be applied.

21.23A. "Enter a sound recording of one work (music, text, etc.) under the heading appropriate to that work. Make added entries under the headings for the principal performers (singers, readers, orchestras, etc.) unless there are more than three. If there are more than three . . . , make an added entry under the one named first." *See* Fig. 16.36.

Fig. 16.36. Rule 21.23A. Sound recording entered under author
of original work.

Main entry   ——▶ Rey, Margret.
under author   Curious George learns the alphabet [sound re-
             cording] / Margret & H. A. Rey.

Note expanding statement of responsibility:
             Read by Julie Harris.

Make added entry for shared author and for reader:
             I. Rey, H. A. (Hans Agusto), 1898-   II.
             Harris, Julie. III. Title.

21.23B. "Enter a sound recording of two or more works all by the same person(s) or body (bodies) under the heading appropriate to those works." Make added entries under the personal headings for the performers as in 21.23A. *See* Fig. 16.37.

Fig. 16.37. Rule 21.23B. Sound recording entered under composer of the
several works performed.

Main entry   ——▶ Chopin, Frédéric, 1810-1849.
under   The 24 preludes [sound recording] / Chopin.
composer

Note expanding statement of responsibility:
             Alexander Brailowsky, pianist.

Make added entry for performer:
             I. Brailowsky, Alexander. II. Title.

21.23C. "Enter a sound recording containing works by different persons under the heading for the person or body represented as principal performer. If there are two or three persons or bodies so represented, enter under the heading for the first named and make added entries under the headings for the others." *See* Fig. 16.38.

Fig. 16.38. Rule 21.23C. Sound recording entered under principal performer.

Main entry ⟶ Boston Pops Orchestra.
under princi-   Greatest hits of the '50s [sound recording].
pal performer
Note expanding statement of responsibility:
          Boston Pops Orchestra; Arthur Fiedler,
          conductor

Make added entry under principal performer:
          I. Fiedler, Arthur, 1894-1979. II. Title.

21.23D.   "Enter under title a sound recording containing works by different persons or bodies performed by more than three principal performers or having no principal performers. For works lacking a collective title that the cataloguer wishes to treat as a unit (see 6.1G), see 21.7C." *See* Fig. 16.39.

Fig. 16.39. Rule 21.23D. Sound recording entered under title.

Main entry ⟶ Firestone presents your favorite Christmas music
under title   [sound recording]

Note expanding statement of responsibility:
          Julie Andrews; Vic Damone; Dorothy Kirsten;
          James McCracken; The Young Americans; with
          the Firestone Orchestra, conducted by Irwin
          Kostal.

Make added entry for first named performer:
          I. Andrews, Julie.

MIXED RESPONSIBILITY IN NEW WORKS

RULE 21.24.   COLLABORATION BETWEEN ARTIST AND WRITER

"Enter a work that is, or appears to be, a work of collaboration between an artist and a writer under the heading for the one who is named first in the chief source of information unless the other's name is given greater prominence by the wording or the layout. Make an added entry under the heading for the one not given main entry. For instruction on texts with illustrations, see 21.11A." *See* Fig. 16.40.

Fig. 16.40. Rule 21.24. Collaborative work entered under artist.

Main entry ⟶ Mair, A. J. (Alice Joy).
under artist   More homes of the pioneers and other build-
named first   ings : pen and wash drawings / by A. J. Mair ;
on title page   with text by J. A. Hendry. --

Make added entry for author:
          I. Hendry, J. A. (John A.). II. Title.

RULE 21.25 REPORTS OF INTERVIEWS OR EXCHANGES

21.25A. "If a report is essentially confined to the words of the person(s) interviewed or of the participants in an exchange (other than the reporter), enter under the principal participant, first named participant, or title as instructed in 21.6. Make an added entry under the heading for the reporter if he or she is openly named in the item." *See* Fig. 16.41.

Fig. 16.41. Rule 21.25A. Interview entered under the first named participant.

Main entry ⟶ Scott, David Randolph.
under first-   Interview from deep space [sound recording] /
named partici-   by David Randolph Scott, Alfred Merrill
pant   Worden, and James Benson Irwin.

Make added entries for other participants:
      I. Worden, Alfred Merrill. II. Irwin, James
      Benson. III. Title.

21.25B. "If a report is to a considerable extent in the words of the reporter, enter under the heading for the reporter." Added entries are made under the headings for the persons interviewed (or for only the first if there are more than three). *See* Fig. 16.42.

Fig. 16.42. Rule 21.25B. Interview entered under reporter.

Main entry ⟶ Schneider, Duane.
under   An interview with Anaïs Nin / Duane
reporter   Schneider.

Make added entry for person interviewed:
      I. Nin, Anaïs, 1903-

RELATED WORKS

RULE 21.28. RELATED WORKS

21.28A. **Scope**

According to Rule 1.9, supplementary items may be described separately or dependently (i.e., described as accompanying material; or in a note; or in a multi-level description, further described in 13.6). This rule (21.28) applies only to separately cataloged works that are related to another work. It includes continuations, sequels, supplements, indexes, concordances, incidental music to dramatic works, cadenzas, scenarios, screenplays, choreographies, subseries, special numbers of serials, and collections of extracts from serials. It does not apply to works that have only subject relationship to other works, or to the particular types of relationship covered in 21.8-21.27.

In *AACR 2* proper, this rule includes librettos, but an alternative rule for librettos is given in a footnote. The Library of Congress has decided to apply the alternative rule for librettos because "librettos are normally sought as an adjunct to the music."[4] Therefore, librettos are entered by LC under the heading for the musical work, with an added entry under the personal heading for the librettist. A name-title added entry is also made under the heading for the original text on which the libretto is based, if this applies. *See* Fig. 16.43.

Fig. 16.43. Rule 21.28A, footnote 7. Libretto entered under heading appropriate to the musical work.

Main entry ⟶ Laderman, Ezra.
for composer   [Galileo Galilei. Libretto. English]
            Galileo Galilei : an opera-oratorio in three acts
      / libretto by Joe Darion ; music by Ezra
      Laderman.

Note providing other title information:
      Original title: The trials of Galileo.

Make added entry for librettist:
            I. Darion, Joseph. II. Title. III. Title: The trials
      of Galileo.

21.28B.   General rule

"Enter a related work under its own heading (personal author, corporate body, or title) according to the appropriate rule in chapter 21. Make an added entry (name-title or title, as appropriate) for the work to which it is related." An added entry is not made, however, for the related work in the case of a sequel by the same author. *See* Figs. 16.44, 16.45, 16.46, and 16.47.

Fig. 16.44. Rule 21.28B. Supplement cataloged separately and entered under author.

Main entry ⟶ Gore, Marvin.
for author   Elements of systems analysis for business data
of   processing. Instructional supplement / Marvin
supplement   Gore, John Stubbe.

Make added entry for co-author of supplement:
            I. Stubbe, John. II. Title.

Note that a name-title added entry is not made because it would, in essence, be a duplication of the main entry and title given before the words "Instructional supplement."

Fig. 16.45. Rule 21.28B. Concordance entered under its own author.

Entry under   ⟶ Williams, Mary.
compiler of   The Dickens concordance, being a compen-
the   dium of names and characters and principal
concordance   places mentioned in all the works of Charles
                Dickens ... / by Mary Williams.

Make added entry for author of works to which this work is related:
           I. Dickens, Charles, 1812-1870. II. Title.

Fig. 16.46. Rule 21.28B. Collection of extracts from a serial entered
as a collection. [Joyce is the subject of these essays].

Main entry appro- James Joyce essays / by Brian O'Nolan ... [et al.].
priate to related
work in hand

Note providing bibliographic history:
           "These essays were first published in Envoy,
           1951."

Make added entry for first-named author and for serial from which essays were extracted:
           I. O'Nolan, Brian, 1911-1966. II. Envoy
(Dublin)

Fig. 16.47. Rule 21.28B. Index entered under its own author.

Main entry   ⟶ Schneider, Ben Ross, 1920-
for compiler   Index to The London stage, 1660-1800 / com-
of index   piled, with an introduction by Ben Ross Schneider, Jr. ;
               foreword by George Winchester Stone, Jr.

Make added entry for serial indexed:
           I. The London stage, 1660-1800. II. Title.

ADDED ENTRIES

RULE 21.29. GENERAL RULE

The preceding rules have indicated the added entries required in typical circumstances to supplement the main entry by providing additional bibliographical access to materials represented in the catalog. In general, added entries are suggested to provide access to other names of persons or titles under which a work may be known and under which catalog users might reasonably search. Persons, corporate bodies, and works related to the work at hand are considered, providing these are openly stated in the work. It is a matter of local library policy to establish certain administrative procedures to make all required added entries, which in turn must be related to the extent of the collection, the needs it serves, and some economic considerations. The Library of Congress has commented on the allowance in 21.29 for more added entries than those prescribed in 21.30.[5] Their feeling is that such "extra" entries may not be needed because *AACR 2* provisions are more generous than those in *AACR 1*. LC cannot decide which extra headings might be of value until *AACR 2* has been in use for some time.

It is prescribed here that if the cataloger believes an added entry is needed, and if the reason for an added entry is not clear from the body of the description, a note should be provided to justify the added entry.

An option provides for explanatory references in place of certain added entries (as in 26.5); the Library of Congress is not applying this option.[6]

RULE 21.30. SPECIFIC RULES

21.30A-21.30H, 21.30K, 21.30M.

These specific rules for added entries for collaborators, writers, editors and compilers, corporate bodies, other related persons or bodies, related works, other relationships, translators, illustrators, and analytical entries have been touched on in the rules for choice of main entry. When particular guidance is needed for one of these cases, these rules in *AACR 2* should be consulted. *See* Figs. 16.48 and 16.50.

Two added entry rules are used with such frequency that they warrant special mention:

21.30J.   Titles

There are only four instances in which an added entry for a title proper (that is not a main entry) should not be made:

> "1)   the title proper is essentially the same as the main entry heading or a reference to that heading

or   2)   the title proper has been composed by the cataloguer

or   3)   in a catalogue in which name-title and subject entries are interfiled, the title proper is identical with a subject heading, or a direct reference to a subject heading used for the work

or   4)   a conventionalized uniform title has been used in an entry for a musical work (see 25.25-25.36)."

Added entries should also be made for any other title (e.g., cover title) that differs significantly (according to 21.2A) from the title proper. *See* Figs. 16.48-16.50.

21.30L.   Series

"Make an added entry under the heading for a series for each separately catalogued work in the series if it provides a useful collocation. *Optionally*, add the numeric or other designation of each work in the series." This option is applied at the Library of Congress.[7]

"Do not make added entries under the heading for a series if:

> 1)   the items in a series are related to each other only by common physical characteristics

or   2)   the numbering suggests that the parts have been numbered primarily for stock control or to benefit from lower postage rates *or* 3)   all the parts of a series are entered under the heading for one person.

In case of doubt, make a series added entry." *See* Fig. 16.49.

Fig. 16.48. Rule 21.30D. Added entry for editor.

———→ Hollindale, Peter.

Shakespeare, William, 1564-1616.
    As you like it / [by William Shakespeare] ; edited by Peter Hollindale.

Added entry noted in tracing:
    I. Hollindale, Peter. II. Title.

Fig. 16.49. Rule 21.30L. Added entry for series.

———→ Studies in folklore ; 2.

Dundes, Alan.
    Analytic essays in folklore / by Alan Dundes.

Use of series area:
    -- (Studies in folklore ; 2)

Added entry noted in tracing:
    I. Title. II. Series.

Fig. 16.50. Rule 21.30K1. Added entry for translator.

———→ Wiemann, Rudolph.

Busch, Wilhelm, 1832-1908.
    The bees : a fairy tale / by Wilhelm Busch ; translated by Rudolph Wiemann.

Notes providing information on translation and summary:
    Translation of: Schnurrdiburr.
    Verse.
    Summary: Relates in verse the adventures and misadventures of a hive of bees and the bee keeper, his daughter, and their neighbors.

Added entry noted in tracing:
    I. Wiemann, Rudolph. II. Title.

SPECIAL RULES

CERTAIN LEGAL PUBLICATIONS

RULE 21.31.   LAWS, ETC.

21.31A.   Scope

This rule is applied to legislative enactments and decrees that have the force of law except for the following cases, which are treated in later rules: administrative regulations (21.32), constitutions and charters (21.33), court rules (21.34), and treaties (21.35).

21.31B.   Laws of modern jurisdictions

21.31B1.   Laws governing one jurisdiction

Laws governing one jurisdiction are entered under the heading for the jurisdiction they govern, with added entries for persons and corporate bodies (other than legislative bodies) that compiled or issued the laws. A uniform title is added as instructed in 25.15A (see chapter 20 of this text). *See* Fig. 16.51.

Fig. 16.51. Rule 21.31B1. Laws governing a single jurisdiction.

Name of ──────→United States.
jurisdiction
Uniform title, ─────→[Tax reduction act of 1975]
see Rule 25.15A   Tax reduction act of 1975, P.L. 94-12, as signed
        by the President on March 29, 1975 : law and ex-
        planation. -- Chicago : Commerce Clearing
        House, [1975]

Make added entry for corporate body issuing or compiling the law:
        I. Commerce Clearing House. II. Title.

21.31B2.   Laws governing more than one jurisdiction

A compilation of laws governing more than one jurisdiction is treated as a collection (see 21.7).

RULE 21.32.   ADMINISTRATIVE REGULATIONS, ETC.

The purpose of this rule is to distinguish between administrative regulations that are promulgated by government agencies under authority granted by one or more laws (as in the United States), and those that are from jurisdictions in which such regulations are laws (as in the United Kingdom and Canada). The former are entered under the promulgating agency, while the latter are entered as instructed in 21.31. *See* Figs. 16.52 and 16.53.

Fig. 16.52. Rule 21.32. U.S. administrative regulation entered under promulgating agency.

Main entry ⟶ United States. Internal Revenue Service.
under promulgat- Estate tax regulations under the Internal
ing agency Revenue Code of 1954 / [United States Treasury
Department, Internal Revenue Service]

Make added entry under heading for uniform title for authorizing law:
I. United States. [Internal Revenue Code of 1954]. II. Title.

Fig. 16.53. Rule 21.32. U.K. administrative regulation entered under the jurisdiction.

Main entry ⟶ Great Britain.
under [Army Code No. 13206]
jurisdiction The Queen's regulations for the Army, 1975 / United Kingdom, Ministry of Defence

Make added entry for promulgating agency:
I. Great Britain. Ministry of Defence. II. Title.

It should be noted that although *AACR 2* uses "United Kingdom" instead of "Great Britain" in all its examples, LC and other national libraries have decided to continue using "Great Britain" on their records. See the discussion in chapter 18 on page 331.

RULE 21.33. CONSTITUTIONS, CHARTERS, AND OTHER FUNDAMENTAL LAWS

21.33A. "Enter the constitution, charter, or other fundamental law of a jurisdiction under the heading for that jurisdiction." *See* Fig. 16.54.

Fig. 16.54. Rule 21.33. Entry for constitution.

Political ⟶ Wyoming.
jurisdiction Constitution of the State of Wyoming, adopted in convention at Cheyenne, Wyoming, September 30, 1889, including all amendments adopted to Nov. 2, 1976 / compiled by Linda Mosley.

Make added entry for compiler:
I. Mosley, Linda.

RULE 21.35.   TREATIES, INTERGOVERNMENTAL AGREEMENTS, ETC.

21.35A.   International treaties, etc.

21.35A1.   "Enter a treaty, or any other formal agreement, between two or three national governments under (in this order of preference):

a)   the heading for the government on one side if it is the only one on that side and there are two governments on the other

b)   the heading for the government whose catalogue entry heading (see 24.3E) is first in English alphabetic order.

"Make added entries under the headings for the other government(s). Add a uniform title (see 25.16B1) to the main and added entries." *See* Fig. 16.55.

Fig. 16.55. Rule 21.35A1. Treaty involving two countries.

¹Entry under country alphabetically first

²Uniform title for main and added entries

Singapore. ←——1
[Treaties, etc. Switzerland, 1969 Feb. 28]
Diplomatic notes modifying the annex to the
2 air services agreement between the Government
of the Republic of Singapore and the Government of the Swiss Confederation signed at
Singapore on 28th February, 1969.

Make added entry for the second-named country: 2
I. Switzerland. [Treaties, etc. Singapore. 1969
Feb. 28]. II. Title: Diplomatic notes modifying
the annex to the air services agreement.

CERTAIN RELIGIOUS PUBLICATIONS

RULE 21.37.   SACRED SCRIPTURES

21.37A.   "Enter a work that is accepted as sacred scripture by a religious group, or part of such a work, under title. For the use of uniform titles for scriptures, see 25.17-25.18. Make an added entry under the heading for any person associated with the work." *See* Fig. 16.56.

Fig. 16.56. Rule 21.37A. Sacred scripture entered under uniform title.

Uniform title ———►Tipiṭaka. Suttapiṭaka. English. Selections.
main entry   Some sayings of the Buddha, according to the
Pali canon / translated [from the Pali] by F. L.
Woodward ; with an introduction by Christmas
Humphreys.

Make added entries for persons associated with the work:
           I. Woodward, F. L. (Frank Lee), 1870 or 71-
1952. II. Humphreys, Christmas, 1901-   III.
Tipiṭaka. Vinayapiṭaka. English. Selections. IV.
Title.

RULE 21.39.   LITURGICAL WORKS

21.39A.   General rule

Liturgical works include "officially sanctioned or traditionally accepted texts of religious observance, books of obligatory prayers to be offered at stated times, and calendars and manuals of performance of religious observances." These are to be entered under the heading for the church or denomination that uses them. An appropriate uniform title, using 25.19-25.23, is added to the main entry. *See* Fig. 16.57.

Fig. 16.57. Rule 21.39A. Liturgical work entered under heading for the church.

Corporate head-   Catholic Church.
ing for specific   ►[Rite of ordination. English]
church   The ordination of deacons, priests, and bish-
Uniform title   ops : provisional text prepared by the International Committee on English in the Liturgy, approved for interim use by the Bishops' Committee on the Liturgy, National Conference of
Catholic Bishops, and confirmed by the
Apostolic See.

Make added entry for title:
           I. Title.

21.39C.   Jewish liturgical works

"Enter a Jewish liturgical work under its title. For the use of uniform titles, see 25.21-25.22. If the work is special to the use of a particular body (association, congregation, synagogue, etc.), make an added entry under the heading for that body." *See* Fig. 16.58.

Fig. 16.58. Rule 21.39C. Jewish liturgical work entered under uniform title.

Main entry
under uniform
title

→Maḥzor (1972). English & Hebrew.
    Maḥzor for Rosh Hashanah and Yom Kippur :
a prayer book for the Days of Awe / edited by
Jules Harlow. -- New York : Rabbinical Assembly,
[1972]

Make added entry for editor and make added entry for body that uses the work:
    I. Harlow, Jules. II. Rabbinical Assembly of
America.

FOOTNOTES

[1]John R. Schroeder, "AACR 2 Abandonment of Corporate Body Main Entry: LC G&M Division Position Paper," photocopy of typescript received Jan. 1980, pp. 2-3.

[2]"Anglo-American Cataloguing Committee for Cartographic Material Formed," *Library of Congress Information Bulletin* 38 (Nov. 2, 1979):456-57.

[3]"AACR 2: Cartographic Materials," *Cataloging Service Bulletin*, no. 7 (Winter 1980):3.

[4]"AACR 2 Options to be Followed by the Library of Congress, Chapters 1-2, 12, 21-26," *Library of Congress Information Bulletin* 37 (July 21, 1978):425.

[5]"AACR 2 Options," p. 425.

[6]"AACR 2 Options," p. 426.

[7]"AACR 2 Options," p. 426.

17 FORM OF HEADINGS FOR PERSONS

INTRODUCTION

The previous chapter dealt with choice of access points; this chapter and the next three chapters will present rules for the form of entry headings and the form of added entries. Once it has been decided what is to be the main entry or heading and what are to be added entries, it must be determined how those entries are to be displayed or written on the record. Choice of entry rules deal with who or what is to be the entry; form of entry rules deal with how an entry is to be written or recorded.

Most headings in American library catalogs consist of a personal name entered under the surname followed by forenames (like the white pages of a telephone directory). However, as the following rules for headings for persons show, there are certain complexities that must be considered in a library catalog. Rules—i.e., principles and practices—must be followed consistently for those persons known by more than one name. There are many possible instances when a person may be known and/or even write under more than one name. Some authors deliberately disguise their real names and write under a pseudonym or pen name—such as Charles Lutwidge Dodgson, who wrote his children's fantasies under the pseudonym of Lewis Carroll. Others consistently write under initialized forenames (e.g., H. G. Wells), while still others, such as Bernard Shaw, consistently omit one of their forenames. If someone's original name is written in a non-roman alphabet, different romanization systems may create different spellings of the name (such as Chekhov, Chekov, or Tchekhov). A married woman has two possible surnames—her maiden surname and her husband's surname. Further compound surnames—i.e., surnames consisting of two or more parts—create problems. Granville-Barker is an example of a compound, hyphenated English surname. Prefixes to surnames create another type of compound surname. De Gaulle and von Goethe are examples of surnames with prefixes; O'Brien and MacPherson are other examples. Individuals who are members of nobility may have two names—a titled name and a common surname (such as Lord Byron, George Gordon Byron). Certain individuals are known under their bynames or forenames rather than their surnames; these include royalty (Elizabeth II), saints (Joan of Arc), popes (Paul VI), and individuals in ancient and medieval periods prior to the development of surnames (Horace). Bynames or forenames often exist in different forms in different languages (such as Horace in English, but Horatius in Latin). The purpose of this chapter is to demonstrate the general rules used to resolve all of these problems. For more complicated problems of personal names, the student should carefully examine *AACR 2*, chapter 22.

The *AACR 2* chapter is divided into four sections, the first three of which suggest the order of the steps taken by the cataloger to establish the form in which the name will appear as a heading in the catalog. The first section, Rules 22.1-22.3, is entitled "Choice of name." This "choice" is a separate action from "choice of access points," discussed in the preceding chapter. Once it has been decided through choice of access points that a person will be given an access point, Rules 22.1-22.3 prescribe the choice of name when that person has used more than one name or different manifestations of the same name. After making a choice of name, the cataloger uses the next section, Rules 22.4-22.11, "Entry element," to decide which element of the chosen name will be the first, and in what order the other elements will follow. The third step is to make any additions to the name that may be necessitated because of the kind of name involved (Rules 22.12-22.17), or because two or more names are identical (Rules 22.18-22.20). The fourth section of *AACR 2*, chapter 22, is "Special Rules for Names in Certain Languages." These are for selected languages in which heading form does not follow the typical "western" style.

It should be noted that the rules in this chapter apply to the choice and form of personal names whether they are access points because of some kind of responsibility for the creation of a work or because they are the subject of a work. That is, a personal name subject heading is constructed in the same manner and according to the same rules as is a personal name main or added entry heading for an author, painter, performer, etc.

The Library of Congress is adopting *AACR 2* for new names and in many cases is changing established heading forms to agree with the prescribed *AACR 2* form. However, in certain defined categories, established names are considered to be "AACR 2 compatible," and the established form will continue to be used even on new records.[1] These categories are identified in this text in conjunction with discussion of the relevant rule. LC's decisions on application of the various options and alternative rules are likewise identified.

CHOICE OF NAME

RULE 22.1. GENERAL RULE

22.1A.   "Choose as the basis of the heading for a person, the name by which he or she is commonly known. This may be the person's real name, pseudonym, title of nobility, nickname, initials, or other appellation."

The principle here is to follow the form customarily used by a person. Thus the following choices might be made:

Pseudonym

> Mathew James
> *not* birth name: James D. Lucey

Nickname

> Billy Graham
> *not* William Franklin Graham

Name in religion

Maria Teresa dell'Eucaristia

not birth name: Maria Teresa Tosi

Short form of name

Virginia Knight Nelson

not Alyce Virginia Knight Nelson

Real name

Sally Benson

not pseudonym: Esther Evarts

22.1B. "Determine the name by which a person is commonly known from the chief sources of information (see 1.0A) of works by that person issued in his or her language. If the person works in a nonverbal context (e.g., a painter, a sculptor) or is not known primarily as an author, determine the name by which he or she is commonly known from reference sources issued in his or her language or country of residence or activity." "Reference sources" include books and articles written about a person.

Throughout this chapter of *AACR 2* there are references to "commonly known" and "predominant" when referring to choosing one name or one form of name. *AACR 2* defines predominant name as, "The name or form of name of a person or corporate body that appears most frequently (1) in the person's works or works issued by the corporate body; or (2) in reference sources, in that order of preference." We are told by the framers of *AACR 2* that "most frequently" should not be taken to mean 51 percent of the instances; yet nowhere is there any firm guideline. For a number of years, the Library of Congress used 75 percent in interpreting the "fullness of name" rule. That is, until a name appeared in a different form in an author's works 75 percent of the time (counting works by the person issued after the person's death as well as during the person's lifetime), the form of heading was not changed. They are continuing to apply this concept with *AACR 2* (within the limits of "compatible" headings explained below), except the percentage is now 66⅔ percent.[2] Perhaps other libraries could follow suit. When a name is first established, "predominant" could be 51 percent or more; but a change would not be called for until the name had appeared differently 66⅔ percent of the time. In the case of pseudonyms (see 22.2C), the cataloger might use the rule for "predominant name" (entry under one of the names used) if one name is used at least 66⅔ percent of the time, but use the rule for "no predominant name" if no one name appears 66⅔ percent of the time.

22.1C.-22.1D.   Terms and punctuation associated with a name

These rules refer to inclusion of titles of nobility or honor, diacritical marks, and hyphens. At first glance it may not be clear how these relate to choice of name. However, the intention here is to give rules for choosing those elements that should be included in the heading. The order in which these elements appear is the subject of Rules 22.4-22.17.

The principal again is to follow the form customarily used by the person. Include titles, words, or phrases that commonly appear with the name. Include accents, other diacritical marks, and hyphens used by the person; except do not include a hyphen that is used between a forename and a surname.

The first of LC's "compatible" headings occurs here. Previous rules did not allow the use of a hyphen between forenames in French names, and in certain other cases. If the only difference between an established heading and its *AACR 2* form is the insertion of a hyphen, the non-hyphenated form will continue to be used. *See* Fig. 17.1.

Fig. 17.1. Rule 22.1D2. Hyphens—LC interpretation.

Established heading: Marcadé, Jean Claude
Writes as: Jean-Claude Marcadé
Established heading retained.

RULE 22.2. CHOICE AMONG DIFFERENT NAMES

Rules 22.2 and 22.3 give more specific guidelines for adhering to the principle stated in 22.1. Rules in 22.2 help choose among different names for the same person, and those in 22.3 help in the choice among different forms of the same name. Both may have to be used in a particular instance, because a name chosen from among different names may itself appear in varying degrees of fullness or with variant spellings. For example, once it has been decided that the name used should be George Novack, not William Warde, one then has to decide whether to use George Novack, George E. Novack, or George Edward Novack.

22.2A.   Predominant name

If a person is *known* by more than one name, and if there is a name that is clearly most common, it is used. If not, the following order of preference is used in making a choice:

"1)   the name that appears most frequently in the person's works

2)   the name that appears most frequently in reference sources

3)   the latest name."

LC has noted that 22.2A or 22.3A, not 22.2C, should be used for an author who simultaneously uses different forms of a *real* name.[3]

22.2B.   Change of name

"If a person has changed his or her name, choose the latest name or form of name unless there is reason to believe that an earlier name will persist as the name by which the person is better known. Follow the same rule for a person who has acquired and become known by a title of nobility (see also 22.6)." *See* Fig. 17.2.

Latest name
used

Jackson, Barbara Ward, Lady, 1914-
    A new creation? : Reflections on the environ-
mental issue / Barbara Ward (Lady Jackson).

Note: Refer from:[4] Ward, Barbara, maiden name used in writings before author's marriage.

LC has noted that this rule applies to authors who have used both a nickname and a real name (e.g., Lucille/Luci). The latest form should be chosen.[5] This should be distinguished from the case where a forename is abbreviated (e.g., Charles/Chas.). In this case, the spelled out form is used, no matter which form was used last.[6]

22.2C.   Pseudonyms

22.2C1.   One pseudonym

"If all the works by a person appear under one pseudonym, or if the person is predominantly identified in reference sources by one pseudonym, choose the pseudonym. If the real name is known, make a reference from the real name to the pseudonym." *See* Fig. 17.3.

Ford, Ford Madox, 1873-1939.
    It was the nightingale / Ford Madox Ford.

Note: Refer from real name: Hueffer, Ford Madox.

The second of LC's "compatible" headings can be associated with this rule. Rules earlier than *AACR 1* required the addition of the term "pseud." to a name entered under pseudonym. Headings established according to those rules have been retained. LC will continue to retain the term "pseud." when it is added to a pseudonym that is not famous. *See* Fig. 17.4.

Established heading: Justinus, pseud.
Judgment: pseudonym is not "famous"
Established heading using "pseud." retained

22.2C2.   Predominant name

"If the works of a person appear under several pseudonyms (or under the real name and one or more pseudonyms), choose one of those names if the person has come to be identified predominantly by that name in later editions of his or her works, in critical works, or in other reference sources (in that order of preference). Make references from the other names." The cataloger is instructed here to ignore reference sources that always enter persons under their real names. *See* Fig. 17.5.

Fig. 17.5. Rule 22.2C2. Entry under pseudonym by which author is predominantly known.

Carroll, Lewis, 1832-1898.
      The hunting of the snark / by Lewis Carroll ;
illustrated by Edward A. Wilson.

Note: Refer from real name: Dodgson, Charles Lutwidge

22.2C3.   No predominant name

"If a person using pseudonyms is not known predominantly by one name, choose as the basis for the heading for each item the name appearing in it. Make references to connect the names (see 26.2C and 26.2D)." As mentioned earlier, a suggested guide to "predominant" is the use of one name 66⅔ percent of the time (see explanation under 22.1B). *See* Fig. 17.6.

Fig. 17.6. Rule 22.2C3. Entry under each pseudonym for the same author.

McBain, Ed.
      The sentries / Ed McBain.

Hunter, Evan
      The blackboard jungle / Evan Hunter

Collins, Hunt
      Cut me in / Hunt Collins

Marsten, Richard
      Murder in the navy / Richard Marsten

Note: The author never wrote using his birth surname, Lombino. He changed his name legally to Hunter. Make explanatory references to connect the various pseudonyms.

22.2C4.   Different names in editions of the same work

"If different names appear in different editions of the same work, or if two or more names of the same person appear in one edition, choose for all editions the name most often used in editions of the work. If that cannot be determined, choose the name appearing in the latest editions of the work. Make name-title references from the other name(s)."

RULE 22.3. CHOICE AMONG DIFFERENT FORMS OF THE SAME NAME

22.3A.   Fullness

"If the forms of a name vary in fullness, choose the form most commonly found. As required, make references from the other forms." *See* Fig. 17.7.

Fig. 17.7. Rule 22.3A. Name entered under form most commonly found.

Hamilton, John P.
    Predominant form: John P. Hamilton
    Occasional form: J. P. Hamilton
    Rare form: "Bud" Hamilton

Note: Because Hamilton is a common surname, the second forename, Peter, may be required in parentheses to distinguish between two identical names (see 22.16). Also, references may be needed from the two forms of name not chosen.

"If no one form predominates, choose the latest form. In case of doubt about which is the latest form, choose the fuller or fullest form." LC has noted that for living people the choice of "latest form" of name cannot be applied.[7]

LC has given a rule interpretation that if a name varies in fullness in the same work, the form found in the chief source of information should be used.[8]

Four of LC's "AACR 2 compatible" categories occur under the auspices of this rule. First, if a name has already been established with a first forename spelled out even though the predominant form uses an initial or deletes the first forename entirely, the established form is kept unless the person is "famous" or the name is being used as an access point on a record for a U.S. imprint. In the case of a famous person, the change to *AACR 2* form is made. The interpretation of "famous" is left to the judgment of the individual cataloger; but in case of doubt, a person is to be considered famous. In the case of the U.S. imprint, the change to *AACR 2* form is made if the first forename should be an initial or should be dropped according to the 66⅔ percent rule.[9] *See* Fig. 17.8.

Fig. 17.8. Rule 22.3A. Fullness—LC practice.

Established heading: McClellan, Bernard Edward, 1939-
    Writes on U.S. imprints as: B. Edward McClellan
    Listed in reference sources as: McClellan, Bernard Edward
    New heading: McClellan, B. Edward (Bernard Edward),
        1939-

Established heading: Marijnissen, Roger H.
    Writes on non-U.S. imprints as: R. H. Marijnissen
    Established heading retained.

Established heading: Wells, Herbert George, 1866-1946.
    Wrote as: H. G. Wells
    Judgment: famous person
    New heading: Wells, H. G. (Herbert George), 1866-1946.

The second "compatible" category having to do with fullness concerns reduction of a second forename to an initial. Except for famous persons, such headings are retained as established.[10] *See* Fig. 17.9.

Fig. 17.9. Rule 22.3A. Fullness—LC practice.

Established heading: McCarthy, John David, 1940-
    Writes as: John D. McCarthy
    Established heading retained.

The third fullness "compatibility" is that an unused second forename or forename initial is not deleted from an established heading. Again, famous names are excepted; famous names are all established in their *AACR 2* forms.[11] *See* Fig. 17.10.

Fig. 17.10. Rule 22.3A. Fullness—LC practice.

Established heading: Miller, Lenore D.
    Writes as: Lenore Miller
    Established heading retained.

The fourth "compatible" category under fullness is that of expansion to a fuller form of name. With the exception of famous names, if forenames are less full than required by *AACR 2*, expansion is not carried out. *See* Fig. 17.11.

Fig. 17.11. Rule 22.3A. Fullness—LC practice.

Established heading: Nechitaĭlo, A. L.
    Has written later as: Annetta Leonidovna Nechitaĭlo
    Established heading retained.

For fullness of names involving surnames, LC applies the 66⅔ percent rule.[12] *See* Fig. 17.12.

Fig. 17.12. Rule 22.3A. Fullness—LC practice.

Established heading: Sánchez E., Rodrigo
    Has now written over 66⅔ % as: Rodrigo Sánchez Enríquez
    New heading: Sánchez Enríquez, Rodrigo

22.3B.   Language

22.3B1.   Persons using more than one language

"If the name of a person who has used more than one language appears in different language forms in his or her works, choose the form corresponding to the language of most of the works." *See* Fig. 17.13.

Fig. 17.13. Rule 22.3B1. Entry for person using more than one language.

Names found on works: William More
                      Guillermo Mora
Lived and worked in both U.S. and Venezuela.
Most works in Spanish.
Entry: Mora, Guillermo

"In case of doubt, choose the form most commonly found in reference sources of the person's country of residence or activity."

LC practice when reference sources cannot be found, or the person is not listed, is to use the form of the name in the person's native language.[13]

Note: The choice made according to this rule may be altered by application of 22.3B2, 22.3B3, or 22.3C.

22.3B2.   Names in vernacular and Greek or Latin forms

"If a name occurs in reference sources and/or in the person's works in a Greek or Latin form as well as in a form in the person's vernacular, choose the form most commonly found in reference sources. . . .

"In case of doubt, choose the Latin or Greek form for persons who were active before, or mostly before, 1400. For persons active after 1400, choose the vernacular form." *See* Fig. 17.14.

**Fig. 17.14. Rule 22.3B2. Entry of name found in both the
vernacular and Latin.**

Name in vernacular: Dante Alighieri (with various spellings)
Name in Latin: Dantes Aligerius
Form most commonly found in reference sources: Dante
  Alighieri
Entry: Dante Alighieri, 1265-1321.

22.3B3. Names written in the roman alphabet established in an English form

"Choose the English form of name for a person entered under given name, etc. (see 22.8) or for a Roman of classical times (see 22.9) whose name has become well established in an English form in English-language reference sources. . . . In case of doubt, use the vernacular or Latin form." *See* Fig. 17.15.

Fig. 17.15. Rule 22.3B3. Entry of name with established English form.

Name of saint in Latin: Justinus
Name in English language reference sources: Justin
Entry: Justin, Saint.

22.3B4. Other names

"In all cases of names found in different language forms and not covered by 22.3B1-22.3B3, choose the form most frequently found in reference sources of the country of the person's residence or activity." *See* Fig. 17.16.

**Fig. 17.16. Rule 22.3B4. Entry of name that is found in different
language forms.**

Name on original work: John Boyer Noss
Name on translation of original work: Jān B. Nūs
Place of author's residence: U.S.
Entry: Noss, John Boyer

22.3C. Names written in a nonroman script

Names that must be romanized or transliterated present many problems. Some languages have a number of systems for romanization, and use of the different systems results in different spellings. In addition, there may be one or more English language forms of some better known names. The rules in 22.3C give some guidance.

22.3C1.   Persons entered under given name, etc.

This rule, like 22.3B3, calls for entry under an English language form, if one exists. (If more than one exists, choose the one that appears most frequently.) *See* Fig. 17.17.

"If no English romanization is found, or if no one romanization predominates, romanize the name according to the table for the language adopted by the cataloguing agency."

Fig. 17.17. Rule 22.3C1. Entry of name originally in nonroman script — given name.

Romanizations of name: Movses Khorenat͡si
                                        Moses Xorenc'i
English language form of name: Moses of Chorene
Entry: Moses, of Chorene

22.3C2.   Persons entered under surname

Unlike the preceding rule, this one directs the cataloger to romanize a name entered under surname according to the table adopted by the cataloging agency. References are made from other romanized forms. If a name is found only in romanized form in the works involved, that form is used.

An alternative rule is given for 22.3C2: "Choose the romanized form of name . . . that has become well-established in English-language reference sources." This corresponds to the treatment of persons entered under given name, but is counter to the principle of entry under the name elements most commonly found in writers' works, or in reference works in the language or country of residence or activity for persons other than writers. The Library of Congress is following the alternative rule.[14] *See* Fig. 17.18.

Fig. 17.18. Rule 22.3C2. Entry of name originally in nonroman script — surname.

Entry in romanized form found in English language reference sources	Scriabin, Alexander N. 12 [i.e. Zwölf] Etüden für Klavier, op. 8 = 12 studies for piano / Alexander Skrjabin ; hrsg. von Günter Philipp. –

Note: Romanized form appearing in the item:
    Alexander Skrjabin

Systematic romanization according to LC's adopted tables:
    Skriabin, Aleksandr N.

Form most often found in English-language reference sources:
    Scriabin, Alexander N.

Refer from:
    Skriabin, Aleksandr N.
    Skrjabin, Alexander

It should be noted that the alternative rule makes no provision for names for which there are no entries in English-language reference sources. Presumably, one should use the provision given in 22.3C1 for persons entered under given name: "If no English romanization is found . . . romanize the name according to the table for the language adopted by the cataloguing agency." *See* Fig. 17.19.

Fig. 17.19.

Romanizations found in chief sources of information, but not in reference sources:
  Matsiute, Regina
  Maciūte, Regina [romanization according to adopted table]
Entry: Maciūte, Regina
Refer from: Matsiute, Regina

Another of the LC "compatible" categories occurs with this rule. Names that were, in the past, established according to a "nonsystematic" romanization, will not be changed to the "systematic" romanization now adopted by the Library of Congress. (This assumes that a well-established English form cannot be found, leaving the name to be romanized according to the table for the language adopted by the cataloging agency.)

22.3D.   Spelling
"If variant spellings of a person's name are found and these variations are not the result of different romanizations, choose the form resulting from an official change in orthography, or, if this does not apply, choose the predominant spelling. In case of doubt, choose the spelling found in the first item catalogued." *See* Fig. 17.20.

Fig. 17.20. Rule 22.3D. Entry of name with variant spellings.

Variant spellings found: Thomas Decker
                          Thomas Dekker
                          Thomas Deckar
Predominant spelling: Thomas Dekker
Entry: Dekker, Thomas, ca. 1572-1632.

ENTRY ELEMENT

RULE 22.4. GENERAL RULE

22.4A.   "If a person's name (chosen according to 22.1-22.3) consists of several parts, select as the entry element that part of the name under which the person would normally be listed in authoritative alphabetic lists in his or her language or country. . . . If, however, a person's preference is known to be different from the normal usage, follow that preference in selecting the entry element." "Authoritative" is defined as meaning "who's who" type publications, not telephone directory type.

22.4B. Order of elements

The entry element is chosen according to Rules 22.5-22.9, but the order of other elements is given here.

22.4B2. If the entry element is the first element, the name is entered in direct order. If that first element is a surname, it is followed by a comma. *See* Fig. 17.21.

Fig. 17.21. Rule 22.4B2. Name entered under first element, which is surname.

Name on chief source of information: Wu Hsin-chung
Surname: Wu
Entry: Wu, Hsin-chung

22.4B3. If the entry element is not the first one, the names preceding it are transposed to follow the entry element and a comma. *See* Fig. 17.22.

Fig. 17.22. Rule 22.4B3. Name entered under third element, which is surname.

Name on chief source of information: Jill S. Slattery
Surname entry element: Slattery
Entry: Slattery, Jill S.

22.4B4. If the entry element is the proper name in a title of nobility, according to 22.6, the personal name follows in direct order, and the term of rank follows last. *See* Fig. 17.23.

Fig. 17.23. Rule 22.4B4. Name entered under proper name of a title of nobility.

Name on chief source of information: Thomas Pitt, 2nd Baron
    Camelford
Entry element: Camelford
Entry: Camelford, Thomas Pitt, Baron, 1775-1804.
Refer from: Pitt, Thomas, Baron Camelford

Note: The part of the term of rank denoting that this is the second person with this title and same common name is not included. Instead, birth and death dates distinguish otherwise identical names.

RULE 22.5. ENTRY UNDER SURNAME

22.5A.   General rule

"Enter a name containing a surname under that surname (see also 22.15A) unless subsequent rules (e.g., 22.6, 22.17, 22.28) provide for entry under a different element." *See* Figs. 17.21 and 17.22.

22.5B.   Element other than the first treated as a surname

"If the name does not contain a surname but contains an element that identifies the individual and functions as a surname, enter under this element followed by a comma and the rest of the name." *See* Fig. 17.24.

Fig. 17.24. Rule 22.5B. Entry under element treated as a surname.

Name on chief source of information: Muḥammad Saʿīd Bāyirlī
Entry: Bāyirlī, Muḥammad Saʿīd
Refer from: Muḥammad Saʿīd Bāyirlī

22.5C.   Compound surname

22.5C1.   Preliminary rule

"The following rules deal with the entry of surnames consisting of two or more proper names (referred to as 'compound surnames') and names that may or may not contain compound surnames. Apply the rules in the order given. Refer from elements of compound surnames not chosen as the entry element."

22.5C2.   Preferred or established form known

"Enter a name containing a compound surname under the element by which the person bearing the name prefers to be entered. If this is unknown, enter the name under the element under which it is listed in reference sources in the person's language or country of residence." *See* Fig. 17.25 below and Fig. 17.30 (page 317).

Fig. 17.25. Rule 22.5C2. Entry under preferred or established form of compound name.

Lloyd George, David, 1863-1945.
War memoirs of David Lloyd George.

Note: Refer from: George, David Lloyd. George is his correct paternal surname.

22.5C3.   Hyphenated surnames

"If the elements of a compound surname are regularly or occasionally hyphenated, enter under the first element." *See* Fig. 17.26.

Fig. 17.26. Rule 22.5C3. Entry under hyphenated surname.

Entry under
first part of
hyphenated
surname

Ward Lock's encyclopedia / edited by Harold
   Boswell-Taylor
   → I. Boswell-Taylor, Harold

Note: Refer from: Taylor, Harold Boswell-

22.5C4.   **Other compound surnames, except those of married women whose surname consists of a combination of maiden name and husband's surname**

"Enter under the first element of the compound surname unless the person's language is Portuguese. If the person's language is Portuguese, enter under the last element." *See* Fig. 17.27.

Fig. 17.27. Rule 22.5C4. Entry of "other compound surnames."

Torres Ramírez, Blanca
   Las relaciones cubanosovieticas / por Blanca Torres
Ramírez.

Note: Refer from: Ramírez, Blanca Torres

22.5C5.   **Other compound surnames. Married women whose surname consists of maiden name and husband's surname**

"Enter under the first element of the compound surname . . . if the woman's language is Czech, French, Hungarian, Italian, or Spanish. In all other cases, enter under the husband's surname. For hyphenated names, see 22.5C3." *See* Figs. 17.28 and 17.29.

Fig. 17.28. Rule 22.5C5. Entry of married French-speaking woman.

Entry under
maiden name

Mendès France, Joan.
   L'anglais juridique et le droit anglais : textes
bilinques et exercises / Joan Mendès France et
Hélène Bourrouilhou.

Note: Refer from: France, Joan Mendès

Fig. 17.29. Rule 22.5C5. Entry of married English-speaking woman.

Graves, Kathleen George
Our Union County heritage : a historical and
biographical album of Union County, people,
places, and events / by Kathleen George Graves
and Winnie Palmer McDonald.

Entry under
husband's
name → I. McDonald, Winnie Palmer

However, if a married woman is known to prefer some other entry element
than prescribed here, 22.5C2 takes precedence. *See* Fig. 17.30.

**Fig. 17.30. Rule 22.5C2. Entry of married English-speaking woman under
preferred entry element.**

Entry under
maiden name

Rutherford Carr, Deborah
Individuals / by Deborah Rutherford Carr and
Thomas J. Carr.

Note: Author is known to prefer combination of maiden name and husband's
surname as compound surname.
Refer from: Carr, Deborah Rutherford

22.5D. Surnames with separately written prefixes

22.5D1. Articles and prepositions

"If a surname includes an article or preposition or combination of the
two, enter under the element most commonly used as entry element in listings
in the person's language or country of residence. See the list of languages and
language groups below."
In *AACR 2* this rule contains many specific examples of names in different languages. Only the most basic of those rules are cited here.

DUTCH. " . . . Enter under the part following the prefix unless the prefix
is *ver*. In that case, enter under the prefix." *See* Fig. 17.31.

Fig. 17.31. Rule 22.5D1. Entry of Dutch name.

Schuit, Steven R.
Dutch business law : legal, accounting, and
tax aspects of business in the Netherlands / by
Steven R. Schuit and Jan M. van der Beek.

Entry under
part follow-
ing prefix

→ I. Beek, Jan M. van der

Note: Refer from: Van der Beek, Jan M.

ENGLISH. "Enter under the prefix." *See* Fig. 17.32.

Fig. 17.32. Rule 22.5D1. Entry of English name beginning with prefix.

Nuclear or not? : choices for our energy future :
a Royal Institution forum / edited by Gerald
Foley and Ariane van Buren.

Entry under
prefix

    I. Van Buren, Ariane

Note: Refer from: Buren, Ariane van

FRENCH. "If the prefix consists of an article or of a contraction of an article and a preposition, enter under the prefix." *See* Fig. 17.33.

Fig. 17.33. Rule 22.5D1. Entry of French name beginning with article.

Entry under
the article

Le Bihan, Alain.
    Francs-maçons   et ateliers parisiens de la
Grande Loge de France au XVIIIᵉ [i.e.
dix-huitième] siècle : 1760-1795 / Alain Le Bihan.
-- Paris : Bibliothèque nationale, 1973.

Note: Refer from: Bihan, Alain le

"Otherwise, enter under the part of the name following the preposition." *See* Figs. 17.34 and 17.35.

Fig. 17.34. Rule 22.5D1. Entry of French names that include prepositions.

Entry under
part of
name follow-
ing the
preposition

Richemont, Jean de.
    L'intégration du droit communautaire dans
l'ordre juridique interne : article 177 du Traité de
Rome / Jean de Richemont ; préf. par Marcel
Ancel.

Fig. 17.35.

Entry under
the article
following the
preposition

La Fontaine, Jean de, 1621-1695.
    Fables / La Fontaine ; préface et commentaires
de Pierre Clarac.

Note: Refer from: Fontaine, Jean de la

GERMAN. "If the prefix consists of an article or of a contraction of an article and a preposition, enter under the prefix." *See* Fig. 17.36.

Fig. 17.36. Rule 22.5D1. Entry of German name under prefix.

Vom Scheidt, Jürgen, 1940-
    Alles über Rauschdrogen / Jürgen vom
Scheidt, Wolfgang Schmidbauer.

Note: Refer from: Scheidt, Jürgen vom

"Otherwise, enter under the part of the name following the prefix." *See* Fig. 17.37.

Fig. 17.37. Rule 22.5D1. Entry of German name with preposition.

Entry under
part of
name follow-
ing the
preposition

Weizsäcker, Carl Christian von.
    Modern capital theory and the concept of ex-
ploitation / Carl Christian von Weizsäcker.

ITALIAN. "Enter modern names under the prefix." *See* Fig. 17.38.

Fig. 17.38. Rule 22.5D1. Entry of modern Italian name.

Entry under
the prefix

De Filippo, Peppino.
    La lettera di mammà : farsa in due parti / Pep-
pino De Flippo.

Note: Refer from: Filippo, Peppino de.

"For medieval and early modern names, consult reference sources about whether a prefix is part of a name." Example:

Medici, Lorenzo de'

SPANISH. "If the prefix consists of an article only, enter under it. . . . Enter all other names under the part following the prefix." *See* Fig. 17.39.

Fig. 17.39. Rule 22.5D1. Entry of Spanish name.

Entry under   Lorenzo, Pedro de.
part of   Libros de la vocación / Pedro de Lorenzo.
name follow-
ing prefix

22.5D2.   Other prefixes

"If the prefix is not an article, or preposition, or combination of the two, enter under prefix." *See* Fig. 17.40.

Fig. 17.40. Rule 22.5D2. Entry under the prefix. "Mac" is an attributive prefix.

MacIntyre, Elisabeth.
    The purple mouse / by Elisabeth MacIntyre. – 1st. ed. –

RULE 22.6. ENTRY UNDER TITLE OF NOBILITY

"Enter under the proper name in a title of nobility (including courtesy titles) if the person is commonly known by that title. Apply this rule to those persons who (1) use their titles rather than their surnames in their works or (2) are listed under their titles in reference sources. . . ." *See* Fig. 17.23 (page 314). "Omit the surname and term of rank if the person does not use a term of rank or a substitute for it" (e.g., John Julius Norwich was born John Julius Duff Cooper and became Viscount Norwich, but the name appears as John Julius Norwich). If the title includes a territorial designation that is an integral part of the title, it should be included. *See* Fig. 17.41.

Fig. 17.41. Rule 22.6. Entry under title of nobility.

Joint Advisory Committee on Pets in Society.
    Dogs in the United Kingdom : report of the Joint Advisory Committee on Pets in Society
Note clarifying statement of responsibility:
    Chairman: Lord Houghton of Sowerby
Make added entry under title of nobility with territorial designation:
    I. Houghton of Sowerby, Douglas Houghton, Baron

This rule is closely related to 22.4B4 and 22.12. The three result in the same form of name, but they approach this type of name from the three viewpoints of order of elements, entry element, and additions to names.

RULE 22.8. ENTRY UNDER GIVEN NAME, ETC.

"Enter a name that does not include a surname and that is borne by a person who is not identified by a title of nobility under the part of name under which the person is listed in reference sources. Include in the name any words or phrases denoting place of origin, domicile, occupation, or other characteristic that are commonly associated with the name in works by the person or in reference sources. Precede such words or phrases by a comma. . . ." *See* Fig. 17.42.

Fig. 17.42. Rule 22.8. Entry of a name under given name.

Paul, of Aleppo.
    The travels of Macarius, patriarch of Antioch / written by
his attendant archdeacon, Paul of Aleppo.

ADDITIONS TO NAMES

GENERAL

RULE 22.12. TITLES OF NOBILITY AND TERMS OF HONOUR AND ADDRESS, ETC.

22.12A.   "Add to the name of a nobleman or noblewoman not entered under title (see 22.6) the title of nobility in the vernacular if the title or part of the title or a substitute for the title [e.g., Lord Byron instead of Baron Byron] commonly appears with the name. . . ." *See* Fig. 17.43.

Fig. 17.43. Rule 22.12A. Addition of title of nobility to given name entry.

Title of   John, of Gaunt, Duke of Lancaster, 1340-1399.
nobility   John of Gaunt's register, 1379-1383 / edited from the original record by the late Eleanor C. Lodge and Robert Somerville.

22.12B.   British titles of honour

"Add the British titles of honour *Sir, Dame, Lord,* and *Lady* if the term commonly appears with the name in works by the person or in reference sources. In case of doubt, add the term of honour." Note that the terms "Hon." and "bart." formerly used in headings are not now authorized. LC will no longer use them and will revise existing headings that contain them.[15]

In *AACR 2* this rule goes on to distinguish the times when such terms should be added after the forenames and when they should be inserted before forenames. However, the Library of Congress, because of the incapability of their computer system to handle nonfiling characters, places all terms of honor and address after the forenames. *See* Figs. 17.44 and 17.45.

Fig. 17.44. Rule 22.12B. Addition of title of honor.

Term of Stephen, James Fitzjames, Sir, 1829-1894.
honor   A digest of the law of evidence / by Sir James Fitzjames
           Stephen. – 5th ed. / by Sir Herbert Stephen and Harry
           Lushington Stephen.

Note: Position of title is LC practice. According to *AACR 2*, heading should be:

Stephen, Sir James Fitzjames, 1829-1894

Fig. 17.45. Rule 22.12B. Addition of title of honor.

Term of Hepworth, Barbara, Dame, 1903-
honor   Barbara Hepworth / J. P. Hodin. -- London : Lund
           Humphries

Note: Position of title is LC practice. *AACR 2* form:

Hepworth, Dame Barbara, 1903-

Another of LC's "compatible" categories occurs with this rule. If a name has been established using an *AACR 2*-authorized term of honor, even though that term does not commonly appear with the name, LC will not revise the heading. *See* Fig. 17.46.

Fig. 17.46. Rule 22.12B. Addition of title of honor—LC compatible heading.

Term of Younghusband, Francis Edward, Sir, 1863-1942.
honor   The heart of a continent : a narrative of travels in Man-
           churia, across the Gobi Desert, through the Himalayas, the
           Pamirs, and Chitral, 1884-1894 / by Frank E. Younghusband.

Note: The *AACR 2* heading for the item in Fig. 17.46 should be:

Younghusband, Frank E., 1863-1942.

LC will retain the established heading, however, because it falls in two "compatible" categories—that of not eliminating unused titles of honor, and that of not reducing a second forename to an initial.

RULE 22.13. SAINTS

"Add the word *Saint* after the name of a Christian saint, unless the person was a pope, emperor, empress, king, or queen, in which case follow 22.17A-22.17B." *See* Fig. 17.47.

Fig. 17.47. Rule 22.13. Addition of "Saint."

Addition
of designa-
tion "Saint"

Jeanne d'Arc eine Heilige? : Sceptische Studien
gelegentlich des Canonisation-processes.
  I. Joan, of Arc, Saint, 1412-1431.

RULE 22.15. ADDITIONS TO NAMES ENTERED UNDER SURNAME

22.15A.   "If the name by which a person is known consists only of a surname, add the word or phrase associated with the name in works by the person
or in reference sources. As required, refer from the name in direct order." *See*
Fig. 17.48.

Fig. 17.48. Rule 22.15A. Addition of phrase associated with surname alone.

Jefferson, Mr., of Gray's Inn.
  Tales of old Mr. Jefferson, of Gray's Inn / collected by
young Mr. Jefferson, of Lyon's Inn.

Note: Refer from: Mr. Jefferson of Gray's Inn

22.15B.   **Terms of address of married women**
    "Add the term of address of a married woman if she is identified only by
her husband's name." *See* Fig. 17.49.

Fig. 17.49. Rule 22.15B. Entry for married woman identified only by
                              husband's name.

1

2

[1] Husband's
name
[2] Term of
address

Bruce, William, Mrs.
    Some intermarriages of some old Springfield,
Ohio, families / compiled by Mrs. Wm. Ultes, Jr.,
as dictated by her mother, Mrs. Wm. Bruce.

Note: Form above is LC practice. *AACR 2* form:

    Bruce, Mrs. William

22.15C.   "Do not add other titles or terms associated with names entered
under surname unless they are required to distinguish between two or more
persons with the same name and dates are not available." *See* Figs. 17.50 and
17.52.

Fig. 17.50. Rule 22.15C. Omission of unneeded term of address.

Name on chief source of information: Dr. Mary Lyon
Entry: Lyon, Mary

RULE 22.16. ADDITIONS TO NAMES CONSISTING OF OR CONTAINING INITIALS

"If part or all of a name is represented by initials and the full form is known, add the spelled out form in parentheses if necessary to distinguish between names that are otherwise identical.

"Refer from the full form of the name." *See* Figs. 17.51 and 17.52.

Fig. 17.51. Rule 22.16. Addition to name containing initials.

Full form of name added in parentheses	Roberts, J. O. (Jack O.) Coal and nuclear : a comparison of the cost of generating baseload electricity by region / J. O. Roberts.

Note: Refer from: Roberts, Jack O.

Fig. 17.52. Rule 22.16. Addition to name containing initials.

Full form of name added in parentheses	Rouse, John E. (John Edward), 1942- Urban housing / by John E. Rouse, Jr.

Note: In addition to use of forenames in parentheses, note that the term "Jr." was omitted from the heading in favor of addition of the birth date.

This rule allows the option of making the above additions even when not necessary to distinguish identical names. LC is following the option when the information is readily available.[16]

Birthdates also are used to distinguish between names that are otherwise identical (*see* 22.18). LC does not search for full forenames if the birthdate is readily available to make the distinction. That is, when two names are identical, readily available forenames and/or birthdates can be used to distinguish them. Only if neither are available does LC then make a search to identify the names for which forename initials stand.[17]

RULE 22.17.   ADDITIONS TO NAMES ENTERED UNDER GIVEN NAME, ETC.

22.17A.   Royalty

This rule in *AACR 2* has many specific subsections with accompanying examples. The essence of the rule is that royal persons are entered under the names by which they are known. These are usually only given names, but if a house, dynasty, or surname is involved, it follows the given name or forename. If there is a roman numeral, it follows the appropriate name. A phrase (in English, if possible) consisting of title and state governed follows next. Other epithets are not added, but are referred from. Consorts, children, and grandchildren of rulers have a title added to their names (again in English, if possible) plus the name of the ruler to whom related. *See* Figs. 17.53 and 17.54.

Fig. 17.53. Rule 22.17A. Entry of royalty.

Entry under royal forename — Nikolaĭ Mikhaĭlovich, Grand Duke of Russia, 1859-1919.

Title and name of state

(Pis′ma vysochaishikh osob k grafinie A. S. Protasovoi)

Письма высочайшихъ особъ къ графинѣ А. С. Протасовой / Великій князь Никогай Михайловичъ. — С.-Петербургъ : Экспедиція заготовленія гос. бумагъ, 1913.

Fig. 17.54. Rule 22.17A. Addition to names of royalty.

Governess.
My life with Caroline / by a governess.

Addition of name of ruler to whom related

1. Caroline, Princess, daughter of Rainier II, Prince of Monaco, 1957-

22.17B.   Popes

22.17C.   Bishops, etc.

22.17D.   Other persons of religious vocation

These rules call for addition of the words *Pope, Bishop, Archbishop, Cardinal,* and other titles in English (if there is an English equivalent) to the names of persons who are high ecclesiastical officials. The name of the latest see is also added to some titles. For other persons of religious vocation who are entered under given name, titles or terms of address are added in the vernacular. Initials of a Christian religious order regularly used by the person, are also added. *See* Figs. 17.55 and 17.56.

Fig. 17.55. Rule 22.17B. Additions to names of popes.

Title
added in
English

John Paul II, Pope, 1920-
    Easter vigil and other poems / translated from
the Polish by Jerzy Peterkiewicz

**Fig. 17.56. Rule 22.17D. Additions to names of persons of
religious vocation.**

Mead, Jude
    Dove in the cleft : the life of Mother Mary
Crucified of Jesus, C.P., the first Passionist nun,
1713-1787 / Jude Mead.
Title added in vernacular
    1. Maria Crocifissa di Gesu, madre, 1713-1787

Two of LC's "compatible" categories occur with these rules. In one category, former rules allowed the abbreviation of "Archbishop" and "Bishop." Where these are the only variations from *AACR 2* in a heading, LC will continue to use the established form. *See* Fig. 17.57.

**Fig. 17.57. Rule 22.17C. Entry of Bishops, etc.—
LC compatible heading.**

Established heading: Baldwin, Abp. of Canterbury, d. 1190.
Judgment: only discord with AACR 2 is abbreviation of
    Archbishop
Established heading retained.

The other compatible category occurring here has to do with the vernacular form of the title. If the heading has used an English title where the vernacular is now prescribed, it will not be changed. *See* Fig. 17.58.

**Fig. 17.58. Rule 22.17D. Entry of "other persons of religious vocation"—
LC compatible heading.**

Established heading: Maria Teresa, Sister, 1901-
AACR 2 would prescribe: "suor" in place of "Sister."
Established heading retained.

ADDITIONS TO DISTINGUISH IDENTICAL NAMES

RULE 22.18. DATES

"Add a person's dates (birth, death, etc.) as the last element of a heading if the heading is otherwise identical to another." *See* Figs. 17.59-17.63.

Fig. 17.59. Rule 22.18. Addition of dates for a living person.

Parkinson, Cyril Northcote, 1909-

Fig. 17.60. Rule 22.18. Addition of dates when references differ as to year of birth; 1496 is probable.

Fox, Edward, Bishop of Hereford, 1496?-1538.

Fig. 17.61. Rule 22.18. Addition of dates when year of birth unknown.

Timberlake, Henry, d. 1626.

Fig. 17.62. Rule 22.18. Addition of dates when years of birth and death unknown, but date of activity is known. (Not used for twentieth century.)

Gardiner, Richard, fl. 1599-1603.

Note: "fl." is the *AACR 2* abbreviation for "flourished"

Fig. 17.63. Rule 22.18. Day, month, and year of birth added to distinguish from others of same name, and same year of birth.

Fischer, John, 1910 Apr. 27-

There is an option to this rule: "Add the dates to all personal names, even if there is no need to distinguish between headings." LC has decided to follow this option *if* the information is readily available.[18]

Two more of LC's "compatible" categories occur with this rule. Earlier rules positioned "ca." within parentheses following the date when a year was uncertain by several years. It should now precede the date and not be enclosed in parentheses. LC will not make this change. *See* Fig. 17.64.

Fig. 17.64. Rule 22.18. Addition of probable dates—
LC compatible heading.

Established heading: Ford, John, 1586(ca.)-1640.
AACR 2 form: Ford, John, ca.1586-1640.
Established heading retained.

The other "compatible" category here involves the *AACR 1* practice of using flourishing dates ("fl.") for twentieth century as well as earlier names. Such headings will not be revised until actual birthdates become available. *See* Fig. 17.65.

Fig. 17.65. Rule 22.18. Addition of "fl." dates—
LC compatible heading.

Established heading: Hollis, John, fl.1976-
AACR 2 form: Hollis, John
[This heading is prescribed even though it does not
distinguish this person from others with the same name.]
Established heading retained until birthdate becomes available.

RULE 22.19. DISTINGUISHING TERMS

RULE 22.20. UNDIFFERENTIATED NAMES

When dates are not available to distinguish between identical names, certain other additions may be made following Rule 22.19. For given names, a brief term may be devised (e.g., "poet") and added in parentheses. For surname entries, a term of address, title of position, initials of academic degree, etc., that appear with the name in works or reference sources may be added. *See* Fig. 17.66. Otherwise, according to Rule 22.20 the same heading is used for all persons with the same name.

Fig. 17.66. Rule 22.19. Distinguishing term added.

Chapman, William H., M.A.

LC's final personal name "compatible" category involves a cataloger-supplied addition of place of residence or field of interest. Such additions are not allowed by *AACR 2*, but will not be removed from established headings. *See* Fig. 17.67.

**Fig. 17.67. Rule 22.20. Additions to undifferentiated names—
LC compatible heading.**

Established headings that will be retained:

Smith, John, of Mountague Close, Southwark.

Edwards, Jan, Librarian.

FOOTNOTES

[1]"Implementation of AACR 2 at the Library of Congress," *Cataloging Service Bulletin*, no. 6 (Fall 1979):5-8.

[2]"Rule Interpretations for AACR 2: Chapter 22," *Cataloging Service Bulletin*, no. 6 (Fall 1979):10.

[3]"Rule Interpretations," p. 9.

[4]For examples of references, see the chapter on references in this text.

[5]"Rule Interpretations," p. 12.

[6]"Rule Interpretations," p. 10.

[7]"Rule Interpretations," p. 10.

[8]"Rule Interpretations," p. 9.

[9]"Rule Interpretations," pp. 10-11.

[10]"Rule Interpretations," p. 11.

[11]"Rule Interpretations," pp. 10-11.

[12]"Rule Interpretations," p. 11.

[13]"Rule Interpretations," p. 12.

[14]"AACR 2 Options to be Followed by the Library of Congress: Chapters 1-2, 12, 21-26," *Library of Congress Information Bulletin*, 37 (July 21, 1978):426.

[15]"Rule Interpretations," p. 13.

[16]"AACR 2 Options," p. 426.

[17]"Rule Interpretations," p. 9.

[18]"AACR 2 Options," p. 426.

18 FORM OF HEADINGS FOR GEOGRAPHIC NAMES

INTRODUCTION

This chapter covers chapter 23 in *AACR 2* which treats the form of heading for any geographic name that may be used as a main or added entry heading. This includes names for places that are now or once were jurisdictional entities. It does not include names that cannot be jurisdictions, such as continents, mountains, and rivers. Yet there is an attempt in *AACR 2* to separate rules for place names that are "only" geographic names from those that are names of jurisdictions. Therefore, one rule in chapter 24, "Headings for Corporate Bodies" (Rule 24.6), deals with what seem to be geographic names; but the rule actually deals with jurisdictions. Another rule, 24.3E, covers "conventional" names of governments and gives instructions to use the geographic name as constructed in chapter 23. Other rules throughout chapter 24 cover additions of geographic names to corporate names for the purpose of identification or distinction. It can be seen, then, that the cataloger cannot rely solely on chapter 23 for the construction of names that appear to be geographic.

In this chapter there are rules for choice of name (23.2-23.3), additions to place names (23.4), and modification of place names (23.5). Problems involved in choice of name generally involve choice between an English form and a form in some other language. Choice may also involve which name to use when the name of a place has changed. For additions to place names, problems involve decisions about which larger place names are most useful for identification. (For example, should the name of the county, state, and/or country be added to the name of a town?) A problem that may require modification of a name involves the use of a term indicating type of jurisdiction. The problem is whether that term comes first, while the name is commonly known or listed under another element of the name (e.g., Kreis Lippe, a county in West Germany, is commonly listed under Lippe). The purpose of this chapter is to demonstrate the rules used to resolve these problems.

RULE 23.2. GENERAL RULES

These general rules involve choice of a name from among variant forms of a name that may be found. The official source used by the Library of Congress for the establishment of geographic names is the U.S. Board on Geographic Names (BGN). However, if the BGN authorizes only a vernacular form when an English form can be determined to be in general use, the English form is used.[1]

23.2A.   English form

"Use the English form of the name of a place if there is one in general use. Determine this from gazetteers and other reference sources published in English-speaking countries. In case of doubt, use the vernacular form (see 23.2B)." *See* Fig. 18.1.

Fig. 18.1 – Rule 23.2A. Geographic name entered under English form of name.

[1]English form
in general use

Forms of name found: Brasil
                              Brazil ←——1
AACR 2 heading: Brazil

Forms of name found: Bucharest ←——1
                              Bucuresti
                              Bucuresci
                              Bukharest
                              Bucarest
AACR 2 heading: Bucharest (Romania)

Forms of name found: Rome ←——1
                              Roma
AACR 2 heading: Rome (Italy)

Certain of the examples given in *AACR 2* for geographic names are not being followed by LC. BGN approves both "Union of Soviet Socialist Republics" (the form used in *AACR 2*) and "Soviet Union" (the form used by LC in the past). LC is continuing to use "Soviet Union." *AACR 2* uses "United Kingdom" in examples where "Great Britain" has been used in the past. However, "Great Britain" can be thought of as the conventional name for "United Kingdom of Great Britain and Northern Ireland." In addition, libraries in Britain wish to continue using "Great Britain." Therefore, LC continues to use the heading "Great Britain." Other decisions include use of "Germany (West)" for Federal Republic of Germany, "Germany (East)" for German Democratic Republic, "Korea (North)" for Democratic People's Republic of Korea, "Korea (South)" for Republic of Korea. For Washington, D.C., LC will use "District of Columbia" as the heading for the government of this name, with "Washington (D.C.)" used only as a location qualifier or as the entry element for cross references from place.[2]

23.2B.   Vernacular form

23.2B1.   "Use the form in the official language of the country if there is no English form in general use." *See* Fig. 18.2 (page 332).

**Fig. 18.2—Rule 23.2B1. Geographic name entered under
vernacular form of name.**

AACR 2 headings: [no English form in use]	Pistoia (Italy) Tétaigne (France) Tromsø (Norway)
AACR 2 heading: [English form not in general use]	Braunschweig (West Germany) [English form: Brunswick]

23.2B2.   "If the country has more than one official language, use the
form most commonly found in English-language sources." *See* Fig. 18.3.

Fig. 18.3.

Forms of name found: Bruxelles
                         Brüssel
                         Brussels

Form most often found in English-language sources:
                         Brussels

AACR 2 heading: Brussels (Belgium)

Note: There is no rule for variations of spelling of the name in the same
language. Because of the close association in the rules of geographic names
and corporate names, it is assumed that needed rules, such as the one for spelling, may be taken from chapter 24 and applied to geographic names:
"If variant spellings of the name appear . . . , use the form resulting from an
official change in orthography, or, if this does not apply, use the predominant
spelling" (24.2C). *See* Fig. 18.4.

Fig. 18.4—Entry of name with variant spellings.

Original spelling: Tandjungpinang, Indonesia
New official spelling: Tanjungpinang, Indonesia
Variants also found: Tandjoengpinang
                      Tandjung Pinang
                      Tanjung Pinang
AACR 2 heading: Tanjungpinang (Indonesia)

RULE 23.3. CHANGES OF NAME

"If the name of a place changes, use as many of the names as are required by:

    a)   the rules on government names (24.3E) . . .

or b)   the rules on additions to corporate names (24.4C6) and conference names (24.7B4) . . .

or c)   other relevant rules in chapter 24."

The essence of this rule is that like corporate bodies, if the name of a place changes, the old name is used for items to which that name is appropriate, and the new name is used for items appropriate to it. The old and new names are connected with "see also" references. *See* Figs. 18.5 and 18.6.

Fig. 18.5—Rule 23.3. Use of more than one name for the same place.

In 1971, the Town of Whitchurch-Stouffville was created, incorporating the Village of Stouffville in Ontario.

    An item requiring Stouffville as a heading prior to 1971 would use the heading:
        Stouffville (Ont.)

    An item requiring Stouffville as a heading in 1971 or later would use the heading:
        Stouffville (Whitchurch-Stouffville, Ont.)

Fig. 18.6—Rule 23.3. Use of latest geographic name as an addition to a corporate body.

In 1971 East Pakistan became Bangladesh. A corporate body whose lifetime spanned the change would have the latest name of the country added, even for items relevant only to the body during the time the country was known as East Pakistan, e.g.,
        Institution of Engineers (Bangladesh)
   not Institution of Engineers (East Pakistan)

RULE 23.4. ADDITIONS TO PLACE NAMES

23.4A.   Punctuation

"Make all additions to place names used as entry elements (see 24.3E) in parentheses."

    e.g., Staunton (Va.)

"If the place name is being used as an addition, precede the name of a larger place by a comma."

> e.g., Second Presbyterian Church (Staunton, Va.)

23.4B.   General rule

"If it is necessary to distinguish between two or more places of the same name . . . , add to each name the name of a larger place as instructed in 23.4C-23.4J. For instructions on abbreviating place names used as additions, see Appendix B.14.

"*Optionally*, apply rules 23.4C-23.4J even if there is no need to distinguish between places.

"*Optionally*, if the name of a state, province, or territory of Australia, Canada, or the United States; of a British county; of a constituent state of Malaysia, the U.S.S.R., or Yugoslavia; or of an island is being used as an addition (see 23.4C-23.4F), do not add to it the name of a larger geographic area."

These two options are being applied selectively by the Library of Congress. The first is applied to all cities and towns, and to all other entities except those named in the second option, with the addition of regions and islands areas in the British Isles (the second option includes only British counties). Then, the second option is applied as stated.[3] The effect of these applications is that all U.S., Canadian, etc., cities have a larger place name added (state, province, etc.), but the larger place name itself does not have yet a larger place name added to *it*.

> e.g., San Francisco (Calif.)
> *not* San Francisco (Calif., U.S.)
> *and* California
> *not* California (U.S.)

It should be noted that if a larger place falling under the second option has a smaller place of the same name within it, a term should be added to the larger place according to 24.6.

> e.g., heading for the city:
> New York (N.Y.)

> e.g., heading for the state:
> New York (State)

The examples in this section are given according to LC's use of the options.

23.4C.   Places in Australia, Canada, or the United States

Add the name of the state, province, or territory of Australia, Canada, or the United States to a place located there. Places located in cities are treated according to 23.4G.

> e.g., Delmont (Pa.)
> Montreal (Québec)
> Melbourne (Vic.)

23.4D.   **Places in the British Isles**

23.4D1.   **Counties, etc.**

"Add to the name of a county, region, or islands area in the British Isles used as entry element in a heading *England, Ireland* (for counties in the Republic of Ireland), *Northern Ireland, Scotland*, or *Wales*, as appropriate."

> e.g., Antrim (Northern Ireland)
> Warwickshire (England)
> Ayrshire (Scotland)

23.4D2.   **Other places (other than places in cities, see 23.4G).**

"If a place is in England, Wales, or the Republic of Ireland, add the name of the county in which it is located."

> e.g., Cambridge (Cambridgeshire)
> Mold (Flintshire)
> Tralee (Kerry)

"If a place is in Scotland, add the name of the region or islands area."

> e.g., Kirkwall (Orkney Islands)

"If a place is in Northern Ireland, add *Northern Ireland*."

> e.g., Londonderry (Northern Ireland)

23.4E.   **Places in Malaysia, the U.S.S.R., or Yugoslavia**

"If a place is in a constituent state of Malaysia, the U.S.S.R., or Yugoslavia, add the name of the state."

> e.g., Moscow (R.S.F.S.R.)
> Kiev (Ukraine)
> Tbilisi (Georgian S.S.R.)

Note: For the constituent republics of the Soviet Union, use the following headings:[4]

Armenian S.S.R.	Lithuania
Azerbaijan S.S.R.	Moldavian S.S.R.
Byelorussian S.S.R.	Russian S.F.S.R.
Estonia	Tadzhik S.S.R.
Georgian S.S.R.	Turkmen S.S.R.
Kazakh S.S.R.	Ukraine
Kirghiz S.S.R.	Uzbek S.S.R.
Latvia	

23.4F.   **Places on islands**

"If a place is on an island and the name of the island or island group is predominantly associated with the name of the place, add the name of the island or island group."

> e.g., Palermo (Sicily)
> Palma (Majorca)
> Mount Stewart (Prince Edward Island)

Note that local places on islands that have previously been established with the name of the country or other jurisdiction as qualifier should now be qualified with the name of the island or island group.

23.4G.   Places in cities

"If a place is in a city, add the name of the city. Refer from the name of the city followed by the name of the place."

> e.g., Bregninge (Svendborg, Denmark)
> Refer from: Svendborg (Denmark). Bregninge
>
> Georgetown (Washington, D.C.)
> Refer from: Washington (D.C.). Georgetown

23.4H.   Other places

"Add to the names of places not covered by 23.4C-23.4G the name of the country in which the place is located."

> e.g., Lund (Sweden)
> Siena (Italy)
> Rio de Janiero (Brazil)

RULE 23.5. PLACE NAMES INCLUDING A TERM INDICATING A TYPE OF JURISDICTION

23.5A.   "If the first part of a place name is a term indicating a type of jurisdiction and the place is commonly listed under another element of its name in lists published in the language of the country in which it is located, omit the term indicating the type of jurisdiction."

> e.g., Kreise Lippe in West Germany is commonly
> listed under Lippe in German lists.
> Heading: Lippe (West Germany)

Note: The examples in *AACR 2*, as mentioned earlier, "are illustrative and not prescriptive" (Rule 0.14). It is worth mentioning that examples in chapter 23 that show "(Germany)" as an addition, are not correct because of the division of the country into two areas that need to be distinguished. For correct example *see* Fig. 18.2 (p. 332) in this text.

"In all other cases include the term indicating the type of jurisdiction."

> e.g., Dutchess County (N.Y.)

Note: The term "county" should be included for U.S. counties, even though many U.S. atlases list counties by name only under the caption "counties" and therefore omit the word "county" with the name. Note that "county" is now spelled out. Most U.S. counties have been established by LC and other libraries in the past using "Co." and will now be changed by LC as new occasions for use of each county name arise.

23.5B.　　　　"If a place name does not include a term indicating a type of jurisdiction and such a term is required to distinguish that place from another of the same name, follow the instructions in 24.6.

　　　　e.g.,　Chimaltenango (Guatemala : Department)

　　　　[there is also a municipality named Chimaltenango]

Note: LC will continue to abbreviate "Department" as "Dept.," even though it is not allowed in *AACR 2*, Appendix B, "Abbreviations."

FOOTNOTES

[1]"Rule Interpretations for AACR 2: Chapter 23," *Cataloging Service Bulletin*, no. 6 (Fall 1979):15.

[2]"Rule Interpretations," p. 15; and personal communication with Paul W. Winkler, Nov. 1979.

[3]"Rule Interpretations," pp. 15-16.

[4]Personal communication with Paul W. Winkler, Jan. 1980.

19 FORM OF HEADINGS FOR CORPORATE NAMES

INTRODUCTION

This chapter covers the rules for construction of names of corporate bodies. "Corporate body" is defined in 21.1B1. In general, entry of a corporate body is under the name the body itself uses except when the rules specify entry under a higher or related body or under the name of a government. Like the principle in use for personal names, the principle for corporate names is to choose the name the corporate body generally uses (including conventional names), even if that name is not the official one. Unlike personal names, however, when the name of a corporate body changes, a new heading is made under that name with cross references to and from various other former and related names.

Following the general rule (24.1) in this chapter, there are rules for choice of names (24.2-24.3), and for additions, omissions, and modifications (24.4-24.11). These are followed by rules for subordinate and related bodies in general (24.12-24.16), for government bodies and officials (24.17-24.26), and for religious bodies and officials (24.27). Problems involved in choice of name include choice among variant forms found in items issued by a body, such as official name or acronym or short form, choice among variant spellings (including differences in romanization), and choice among different languages. Problems requiring additions, omissions, or other modifications include the need to distinguish two or more bodies with the same name, the need to provide adequate identification for a name that does not convey the idea of a corporate body, the desire to omit unnecessary or excess terms such as "incorporated" or "biennial." In dealing with a subordinate body, the cataloger must decide whether the body can be entered directly under its own name or must be entered under a higher body, and because government and religious bodies present special problems in this area, the cataloger must know whether a subordinate body belongs in one of these two groups before applying the rules. The purpose of this chapter is to demonstrate only the most important problems of corporate entry. For more detail, the cataloger should consult *AACR 2*, chapter 24.

As with personal names, there are certain previously established headings for corporate bodies that LC is considering "*AACR 2* compatible." These are discussed with the pertinent rule.

GENERAL RULES

RULE 24.1. BASIC RULE

"Enter a corporate body directly under the name by which it is predominantly identified, except when the rules that follow provide for entering it under the name of a higher or related body (see 24.13) or under the name of a government (see 24.18).

"Determine the form of name of a corporate body from items issued by that body in its language (see also 24.3A), or, when this condition does not apply, from reference sources.

"If the name of a corporate body consists of or contains initials, omit or include full stops and other marks of punctuation according to the predominant usage of the body. In case of doubt, omit the full stops, etc. Do not leave a space between a full stop, etc., and an initial following it. Do not leave spaces between the letters of an initialism written without full stops, etc.

"Make references from other forms of the name of a corporate body as instructed in 26.3."

> e.g., Lawyer's Committee for Civil Rights Under Law.
>
> W. K. Kellogg Arabian Horse Center.
> Refer from: Kellogg Arabian Horse Center
> *and* Kellogg (W.K.) Arabian Horse Center
>
> Nelliston Community Group.

One of LC's compatible categories occurs under this rule. The rule calls for including punctuation according to the predominant usage of the body. This was not necessarily done in the past. Headings previously established without quotation marks that the body commonly uses will continue to appear without quotation marks. *See* Fig. 19.1.

Fig. 19.1—Rule 24.1. Use of punctuation—LC Compatible heading.

[1]**Heading without quotation marks** Symposium Pro Musica Antiqua Prag.
        Musik am Kaiserhof [sound recording] / Symposium
        "Pro Musica Antiqua" Prag.

[2]**Usage of performing group includes quotation marks**

New headings *will* be established with quotation marks, but if other languages use a different style of quotation marks from ours, LC will establish the name using American-style double quotation marks.[1]

It should also be noted here that for a corporate name that includes the name of a place at the end, the punctuation used by the body will be retained. This means that some names may be established ending with a place preceded by a comma and a space, and others may be established with a place enclosed in parentheses. These have nothing to do with the additions prescribed in 24.4 and should not be interpreted as "errors,"

> e.g., University of California, San Diego
> *not* University of California (San Diego)

24.1A.   Romanization

"If the name of the body is in a language written in a nonroman script, romanize the name according to the table for that language adopted by the cataloguing agency. Refer from other romanizations as necessary." This means that even if a romanized form of the name appears in items issued by a body, that form may be used only if it corresponds to the table adopted by the cataloging agency.

A footnote in *AACR 2* allows an alternative to this rule: a romanized form appearing in items issued by the body is used with references from other romanizations. The Library of Congress is not applying the alternative rule.[2] *See* Fig. 19.2.

Fig. 19.2 — Rule 24.1A. Romanization of names originally in nonroman script. Also illustrates Rule 24.3A: Use of the form in the official language of the body. Refer from the English form of the names.

Corporate names entered under romanized form

Akademiĭa nauk SSSR. ←

Noctilucent clouds : optical properties / Academy of Sciences of the U.S.S.R., Soviet Geophysical Committee, and Institute of Physics and Astronomy of the Academy of Sciences of the Estonian S.S.R.

Make added entries for romanized forms of names:

I. Akademiĭa nauk SSSR. Mezhduvedomstvennyĭ geofizicheskiĭ komitet. II. Eesti NSV Teaduste Akadeemia. Füüsika ja Astronoomia Instituut.

24.1B.   Changes of name

"If the name of a corporate body has changed (including change from one language to another), establish a new heading under the new name for items appearing under that name. Refer from the old heading to the new and from the new heading to the old (see 26.3C)." *See* Fig. 19.3.

Fig. 19.3—Rule 24.1B. Entry under each name a
corporate body has used.

Entry under   The Long Range Planning Service of the Stanford Research
three names   Institute became the Business Intelligence Program in April
1976. On May 19, 1977, the Institute changed its name to
S.R.I. International.

Works by these bodies are found under the following headings according to the name used at the time of publication:

⟶ Stanford Research Institute. Long Range Planning Service.

⟶ Stanford Research Institute. Business Intelligence Program.

⟶ S.R.I. International. Business Intelligence Program.

RULE 24.2.   VARIANT NAMES.   GENERAL RULES

Variant names here do not include those resulting from official changes of
names. Such changes are covered by 24.1B.

24.2B.   "If variant forms of the name are found in items issued by the
body, use the name as it appears in the chief sources of information. . . ." *See*
Fig. 19.4.

Fig. 19.4—Rule 24.2B. Entry of name having variant forms.

Name on title page: Michael Bradner Associates
Forms of name found elsewhere in work:
   Mike Bradner & Associates
   Mike Bradner and Associates
AACR 2 heading: Michael Bradner Associates
Refer from: Mike Bradner and Associates
         Bradner Associates

24.2C.   "If variant spellings of the name appear in items issued by the
body, use the form resulting from an official change in orthography, or if this
does not apply, use the predominant spelling." *See* Fig. 19.5.

Fig. 19.5—Rule 24.2C. Entry of name having variant spellings.

Name on some title pages:
   Allgemeines deutsches Commersbuch
Name on most title pages:
   Allgemeines deutsches Kommersbuch
AACR 2 heading: Allgemeines deutsches Kommersbuch
Refer from: Allgemeines deutsches Commersbuch

24.2D.   "If variant forms appear in the chief source of information, use the form that is presented formally. If no form is presented formally, or if all forms are presented formally, use the predominant form.

"If there is no predominant form, use a brief form (including an initialism or an acronym) that would differentiate between the body and others with the same or similar brief names." *See* Fig. 19.6.

Fig. 19.6 — Rule 24.2D. Entry under brief form of name.

Names on title page: GAAG, the Guerrilla Art Action
    Group
Neither form formally presented. No predominant form.
AACR 2 heading: GAAG.
Refer from: Guerrilla Art Action Group

Another of LC's compatible headings is related to this rule. When the brief form of name consists of initials, Appendix A, Rule 1 instructs the cataloger to capitalize such initials according to the predominant usage of the body. Older rules, however, required construction of such headings as a "word" with only the first letter capitalized. When such already-established headings would be formed with all the letters capitalized, LC will continue to use the established form unless the initials are "famous." *See* Fig. 19.7.

Fig. 19.7 — Rule 24.2D. Capitalization (Appendix A.1).
Capitalization of acronym — LC compatible heading.

Established heading: Arel.
Usage of body: AREL [initials of Agenzia di recerche e
    legislazione]
Judgment: initials are not famous
Established heading retained.

RULE 24.3. VARIANT NAMES. SPECIAL RULES

24.3A.   **Language**

"If the name appears in different languages, use the form in the official language of the body. . . .

"If there is more than one official language and one of these is English, use the English form. . . ."

If the above does not apply, the order of preference is as follows: the predominant language; then English, French, German, Spanish, or Russian; then the language that comes first in English alphabetic order. *See* Fig. 19.8.

Fig. 19.8 — Rule 24.3A. Entry of name found in different languages.

Names on publications:
  Schweizerische Hochschulrektoren-Konferenz,
      Kommission für Hochschulplanung
  Commission de planification de la Conférence
      des recteurs des unwersites suisses
Official language: German
AACR 2 heading: Schweizerische Hochschulrektoren
    -Konferenz. Kommission für Hochschulplanung.
Refer from French form.

An alternative to this rule allows use of a form of language appropriate to the catalog's users if the application of the rule results in a language not familiar to the users. LC is not following this alternative because a national library cannot cater to individual library users.[3]

24.3B.   Language. International bodies

"If the name of an international body appears in English on items issued by it, use the English form. In other cases, follow 24.3A." *See* Figs. 19.9 and 19.10.

**Fig. 19.9 — Rule 24.3B. Entry of international body
when the name appears in English.**

Names on title page:
  al-Maṣrif al-'Arabī lil-Tanmiyah al-Iqtiṣādīyah
      fī Afrīqiyā
  Arab Bank for Economic Development in Africa
  Banque Arabe de développement économique en
      Afrique
AACR 2 heading: Arab Bank for Economic Development
    in Africa
Refer from the names in Arabic and French.

**Fig. 19.10 — Rule 24.3B. Entry of international body when the
name is not in English on its publications.**

Forms of name used on publications:
  Nederlandse Vereniging voor Internationaal
      Recht
  NVIR [full form predominant]
English equivalent: Netherlands Branch of the International
    Law Association
    [English not used on its publications]
AACR 2 heading: Nederlandse Vereniging voor
    International Recht
Refer from English equivalent.

24.3C.   Conventional name

24.3C1.   General rule

"If a body is frequently identified by a conventional form of name in reference sources in its own language, use this conventional name." *See* Fig. 19.11.

Fig. 19.11 — Rule 24.3C1. Entry under conventional name.

[1] Conventional name

[2] Official name

Bury St. Edmunds Abbey.
    The customary of the Benedictine Abbey of Bury St. Edmunds in Suffolk : (from Harleian MS. 1005 in the British Museum) / edited by Antonia Gransden.

24.3C2.   Ancient and international bodies

"If the name of a body of ancient origin or of one that is international in character has become firmly established in an English form in English language usage, use this English form." A footnote comments that this rule applies to such bodies as religious bodies, fraternal and knightly orders, Church councils, and diplomatic conferences. *See* Fig. 19.12.

Fig. 19.12 — Rule 24.3C2. Entry under English form of conventional names of international bodies.

Orthodox Eastern Church, Greek.
    [Hēmerologion tēs Ekklēsias tēs Hellados]
    Ἡμερολόγιον τῆς Ἐκκλησίας τῆς Ἑλλάδος.

English form of names

Catholic Church. Canadian Catholic Conference.
    Messages des évêques canadiens à l'occasion de la Fête du travail (1956-1974) / présentation de Richard Arès.

24.3D.   Religious orders and societies

"Use the best-known form of name for a religious order or society." An English form is preferred, if one exists. Otherwise, the language of the country of origin is used. *See* Fig. 19.13.

Fig. 19.13—Rule 24.3D. Entry of religious orders and societies.

White Fathers.
   Annexes des Archives de la Maison généralice des Pères blancs = Documents in the Annexe of the Archives of the Generalate of the White Fathers.

Name of religious order or society

Société de Saint Vincent de Paul à Marseille.
   La Société de Saint-Vincent de Paul à Marseille : histoire d'un siècle (1844-1944).

24.3E.   Governments

"Use the conventional name of a government, unless the official name is in common use. The conventional name of a government is the geographic name (see chapter 23) of the area (country, province, state, county, municipality, etc.) over which the government exercises jurisdiction."

   e.g., Jersey City (N.J.)
   not   City of Jersey City

   Korea (North)
   not   Democratic People's Republic of Korea

   San Marino
   not   Most Serene Republic of San Marino

24.3F.   Conferences, congresses, meetings, etc.

"If the variant forms of a conference name appearing in the chief source of information include a form that includes the name or abbreviation of the name of a body associated with the meeting, use this form. . . .

"If, however, the name or abbreviation of a name is of a body to which the meeting is subordinate (e.g., the annual meeting of an association), see 24.13." *See* Fig. 19.14.

Fig. 19.14—Rule 24.3F. Entry of a conference under form of name that includes initials of the bodies associated with the meeting.

Name of meeting: ALI-ABA Course of Study : Legal
   Issues in the Coal Industry
Name appears both with and without the initials of the
   American Law Institute and the American Bar
   Association
AACR 2 heading: ALI-ABA Course of Study : Legal Issues
   in the Coal Industry (1978 : Washington, D.C.)
Refer from: Course of Study : Legal Issues in the Coal
   Industry (1978 : Washington, D.C.)

ADDITIONS, OMISSIONS, AND MODIFICATIONS

RULE 24.4. ADDITIONS

24.4A.　　General rule

"Make additions to the names of corporate bodies as instructed in 24.4B-24.4C.

"For additions to special types of corporate bodies (e.g., governments, conferences), see 24.6-24.11. Enclose in parentheses all additions required by these and other rules in this chapter."

24.4B.　　Names not conveying the idea of a corporate body

"If the name alone does not convey the idea of a corporate body, add a general designation in English."

> e.g.,　ABBA (Musical group)

> Prévention routière internationale (Association)

> But (Yacht)

This is another category in which LC has decided to consider an already-established heading as compatible. If an established heading includes such a term that would not now be considered necessary, or conversely, if an established heading lacks such a term now thought to be needed, the established heading will be retained. *See* Fig. 19.15.

Fig. 19.15 — Rule 24.4B. Addition of term to convey idea of corporate body — LC compatible heading.

Established heading: Desert Bicyclists
Term needed to convey idea of a corporate body:
　Desert Bicyclists (Society)
Established heading retained.

24.4C.　　Two or more bodies with the same or similar names

24.4C1.　　General rule

"If two or more bodies have the same name, or names so similar that they may be confused, add a word or phrase to each name as instructed in 24.4C2-24.4C10. . . .

"*Optionally*, apply rules 24.4C2-24.4C10 even if there is no need to distinguish between bodies."

The Library of Congress is following the option given here "on a limited, case-by-case basis, [because they] feel that certain corporate headings, although not conflicting, would be more identifiable to the user if they were qualified, primarily by means of a geographic qualifier."[4] However, if a name is already established without a qualifier, the qualifier will not be added (in a non-conflict situation) even if the name is one to which the option would now be applied. Such an established heading will be considered "compatible" and retained. *See* Fig. 19.16.

Fig. 19.16—Rule 24.4C1. Optional addition of qualifier to corporate name—LC compatible heading.

Established heading: Psychological Research Academy
More useful for identification would be:
    Psychological Research Academy (Calcutta, India)
Established heading retained.

Further explanation of LC's application of the option to new names has been published in *Cataloging Service Bulletin*. The appropriate qualifier is added to a name "if it is judged likely that a conflict may arise in the future." This judgment is made if a name lacks distinctive elements. Examples given include: Computer Hardware Management Center, Institute of Strategic Studies, and National Irrigation Research Station. When in doubt about whether names are indistinctive, the qualifier is added. Exception, however, is made for business firms. LC does not add qualifiers to such names unless there is a conflict.[5]

24.4C2-24.4C10.

Rules 24.4C2-24.4C7 authorize addition of place names—country, state, province, etc.—for a body that is national, provincial, etc., in character, or of local place names for a body whose character is essentially local. If a place is not appropriate, 24.4C8-24.4C10 provide for addition of the name of an institution, the inclusive years of existence, or some other appropriate general designation in English. *See* Figs. 19.17 and 19.18.

Fig. 19.17—Rule 24.4C2. Addition of country to corporate name.

National Committee on the Status of Women (India).
    Status of women : report to the Government / National Committee on the Status of Women.

Note: This name could be held by similar groups in several countries. Therefore the name of the country is added.

(Fig. 19.18 is on page 348)

Fig. 19.18—Rule 24.4C4. Addition of local place name to corporate name.

Valley Medical Center (Fresno, Calif.)
    Recent advances in burn therapy / Valley
Medical Center.

Note: This name is more identifiable with the addition of its location.

It should be noted that when a place is used as a qualifier, if it is a place that is itself qualified by a larger place according to chapter 23, the smaller and the larger place are both used in the qualifier of the corporate body. Thus, for a corporate body in Oklahoma City, the name of the city alone cannot be used as qualifier. It must be: (Oklahoma City, Okla.). *See also* Fig. 19.18.

RULE 24.5. OMISSIONS

24.5A-24.5C.

These rules require omission of certain elements from corporate names: initial articles are omitted unless required for grammatical reasons; terms indicating incorporation, etc., are omitted unless they are an integral part of the name or are needed to clarify the fact that the name is that of a corporate body. Other required omissions occur in rare instances, and the cataloger should consult *AACR 2* for them. *See* Figs. 19.19, 19.20, and 19.21.

Fig. 19.19—Rule 24.5A. Entry of name omitting initial article.

**Initial
article
omitted**
   / News (New York, N.Y.)
      European round trip / The News.

**Fig. 19.20—Rule 24.5C1. Entry of name omitting term
indicating incorporation.**

Name appearing on publications:
    Firestone Tire and Rubber Company, Inc.
Judgment: "Inc." not necessary for clarification as a
    corporate body
Heading: Firestone Tire and Rubber Company

**Fig. 19.21—Rule 24.5C1. Entry of name retaining term
indicating incorporation.**

**Term of
incorporation
retained**
  A Week full of Saturdays [motion picture]

      [Produced and distributed by Alternate Choice, Inc.]
    I. Alternate Choice, Inc.

Another of LC's "compatible" categories is associated with this rule. If a heading has been established using a term of incorporation that should now be deleted, the established heading will be retained. Even if such a term should be included, all headings of this type established prior to *AACR 2* are considered "compatible" because "inc." and "ltd." were used with lower case letters but would now be capitalized. *See* Fig. 19.22.

Fig. 19.22 — Rule 24.5C1. Entry of name with term of incorporation not capitalized — LC compatible heading.

Established heading: Volkswagen of America, inc.
AACR 2 heading: Volkswagen of America, Inc.
Established heading retained.

RULE 24.6. GOVERNMENT ADDITIONS

As mentioned in the chapter on geographic names, this rule is an attempt to give directions for entry of names of jurisdictions — distinct from the rules given for strictly geographic names. However, they are not totally separate, because this rule says that if names have not been differentiated by use of Rule 23.4, then further addition according to this rule should be made.

LC has elaborated upon how it will interpret this rule, because it is not clear from the rule whether additions should be made to *both* conflicting names in all cases:

"When a succession of jurisdictions would be entered under the same name, use one heading for all, no matter what differences there are between the jurisdictions.

	North Carolina		Hawaii
not	North Carolina (Colony)	*not*	Hawaii (Kingdom)
	North Carolina (State)		Hawaii (Republic)

"Do not qualify the name of a sovereign nation when it conflicts with the name of another place that is not a sovereign nation.

Italy
Italy (Tex.)."[6]

A third elaboration on this rule distinguishes between situations where the name of a place within a jurisdiction conflicts with the name of the jurisdiction, and situations where the name of a jurisdiction conflicts with the name of a place in another jurisdiction. In the first situation, the name of the larger jurisdiction is qualified with the name of the type of government, e.g.:

	Québec (Québec)	[name of city]
not	Québec (Province)	[name of larger jurisdiction]

In the second situation, only the name of the place in another jurisdiction is qualified,

> e.g., Alberta (Va.)
> Alberta
> *not* Alberta (Province)

An exception is made for the state of Washington. It is entered:

> Washington (State)[7]

24.6B. "Add the type of jurisdiction in English if other than a city or a town. If there is no English equivalent for the vernacular term, use the vernacular term."

> e.g., São Paulo (Brazil)
> São Paulo (Brazil : State)
> Alessandria (Italy : Province)
> Esberg (Denmark : Kommune)
> Detmold (West Germany : Landkreis)

RULE 24.7. CONFERENCES, CONGRESSES, MEETINGS, ETC.

24.7A. Omissions

"Omit from the name of a conference, etc. words that denote its number, frequency, or year of convocation." *See* Fig. 19.23.

Fig. 19.23—Rule 24.7A. Omission of number from name of conference.

Name on title page: II Jornadas de Derecho Natural
Heading: Jornadas de Derecho Natural . . .

24.7B. Additions

24.7B1. General rule

"Add to conference, etc., headings (including headings for conferences entered subordinately, see 24.13) the number of the conference, etc., the year, and the place in which it was held." If any of these elements are not known, they are omitted. *See* Figs. 19.24 and 19.25.

Fig. 19.24—Rule 24.7B. Additions to names of conferences.

[1]Name of
conference   Symposium on Viral Hepatitis (2nd : 1978 : University
[2]Number   of California San Francisco) ◄——— 4
[3]Date   Second Symposium on Viral Hepatitis, University
[4]Place   of California San Francisco, Mar. 16-19, 1978.

Fig. 19.25—Rule 24.7B. Additions to names of conferences.

¹Name of conference

²Date

³Place

International Congress on Ocular Trauma (1976 : Boston, Mass.)

Ocular trauma : International Congress on Ocular Trauma at Boston

RULE 24.10. LOCAL CHURCHES, ETC.

24.10A. "If the name of a local church, etc. does not convey the idea of a church, etc., add a general designation in English."

> e.g., Santa Maria Bianca della Misericordia (Parish church : Milan, Italy)

24.10B. "Add to the name of a local church, etc., the name of the place or local ecclesiastical jurisdiction (parish, Pfarrei, etc.) in which it is located (see 24.4C4-24.4C6) unless the location is clear from the name itself."

> e.g., Mt. Enon Baptist Church (Mitchell County, Ga.)

LC has noted that it will use any rules in 24.4, not just 24.4C4-24.4C6, in choosing the qualifier to be added to the name of a local church, etc.[8]

SUBORDINATE AND RELATED BODIES

The problem of entry of corporate bodies that are subordinate to or closely related to other bodies is a difficult one. No completely unambiguous set of rules (including *AACR 2*) has yet been devised to handle it. The remainder of chapter 24 of *AACR 2* (Rules 24.12-24.27) deals with such rules; yet even with this exhaustive treatment the end result may still depend upon the judgment of the individual cataloger.

There are three parts to this section: general rules, government body rules, and religious organization rules. The cataloger must first know if a body is a government or religious body. This is important because, in some cases, the results of applying the non-government rules to a government body yield a heading not intended by the makers of the code (e.g., "University of Natal," entered directly according to the sequence of government body rules, would be entered "Natal. University" if the general sequence of rules were applied). However, once into the sequence for government or religious bodies, the cataloger may be referred back to the general sequence for further instructions.

If it is determined that a body is a government body, Rules 24.17-24.26 must be consulted before any others in chapter 24, because a government body is always a subordinate body—that is, it is always subordinate to a jurisdiction. Once into the rules, the result may be the same as if subordination were not involved—that is, the body may be entered under its own name. (For example, the University of California, Los Angeles, a state institution, and the University of Southern California, a private institution, both end up entered under "University of. . . .") But if the body is one of the types listed in 24.18, it will be entered subordinately. If it *is* one of the types listed, then Rule 24.19 for direct or indirect subheading must be consulted; and if it is one of Types 5 through 10, one of Rules 24.20-24.26 must also be consulted. The cataloger must also be concerned with the level of subordinate body involved. If it is subordinate to another government body that is entered under its *own name* because it is not one of the types listed in 24.18, then general Rules 24.12-24.14 must be consulted for formulation of the heading for the subordinate body. If it is subordinate to another body that is entered under *jurisdiction*, then the cataloger continues to use government body Rules 24.17-24.19 for formulation of the heading for the subordinate body.

If it is determined that a body is a religious body, Rule 24.27 and its subparts are consulted first. Certain kinds of religious subordinate bodies are specified for subordinate entry in these rules. All others are to be treated according to general Rules 24.12-24.14.

For all subordinate bodies other than government or religious, the cataloger uses general Rules 24.12-24.16, which refer back to 24.1-24.3 for construction of headings for subordinate bodies that should be entered under their own names.

RULE 24.12. GENERAL RULE

"Enter a subordinate body (other than a government agency entered under jurisdiction, see 24.18) or a related body directly under its own name (see 24.1-24.3) unless its name belongs to one or more of the types listed in 24.13. Refer to the name of a subordinate body entered independently from its name in the form of a subheading of the higher body (see 26.3A7)." *See* Figs. 19.26 and 19.27. [Note the similarity of this rule to 24.17 for government bodies.]

Fig. 19.26—Rule 24.12. Entry of subordinate body under its own name.

Information on title page of exhibition catalog:
    Baxter Art Gallery, California Institute of Technology,
        Pasadena
AACR 2 heading: Baxter Art Gallery.
Refer from: California Institute of Technology, Pasadena.
    Baxter Art Gallery

Fig. 19.27.

Information on title page: National Affiliation for Literacy
    Advance, Laubach Literacy International's pro-
        gramming arm in the U.S. and Canada.
AACR 2 heading: National Affiliation for Literacy Advance.
Refer from: Laubach Literacy International. National
    Affiliation for Literacy Advance

RULE 24.13. SUBORDINATE AND RELATED BODIES ENTERED SUBORDINATELY

"Enter a subordinate or related body as a subheading of the name of the body to which it is subordinate or related if its name belongs to one or more of the following types. Make it a direct or indirect subheading as instructed in 24.14. Omit from the subheading the name or abbreviation of the name of the higher or related body in noun form unless this does not make sense." [Note the similarity of this rule to 12.18 for government bodies. Note also that Types 1-3 in the two rules are nearly identical, but that the other types are quite different.]

TYPE 1. "A name that contains a term that by definition implies that the body is part of another, e.g., department, division, section, branch." *See* Fig. 19.28. LC has identified two additional terms that will be considered to imply that a body is part of another. These are "administrative office" and "secretariat."[9]

Fig. 19.28 — Rule 24.13, Type 1. Subordinate entry of body that is part of another.

Current legal aspects of doing business in the Far East / Section of International Law, American Bar Association.

I. American Bar Association. Section of International Law.

A major category of LC "compatible" headings affects headings constructed by many rules, but it can be illustrated here. LC will continue to abbreviate Department as "Dept." even though this is not authorized by *AACR 2* Appendix B, "Abbreviations." A difference here from other "compatible" headings is that "Dept." will be used in new headings as well as on previously established ones. *See* Fig. 19.29.

Fig. 19.29 — Rule 24.13. Illustration of LC's decision on use of the abbreviation "Dept."

Previously established heading: Notre Dame, Ind. University. Dept. of Economics
LC's new heading under *AACR 2*: University of Notre Dame. Dept. of Economics.
Note: Even though the heading must be reconstructed for other reasons, the abbreviation "Dept." is retained.

TYPE 2. "A name that contains a word normally implying administrative subordination (e.g., committee, commission), providing the name of the higher body is required for the identification of the subordinate body." *See* Fig. 19.30. Note that the two words given in parentheses are only examples. Other terms mentioned by LC for this rule are "administration" and "board." (*See also* the list under 24.18, TYPE 2.) For the second part of the rule, judgment is to be used by LC's catalogers to determine whether the name of the higher body is required for identification. If problems arise with this, LC may develop a rule interpretation.[10]

Fig. 19.30—Rule 24.13, Type 2. Subordinate entry of body that is administratively subordinate to another.

Information on title page: NAIS Teacher Services
   Committee.
Heading: National Association of Independent Schools.
   Teacher Services Committee.
Refer from: NAIS Teacher Services Committee.

TYPE 3. "A name that has been, or is likely to be, used by another higher body for one of its subordinate or related bodies." *See* Fig. 19.31. LC has pointed out that if searching the catalog reveals another body of the same name, then this rule arbitrarily requires subordinate entry no matter how distinctive the name is.[11] Thus, the National Portrait Gallery must be entered subordinately under the Smithsonian Institution because there is also a National Portrait Gallery in London. But the National Collection of Fine Arts, also subordinate to the Smithsonian Institution, can be entered under its own name because there is no other National Collection of Fine Arts.

Concerning the "or is likely to be" provision, LC has commented that this should be applied to "names that one knows are repeated from organization to organization even without any concrete evidence."[12] If too much falls in the "gray area," LC may develop a rule interpretation.

Fig. 19.31—Rule 24.13, Type 3. Subordinate entry of body that has a name likely to be used by another body.

Name in credits of motion picture: Brigham Young University, Media Productions.
Judgment: "Media Productions" is likely to be used by
   many colleges for such a subordinate unit.
Heading: Brigham Young University. Media Productions.

It is TYPE 3 in both 24.13 and 24.18 that is likely to cause the most difficulty in judgment for catalogers. For example, the University College of Botswana has a subordinate body named "National Institute of Development and Cultural Research." Because University College of Botswana, a government body, is entered under its own name, its subordinate bodies are entered according to 24.12 and 24.13. If the cataloger decides that other English language countries are likely to have a "National Institute of Development and Cultural Research," then the heading will be "University College of Botswana. National Institute of Development and Cultural Research." If the judgment is that the name is *not* likely to be used elsewhere, the subordinate body is entered under its own name. In the latter case, the cataloger must then decide whether to add "(Botswana)" to the name according to 24.4C. The difficulty is that if the name seems to need "(Botswana)" for identification, then it seems also to be a "Type 3" heading. Catalogers should watch for further rule interpretations on this issue.

TYPE 4. "A name of a university faculty, school, college, institute, laboratory, etc., that simply indicates a particular field of study." *See* Fig. 19.32.

Fig. 19.32—Rule 24.13, Type 4. Subordinate entry of body that has a name that simply indicates a field of study.

Name on title page: School of Graduate and Professional
    Studies, Emporia State University
Heading: Emporia State University. School of Graduate
    and Professional Studies.

TYPE 5. "A name that includes the entire name of the higher or related body." *See* Fig. 19.33. LC will "base the determination of 'entire name' on the form used in the heading for the higher or related body."[13]

Fig. 19.33—Rule 24.13, Type 5. Subordinate entry of body that has a name that includes the name of the higher body.

Name on title page: Chaucer Group of the Modern
    Language Association
Heading: Modern Language Association of
    America. Chaucer Group.
Note: "of America" is determined from other sources to
    be included in the predominant usage of the higher
    body.

RULE 24.14. DIRECT OR INDIRECT SUBHEADING

"Enter a body belonging to one or more of the types listed in 24.13 as a subheading of the lowest element in the hierarchy that is entered under its own name. Omit intervening elements in the hierarchy unless the name of the subordinate or related body has been, or is likely to be, used by another body entered under the name of the same higher or related body. In that case, interpose the name of the lowest element in the hierarchy that will distinguish between the bodies. . . .

"Refer from the name in the form of a subheading of the name of its immediately superior body when the heading does not include the name of that superior body." [Note the similarity of this rule to 24.19 for government bodies.] *See* Figs. 19.34 and 19.35.

Fig. 19.34—Rule 24.14. Indirect subordinate entry of a section.

Name on title page: University of Washington Libraries, Manuscripts Section
Heading: University of Washington. Libraries. Manuscript Section.

Note: Even though the University of Washington is a government body, its subordinate bodies are entered according to 24.12-24.14 because the University is entered under its own name, not under jurisdiction.

Fig. 19.35—Rule 24.14. Direct subordinate entry of a laboratory.

Name on title page: Radiological Research Laboratory, Department of Radiology, Columbia University, New York, N.Y.
Heading: Columbia University. Radiological Research Laboratory.
Refer from: Columbia University. Dept. of Radiology. Radiological Research Laboratory

---

Omission of elements of a hierarchy is another area where the results of various catalogers' judgments may vary. The words "or is likely to be" will mean differences in judgment. The Library of Congress has identified for its catalogers two categories where judgment should not vary.[14] In the first category, names of bodies performing functions common to many higher bodies (e.g., Personnel Office; Planning Dept.), the hierarchy should be included. In the second category, names of bodies performing major functions unique to the higher body (e.g., Division of Fisheries; Division of Transport [under the Ministry of Transport, Industry, and Engineering]), intervening elements of the hierarchy should be omitted. Common sense must dictate the inclusion of hierarchy for the great middle ground. The cataloger should consider whether the name would be appropriate for another subordinate body within the same higher body structure and whether some word or phrase in a name in the hierarchy expresses an idea necessary to the identification of the subordinate body.

GOVERNMENT BODIES AND OFFICIALS

RULE 24.17. GENERAL RULE

"Enter a body created or controlled by a government under its own name (see 24.1-24.3) unless it belongs to one or more of the types listed in 24.18. However, if a body is subordinate to a higher body that is entered under its own name, formulate the heading for the subordinate body according to 24.12-24.14. Refer to the name of a government agency entered independently from its name in the form of a subheading of the name of the government (see 26.3A7)." *See* Fig. 19.36.

Fig. 19.36—Rule 24.17. Entry of a government body under its own name.

Heading: Warren Commission (U.S.)
Refer from: United States. Warren Commission
　　　　　　United States. President's Commission on the
　　　　　　　　Assassination of President Kennedy
　　　　　　President's Commission on the Assassination of
　　　　　　　　President Kennedy.

Note: Because this rule refers back to 24.1-24.3, the conventional name of the body is chosen according to 24.3C, rather than the official name.

RULE 24.18. GOVERNMENT AGENCIES ENTERED SUBORDINATELY

"Enter a government agency subordinately if it belongs to one or more of the following types. Make it a direct or indirect subheading of the heading for the government as instructed in 24.19. Omit from the subheading the name or abbreviation of the name of the government in noun form unless such an omission would result in an objectionable distortion."

TYPE 1. "An agency with a name containing a term that by definition implies that the body is part of another, e.g., department, division, section, branch, and their equivalents in other languages." *See* Fig. 19.37 (page 358). As under 24.13, TYPE 1, the words, "administrative office" and "secretariat," should be added to the list of terms suggested here.

**Fig. 19.37—Rule 24.18, Type 1. Entry of subordinate government body
that has a name implying it is part of another body.**

Name on title page: Division of Planning, City of
Jersey City
Heading: Jersey City (N.J.). Division of Planning.

TYPE 2. "An agency with a name containing a word that normally
implies administrative subordination (e.g., committee, commission), providing the name of the government is required for the identification of the
agency." *See* Fig. 19.38.

**Fig. 19.38—Rule 24.18, Type 2. Entry of subordinate government body
that has a name implying administrative subordination.**

Information on title page: Legislative Commission on
Medical Cost Containment, Raleigh; [seal]:
The Great Seal of the State of North Carolina.
Heading: North Carolina. Legislative Commission on
Medical Cost Containment.

LC has issued a rule interpretation for catalogers at LC. There are two
tests to be applied here. One is a judgment as to whether the name contains a
word that implies "administrative subordination." The cataloger should ask
whether the word is commonly used in a particular jurisdiction for names of
government subdivisions. If in doubt, the word is considered *not* to have such
an implication. For U.S. government bodies, a list of such words has been
started:

administration
advisory . . . (e.g., advisory panel)
agency
authority
board
bureau
commission
committee
office
service
task force[15]

A list of such words that LC has rejected as TYPE 2 has also been started:

council
project
program[16]

If the name passes the first test, it is then evaluated as to whether the name of the government is required for identification. "If either the name of the government is stated explicitly or implied in the wording of the name, or the name contains some other element guaranteeing uniqueness absolutely (usually a proper noun or adjective), enter it independently; in all other cases, enter the name subordinately."[17] Thus, the United States Travel Service, which includes the government in its name, is entered independently: United States Travel Service. The Soil Conservation Service, however, is entered subordinately: United States. Soil Conservation Service.

If the body is entered independently according to this interpretation, the name of the government is added as a qualifier unless the name or an understandable surrogate for the name of the government (e.g., "American" for U.S.) appears in the name.[18] *See* Fig. 19.36 (page 357).

TYPE 3. "An agency with a name that has been, or is likely to be, used as the name of another agency, providing the name of the government is required for the identification of the agency." *See* Fig. 19.39.

Fig. 19.39 — Rule 24.18, Type 3. Entry of subordinate government body that has a name likely to be used by another agency.

Name on title page: Minnesota Energy Agency, St. Paul, MN.
Judgment: Energy Agency is a name likely to be used in other states, or cities or countries.
Heading: Minnesota. Energy Agency.

As under Rule 24.13, TYPE 3, this rule will cause difficulty for catalogers. However, LC has established a policy for interpreting this rule. If there is actually conflict, and the name of the government is required for identification, entry must be under the name of the government. The "or is likely to be" part of the rule is interpreted in the following way:

"If the body is at the national level of government, enter the name under the heading for the government only if the name indicates no more than a type of body. For example, enter subordinately:

Research Center
Library
Technical Laboratory

but enter independently:

Population Research Center (U.S.)
Nuclear Energy Library (U.S.)
Technical Laboratory of Oceanographic Research (U.S.)
National Institute on Alcohol Abuse and Alcoholism (U.S.)
. . .

"If the body is below the national level, enter it subordinately unless either the name of the government is stated explicitly or implied in the wording of the name or the name contains some other element guaranteeing uniqueness absolutely (usually a proper noun or adjective)."[19]

As under 24.18, TYPE 2, a body entered independently under TYPE 3 will have the name of the government added as a qualifier unless it is already part of the body's name.

TYPE 4. "An agency that is a ministry or similar major executive agency (i.e., one that has no other agency above it) as defined by official publications of the government in question." *See* Fig. 19.40.

Fig. 19.40—Rule 24.18, Type 4. Entry of a major executive agency.

Name on title page: Oyo State Executive Council
Heading: Oyo (Nigeria : State). Executive Council.

TYPE 5. "Legislative bodies (see also 24.21)." *See* Fig. 19.44 (page 362).

TYPE 6. "Courts (see also 24.23)." *See* Fig. 19.45 (page 362).

TYPE 7. "Principal armed services (see also 24.24)." *See* Fig. 19.46 (page 363).

TYPE 8. "Chiefs of state and heads of government (see also 24.20)." *See* Fig. 19.43.

TYPE 9, "Embassies, consulates, etc.," and TYPE 10, Delegations to international and intergovernmental bodies," are also entered subordinately.

RULE 24.19. DIRECT OR INDIRECT SUBHEADING

This rule is the same as 24.14 except that the body is entered under the heading for the government instead of the lowest element in the hierarchy that is entered under its own name. Other elements in the hierarchy are interposed or omitted in the same way and with the same difficulties in judgment. (*See* discussion under 24.14.) *See* Figs. 19.41 and 19.42.

Fig. 19.41—Rule 24.19. Indirect subordinate entry of an office.

Name on title page: Office of the Executive Director,
    Colorado Department of Natural Resources.
Heading: Colorado. Dept. of Natural Resources. Office
    of the Executive Director.

Fig. 19.42—Rule 24.19. Direct subordinate entry of an office.

Name on title page: U.S. Department of Commerce
Maritime Administration, Office of Port and
Intermodal Development.
Heading: United States. Office of Port and Intermodal
Development.
Refer from: United States. Maritime Administra-
tion. Office of Port and Intermodal Development.

SPECIAL RULES

RULE 24.20. GOVERNMENT OFFICIALS

24.20B.   Heads of state, etc.

"The subheading for a sovereign, president, other head of state, or governor acting in an official capacity (see 21.4D) consists of the title of the office in
English (unless there is no equivalent English term), the inclusive years of the
reign or incumbency, and the name of the person in a brief form and in the
language of the heading for that person." Use non-sexist terminology, e.g.,
"Sovereign," not "Queen" or "King." *See* Fig. 19.43.

Fig. 19.43—Rule 24.20B. Entry of governor as an official.

¹Government   New Jersey. Governor (1974-   : Byrne)
²Title   A plan for education and tax reform in New Jersey :
³Dates   special message to the Legislature, June 13, 1974 / Brendan
⁴Surname   T. Byrne, Governor.

An explanatory reference should be made to the incumbent as a person (*see*
26.3C1).

24.20C.   Heads of governments and of international governmental bodies

For heads of governments who are not also heads of state and for heads
of international intergovernmental organizations, the subheading is the title of
the office in the vernacular or in the official language of the organization,
without dates or names.

RULE 24.21. LEGISLATIVE BODIES

Chambers of legislative bodies are entered subordinately to the legislative body, and committees are entered subordinately to the legislature or to a chamber, whichever is appropriate. A subcommittee of the U.S. Congress is entered as a subheading of the committee to which it is subordinate. If legislatures are numbered, the number and year(s) are added [e.g., United States. Congress (95th : 1977-1978).]. Session numbers may also need to be added. *See* Fig. 19.44.

Fig. 19.44—Rule 24.21. Entry of a state legislative committee.

Name on title page: Committee on Motor Vehicles,
Illinois House of Representatives
Heading: Illinois. General Assembly. House of
Representatives. Committee on Motor Vehicles.

It should be noted that, although *AACR 2* shows in its examples "United States. Congress. House of Representatives" which is the official name of that body, the Library of Congress will continue to use the conventional name "House" in its headings for the body.

RULE 24.23. COURTS

Civil and criminal courts are entered as subheadings of the jurisdiction. A place name for the place a court sits or the area it serves is omitted but added as a conventional addition if needed to distinguish it from others of the same name. *See* Fig. 19.45.

Fig. 19.45—Rule 24.23. Entry of a court under jurisdiction with addition of area it serves.

Name on title page: Franklin County branch of the
Court of Common Pleas of the 39th Judicial
District of Pennsylvania
Heading: Pennsylvania. Court of Common Pleas (39th
Judicial District).

RULE 24.24. ARMED FORCES

A principal service of the armed forces of a government is entered as a subheading of the government. A branch, district, or unit is entered as a subheading for the principal service; and if it is numbered, the numbering in the style used in the name follows the name. *See* Fig. 19.46.

**Fig. 19.46—Rule 24.24. Entry of an armed service branch under
the principal service.**

Name on chief source of information:
    Air Defense Command, U.S. Air Force
Heading: United States. Air Force. Air Defense
    Command.

RELIGIOUS BODIES AND OFFICIALS

RULE 24.27. RELIGIOUS BODIES AND OFFICIALS

24.27A.   Councils, etc., of a single religious body

Councils, etc., of a single religious body are entered as subheadings of
that body. Appropriate additions may be made as for conferences, etc.,
(24.7B). General councils are entered according to the general rules for subordinate bodies (24.12-24.13). *See* Fig. 19.47.

Fig. 19.47—Rule 24.27A. Entry of a religious council.

Name on title page: Il Concilio romano del 1725
Heading: Catholic Church. Concilio romano (1725).

24.27B.   Religious officials

The heading for a religious official acting in an official capacity looks
very much like the heading for a head of state (24.20B). It consists of the
heading for the diocese, order, patriarchate, etc., followed by the title in
English (unless there is no English equivalent), the inclusive years of incumbency, and the name of the person. *See* Fig. 19.48.

Fig. 19.48—Rule 24.27B. Entry of a religious official.

Name on title page: His Holiness John Paul II
Heading: Catholic Church. Pope (1978-   : John
    Paul II)
Refer in an explanatory reference to the personal
    heading for John Paul II.

24.27C.   Subordinate bodies

Provinces, dioceses, synods, and other subordinate units having jurisdiction over geographic areas are entered as subheadings of the religious body. For the Catholic Church, the English form of name should be used. *See* Fig. 19.49.

Fig. 19.49—Rule 24.27C. Entry of religious subordinate body.

Name on title page: Arzobispado del Cuzco
Heading: Catholic Church. Archdiocese of Cuzco (Peru).
Refer from: Catholic Church. Arzobispado del Cuzco
        (Peru).

FOOTNOTES

[1]Personal communication with Paul W. Winkler, Nov. 1979.

[2]"AACR 2 Options to be Followed by the Library of Congress: Chapters 1-2, 12, 21-26," *Library of Congress Information Bulletin* 37 (July 21, 1978):426-27.

[3]"AACR 2 Options," p. 427.

[4]"AACR 2 Options," p. 427.

[5]"Rule Interpretations for AACR 2: Chapter 24," *Cataloging Service Bulletin*, no. 6 (Fall 1979):17.

[6]"Rule Interpretations," pp. 18-19.

[7]"Rule Interpretations," pp. 18-19.

[8]"Rule Interpretations," p. 19.

[9]"Rule Interpretations," p. 19.

[10]"Rule Interpretations," p. 19.

[11]"Rule Interpretations," p. 19.

[12]"Rule Interpretations," p. 19.

[13]"Rule Interpretations," p. 19.

[14]"Rule Interpretations," pp. 21-22.

[15]"Rule Interpretations," p. 20.

[16]Personal communication with Paul W. Winkler, Nov. 1979.

[17]"Rule Interpretations," p. 20.

[18]"Rule Interpretations," p. 20.

[19]"Rule Interpretations," pp. 20-21.

20 UNIFORM TITLES

INTRODUCTION

When a work has appeared under more than one title, a uniform or conventional title may be used for cataloging purposes in order to bring all editions of the work together. Uniform titles are commonly used for sacred scriptures, creeds, liturgical works, and anonymous classics. "Bible" is a very common example of a uniform title in library catalogs; similarly, editions of the Mother Goose verses are assembled under the uniform title "Mother Goose." In these cases the uniform titles represent main entry headings. In other instances the uniform title is bracketed and placed between the main entry and the body of the card, as in the case of music, laws, liturgical works, and translations. *AACR 2*, chapter 25, contains many further suggestions for extending these rules to other instances. The Library of Congress, on its printed cards, has used uniform titles consistently only in those instances listed above; so libraries that apply these rules fully must also assume responsibility for revising many LC printed cards. MARC records formulated by LC according to *AACR 2*, however, will contain all uniform titles provided by the rules. These will not necessarily appear on LC's printed cards, but may be available to a library depending upon the type of access the library has to machine-readable records.[1]

One of the problems faced in constructing uniform titles is the choice of a title when titles of a work appear in more than one form. Titles may be in different languages, in one or more long forms and one or more short forms, or in two simultaneous versions (as when a work is published simultaneously in England and the United States under different titles). Some works may be published in parts and need identification of the part *without* identification of the whole (as in the case of one title from a trilogy), or *with* identification of the whole (as in the case of a book from Homer's *Iliad*, called only "Book 1"). Further additions may be needed to distinguish uniform titles from each other or from other headings, to identify the language in which the work appears, to identify the version, or to date the particular edition. The purpose of this chapter is to demonstrate the general rules used to resolve these problems. Much more detail can be found in *AACR 2*, chapter 25.

It has also been discovered that there is a major omission from this chapter. The problem relates to situations where two or more items or series of items have the same title proper but are not editions of the same work. When added entries are called for, there is, with *AACR 2*, no way to distinguish the added entries if entry is under title. In response to this problem the Library of Congress and the National Library of Canada have jointly proposed a set of guidelines for creating "unique titles" [i.e., uniform titles] as a means of distinguishing between titles that are identical. This proposal has been published in *Cataloging Service Bulletin*.[2] It will be put forward to the proper authorities as a proposal for official addition to *AACR 2*. It is consistent with the rules in *AACR 2*, chapter 25, and its application results in headings enclosed in square brackets and given before the title proper; if approved, it presumably will become part of chapter 25.

In addition to the first rule, which sets down the conditions for use of uniform titles, the *AACR 2* chapter comprises three groups of rules: basic rules for choice and form of the title itself (Rules 25.2-25.4, and 25.12), rules for additions to uniform titles (Rules 25.5-25.11), and special rules for certain materials (Rules 25.13-25.36). The materials given special treatment are manuscripts (25.13), incunabula (25.14), legal materials (25.15-25.16), sacred scriptures (25.17-25.18), liturgical and other religious works (25.19-25.24), and music (25.25-25.36).

RULE 25.1. USE OF UNIFORM TITLES

" . . . The need to use uniform titles varies from one catalogue to another and varies within one catalogue. Base the decision whether to use uniform titles in a particular instance on:

    a)   how well the work is known

    b)   how many manifestations of the work are involved

    c)   whether the main entry is under title

    d)   whether the work was originally in another language

    e)   the extent to which the catalogue is used for research purposes."

In essence this rule states that the entire set of rules on uniform titles is optional, and a policy decision should be made in each cataloging agency as to whether some or all of the rules should be applied.

GENERAL RULES

RULE 25.2. BASIC RULE

25.2A.   "When the manifestations (other than revised editions) of a work appear under various titles, select one title as the uniform title as instructed in 25.3-25.4.

"Use a uniform title for an entry for a particular item if

    1)   the item bears a title proper that differs from the uniform title

or 2)   the addition of another element (e.g., the name of the language of an item, see 25.5D) is required to organize the file.

"Enclose the uniform title in square brackets, and give it before the title proper. If the work is entered under title, give the uniform title as the heading with square brackets. *Optionally*, record a uniform title used as main entry heading without square brackets."

The Library of Congress is following the option, which is a continuation of LC's past practice.[3] The examples in this text also follow the option. *See* Fig. 20.1.

Fig. 20.1. Rule 25.2A. Uniform title as main entry without square brackets—LC practice.

Uniform title ——▶ Beowulf.
as main   Beowulf : an edition with manuscript spacing
entry   notation and graphotactic analyses / Robert D.
        Stevick.

25.2B. "Do not use a uniform title for a manifestation of a work in the same language that is a revision or updating of the original work. Relate editions not connected by uniform titles by giving the title of the earlier edition in a note on the entry for the revision or updating (see 1.7B7, 2.7B7, etc.)." *See* Fig. 20.2.

Fig. 20.2. Rule 25.2B. New title, not uniform title, is used for new edition in the same language.

Note giving   Hawker, Pat.
title of   Amateur radio techniques / Pat Hawker. -- 6th
earlier   ed. -- London : Radio Society of Great Britain,
edition   1978.

        336 p. : ill. ; 25 cm.

        First ed. published with title: Technical topics
for the radio amateur.

INDIVIDUAL TITLES

RULE 25.3. WORKS CREATED AFTER 1500

25.3A. "Use the title or form of title in the original language by which a work created after 1500 has become known through use in manifestations of the work or in reference sources." *See* Fig. 20.3.

Fig. 20.3. Rule 25.3A. Uniform title in original language.

Suder, Joseph, 1892-
   [Dona nobis pacem]
   Festmesse in D [sound recording] / Joseph Suder.

Other titles given to this work:
  Messe Dona nobis pacem
  Grosse Messe Dona nobis pacem

LC catalogers will delete the initial article from a uniform title if it is in the nominative case, even when the uniform title is under a name. This provision also applies to Rule 25.4A.[4] With this provision, the first, third, and fifth examples under this rule in *AACR 2* would not begin with "The" (e.g., [Pickwick papers], not [The Pickwick papers]).

25.3B. "If no one title in the original language is established as being the one by which the work is best known, or in case of doubt, use the title proper of the original edition. . . ."

25.3C. **Simultaneous publication under different titles**

25.3C1. "If a work is published simultaneously in the same language under two different titles, use the title of the edition published in the home country of the cataloguing agency. If the work is not published in the home country, use the title of the edition received first." *See* Fig. 20.4.

Fig. 20.4. Rule 25.3C. American title used as uniform title for work whose British title is different.

Mansfield, Peter, 1928-
   [The Arab world]
   The Arabs / Peter Mansfield. -- Harmondsworth : Penguin, 1928.

Note explaining uniform title:
   American ed. published under title: The Arab world.

RULE 25.4. WORKS CREATED BEFORE 1501

25.4A. "Use the title, or form of title, in the original language by which a work created before 1501 . . . is identified in modern reference sources. If the evidence of modern reference sources is inconclusive, use the title most frequently found in (in this order of preference):

1)   modern editions

2)   early editions

3)   manuscript copies." *See* Fig. 20.5.

"Omit initial articles if not required for reasons of grammar." LC, however, is deleting all initial articles as described under 25.3A.

Fig. 20.5. Rule 25.4. Uniform title for pre-1501 work as identified in reference sources.

Uniform ⟶ Gawain and the Grene Knight.
title   Sir Gawain and the Green Knight / translated with an introduction by Brian Stone.

In general, a well-established English title, if there is one, is used for a pre-1501 Greek work or anonymous work in non-roman script. *See* Fig. 20.7.

RULE 25.5. ADDITIONS TO UNIFORM TITLES

25.5B. "Additions are made in parentheses to distinguish between identical uniform titles, or to distinguish the uniform title from an otherwise identical form used as the heading for a person, a corporate body, or a reference. *See* Fig. 20.6.

Fig. 20.6. Rule 25.5B. Additions in parentheses to distinguish between two otherwise identical uniform titles.

Jungle book (1942)
　Jungle book [motion picture]

Jungle book (1967)
　The jungle book [motion picture]

In the case of radio and television programs, LC adds the qualifier "(Radio program)" or "(Television program)" to all such titles even if there is no conflict.[5]

25.5C. "Add in parentheses an appropriate designation to distinguish between identical uniform titles for works entered under the same personal or corporate heading."

e.g., 　United States.
　　　　　[Census (1960)]

　　　　United States.
　　　　　[Census (1970)]

25.5D. "If the linguistic content of the item being catalogued is different from that of the original (e.g., a translation, a dubbed motion picture), add the name of the language of the item to the uniform title. Precede the language by a full stop." *See* Figs. 20.7 and 20.8.

Fig. 20.7. Rules 25.4 and 25.5D. Anonymous pre-1501 work originally in non-roman script entered under established English title with the language of the translation in hand added.

[1] Uniform title

[2] Language

Arabian nights. English.
　More fairy tales from the Arabian nights /
　edited and arranged by E. Dixon ; illustrated by
　J.D. Batten.

**Fig. 20.8. Rule 25.5D. Modern translation with original title as
uniform title, followed by language of translation.**

¹Uniform
title

Leys, Simon.
  [Les habits neufs du président Mao. English]
²Language
  The Chairman's new clothes : Mao and the
cultural revolution / Simon Leys ; translated by
Carol Appleyard and Patrick Goode.

RULE 25.6. PARTS OF A WORK

This rule is not applied to parts of the Bible and certain other sacred scriptures (*see* Rules 25.17-25.18) or to parts of musical works (*see* Rule 25.32).

25.6A.   Single parts

25.6A1.   "If a separately catalogued part of a work has a title of its own, use the title of the part by itself as the uniform title. Make a *see* reference from the heading for the whole work and the title of the part as a subheading of the title of the whole work. . . ." *See* Fig. 20.9.

**Fig. 20.9. Rule 26.6A1. Separately cataloged part with its own
title as uniform title.**

Hesse, Hermann, 1877-1962
  [Tractat vom Steppenwolf. English]
  Treatise on the Steppenwolf / Hermann Hesse ; [translated from the German] ; paintings by Jaroslav Bradac.

Note: The title of the whole work is *Der Steppenwolf.*

25.6A2.   "If a separately catalogued part of a work is identified only by a general term (with or without a number) such as

  Preface

  Detail

  . . .

  Book 1

  . . .

use the designation of the part as a subheading of the title of the whole work. Use arabic numerals to record the number of the part." *See* Fig. 20.10.

Fig. 20.10. Rule 25.6A2. Separately cataloged part given as subheading of the title of the whole work.

¹Whole
work   Milton, John, 1608-1674.   2
                          [Paradise lost. Book 4]
²Part   1   Paradise lost, book IV / John Milton ; edited
                        by S. E. Goggin.

25.6B.   Several parts

25.6B1.   "If the item being catalogued consists of consecutive parts of a work and the parts are numbered, use the designation of the parts in the singular as a subheading of the title of the whole work followed by the inclusive numbers of the parts." *See* Fig. 20.11.

Fig. 20.11. Rule 25.6B1. Separately cataloged consecutive parts of a work given as subheading of the title of the whole work.

¹Whole   Milton, John, 1608-1674.   2
work   1   [Paradise lost. Book 9-10]
²Singular   Paradise lost, books IX and X / John Milton ;
form of   edited by Cyril Aldred.
name of part

COLLECTIVE TITLES

Collective titles can be general (e.g., "Works," "Selections") or more specific (e.g., "Novels," "Poems," "Laws, etc."). When these are used alone, the effect is to separate originals from translations, different editions from each other, etc., if the titles proper are different. They also are inadequate when being used in added entries. Therefore, LC has emphasized using Rule 25.5C in conjunction with collective titles when needed to bring together items with different titles proper or to refer to a work in an added entry. The designation to be enclosed in parentheses may be title proper, editor, translator, publisher, etc. — whichever best fits each case. Two of the examples given are:

United States.
[Laws, etc. (U.S. code)]
United States code . . .

Maugham, W. Somerset (William Somerset), 1874-1965.
[Short stories (Heinemann)]
Complete short stories . . .

This technique is applied only after the need arises; thus, earlier entries must be revised.[6]

RULE 25.8. COMPLETE WORKS

"Use the collective title *Works* for an item that consists of, or purports to be, the complete works of a person, including those that are complete at the time of publication." *See* Fig. 20.12.

Fig. 20.12. Rule 25.8. Collective title "Works" used as uniform title.

Posada, José Guadalupe, 1852-1913.
[Works. English & German]
Das Werk von José Guadalupe Posada = The works of José Guadalupe Posada / edited and with an introduction by Hannes Jähn.

RULE 25.9. SELECTIONS

"Use the collective title *Selections* for items consisting of three or more works in various forms, or in one form if the person created works in one form only, and for items consisting of extracts, etc., from the works of one person." *See* Fig. 20.13.

Fig. 20.13. Rule 25.9. Collective title "Selections" used as uniform title.

Twain, Mark, 1835-1910.
[Selections]
The best of Twain / selected and introduced by Mike Kalmbach.

SPECIAL RULES FOR CERTAIN MATERIALS

LEGAL MATERIALS

RULE 25.15. LAWS, ETC.

25.15A.   Modern laws, etc.

25.15A1.   Collections
"Use *Laws, etc.* for complete or partial collections of legislative enactments other than compilations on a particular subject." *See* Fig. 20.14.

Fig. 20.14. Rule 25.15A1. Collective title "Laws, etc." used as uniform title.

India.
[Laws, etc.]
The Code of civil procedure, 1908 (5 of 1908), as modified up to the 1st May 1977.

25.15A2.   Single laws, etc.

"Use as the uniform title for a single legislative enactment (in this order of preference):

a)   the official short title or citation title

b)   an unofficial short title or citation title used in legal literature

c)   the official title of the enactment

d)   any other official designation (e.g., the number or date)."
See Fig. 20.15.

Fig. 20.15. Rule 25.15A2. Official short title used as uniform title.

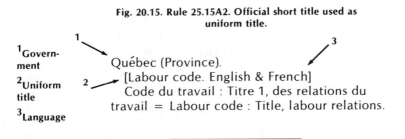

¹Govern-
ment

²Uniform
title

³Language

Québec (Province).
[Labour code. English & French]
Code du travail : Titre 1, des relations du travail = Labour code : Title, labour relations.

RULE 25.16. TREATIES, ETC.

The uniform title for treaties is "Treaties, etc." Various additions are made depending upon the circumstances: the second party for a collection or single treaties between two parties; the date or earliest date of signing (in the form: year, abbreviated name of the month, number of the day) for a single treaty. A single treaty between four or more parties is entered under the name by which the treaty is known (in English, if possible) followed by the year of signing in parentheses. Added entries for individual signers, if made, are formulated with the uniform title "Treaties, etc." followed by date of signing. *See* Fig. 20.16.

Fig. 20.16. Rule 25.16. Uniform title for a treaty between
two parties.

¹Conven-
tional uniform
title

²Second
Country

³Date

United States.
[Treaties, etc. Vietnam, 1972 Oct. 2]
Agricultural commodities : agreement be-
tween the United States of America and Viet-
Nam signed at Saigon October 2, 1972.

SACRED SCRIPTURES

RULE 25.17. GENERAL RULE

"Use as the uniform title for a sacred scripture (see 21.37) the title by which it is most commonly identified in English-language reference sources dealing with the religious group to which the scripture belongs. . . . "

RULE 25.18. PARTS OF SACRED SCRIPTURES AND ADDITIONS

25.18A.   Bible

When appropriate, the testaments (designated O.T. and N.T.) are added after the word "Bible." Then books are designated. If the books are numbered, the number is given as an ordinal arabic numeral after the name. The name of a group of books may also be a subdivision of the testament (e.g., Minor Prophets, Apocrypha, Gospels). Next are added, as appropriate: 1) language; 2) version, translator, name of manuscripts or repository, or reviser; and 3) year. Examples are:

Bible.   *N.T. Gospels* . . .
Bible.   *O.T. Historical books* . . .
Bible.   *O.T. Genesis XII, 1 – XXV, 11* . . .
Bible.   *N.T. Corinthians, 1st* . . .

Bible.   [parts] [language] [versions] [selections] [date]
Bible.   English. Knox. 1956.
Bible.   *N.T.* English. Goodspeed. 1943.
Bible.   *O.T. Leviticus.* Hebrew. Samaritan. 1959.
Bible.   English. Authorized. Selections. 1947.

Note: Enter combinations of selections or excerpts under the most specific Bible heading and insert subheading "Selections" after language and version but before date (Rule 25.18A9).

Fig. 20.17. Rule 25.18A. Uniform title entries for the Bible.

¹Uniform
title

²Language

Bible. English. Selections. 1931.
Readings from the Bible.

Contents note to clarify subheading:

³Selections

⁴Date

Contents: The birth of Jesus.–The Lord's
Prayer.–XXIII Psalm.–Ten Commandments.

Fig. 20.18.

¹Uniform
title

²Parts

³Language

⁴Date

Bible. O.T. Ecclesiastes. Ethiopic. 1931.
The Ethiopic text of the Book of Ecclesiastes /
edited by Samuel A. B. Mercer.

25.18B.-25.18M. These are special rules for the Talmud, Mishnah and Tosefta, Midrashim, Buddhist scriptures, Vedas, Aranyakas, Brahmanas, Upanishads, Jaina Āgama, Avesta, and Koran. Rules are given for parts and additions as for the Bible.

LITURGICAL WORKS

RULE 25.19. FORM AND LANGUAGE OF TITLE OF LITURGICAL WORKS

"If the name of a body under which a liturgical work is entered is given in English, use as uniform title a well-established English title if there is one. Otherwise, use a brief title in the language of the liturgy." *See* Fig. 20.19.

Fig. 20.19. Rule 25.19. Uniform title for a liturgical work.

¹Corporate
name

²Uniform
title

³Language

Catholic Church.
[Mass, Epiphany. German]
Messe an Epiphanias.

MUSIC

RULE 25.25. GENERAL RULE

"Formulate a uniform title for a musical work as instructed in 25.26-25.36. Use the general rules 25.1-25.7 insofar as they apply to music and are not contradicted by the following rules."

RULE 25.26. DEFINITIONS

AACR 2 carefully distinguishes here between the use of the word "title" and the use of the word "work" in these rules. Essentially, "title" refers to the words used to name the "work," which refers to a whole unit, a set of works with a group title, or a group of works with a single opus number.

RULES 25.27-25.36

Uniform titles are frequently used in cataloging music because the same musical composition is often issued in numerous editions with variations in the language and the wording of the title pages. A uniform title may also be used whenever a filing device is needed for music entered under a person other than a composer, e.g., arranger. Composer-title cross references are made from forms of the title not used as uniform title, as may be advisable. The following examples are typical:

> Beethoven, Ludwig van, 1770-1827.
> > Battle of Vittoria
> > see
> Beethoven, Ludwig van, 1770-1827.
> > Wellingtons Sieg.

> Beethoven, Ludwig van, 1770-1827.
> > Cantata on the death of Emperor Joseph II
> > see
> Beethoven, Ludwig van, 1770-1827.
> > Kantate auf den Tod Kaiser Josephs II.

In the selection and construction of uniform titles the most reliable bibliographical sources are consulted, such as thematic indexes, bibliographies, music encyclopedias, etc. Information given in the work cataloged is not used without an attempt at verification. The Library of Congress catalogs are certainly useful in constructing a uniform title, but only after the cataloger has identified the work in thematic or other musical sources.

Rules 25.25-25.33, which give the principles of construction of a uniform title for a single work or type of work, are not fully quoted here. The most basic type of uniform title is generally that of the first edition of the work, modified as stated in Rule 25.27, with the choice of language dependent on the type of composition. The next element is the medium of performance, the instruments for which it was written (Rule 25.29); this is followed by further identifying elements to distinguish the work from other compositions by the same composer, generally the serial number, opus (or thematic index) number, and the key (Rule 25.31). Examples of such entries follow:

Bach, Johann Sebastian, 1685-1750.
[Die Kunst der Fuge]
The Art of the fugue

Bach, Johann Sebastian, 1685-1750.
[Lobet den Herrn, alle Heiden, S. 230]
Motet no. 6: Praise the Lord, all ye heathen

Haydn, Joseph, 1732-1809.
[Quartets, strings, no. 83, op. 77, no. 2, F major]
Quartet, op. 77, no. 2, in F major

Dvořák, Antonín, 1841-1904.
[Symphonies, no. 8, op. 88, G major]
From the new world: symphony no. 8 by Dvořák.

Uniform titles for separately published parts of a work, collections, excerpts, arrangements, and adaptations are constructed basically to provide the most reasonable filing location (see Rules 25.32-25.36). For example:

[Organ music]
[Organ music. Selections]
[Sonatas, piano]
[Artaxerxes. The soldier tir'd]
[Fantasiestücke, piano, op. 12. Traumes Wirren]
[Quartets, strings, no. 8-13, op. 2]
Note that separately published parts of a musical work use the title of the whole work, followed by the title of the part. This is counter to 25.6A1 for other types of works.

Cowell, Henry, 1897-1965.
[Concerto brevis, accordion; arr.]
Concerto brevis, for accordion and orchestra; piano reduction by the composer.

Titles of works in the larger vocal forms (operas, oratorios, etc.) generally require additional modification because of the various versions in which they are likely to be issued. For example:

Puccini, Giacomo, 1858-1924.
[Manon Lescaut]

[Manon Lescaut. Piano-vocal score]

[Manon Lescaut. Libretto. English]

FOOTNOTES

[1]"AACR 2 Options to be Followed by the Library of Congress: Chapters 1-2, 12, 21-26," *Library of Congress Information Bulletin* 37 (July 21, 1978): 427.

[2]"Unique Serial Identifiers," *Cataloging Service Bulletin*, no. 5 (Summer 1979): 4-9.

[3]"AACR 2 Options," p. 427.

[4]"Rule Interpretations for AACR 2: Chapter 25," *Cataloging Service Bulletin*, no. 6 (Fall 1979): 24-25.

[5]"Rule Interpretations," p. 25.

[6]"Rule Interpretations," p. 25.

21 REFERENCES

INTRODUCTION

All the rules in the preceding four chapters have referred to "references" needed when one name or form of heading is chosen from among more than one possible name or form of heading. This chapter is a summary of all those situations where cross references are called for explicitly or implicitly in the earlier rules. This chapter also gives examples of the different types of references. Chapter 26 of *AACR 2*, "References," begins with introductory notes that define different kinds of references, explain the form to use, and set up the conditions under which references should be made. Following this introduction are specific rules for and examples of references for persons, corporate bodies and geographic names, and uniform titles. Finally, there is a rule allowing references instead of certain added entries that are common to many editions.

RULE 26.0. INTRODUCTORY NOTES

"See" references. "The function of a *see reference* is to direct the user of a catalogue from a form of the name of a person or a corporate body or the title of a work that might reasonably be sought to the form that has been chosen as a name heading or a uniform title." A *see* reference says to the user, "No, you won't find what you're looking for here; but if you'll look under _____ , you will find something."

"See also" references. "The function of a *see also reference* is to direct the user from one name heading or uniform title to another that is related to it." A *see also* reference says to the user, "Yes, there is some information here, and you may also be interested in related information that you can find under _____ ."

Name-title references. "When a *see* or *see also reference* is made from a title that has been entered under a personal or corporate heading, it is made in the form of a *name-title reference* beginning with the personal or corporate heading followed by the title concerned."

Explanatory references. "When a simple *see* or *see also reference* does not give adequate guidance to the user of the catalogue, an *explanatory reference* giving more detailed guidance is made."

Forms of references. "In general the form of name of a person or corporate body from which reference is made has the same structure as it would have as a heading. . . .

"When reference is made to two or more different headings or titles from the same form, make one reference, listing in it all headings to which reference is being made." For example:

> Taylor, J. R.
>> see also
> Taylor, James Robly, 1925-
> Taylor, John Roberts.

> ACU
>> see
> Arbeitskreis Computer im Unterricht.
> Arbeitskreis Computer-Unterstützter Unterricht.
> Association of Commonwealth Universities.

Conditions for making references. "In making references, bear the following points in mind:

a) There must be an entry in the catalogue under the name heading or uniform title to which any type of reference is made.

b) There should normally be an entry in the catalogue under the name heading or uniform title from which a *see also* reference is made.

c) It is necessary to make a record of every reference under the name heading or uniform title to which it refers in order to make possible a correction or deletion of that reference.

d) When in doubt about making a reference, make it."

Note the word "normally" under "b." Few libraries with manual catalogs find it feasible to make a "see" reference where a "see also" reference would be made if the catalog contained the heading referred from, only to change to a "see also" reference when that heading is added to the catalog.

The wording of the examples of explanatory references in *AACR 2* and in this text is not intended to be prescriptive, but only to provide examples.

RULE 26.1. BASIC RULE

Make a reference from a form not used to the one that is used unless the form is so similar as to make the reference unnecessary. Use appropriate additions to distinguish the form in the reference from other headings or references.

RULE 26.2. NAMES OF PERSONS

26.2A. "See" references

26.2A1. Different names

"Refer from a name used by a person, or found in reference sources, that is different from that used in the heading for that person. (For persons entered under two or more different headings, see also 26.2C1 and 26.2D1.)" For example:

> Tosi, Maria Teresa
> see
> Maria Teresa dell'Eucaristia, suor, 1918- .

> Beyle, Marie Henri
> see
> Stendhal, 1783-1842.

> Sklodowska, Marie
> see
> Curie, Marie, 1867-1934.

26.2A2. Different forms of the name

"Refer from a form of name . . . [that] differs significantly from the form used in the heading for that person." For example:

> Burt, Stanley G.
> see
> Burt, S. G. (Stanley G.).

> Abe, Suehisa
> see
> Abe, Suenao, 1622-1709.

> Ruth, George Herman
> see
> Ruth, Babe, 1895-1948.

> Homerus
> see
> Homer.

26.2A3. Different entry elements

"Refer from different elements of the heading for a person under which that name might reasonably be sought." For example:

> Van Zuidam, R. A.
> see
> Zuidam, R. A. van.

Buren, Ariane van
see
Van Buren, Ariane.

Damas, Bernardo Valverde
see
Valverde Damas, Bernardo.

Ram Acharya
see
Acharya, Ram.

Wellesley, Arthur, Duke of Wellington, 1769-1852
see
Wellington, Arthur Wellesley, Duke of, 1769-1852.

26.2B.   Name-title references

Name-title references involving personal name differences are prescribed in four cases. The most common of these is a name-title reference from the inverted form of initials for each item entered under initials in direct order. For example:

N., A. R.
The right way and the wrong way
see
A. R. N.
The right way and the wrong way.

26.2C.   "See also" references

26.2C1.   "If the works of one person are entered under two different headings, make a *see also* reference from each heading to the other (see also 26.2D1)." For example:

Baker, Ray Stannard
see also
Grayson, David

Grayson, David
see also
Baker, Ray Stannard

26.2D.   Explanatory references

26.2D1.   General rule

"When more detailed guidance than a simple *see* or *see also* reference is required, make explanatory references." For example:

Stone, Rosetta
 The joint pseudonym of Michael K. Frith and Dr. Seuss.
For separate works entered under each name see
 Frith, Michael K.
 Seuss, Dr.

Hunter, Evan
 For works of this author written under pseudonyms, see
 Collins, Hunt
 McBain, Ed
 Marsten, Richard

26.2D2. *"Optionally*, make explanatory references under the various separately written prefixes of surnames to explain how names with such prefixes are entered in the catalogue." For example:

Van
 Names beginning with this prefix are also entered under the
 name following the prefix (e.g., Zuidam, R. A. van)

The Library of Congress is not applying this option because it is felt that such references provide the user with less help than do specific references.[1]

RULE 26.3. NAMES OF CORPORATE BODIES AND GEOGRAPHIC NAMES

26.3A.   **"See" references**

26.3A1.   **Different names**
 "Refer from a name used by a body, or found in reference sources, that is significantly different from that used in the heading for that body. For references to be made in connection with changes of name, see 26.3C1." For example:

God Squad
 see
Detroit (Mich.). Police Dept. Chaplain Corps.

26.3A3.   **Different forms of the name**
 "Refer from a form of name used by a body or for a place, or found in reference sources, or resulting from a different romanization of the name. . . ." For example:

A.B.E.D.I.A.
 see
Arab Bank for Economic Development in Africa.

Wien (Austria)
   see
Vienna (Austria).

Pharmaceutical Society of Korea
   see
Taehan Yakhakhoe.

Guerrilla Art Action Group
   see
GAAG.

Carlsruhe (West Germany)
   see
Karlsruhe (West Germany)

Kellogg (W. K.) Arabian Horse Center
   see
W. K. Kellogg Arabian Horse Center.

General Aniline and Film Corp. Ansco
   see
Ansco

Jesus, Society of
   see
Jesuits.

Bradner Associates
   see
Michael Bradner Associates.

Torup (Denmark)
   see
Hammer-Torup (Denmark).

26.3A5.   **Numbers**

If the catalog is filed so that numbers expressed as words are in a different place than numbers expressed as numerals, make references from the opposite form to the one used in the heading, if the number is in a position to affect the filing. For example:

Three M Company
   see
3M Company

3 Bridges Reformed Church (Three Bridges, N.J.)
   see
Three Bridges Reformed Church (Three Bridges, N.J.)

26.3A6. Abbreviations

If the catalog is filed so that abbreviations are in a different place than the equivalent words, refer from the full form to an abbreviation, if the abbreviation is in a position to affect the filing. For example:

> Mount Auburn Cemetery (Cambridge, Mass.)
>> see
> Mt. Auburn Cemetery (Cambridge, Mass.)

26.3A7. Different forms of heading

"Refer from different forms of heading under which a corporate body might reasonably be sought." For example:

> Cambridge. University
>> see
> University of Cambridge.

> California Institute of Technology, Pasadena. Baxter Art
> Gallery
>> see
> Baxter Art Gallery.

> Virgin Islands of the United States. Division of Curriculum
> & Instruction. Project Introspection
>> see
> Project Introspection.

> United States. Maritime Administration. Office of
> Commercial Development. Office of Port and Intermodal
> Development
>> see
> United States. Office of Port and Intermodal
> Development.

> Concilio romano (1725)
>> see
> Catholic Church. Concilio romano (1725).

26.3B. "See also" references

26.3B1. "Make *see also* references between independently entered but related corporate headings." For example:

> Amsterdam (Holland). Gemeentelijke-Archiefdienst
>> see also
> Amsterdam (Holland). Gemeente-Archief.

> Treaty of Versailles, 1919
>> see also
> Paris Peace Conference, 1919.

26.3C.   Explanatory references

26.3C1.   General rule

"When more detailed guidance than a simple *see* or *see also* reference is required, make explanatory references." For example:

> United Nations. Missions.
>   Delegations, missions, etc. from member nations to the United Nations and to its subordinate units are entered under the name of the nation followed by the name of the delegation, mission, etc., e.g.
> United States. Mission to the United Nations.
> Uruguay. Delegación en las Naciones Unidas.

> Automotive Transport Association of Ontario
>   see also the later heading
> Ontario Trucking Association.

> Ontario Trucking Association
>   see also the earlier heading
> Automotive Transport Association of Ontario.

> A. Harris & Co.
>   Sanger Brothers was established in 1857. A. Harris & Co. was established in 1886. In 1961 they merged to form Sanger-Harris.
>   Works by these bodies are found under the following headings according to the name used at the time of publication:
>   Sanger Brothers.
>   A. Harris & Co.
>   Sanger-Harris.

> Oceans '78 Conference (4th : 1978 : Washington, D.C.)
>
>   Publications of this series of meetings are found under the following headings or titles:
>   1970: IEEE International Conference on Engineering in the Ocean Environment (1970 : Panama City, Fla.)
>   1971: Conference on Engineering in the Ocean Environment (1971 : San Diego, Calif.)
>   1972: IEEE International Conference on Engineering in the Ocean Environment (1972 : Newport, R.I.)
>   1974: IEEE International Conference on Engineering in the Ocean Environment (1974 : Halifax, N.S.)
>   1975: Conference on Engineering in the Ocean Environment (1975 : San Diego, Calif.)
>   1976: Oceans '76.
>   1977: Oceans '77 conference record.
>   1978: Oceans '78 Conference (4th : 1978 : Washington, D.C.)

26.3C2.   Acronyms

"If the filing system used in the catalogue distinguishes between initials with full stops and initials without full stops, and more detailed guidance than a simple *see* reference is called for, make an explanatory reference under each form." For example:

> N.A.C.
> see
> Naval Avionics Center.
> Neighbourhood Advice Council.
>> In this catalog, titles and other entries may be found under the acronym filed as a word.

Note: Make the same explanatory reference under NAC.

RULE 26.4. UNIFORM TITLES

26.4A.   "See" references

26.4A1.   Different titles or variants of the title

"Refer to the uniform title from the different titles and variants of the title under which a work has been published or cited in reference sources. Refer from and to a name heading and title when appropriate." For example:

> Laderman, Ezra.
> The trials of Galileo
> see
> Laderman, Ezra.
> Galileo Galilei

> Córdoba (Argentina : Province).
> Ley no. 4051
> see
> Córdoba (Argentina : Province).
> Ley orgánica del poder judicial (1942)

> Suder, Joseph, 1892-
> Festmesse, in D
> see
> Suder, Joseph, 1892-
> Dona nobis pacem

> Revueltas, Silvestre, 1899-1940.
> Chit-chat music
> see
> Revueltas, Silvestre, 1899-1940.
> Música para charlar

[Title page title: Música para charlar = Chit-chat music. Title added entries would be made for both titles. In the other cases, a title added entry would be made for the title proper of the edition being cataloged.]

"In the case of translated titles, refer to the uniform title and the appropriate language subheading, when appropriate." For example:

Song of Roland
see
Chanson de Roland. English

Naft, Stephen, 1878-1956.
Kyōsanshugi ni taisuru nijū no shitsumon
see
Naft, Stephen, 1878-1956.
Answer please! Questions for communists. Japanese

26.4A2.   Titles of parts of a work cataloged independently
" . . . Refer from the titles of such parts in the form of subheadings under the uniform title for the whole work." For example:

Hesse, Hermann, 1877-1962.
Der Steppenwolf. Tractat vom Steppenwolf
see
Hesse, Hermann, 1877-1962.
Tractat vom Steppenwolf

26.4A3.   Titles of parts cataloged under the title of the whole work
" . . '. Refer from the titles of such parts, if they are distinctive, to the uniform title under which they will be found." For example:

Strauss, Richard, 1864-1949.
Breit über mein Haupt dein schwarzes Haar
see
Strauss, Richard, 1864-1949.
Lieder, op. 19. Breit über mein Haupt dein
schwarzes Haar

al-Muʿawwidhatān
see
Koran. ạl-Muʿawwidhatān.

26.4A4.   Collective titles
"When a collection of, or a selection from, a person's works is catalogued under a conventional collective title, refer from the name and title taken from the chief source of information . . . [if the title is distinctive]." For example:

Shepp, Archie.
   Further fire music
     see
Shepp, Archie.
     Instrumental music. Selections

FOOTNOTES

[1]"AACR 2 Options to be Followed by the Library of Congress: Chapters 1-2, 12, 21-26," *Library of Congress Information Bulletin* 37 (July 21, 1978): 427.

22 SUBJECT ARRANGEMENT OF LIBRARY MATERIALS

INTRODUCTION

Collections in libraries of any appreciable size are arranged according to some system, and the arrangement is generally referred to as classification. Classification provides formal, orderly access to the shelves. Many different arrangements of books have been used. The *Pinakes* was a catalog of general subject locations devised by Callimachus for the Alexandria Library in Hellenic Egypt. Many medieval and early New England libraries used fixed location by size. Today's subject classification systems, with their relative notation, permit interfiling of new materials at the proper places as they are added to the collection.

No matter what scheme is chosen, or how large the library, the purpose of classification is to make each item readily available. Ease of access is especially important if the collection is heterogeneous. It is convenient and desirable — particularly in the open-shelf collections to which many libraries in the United States are committed — to have, for example, all histories of the United States together, or all books on symbolic logic, or all symphony scores together, so that the patron, who may or may not have one title in mind, can find related works in one location.

The ultimate aim of any classification system is to lead the patron to the items required, either through direct search of the shelves (open stacks), or through the help of a library attendant whose duty it is to retrieve the materials on demand (closed stacks). Each system has its virtues. Open stacks encourage browsing, and thus stimulate intellectual awareness and foster serendipity. They work best with a logical, fairly comprehensible system of classification that encourages the patron's self-reliance in seeking items on a particular subject or its specific aspects. Closed stacks lessen the chances that materials will be mishandled, misplaced, or stolen, but they force the patron to limit his or her own searching to the catalog (and perhaps the shelflist), and to wait for a library employee to bring items specifically requested. Closed stacks still have a use in a storage library situation where items may not be shelved in subject groups at all, but ranged in more or less fixed location by size, with consecutive numbers assigned as addresses. "Fixed location" means that each item has one specific, fixed position on the shelf in the library as was the case in many libraries prior to the mid-nineteenth century. "Relative location" is a fluid, constantly changing arrangement of items according to their relationship to one another and resulting from the addition of new materials or the removal of old, weeded or lost, materials. In this system items may be moved from shelf to shelf without altering or disturbing their classified sequence.

No matter what the classification scheme or the type of shelving, the library catalog, as primary source of reference, must be complete and current. It provides information about particular items or types of items in various ways, usually by author, title, and subject, and gives in the form of call numbers the shelf addresses where they may be found.

PHILOSOPHICAL PROPERTIES OF CLASSIFICATION

It must be remembered that the term "classification" refers to two processes: 1) devising a scheme by which materials (or concepts) are classified or arranged in a consistent or systematic order on the basis of some stated principles, and 2) applying this particular scheme of classification (classification system) in the actual process of classifying a specific document or item at hand. Before we can discuss theoretical problems of literary classification, we must briefly touch on the process of classification in general, particularly as it applies to the classification of knowledge, or, as it is sometimes called, philosophical classification.

A classification scheme is defined as an orderly distribution of the universe into groups of main subjects or classes. A class is, broadly speaking, any group of entities exhibiting one or more common characteristics or traits. As a technical term, it is normally limited to comprehensive concepts or categories, as distinct from divisions, subclasses, sections, etc. A concept is, for present purposes, an idea encompassing the essential attributes of a class, subclass, etc. It includes all that is characteristically associated with, or suggested by, a general term. A characteristic is a conceptualized attribute by which classes may be identified and separated into groups, or further subdivided by topic, form, location, chronology, etc.

Kant finds that there are always two factors in genuine knowledge—the raw materials, which are sense experiences, and the synthetic, organizing, or ordering activity of the mind. To the understanding or to the faculty of making judgments—that is, the faculty of forming the concepts and laws that constitute order and sequence—belong the native forms of judgment, or the universal ways in which the mind synthesizes or orders the contents of sense perception. These forms are the categories—that is, the fundamental and universal forms of thinking objects and their relations. Through the use of these categories, the mind builds up the material of sense perception into a systematized or orderly whole of intelligible experience. Kant's categories correspond to the classification of judgment forms in traditional logic. They are as follows:

1. Categories of quantity
   Unity
   Plurality
   Totality

2. Categories of quality
   Reality
   Negation
   Limitation

3.   Categories of relation
     Inherence and subsistence, or substance
     Causality and dependence
     Community, or reciprocity of causal influence

4.   Categories of modality
     Possibility — Impossibility
     Existence — Nonexistence
     Necessity — Contingency

In order to illustrate Kant's argument and theory it will suffice to show the application of a few of these categories:

1. **Unity.** The mind unites various sensations — for example, color, form, weight, size, taste, etc. — into the unity or identity of an orange.

2. **Plurality.** The mind, in order to count a bag of oranges, must repeat, say twelve times, its identification of unity and must add or synthesize each one to the previously recognized number, as it goes along.

3. **Substance.** The mind can recognize change only by reference to something permanent. Without consciousness of permanence there is no consciousness of change, and vice versa. Thus, when we think of any object — for example, a table — we can say its appearance changes only if we recognize an identical "it" that changes. If we go back to the old childhood home, we can say it has not changed much only if we recognize that we and other things have changed, while remaining recognizably the same.

4. **Causality.** A causal relation is one of necessary and irreversible sequence. "*A* is the cause of *B*" means that it is necessary that *A* should first occur if there is to be an occurrence of *B*.

Now, the use or application of any category means always synthesis, organization or unification, in some fashion, of the chaotic manifold of sense experience. Knowledge involves both analysis and synthesis. We must first see things together before we can take them apart, and we cannot see things together unless we put them together.

This seems to be one of the main problems of a logical classification. In view of the vast field of knowledge yet to be discovered, how successfully can we proceed with the mental grouping of "known" and often fragmentized pieces of information, fitting them into existing (or non-existing) patterns in our attempt at a synthesis? To Aristotle, scientific knowledge consists of arranging these particulars under class concepts (he called them "universals"), and combining these concepts into a system. For him, science was definition, or explanation of a concept, first in terms of its essential properties, then in terms of those differentiating properties which set it apart from other conceptualized groups. The ultimate purpose of Aristotelian science was a complete classification of objects of knowledge into concepts exhibiting all the resemblances and differences essential to their full comprehension. Definition of a term or a class concept must be a complete statement of:

a)   the *essential attributes* of the class, e.g., "Man is an animal with powers of rational speech"

b) the *peculiar attributes* of the class, e.g., "Man is capable of laughter"

c) the *next higher genus*, e.g., "Man is an animal"

d) the *differentiating properties*, e.g., "Man is the only animal capable of speech"

e) the *accidents* or properties not included in the definition, but common to this and other classes, e.g., "Man is a material object."

Modern science views the Aristotelian synthesis as incomplete but generally valid. If classification per se is not knowledge, it is certainly the most important method of dealing with knowledge. It enables us to observe objects and events, and to abstract from their various qualities those characteristics that they have in common and that show how they are related. This is the process by which we arrive at all scientific generalization.

TYPES OF CLASSIFICATION

Philosophical classification, which is based on the essential characteristics of the phenomena classified, is frequently called natural classification, because it is closely linked with natural language and its semantic context. Contrasted with it is artificial classification, which adopts some chance property or trait as the criterion of arrangement. However, certain traits dependent on such things as the random consequences of naming can give rise to orderly arrangements of considerable value, such as alphabetical lists of names, or conventionalized (mnemonic) series of numbers. These artificial traits are quite commonly used as auxiliary techniques of practical classification.

From another point of view, classes are logically characterized by their extension and their intension. The extension of a class is the aggregate of things (actions, events, etc.) which it includes or denotes. The class of "trees" has greater extension than that of "maples" because it denotes more members. The intension of a class is the sum of its unique attributes, qualities, or identifying marks which, taken together, imply the concept signified by its name. The name, in this sense, connotes the essence, the *sine qua non*, without which the thing (action, event, etc.) cannot be a member of the class. Thus a tree cannot be "deciduous" unless it sheds its leaves at the end of each growing season. Clearly the terms "extension" and "intension" are correlative. That is, they complement one another by reciprocally delimiting concepts and explicating definitions.

The notions of extension and intension are especially illuminating in discussions of hierarchical, as distinct from referential classification. Hierarchical classification is based on the assumption that the process of subdivision and collocation must exhibit as much as possible the "natural" organization of the subject, proceeding from classes of greater extension and smaller intension to those of smaller extension and greater intension. It represents knowledge "as a 'family tree' following, at least in part, the rules of division accepted by logicians."[1] Its principles may be summarized as follows:

1. It proceeds by assembling the groups of sciences of the principal fields of knowledge into main classes or divisions which are dictated by the accepted theory of knowledge.

2. It continues by the designation of differentiating qualities within each main class, thus producing subclasses and subdivisions.

3. Each subgroup is divided by further differentiating qualities to produce successively sections and subsections until further differentiation is impossible or impracticable.

4. Each differentiated subgroup of a class is subordinate to the class heading. The sum of these subgroups is the whole meaning of the class term.[2]

Referential classification may appear to group categories and topics in hierarchical arrays, but in contrast to "natural," scientifically determined subordination, it ranks them more or less artifically according to one or more traits arbitrarily chosen for the purpose. Essentially it is,

> . . . a pragmatic and empirical system in which the constituent elements are related with reference to a single isolated trait, property, or use, without respect to other characteristics. Referential classification admits the possibility of regrouping the same universe of things according to a different trait, property, etc. Such a classification is predicated upon the obvious truth that any single unit may be meaningful in any number of different relationships, depending upon the immediate purpose. In referential classification it is the external relations, the environment, rather than the "essence" of concepts, that are all important to the act of classifying.[3]

The cross-fertilization concepts in information retrieval that are based on the multidimensional approach make more use of referential than of hierarchical classification. They also rely on a minimum of enumeration, and tend to be synthetic in nature. Enumerative classification attempts to assign designations for (to enumerate) all the single and composite subject concepts required in the system. The individual classifier is more or less expected to fit his entire collection into the Procrustean bed of the schedule listings, having little opportunity to insert new concepts because no mechanism is provided with which to do so.[4] Synthetic classifications are more likely to confine their explicit lists of designations to single, unsubdivided concepts, giving the local classifier generalized rules with which to construct headings for composite subjects.

> . . . the older general bibliographical schemes tended to enumerate all subjects . . . and to provide symbols as a ready-made class-mark for each subject identified and listed. A different approach is now favoured by many classificationists, but widely-used schemes — particularly LC and to a somewhat lesser extent DC — adhere strongly to the idea of the systematic listing or enumeration of subjects in a gigantic classificatory map. They are thus sometimes referred to as *enumerative classifications*.

The newer method relies on *synthesis*—the fitting together of various components to specify a subject—rather than an enumeration. It is often associated with the eminent Indian librarian, S. R. Ranganathan, and was put forward, somewhat tentatively, in 1933 in the *Colon Classification*. . . .

The distinction between the two approaches may be clarified by means of examples. Consider the specific subject: *"The doctrine of Grace in Methodism in Britain during the eighteenth century."* A *completely enumerative* classification would try to provide the *classifier* with a complete class-mark for this, as for all other subjects. (It may be noted that the older schemes are rarely enumerative to this degree, but the method of listing all topics is essentially the major principle which they try to follow.) A *completely synthetic*, or *faceted*, scheme on the other hand would instruct the classifier to break down the subject into its component parts and then to build the required class-mark by linking together the part representing Methodism (as a branch of Christianity in the Religion class), the part representing Grace (from the Doctrines facet of that class), the part representing Britain (from the geographical facet common to all classes), and the part representing the eighteenth century (from the Chronological facet applicable to each class).[5]

LIBRARY CLASSIFICATION

Organized documentary collections have existed since early civilizations learned to convert their spoken languages to written form. Even before the codex book appeared, early record depositories received some form of utilitarian arrangement. Groupings were made by title, by broad subject, by chronology, by author, by order of acquisition, by size, etc. But, the most substantive developments in the arrangement of library collections were concurrent with the rapid growth of libraries and their use during the nineteenth century. At that time librarians felt a definite need for better methods of arrangement, so that the content of their holdings would be available, and more apparent, to the user.

The history of modern library classification corresponds to the various attempts to adapt and modify existing philosophical systems of knowledge to the arrangement of materials and to users' needs. One of the best known early American classifiers was Thomas Jefferson, third President of the United States. He adapted certain elements of Francis Bacon's outline of knowledge, not only to his own library, but also to his plans for the organization of the University of Virginia and the reorganization of the College of William and Mary.

Bacon's system classified materials as functions of the three basic faculties: history (natural, civil, literary, ecclesiastical) as the function of memory; philosophy (including theology) as that of reason; and poetry, fables, and the like, as that of imagination.[6] Its influence was widespread. Jean Le Rond d'Alembert used the Baconian system for the arrangement of the famous *Encyclopédie ou dictionnaire raisonné des sciences des arts et des métiers* of the French Enlightenment (1751-1765). Jefferson's classification was based on that modification as was the *Catalogue* of Benjamin Franklin's Library Company of Philadelphia (1789). Three years before Jefferson's *Catalogue of the Library of the United States* was installed at the Library of Congress, a variant of the Philadelphia scheme was used to produce the 1812 *Catalogue of the Library of Congress.*[7]

Among other early followers of the Baconian system were Thaddeus Mason Harris, librarian at Harvard (1791-1793); Edward William Johnson, librarian of the College of South Carolina and later of the St. Louis Mercantile Library; and, finally, Johnson's successor, William Torrey Harris, a Hegelian who inverted the Baconian system, creating an independent American classification. At the same time, various adaptations of the Brunet utilitarian classification scheme existed in several American libraries as a direct result of its use to arrange parts of the British Museum and the Bibliothèque Nationale.[8]

In 1876 Melvil Dewey devised his famous Dewey Decimal Classification (DDC), based in large part on W. T. Harris's system, with a decimal notation. Soon DDC was spreading its influence throughout the world. At about the same time, Charles A. Cutter began his work at the Boston Athenaeum. Cutter sought to achieve, not a classification of knowledge, but a practical, useful method for arranging library materials. Nevertheless, his Expansive Classification shows the definite influence of Spencer and Comte, especially in the development of its subordinate classes.

At the beginning of the present century, when the Library of Congress had grown from several thousand books to nearly one million, it was apparent that the library would need a new classification system. After much deliberation, J. C. M. Hanson and Charles Martel decided to design an independent system governed by the actual content of the collection (literary warrant). This form of classification differs from a purely philosophical approach in that it is based on the books as entities. For this reason it is enumerative yet referential.

In contrast to more hierarchical and enumerative classifications, such as the DDC, LC, Cutter, and Brown schemes, the Colon system is more referential and synthetic, while the Universal Decimal Classification (UDC) and Bliss's Bibliographic Classification, especially in its new second edition, are interesting blends of the two types. As indicated earlier, traditional schemes were never completely enumerative. Dewey made use of a table of "form divisions"; Cutter introduced supplementary tables of geographic and chronological numbers; and the internal and external tables in the LC schedules borrowed all these devices from the earlier schemes. Recent editions of DDC and LC schedules show increased emphasis on auxiliary displays as a means of synthesizing possible class numbers. Brown's Subject Classification had its Categorical and Biographical Tables. The distinction between enumerative and synthetic approaches to classification is a matter of degree, but serves as a guiding principle for charting the progress of modern theory.

In summary, established philosophical systems of knowledge, with various modifications, underlie most traditional library classifications. The frequent distinction between classification of knowledge and classification of materials seems to have confused the thinking of many librarians. The two processes have important interactions. Even cursory examination of any library classification, including those purporting to organize "the items themselves," reveals an intellectual concept of the item as an expression of certain ideas in one of many available media. Philosophical classification organizes knowledge itself — registering, evaluating, and classifying thoughts, ideas, and concepts for the universal purpose of adequately representing the field of human learning. Library classification arranges the records which express and preserve knowledge, making adjustments as needed because of the physical format of such records. Henry Bliss took this view as a fundamental premise of his own work in bibliographic classification:

> The distinction so often drawn between the classification of knowledge and the classification of books should not lead us to negative conclusions, such as those of the logician Jevons, the bibliographer Schneider, and the classificationer, Melvil Dewey. There are indeed two kinds of classification, on the one hand the logical, natural, and scientific, on the other hand the practical, the arbitrary, the purposive; but for library classification we should join these two hands; the two purposes should be combined. To make the classification conform to the scientific and educational organization of knowledge is to make it the more practical. A logical and scientific organization of knowledge should be adapted to the practical requirements, the various bibliographic services, and the necessary economies. It were well too that we should bear in mind that a library is, in a higher view, a temple of knowledge, and its classification should be, not a haphazard, ramshackle structure, but an internal edifice worthy of its environment and itself of intellectual and educational value.[9]

The natural order of any subject, according to Bliss, is to put the general works first. These should be followed by works on general subjects treated specially, then by works on special subjects treated generally, and lastly by works on special subjects treated specially. The "natural" hierarchy of the discipline or topic is thus preserved:

1. The general treated generally: *Locomotives*
2. The general treated specially: *Loco-design*
3. The special treated generally: *Electric locomotives*
4. The special treated specially: *Electric loco-design*

Bliss designed a table to show graded specifications applicable to the systematic subdivision of most subjects, general or special:[10]

GENERAL IN SCOPE
    Bibliographical
    Historical and critical
        Historical
        Method, scope, and relations of the subject to others
        Critical
        Biographical
        Ancillary: statistics, illustrations, etc.; documents, reports, etc.
    Miscellaneous
        Periodicals and serials of societies, etc.
        Collections, selections, readings, miscellanies, essays

GENERAL IN SCOPE AND TREATMENT
  Elementary, introductory
  Manuals, compends
  Treatises, principles, comprehensive studies
  Discourses

GENERAL IN SCOPE AND SPECIAL IN TREATMENT
  Theoretical treatises
  Aspects of general subject
  Treatment for special purposes, interests, professions, etc.
  Technical
  Experimental and laboratory

SPECIAL IN SCOPE AND TREATMENT
  Special subjects
  Special theories
  Aspects in special interests
  Special topics
  Special methods, experiments, etc.
  Statistical treatment
  Pamphlets of special content, and other special materials

FUNCTIONAL PROPERTIES OF
TRADITIONAL CLASSIFICATION SCHEMES

Most traditional classification systems are basically enumerative. By contrast, the more recent schemes tend to be synthetic. In this introductory text the discussion of functional properties will apply quite generally to both kinds of order. All printed schedules of library classifications reflect adjustments to the media in which the information may appear and provide detailed analysis of the scope and sequence of topics covered. But it is well to remember that materials on shelves or in files are arranged in a single order. Most items can be requested by author, title, subject, or form, but they can be organized by only one of these at a time. Linear arrangement imposes certain limitations on the classifier. Over the years efforts to meet such limitations have resulted in techniques or features which are characteristic of nearly every worthwhile library classification.

One such feature is a generalia or general works class, which accommodates items that are too broad in scope for inclusion in any single class. Such works usually overlap several traditional disciplines or "classes," e.g., encyclopedias, dictionaries, general periodicals, etc.

In addition, form classes organize materials according to their form of presentation rather than to their subject content. Literary works, e.g., poetry, drama, fiction, etc., are the most obvious, but books of etchings, photographs, musical scores, etc. also fall into this group.

Form divisions group items dealing with different subjects in the same mode of presentation. The "standard subdivisions" of the Dewey Decimal Classification, for instance, can be used to subdivide most disciplines or topics. It should be recognized, however, that some are "modes of treatment" rather than "form divisions." So, for example, "compends," "outlines," "dictionaries," or "periodicals" belonging to a subject do embody physical forms. Other groups such as philosophical or theoretical treatments, works dealing with study and teaching or research in a subject, histories, and biographies, etc., are classified rather by their "inner form."

A notation translates the meaning of a specific class, division, or subdivision into a shorthand symbol or code to be used as a shelf or file address and a convenient reference to the arrangement and identification of the parts of the system. It must be simple, brief, and flexible. It may be composed of letters, numerals, arbitrary signs, or a mixture of these. In general, there are two basic types of notation. Pure notation uses one kind of symbol, such as the Roman alphabet or Arabic numerals, consistently and exclusively, or nearly so (although one might question whether a pure letter notation would permit both upper and lower case symbols denoting variations of signification). The Dewey Decimal Classification is known for its "pure" notation, but it employs a decimal point as well as the ten digits. Mixed notation uses two or more kinds of symbols, e.g., a combination of letters and numerals. Notation plays an important role in any classification scheme, especially with the modern emphasis on relative location. A notation that serves as a guide to the arrangement of items on the shelf helps to preserve orderly sequence by topic, or form, or whatever the principle of organization may be. A summary of some of the functions and properties of notation follows:

1) A notation stands in place of terms used in the classification schedules. It shows the sequence of classes, and in some cases (e.g., the Dewey Decimal Classification) hierarchical subordination of subjects. Thus it is not only a location device representing the classification terminology in a symbolic language, but it may also guide the user to the position of actual subjects in the array, indicating subject relationships.

2) A notation serves to connect the alphabetical order of terms listed in the index with the systematic order of classification.

3) A notation should be simple and brief in order to provide such guidance functions efficiently. It should contain some mnemonic features or easily identified aids to the memory. In addition, it should be flexible, reflecting the hospitality of the classification system to new topics, aspects of topics, inter-relationships, etc. That is, it should provide one or more techniques for being expanded according to need.

Another feature of the library classification is the index, which provides a means of efficient alphabetical reference to all the terms used in the classification schedules. Some indexes are specific, e.g., that in Brown's Subject Classification, which claims to provide but a single place for each subject (cf. p. 466). Other indexes are relative, in that they not only provide alphabetical references to all terms used in the schedules, but also show the relation of each specific subject to other related subjects or their aspects. Perhaps the best known of this type is the relative index to the Dewey Decimal Classification, where the disciplinary organization makes it likely that a single topic will be subordinated under more than one class or subclass, according to its different features or characteristics. No doubt a relative index is a useful aid for the beginning student of classification; in the classification process it is important not only to locate specific topics in the index and the schedules, but also to learn how to relate specific items to the rest of the collection. The key to successful classification is realization that library materials are arranged according to specific subjects or forms, but are also arranged in relation to the subject and forms of other materials.

CRITERIA FOR A
SUCCESSFUL CLASSIFICATION SCHEME

Classification schemes, as indicated earlier, vary widely. Besides providing for the subject organization of the collection, a successful classification scheme may consist of such devices as:

Classification by method of treatment or form of materials treated. Both of these considerations are open to the classifier's prejudices.

Classification according to an alphabetical arrangement of subjects. In this method the notation must be manipulated rather carefully to allow for expansion to include new subjects.

Classification according to a variety of bibliographic details, such as place of printing, publication, date, or type of binding.

Any or all of these techniques may be justifiably and successfully used for a special situation such as a rare book collection or a collection concerned with a particular subject area or period. Assuming, however, that the library is neither highly specialized nor its collection exceedingly rare, it is well to list a few criteria which may be generally applied to judge a successful classification system:

1. It must be inclusive as well as comprehensive. That is, it must encompass the whole field of knowledge as represented in collectible media of communication and information. It must therefore include all subjects that are, have been, or may be recognized, allowing for possible future additions to the body of knowledge. It must make provision, not only for the records themselves, but for every actual and potential use of the records.

2. It must be systematic. Not only must the division of subjects be exhaustive, but it must bring together related topics in logical, comprehensible fashion, allowing its users to locate easily whatever they want that is available. It must be so arranged that each aspect of a subject can be considered a separate, yet related, part of the scheme, and it must be so arranged that new topics and aspects can be added in a systematic manner.

3. It must be flexible and expansible. It must be constructed so that any new subject may be inserted without dislocating the general sequence of classification. It must allow for recognized knowledge in all its ramifications, and it must be capable of admitting new subjects or new aspects of well-established subjects. The flexibility of the notation is of first importance if the classification scheme is to be expansive and hospitable in the highest degree. It should also be current. Both the Dewey Decimal Office and the Library of Congress send subscribing libraries periodic lists of all changes in their schedules, noting additions and deletions. These notices and revisions are especially important in subject areas in which a great deal of new work is being done.

4. It must employ terminology that is clear and descriptive, with consistent meaning for both the user and the classifier. The arrangement of terms in the schedule and the index should help reveal the significance of the arrangement. The terms themselves should be unambiguous and reasonably current, correctly identifying the concepts and characteristics present in the materials being classified.

BROAD AND CLOSE CLASSIFICATION

Close classification means classing each work as specifically as possible, using all available subdivisions in the classification scheme. Broad classification groups works under the main divisions and subdivisions of the scheme, without using its minute breakdowns into narrower concepts. The classifier using the schedules should understand that when a library has relatively few items in a given subject area, broad classification might actually be more useful than isolating each item under its own specific call number, since many graduated progressions of the full scheme are not represented in the collection. A library using the Dewey Decimal Classification with a large collection of Bibles, for example, may need to classify the King James Version in 220.5203, whereas a smaller collection might cut back to the broad number 220. Generally speaking, DDC provides small libraries with more opportunities than does the LC Classification to cut back to broader numbers, because its enumeration stresses logical progress through the natural hierarchies of subject matter, while the Library of Congress bases its enumeration more on the large quantities of materials represented on its shelves and has relatively few numbers that signify broad categories. Larger libraries, having more titles to arrange in a given subject area, often prefer the LC opportunities for close classification.

GENERAL PRINCIPLES OF CLASSIFYING

In discussing the philosophical properties of classification, a distinction was drawn between making a more or less comprehensive scheme, and applying it piecemeal in the actual process of classifying each new document. Most of this chapter has been directed to the broad principles, methods, and problems of constructing classification systems. Some attention should now be given to the application of any one such system to the ordering of a library collection and to the necessity of choosing the optimum location for each item.

When classifying an item with respect to the particular library's holdings, the classifier should, as well as the system allows, observe and translate that item's characteristics of discipline, topic, form, etc. into the conceptual frame of the system. To do so, it may be necessary to by-pass existing minute or narrow concepts and class numbers, or to insert new ones into the existing schedules. We noted earlier that both of these modifications are usually possible in some degree, but classification schemes vary in their hospitality to local manipulation. It is assumed that such possibilities and difficulties were considered when the choice was made of one scheme over all others for use in a local library.

Once the particular system of arrangement is chosen, certain general precepts enable the classifier to apply it meaningfully and consistently to the separate items and groups of items acquired by the library. The following summary is designed to aid that process of continuous, cumulative application. These principles apply primarily to such linear (shelf) classifications as the Dewey Decimal and the Library of Congress schemes.[11]

1. **Class the item first according to subject, then by the form in which the subject is represented, except in the generalia class and in literature, where form might be paramount.** In most cases the classifier has to determine the subject matter of the item using the classification schedules as the matrix. This is no easy task, especially when the item does not cover a specific, easily recognized topic. Chapter 1 of this text provides a short summary of procedures used by catalogers in "reading an item technically." The technique is helpful in subject, as well as in descriptive, cataloging. Such features as the preface, introduction, table of contents, or even the index may help the classifier to recognize the subject matter.

Following the principle of generally classifying an item by subject, one entitled *History of Mathematics* should be classified with mathematics, not with history. Similarly, *Nature in Italian Art, a Study of Landscape Backgrounds from Giotto to Tintoretto* would be classified under landscape painting, not under the history of Italian art. In some cases, however, the subject is elusive and the classifier must rely on his or her judgment. The problem, well described by Bliss, has been elaborated upon by Sayers:

> If the book on Scotland is not mainly geographic and historical, but consists of descriptive and narrative chapters together with a melange of literary and scientific observations and reflections on the national traits and institutions, also considerable social philosophy in the last chapters, the judgment is indeed complex and the decisions may be uncertain.[12]

Given these conditions, several other general principles must be considered in selecting the proper alternative.

2. **Class an item where it will be most useful.** The classifier has to consider the nature of the collection (see the previous discussion of broad versus close classification) and the needs of the user. Generally speaking, this second principle is a part of the fundamental rule that characteristics chosen for classification are essential to the purpose for which the scheme was developed. At least two questions can be raised in this context:

a. What is the subject matter of the item and how does it relate to the nature of the collection? The procedures in a highly specialized library with a professional clientele will be different from those used in a public library.

b. What is the form in which the subject is presented, or its method of treatment? For example, subject bibliographies can be classed in one of two ways. If they are put with related subject materials they will be more useful to a patron who wants titles on a given subject already represented in the library's holdings. If, as in both the DDC and LC classifications, the preferred location is in a separate bibliography section which is further subdivided into author bibliographies, national bibliographies, subject bibliographies, etc., then the "user" who benefits most is the librarian doing bibliographic verification, book order preparation, and the like.

3. **Place the item in the most specific subject division that will contain it, rather than with the general topic.** In this respect it is helpful to study the morphology of the entire scheme, in order to answer such questions as:

a. What is the specific heading embracing the subject?

b. How is this subject subdivided in the classification schedule?

Obviously if most libraries of any size would assign a single number to all books dealing with the history of France, failing to subdivide them by time periods and places, the result would be a discouragingly large assortment of volumes under one number. On the other hand, the uses of broad classification for definite, clearly recognized objectives, should not be overlooked.

4. **When the book deals with two or three subjects, place it with the predominant subject or with the one treated first. When the book deals with more than three subjects, place it in the general class that combines all of them.** This principle requires little explanation. The subject that is treated most fully should take predominance over secondary subjects. If two subjects are coordinate (e.g., electricity and magnetism treated equally in the same volume) the item should be placed with whichever topic comes first.

There are some refinements to this general principle. For example, if the work covers two subjects, one of which is represented as acting upon or influencing the other, such a work should be classed under the subject influenced or acted upon. Thus a work discussing French influence on English literature should be classed with English literature. On similar grounds a work such as *Religious Aspects of Philosophy* should be classed under philosophy, not religion, since a treatment of some particular aspect of a subject should be classed with the subject, not with the aspect.

Another, perhaps more involved difficulty arises with the monographic series or collected set. (*See* pages 261-62.) Will Durant's *Story of Civilization* can be classed as an author's collection of six related volumes under a broad "history of civilization" number. Or the classifier can place volume 1 with other works on oriental civilization, volume 2 with those on Greek civilization, and so on. The Library of Congress traditionally prefers to shelve series and collected sets together, but has in recent years provided, for optional use by other libraries, an alternative, volume-specific class number in brackets on most of its separate records for monographs belonging to serial sets. Since 1974 the quarterly *Monographic Series* lists all such records alphabetically under their respective series names.

CONCLUSION

Critics have noted limitations in existing classification systems used by most libraries today.[13] A few are summarized here only as a basis for further study. There is a long-standing argument over the logical arrangement of various systems. Though a scheme may be logical within itself, it can also have inconsistencies. For example, in Dewey Decimal Classification, language is separated from literature, and history from social sciences. In the Library of Congress scheme language is classified with literature, as history is shelved close to the social sciences. Arguments can be advanced for both approaches. Language is closely related to literature, but it is also an essential to all disciplines. History throws much light on the social sciences, but every discipline and every literature has its own history which influences, and is influenced by general social history. There is some evidence that the current trend away from hierarchical enumeration toward referential synthesis has lessened concern over achieving the one incontestibly correct logical arrangement.

Again, DDC and LC, the two most popular library classifications, are both linear, and therefore uni-dimensional. Yet the relationships among works are multi-dimensional and cannot be represented as the projection of a straight line. Linear arrangement, plus the expense and potential confusion of classing different copies of the same item in different places, requires that one classification number be assigned to each title whether it covers one subject or many. A supplementary subject approach to classified materials through separate subject lists with references was developed in an attempt to solve this and related problems. See chapters 26-28 for extended discussions of the technique.

Other limitations include problems of reorganization and relocation arising from the need to keep any classification scheme up to date. One of the most obvious of these problems is the tendency of the notation to become more complex and awkward as the schedules are expanded to include new subjects and to define old topics more specifically.

In chapters 23-25 seven of the better-known modern classifications devised by librarians and used in various library contexts will be discussed. Their resemblances and differences will be briefly examined, to show their actual and possible uses, strengths, and limitations.

'FOOTNOTES

[1]W. C. Berwick Sayers, *Sayers' Manual of Classification for Librarians*, 5th ed. rev. by Arthur Maltby (London, Andre Deutsch, 1975), pp. 33-34.

[2]Jesse H. Shera and Margaret E. Egan, *The Classified Catalog* (Chicago, American Library Association, 1956), pp. 38-39.

[3]Shera and Egan, *Classified Catalog*, pp. 39-40.

[4]A. C. Foskett, *The Subject Approach to Information*, 3rd ed. (London, Clive Bingley; Hamden, CT, Linnet Books, 1977), p. 96.

[5]Sayers, *Manual of Classification*, 5th ed., pp. 34-35.

[6]Cf. Bacon's *Advancement of Learning* (1605) and *De augmentis scientarium* (Bacon's influence on the Dewey and Library of Congress classification is discussed briefly on pages 406 and 429).

[7]LaMontagne, Leo E., "Historical Background of Classification," in *The Subject Analysis of Library Materials* (New York, Columbia University School of Library Service, 1953), p. 20.

[8]Further historical information about the development of modern classification schemes can be found in chapters 23-25.

[9]Henry Evelyn Bliss, *The Organization of Knowledge in Libraries*, 2nd ed. rev. and partly rewritten (New York, H. W. Wilson, 1939), pp. 36-37.

[10]Bliss, *Organization of Knowledge*, p. 93.

[11]This discussion summarizes the principles stated by several authors, including William Stetson Merrill, *Code for Classifiers, Principles Governing the Consistent Placing of Books in a System of Classification*, 2nd ed. (Chicago, American Library Association, 1939) and W. C. Berwick Sayers, *A Manual of Classification for Libraries and Bibliographers*, 3rd ed. (London, Andre Deutsch, 1955). These principles apply primarily to such linear classifications as Dewey Decimal. The reader will also observe that for the purpose of this discussion we selected Sayers' third edition and not the fifth, quoted earlier.

[12]Quoted in Sayers, *Manual of Classification*, 3rd ed., pp. 235-36.

[13]A helpful list of articles and books on classification theory can be found in the brief bibliography: Phyllis A. Richmond, "Reading List in Classification Theory," *Library Resources & Technical Services* 16 (Summer 1972):364-82.

23 DEWEY DECIMAL CLASSIFICATION

INTRODUCTION

Of modern library classification schemes, the Dewey Decimal Classification is both the oldest and the most widely used in the United States. It also has a substantial following abroad. Such widespread use is a tribute to Melvil[le Louis Kossuth] Dewey, whose original plan was adaptable enough to incorporate new subjects as they emerged, and flexible enough to withstand the changes imposed by the passage of time. Born on December 10, 1851, and graduated from Amherst in 1874, Dewey became assistant college librarian. He developed the first draft of his system for arranging books at that time. He soon became a leader in American librarianship, helping to found both the American Library Association and the first American library school at Columbia University. Being a man of many interests, he was also an advocate of spelling reform. He shortened his forename to "Melvil," dropped his two middle names, and even attempted to change the spelling of his surname to "Dui." Throughout his career he promoted librarianship by his teaching, writing, and speaking. In recognizing and acting upon the need to systematize library collections for effective use, he knew of various previous attempts, but found them inadequate.

In 1870 W. T. Harris, of the St. Louis public schools, suggested a general classification based on an inversion of the Baconian order, which divided all knowledge into two broad categories: human and divine. Bacon subdivided each of these categories into history, poesy, and philosophy (discussed in chapter 22 of this text, Subject Arrangement of Library Materials). History derived from memory; poesy from imagination; and philosophy from reason. Only the first category, human knowledge, was used by Bacon's followers, until William Harris incorporated the second category (revealed theology) into the class "religion." Inverting the three main classes of the first category, Harris started his outline with science, including philosophy, religion, etc. He then added art (including fine arts, poetry, and pure fiction), and finally history (including geography, civil history, and biography). In general, Dewey's outline approximates that of Harris, as the following table shows:

Bacon		Harris	Dewey
Original	**Inverted**		
		Science	
History	Philosophy	Philosophy	General Works
		Religion	
		Social and Politi-	Religion
		cal Science	Sociology
		Natural Sciences	Philology
		and Useful Arts	Science
			Useful Arts
Poesy	Poesy	**Art**	
		Fine Arts	Fine Arts
		Poetry	Literature
		Pure Fiction	
		Literary Miscellany	
		History	
Philosophy	History	Geography and	History
		Travel	Biography
		Civil History	Geography and
		Biography	Travel
		Appendix	
		Miscellany	

Dewey never claimed to have originated decimals for classification nota-tion, but earlier systems used them merely as shelf location devices with no significant relation to the subject matter. What Dewey did claim, and with some justification, was his "relative index," compiled as a key to the "diverse material" included in his tables. His most significant contribution was perhaps the use of decimals for hierarchical divisions. Combined with the digits 0 to 9, decimals provide a pure notation which can be subdivided indefinitely. Through the inclusion of lead zeros, the decimal principle dominates even the three notational places to the left of the decimal point.

The first edition of Dewey's scheme, prepared for the Amherst College Library, was issued anonymously in 1876 under the title *A Classification and Subject Index for Cataloguing and Arranging the Books and Pamphlets of a Library*. It included schedules to 1,000 divisions numbered 000-999, together with a relative index and prefatory matter—a total of forty-four pages. The second, "revised and greatly enlarged" edition was published under Dewey's name in 1885. Since that time seventeen more full editions and eleven abridgments have appeared. The fourteenth edition, published in 1942, remained the standard edition for many years because an experimental index to the fifteenth edition, published in 1951, was unsuccessful. In 1958 the six-teenth edition appeared with many changes and additions, including a com-plete revision of sections 546-47, "Inorganic and Organic Chemistry." Since that time each successive edition has carried, besides other, less sweeping changes, one or more "phoenix schedules," which are totally new developments of targeted portions of the system. The present nineteenth edition, and its associated eleventh abridged edition, was published in 1979.[1]

BASIC CONCEPTS

The system is called "decimal" because it arranges all knowledge as represented by library materials into ten broad subject classes numbered from 000 to 900. Using Arabic numerals for symbols, it is flexible only to the degree that numbers can be expanded in linear fashion to cover special aspects of general subjects. Theoretically, expansions may continue indefinitely. The more specific the work being classified, the longer the number combination will tend to grow. At least one Library of Congress record carries a suggested Dewey number containing twenty-one digits, i.e., eighteen decimal places (cf. LC card number 72-90701 — *American Indian Art: Form and Tradition*). But such long numbers, however accurate, are unwieldy; it is hard to crowd them onto book spines and catalog cards, and dangers of miscopying and misshelving are multiplied. For these and related reasons many larger libraries have turned from DDC to some other system, such as LC, which has a more economical notation.

Nevertheless, the Dewey Decimal Classification System has many advantages. Its content is compact, consisting in the eighteenth and nineteenth editions of a volume for introductory matter, auxiliary tables, a list of relocations and schedule reductions, and a series of three schedule summaries, plus a second volume for schedule development and a third for the relative index. It incorporates many mnemonic devices that can be transferred from one class to another (e.g., "-03" at the end of a class number of any length often indicates a dictionary of the subject at hand). The classifier, once familiar with the system, can apply it to incoming materials quite rapidly. It provides a limited number of optional alternative locations and allows for great detail of specification. The patron is likely to be familiar with it, because it is the system most frequently used in school and small public libraries. Furthermore, it arranges subjects from the general to the specific in a logical order, which often can be traced by analogy through more than one class. It is philosophical in conception, being based on a systematic outline of knowledge that allows for subjects not yet known to man. Even so, the overall arrangement is not preemptively theoretical or logical. Dewey's intent was to provide a practical system for classifying books. This primary application to the books generally found in American libraries remains one of its notable limitations, although efforts have been made in later editions to rectify that bias.

SCHEDULE FORMAT

At the close of volume 1, DDC provides three summaries, showing successively the ten main classes, the 100 divisions, and the 1,000 sections of the basic scheme. Each class from 100 to 900 consists of a group of related disciplines. The 000 class is reserved for materials too general to fit anywhere else.

The Ten Main DDC Classes

000 Generalities
100 Philosophy & related disciplines
200 Religion
300 Social sciences
400 Language
500 Pure sciences
600 Technology (Applied sciences)
700 The arts
800 Literature (Belles-lettres)
900 General geography & history

Each main class is separated into ten divisions, although a few of these, and of further subdivisions, may seem to be rather artifically located within the class:

The Divisions of a Typical DDC Class

600-609 Technology (Applied sciences)
610-619 Medical sciences   Medicine
620-629 Engineering and allied operations
630-639 Agriculture and related technologies
640-649 Home economics and family living
650-659 Management and auxiliary services
660-669 Chemical and related technologies
670-679 Manufactures
680-689 Manufacture of products for specific uses
690-699 Buildings

As a hierarchical classification, DDC applies the principle of developing disciplinary and subject relationships sequentially, from the general topic to the special/specific subdivision. Within most subdivisions the first portion covers general works on the given topic:

The Sections of a Typical DDC Division

610 Medical sciences   Medicine
611 Human anatomy, cytology, tissues
612 Human physiology
613 General & personal hygiene
614 Public health & related topics
615 Pharmacology & therapeutics
616 Diseases
617 Surgery & related topics
618 Other branches of medicine
619 Experimental medicine

In volume 2 the full schedules present in detail those subjects identified by the primary sections:

The Subdivisions of a Typical DDC Section

612	Human physiology
612.1	Blood and circulation
612.2	Respiration
612.3	Nutrition
612.4	Secretion, excretion, related functions
612.6	Reproduction, development, maturation
612.7	Motor functions and integument
612.8	Nervous and sensory functions
612.9	Regional physiology

Decimals may of course be, and usually are, further subdivided, although, as in the section subdivisions listed above, there are often asymmetrics attesting to the fact that the phenomena of the world cannot always be subdivided and re-subdivided into groups of ten:

Extended Decimal Subdivision of a DDC Topic

612	Human physiology
612.1	Blood and circulation
612.11	Blood
612.12	Blood chemistry
612.13	Blood vessels and vascular circulation
612.14	Blood pressure
612.17	Heart
612.18	Vasometers

Successive lengthening of the base number by one (occasionally two or three) digit(s) achieves step-wise division. This pyramidal structure means that, in subject relationships, what is true of the whole is true of the parts. For instance, the medical sciences are a branch of technology; physiology is a medical science, etc.

A Typical DDC Hierarchical Sequence

600	Technology (Applied sciences)
610	Medical sciences Medicine
612	Human physiology
612.1	Blood and respiration
612.11	Blood
612.112	White corpuscles

As the notation expands beyond the decimal point, DDC editors introduce a space after every third number. Thus the schedules show "331.873 2 Membership and membership policies in labor unions," or "001.644 04 Electronic data processing network systems." The schedules rarely display numbers with more than four decimal places, although the relative index sometimes expands numbers to eight or even nine decimals. Thus in the index we find "Radiations — biophysics — terrestrial — med. sci. — animals 636.089 201 448." Yet the schedules proper expand "636 - Animal husbandry" only as far as "636.089 Veterinary sciences; veterinary medicine." The decimal spaces are inserted merely to facilitate reading the closely-listed digits. On library materials and bibliographic records they should be omitted, so that the number will occupy no more space than is absolutely necessary.

Certain places in the schedules where fully symmetrical expansion cannot be maintained are given centered headings, which represent concepts for which there is no specific number in the notational hierarchy, and which, therefore, cover an abbreviated span of numbers. These appear with centered inch-long lines immediately above them, and with triangular arrow-head indicators at their left margins, e.g.,

A Typical DDC Centered Heading

▶   439.7-439.8   East Scandinavian languages

If the sequential development of subdivisions is spread over several pages in such a way that the original broad relationships are obscured, a summary introduces the governing steps of the sequence, e.g.,

Summary

332.1	Banks and banking
332.2	Specialized banking institutions
332.3	Credit and loan institutions
332.4	Money
332.5	Other mediums of exchange
332.6	Investment and investments
332.7	Credit
332.8	Interest and discount
332.9	Counterfeiting, forgery, alteration

Other useful formatting devices are the section numbers and running titles at the top of each page of volume 2 (the schedules), the use of bold-face and light-face type in various sizes, plus lefthand marginal indentions, to indicate hierarchical structure, the use of square brackets for numbers from which a topic has recently been shifted (or "relocated") and the use of italics for "reused" numbers. In the nineteenth edition there are only eleven individually reassigned topics for which italics warn the user that the number has been only recently vacated (*see* DDC edition 19, Editor's Introduction, volume 1, sections 14.23 and 2.4).

PHOENIX SCHEDULES

In the nineteenth edition there are also three relatively confined, but significant areas which have undergone complete remodeling. Sociology, which in edition 18 occupied number 301, is now recast into the span 301-307. Similarly, topics covering the political process (formerly subdivisions of "324 Electoral process" and "329 Practical politics. Political parties") have now been combined and reordered under 324 alone, leaving 329 vacated. The third broad change is in area notations -41 and -42, where subdivisions are revised to conform to the reorganized local administrative pattern of the United Kingdom. All these changes are summarized at the close of volume 1, where the edition 18 and 19 numbers are listed in parallel columns.

A fourth phoenix schedule was at one time contemplated for "560-590 Life sciences" but it was postponed, to allow more careful study, and to concentrate efforts in the three areas cited above.

CLASSIFICATION BY DISCIPLINE

A basic premise of the Dewey approach is that there is no one class for any given subject. The primary arrangement is by discipline. Any specific topic may appear in any number of disciplines. Various aspects of such a topic are usually brought together in the relative index. For example, a work on "families" may be classed in one of several places depending on its emphasis. Moreover, the phoenix schedule for sociology included in edition 19 has significantly changed some of these assignments, as can be seen in the table below. Besides the aspects shown there, other material on families may be found in still different DDC numbers. Use of the relative index would lead the classifier to some of them.

DDC Class Numbers Pertaining to the Family

19th ed.		18th ed.
155.924	Psychological influences of family members	155.924
173	Ethics of family relationships	173
241.63	Christian family ethics	241.63
249	Christian observances in family life	249
261.835	Christian attitudes on sex, marriage, family	261.8342
291.17835	Various religious attitudes on sex, family, etc.	291.178342
291.563	Moral theology and family relationships	291.563
294.3563	Buddhist attitudes on family relationships	294.3563
294.54863	Hindu attitudes on family relationships	294.54863
296.4	Religious family rites, celebrations, services	296.7
304.66	Population control, including family planning	301.426
306.8	Marriage and family	301.42
306.84	Types of marriage, monogamous, polygamous, etc.	301.422
306.85	Types of families, patriarchal, nuclear, etc.	301.421
306.87	Intrafamily relationships	301.427

306.88	Family dissolution	301.428
346.015	Domestic relations (Family law)	346.015
351.815	Population control and family planning	
362.82	Families with specific problems	362.82
364.253	Influence of family and peer groups on causes of crime and delinquency	364.253
392.3	Customs of the home and domestic arts	392.3
613.94	Family planning and birth control	613.94
616.89156	Family psychotherapy	616.8915
640.42	Family budgeting, expenditure control, etc.	640.42
646.78	Family living, harmonious relations, etc.	
790.191	Recreational activities for families	790.191
793.0191	Indoor activities and programs for families	793.0191
796.0191	Sports for families	796.0191
796.78	Driving family cars for pleasure	796.78
929.2	Family histories	929.2

SCOPE NOTES AND "ADD" INSTRUCTIONS

The schedules employ several instructional devices that will aid the classifier. One such device is the scope note, which appears frequently under a specific classification category, identifying what is to be classed in that number, or what should be classed elsewhere. For instance, under the centered heading 913-919 are found a cluster of scope notes and classing instructions as follows:

913-919   Geography of and travel in ancient world; specific continents, countries, localities; extraterrestrial worlds
      If preferred, class elementary geography textbooks on ancient world, on specific continents, countries, localities in 372.8913-372.8919

      Class interdisciplinary works on geography and history of ancient world, of specific continents, countries, localities [*all formerly* 913-919] in 930-990

      Class comprehensive works, geography of and travel in more than one continent in 910; geography of and travel in areas, regions, places not limited by continent, country, locality in 910.09; historical geography in 911; graphic representations in 912

Another type of scope note is the definition which helps the classifier understand the meaning of a particular topic, e.g.,

330   Economics
      The science of human behavior as it relates to utilization of scarce means for satisfaction of needs and desires through production, distribution, consumption

     For commerce, see 380.1

Still other headings are followed by notes enumerating specific qualifications, such as:

> 331   Labor economics
>   Class here industrial relations
>
>   Class sociology of laboring classes in 305.56, economic conditions of laboring classes in 330.9; personnel management in 658.3
>
> 331.1   Labor force and market
>   Class labor force and market with respect to workers with specific personal characteristics in 331.3-331.6

"Add" instructions appear under some simple numbers or sequences of numbers to serve as means of further subdivision through analogy. They refer the classifier to still another number or number sequence where subdivisions are spelled out, and give instructions on how to transfer the subdivisions into the analogue number or sequence. The following example will illustrate:

> 574.921-.928   Marine biology (Biological oceanography)
>   Add to base number 574.92 the numbers following 551.46 in 551.461-551.468, e.g. Mediterranean Sea life 574.922; however, class Antarctic waters of Atlantic Ocean in 574.924, of Pacific Ocean in 574.9258, of Indian Ocean in 574.927; comprehensive works on Antarctic waters in 574.924

Under "551.46   Oceanography" we find that the full sequence referred to may be summarized as follows:

> 551.461   Atlantic Ocean
> 551.4611   North Atlantic
> 551.4612-.4614   Northeast and northwest Atlantic
> 551.462   Mediterranean Sea
> 551.463   Caribbean Sea and Gulf of Mexico
> 551.464   South Atlantic Ocean
> 551.465   Pacific Ocean
> 551.466   East Pacific Ocean
> 551.467   Indian Ocean
> 551.468   North Polar Sea (Arctic Ocean)

A more complicated add instruction may take the following form:

> 616.99411-.99415   Malignant neoplasms (Cancers) of cardiovascular organs
>   Add to base number 616.9941 the numbers following 611.1 in 611.11-611.15, e.g. cancer of heart 616.99412; then add further as instructed under 618.1-618.8

This process of number building is explained in detail in the Editor's Introduction to DDC edition 19 (volume 1, section 8.542, pp. xlv-xlvi).

Several other types of notes help to determine a needed classification number, and occasionally clarify a given terminology with helpful examples. Under "693.98 Construction in nonrigid materials" we find the note "Example: pneumatic construction." There are also numerous "class here" notes throughout the schedules, e.g.,

711.6 Plans and planning of structural elements in civic art
Adaptation to site and use
Class here comprehensive works on plans and planning of specific elements
For utilities, see 711.7

To meet the increasing use of the Dewey Decimal Classification on an international scale a greater number of optional provisions has characterized recent editions. In the nineteenth edition new options emphasize favored languages, religions, and the like. This edition also returns to conventional American spelling from the earlier efforts to retain some vestige of simplified spelling forms, such as "divorst," "publisht," and the like. Even these few remnants of Dewey's preferences tended to perplex users whose native language was not English, say the editors.

AUXILIARY TABLES

Auxiliary tables 1 through 7 give the classifier still another way to expand existing numbers in the schedules. In many instances the use of these tables eliminates the "add" instructions (formerly called "divide-like notes") which usually require frequent back-and-forth paging to determine an appropriate number sequence. Note that in either case a base number is always provided, to which the indicated sequence of numbers is to be added.

STANDARD SUBDIVISIONS

As was noted under the "General Principles of Classifying" section of chapter 22, all shelf classifications provide a dual approach. Some books are grouped on the basis of their subject content, while others will be placed according to their physical format. The standard subdivisions supplied in auxiliary Table 1 of the Dewey Decimal Classification derive from what was called in earlier editions a table of "form divisions." The present-day "standard subdivisions" include examples other than form. Some actually do treat physical form (e.g., dictionaries, encyclopedias, periodicals, etc.). Others represent "modes of treatment," covering theoretical or historical aspects of the subject, such as philosophy and theory, history, etc. To show that none can stand alone as a complete class number, each is preceded in the table by a dash, which should be omitted when that number is attached to a bona fide class number. The following is a summary description of Table 1 as presented in volume 1 of DDC edition 19:

-01   **Philosophy and theory.** An exposition of any subject treated from the theoretical point of view.
Example: 701   Philosophy of the arts

-02   **Miscellany.** A subject treated briefly or in outline only, as in synopses, outlines, manuals, etc. This subdivision also includes material treated in tabular form, illustrations and models, directories, patents, techniques, equipment, price lists, etc.
Example: 621.15027   Patents on portable steam engines

-03   **Dictionaries, encyclopedias, concordances.**
Example: 720.3   Dictionary of architecture

-04   **Special topics of general applicability.**
Example: 364.042   Extent, incidence, distribution of crime

-05   **Serial publications.** Used for publications of a literary nature or in which the subject is treated in articles, papers, etc.
Example: 720.5   Architectural Record

-06   **Organizations and management.** Official publications of international, national, state, provincial, and local organizations such as reports, proceedings, regulations, membership lists, etc.
Example: 720.6   Transactions of the Royal Institute of British Architects

-07   **Study and teaching.** Methods of studying and teaching (including research).
Example: 707   Pearson's The New Art Education

-08   **History and description of the subject among groups of persons.** This number is italicized in edition 19, signifying that its use for collections has been discontinued.

-09   **Historical and geographical treatment.**
Example: 720.9   Fletcher's History of Architecture

Most of the standard subdivisions are further subdivided in Table 1. For example, under "-01 Philosophy and theory" the following subtopics are listed:

-012   Classification
-013   Value
-014   Languages (Terminology) and communication
-015   Scientific principles
-016   Indexes
-018   Methodology
-019   Psychological principles

The -09 can be geographically divided, through the addition of area digits from Table 2, e.g., "720.973   History of architecture in the United States." This type of complex number building will be explained later in this chapter in the section on "Area Tables."

Unless specific instructions indicate otherwise, standard subdivisions may be used with any number if such application is meaningful. Although in the table each is preceded by a single zero, e.g., "-03 Dictionaries, etc.," it is sometimes necessary in the schedules to apply a double or triple zero to introduce the subdivision. It happens when single zero subdivisions are already appropriated in the schedules for special purposes. The instructions which cover such situations are explicit and should be followed carefully. A few examples will illustrate certain basic principles:

a)   **Standard subdivisions contained as a part of a complete heading**

In some parts of the schedules a concept that is ordinarily expressed as a standard subdivision has its own number, e.g., a dictionary of literature is classed in 803 (800 for literature, 803 for dictionary), rather than in 800.3 or 800.03.

b)   **0-divisions utilized for a specific purpose; standard subdivision to be introduced by a double-0**

An example of the double-0 appears at "271   Religious congregations and orders in church history." Here the instruction is to use 271.001-271.009 for standard subdivisions. Single-0 subdivisions are used for specific kinds of religious congregations, e.g., "271.01   Contemplative," "271.03   Teaching," "271.04   Preaching," etc. Therefore, a dictionary of religious congregations and orders in general is classed in 271.003.

c)   **00-divisions utilized for special purposes; standard subdivisions to be introduced by a triple-0**

An example of the triple-0 appears at "350   Public administration." Here the instruction is to use 350.0001-350.0009 for standard subdivisions of this general subject. 350.001-350.009 are reserved for bureaucracy and specific aspects of the chief executive, while 350.01-350.08 are used for specific executive departments and ministries of cabinet rank. 350.1-350.9 encompass specific aspects of public administration such as personnel management, lists of officials and employees, civil service examinations, etc. Therefore, a dictionary of public administration in general is classed 350.0003.

AREA TABLES

When a given heading can be subdivided geographically and the library has many books dealing with that subject, it is recommended that the classifier use Table 2 (the area table) which allows one to expand the number systematically by region or site. Until the seventeenth edition of DDC, geographic subdivision was indicated by means of a note to "Divide like 930-999." However, as the schedules grew the use of their historical sequences to form geographic aspects for other numbers became cumbersome and confusing. In the seventeenth edition the area table replaced 930-999 for number building, leaving the history numbers solely for history. It is by far the bulkiest of the seven auxiliary tables accompanying the DDC schedules. Its general arrangement is as follows:

-1   Areas, regions, places in general
-2   Persons regardless of area, region, place
-3   The ancient world
-4   Europe Western Europe
-5   Asia Orient Far East
-6   Africa
-7   North America
-8   South America
-9   Other parts of world and extraterrestrial worlds
        Pacific Ocean islands (Oceania)

For example, area -1 is used for the treatment of any subject geographically, but not limited by continent, country, or locality. It allows diverse elements that have natural ties to regions or groups (e.g., frigid zones, temperate zones, land forms, or types of vegetation) to be brought together under certain subjects. Area -2 permits subdivision by biography, diaries, reminiscences, correspondence, and the like of persons associated with any subject for which the schedule instructions say to add the "areas" notation directly instead of adding "standard subdivision" notation -092 from Table 1. Area -3 offers specific subdivisions for ancient countries and areas up to the fall of the Roman Empire. Area notations -4 through -9 are for specific continents, and modern countries. For example, area number "-4 Europe" has the following summary subtopics:

-41   British Isles
-42   England and Wales
-43   Central Europe Germany
-44   France and Monaco
-45   Italy
-46   Iberian Peninsula and adjacent islands Spain
-47   Union of Soviet Socialist Republics (Soviet Union)
-48   Scandinavia
-49   Other parts of Europe

The area notations -41 and -42 have been extensively revised in the nineteenth edition to reflect a thorough reorganization of British local administration. The area concepts of "British Isles," "United Kingdom," and "Great Britain" were at the same time relocated from area -42 to area -41. For the convenience of those wishing to compare the edition 19 table with the one it replaces, a list of the number changes between the eighteenth and nineteenth editions is printed near the close of volume 1. The primary divisions, with a few illustrative subtopics, may now be summarized as follows (notice the failure of the notation to reflect hierarchical equivalencies precisely, as where Scotland requires a longer number than does England):

-41	British Isles
-411	Scotland
-412	Northeastern Scotland
-4127	City of Dundee district. Including Monifieth
-42	England and Wales
-421	Greater London
-4213	West London
-42132	Westminster. Including Paddington, Saint Marylebone
-422	Southeastern England

For example, a general treatise on higher education in Dundee, Scotland, will be classed in 378 in the Dewey Decimal Classification. The schedule at 378.4-.9 instructs "Add 'Areas' notation 4-9 from Table 2 to base number 378." The index refers to "*area*-4127" as the number for "Dundee Tayside Scot." This number is therefore applied to 378, giving 378.4127, as the following analysis shows:

378	Higher education
378.4	Europe
378.41	British Isles
378.412	Northeastern Scotland
378.4127	Dundee, Scotland

There is no provision in Table 2 for separating Dundee from Monifieth or the rest of Tayside, so this is the most specific number which can be applied.

Where specific instructions (as in 378.4-.9) are not given for geographical treatment in the schedules, the classifier can apply the standard subdivision "-09 Historical and geographical treatment" to any number which lends itself to that approach, unless localized instructions mandate a double- or triple-0 in place of the single-0. For example, the specific DDC number for savings banks is 332.21. To class a work on savings banks in Westminster, London, the schedule gives no specific direction to use Table 2, and also that single-0 is not assigned to any specific subdivisions. So the standard subdivision -09 may be used directly. In Table 1 a note under "-093-099 Treatment by specific continents, countries, localities; extraterrestrial worlds" says to "Add 'Areas' notation 3-9 from Table 2 to base number -09." So books on savings banks in Westminster, London, will be classed in 332.210942132. The number may be analyzed to show:

332.21	Savings banks
332.2109	Standard subdivision for historical and geographical treatment
332.21094	In Europe
332.210942	In England and Wales
332.2109421	In Greater London
332.21094213	In West London
332.210942132	In Westminster

It should be noted by the beginning student that although both of these examples result in very long numbers, they are quite simple to construct.

The nineteenth edition includes five additional auxiliary tables, which are used less frequently than the standard subdivision or the area tables, and often are limited to individual classes. Like those first two tables, they incorporate basic mnemonic features.

INDIVIDUAL LITERATURES

In Table 3, "Subdivisions of Individual Literatures," a detailed and specialized development of subdivision "-08   Collections" makes use of a supplementary Table 3-A, which is new in edition 19. The notation "-09   History, description, critical appraisal" is adapted from the Table 1 standard subdivision -09, and developed for use with divisions 810-890 from the full schedules. In addition, numbers "-1-8   Specific forms" develop and expand the summary form numbers which appear in the full schedules under "810   American literature in English." These mnemonic form divisions for kinds of literature are:

-1	Poetry	(e.g., 831 German poetry)
-2	Drama	(e.g., 842 French drama)
-3	Fiction	(e.g., 839.313 Dutch fiction)
-4	Essays	(e.g., 869.4 Portuguese essays)
-5	Speeches	(e.g., 845 French speeches)
-6	Letters	(e.g., 836 German letters)
-7	Satire and humor	(e.g., 869.7 Portuguese satire & humor)
-8	Miscellaneous writings	(e.g., 839.318 Dutch miscellaneous writings)

INDIVIDUAL LANGUAGES

Table 4, "Subdivisions of Individual Languages," is used with base numbers for individual languages, as explained under 420-490. In a fashion similar to that of Table 3 it provides mnemonic form divisions for languages, e.g.,

-1   Written and spoken codes of the standard form of the language.
   (e.g., 431   Written and spoken codes of standard German)
-2   Etymology of the standard form of the language.
   (e.g., 442   Etymology of the standard form of French)
-3   Dictionaries of the standard form of the language.
   (e.g., 439.313   Dictionaries of the standard form of Dutch)
-5   Structural system (Grammar) of the standard form of the language.
   (e.g., 469.5   The grammar of the standard form of Portuguese)
-7   Nonstandard forms of the language.
   (e.g., 437   Nonstandard German)
-8   Standard usage of the language.
   (e.g., 448   Standard French usage)

RACIAL, ETHNIC, NATIONAL GROUPS

Table 5, "Racial, Ethnic, National Groups," is used according to specific instructions at certain places in the schedules, or through the interposition of "-089 Treatment among specific racial, ethnic, national groups" from Table 1. These applications are exactly parallel to the use of Table 2, either on direct instructions in the schedule, or on interposition of "-09 Historical and geographical treatment" from Table 1. The Table 5 summary is:

-1	North Americans
-2	Anglo-Saxons, British, English
-3	Nordics
-4	Modern Latins
-5	Italians, Romanians, related groups
-6	Spanish and Portuguese
-7	Other Italic peoples
-8	Greeks and related groups
-9	Other racial, ethnic, national groups

An example to illustrate the use of Table 5 could be a work dealing with special education for American blacks. The number for special education, as found in the index and the schedules, is 371.9. An instruction under subdivision "371.97 Students exceptional because of racial, ethnic, national origin" says "Add 'Racial, Ethnic, National Groups' notation 01-99 from Table 5 to base number 371.97." The number in Table 5 for "United States blacks (Afro-Americans)" is -96073. Thus the full class number 371.9796073 may be analyzed as follows:

371.9	Special education
371.97	Students exceptional because of racial, ethnic, national origin
371.979	Racial, ethnic, national groups other than North American or major European nationalities
371.9796	Africans and people of African descent
371.97960	Digit used to expand the notation, here geographically
371.979607	In North America
371.9796073	In the United States

LANGUAGES

Table 6, "Languages," is a basic mnemonic table used to indicate the particular language of a work, or which is the subject matter of a work. It is used as instructed in the tables, and is particularly relevant to classes 400 and 800. The summary is:

-1   Indo-European (Indo-Germanic).languages
-2   English and Anglo-Saxon languages
-3   Germanic (Teutonic) languages
-4   Romance languages
-5   Italian, Romanian, Rhaeto-Romanic
-6   Spanish and Portuguese
-7   Italic languages
-8   Hellenic languages
-9   Other languages

To illustrate the application of this table let us class a Bible in French, starting from the entry given in both index and schedules "220.5   Modern versions and translations of the Bible." For "220.53-59   Other languages than English" the schedule direction says "Add 'Languages' notation 3-9 from Table 6 to base number 220.5." The notation for French in Table 6 is -41. The resulting whole number for a modern French Bible may be analyzed as follows:

220   The Bible
220.5   Modern versions
220.54   In the Romance languages
220.541   In modern French

PERSONS

Table 7, "Persons," is used when the schedules say to add the "Persons" notation to a base number. This table deals with various characteristics of persons, as the following summary shows:

-01   Individual persons
-02   Groups of persons
-03-08   Persons by various nonoccupational characteristics
    -03   Persons by racial, ethnic, national background
    -04   Persons by sex and kinship characteristics
    -05   Persons by age
    -06   Persons by social and economic characteristics
    -08   Persons by physical and mental characteristics
-09-99   Persons by various occupational characteristics
    -09   Generalists and novices
-1-9   Specialists
    -1   Persons occupied with philosophy and related disciplines
    -2   Persons occupied with or adherent to religion
    -3   Persons occupied with the social sciences and socioeconomic activities
    -4   Persons occupied with linguistics and lexicography
    -5   Persons occupied with pure sciences
    -6   Persons occupied with applied sciences (Technologists)
    -7   Persons occupied with the arts
    -8   Persons occupied with creative writing and speaking
    -9   Persons occupied with geography, history, related disciplines and activities

Obviously, from -09 to -9 this table is based on the ten main classes of DDC. A book on Shakers as a social group furnishes the following example. The number for adherents of religious groups in social contexts is now 305.6. This number represents a phoenix schedule change in the nineteenth edition from "301.452 Adherents to religious organizations" in the eighteenth edition. The directions in the schedule at the new number say "Add to base number 305.6 the numbers following 2 in 'Persons' notation 21-29 from Table 7." The Table 7 number for Shakers is -288. Thus our book would be classed 305.688. The analysis of the number proceeds as follows:

305   Social stratification (Social structure)
305.6   Adherents of religious groups
305.68   Nondominant Christian churches
305.688   Shakers

THE RELATIVE INDEX

The DDC "relative" index enumerates alphabetically all the main headings in the classification schedules, plus certain other specific entries not actually listed in the schedules. One such instance was discussed on page 411. In another, the index carries the subordinated entry "Halogenated compounds — synthetic drugs pharm. 615.312." Yet there is no 615.312 listed as such in the schedules. Only an "add to" instruction under 615.31 shows how to expand the schedules to obtain the more specific 615.312.

In other places index terminology varies from that found in the schedules for the same class number, although the general meanings coincide. Thus, the schedule entry "612.7921 Glands and glandular secretions, including perspiration" is a generalized representation of the index entry "Sebaceous glands — biochemistry — human phys. 612.7921." Synonyms which appear in the schedules in scope notes or parentheses are represented by *see* references in the index. For example, the index alphabetizes "Blackjack (game) *see* Twenty-one (game)," as well as "Twenty-one (game) — recreation 795.42." The corresponding entry in the schedules is "795.42 Games based chiefly on chance. Examples: baccarat, faro, twenty-one (blackjack)."

The "relative" index is so-called because it is claimed to show relationships of each specific topic to its discipline, and to other topics. Terminological subdivisions are indicated, not by hyphens, as the above examples use, but by lists of entries successively indented from the left margins of each column. Many *see also* references are given in italics (e.g., "Organizations . . . *s.a. spec. kinds e.g.* Labor unions; Corporations"). There are also *see* references to "other aspects" (e.g., "Prairies . . . *other aspects see* Plane regions"). Geographic name entries usually refer the user to the appropriate area table (e.g., "Macerata Italy *area*-45673"). A few referrals occur to the standard subdivisions and to other auxiliary tables (e.g., "Repairs & repairing . . . *s.a. s.s.*-0288").

The classifier should, of course, consult the index, especially in cases in which the location of the desired topic, or the precise nature of its relation to other topics, is in doubt. Yet the relative index should never become a substitute for the schedules. It is coordinated with them, but is limited for reasons of space, and cannot show hierarchical progressions or topical groupings. It will guide the classifier to some, but not necessarily all, aspects of a given subject. The next important step in the classification process is to consult the schedules for verification, perspective, and possible further instructions. Only by using the two types of display together can the full potential of the scheme be realized.

BROAD AND CLOSE CLASSIFICATION

Since it offers a wide variety of techniques and nearly limitless expansions in number building, Dewey Decimal Classification is hospitable to all the titles which a large library might add in any subject. It also offers various ways to meet the limited needs of smaller libraries. The classifier must remember that, in general, when there are relatively few books in a given subject area, DDC encourages broad classification. Digits in class numbers after decimal points may be cut off at any appropriate place. The present policy of the Library of Congress is to provide bibliographic records with Dewey Decimal numbers of from one to three segments. The segments are indicated by prime marks, e.g., "513'.93'028," which number stands for "Arithmetic – Business mathematics – Techniques, procedures, apparatus, etc." A small public library with a limited collection of mathematics books might prefer to keep them all together under 513. If the library has several dozen books on mathematics, it might keep the business-oriented ones together by using the number 513.93. If it maintains a separate resource collection for use by business and commercial clients, it could add the standard subdivision -028 to distinguish the "how-to-do-it" manuals. When a library decides to retain one or more of the DDC segments to achieve close classification at a particular point in the collection, it omits the prime marks, which were used in the LC record merely to suggest break-points.

ABRIDGED EDITIONS

The first *Abridged Decimal Classification and Relativ Index for Libraries, Clippings, Notes, etc.* appeared in 1894, the year in which the fifth edition of the full schedules was published. Abridged edition 11 is based on DDC edition 19, and followed its publication in 1979 by only a few months. Like its predecessors, it is designed primarily for general collections of 20,000 titles or less, such as are found in small public and school libraries. Abridged edition 10 was an adaptation, using not only shorter, but some slightly different numbers than its companion eighteenth edition. But the widespread use of segmentation marks for Dewey class numbers in Library of Congress records and other centrally produced bibliographic entries vitiated the usefulness of this approach. Abridged edition 11 is therefore once again a true abridgment of its parent nineteenth edition. Yet it continues the trend in the ninth and tenth abridged editions toward fewer entries, while the full seventeenth, eighteenth, and nineteenth editions increase their entries, as the following brief table shows:

Edition	Total entries
DDC 17th edition	22,355
DDC abridged 9th edition	2,838
DDC 18th edition	26,141
DDC abridged 10th edition	2,542
DDC 19th edition	29,528
DDC abridged 11th edition	2,516

CONCLUSIONS

Among the difficulties built into the Dewey Decimal Classification System are its long numbers, which increase rather than diminish as the system grows, nullifying much of the mnemonic character of the basic system. Thus the number 636.089201448, which was cited previously on page 411 as coming from the relative index entry for medical radiation of terrestrial animals is so long that any mnemonic associations between it and the number 612.01448 (from which it was built) are obscured. Librarians who wish to retain these long numbers because of extensive holdings in one or more fields should write them on books and cards in several lines. The above numbers could be written in short meaningful segments as follows:

```
636   and   612
.089         .01
201          448
448
```

Related to the long number difficulties are the rapid, often sweeping, topical relocations from one edition to another. Such drastic surgery is forced upon the system by its limited notational base and the swift growth and change in the world of knowledge and of publication. An earlier edition of this text discussed in some detail the problem of reclassification faced by libraries attempting to keep abreast of schedule changes. DDC 19 suggests in volume 1, section 14, pages lxxii-lxxiv, various ways of adjusting to its expansions, reductions, relocations, reused numbers, and phoenix schedules. Its relative index is designed to facilitate updated classification by containing an entry for every significant term in the schedules and tables, with numerous cross references to assist the user who is not familiar with the terminology. While the big rush, particularly in academic libraries, to change from Dewey to the Library of Congress classification seems to have run its course, no library can afford to ignore all efforts to keep shelf arrangement contemporary with the shifts in knowledge as reflected in the literature.

DDC editors are already compiling data in anticipation of the twentieth edition, but that work is still some years in the future. For the present, libraries are getting acquainted with the nineteenth edition. Their reactions will carry significant impact for the future of the Dewey Decimal system, both here in the United States and Canada, and abroad.

CUTTER NUMBERS

Providing a classification number with a supplementary book number enables the cataloger to design a fully unique call number for each title in a collection. The book numbers most often used with DDC class numbers are taken from a set of tables devised by Charles Ammi Cutter. These tables equate surnames and other words with alphanumeric sequences in such a way as to keep all materials with the same class number arranged alphabetically within the class by main entry. Cutter initially produced a table in a single alphabet of all consonants except "S," followed by an alphabet of vowels and the letter "S."[2] This "two-figure" table (most of its combinations consist of a capital letter plus two digits) was later expanded by Kate E. Sanborn to provide more differentiation among names for use with larger collections.[3] However, since she did not adhere to Cutter's schema, Cutter then developed his own expansion to permit growing libraries to assign more specific book numbers without disrupting the sequences they had already established from his two-figure table.[4] There are thus three different "cutter" tables. The Cutter-Sanborn version is perhaps the most widely used today, being preferred by many larger libraries because of its simpler design and notation.

While Cutter numbers are most commonly used to arrange material by main entries (usually authors' surnames, but occasionally forenames, corporate names, or titles), they are also used in some instances to alphabetize material by subject, as in the case of biography. To illustrate the use of each table, let us suppose that we wish to assign a book number for the English poet John Donne. The three tables carry the following sequences:

Cutter Two-figure Table

Doll	69	Foh
Dom	71	Folg
Doo	72	Foll

Cutter Three-figure Table

Donk	718	Folk
Donnet	719	Folke
Doo	72	Foil

Cutter-Sanborn Table

Donk	684	Fonti
Donn	685	Fontr
Donner	686	Foo

According to the Cutter two-figure table, the number for Donne is D71. By the Cutter three-figure table it is D718 (an expansion of the D71 assignment). But by the Cutter-Sanborn table it is D685. The above examples also demonstrate the typical three-column display used in the original form of the tables. In 1969 Paul K. Swanson of the Forbes Library, Northampton, Massachusetts, and Mrs. Esther M. Swift, editor of the H. R. Huntting Company, revised this arrangement into single continuous alphabets of two columns, with letters on the left corresponding to numbers on the right. The new arrangement appears to be easier to use.

The work letter (or work mark) is the first letter of the title of the work, exclusive of articles. It follows the cutter number on the second line of the call number. Thus, the complete call number of Henry James's novel *Wings of the Dove* is 813.4 J27w. Work letters do not inevitably ensure that a book will be placed in alphabetical sequence within the author grouping; this depends upon the sequence of acquisition of the books. One additional letter from the title may be added if necessary. Thus, a copy of James's *Washington Square* might be classified 813.4 J27wa. If the third acquisition is a volume entitled *The Works of Henry James*, it can be classified 813.4 J27wo.

With an author such as Erle Stanley Gardner, who began the title of all of his Perry Mason mysteries with *The Case of the . . .* , such a scheme is not feasible. Depending on the library's policy, the cataloger can choose one of several alternatives. For example, the cataloger can ignore completely the common phrase "the case of the" and proceed directly to the distinctive part of the title, or use two work letters: "c" for "case," plus an additional letter for the distinctive title (e.g., *The Case of the Mischievous Doll* might be assigned the work letters "cm").

Biographies and criticism of a specific author pose a particular problem of library policy. Two procedures are common. In the Dewey schedule, 928 is the biography number for literary figures (920 for Biography; 8 for Literature). Thus, biographies of authors might be classified in 928, with subdivision for nationality. Another way of classifying biography is to use the standard biography subdivision, 092. A third possibility is to classify biographies of authors with their work, in order to keep everything by and about a literary figure in one place. In such cases, a common method of distinguishing works "by" from works "about" an author is to insert an arbitrary letter — usually one toward the end of the alphabet — after the cutter number and to follow it with the initial of the author of the biography. This device puts all books about an author directly behind all books by him. Thus, if the letter "z" is chosen as the biographical letter, a biography or criticism of Henry James by Leon Edel would be cuttered J27zE; and it would follow, in shelflist order, J27w. If James had written a novel beginning with the letter "z" only the work letter "z" would be used for the novel; thus, the novel would still come before all criticism and biography.

The problem of a variety of editions occurs most frequently in literature, but classic works in all other fields are also reprinted by the same or another publisher, especially now that paperbacks have revived many worthwhile books that have been long out of print.

One cataloging practice is to assign the date of publication as part of the call number to all editions of a single work issued by the same publisher, and to assign a number following the work letter to all editions of the same work published by different publishers. Thus, the first acquired copy of *Wings of the Dove* would be classified 813.4 J27w. If the library acquired a second copy of the novel, issued by a different publisher, the number would be 813.4 J27w2. Assume that the second publisher was Modern Library, and that the library received another edition of the novel, also published by Modern

Library in 1955. The call number might then be 813.4 J27w2 1955. A completely different edition published by a third publisher would be classified 813.4 J27w3.

FOOTNOTES

[1]Melvil Dewey, *Dewey Decimal Classification and Relative Index*, 19th ed., edited under the direction of Benjamin A. Custer (Albany, NY, Forest Press, 1979), 3v.

Melvil Dewey, *Abridged Dewey Decimal Classification and Relative Index*, 11th ed. (Albany, NY, Forest Press, 1979).

[2]Charles Ammi Cutter, *Two-Figure Author Table*, Swanson-Swift revision, 1969. Distributed by Libraries Unlimited, Inc., Littleton, CO (formerly distributed by H. R. Huntting Co.).

[3]*Cutter-Sanborn Three-Figure Author Table*, Swanson-Swift revision, 1969. Distributed by Libraries Unlimited, Inc., Littleton, CO (formerly distributed by H. R. Huntting Co.).

[4]Charles Ammi Cutter, *Three-Figure Author Table*, Swanson-Swift revision, 1969. Distributed by Libraries Unlimited, Inc., Littleton, CO (formerly distributed by H. R. Huntting Co.).

24 LIBRARY OF CONGRESS CLASSIFICATION

INTRODUCTION

The Library of Congress was founded in 1800. Its earliest classification system was by size (folios, quartos, octavos, etc.), subdivided by accession numbers. But by 1812 the collection had grown to about 3,000 volumes, and a better method of classification was needed. The solution was to arrange the works under eighteen broad subject categories similar to the Bacon-d'Alembert system used in the 1789 *Catalogue* of Benjamin Franklin's Library Company of Philadelphia. Soon after, in 1814, British soldiers burned the Capitol where the collection was housed. To re-establish it, Thomas Jefferson offered to sell Congress his library of around 7,000 volumes. Jefferson had cataloged and classified the works himself, using forty-four main classes and divisions based on a different interpretation of the Bacon-d'Alembert system. After some debate, Congress agreed to purchase the Jefferson books. Although many were destroyed in a later fire, the classification which came with them was used until the end of the nineteenth century. By that time it had undergone so much ad hoc modification, largely based on shelving and other physical limitations, that it was barely recognizable, and completely inadequate.

Many significant changes occurred at the Library of Congress near the turn of the century. In 1899 Dr. Herbert Putnam, the new Librarian, with many new staff appointments and a brand new building, decided to reorganize and reclassify his rapidly growing collection. Since it was to be moved into more adequate shelving areas, the time was right to develop a better, more detailed classification system. There were already in existence the first five editions of the *Dewey Decimal Classification* and the first six expansions of Cutter's *Expansive Classification*. LC classifiers studied both, as well as the German *Halle Schema* devised by Otto Hartwig. They did not adopt any in full, but the experience they gained was invaluable, and their debt, especially to Cutter, is implicit in the basic structure of their system. While the outline and notation of their main classes is very similar to the *Expansive Classification*, there are no main classes I, O, W, X, or Y, as there are in the Cutter system.[1] All five letters do appear, however, as second or third symbols in the notation for various Library of Congress subclasses. The other major similarity to the *Expansive Classification* is in the structure of class "Z — Bibliography and Library Science," which was the first class devised, and was adopted from Cutter with only minor variations.

After Putnam and his Chief Cataloger, Charles Martel, determined the broad outlines of the new classification, different subject specialists were asked to develop each individual schedule, or portion of the system. Within a broad general framework set up to ensure coordination, each topic or form of presentation identified as a class or subclass was further organized to display the library's holdings and to serve anticipated research needs. Schedules comprising single classes or parts of classes were separately published as they were completed. Most of them first appeared between 1899 and 1940. Many have since gone through several editions. In one sense, the scheme represents a series of special classifications. Yet special libraries, with narrowly defined collecting and service goals, often find the LC Classification, which serves broader, more interdisciplinary uses, unsatisfactory for their purposes.

To keep the system functionally up-to-date, individual schedule volumes are frequently reviewed in committee. Revisions, reallocations, and additions keep it flexible and hospitable to new subjects or points of view. For example, recent interest in eastern religions and the increase in materials from Asia occasioned a reallocation in 1972 of the topic "Buddhism" from the span BL1400-1495 into a whole new subclass, BQ. Revisions were likewise made in subclass PL, particularly in the sections for Chinese, Japanese, and Korean literatures. Also recent are block revisions in the "D — General and Old World History" class. In subclass DZ, Hungary has been released at last from Austrian captivity. Number spans now reflect political changes in Albania, Bangladesh, Korea, Namibia, Somalia, and the like. A new triple-letter subclass "DJK — Eastern Europe" was developed in 1976. Further steps are underway to counter the old tendency to equate that region with the Soviet Union or the Balkan Peninsula. Intensified foreign acquisitions programs under PL480, the National Program for Acquisitions and Cataloging (NPAC) initiated by Title II of the Higher Education Act of 1965, the revised Copyright Law, and other developments, stimulate increased expansion and revision of the system.

Hundreds of different number-letter combinations compatible with the notation have not yet been employed, or have been retired in favor of new locations. The scheme will continue to accommodate for a long time the many new subjects and aspects of subjects not yet anticipated. It is particularly useful for large university and research collections because of its hospitality and inherent flexibility. It has been used effectively in smaller academic and public libraries, although its adaptability for broad classification is limited. Even special libraries frequently base their own more technical constructs on it, extending its schedules or parts of schedules to cover their unique materials. Some foreign libraries also use the system, although, in spite of LC's large foreign holdings, it is primarily designed from an American perspective.

CLASSIFICATION TOOLS AND AIDS

The working schedules are contained in thirty-three separate volumes. Besides the basic schedules, there is a separately published partial index for P-PM subcategories in the Language and Literature class, and a short general *Outline*, now in its fourth edition, which gives the secondary and tertiary subclass spans for most classes. Several volumes are devoted to subclass coverage of broad areas, such as related language and literature groups. They comprise:

A   General Works; Polygraphy (4th ed., 1973)

B, pt. 1, B-BJ   Philosophy; Psychology (3rd ed., 1979)

B, pt. 2, BL-BX	Religion (2nd ed., 1962)
C	Auxiliary Sciences of History (3rd ed., 1975)
D	General and Old World History (2nd ed., 1959; Reissue with supplementary pages, 1966)
E-F	American History (3rd ed., 1958; Reissue with supplementary pages, 1965)
G	Geography; Maps; Anthropology; Recreation (4th ed., 1976)
H	Social Sciences (3rd ed., 1950; Reissue with supplementary pages, 1965)
J	Political Science (2nd ed., 1924; Reissue with supplementary pages, 1966)
K subclass	Law (General) (1st ed., 1977)
KD	Law of the United Kingdom and Ireland (1st ed., 1973)
KE	Law of Canada (1st ed., 1976)
KF	Law of the United States (Prelim. ed., 1969)
L	Education (3rd ed., 1951; Reissue with supplementary pages, 1966)
M	Music; Books on Music (3rd ed., 1978)
N	Fine Arts (4th ed., 1970)
P-PA	General Philology and Linguistics; Classical Languages and Literatures (1st ed., 1928; Reissue with supplementary pages, 1968)
PA supplement	Byzantine and Modern Greek Literature; Medieval and Modern Latin Literature (1st ed., 1942; Reissue with supplementary pages, 1968)
PB-PH	Modern European Languages (1st ed., 1933; Reissue with supplementary pages, 1966)
PG	Russian Literature (in part) (1st ed., 1948; Reissue with supplementary pages, 1965)

PJ-PM	Languages and Literatures of Asia, Africa, Oceania; American Indian Languages; Artificial Languages (1st ed., 1935; Reissue with supplementary pages, 1965)
P-PM supplement	Index to Languages and Dialects (2nd ed., 1957; Reissue with supplementary pages, 1965)
PN, PR, PS, PZ	General Literature; English and American Literatures; Fiction in English; Juvenile Literature (2nd ed., 1978)
PQ, pt. 1	French Literature (1st ed., 1936; Reissue with supplementary pages, 1966)
PQ, pt. 2	Italian, Spanish, and Portuguese Literatures (1st ed., 1937; Reissue with supplementary pages, 1965)
PT, pt. 1	German Literature (1st ed., 1938; Reissue with supplementary pages, 1966)
PT, pt. 2	Dutch and Scandinavian Literatures (1st ed., 1942; Reissue with supplementary pages, 1965)
Q	Science (6th ed., 1973)
R	Medicine (3rd ed., 1952; Reissue with supplementary pages, 1966)
S	Agriculture (3rd ed., 1948; Reissue with supplementary pages, 1965)
T	Technology (5th ed., 1971)
U	Military Science (4th ed., 1974)
V	Naval Science (3rd ed., 1974)
Z	Bibliography; Library Science (4th ed., 1959; Reissue with supplementary pages, 1965)
A-Z	Outline (4th ed., 1978)

Updating is accomplished by a variety of publications, most of which are available directly from the Library of Congress.

1. **Revised editions of individual schedules.** As the above list shows, the various schedules differ widely in the number and kind of revisions made. Pre-1970 volumes were letter-press printed on both sides of each leaf, and issued in beige paper covers. As changes came, some schedules were

thoroughly revised and issued in new editions. In other cases, "reissues" showed the new material cumulated at the back in a separate sequence, with a separate index. Users had to remember to look in both sections each time they consulted one of these "reissues." Since 1970 all revisions show a new format. They are photo-offset from keyboarded copy, printed on only one side of each leaf, and bound in blue-and-white paper covers. Automated production techniques now make fully integrated revisions more feasible, so the confusing double-sequence reissues no longer appear. However, the new editions do not always render prior editions obsolete. A notable instance is the second edition of the PN, PR, PS, PZ schedule, which omits not only the first edition index entries for personal names, but also long-established, heavily-used author cutters from the *Additions and Changes* because they were never incorporated into the "official schedules."[2] Instructive prefaces are frequently dropped from new editions. When buying recent editions of the schedules, classifiers should check their older issues, to ensure that no valuable information would be inadvertently lost if they were discarded. All schedules and the *Outline* are sold individually by the Library's Cataloging Distribution Service at nominal prices.

2. **Library of Congress Additions and Changes.** This stapled paper publication reports quarterly on the latest adjustments in all schedules and schedule indexes of the LC Classification. Subscriptions may be placed with the Cataloging Distribution Service.

3. **Library of Congress Classification Schedules: A Cumulation of Additions and Changes.** These periodic cumulations of the quarterly *Additions and Changes* have been published since 1972 by Gale Research Company on contract with the Library of Congress.[3] The class and subclass coverage of each separate booklet corresponds to that of the basic schedule volumes. Each new set updates previous cumulations from their final cutoff date to the close of a given year. Their chief value is to reduce and consolidate the number of places one must look to get full information about the system. Each new series or individual volume is available from the publisher.

4. **Cataloging Service Bulletin.** This channel for recent decisions and experiments in technical processing at the Library of Congress has been offered free since 1945 to all subscribers to various cataloging distribution services, such as LC printed cards, MARC tapes, etc. It now has a regular quarterly publication schedule, carrying valuable data on LC classification and shelflisitng practice, as well as other aspects of subject and descriptive cataloging.

5. **Library of Congress Subject Headings.** There is no official comprehensive index to the LC classification scheme. Most of the schedules carry their own indexes, which are largely self-contained, although they occasionally refer to other schedules where related materials can be found on an indexed topic. For example, the index to class "T – Technology" provides the following sequence of entries under "Automobiles":

Automobiles: TL1-390
  Accidents: HE5614-5614.5
  Pollution control devices: TL214.P6
  Racing: GV1029-1029.8

At best, this type of cross-schedule indexing is spotty. The class "H — Social Sciences" index entries under "Automobiles" read:

Automobiles
  Industry and statistics: HD9710
  Insurance: HG9970.A4-68
  Law: HE5619-20, etc.
  Pools, *see* Car pools
  Selling: HF5439.A8
  Taxation: HD9710
  Transportation
    Railroad: HE2321.A8
    Water: HE595.A8

The most obvious substitute for an official comprehensive index is *Library of Congress Subject Headings.*[4] While it was never designed to function as a true index, many entries and subdivisions refer in parentheses to one or more class numbers, often including terminology used in the schedules. In it, under the term "AUTOMOBILES" (including subdivisions and inverted modifications) there are no less than sixty-three specific LC class number associations. One of these is from the "R — Medicine" schedule, three each come from the "H — Social Sciences" and "U — Military Science" schedules, seven from "G — Geography, etc.," and the rest from "T — Technology." The following comparison shows how most, but seldom all, LC class numbers relating to a given concept can be grouped more quickly through *LCSH* than through the many schedule indexes:

Schedule B-BJ — Philosophy; Psychology:

Hypnotism (Parapsychology): BF1111 +
  [of 3d ed. (1979) schedule]

Schedule BL-BX — Religion:

Hypnotism
  and religion: BL65.H9
  Moral theology
    Roman Catholic Church: BX1759.5.H8

Schedule H — Social Sciences:

Hypnotism and crime: HV6110

Schedule Q — Science:

Hypnotic conditions (Neurophysiology): QP425

Schedule R — Medicine:

Hypnotism and hypnosis
    Forensic aspects: RA1171
    Psychiatry: RC490-499; RM(917-926)
    Surgery: RD85.H9
    System of healing: RZ430

LCSH8 and supplements:

HYPNOTISM (BF1111-1156; Hypnotism and crime, HV6110;
    Psychiatry, RC490-499)
HYPNOTISM — MORAL AND RELIGIOUS ASPECTS (Catholic
    Church, BX1759.5.H8)
HYPNOTISM IN SURGERY (RD85.H9)

6. **LC Catalog, Books: Subjects.**[5] This part of the *National Union Catalog* series has been published since 1950. Its reproductions of printed cards, in alphabetical order according to their assigned subject headings, associate subject terms with actual LC classification assignments. However, since both primary and secondary subject terms are indexed, the class numbers often appear to have only tangential relation to the subjects under which they are indexed.

7. **Library of Congress Shelflist in Microform.** In 1978 the six and one-half million cards of the LC shelflist, arranged by call number, were offered for purchase in various microformats (35mm. roll film, 16mm. cartridge, and microfiche) as well as in Copyflo hard copy. The United States Historical Documents Institute, Inc. and University Microfilms International jointly sponsored the filming, and respectively sell different formats of the full shelflist, or selected portions of it. This tool can be used most effectively for fine-tuning class number and shelflist assignments through comparison of proposed numbers for new materials with those already grouped in a given area.

8. **Commercially prepared indexes.** Just as the Gale *Additions and Changes* cumulations and the LC shelflist reproductions are commercial aids based on official, publicly accessible LC data, so a number of new indexing ventures reflect similar trade manipulation of publications or automated processing available from the Library of Congress. They are designed to give broader scope and greater depth to the primary access materials on which they draw. Notable among these are:

Williams, James G., Martha L. Manheimer, and Jay E. Daily. *Classified Library of Congress Subject Headings.* New York, Marcel Dekker, 1972. v. 1 — Classified List; v. 2 — Alphabetic List. Based on a computer tape of *LCSH7* (1966) and its supplements to June 1967.

Elrod, J. McRee, Judy Inouye, and Ann Craig Turner. *An Index to the Library of Congress Classification. With Entries for Special Expansions in Medicine, Law, Canadiana, and Nonbook Materials.* Preliminary edition. Ottawa: Canadian Library Association, 1974. Based on schedule indexes, *Additions and Changes* through 1973, and some non-official Canadian, British, and American expansions of the LC Classification.

Olson, Nancy B. *Combined Indexes to the Library of Congress Classification Schedules.* Washington: United States Historical Documents Institute, 1974. These fifteen volumes comprise five major subsets based on schedule indexes to the close of 1973, proper names with associated LC class numbers from the *LC Catalog, Books: Subjects* for 1965-1969, and portions of the official LC shelflist as microfilmed on a variety of dates from early 1970 through mid-1974:

Set I: Author/number index. Alphabetical by literary authors' names. 2v.

Set II: Biographical subject index. Alphabetical by subjects' names. 3v.

Set III: Classified index to persons. All entries from Set II arranged in LC class number order. 3v.

Set IV: Geographical name index. Nouns only, in permuted alphabetical order. 1v.

Set V: Subject keyword index. Includes all entries from Set IV as well as topical subjects. 6v.

9. **Texts and general discussions.** Through the years many perceptive discussions of the LC Classification System have appeared. The following selection gives those titles which are most recent or most likely to help introduce the scheme to the beginning student:

Chan, Lois M. *Immroth's Guide to the Library of Congress Classification.* 3rd ed. Littleton, CO: Libraries Unlimited, 1980.

Immroth, John Phillip. "Library of Congress Classification," in *Encyclopedia of Library and Information Science*, v. 15, pp. 93-200. New York, Marcel Dekker, 1975.

Matthis, Raimund E., and Desmond Taylor. *Adopting the Library of Congress Classification System: A Manual of Methods and Techniques for Application or Conversion.* New York, R. R. Bowker, 1971.

Swanson, Gerald L. *Dewey to LC Conversion Tables.* New York, CCM Information Corporation, 1972.

Use of the Library of Congress Classification: Proceedings of the Institute . . . New York City, July 7-9, 1966. Edited by Richard H. Schimmelpfeng and C. Donald Cook. Chicago, American Library Association, 1968.

BASIC FEATURES

Since the LC Classification was developed as a utilitarian scheme for books at the Library of Congress, it is an enumerative, rather than a deductive, system. Among the basic features borrowed from C. A. Cutter are its order of main classes, its use of capital letters for main and subclass notation, its use of Arabic numerals for further subdivision, and its modification of the Cutter author-mark idea to achieve alphabetic subarrangements of various kinds. While most LC call numbers follow a simple, recurring letter-number-letter-number pattern, various other combinations sometimes reflect special situations, or more detailed subdivisions. Twenty large main classes represent the traditional disciplines, plus an additional class for general works.

All the LC schedules have similar, but not identical, sequencing arrangements and physical appearance. Within each sequence of class numbers the order proceeds as a rule from general aspects of the topic or discipline to its particular divisions and subtopics. Chronological sequences may trace historical events, publication dates, or other useful time frames. Geographical arrangements are frequently alphabetical, but just as frequently are given in a "preferred order," starting with the Western Hemisphere and the United States. Class "G—Geography, etc." is distinct from the history classes, although located next to them. This distribution is more effective than the DDC location of "910—Geography and Travel" within class "900—History." Neither scheme quite succeeds in solving the problem of ambiguous relationships between popular works of description and travel, and other, perhaps more scholarly, books on national or regional social life and customs. The user must search both the history and the geography shelves to find all available materials on these topics.

There are other significant differences from the Dewey Decimal theory of organizing some materials. In class "J—Political Science," which is largely devoted to constitutional history of various modern governments, the primary groupings are national or jurisdictional. Each topical aspect (e.g., political parties or electoral systems) is treated as a subdivision of the governmental unit under which it functions. In DDC materials are grouped first by topic (e.g., "324—The political process," *formerly* "329—Practical Politics") and then subdivided by geography or jurisdiction.

Similarly, the Library of Congress provides broad subclasses in class P for the various national literatures, subdividing next by chronology and then by individual author. Seldom, except for anthologies, does it group literary works by form. DDC also starts in its 800 class with a basic separation into national literatures, but it subdivides next by form, e.g., poetry, drama, fiction, etc. Only subordinately does it provide for time divisions or individual authors.

The LC preference for grouping national literatures by time period and author extends to class "B—Philosophy" but not to music or the graphic arts. In subclass "M—Music and Scores" works are classed first by form (e.g., opera, oratorio, symphony, chamber music), then by composer. There is no attempt to keep time periods, national schools, or genres of expression (e.g., classical, romantic, modern) distinct. Subclass "ML—Literature, History and Criticism of Music" does use national, chronological, and similar groupings. In class "N—Fine Arts" materials are grouped first by form (e.g., sculpture, drawing, painting), then by nationality or chronology, and finally by artist.

The major LC use of literary grouping by form is its infamous subclass "PZ—Fiction in English; Juvenile Belles Lettres." Here a concession was made to a "reader interest" orientation which proved to be most controversial, and a stumbling block to the full use of LC Classification by other research libraries with large holdings in literature. But for this one aberration, LC's handling of literature has met with general approval. A recurring pattern of organization within each literature affords the shelf or shelflist browser a useful guide:

1. History and criticism, subdivided
   a. Chronologically
   b. Then by form
2. Collections or anthologies, subdivided by form
3. Individual authors, subdivided
   a. Chronologically
   b. Then alphabetically by author
      1) Collective works
      2) Individual works
      3) Biography and criticism

The LC Classification breaks the "Generalia" class familiar to DDC users into two classes at opposite ends of the alphabet. The "A—General Works" schedule employs for its subclasses rare instances of mnemonic notation. General encyclopedias are located in subclass AE, general indexes in AI, general museum publications in AM, and so forth. By contrast, the Z class, containing bibliographies and works on the book industries and on libraries, has no two-letter subclasses at all. While its subject bibliographies are arranged alphabetically by topic in the Z5001-Z8000 span, there is nothing mnemonic about their notation. The only other notable instances of mnemonic class letter associations are for class "G—Geography, etc.," class "M—Music," subclass "ML—Music Literature," and class "T—Technology."

SCHEDULE FORMAT

Most of the LC schedules exhibit certain common features of external and internal format to help the classifier find his way. Many of these format features are missing from certain schedules, a reminder that the scheme was intentionally decentralized in its development. Subject specialists were encouraged to adopt standard modes of organization, but were never forced to maintain a rigid formal pattern.

EXTERNAL FORMAT

The gross physical format, or external appearance of the schedules has already been described. Both old and new editions, regardless of typography or binding, tend to follow a familiar pattern of organization:

1. **A preface or prefatory note** nearly always follows the title page. As was said, these introductory remarks in recent editions have become briefer and less helpful for classification purposes than they formerly were.

2. **Brief synopses** next appear in over one-third of the schedules, to show the primary subdivisions contained in those volumes. In most cases these broad subclasses are readily identifiable by their brief double-letter notation, but the newly developed class "K — Law" is issued in double-letter subclass volumes with synopses that frequently show mnemonic triple-letter divisions. We can learn at a glance that the law of Ontario is found in subclass KEO, while that of Quebec is in KEQ. A similar mnemonic arrangement applies to the American states in subclass KF, but their notation is more complicated since several states share certain initial letters. Moreover the KF schedule is one of those which carries no synopsis. By contrast, the class H synopsis reproduced here is perhaps the longest to be found in any schedule:

SYNOPSIS

SOCIAL SCIENCES

H	General works
HA	Statistics

ECONOMICS

HB	Economic theory
HC-HD	Economic history and conditions
HC	National production and economic conditions (by country)
HD	Agriculture and industry
	Land
	Agriculture
	Corporations
	Labor
	Industries
HE	Transportation and communication
HF	Commerce, including tariff policy
HG	Finance (General). Private finance
	Money
	Banking
	Insurance
HJ	Public finance

SOCIOLOGY

HM	General works. Theory
HN	Social history and conditions. Social problems. Social reform
HQ-HT	Social groups
HQ	Family. Marriage. Woman
HS	Soceties: Secret, benevolent, etc. Clubs
HT	Communities. Classes. Races
HV	Social pathology. Social and public welfare. Criminology
HX	Socialism. Communism. Anarchism

3. **An outline,** consisting not only of alphabetic subclasses, but of significant alphanumeric subspans, is present in nearly every schedule. In schedules without synopses the outlines tend to be briefer and to show broader subdivisions; in schedules with synopses, they are longer and more detailed. Occasionally, as in the schedule for class "J — Political Science," the "synopsis" is really an outline. These two kinds of preliminary overview lend a counterweight to the detail of the schedule indexes. They offer the user supplementary techniques for arriving quickly at any given portion of the schedules. The outline for the first two subclasses of class H appears in the schedule as follows:

OUTLINE

H   **SOCIAL SCIENCES**

General

1-8	Periodicals.
9	Yearbooks
20-29	Societies
21-29	Congresses. Exhibitions.
31-39	Collections
41-49	Encyclopedias
51-53	History
57-59	Biography
61	Theory. Method
62-69	Study and teaching: Museums. Schools. Debates
71-95	General works

HA   **Statistics**

1-23	General
29-33	Theory. Method
35	Study and teaching
36-40	Organization
41-48	Annuals. General works. Albums, etc.
155-173	Universal statistics.
175-4010	By country

One cannot assume that the numbers and spans given in a schedule outline will coincide precisely with those in the corresponding portion of the general

Outline (4th edition). Decentralized classification and intermittent revisions of the different publications results in slightly varying "summaries" of schedule contents in print at the same time. The section of the H and HA subclasses in the fourth edition of the *Outline* reads like a synopsis:

SOCIAL SCIENCES

H   Social sciences (General)
HA   Statistics
       Including collections of general and census statistics
       of special countries. For mathematical statistics, *see* QA

4. **The schedule proper** enumerates specific class number assignments and sequences in their most explicit form. Page formatting devices, standard in most published schemes, demonstrate hierarchical subordinations and progressions. LC schedules show left-margin indentions, with nested running titles on nearly every page to demonstrate hierarchy. These devices are not so carefully worked out, nor so consistently displayed, as they are in the Dewey Decimal Classification. Size and quality of typeface also indicate levels of subordination in the pre-1970 letter-press LC schedules, as well as in DDC. But current production from typed copy permits the use of only two typographical devices (underlining and full capitals) to identify topics of greater generality or inclusiveness. Many broad headings not listed in the schedule outline, but which offer a useful survey of subtopics, are interpolated just ahead of the specific numbers which they embrace. They often carry no single class number of their own. For this and related reasons the LC scheme does not work well for classifying small general collections, or parts of collections. Nor are these spans very often accompanied by internal summary tables such as DDC uses.

Most schedules do carry internal tables at key junctures, to provide schematic patterns for further localized development of class numbers or sequences. While the LC system is basically enumerative (that is, its topical number assignments are usually not made until there is at least one book to go into the category), these generalized tables open up patterned arrangements which are usually not fully realized on the shelves.

A related space saver is the "Divide like" or "Subarranged like" note, which appears infrequently, but very specifically, in simple one-to-one equivalencies, without the complications encountered in the more abstractly contrived DDC notation. Scope notes and footnotes occasionally refer to auxiliary tables, etc., or they sometimes give useful instructions for number building. The following page from the "T — Technology" schedule shows most of these features:

TD   ENVIRONMENTAL TECHNOLOGY. SANITARY ENGINEERING

⟶   The promotion and conservation of the public health, comfort and convenience by the control of the environment
Cf. GF, Human ecology
    HC68, HC95-710, Environmental policy (General)
    HD3840-4730, Economic aspects (Government ownership, municipal industries, finance, etc.)
    QH75-77, Landscape protection
    RA565-604, Public health
    S622-627, Soil conservation
    S900-972, Conservation of natural resources
    TC801-978, Reclamation of land
    TH6014-7975, Building environmental engineering

	Periodicals and societies, by language of publication
1	English
2	French
3	German
4	Other languages (not A-Z)
5	Congresses
6	Exhibitions. Museums
⟶	Subarranged like TA6
7	Collected works (nonserial)
9	Dictionaries and encyclopedias
12	Directories
	History
15	General works
16	Ancient
17	Medieval
18	Modern to 1800
19	Nineteenth century
20	Twentieth century
21-126	Country and city subdivisions. Table I[1]
⟶	Including municipal reports of public sanitary works
	Under each country (except as otherwise specified):
	(1) .A1A-Z General works
	.A6-Z States, provinces, etc.
	(2) Local (Cities, etc.), A-Z
	Biography
139	Collective
140	Individual, A-Z
	General works
144	Early to 1850
145	1850-
146	Elementary textbooks
148	Popular works
151	Pocketbooks, tables, etc.
153	General special
155	Addresses, essays, lectures
156	Environmental and sanitary engineering as a profession
157	Study and teaching
.5	Research
158	Municipal engineering organization and management

⟶ [1]For Table I, *see* pp. 263-65. Add country number in table to 0

5. **Auxiliary tables** designed for use with more than one specific class number or span are located externally to the schedules proper in many volumes. If, as in the "B—Philosophy" and "J—Political Science" schedules, they apply to only one subclass, they follow that subclass. Otherwise, they appear after the full schedule, immediately preceding the index. Sometimes a table number is given in parentheses beside an entry in the schedule, to warn the user that the entry should be further subdivided. More often a footnote cites the table with its page number, and occasionally indicates how the interpolation should be made. Such a footnote can be seen on the subclass TD page reproduced above. A part of the table to which it refers appears here:

T   TABLES OF SUBDIVISIONS

                                  TABLE I

                    HISTORY AND COUNTRY DIVISIONS
          History
15   General works
16   Ancient
17   Medieval
18   Modern
19   19th century
20   20th century
          Special countries

                  Under each country with two numbers:
                  (1)   General works
                  (2)   Local or special, A-Z
                  The numbers for "Cities or other special," "Local or special," "Prov-
                  inces or special" may be used in some cases for the local subdivision,
                  in other cases for special canals, rivers, harbors, railroads, or bridges,
                  as specified in the particular scheme to which this table is applied
                  Under both general and local subdivisions arrange as follows:
                  .A1-5   Official documents
                  .A6-Z   Nonofficial. By author, A-Z
                  e.g. TD257.A5, 1966, Gt. Brit. Water Resources Board.
                      Water supplies in South East England
                      TD264.T5P6, 1967, Port of London Authority.   The cleaner
                  Thames.
                      TD224.C3A53, 1963, California.   Dept of Water Resources.
                  Alameda County investigation

21   America
22   North America
23   United States
  .1   Eastern states. Atlantic coast
  .15   New England
  .2   Appalachian region
  .3   Great Lakes region
  .4   Midwest. Mississippi Valley
  .5   South. Gulf states
  .6   West

.7	Northwest
.8	Pacific coast
.9	Southwest
24	States, A-W ⟵
	e.g. .A4 Alaska
	.H3 Hawaii
25	Cities (or other special), A-Z
26	Canada
27	Provinces (or other special), A-Z
.5	Latin America
28-29	Mexico ⟵
30	Central America
31	Special countries, A-Z

This auxiliary Table I from the T schedule is "simple" because it carries only one sequence of numbers which can be interpolated directly into the corresponding number spans in the schedule. Other tables are "compound." That is, they supply more than one number sequence for the same list of subtopics. Number spans from the schedule and the table are matched according to the quantity of materials which the LC classifiers anticipate at any given location. The following excerpt from the "N—Fine Arts" external Tables I to III-A shows how spans of from one hundred to three hundred numbers can be distributed by reference to the same list of terms.

N   TABLES OF SUBDIVISIONS

Tables I to III-A

I (100)		II (200)	III (300)	III-A (300)
01	America	01	01	01
	Latin America	02	02	02
02	North America	03	03	03
03	United States	05	05	05
.5	Colonial period; 18th (and early 19th) century	06	06	06
.7	19th century	07	07	07
04	20th century	08	08	08
05	New England	10	10	10
.5	Middle Atlantic States	.5	.5	.5
06	South	11	11	11
07	Central	14	18	18
08	West	17	23	23
09	Pacific States	19	25	25
10	States, A-W	25	35	35
11	Cities, A-Z	27	38	38
12	Special artists, A-Z	28	39	39
13	Canada	29	41	41
14	Mexico	31	44	44

15	Central America	33	47	47
16	British Honduras	35	50	50
17	Costa Rica	37	53	53
18	Guatemala	39	56	56
19	Honduras	41	59	59
20	Nicaragua	43	62	62
21	Panama	45	65	65
22	Salvador	46	67	67
23	West Indies	47	68	68
24	Bahamas	49	71	71
25	Cuba	51	74	74
26	Haiti	53	77	77
27	Jamaica	55	80	80
28	Puerto Rico	57	83	83
29	Other, A-Z	58	86	86
30	South America	59	89	89
31	Argentine Republic	61	92	92
32	Bolivia	63	95	95
33	Brazil	65	98	98
34	Chile	67	101	101

For instance, the span "N5801-5896—Classical Art in Other [i.e. Non-Greek or Italian] Countries" is to be distributed according to Table I, starting from class number N5800. On the other hand, "NB1501-1684—Sculptured Monuments in Special Countries" uses Table II as a guide for adding country numbers to NB1500. Similarly, "ND2601-2876—Mural Painting in Special Countries" uses Table III to add country numbers to ND2600.

Geographical and chronological subdivisions are often relegated to auxiliary tables. Frequently the two concepts are combined, as in the above excerpt from the N schedule. But other principles of division may also be found in tabular form. A compound table external to subclass "JS—Local Government" contains such categories as "Periodicals," "Executive administration," "Legislative organization," and the like. The heavily-used PN, PR, PS, PZ schedule closes with an extensive set of simple and compound tables designed for use with literary author numbers, running the gamut from long spans for prolific, often translated and discussed authors to brief expansions of cutter designations for recent or little-published authors.

A few auxiliary tables, especially certain geographic lists from the H schedule, are said to "float." That is, they appear, usually in slightly variant forms, in other schedules. Thus the Table of Countries in One Alphabet from the H schedule shows up in mutation as an auxiliary table for schedules C, D, E-F, T, U, and V.

6. **A detailed index** accompanies each schedule except PA Supplement, PB-PH, PG, PJ-PM, P-PM Supplement (which is itself an index), and Parts 1 and 2 each of the PQ and PT subclasses. These indexes vary in coverage and depth, but most of them list specific topics from their schedule. Cross references from synonyms or related terms, alphabetized and indented subordinate topical lists, and suggestions for placing related materials in other schedules are occasionally included. Excerpts from the class "T—Technology" and class "H—Social Sciences" indexes are given on page 434.

7. **Supplementary pages of additions and changes** appear at the back of many schedules published before 1970. These were discussed under "Revised editions of individual schedules" on pages 432-33.

INTERNAL FORMAT

While Herbert Putnam and Charles Martel left the local arrangement of topical and form divisions very much to the discretion of their subject specialists, they nevertheless identified certain basic orientation features for use throughout the system. These organizational concepts were generally known as "Martel's Seven Points" of internal format. They could be incorporated into the schedules at any level of hierarchical subdivision appropriate within the given context. They encompassed:

1. **General form divisions.** The approach here was similar to Dewey's Form Division Table, which has evolved in recent DDC editions into the Table of Standard Subdivisions. It assumes that library materials can often be effectively grouped according to their mode of presentation. Examples are periodicals, society publications, collections, dictionaries or encyclopedias, conference, exhibition, or museum publications, annuals or yearbooks, directories, and documents. Because of their general application they belong near the beginning of any disciplinary or topical section, but the LC system imposes no rigid order upon their location. Their importance in subclass "L—Education (General)" is best observed in the following schedule outline:

L	EDUCATION (GENERAL)
7-97	Periodicals. Societies
101	Yearbooks
106-107	Congresses
111-791	Documents. Reports
797-899	Exhibitions. Museums
900-991	Directories

By contrast, subclasses "LD-LG—Individual Educational Institutions" show no obvious use of the form division concept. Only in their auxiliary tables do a few of the forms emerge as useful ordering concepts.

2. **Theory. Philosophy.**

3. **History. Biography.**

4. **Treatises. General works.** Works falling under these three of Martel's Seven Points are often intermixed with those arranged according to physical form, and with other locally useful groupings, as the following excerpt shows:

QC	**PHYSICS**
1	Periodicals, societies, congresses, serial collections, yearbooks
3	Collected works (nonserial)
5	Dictionaries and encyclopedias
.3	Communication in physics
.45	Physics literature
.5	Abstracting and indexing
6	Philosophy
	Unified field theories, *see* QC173.7-75
	Relativity physics, *see* QC173.5-65
.8	Nomenclature, terminology, notation, abbreviations
	History
7	General works
9	By region or country, A-Z
	Biography
15	Collective
16	Individual, A-Z
	e.g. Curie, Marie and Pierre, *see* QD22
	.E5 Einstein
	.N7 Newton
.2	Directories
	Early works
17	1501-1700
19	1701-1800

5. **Law. Regulation. State relations.** Until the publication in 1969 of the first "K—Law" subclass, this ordering principle was handy for grouping legal materials with their related topics, especially in the social sciences. The belated, still unfinished development of class K inverts the relationship. Whenever possible we now classify such works first as legal materials, and only subordinately as being discipline-oriented. For example, books dealing with government regulations for control of drugs as economic commodities were originally classed in HD9665.7-9. Those dealing with regulations for the manufacture, sale, and use of drugs were classed in RA402. Subclass "KF—Law of the United States" now places drug laws in KF3885-3894. In years to come, most works dealing with U.S. drug legislation and regulation will be placed there.

6. **Study and teaching. Research. Textbooks.** Unlike DDC, the LC scheme sometimes allows a unique place for textbooks, as well as for more theoretical works on how to study, teach, or research a topic. Thus under "QL—Zoology" there appears the following sequence:

QL   **ZOOLOGY**

General works and treatises
41   Early through 1759
45   1760-1969
.2   1970-
46   Pictorial works and atlases
.5   Zoological illustrating
——→   Textbooks
Advanced
47   Through 1969
.2   1970-
Elementary
48   Through 1969
.2   1970-
49   Juvenile works
Cf. SF75.5, Domestic animals
50   Popular works
For stories and anecdotes, *see* QL791-795
.5   Zoology as a profession
——→ 51   **Study and teaching. Research**
.5   Problems, exercises, examinations
52   Outlines, syllabi
53   Laboratory manuals
Cf. QL812, Anatomy
QP44, Physiology
55   Laboratory animals
——→   General works only. Prefer systematic divisions for particular groups of animals.
Cf. SF405.5-407, Breeding and care.
57   Audiovisual aids
58   Other special

In other disciplines LC Classification explicitly groups textbooks with
general works and treatises. Under one subtopic we find:

QH   **ECOLOGY**

540   Periodicals, societies, congresses, serial collections, yearbooks
.3   Collected works (nonserial)
.4   Dictionaries and encyclopedias
——→ 541   General works, treatises, and textbooks
.13   Popular works
.14   Juvenile works
.145   Addresses, essays, lectures
——→   .15   Special aspects of the subject as a whole, A-Z
.M3 Mathematical models
.R4 Remote sensing
——→   .2   Study and teaching. Research
.3   Biological productivity
.5   By type of environment, A-Z

7. **Subjects and subdivisions of subjects.** Most modern classification systems are disciplinary rather than topical. That is, they normally proceed from broad general divisions of knowledge to narrower subdivisions, with more or less comprehensive coverage provided for each special topic in relation to the hierarchy. Any linear arrangement of books or other materials on shelves must resort to a series of cyclic progressions if it displays subject-related groupings based on logical considerations or practical associations. Just as Martel's fifth point reminds classifiers that "general works" should be shelved together, usually near the beginning of each new topical group, so this seventh point provides for further subject breakdown based on "literary warrant" or the amount of material requiring classification in such a group. One intermediate type which the LC system frequently places just after "general works" is a potpourri called "general special" or "special aspects." These works treat the topic from particular points of view. Sometimes, as in TD153 (see page 442) and QH541.15 (above), such books have a single class number. At other places they must be spread out over several pages of the schedules. Example 4 at the close of this chapter shows a "general special" assignment.

NOTATION

1. **Class numbers.** The typical LC class number contains a mixed notation of one to three letters, followed by one to four integers, and possibly a short decimal. Decimal numbers were not used much until it became necessary to expand certain sections where no further integers were available. Decimals do not usually indicate subordination, but allow a new topic or aspect to be inserted into an established context. In the above excerpt from the "QH540-549 — Ecology" schedule the decimals belie the left-margin indentions of their associated topics. Clearly, "QH541.145 — Addresses, Essays, Lectures" is hierarchically equivalent to "QH541 — General Works, Treatises, and Textbooks."

Another method of expanding LC class numbers is by means of mnemonic letter-number combinations, which look like Cutter's "Author numbers," but are derived from a different matrix (*see* "Book numbers" below). These "cutter numbers" may represent geographic, personal, corporate, or topical names. They are subordinated to schedule numbers where an instruction to subdivide "A-Z" appears. Since they are part of the class number, most of the actual LC assignments, or at least a significant number of examples, are usually included within the schedule (*see* "QH541.15 — Special Aspects of Ecology as a Whole, A-Z" and "QC16 — Individual Biography of Physicists, A-Z" above). Geographic cutter numbers are generally omitted, however, unless they happen to be available in an auxiliary table to one or another of the schedules. In the excerpt from class T, Table I above, the table number 24 is associated with American states "A-W," together with a rare inclusion of two examples. The class T user will find that auxiliary Table III is a complete list of state cutter numbers which corroborates the examples in Table I.

Alphabetic geographic sequences normally appear at subordinate places in the schedules, where they subdivide a single integer or decimal number. For broader disciplines or subjects, where the geographic arrangement covers an extensive number span, the organization follows a "preferred pattern" as was noted in the section on basic features (page 444). The excerpt from class N, Tables I to III-A, shows how such sequences begin with "home base" (i.e., the Western Hemisphere and the United States), following a pattern which covers the earth pretty much according to our American perceptions of the nearness and importance of our neighbors.

Library of Congress interpretation of "cutter numbers" is always decimal. In a typical letter(s)-number(s)/letter-number(s) combination, the primary letter(s)-number(s) group should be arranged first alphabetically, then by integer(s) until a fifth digit is introduced following a decimal point. All schedules make the basic ordering by integer quite evident, as when PR509 follows PR51, but precedes PR5018. The secondary letter-number(s) combination, by contrast, should be filed decimally. The Library of Congress carefully inserts a decimal point in front of it, even if, as at "QH541.15.M3 — Mathematical Models in Ecology," a decimal is already part of the primary number. Some libraries using the LC system drop the cutter decimal from their notation, on the premise that users will remember to follow the convention. The practice may possibly cause confusion in long cutter number runs where it is not clearly understood that a class number like PR4972.M33 should follow PR4972.M3 but precede PR4972.M5.

Occasionally a class number, or series of numbers, appears in the schedules in parentheses. These were formerly termed "shelflist numbers," but today more often called "alternative class numbers." Some of them represent locations once actively used, but now retired by the Library of Congress. Class number G1020, for instance, was assigned to school atlases in schedule G, third edition (1954). By 1966 the *Additions and Changes* showed it as G(1020) with an instruction to see G1019 for school atlases. In the 1976 fourth edition of class G, there is no G1020 at all. *See* the schedule R index example on page 435.

Other class numbers appear to have been reserved in parentheses for possible future use, and have since been activated. The span "PA2023 — 2027 — Congresses and collections of Papers Dealing with Latin Philology and Language" was so reserved in the original 1928 edition of the P-PA schedule, but all parentheses were removed by 1962. Alternative class numbers are nearly always accompanied by "prefer notes." Thus subclass SF (Animal culture) has an entry "SF(112) Weight tables, see HF5716.C2, etc." Libraries using the LC system are welcome to adopt these alternative class numbers if their own classification needs are better realized by so doing.

2. **Book numbers.** Library call numbers serve a double function. The class number portion groups related materials together. The book number, which forms the second portion of the complete call number, uniquely identifies different works in the same class. Traditionally, the book number is based on the main entry, which has been chosen for the work through descriptive cataloging. Various terms such as "author number" and "cutter number" have been applied, but "author number" does not allow for those works with title main entries, while "cutter number" is misleading on two counts. First, the LC method of deriving it differs from the original tables devised by C. A. Cutter. Second, as we already know, LC often uses "cutter numbers" as secondary parts of its class number notation. The latest version of the LC "book number table" reads as follows:

Library of Congress call numbers consist, in general, of two principal elements: class number and book number, to which are added, as required, symbols designating a particular work.

Library of Congress book numbers are composed of the initial letter of the main entry heading, followed by Arabic numerals representing the succeeding letters on the following basis:

```
1) After initial vowels
      for the second letter: b  d  l,m  n  p  r  s,t  u-y
               use number: 2  3   4   5  6  7   8    9

2) After the initial letter S
      for the second letter:  a  ch  e  h,i  m-p  t   u
               use number:   2   3   4   5    6   7-8  9

3) After the initial letters Qu
      for the third letter:  a  e  i  o  r  y
              use number:   3  4  5  6  7  9
      for names beginning Qa-Qt
                use: 2-29

4) After other initial consonants
      for the second letter:  a  e  i  o  r  u  y
               use number:   3  4  5  6  7  8  9

5) When an additional number is preferred
      for the third letter:  a-d  e-h  i-l  m  n-q  r-t  u-w  x-z
               use number:   2*    3    4   5   6    7    8    9
      (*optional for third letter a or b)
```

Letters not included in these tables are assigned the next higher or lower number as required by previous assignments in the particular class.

The arrangements in the following examples illustrate some possible applications of these tables:

```
1) Names beginning with vowels

   Abernathy  .A2    Ames       .A45   Astor     .A84
   Adams      .A3    Appleby    .A6    Atwater   .A87
   Aldrich    .A4    Archer     .A7    Austin    .A9

2) Names beginning with the letter S

   Saint      .S2    Simmons      .S5   Steel     .S7
   Schaefer   .S3    Smith        .S6   Storch    .S75
   Seaton     .S4    Southerland  .S64  Sturges   .S8
   Shank      .S45   Springer     .S66  Sullivan  .S9
```

3) Names beginning with the letters Qu

Qadriri	.Q2	Quick	.Q5	Qureshi	.Q7
Quabbe	.Q3	Quoist	.Q6	Quynn	.Q9
Queener	.Q4				

4) Names beginning with other consonants

Carter	.C3(7)	Cinelli	.C5(6)	Cullen	.C8(4)
Cecil	.C4(2)	Corbett	.C6(7)	Cyprus	.C9(6)
Childs	.C45	Croft	.C7(6)		
	( ) = if using two numbers				

5) When there are no existing conflicting entries in the shelflist, the use of a third letter book number may be preferred:

Cabot	.C3	Callahan	.C34	Carter	.C37
Cadmus	.C32	Campbell	.C35	Cavelli	.C38
Daffrey	.C33	Cannon	.C36	Cazalas	.C39

The numbers are decimals, thus allowing for infinite interpolation of the decimal principle.

Since the tables provide only a general framework for the assignment of numbers, the symbol for a particular name or work is constant only within a single class. Each entry must be added to the existing entries in the shelflist in such a way as to preserve alphabetic order in accordance with Library of Congress filing rules.[6]

Some points need further comment. Note first of all that the numeral "1" appears nowhere in the table. The Library of Congress avoids its use, and the use of zeros, as decimals to preserve alphabetic order. If, for instance, the name "Abbott" were given the cutter ".A1," a subsequent cutter at the same location for "Aamodt" would have to be, say, ".A09," while "Aagard" would go to ".A085" or something like it. While most type-fonts and computer print-chains distinguish between the digit zero and the capital letter "O," typewriters as a rule do not. In actual practice, LC shelflisters would more likely give "Abbott" a cutter such as ".A15" so later assignments for names such as "Aagard" and "Aamodt" could have ".A12" and ".A128," or similar decimals to insure space for unlimited further alphabetical expansion if needed.

All this brings out another trait of LC shelflisting. There is nothing sacrosanct about the above table. It has been officially changed as shelflisting problems were encountered and new needs were perceived. The present LC shelflist contains a jumble of old and new assignments. Recently devised numbers may reflect accommodation to outmoded practices, to avoid extensive re-shelflisting, rather than following current practice as outlined in the table. Author numbers assigned for the same person may also vary significantly from one class number to another. The examples below illustrate such a variation:

TL561   Splaver, Sarah, 1921-
.S65   Some day I'll be an aerospace engineer . . . 1967.
                                                            67-23997

T   Technology
TL   Motor vehicles. Aeronautics. Astronautics
561   Aeronautics as a vocation
.S65   The author number for Splaver

. . . .

Z682   Splaver, Sarah, 1921-
.S735   Some day I'll be a librarian . . . 1967.
                                                            67-23998

Z   Bibliography and Library science
682   Personnel in library science
.S735   The author number for Splaver

Since cutter numbers are used by the Library of Congress to extend some class numbers, as well as for book number shelflisting, many works have at least two cutter segments in their call numbers. One example is Niles M. Hansen's *French Regional Planning* (LC card number 68-14603) for which the LC call number HT395.F7H35 can be analyzed as follows:

H   Social sciences
HT   Communities. Classes. Races
395   Regional planning: countries or regions other than the
              United States, A-Z
.F7   France
H35   The author number for Hansen

While double cutters are commonplace, triple "cutters" are exceedingly rare. They have been used in class G for certain kinds of subject maps, but with a special disclaimer added. An example is the *Urban Atlas, Tract Data for Standard Metropolitan Statistical Areas: Hartford, Connecticut* from the U.S. Bureau of the Census (LC card number 75-603461). Its call number G1242.H3E25U5 1974 signifies:

G   Geography. Maps. Anthropology. Recreation
1242   Connecticut sub-area atlas
.H3   Hartford metropolitan area
E25   Statistical areas. Census tracts [see Table IV - Subject sub-
              divisions: "These numbers are not Cutter numbers and have
              no alphabetical significance."]
U5   Cutter number for United States. Bureau of the Census,
              the authority responsible for the atlas
1974   Date of atlas publication

3. **Reserved cutter numbers.** The LC schedules and tables frequently set aside the first few ".A" or the last several ".Z" possibilities in a cutter sequence for special purposes. Observe the example at "TD21-126 — Country and City Subdivisions of Environmental Technology and Sanitary Engineering" on page 442. Assume that class T, Table I and the internal table in the schedule have been applied to derive the class number TD28.A1 for a general work on sanitary engineering in Mexico. Let us suppose that the first book classified here was written by a Ricardo Gomez. Using the LC book number table, we would probably complete the full call number as TD28.A1G6, or TD28.A1G65. A second work on the same topic by a Werner Goode might then receive the call number T28.A1G66, while still a third treatise by a Ralph Goddard could be given something like T28.A1G58.

Assume now that we have a book on sanitary engineering in the Mexican state of Aguascalientes. It cannot receive the usual book cutter ".A3" or ".A33" because the internal table at TD21-126 has "reserved" .A1 through .A5 for general works and other possible future needs. Therefore we must accommodate the reservation by assigning the class number T28.A68 or T28.A7, followed by an appropriate book number. Now suppose that still another book covers sanitary engineering in the city of Aguascalientes. Our class number will probably be T29.A33, plus a second cutter for the main entry.

".A" cutters are likely to be reserved for serials, society publications, documents, etc., where these general forms of material have not been given integer or decimal class numbers. Such special reservations are often called "official" cutters. The following schedule excerpt, with two LC call number assignments, illustrates this practice:

HA   **STATISTICS**

175-4010	By country
195-730	United States
730	Cities, A-Z
	Under each:
	.A1-5 Official
	.A6-Z Nonofficial

. . . .

HA730   Houston, Tex. Division of Vital Statistics.
.H67A3   Facts about Houston : population, births, deaths, maternal and infant deaths . . . 1958.   77-350875

HA730   Houston, Tex. Chamber of Commerce. Census Tract
.H67H6   Division.
             1970 Census data for the Houston area . . . 1971
                                                      78-31293

In both of the above call numbers ".H67," identifying the city of Houston, is a geographical extension of the class number. Publications of the city government's Division of Vital Statistics are considered to be "official publications." Therefore "A3" is added in accordance with schedule instructions and the LC shelflist entries, to serve as the book number. Houston Chamber of Commerce publications, not being considered "official," have their book cutters based on the traditional first word of the main entry.

".Z" cutter reservations are most common in class P, where researchers like to have biography and criticism of an author shelved immediately following his works. In this class, separate integers frequently designate all authors of a given period whose surnames start with the same initial. The first cutter number is then based on the second letter of the surname. A second cutter, based usually on an auxiliary table of reserved numbers, identifies collected works, selections, titles of separate works, adaptations, translations, or biography and criticism. *The Selected Letters of Robinson Jeffers, 1897-1962* (LC card number 67-29318) carries the LC call number PS3519.E27Z53, exemplifying application of auxiliary Table IXa.

Workmarks, in the traditional sense of lower-case letters added to book numbers to alphabetize titles or writers of biographies, are not used by the Library of Congress. Lower-case letters do serve a few special purposes in LC call numbers, but they are comparatively rare. In subclass "PZ — Fiction in English. Juvenile Literature" a unique combination of upper- and lower-case letters (instead of second cutter numbers) alphabetizes the titles of a given author, while Arabic numerals (instead of dates) designate reissues or new editions. Thus Colin Spencer's *The Tyranny of Love* published in New York by Weybright and Talley (LC card number 68-28267) has the LC call number PZ4.S7446Ty3.

4. **Additions to call numbers.** The adding of dates to LC call numbers has increased with multiple publication in more than one country, in different imprints, in paperback as well as hard cover, in later editions, and in reprints. The Library of Congress now gives rather explicit guidelines for adding dates to call numbers.[7] One use of lower-case letters is to identify bibliographically distinct issues of the same title published in the same year. For example, when Brian Jackson's *Working Class Community: Some General Notions Raised by a Series of Studies in Northern England* was simultaneously published in London and New York by Routledge & Kegan Paul, and by Humanities Press (LC card number 68-101992) it was given the LC call number "HN398.Y6J3 — Social History and Conditions in Yorkshire" plus author or book number. Later that year (1968), a second New York issue by F. A. Praeger (LC card number 68-25543) received the same call number with an added element "1968b." Note: LC card numbers do not necessarily show the precise order in which successive issues of the same title are to be shelflisted. Card numbers may be assigned in advance of publication, or other shelflisting conditions may dominate.

A few other exceptional notations show up in some schedules. For example, dates are used not only as final elements, to distinguish issues of the same title. They occasionally become secondary elements of class numbers, taking precedence over book numbers. Class numbers "BX830-831 — Medieval and Modern Councils Within Roman Catholicism" use this device to arrange church councils by date of opening. An example is Xavier Rynne's *Vatican Council II* (LC card number 67-21527), which carries the LC call number BX830 1962 .R94. Also, in schedule "BL-BX — Religion" some Bible texts are so specifically classed that LC shelflisters add merely dates (no book numbers) to keep them in order. A recent example is:

BS391.2   Bible. English. Revised Standard. Selections. 1975.
1975   Christianica : the basic teachings of the Christian faith ar-
            ranged for prayer and meditation . . . 1975.
                                                                74-13005

    BS   Bible
370-399   Selections. Quotations
390-391   English
    391   General
        .2   1951-
    1975   The publication date of this anthology

CONCLUSIONS

Most libraries using the LC classification system will continue to appropriate officially assigned call numbers for any of their own materials which the
Library of Congress has already classified. However, it is a rare library which
holds only titles, editions, and issues available in the Library of Congress collection. Librarians and library users should be able to break down an LC call
number into its components. Classifiers should be able to create reasonably
consistent supplementary numbers with which to fit their unique holdings into
the system. Users may stumble over special practices at local points, but the
general principles of arrangement are nearly always decipherable, especially if
a shelflist of LC call numbers is available to compare with the schedules.
Highly specific shelflisting (i.e., the rationale underlying many book numbers)
is, on the other hand, not always so easy to explain. The perfectionist
classifier, geared to the invariabilities of DDC, must remember that the LC
system is loosely coordinated and essentially pragmatic. It aims first to class
closely, then to identify uniquely, particular works, or issues of works, using
the most economical notation available within its broad parameters of theory
and practice.
    A few examples of number building have been analyzed earlier in this
chapter. The following illustrations serve primarily for review:

EXAMPLE 1

DC203.4   Ashton, John, b. 1834.
A82   English caricature and satire on Napoleon I . . . 1968.
1968   67-24349

    D   History and Topography (except America)
    DC   France
139-249   Revolutionary and Napoleonic period, 1789-1815
203-212   Biography of Napoleon
    203   General works
        .4   Caricature and satire
    .A82   The personal author number for Ashton
    1968   Date of this publication   [Originally
                                    published in 1888]

EXAMPLE 2

JX1977.8 Asamoah, Obed Y.
.G4A8 The legal significance of the declarations of the general assembly of the United Nations . . . 1966.
                 67-81320

J Political science
JX   International law
1901-1991   Procedure in international disputes. International arbitration. Peace literature, etc.
1977   United Nations, 1946-
 .8   Special topics, A-Z
.G4   General Assembly
A8   The personal author number for Asamoah

EXAMPLE 3

KFM2929 Massachusetts. Courts.
.A2   Massachusetts rules of court, 1975, with amendments to Nov. 15, 1974 . . . 1975
1975
                 75-315486

K Law
KF   Law of the United States
KFM   Law of the states with the initial letter M
2400-2999   Massachusetts [see auxiliary state table for sub-divisions]
2908-2960   Courts. Procedure
2928-2960   Civil procedure
2929   Court rules
.A2   Official cutter number for this work
1975   Date of publication

EXAMPLE 4

NA7125 Affordable houses designed by architects / [edited] by Jeremy Robinson and the editors of Architectural record . . . 1979.   78-11471
.A35

N Fine arts
NA   Architecture
4100-8480   Special classes of buildings
4170-8480   Classed by use
7100-7880   Domestic architecture
7125   General special [i.e. particular aspects of the topic]
.A35   The title main entry number

EXAMPLE 5

RA407.3	American Hospital Association
.A73	Comparative statistics on health facilities and popula-
1978	tion : metropolitan and nonmetropolitan areas. 1978 ed.
	. . . c1978. 78-7259

R	Medicine
RA	Public aspects of medicine
407-409	Medical statistics
407	General
.3-.5	By country
.3	United States
.A73	The corporate author number for American Hospital Association
1978	The edition date

FOOTNOTES

[1]A table comparing the main classes of the Cutter and the LC schemes is given on page 461.

[2]*Cataloging Service Bulletin*, no. 2 (Fall 1978):45.

[3]Library of Congress, *Library of Congress Classification Schedules: A Cumulation of Additions and Changes through 1973* (Detroit, Gale Research Company, 1974), 32 vol.; *Library of Congress Classification Schedules: A Cumulation of Additions and Changes 1974-77* (Detroit, Gale Research Company, 1978), 28 vol.

[4]Library of Congress, Subject Cataloging Division, *Subject Headings*, 8th ed. (Washington, The Library, 1975), 2 vol. and suppls. For a detailed discussion of this work, *see* chapter 24.

[5]Library of Congress, *Library of Congress Catalog, Books: Subjects* (Washington, The Library, 1950-date).

[6]*Cataloging Service Bulletin*, no. 3 (Winter 1979):19-20.

[7]*Cataloging Service Bulletin*, no. 3 (Winter 1979):20-23.

25 OTHER GENERAL CLASSIFICATION SYSTEMS

INTRODUCTION

This chapter provides a brief overview and comparison of some of the more significant modern classifications besides DDC and LC. Those discussed will be Cutter's Expansive Classification, Brown's Subject Classification, Bliss's Bibliographic Classification, the Universal Decimal Classification, and Ranganathan's Colon Classification. While these by no means exhaust modern classification research and practice, they do illustrate many of the problems and solutions, or failures, of both the seminal and the well-entrenched systems discussed in the contemporary literature.[1]

CUTTER'S EXPANSIVE CLASSIFICATION

The Expansive Classification, like the Dewey Decimal Classification, is the brainchild of an eminent library pioneer. Charles Ammi Cutter (1837-1903) was fifteen years older than Melvil Dewey (1851-1931) but took fifteen years longer to publish his scheme. Both men devised their systems as practical efforts to organize collections which they knew and served. Just as DDC came out of Dewey's student employment in the Amherst College Library, so Cutter's cataloging efforts in the Harvard College Library, and for much longer at the Boston Athenaeum, flowered into his Expansive Classification.

While the lives and achievements of the two men show many parallels, there are also significant differences. In classification, Dewey chose his pure decimal notation early on, making it such a key feature of his approach that it more or less governed all subsequent growth patterns. He saw that a simple basic design, easy-to-master mnemonic devices, and a certain sturdy inflexibility could provide a general system that would be applicable to the many libraries which were being established. With characteristic energy, he started a schedule of periodic revision to keep his system responsive to the rapidly changing cultural and publishing milieu. And he marketed his invention with zest and conviction. Cutter was of a more delicate physique and temperament, less exuberant, more institution-oriented. But he too, imbued with the gregarious optimism of his era, worked diligently to establish librarianship as a helping profession, with "scientific" organization as one of its basic assumptions.

Unlike DDC, Cutter's notation was a secondary feature. His scheme has often been praised for an essential logic and balance that was unaffected by his ready change of notation in response to professional criticism. For instance, when he adapted his Athenaeum arrangement to the Cary Library in Lexington, Massachusetts, he retained its intrinsic order, but substituted a different, more popular alphanumeric notation.[2]

DDC is part of the long historical tradition running from Aristotle through Francis Bacon to the early 1870s classifiers, Natale Battezzati and William Torrey Harris. Cutter appears to have been most directly influenced by the seventeenth century French work of Gabriel Naudé, and by Ismael Bouilliau's System of the Paris Booksellers, as reflected in Jacques Charles Brunet's 1804 *Manuel du librairie et de l'amateur de livres*,[3] although the general ferment makes it difficult to trace derivations precisely. Ingenious scientific thinkers such as Auguste Comte, André Marie Ampère, and Herbert Spencer, and systematic philosophers such as Immanuel Kant and G. W. F. Hegel published schemes of knowledge which, while largely ignoring older, more scholastic views, commanded well-deserved attention from library classifiers.

Both Dewey and Cutter made use of such synthetic devices as a place for materials broadly distinguished by their form of presentation, rather than their specific content, and for systematic subdivision of topics, when useful, by form, chronology, or geographic location.

Cutter's scheme stressed a sequence of "classifications," or expansions, from a very simple set of categories for a small library to an intricate network of interrelated, highly specific subdivisions for the library of over a million volumes. He did not live to finish his ultimate seventh expansion, or to embark on a successive-edition program, but he did have the satisfaction of seeing the Library of Congress prefer many features of his scheme to that of his friendly rival. As with switching notation, his willingness to take suggestions, and to compromise, worked to his credit and to the continuing influence of his system in spite of its limited adoption.

Cutter found the ten broad classes of DDC too narrow a base for large collections. He therefore turned to the alphabet, with its easily ordered sequence of up to twenty-six primary groupings. For collections which "could be put into a single room" his first "classification" used only seven letters, with an eighth double-letter subclass, as follows:

A	Works of reference and general works which include several of the following sections, and so could not go to any one
B	Philosophy and Religion
E	Biography
F	History and Geography and Travels
H	Social sciences
L	Natural sciences and Arts
Y	Language and Literature
YF	Fiction

If a small library should grow to require closer, more specific classes, Cutter's second classification, or expansion, introduced a mixed alphanumeric notation. It also subdivided the "F — History" and the new "G — Geography" classes by adding two Arabic numerals to the letter to signify identical geographic areas for each class. For example, F30 means History of Europe, while G30 means Geography of Europe. Another change is the splitting of the "L — Natural sciences and Arts" group. The second expansion holds fourteen main classes, some redefinition of the original seven, and further differentiation of two classes along geographic lines. Its outline is:

A   Works of reference, etc.
B   Philosophy and Religion
E   Biography
F   History [subdivided geographically by use of two digits]
G   Geography and Travels [subdivided in the same way as the F class]
H   Social sciences
L   Physical sciences
M   Natural history
Q   Medicine
R   Useful arts
V   Recreative arts, Sports and games, Theatre, Music
W   Fine arts
X   Language
Y   Literature
YF   Fiction

The third expansion completes all but "P—Vertebrates" of the base twenty-six divisions, and separates Religion from Philosophy, moving it to a second double-letter subclass. Part of the debt which LC Classification owes to Cutter can easily be traced through the following outline comparison:

Cutter's Expansive		**Library of Congress**	
A	General works	A	General works
B	Philosophy	B	Philosophy — Religion
BR	Non-Judaeo-Christian religions		
C	Judaism and Christianity	C	History — Auxiliary sciences
D	Ecclesiastical history	D	History (except America)
E	Biography	E-F	History of the Americas
F	History		
G	Geography	G	Geography — Anthropology
H	Social sciences	H	Social sciences
I	Sociology		
J	Political science	J	Political science
K	Law	K	Law
L	Natural sciences	L	Education
M	Natural history	M	Music
N	Botany	N	Fine arts
O	Zoology		
		P	Language and literature
Q	Medicine	Q	Science
R	Technology	R	Medicine
S	Engineering	S	Agriculture
T	Manufactures and Handicrafts	T	Technology
U	Defensive and preservative arts	U	Military science
V	Athletic and recreative arts	V	Naval science
W	Fine arts		
X	Languages		
Y	Literature		
YF	Fiction		
Z	Book arts	Z	Bibliography and Library science

The fourth expansion subdivides twelve main classes for the first time, increasing the double-letter subclasses to fifty. It also carries an extensive supplementary table expanding the double-digit geographic numbers from the F and G classes into a "place" or "local" list. Portions of this table are to be used as needed, by following instructions in the schedule proper. For example, the X class carries double-letter subclasses signifying form divisions. It also has a note that "any other language than English will be marked from the local list." There follow examples. Numbers fully spelled out in the fourth expansion are given below:

X	ENGLISH LANGUAGE	Y	ENGLISH AND AMERICAN
XD	Dictionaries		LITERATURE
XG	Grammars	YD	English drama
		YF	English fiction
		YJ	English juvenile literature
		YP	English poetry
X11	LANGUAGE IN GENERAL	Y11	LITERATURE IN GENERAL
X35	Italian language	Y35	Italian literature
		Y36	Latin literature
X39	French language	Y39	French literature
		Y39F	French fiction
		Y40	Spanish literature
		Y40D	Spanish drama
		Y41	Portuguese literature
X46	Dutch language		
X467	Flemish language		
X47	German language	Y47	German literature
		Y47P	German poetry
		Y54	Russian literature

The fifth expansion introduces the twenty-sixth single-letter class "P — Vertebrates," and subdivides all remaining undivided classes, using many triple- and a few quadruple-letter sections. It also provides a new use for Arabic number series, to indicate chronological periods. Under "W — Fine Arts," we find:

W11	HISTORY OF ART
W119	Prehistoric art
W12	Ancient art
W122	Egypt
	Chaldea, Babylonia, Assyria
. . . .	
W129	Rome
W13	Modern art (as opposed to Ancient art)
W14	Christian art
W141	Catacombs
W144	Christian symbolism and iconography
W149	Dance of Death
W15	Medieval art (476-1450 A.D.)
W16	Renaissance art
W17	Modern modern art

The sixth "classification" introduces no new techniques — only new expansions of existing classes and subclasses.

Other synthetic devices are appended to the volume carrying the first six expansions. Cutter explains his use of decimal author marks in a section which assumes that the user has access to his two-figure author table. He goes on to suggest the use of alphabetic workmarks based on introductory letters of titles, as well as other special markings for size, copy, edition, translation commentary, and special format (e.g., a dictionary of a topic). In another section he supplies a rudimentary table of single digits for addition "to any class number" to keep certain typical formats together. It reads as follows:

- •1   Theory of the subject
- •2   Bibliography of the subject
- •3   Biography of the subject, i.e., lives of persons connected with it
- •4   History of the subject
- •5   Dictionaries of the subject
- •6   Hand-books, etc., of the subject
- •7   Periodicals limited to the subject
- •8   Societies devoted to the subject
- •9   Collections of works on the subject by several authors

The notation of some common formats, such as dictionaries, varies according to the relationship of that format to the class or section as a whole. In the fifth and sixth classifications, subclass AD is introduced for general dictionaries "except those which are put in X." For most topics, however, the digit 5 from the table above means a dictionary when it follows the class number and precedes the author number. Cutter's example is "E83•5A1 - Allen's American biographical dictionary." Again, according to the table of special marks, dictionaries may be identified by placing a capital Z after a decimal point, following the workmark. Cutter cites "•sH1•Zc5 - Clarke's Shakespere concordance (in a library which has no special mark for Shakespere)."

Biscoe Date-letters are recommended for certain chronological situations, but no very specific instruction or examples are given. A considerable discussion of the ways to arrange biography, and Greek and Latin authors, is included.

The seventh classification was published in eighteen parts, edited and to some extent developed by William Parker Cutter after the originator's death.[4] All expansions were prepared on the theory that as a library outgrew its simpler modes of organization, partial dislocation and reclassification of the existing collection was preferable to complete reorganization. Although some books would have to be reclassed and relocated, not all would be, and certainly not all at once. To demonstrate the notational shifts required for one topic, if a growing library should decide to adopt a fuller expansion after using a lesser one, the following examples show how a book on corporal punishment of school children would be classed in each of the seven expansions:

1st and 2nd classification:	H Social sciences (including Sociology)
3rd classification:	I Sociology
4th classification:	I Sociology
	IK Education
5th classification:	IK Education
6th classification:	IK Education
	IP Pedagogics

7th classification:	IP	Pedagogics
	IPD	Discipline
	IPDC	Corporal punishment

Various later authorities have examined the system against a background of theory and modern development.[5] While it was never widely adopted, some sixty-seven American, Canadian, and British libraries have been identified as past or present Cutter System users.[6] Perhaps even more important is the influence it exerted on later, more popular classifications, such as that developed soon after at the Library of Congress.

BROWN'S SUBJECT CLASSIFICATION

Next in chronological development is a British scheme. James Duff Brown (1864-1914) was a Scottish counterpart of Dewey and Cutter, if somewhat younger. Coming to the profession from an early apprenticeship to publishers and booksellers, he became deeply involved in the public library movement in Great Britain. It is debatable whether his advocacy of open stacks was directly influenced by his travels in the United States, in 1893. Without benefit of a university education, his breadth of knowledge was legendary, and his interest in music resulted in several music reference tools which he either compiled or sponsored.

Brown recognized the lack of good organization of materials in most British libraries. To make open stack access feasible he and John Henry Quinn published in 1894 a "Classification of Books for Libraries in Which Readers Are Allowed Access to Shelves." Brown's own "Adjustable Classification" followed in 1898. As the name implies, it allowed for insertion of new divisions or topics as needed, but it was not worked out or indexed in much detail. Growing out of it, in 1906, was the first edition of the *Subject Classification.* In 1914, shortly after Brown's death, came a second edition, and in 1939 James Douglas Stewart issued a revised and enlarged third edition.[7]

The basic scaffold of Brown's *Subject Classification* consists of eleven main classes, expressing four broad divisional concepts in orderly sequence. Primary notation is alphabetical, with some classes assigned more than one capital letter, to cover all subtopics without making the notation unduly long:

A	Generalia	} Matter and Force
B C D	Physical Science	
E F	Biological Science	
G H	Ethnological and Medical Science	} Life
I	Economic Biology and Domestic Arts	
J K	Philosophy and Religion	} Mind
L	Social and Political Science	
M	Language and Literature	
N	Literary forms	} Record
O - W	History, Geography	
X	Biography	

Each initial letter is followed by three Arabic numerals. Sequence, rather than length of number reveals hierarchy, e.g.,

D600	METALLURGY
601	Smelting
602	Blast Furnaces
603	Open Hearth Furnaces
604	Ores

These schedule numbers may be expanded like decimals (without the decimal point) when new topics require insertion. If further topics will likely need space, Brown suggests using odd numbers first, but he finds "no reason apart from a long symbol, why . . . the additions to the decimal main numbers should not run to 100 or even 1000 places."[8] His illustration starts from "K951 - Catholic Apostolic Church (Irvingites)" in the schedule. To intercalate, one might add "K9510 - Christadelphians" and "K9511 - Christian Strugglers," or, if preferred, add "K9511 - Christadelphians" and "K9513 - Christian Strugglers," leaving the even expansions for possible future use.

National (i.e., geographic) numbers from the O - W classes may be attached to topical numbers when needed, using only the class letter and first figure of the place letter in most cases. Thus "S000 - Russia" can be added to "M906 -Municipal Libraries" to give the general number "M906S0 - Libraries in Russia."

A Categorical Table of "forms, etc. for the subdivision of subjects" makes use of a dividing point which is not a decimal. From it ".954 - Essays" can be added to "D705 - Physical Chemistry" to give "D705.954 - Essays on Physical Chemistry." Besides the dividing point to introduce a number from the Categorical Table, other relational signs appear. The plus mark usually indicates two facets from the same class:

Example 1:	A639	Landscape
	A616	Water Colour Painting
Result:	A639 + 616	Landscape Painting in Water Colours

Example 2:	C612	Violoncello
	C475	Gavottes
Result:	C612 + 475	Gavottes for Violoncello
		[*Not* C475 + 612. Brown thought it more useful to number the instrument and divide by form]

Another relational symbol is the underscore, used to separate parts of a stacked number. The purpose is to keep the extended notation compact, with the author or book number subordinate to the class number. A "Table for the Sub-division of Subjects, and the Arrangement of Individual Biography, Fiction, Poetry, Drama, Essays and Other Alphabetic Classes" (often referred to as the "Biography Table") is appended to the X class. In the tradition of the Cutter Author Tables, it associates an alphabetical with a numerical sequence, but unlike Cutter, Brown uses four-digit decimal interpolation into integral three-digit progressions, again without inserting a decimal point. We saw this rather confusing practice in his provisions for expanding class numbers:

Example 1:   E100   BOTANY
            .3   Textbooks, Systematic [Categorical Table]
           3408   Surname "Bow. . ." [Biographical Table]

Result: E100.3
           3408   Bower. Practical Instruction in Botany.

Example 2:   N250   Individual dramatists, arranged by number from
                    the Biographical Table
           .919   Criticism [Categorical Table]
           7860   Surname "Sha. . ." [Biographical Table]

Result: N250.919
           7860   Any criticism of a particular Shakespeare play.

Brown admits difficulties in determining the "most constant place" for criticism on Shakespeare and his works, in whole or in part. He suggests that a book carrying the above call number might be placed alphabetically by author with other, more general Shakespeare criticisms, in class X7860.

A number of other devices are offered for adaptation according to the needs of the local library. Biscoe and other alternative chronology tables are included. The use of introductory lower-case letters to show special collections or locations is suggested, e.g.,

Example: j   Juvenile work
           F881   Elephants
           .4   Text-Books, popular (non-scientific)
                   [CategoricalTable]

Result: jF881.4   A non-technical book on elephants in the
                      children's collection

Brown carried this typing device one step further by recommending symbols for polemic or controversial treatments. He suggested two asterisks or an "a" (against) for an unfavorable view, and a single asterisk or "f" (for) in the case of a favorable discussion, e.g.,

Example: I714   Smoking
Result: **I714 *or* aI714   Johnston. Is Smoking Injurious?
         *I714   *or* fI714   Russell. The Smoking Habit.

Brown's Generalia class was broader in scope than most other systems allow (e.g., "A100 - Education," and "A400 - Logic and Mathematics"). Theoretically, he believed that every form of knowledge could be traced to a principle from which it develops. He attempted to provide a matrix in which everything relating to a single topic could be assembled at "one constant or unmistakeable place." He argued that "every science and art springs from some definite source, and need not, therefore, be arbitrarily grouped in alphabetical, chronological, or purely artificial divisions."[9] He was particularly suspicious of the disciplinary "Fine Arts, Useful Arts, Science" divisions. Instead he associated Building with Architecture, Music with Acoustics, Fire Engines with Heat, Air-Craft with Meteorology, Sports with Biology, and so on. His grouping of material around "concrete" themes, and his "specific" one-place-per-subject index repudiates the widely-recognized principle of classification by discipline. Instead, it fosters what has been called "classification by attraction."[10]

Similarly, his attempt to equate science with technology is no longer deemed fruitful. His undue emphasis on British history and geography should surprise no one who sees analogous skews in DDC and LC, for similar reasons. While Brown's *Subject Classification*, like Cutter's *Expansive Classification*, never received the widespread adoption received by their American rivals, timing and the lack of a consistent, continuing update program may be the explanation, rather than the comparative merits of the four schemes. Brown's system stimulated research and development in British classification theory, much as Cutter's did in the United States. Both are now milestones of classification history, rather than popular modern schemes for arranging library materials.

BLISS' BIBLIOGRAPHIC CLASSIFICATION

Henry Evelyn Bliss (1870-1955) was Librarian of the College of the City of New York, where he spent some thirty years developing and testing his ideas on library classification. After several periodical articles and books, he finished publication of his magnum opus only two years before his death.[11]

A "bibliographic" classification is, in Bliss' terminology, one designed to organize documentary materials (i.e., library collections, chiefly in print format). The sequence of main classes nonetheless preserves the discipline (rather than topical) orientation which Bliss interpreted as the basic structure of knowledge. Paul Dunkin called it "a sort of reader interest classification for scholars."[12] It is based on three major principles:

1. Collocation of related subjects: closely related subjects placed in close proximity, e.g., chemical technology with chemistry, plant pathology with plant eugenics, etc.

2. Subordination of special to general: placement according to the principle of decreasing extension, so the general subject is followed by the more specific subject.

3. Graduation by specialty: "the generalizations and laws of each more general science are true in some measure of all the more special sciences. . . . But the laws or truths of the more special sciences rarely apply to the more general sciences or solve their problems."[13]

According to Bliss, it is important in classifying a book to decide in what main classes it falls. The literature on concrete topics like "bees" is not kept in one place (as Brown would try to do) but is distributed according to the "aspect" from which it is viewed. For example, a book on bees from a scientific aspect goes to class "G - Zoology," whereas a book on beekeeping is classed in "U - Useful Arts."

The Bliss system soon grew more popular in Great Britain than in the United States.[14] A British Committee for the Bliss Classification, which changed its name in 1967 to the Bliss Classification Association, draws its membership largely from libraries using the scheme. It publishes an annual *Bliss Classification Bulletin*, formerly issued by H. W. Wilson and has commissioned its chairman, Jack Mills, to edit a thoroughly revised and enlarged second edition in twenty separate parts. After various delays, the first volumes of this edition appeared in 1977.[15] No further classes or parts have come since, but they are promised at the earliest opportunity. Their format will be:

Part

1　Introductory volume, with full instructions on use; the common auxiliary schedules of Place, Time, etc.; and a substantial outline of the whole scheme, etc.

2　Classes 1-9 — Generalia; Universe of knowledge; Communications, including library and information science.

3　Class A — Philosophy ; Logic; Mathematics; Statistics.

4　Class B — Physics; Physics based technology.

5　Class C — Chemistry; Materials technology.

6　Class D — Astronomy and Space science; Earth sciences; Geography.

7　Classes E-G — Biology; Botany; Zoology.

8　Classes H-I — Health sciences; Psychology.

9　Class J — Education.

10　Class K — Sociology; Customs; Folklore; Ethnography.

11　Classes L-O — History.

12　Class P — Religion; the Occult; Morals and Ethics.

13　Classes Q-S — Social studies; Social administration and welfare; Political science and Law.

14　Class T — Economics; Management.

15　Classes UA-D — Agriculture and Animal husbandry.

16　Classes UE-N — Environmental technologies; Civil engineering; Constructional industries; House and home.

17　UO-W — Industrial, production, and mechanical engineering.

18　Class V — Fine arts, including Music.

19　Class W/Y — Language and literature.

20　Consolidated A/Z index to the whole scheme.[16]

The second edition makes full use of principles which Bliss developed over the years but had little opportunity to apply consistently to his original edition. It also derives techniques of facet analysis, as well as of explicit citation and filing orders from Ranganathan's monumental contributions to classification theory.[17]　The citation order, or sequence of aspects, is standardized as far as possible throughout the system. In special contexts it is precisely determined and fully explained in the schedules:

For example, not only is the user told whether, in the class Education, to cite the facet of Person taught before or after the facet subject taught, but in the former he is also told whether to cite the array Person by degree of handicap before or after the array Person by age.[18]

Because of the unpredictable progress of knowledge, with its effect on the numbers and content of published books and serials, certain relocations, amendments, and new subjects appear in the second edition schedules. Each class will receive rigorous analysis to determine and display explicitly its aspects or facets and arrays. More consistent and generally applicable tables of common subdivisions replace the former auxiliary schedules for geographical subdivisions, historical periods, etc. Use of the Anterior Numerical Classes 1-9 as prefixes to topical or disciplinary class letters (e.g., "6—Periodicals" prefixed to "A2J—Technology in General" to create "6A2J—Periodicals in General Technology") will be dropped.

Second edition notation consists of capital letters and numerals, omitting zero because of its similarity to the letter "O". Lower case letters, commas (formerly used as facet indicators), and hyphens (formerly used to link elements derived from different subject areas rather than from different facets of the same class) have been eliminated. Bliss wished to keep his numbers as brief as possible, consistent with full expression of the various aspects of a topic. He was not interested much in expressiveness, that is, showing position in the logical hierarchy of the system by the length or configuration of the individual class number. Rather, he tried to make his notation show flexibly, but specifically, all the auxiliary features (facets and arrays) which might be used to modify the basic subject of a work. He further strove to provide alternative locations and treatments so that the individual classifier could select the one most appropriate to the library's holdings. Mills substitutes "retroactive" notation for Bliss' relational commas and hyphens:

> . . . the subject Audio visual aids in teaching foreign languages in primary schools gets the classmark JMK OIE (from JM Primary Schools, JKO Foreign languages in the curriculum, JIE Audio visual aids).[19]

For the library using a classified catalog, on the other hand, the hyphen may still be invoked to achieve permuted multiple entry:

> . . . the subject above could be given the notation JM-JKO-JIE and entries then made also (by clerical procedures) under JKO-JIE-JM and JIE-JM-JKO. Alternatively, the briefer and simpler classmark achieved by retroactive notation could be used for the shelf mark and the longer ones for the catalogue.[20]

The future of the *Bibliographic Classification* is dependent in large part on the timing and public acceptance of the new edition. That Bliss' theory and practice had many advantages is a fact recognized by anyone who knows it well enough to compare it with more widely accepted schemes. That it badly needed updating and further development is also clear. The gargantuan job of complete overhaul by a few aficionados on a shoestring budget, if finished, should permit future sequential revision of different class schedules as needed (somewhat resembling the present revision program at the Library of Congress). Meanwhile, some libraries using the original schedules are falling away.[21] Establishment of the Bliss scheme as a major contender for library adoption will require not only efficient, dedicated work, but a great deal of luck.

UNIVERSAL DECIMAL CLASSIFICATION

The UDC, an expansion of the Dewey Decimal Classification, was first published in French in 1899 as the *Manuel du répertoire universel bibliographique.* Over the years it has been expanded in great detail by the Fédération Internationale de Documentation (FID), and published in several languages, including English.[22] It is primarily designed for subject indexing of all branches of knowledge, with decimal notation to specify what are frequently hierarchic levels of treatment. The broader subject divisions are similar to those of DDC, but in its detail and use of synthetic devices UDC has moved a long way from Dewey. Presently its main classes, forswearing the three-digit notation of DDC, are:

0. Generalities of Knowledge
1. Philosophy; Metaphysics; Psychology
2. Religion; Theology
3. Social Sciences
4. [Vacant. Formerly, Linguistics]
5. Mathematics; Natural Sciences
6. Applied Sciences; Medicine; Technology
7. Arts; Recreation; Entertainment; Sport
8. Literature; Belles-Lettres
80. Philology; Linguistics; Languages
9. Geography; Biography; History

The basic notation of UDC consists of Arabic numerals used decimally, proceeding from shorter numbers signifying broader topics or disciplines to longer numbers for more specific topics. This practice of using simple, progressive enumeration to display the various aspects or facets of a major discipline is reminiscent of DDC, e.g.:

3	SOCIAL SCIENCES
34	Law. Jurisprudence. Legislation
347	Private Law. Civil law
347.7	Commercial and company law
347.74	Commercial contracts
347.746	Bills of exchange

But UDC tends toward greater flexibility, heavier use of synthetic classification, and even longer call numbers than DDC. Fourteen "facet indicators"—symbols of connection, addition, and consecutive extension—make it hospitable to highly specific topical denotations. For this reason it is considered by some to be more adapted to indexing uses than to shelf arrangements. The devices are of two kinds: common auxiliaries, which are applicable in any class, and special auxiliaries, which are used only in certain parts of the schedules, with different meanings, according to the class with which they are used. The following appear most frequently:

The plus sign (+) to show addition to, or extension of, general categories, both consecutive and nonconsecutive.

Examples: 539.1 + 621.039 - Nuclear science and technology
622 + 669 - Mining and metallurgy

This sign was very common prior to 1952, when FID began to counsel its avoidance, usually in favor of one of the two following signs:

The slash (/) to join consecutive UDC numbers, achieving a broader heading than either alone would warrant.

Examples: 22/28 - The Christian religion
624/628 - All branches of civil engineering

The colon (:) to link any two independent class numbers to form a more specific subject. It allows the classifier to make permuted multiple entries for a classed catalog.

Example: 621.785:669.14 - Heat treatment of steel (under
621.785 -Heating and heat treatment
processes),

or: 669.14:621.785 - Heat treatment of steel (under
669.14 -Steel. Special carbon steels).

The square brackets ([ ]) to denote subordination.

Example: 622[31] - Mining statistics.

The equal sign (=) to specify the language (other than that of the basic collection) in which a document is written.

Example: 678(038) = 82 = 20 - A Russian-English dictionary
of rubber and plastics.

Place digits (1/9) to specify location. They resemble the familiar geographic numbers of both DDC and UDC, without the initial numbers "9" for the History class, or "91" for the Geography subclass. They are used within brackets.

Example: 327[42:44] - International relations between Britain and France.

With its detailed enumeration of subdivisions and its auxiliary signs UDC can specify almost any topic or phase of a topic which the classifier wishes. The price is a notation which can produce even longer numbers than the most notorious of DDC examples. With its more than 100,000 divisions in the main tables, compared to some 11,000 in the DDC schedules, it is a most comprehensive classification scheme. Moreover, its international appeal, publication in various languages, well designed index, and organized, financially stable programs for revision and expansion make of it a practicable system based on a solid foundation of widespread use. A number of manuals and supplementary tools are available to the inquirer who wishes to study it in more detail.[23]

COLON CLASSIFICATION

S. R. Ranganathan, an Indian mathematician studying library science in England, became one of the foremost theoreticians in library classification, publishing *Prolegomena to Library Classification* (3rd ed., 1967), *Library Classification Fundamentals and Procedure* (1944), *Elements of Library Classification* (1953), and many other treatises and hundreds of articles and short essays, most of which deal with "facet" classification or indexing.[24] His influence can be compared to that of Dewey or Cutter in this country, or James Duff Brown in Great Britain. A whole school of thought developed from his basic concepts, and there has been growing interest, particularly in Europe, in adapting them to special "faceted" indexing schemes.

It is impossible to present all the important features of Colon Classification in a brief discussion. We will limit this presentation to a few fundamentals, referring the reader to the voluminous literature on the subject.[25] The primary thrust of Ranganathan's approach is to analyze subject matter into constituent elements or facets. He argued that the actual intuitive process of classifying a book consists of eight steps.[26]

0. **The raw title** is the one appearing on the title page of the work being classified, for example, *Japanese High School Education.*

1. **The expressive title** is the cataloger's title based on the actual subject content of the work. For instance, perusal of *Japanese High School Education* might show that it is really a descriptive account of the state of high school education in Japan and adjacent islands from 1950 to 1960.

2. **The kernel title** states the expressive title in nuclear units, usually nouns and descriptive adjectives, e.g., "High school level. Education. Japan and adjacent islands. 1950-1960."

3. **The analyzed title** identifies the function of each kernel or element. This is a particularly important step in Colon Classification, but it can be applied to any scheme, e.g.,
   High school level (Subject subdivision)
   Education (Main class)
   Japan and adjacent islands (Geographic division)
   1950-1960 (Chronological division)

4. **The transformed title** rearranges the kernels and labels into a sequence helpful to the user, or according to a prescribed order in the particular classification system. The Colon labels used in this example will be explained subsequently:
   Education (Basic facet)
   High school level (Personality facet, round 1, level 1)
   Japan and adjacent islands (Space facet, level 1)
   1950-1960 (Time facet, level 1)

5. **The title in standard terms** replaces the kernel title terms with terminology from the schedules of the particular classification system (here, the Colon Classification), e.g.,
    Education (Basic facet)
    Secondary (Personality facet, round 1, level 1)
    Japan (Space facet, level 1)
    1950s (Time facet, level 1)

6. **The title in kernel numbers** replaces the schedule terminology with the appropriate notation from the particular schedules, e.g.,
    T (Basic facet)
    2 (Personality facet, round 1, level 1)
    42 (Space facet, level 1)
    N5 (Time facet, level 1)

7. **The class number** is generated by the removal of the schedule terminology, and the insertion of identifying punctuation, as required by the schedule, e.g.,
    T,2.42'N5

Reliable definitions of systematic features in the Colon Classification are not easy to come by. Terminology shifts from edition to edition, and from explanation to explanation. Some of the more frequently encountered terms are:

Main class. These are more or less traditional disciplinary divisions, but their notation is mixed, and slightly confusing. Moreover, if and when the seventh edition (originally promised for 1972) is published, they may be modified.[27] In edition six, they are given as follows:

(See example on page 474)

CHAPTER 1

MAIN CLASS

z	Generalia	Δ	Spiritual Experience and Mysticism
1	Universe of Knowledge	MZ	Humanities and Social Sciences
2	Library Science		
3	Book Science	MZA	Humanities
4	Journalism	N	Fine Arts
		NX	Literature and Language
A	Natural Sciences	O	Literature
AZ	Mathematical Sciences	P	Linguistics
B	Mathemetics	Q	Religion
		R	Philosophy
BZ	Physical Sciences	S	Psychology
C	Physics	Σ	Social Sciences
D	Engineering	T	Education
E	Chemistry	U	Geography
		V	History
F	Technology	W	Political Science
G	Biology	X	Economics
H	Geology	Y	Sociology
HX	Mining	YX	Social Work
I	Botany	Z	Law
J	Agriculture	*Illustrative*	
K	Zoology	(: g)	Criticism technique
KX	Animal Husbandry	(p)	Conference technique
L	Medicine	(r)	Administration report technique
LX	Pharmocognosy	(P)	Communication theory
M	Useful Arts	(X)	Management

2·4

Facet. Main classes, and some specially identified secondary (Canonical) classes, are subdivided by one or more Trains of Characteristics. The totality of possible divisions of a single characteristic is said to constitute an Array. For example, libraries may be divided into various "arrays" such as categories of ownership (public, private, etc.), educational status (school, special, etc.), physical status of user (hospital, juvenile, etc.), subject covered (medicine, engineering, etc.), or other characteristics. The whole series of such arrays composes the "library facet."

Technically, each facet manifests one of five Fundamental Categories. These are usually listed in decreasing sequence of "concreteness": Personality, Matter, Energy, Space, and Time ("PMEST"). Personality usually covers things, types of things, or types of action, but in main classes, like History or Political Science, it can involve geographical region, while under Literature it includes literary periods, movements, and the like. Matter generally signifies constituent elements: instruments in Music, periodicals in Library Science, gold in Economics (Money). (Yet under Metallurgy, gold and other metals are interpreted as a Personality facet.) Energy most often involves operations, problems, processes, techniques, etc., such as grammar under Linguistics, curriculum in Education, physiology under Biology, and exports in Economics. Space and Time are in most cases self-explanatory facets. The sequence in which facets appear in call numbers depends on the rather arbitrary facet formula established for each main class.

Focus. While the terms "focus" and "facet" both convey the notion of aspect, "focus" is used less specifically than "facet." One may refer to "Basic focus" as a synonym for "Basic facet." But then each division in a facet can be called an "Isolate focus" or simply an "Isolate." And under certain conditions Compound foci express intricate relationships for complex topics.

Levels of Manifestation. Two or more foci relating to the same facet of a main class or topic may be expressed in a facet formula. They represent variations on the PMEST theme, and are devised to provide a citation order which is valid for the whole field of knowledge, using only the five Fundamental Categories. For instance, under "Chapter I - BOTANY" the facet formula is:

I [P], [P2]: [E] [2P].

This formula means that two levels of the Personality category precede the Energy category in a botany class number according to the following arrays:

Foci in P		Foci in P2	
1	CRYPTOGAMIA	1	BASIC AND REGIONAL
2	THALLOPHYTA	11	Cell
21	Protophyta (bacteria, yeast, microbes)	12	Tissue
22	ALGAE (SEA-WEEDS)	13	Root
221	Cyanophyceae (blue-green algae)	131	Root hair
223	Chlorophyceae (green algae)	132	Secondary root
225	Phaeophyceae (brown algae)	133	Primary root
227	Rhodophyceae (red algae)	14	Stem
23	FUNGI		[etc.]
	[etc.]		

Rounds of Manifestation. The above facet formula also means that the Energy facet introduces a new "round" of the Personality facet. The schedule says: "Foci in [E] cum [2P] as in G BIOLOGY with the following addition: 8 PALEOBOTANY." In "Chapter G - BIOLOGY" we find:

Foci in [E] cum [2P]

1	PRELIMINARIES	19	MICROSCOPY
11	Nomenclature, classification	192	Sectioning
12	Natural history	195	Fixing
13	Popular description	196	Mounting
14	Picture	198	Staining
17	Collecting	1995	Microphotography
18	List	2	MORPHOLOGY
			[etc.]

Following these instructions, we would give a book on the microphotography of algae tissue the call number I,22,12:1995.

The Colon Classification is equipped with numerous mnemonic and other notational devices. The main classes, as we have seen, are usually denoted by capital letters. Arabic numbers are used for divisions of their facets. Lower-case letters signify common bibliographical forms and subject divisions, etc. Facet indicators introduce the Fundamental Categories: a comma (,) precedes Personality, a semicolon (;) precedes Matter, a colon (:) precedes Energy, a period (.) precedes Space, and an apostrophe (') precedes Time. Thus the notation can become lengthy and complex. In addition there are four cumbersome indexes to the scheme and three orders (with their own page numbers) to the main schedules.

Colon Classification has not been widely used, even in India, because it is difficult to comprehend and apply. Nevertheless, Ranganathan's ideas provided much grist for current research on classification theory. At the time of his death in 1972, he was nearly ready to issue serially a seventh edition of his seminal work, but none of its projected parts have yet appeared.

CONCLUSION

The five classification systems briefly reviewed here differ from each other, and from the better known DDC and LC systems, in many ways. In basic theory of the organization of knowledge, some emphasize the specific subject approach, clustering these unitary topics in related sequences, whereas most start from a broad disciplinary orientation, subdividing hierarchically, so that the various aspects or unitary topics become scattered to different parts of the system. In providing a schedule framework to arrange books on shelves, some systems (the more traditional) are primarily enumerative, whereas most newer ones are synthetic or faceted. Some maintain a comparatively pure notation, whereas others use combinations of letters and Arabic numerals, while upper- and lower-case letters, Roman numerals, Greek letters, and a variety of arbitrary relational signs and symbols appear in still others. Timeliness is a constant problem. Some systems maintain a serials program to announce additions and changes, or issue new editions at intervals of five to twenty-five years. All have outlived their originators, but some suffer more than others from age and lack of funds or organized promotion. Each has unique attractive features; each has practical and theoretical problems. Some are more useful for shelf arrangement of books and related formats. Others are better suited to in-depth indexing of periodical articles, technical reports, books, and the like. Centripetal forces such as networking seem at the moment to favor general acceptance of one or two well-known, widely-used schemes, overlooking functional disadvantages to achieve standardization and administrative coherence. Yet classification research, like that in all other areas of bibliographic organization, is very brisk and busy in the modern world of information science. Time may show that all the schemes we study and use today, regardless of their present achievements or popularity, are chiefly important for the historic part they play as heralds of still better solutions to the problems of subject access.

FOOTNOTES

[1]Four examples of specific applications using the five systems discussed in this chapter, as well as DDC and LC, are given in:
Bohdan S. Wynar, *Introduction to Cataloging and Classification*, 5th ed., prepared with the assistance of John Phillip Immroth (Littleton, CO, Libraries Unlimited, 1976), pp. 314-28.

[2]Charles Ammi Cutter, *Expansive Classification, Part I: The First Six Classifications* (Boston, Cutter, 1891-1893).

[3]The *Table méthodique en forme de catalogue raisonné*, or classified portion of the *Manuel* made use of five main classes: Theology, Jurisprudence, Sciences and Arts, Belles-Lettres, and History.

[4]Charles Ammi Cutter, *Expansive Classification, Part 2: Seventh Classification*, largely edited by William Parker Cutter (Boston and Northampton, MA, 1896-1911), 2v. with supplementary pages.

[5]Henry Evelyn Bliss, *The Organization of Knowledge in Libraries*, 2nd ed. (New York, H. W. Wilson, 1939), Chapter XI.
W. C. B. Sayers, *A Manual of Classification*, 3rd rev. ed. (London, Andre Deutsch, 1955), Chapter XV.
John Phillip Immroth, "Expansive Classification," in *Encyclopedia of Library and Information Science*, vol. 8 (New York, Marcel Dekker, 1972), pp. 297-316.

[6]Robert L. Mowery, "The Cutter Classification: Still at Work," *Library Resources & Technical Services* 20 (Spring 1976):154.

[7]James Duff Brown, *Subject Classification: With Tables, Indexes, etc. for the Subdivision of Subjects*, 3rd ed., rev. and enl. by James Douglas Stewart (London, Grafton, 1939).

[8]Brown, *Subject Classification*, p. 14.

[9]Brown, *Subject Classification*, p. 11.

[10]A detailed analysis of *Subject Classification* can be found in:
Jack Mills, *A Modern Outline of Library Classification* (London, Chapman & Hall, 1968), pp. 103-116.

[11]Bliss's major works are the following: *The Organization of Knowledge and the System of the Sciences* (New York, Holt, 1929); *The Organization of Knowledge in Libraries*, 2nd ed. rev. and partly rewritten (New York, H. W. Wilson, 1939), see page 405 for further citations; *A Bibliographic Classification: Extended by Systematic Auxiliary Schedules for Composite Specification and Notation* (New York, H. W. Wilson, 1940-1953), 4v. in 3.

[12]Paul S. Dunkin, *Cataloging U.S.A.* (Chicago, American Library Association, 1969), p. 126.

[13]Bliss, *Organization of Knowledge in Libraries*, pp. 42-43.

[14]See, for instance: School Library Association (England), *The Abridged Bliss Classification: The Bibliographical Classification of Henry Evelyn Bliss Revised for School Libraries* (London, The Association, 1967).

[15]*Bliss Bibliographic Classification*, 2nd ed., edited by Jack Mills (London, Butterworths, 1977-).
    Part 1 — Introduction and Auxiliary Schedule. 1977.
    Class J — Education. 1977.
    Class P — Religion; the Occult; Morals and Ethics. 1977.
    Class Q — Social welfare. 1977.

[16]Jack Mills, "The New Bliss Classification," *Catalogue & Index: Periodical of the Library Association Cataloguing and Indexing Group*, no. 40 (Spring 1976):6.

[17]For a discussion of Ranganathan's Colon Classification, see pages 472-477.

[18]Mills, "New Bliss Classification," p. 3.

[19]Mills, "New Bliss Classification," p. 4.

[20]Mills, "New Bliss Classification," p. 14.

[21] See, for instance: "Ibadan Abandons Bliss," *Library Association Record* 79:241 (May 1977), which tells how the University of Ibadan (Nigeria) after using Bliss for twenty-five years, is converting to the LC scheme because of the inadequacy of outdated, unrevised Bliss schedules.

[22]Fédération Internationale de Documentation, *Classification Décimale Universelle*, 2e ed. (Bruxelles, Institute International de Bibliographie, 1927-1953), 4v.; *Universal Decimal Classification, Complete English Edition*, 4th International ed. (London, British Standards Institution, 1943-), in progress; *Universal Decimal Classification: Abridged English Edition*, 3rd rev., 1961. (London, British Standards Institution, 1963).

[23]*Guide to the Universal Decimal Classification* (London, British Standards Institution, 1963).

International Federation for Documentation, *10-Year Supplement to Abridged UDC Editions: 1958-1968* (The Hague, F.I.D./UNESCO, 1969) (in English, French and German).

International Federation for Documentation, *UDC Revision and Publication Procedure* (The Hague, F.I.D., 1968) (in English, French and German).

A. C. Foskett, *The Subject Approach to Information*, 3rd ed. (London, Clive Bingley; Hamden, CT, Linnet Books, 1977), Chapter 18—"The Universal Decimal Classification," pp. 306-26.

Jack Mills, *The Universal Decimal Classification* (New Brunswick, NJ, Rutgers, The State University School of Library Science, 1964).

Jean Perrault, *An Introduction to U.D.C.* (Hamden, CT, Archon Books, 1969).

[24]The work comprising the schedules proper is:
Colon Classification, 6th rev. ed. (London, Asia Publishing House, 1963). The seventh edition will appear in parts.

[25]The student will be well advised to read:
C. D. Batty, *Introduction to Colon Classification* (Hamden, CT, Archon Books, 1966).

B. I. Palmer, and A. J. Wells, *The Fundamentals of Library Classification* (London, Allen & Unwin, 1951). (Rather dated, but still one of the best presentations).

B. C. Vickery, *Classification and Indexing in Science*, 2nd ed. (London, Butterworths, 1959).

[26]A. Neelameghan, "Classification, Theory of," *Encyclopedia of Library and Information Science*, Vol. 5 (New York, Marcel Dekker, 1971):167-73.

[27]P. Jayarajan, "The Schedule of Main Subjects Proposed for Edition 7 of the Colon Classification," *Library Resources & Technical Services* 16 (Summer 1972):359-63.

26 VERBAL SUBJECT ANALYSIS

INTRODUCTION

We have seen in the preceding chapters that classification provides a library with a systematic arrangement of materials according to their subject content, mode of treatment, or even their physical format. In addition to classification, there is another commonly used means of access to the intellectual contents of a library—namely indexing through the use of a subject heading list of controlled vocabulary terms and cross references. Whereas classification provides a logical, or at least a methodical, approach to the arrangement of documentary materials, subject headings give a more random alphabetic approach to the concepts inherent in those materials, thus adding another dimension to the linear arrangement characteristic of classification. The two techniques offer alternative, and to some extent complementary, modes of access to the collection, comprising that aspect of bibliographic control and access known as subject cataloging.

There are many theoretically sound objectives for subject cataloging. Shera and Egan summarized them as follows:

1. To provide access by subject to *all* relevant material.

2. To provide subject access to materials through all suitable *principles of subject organization*, e.g., matter, process, applications, etc.

3. To bring together references to materials which treat of substantially the *same subject* regardless of disparities in terminology, disparities which may have resulted from national differences, differences among groups of subject specialists, and/or from the changing nature of the concepts with the discipline itself.

4. To show *affiliations among subject fields*, affiliations which may depend upon similarities of matter studied, or method, or of point of view, or upon use or application of knowledge.

5. To provide entry to any subject field at any *level of analysis*, from the most general to the most specific.

6. To provide entry through any *vocabulary* common to any considerable group of users, specialized or lay.

7. To provide a *formal description of the subject content* of any bibliographic unit in the most precise, or specific, terms possible, whether the description be in the form of a word or brief phrase or in the form of a class number or symbol.

8. To provide means for the user to make *selection* from among all items in any particular category, according to any chosen set of criteria such as: most thorough, most recent, most elementary, etc.[1]

CLASSIFIED VERSUS ALPHABETIC APPROACH
TO INFORMATION

We have already observed some of the limitations of library classification. These limitations are inherent not only in the philosophical characteristics of the classification process, but also in the dual manifestations of the collected materials, which are both intellectual and physical entities. For the sake of inventory control, classifiers traditionally choose only one place on the shelves for all copies of a given item. They strive for the optimum location in view of its content, the accepted classification schedule, and the needs of the clientele. Such decisions are not always easy to make. For instance, the same historical treatise might go equally well into political or economic history, or perhaps under social history or biography. While its physical station is unique, a subject index or catalog can offer more than one citation to it, each emphasizing a different aspect of its contents.

The inquirer who wants information on a certain subject will approach the catalog with questions formulated in his own words. These terms must be translated into the predetermined access categories of the catalog. Such communication between inquirer and catalog, with the possible intervention of a librarian, must take place regardless of the type of catalog consulted or the arrangement of its entries. Three systems of arranging entries in a library catalog were discussed in chapter 1. Classified catalogs were said to be the oldest of the three, although in present-day libraries they are less numerous than alphabetical catalogs of either the dictionary or the divided mode. In the case of the classified catalog, the user's verbalization is diverted into the retrieval channels of the accepted classification. More than one category of the schedules may represent a significant aspect of the same item, thus allowing more than one entry or access point for that item. A skilled user may know the schedules well enough to go directly to those categories which correspond to his needs. However, all good classified catalogs are accompanied by an alphabetical index, to help users translate their needs into the formal search matrix.

The alphabetical catalog might facilitate the information retrieval process for most users, but it is identical in principle to the classified catalog index. In either case, the search for relevant information usually starts with an alphabetical list of subject terms. If the user's terminology coincides with that of the list, the search process will be quite direct. If not, the user must follow cross references, or try to adjust his or her vocabulary to that of the accepted system.

Still, each type of catalog requires a different pattern of communication. The classified catalog offers a vertical (hierarchical) approach to the collection through its closely related classes and categories, under which materials can be identified by means of logical, orderly sequences from general to specific. The alphabetical catalog gives a horizontal approach through its random scattering of access points throughout the entire linguistic finding apparatus.

Classified Arrangement

Certain advantages of a classified catalog were cited in chapter 1. They include:

1. *A controlled order of academic disciplines, as well as of popular topical sequences.* This order fosters direct, efficient searching at either catalog or shelf for those users familiar with the classification scheme. A reader interested in psychology, for instance, can initially consult and study a single section of the catalog with assurance of its relevance.

2. *Extensive opportunities for in-depth searching.* Based on logical relationships rather than linguistic associations, this arrangement not only offers a better comprehension of subject matter, but also directly stimulates the learning experience. It expands the frequently-discussed values of browsing in an open-shelf library.[2] Directly related is the opportunity to search in both directions, from general to specific as well as from specific to general.

3. *Denotative symbols (notation) objectively signifying topics and categories.* They reduce to a minimum the connotative implications and prejudices often associated with linguistic terms. The notation further allows one class number to be used for shelving, while others may designate supplementary entries in the catalog.

There are, on the other hand, ineluctable disadvantages which account for the relatively few classed catalogs in modern libraries:

1. *Much of our cultural heritage, as recorded in documentary collections, cannot be satisfactorily systematized.* Any classification scheme, as we have seen, has inherent deficiencies. The most effective classed catalogs are in special libraries, chiefly those for one or more scientific or technological disciplines. These areas are the most susceptible to rigid logical systematization. Even traditional academic disciplines tend to crumble nowadays before the onslaught of inter- and multi-disciplinary studies. Systems of arrangement within any subject field can be made obsolete by the advancing frontiers of knowledge.

2. *Systematic arrangements are almost never such ready vehicles of common knowledge as is the alphabet.* While factual information, study, and research slowly renounced their aristocratic prerogatives for the uses of democracy and popular education, the older, more esoteric patterns of organization, however worthy, were often sacrificed to the mechanical, rote mechanisms of arithmetic and alphabetic progression.

The alphabetic index accompanying a classified catalog usually gives access only to spans and categories of classification, unlike a true catalog, which identifies specific titles. It points the user to both the classified catalog, where *all* the library's holdings are recorded, and to the shelves, where actual documents can be examined, but where items may be inadvertently missing, being at the moment in use elsewhere. It may be a published index to the particular classification scheme, e.g., the "relative index" of the Dewey Decimal Classification. It may be a list of separately published subject headings that are locally associated with class numbers from a given system, e.g., *Library of Congress Subject Headings*, which carries many LC classification numbers, although it is not specifically designed to be a classification index. Or it may be a specially generated index, such as a chain index, based on the extracted vocabulary of the classification used. (Chain indexing will be described in full detail in chapter 29.) Its major advantage in this context is that specific rules for controlling the index vocabulary may be based on the classification scheme being used. For example, the concept "whiskey" is classed in at least four places in three LC classification schedules.[3] The various contexts are outlined below:

H	Social sciences
HD	Economic history
HD9000-9490	Agricultural products
HD9395	Whisky
K	Law
KF	United States law
KF1601-1666	Trade regulation
KF1619-1620	Labeling
KF1620.A57	Whiskey
KF6200-6795	Public finance
KF6251-6708	Revenue
KF6271-6645	Taxation
KF6600-6645	Excise taxes
KF6612-6613	Liquor taxes
KF6613.W4	Whiskies
T	Technology
TP	Chemical technology
TP500-659	Fermentation industries
TP589-617	Distilling
TP597-617	Distilled liquors
TP605	Whiskey

From these sequences and categories, the following chain index entries could result:

Agricultural products: Economic history, HD9000-9490
Chemical technology, TP
Distilled liquors: Fermentation industries, TP597-617
Distilling: Fermentation industries, TP589-617
Economic history, HD
Excise taxes: Revenue: U.S. law, KF6600-6645
Fermentation industries: Chemical technology, TP500-659

Labeling: Trade regulations: U.S. law, KF1619-1620
Law, K
Liquor taxes: Revenue: U.S. law, KF6612-6613
Public finance: U.S. law, KF6200-6795
Revenue: Public finance: U.S. law, KF6251-6708
Social sciences, H
Taxation: Revenue: U.S. law, KF6271-6645
Technology, T
Trade regulations: U.S. law, KF1601-1666
United States law, KF
Whiskey: Economic history, HD9395
Whiskey: Excise taxes, KF6613.W4
Whiskey: Fermentation industries, TP605
Whiskey: Labeling, KF1620.A57
Whiskies, *see* Whiskey
Whisky, *see* Whiskey

Alphabetical Arrangement

Some of the more obvious advantages of an alphabetical catalog or index
are:

1. *Simplicity and popularity.* The apparent simplicity of alphabetical
   filing can be deceptive, however. Filing problems inevitably arise,
   especially in dictionary catalogs, where interfiling personal and corporate authors, titles, subjects, cross references, etc., becomes
   something like the old dilemma of adding apples and oranges to
   pears. (The filing of LC subject headings is discussed in chapter 27,
   and chapter 31 is addressed to general filing systems and problems.)

2. *Direct access to bibliographic data and holdings.* In spite of its filing pitfalls, a consolidated, single-strike catalog is in many ways
   more efficient. The "double look-up," and even more extended,
   serial searching, are reduced to a minimum. The user may in most
   cases move directly from the catalog to the shelves.

3. *Greater freedom in introducing new groupings.* Descriptive subject
   headings, being more linguistic in nature, need not bear the same
   logical relationship to one another as do classes in a systematic
   arrangement.

4. *More efficient automated information retrieval.* With such
   sophisticated techniques as Boolean logic, and the hope of still
   more powerful modes of random access, computer programming
   appears to be more effective in alphabetical than in systematic
   searches.

On the other hand, the alphabetic approach has serious drawbacks:

1. *Fragmentation of subject matter.* Most published subject heading lists for libraries indulge in a kind of surreptitious "classing" through the use of inversions, subdivisions, and the like. The urge to group like topics in one place, to make subject searching more efficient, is almost irresistible.

2. *Exacerbation of semantic problems.* In the absence of short, specific words for many subject concepts, awkward compound and prepositional phrase headings soon appear, to complicate the filing and confound the user.

3. *Inherent weakness in the conceptual structure of subject headings.* With no systematic framework to regulate its growth, an alphabetic subject list inevitably stumbles over the problems of the plurality and specificity of its terms. The concept of specific entry is difficult to control, as we shall see in a later section of this chapter.

BASIC CONCEPTS AND STRUCTURE OF SUBJECT HEADINGS

Subject heading has been defined as "a word or a group of words indicating a subject under which all material dealing with the same theme is entered in a catalog or a bibliography, or is arranged in a file."[4] Today, information analysts distinguish pre-coordinate indexing, by which appropriate terms are chosen and coordinated at the time of indexing, from post-coordinate indexing, with which coordination takes place after the encoded documents have been stored.[5] The distinction will be explored in chapter 29, Other Forms of Verbal Analysis. Libraries traditionally prefer the former method of compiling alphabetical subject catalogs. All standard published lists of "subject headings" were developed with pre-coordinate indexing techniques.

Obviously, subject headings have dual objectives: 1) to identify pertinent material on a given subject or topic, 2) to enable the inquirer to find material on related subjects. Both objectives pose problems of communication; both demand a set of terms that match, as far as possible, the terms likely to be in the minds of inquirers wishing to locate material on a given topic or in a given discipline. E. J. Coates warns:

> This would be fairly simple to achieve if there were an uncomplicated, one-to-one relationship between concepts and words: that is to say, if there were a single word corresponding to each separate concept and a single concept corresponding to each separate word. In fact, we have on the one hand concepts that can be rendered by any one of a number of words, and on the other hand, concepts for which no single word equivalent exists in the natural language.[6]

Modern subject heading practice has its roots in Charles A. Cutter's *Rules for a Dictionary Catalog*.[7] Immroth reminds us that Cutter's "rules for subject entries are the basis for two·major American lists of subject headings—the *Library of Congress Subject Headings* and the *Sears List of Subject Headings*."[8] Later theorists refined and expanded Cutter's work in various ways. David Judson Haykin, former Chief of the Library of Congress Subject Cataloging Division, enumerates the principles on which the choice of terms for a subject list must rest.[9] They may be summarized as follows:

1. *The reader as focus.* The heading, in wording and structure, should be that which the reader will seek in the catalog, if we know or can presume what the reader will look under. In the face of a lack of sufficient objective, experimental data, we must rely for guidance in the choice of terms upon the experience of librarians and such objective findings as are available.

2. *Unity.* A subject catalog must bring together under one heading all the books which deal principally or exclusively with the subject, whatever the terms applied to it by the authors of the books, and whatever the varying terms applied to it at different times. [It] must [use] a term which is unambiguous and does not overlap in meaning other headings in the catalog, even where that involves defining the sense in which it is used.

3. *Usage.* The heading chosen must represent common usage or, at any rate, the usage of the class of reader for whom the material on the subject within which the heading falls is intended. Whether a popular term or a scientific one is to be chosen depends on several considerations. If the library serves a miscellaneous public, it must prefer the popular to the scientific term.

4. *Specificity.* The heading should be as specific as the topic it is intended to cover. As a corollary, the heading should not be broader than the topic; rather than use a broader heading, the cataloger should use two specific headings which will approximately cover it.

The following discussion touches on some of the most important problems encountered in construction and use of subject headings. Library literature is replete with detailed treatments of the various aspects of these problems. It should be noted, however, that literature on theoretical concepts of subject headings is practically non-existent.[10]

THE CHOICE OF SUBJECT HEADINGS

Linguistic usage determines correctness of form in natural language, as all grammarians and dictionary compilers well know. Language changes constantly, not only in response to new discoveries and formulations of knowledge, but also in response to dynamic forces of its own, some but not all of which have been codified by linguists. In choosing subject terms, librarians try to consider both the author's usage and the patron's needs and preferences. But authors and patrons are likely to use different terms for the same subject. Without a record of choices, the cataloger may enter the same subject under two or more different headings. Two types of decision are especially likely to miscarry: those for which more than one adequate term is available, and those for which no adequate term is available.

Selecting a term from among verbal equivalents. The cataloger or compiler of a subject heading list must sometimes choose one subject term from among several synonyms or very similar terms. Cutter suggests the following sequence of preferences when selecting from synonymous headings:[11]

1. *The term most familiar to the general public.* Cutter no doubt was thinking of the local library's public. We shall see that one of the major differences between *LCSH* and *Sears* is that *LCSH*, being designed for use in a comprehensive research library, favors scientific terminology (e.g., "ARACHNIDA *see also* SPIDERS"), whereas *Sears* tends to use more popular terms (e.g., "Arachnida *see* SPIDERS").

2. *The term most used in other catalogs.* Since patrons frequently change libraries, or consult more than one library catalog, it is comforting to find that terminology remains stable, even standardized, so long as it does not violate the usage of the local library's public. Broad automated networks, using consolidated machine-readable data bases, make reliably standardized terminology even more desirable. A different, but related, argument is that new concepts and terms are often introduced into the periodical literature before they form the topics of full-scale books. If a library's subject heading list does not yet include such a term, the cataloger might well consult the *New York Times Index*, or commonly-used periodical indexes and abstracting tools, to discover what usage, if any, has been established.

3. *The term that has fewest meanings.* The clear intent here is to avoid ambiguity wherever possible.

4. *The term that comes first in the alphabet.* This is the type of arbitrary, procedural decision which can and should be invoked when semantic considerations have been exhausted.

5. *The term that brings the subject into the neighborhood of other, related subjects.* It was previously noted that a serious drawback of alphabetic arrangement is its fragmentation of subject matter, and that most alphabetic subject lists indulge in some "classing." Here is Cutter's recognition that the technique is valid, but only after all other modes for choosing terms have been exhausted.

Supplying a term which is not contained in a single word. Some concepts must be expressed by phrases (combinations of words). Phrase headings present certain disadvantages. As Coates indicates, most catalog users try to formulate search topics in single words, even when a phrase would be used in natural language.[12] Various uncertainties shadow the introduction of phrases into a controlled vocabulary. In determining the order of words, should a heading always retain the order of natural language, or should modifications and transpositions be allowed in the interests of brevity and clarity? Should a variety of syntactic forms be used, or should the syntax of phrase headings be confined to a few simple forms which occasionally make them seem awkward and artificial? Some theorists feel that, lacking cleanly enunciated rules, phrase-makers have produced a number of troublesome headings. Modern usage condones several varieties which different subject lists usually adapt to their own uses. The specific rules printed in *Sears List of Subject Headings* and in *Library of Congress Subject Headings* simplify but do not solve this problem, since they are purely arbitrary.[13] The problem of communication still exists. Many books are listed under subject headings that patrons would not immediately think of as the appropriate ones under which to search. For the most part they can be roughly categorized as follows. All examples are taken from either the *Sears* or the Library of Congress list:

1. *Modified nouns.* Modifiers can take different syntactic forms:
   a) Nouns preceded by adjectives or other modifiers, e.g., "Regional planning," "Furbearing animals," or "Country life"
   b) Nouns followed by adjectives or other modifiers, e.g., "Occupations, Dangerous," "Insurance, Malpractice," or "Molds (Botany)"

2. *Conjunctive phrases.* The conjunction is nearly always "and," e.g., "Mills and millwork," "Instrumentation and orchestration," or "Mind and body"

3. *Prepositional phrases.* "In" and "of" are most common, but other prepositions may be used to form phrases, e.g., "Segregation in education," "Freedom of conscience," or "Missions to Hottentots"

4. *Serial phrases*, e.g., "Hotels, motels, etc.," "Rewards (Prizes, etc.)," or "Plots (Drama, fiction, etc.)"

5. *Complex phrase forms*, e.g., "Artificial satellites in telecommunication," "Glass painting and staining," "Libraries, College and university," "State aid to libraries," "Cities and towns, Ruined, extinct, etc.," "Justice, Administration of," "Music, Popular (Songs, etc.)," "Right and left (Political science)," or "Fortune-telling by tea leaves"

6. *Subdivided topical phrases*, e.g., "Book industries and trade — Exhibitions," "Mines and mineral resources — United States," or "Military service, Compulsory — Draft resistors"

THE NUMBER OF SUBJECT HEADINGS

The number of subject headings entered into a catalog for a single item depends on many factors. As long as most library catalogs are in card form, rapidly increasing bulk is both an economic and a use hazard. Maintenance costs (housing, filing, revising) are high, while users grow confused, or waste considerable time, moving from one point to another in a roomful of several thousand trays. The larger the number of subject entries provided, the greater is the cost of cataloging a title. On the other hand, the assignment of more headings per item makes the total resources of the library more available, and may bring out special aspects and bits of unusual or significant information.

The modern trend toward storing catalogs in machine-readable data banks makes increasing the number of subject entries proportionately less expensive in time, effort, or cost of retrieval. Print-outs in either book form or microform occupy little space and can be consulted in one spot, as can a cathode ray tube (CRT) giving online access. Moreover, the simultaneous display of either complete or truncated entries in an ordered column often makes filing practices self-evident. The Library of Congress presently adds an average of 2.3 subject entries per cataloged item. This figure includes those titles for which no subject headings are assigned (e.g., individual works of drama, fiction, poetry, and the like). The tendency over past decades has been to reduce the average number of subject entries, especially subject analytics. Indexes and abstracting tools in science and technology, by contrast, tend to use specific subject entries to a point of minute analysis. Twenty to forty subject terms for one brief article are not rare. It is possible that subject analysis of library titles will expand in the future, given the increased use of automated bibliographic control. The computer may at the same time facilitate more, and better, studies of library use, to discern optimum types and quantities of subject headings for full subject retrieval.

LOCATION OF MATERIAL ON RELATED SUBJECTS

Consistency is one of the most important criteria for assigning subject headings. The cataloger should choose one subject term, and one alone, to index all materials on the same topic. References should then be made to the chosen heading from all other likely headings. They help the inquirer to locate available material on the topic, plus collateral topics, at the level of specificity and from the point of view most useful for the particular need. Cross references consist primarily of two types: *see* references refer from a name or term under which no items are entered to the relevant term under which items are listed, e.g., "Lunar expeditions *see* SPACE FLIGHT TO THE MOON"; *see also* references suggest that not only is the already located heading more or less relevant, but the user might wish to look under other, similar or closely related terms, e.g., "DEAFNESS *see also* HEARING AIDS."

Hierarchical references move vertically, rather than horizontally, leading the user to topics at a different level of specificity. *See also* references of this type nearly always move "down" from a general term to one or more specific topics subsumed under it, e.g., "CRUELTY *see also* ATROCITIES." A few *see* references, however, move "up" from a specific term which is not used to the broader term which contains it, e.g., "Heirs *see* INHERITANCE AND SUCCESSION."

Coordinate references may be of either the *see* or the *see also* variety. The connections they make, and the relationships they show are horizontal rather than vertical. They occasionally overlap in such ways that reciprocal or multi-lateral entries are deemed to be necessary. Some direct the user from a term not used (i.e., where no material is listed) to a synonymous or closely related term, where materials are listed, e.g.:

Synonymous terms:
"Civic art *see* ART, MUNICIPAL"

Closely related terms:
"REFORESTATION *see also* TREE PLANTING"
"TREE PLANTING *see also* REFORESTATION"

Others suggest "associative" (not necessarily related) or "illustrative" (not, strictly speaking, synonymous) terms, e.g.:

Associative, unrelated terms:
"CORRUPTION IN POLITICS *see also* LOBBYING"
"LOBBYING *see also* CORRUPTION IN POLITICS"

Illustrative, non-synonymous terms:
"Economic entomology *see* INSECTS, INJURIOUS
AND BENEFICIAL"

Besides simple cross references, subject heading lists sometimes include scope notes to define and delimit a subject term. These may or may not suggest further terms for the user to consult. Some libraries copy these notes for guides to precede all subject entries under those given terms in their catalogs. Other libraries, wishing to avoid unnecessary catalog entries, keep one or more copies of the printed list near the catalog for public consultation. The following two examples come from *Sears*, but nearly verbatim scope notes for the same terms can be found in *LCSH*:

COMMUNITY AND SCHOOL
Use for materials on ways in which the community at large, as distinct from government, may aid the school program.

MIGRANT LABOR
Use for materials dealing with casual or seasonal workers who move from place to place in search of employment. Materials on the movement of population within a country for permanent settlements are entered under MIGRATION, INTERNAL.

Some lists include key headings or pattern headings, with instructions to the cataloger on how to construct other headings of similar form which have been omitted from the list for reasons of brevity. The following example is from *Sears*:

HIJACKING OF AIRPLANES
Use same form for the hijacking of other modes of transportation.

To assure maximum consistency, a careful, up-to-date record of all subject term selections and cross references should be kept, either by checking the terms used and the additions made in a standard printed list, or by maintaining a separate subject authority file. Such a record can save the cataloger time in the long run, and provide the following summary information:

1. Unused terms from which *see* references have been made.

2. Scope notes describing a heading, or distinguishing its use in instances where one of its two or more meanings has been chosen.

3. Less comprehensive, subordinate headings, to which *see also* references have been made from more comprehensive terms.

4. More comprehensive, broad headings, from which *see also* references have been made to more specific headings.

5. Coordinate headings from which and to which cross references have been made from related or associated headings.

THE CONCEPT OF SPECIFIC ENTRY

One of Haykin's principles on which the choice of terms for a subject list must rest was "specificity."[14] The idea had been enunciated a good half century earlier by Cutter:

> Enter a work under its subject heading, not under the heading of the class which includes that subject. . . . Put Lady Cust's book on "the cat" under "Cat," not under Zoology or Mammals, or Domestic animals. . . . Some subjects have no name. They are spoken of by a phrase or phrases not definite enough to be used as headings. It is not always easy to decide what is a *distinct* subject. . . . Possible matters of investigation . . . must attain a certain individuality as objects of inquiry and be given some sort of *name*, otherwise we must assign them class-entry.[15]

A great weakness of the concept of specific entry is that subjects must be described in terms that are constantly changing. Material very often has to be cataloged before a suitable term has been found in any standard list. Many subjects now represent a cross-fertilization among once traditional disciplines. As Coates indicates,

> New subjects are being generated around us all the time, and while subjects may still be more or less distinct, there can be no hard and fast separation of the "distinct" subjects from the others.[16]

Not only do particular terms fluctuate in meaning, but a constant, obtrusive tendency of any alphabetic subject list based on the ideal of specific entry is to develop sequences of topical subdivisions or modifications which, as was previously noted, convert true random access into an inadvertent classing device. All such lists show marks of a split personality in this respect. The two most popular American lists, *LCSH* and *Sears*, will be reviewed in the next two chapters; later chapters will present some indexing systems which have been proposed as supplements to, or replacements for, these two lists as a primary mode of subject access to organized library collections.

FOOTNOTES

[1]Jesse H. Shera and Margaret E. Egan, *The Classified Catalog* (Chicago, American Library Association, 1956), p. 10.

[2]Unfortunately, the problems and values of browsing have not been sufficiently researched. One can also raise the question why, in most libraries, the shelf list, which functions as a limited classed catalog, is not made readily accessible to the users. Precisely because of its usefulness to the entire library staff, the shelf list is often sequestered away from public reach. But the patron who has a sufficient grasp of his or her field of interest, and who is willing to learn something about the classification scheme, surely would reap similar benefits from having access to it.

[3]It bears witness to the decentralized development of the LC Classification that the term is spelled "whiskey" in the KF and T schedules, but "whisky" in the H schedule. Schedule spellings are retained in the examples, but require cross referencing in the completed chain index.

[4]*A.L.A. Glossary of Library Terms, With a Selection of Terms in Related Fields* (Chicago, American Library Association, 1943), p. 136.

[5]A. C. Foskett, *The Subject Approach to Information*, 3rd ed. (London, Clive Bingley; Hamden, CT, Linnet Books, 1977), p. 73.

[6]E. J. Coates, *Subject Catalogues: Headings and Structure* (London, Library Association, 1960), p. 19.

[7]Charles Ammi Cutter, *Rules for a Dictionary Catalog*, 4th ed. (Washington, GPO, 1904).

[8]John Phillip Immroth, "Cutter, Charles Ammi," in *Encyclopedia of Library and Information Science*, vol. 6 (New York, Marcel Dekker, 1971), p. 382.

[9]David Judson Haykin, *Subject Headings: A Practical Guide* (Washington, GPO, 1951), pp. 7-9.

[10]For a fuller understanding of theoretical as well as practical applications of subject headings, we recommend in addition to other citations:

Jessica Lee Harris, *Subject Analysis: Computer Implications of Rigorous Definition* (Metuchen, NJ, Scarecrow Press, 1970).

Julia Pettee, *Subject Headings, the History and Theory of the Alphabetical Approach to Books* (New York, H. W. Wilson, 1946).

Subject Retrieval in the Seventies: New Directions, edited by Hans (Hanan) Wellisch andThomas D. Wilson (Westport, CT, Greenwood Publishing Co., 1972).

B. C. Vickery, *Techniques of Information Retrieval* (Hamden, CT, Archon books, 1970).

[11]Cutter, *Dictionary Catalog*, p. 19.

[12]Coates, *Subject Catalogues*, p. 19.

[13]For the development of phrase heading forms in *Sears List of Subject Headings* and in *Library of Congress Subject Headings* see chapters 27 and 28.

[14]See p. 486.

[15]Cutter, *Dictionary Catalog*, pp. 66-67.

[16]Coates, *Subject Catalogues*, p. 32.

27 LIBRARY OF CONGRESS SUBJECT HEADINGS

INTRODUCTION

The official list of Library of Congress subject headings consists of some 50,000 terms, with cross references, which have been established over the years since 1897 for use in that library's subject catalogs. A basic two-volume eighth edition appeared in 1972.[1] Quarterly supplements announce changes, including cancelled terms, added new terms, and revisions. They are later cumulated into volumes spanning one or more years. Eventually, a ninth edition will incorporate all changes into a basic list. Meanwhile, a fully updated list can be purchased each quarter on microfilm or microfiche. It saves the bother of consulting several alphabets to find the most current status of any given term. Machine-readable tapes of the basic list and its supplements are also available for purchase from LC's Cataloging Distribution Service by those users developing their own automated catalog programs.

Though developed to give subject access to the vast collections of one particular library, this list can be, and has been, adopted by libraries of all sizes, including many with non-LC classification schemes. The National Library of Canada, for example, has for many years used it as basic, supplementing it with a special set of terms for Canadian material.[2] It is used by most large public libraries, college and university libraries, and special libraries that do not have more technical subject lists of their own. Since LC printed cards and MARC tapes usually carry Dewey Decimal classification numbers as well as LC call numbers, but have only LC subject headings, some smaller libraries also use the LC subject list. Others retain the shorter, less frequently revised *Sears* list as their primary source, but consult the LC list for suggestions when *Sears* cannot provide the specificity or the diversity they want.[3]

Supplementary grafting of portions of one list onto the other should be carefully monitored, to avoid inconsistencies or contradictions. For instance, LC uses the term "UNIVERSITIES AND COLLEGES—Insignia," whereas *Sears* uses "COLLEGES AND UNIVERSITIES" but does not include the subdivision "—Insignia." If a library using *Sears* headings wishes to use the subdivision, it should retain its Sears form of the primary segment, i.e., "COLLEGES AND UNIVERSITIES—Insignia," or else convert all its "COLLEGES AND UNIVERSITIES" headings to the LC form.

Again, LC uses the terms "LIBERTY OF SPEECH" and "PERSONALITY (LAW)." *Sears*, by contrast, uses "FREE SPEECH," and has no term corresponding to "PERSONALITY (LAW)." If a library following *Sears* has need of the heading "PERSONALITY (LAW)," and wishes to follow the LC cross references connecting the two concepts, it should be consistent with *Sears* by translating the first term, so that its reference card will read: "PERSONALITY (LAW) *see also* FREE SPEECH" (not "PERSONALITY (LAW) *see also* LIBERTY OF SPEECH," as the LC reference reads).

BACKGROUND

The current eighth edition of *LCSH* is heir to a long tradition of theory and practice which is generally held to begin with Charles Ammi Cutter's *Rules for a Dictionary Catalog*.[4] A brief review of Cutter's approach, and of the major developments stemming from his work can be found in chapter 26, "Verbal Subject Analysis." The purpose in the present chapter is to highlight trends leading directly to *LCSH* in its present form.[5]

On July 1, 1909, J. C. M. Hanson, Chief of the Catalog Division of the Library of Congress, addressed the Catalog Section of the American Library Association at its Bretton Woods Conference on "The Subject Catalogs of the Library of Congress."[6] He alluded to a two-volume subject catalog published by the Library in 1869, but called the subject heading developments of the intervening forty years too radical to permit a meaningful comparison. The many changes attendant upon the new classification scheme and the move into the new building required a new approach to subject indexing. LC catalogers agreed to start from the *ALA List of Subject Headings for Use in Dictionary Catalogs (1895)*, which embodied much of Cutter's theory, and which originally formed an appendix to his *Rules*. It was designed for smaller libraries of "generally popular character," but with LC's printed card distribution plans, such an orientation was not altogether disadvantageous.

The first cards carrying the new headings were published in July 1898, although subject terms were given only if an LC call number was available to print. Since many class schedules were still undeveloped, the list of subject headings grew slowly in the first decade. Proposed new headings were compared to those in the *ALA List* before final selection. Separate publication of the new list did not start until 1909, when the annotated and interleaved copies of the *ALA List* grew unwieldy. It was assumed from the first that cumulations of additions and changes would be issued periodically to supplement the main list, which itself appeared in parts until March 1914.

The practice of subordinating place to subject in scientific and technical headings, as well as under many economic and educational topics, was established at this time. But other subjects—historical, political, administrative, social, and descriptive—were to be subordinated to place, although Hanson admitted to "a number of subjects so nearly on the border line, that it has been difficult in all cases to preserve absolute consistency in decisions" (p. 387). Besides the place/subject versus subject/place precedents, other syntactic forms evolved:

> There is undeniably a strong tendency in the Library of Congress catalog to bring related subjects together by means of inversion of headings, by combinations of two or more subject-words, and even by subordination of one subject to another (p. 389).

Hanson recognized that subordination within the dictionary arrangement of his new subject list was a concession to the alphabetic-classed or systematic organization of the 1869 catalog. He argued:

. . . the student and the investigator . . . are best served by having related topics brought together so far as that can be accomplished without a too serious violation of the dictionary principle (p. 390).

TYPES OF SUBJECT HEADINGS

Library of Congress subject headings are constructed in a variety of ways, ranging from a single noun to complex descriptive phrases. As was discussed in chapter 26, Cutter enumerated six varieties according to their grammar or syntax.[7] They covered only primary headings, i.e., headings without further subdivision. The categories below are his, but the examples come from the current LC list:

1. A single word (e.g., "SKATING")
2. A noun preceded by an adjective (e.g., "ADMINISTRATIVE LAW")
3. A noun preceded by another noun used like an adjective (e.g., "ENERGY INDUSTRIES")
4. A noun connected with another by a preposition (e.g., "RADIOISOTOPES IN CARDIOLOGY")
5. A noun connected with another by "and" (e.g., "LIBRARIES AND SOCIETY")
6. A phrase or sentence (e.g., "SHOW DRIVING OF HORSE-DRAWN VEHICLES")

While Cutter did tolerate modifier inversions (e.g., "ETCHING, ANONYMOUS") "only when some other word is decidedly more significant or is often used alone with the same meaning as the whole name," he made no explicit provision for parenthetical qualifiers (e.g., "KAIROS (THE GREEK WORD)") or other such complicated forms as "INTERNAL COMBUSTION ENGINES, SPARK IGNITION," which, like subdivisions, are usually reminiscent of the alphabetico-classed approach. There are various alternative groupings. This discussion will follow those used by Lois Mai Chan in her recent treatise on LC subject headings.[8]

SINGLE NOUN OR SUBSTANTIVE

Cutter's Rule No. 172 reads: "Enter books under the word which best expresses their subject, whether it occurs in the title or not." He worked primarily in terms of the simple concept-name relationship on which the noun forms of all languages are based. The Library of Congress over the years has experimented with slight variations of this single-word heading, for example, inclusion of an initial article (e.g., "THE WEST"), sometimes inverted (e.g., "STATE, THE") in the interests of clarity. Such forms were always rare, and seem to be growing rarer. Automated filing problems permit no new headings starting with "THE . . ." and force elimination of the initial article from others previously established.

Another variation was the distinction drawn, particularly in literature and art, between singular nouns (denoting the activity or the form, e.g., "ESSAY" and "PAINTING") and plural nouns (denoting the objects, e.g., "ESSAYS" and "PAINTINGS"). No new plural noun headings are being established, and some old plurals (e.g., "PAINTINGS") have recently been cancelled in favor of the singular form.

ADJECTIVAL HEADINGS

These headings start with a modifier followed by a noun or noun phrase (e.g., "MUNICIPAL OFFICIALS AND EMPLOYEES"). Chan lists nine types of modifiers, quoting Haykin to the effect that they require *see* references only when the modifier rather than the substantive carries the primary meaning:[9]

1. Common adjective (e.g., "DENTAL RECORDS")
2. Ethnic, national, or geographic adjective (e.g., "AFRO-AMERICAN LIBRARIANS")
3. Eponymic adjective (e.g., "BERNOULLIAN NUMBERS")
4. Participial modifiers (e.g., "APPLIED ANTHROPOLOGY" or "HEARING AIDS")
5. Common noun (e.g., "HOUSEHOLD PESTS")
6. Proper noun (e.g., "BERNSTEIN POLYNOMIALS" or "SHANGHAI GESTURE")
7. Common noun, possessive case (e.g., "SAILORS' SONGS")
8. Proper noun, possessive case (e.g., "BERGMANN'S RULE")
9. Combination (e.g., "WOMEN'S LIBERATION MOVEMENT" or "ERHARD SEMINARS TRAINING")

CONJUNCTIVE PHRASE HEADINGS

Headings composed of two or more nouns, with or without modifiers, connected by "and" or ending with "etc." belong in this group. Those which are additive may comprise similar elements (e.g., "WIT AND HUMOR" or "HOTELS, TAVERNS, ETC."), or the elements may be contradictory (e.g., "RIGHT AND WRONG"). Headings of this type are no longer established. If needed, separate headings are made for each element. Some older additive headings, such as the former "BUDDHA AND BUDDHISM," have been separated, to the dismay of certain local catalogers with large files of material affected.[10]

Still being added are conjunctive headings expressing cause and effect, influence, or similar reciprocal relationships (e.g., "ALCOHOLISM AND CRIME" or "ASTRONAUTICS AND CIVILIZATION").

PREPOSITIONAL PHRASE HEADINGS

Prepositions sometimes enable the subject cataloger to express single but complex ideas for which there is no one word. Some express reciprocal relationships for which an "and" phrase would be artificial (e.g., "PHOTOGRAPHY IN PSYCHIATRY" or "POLICE SERVICES FOR JUVENILES"). Some are inverted (e.g., "DRUG ABUSE, PREDICTION OF"). Prepositions so used include:

against (e.g., "OFFENCES AGAINST THE PERSON")

as (e.g., "ALFALFA AS FEED")

for (e.g., "CAMPS FOR THE HANDICAPPED")

from (e.g., "THEFT FROM MOTOR VEHICLES")

in (e.g., "HUMAN EXPERIMENTATION IN MEDICINE")

of (e.g., "FREE ELECTRON THEORY OF METALS")

on (e.g., "METALLIC OXIDES, EFFECT OF RADIATION ON")

to (e.g., "CERAMIC TO METAL BONDING")

with (e.g., "DOUBLE BASS WITH BAND")

Many of these circumlocutions are replaced when a simpler expression gains currency (e.g., "PSYCHOANALYSIS IN HISTORIOGRAPHY" was recently replaced by "PSYCHOHISTORY"). "As" headings for classes of persons have recently been restricted to persons not normally considered to have a profession (e.g., "CHILDREN AS COLLECTORS" or "ANIMALS AS ARTISTS"), or to situations involving two professions (e.g., "PHYSICIANS AS AUTHORS"). Old headings in which men or women are identified as professionals (e.g., "MEN AS COLLECTORS" or "WOMEN AS TEACHERS") are being replaced by adjectival phrases (e.g., "MEN COLLECTORS" and "WOMEN TEACHERS"). "In" headings are used broadly to designate persons from one particular discipline or activity treated "in" a different capacity (e.g., "MUSICIANS IN LITERATURE").[11]

PARENTHETICAL QUALIFIERS

Nouns or phrases in parentheses following primary terms have in the past occasioned a variety of linguistic ineptitudes. The Library of Congress no longer adds them to designate special applications of a general concept, although it has no plans to change established headings such as:

VIBRATION (MARINE ENGINEERING)

COOKERY (FROZEN FOODS)

EXCAVATIONS (ARCHAEOLOGY)

SYMMETRY (BIOLOGY)

ENVIRONMENTAL ENGINEERING (BUILDINGS)

For newly established situations, three different techniques are available:

1. "In" and "of" headings:

    INFORMATION THEORY IN BIOLOGY (*not* INFORMATION THEORY (BIOLOGY))

    ANESTHESIA IN CARDIOLOGY (*not* ANESTHESIA (CARDIOLOGY))

    ABANDONMENT OF AUTOMOBILES (*not* ABANDONMENT (AUTOMOBILES))

2. Adjectival headings:

    COMBINATORY ENUMERATION PROBLEMS (*not* ENUMERATION PROBLEMS (COMBINATORIAL ANALYSIS))

    INDUSTRIAL DESIGN COORDINATION (*not* DESIGNS (INDUSTRIAL PUBLICITY))

    SERIALS CONTROL SYSTEMS (*not* CONTROL SYSTEMS (SERIALS))

3. Subdivisions under a primary heading (preferred when practicable):

    GEOGRAPHY — NETWORK ANALYSIS (*not* NETWORK ANALYSIS (GEOGRAPHY))

    PUBLIC HEALTH — CITIZEN PARTICIPATION (*not* CITIZEN PARTICIPATION (PUBLIC HEALTH))

Where primary headings express concepts in more than one discipline, parenthetical qualifiers are used, although not always does more than one such qualifier appear with the potentially confusing word — e.g., "BANDS (MUSIC)."

Three situations are recognized in which it may be necessary to use parenthetical qualifiers:

1. To specify a definition if several can be found in the dictionary (e.g., "ANALYSIS (PHILOSOPHY)")

2. To remove ambiguity if other actual or possible terms or phrases exist (e.g., "CLUTTERING (SPEECH PATHOLOGY)")

3. To make an obscure word or phrase more explicit (e.g., "PAPST (THE GERMAN WORD)").[12]

INVERTED HEADINGS

We have already cited Haykin's emphasis on primary meaning in adjectival phrases. Inversions, while awkward syntactically (e.g., "AGED, WRITINGS OF THE, AMERICAN"), serve the alphabetico-classed function of subordinating specific descriptors under their broad generic categories (e.g.,

"EDUCATION, BILINGUAL" or "ASYLUM, RIGHT OF"). Here too, much inconsistency is apparent. It is hoped that the Library of Congress will be able to address this difficulty in the course of its efforts to modernize and systematize its subject list.

SEMANTICS

Not only have syntactic forms of LC subject headings come under close scrutiny and revision in recent years, but *LCSH* terminology has been reconsidered. Word meanings, particularly their connotative aspects, mutate rapidly; social and political upheavals cause many changes, and scientific and technological developments account for many more. The problem of shifting terminology is particularly troublesome for a subject access list based on specific entry, avoidance of synonyms, and controlled cross references, designed for use with card or printed book catalogs.

A ringing complaint that *LCSH* terminology was obsolete and prejudicial came from Sanford Berman in 1971.[13] As Head of the Hennepin County, MN, Catalog Department, Berman now edits the *HCL Cataloging Bulletin*, a widely-read, mimeographed bi-monthly carrying lists of subject headings and cross references currently added to the HCL catalogs.[14] Most of these are considerably more responsive to changes in usage than are the official additions and changes in *LCSH*, which reflects dread of a serious loss of control through irresponsible proliferation. Sections in the *HCL Cataloging Bulletin* on subject precedents, usage examples, and authorities; on DDC and *AACR* interpretations; and on book reviews, as well as brief articles or summaries of speeches, are all of interest to many catalogers.

Other writers have criticized the pedantic stance at the Library of Congress on conceptual and linguistic shifts. Doris Clack's 1975 analysis of black literature resources starts from a critique of LC subject analysis. She reminds us that:

> Inadequate subject analysis is not just a problem with black literature — though admittedly there the level of adequacy is critically low — nor has it only in recent years been brought to the attention of the library world.[15]

Clack devotes the bulk of her treatise to various lists of LC class numbers and subject terms from the black perspective. A classified "List of Relevant Subjects Included in the Library of Congress Classification Schedules and Appropriate Subject Headings" is followed by the list of "Relevant Library of Congress Subject Headings" (first in alphabetic, then in classified order) and then by lists of non-relevant LC class numbers and subject headings. Since her book was published the Library of Congress has made some changes. The one cited below involved changing approximately 12,000 cards:

> A basic function in the maintenance of a subject heading system is that of updating headings to conform to changing terminology or altered concepts. In general, the Library of Congress is and has been conservative in making changes since it involves altering reference structures surrounding a given heading as well as

accommodating the change in both the card catalogs and the machine-readable data base. However, after a long period of great reluctance in effecting major changes, the Library has recently been involved in a number of changes represented in the following list . . .

> NEGROES. This heading discontinued February 1976. See AFRO-AMERICANS for later materials on the permanent residents of the United States. See BLACKS for later materials on persons outside the United States. . . .[16]

Reflecting a similar socio-linguistic revolution is Joan K. Marshall's 1977 critique of sex bias in *LCSH*.[17] She uses six principles developed by the SRRT Task Force Committee on Sexist Subject Headings to replace logically and consistently the guess-work which evolved over the years from Cutter's concern for the "convenience of the public." Based on the six principles, she submits an alphabetical, annotated "Thesaurus for Nonsexist Indexing and Cataloging." As in the case of blacks, the Library of Congress has overhauled some of its more obsolete or offensive sexist headings, and promises to undertake more sweeping revisions as soon as its present catalogs are closed in 1981. Annual *LCSH* supplements usually carry lists of the significant heading changes made during the year.

GENERAL PHYSICAL CHARACTERISTICS OF THE LIST

The present eighth edition carries an extensive introduction and several lists of pattern headings and subdivisions, to help local catalogers construct LC-type subject terms consistent with its basic principles. There is also a discussion of, and a list of, terms used by the Library of Congress in its Annotated Card Program for children's literature. Both the pattern headings and the Annotated Card Program will be discussed later in this chapter. The entire introduction may be purchased separately, since it does not appear on the microforms or the machine-readable formats.

FILING

The list proper is given in alphabetical order, three columns to a page. Filing rules were revised for the eighth edition, to facilitate computer manipulation. Basic arrangement is word by word. Numbers given in digits precede alphabetic characters in the order of increasing value. Initials separated by punctuation file as separate words. Abbreviations without interior punctuation file as single whole words:

Old Format	New Format
ACI test *See* ADULT-CHILD INTER- ACTION TEST	4-H CLUBS
ACTH	A-36 (Fighter-bomber planes) *See* MUSTANG (FIGHTER PLANES)
A.D.C. *See* CHILD WELFARE	A.D.C. *See* CHILD WELFARE
A4D bomber *See* SKYHAWK BOMBER	A PRIORI
AK8 MOVING-PICTURE CAMERA	A3D bomber *See* SKYWARRIOR BOMBER
ALGOL (COMPUTER PROGRAM LANGUAGE)	A4D bomber *See* SKYHAWK BOMBER
A PRIORI	
A-36 (Fighter-bomber planes)	AACHEN
See MUSTANG (FIGHTER PLANES)	ACI test *See* ADULT-CHILD INTER- ACTION TEST
A3D bomber *See* SKYWARRIOR BOMBER	ACTH
AACHEN	AK8 MOVING-PICTURE CAMERA
ALASKA	ALASKA
FLUTE MUSIC	ALGOL (COMPUTER PROGRAM LANGUAGE)
	FLUTE MUSIC
4-H CLUBS	

Punctuation of subject terms affects filing order more immediately than it does in lists such as *Sears*, which sacrifice categorical to straight alphabetical arrangement. LC subject headings which contain subordinate elements preceded by one or more dashes fall into three groups:

a) period subdivisions, arranged chronologically according to explicit dates, regardless of whether a descriptive term is used,

b) form and topical subdivisions, arranged alphabetically, and

c) geographical subdivisions, arranged alphabetically.

The secondary subdivisions under "UNITED STATES—Foreign relations" faithfully illustrate all three groups in order:

a) UNITED STATES—Foreign relations—Revolution, 1775-1783
UNITED STATES—Foreign relations—1783-1865
UNITED STATES—Foreign relations—Constitutional period, 1789-1809
UNITED STATES—Foreign relations—War of 1898

b) UNITED STATES—Foreign relations—Executive agreements
UNITED STATES—Foreign relations—Historiography
UNITED STATES—Foreign relations—Juvenile literature
UNITED STATES—Foreign relations—Law and legislation
UNITED STATES—Foreign relations—Speeches in Congress
UNITED STATES—Foreign relations—Treaties

c) UNITED STATES—Foreign relations—Canada
UNITED STATES—Foreign relations—France
UNITED STATES—Foreign relations—Japan
UNITED STATES—Foreign relations—Russia

In actual practice these three groups generally collapse into two, for nearly all period subdivisions follow such topical subdivisions as "—Civilization," "—Economic conditions," "—Politics and government," or "—History." All period subdivisions now have explicit dates to allow for computer filing:

Old Format	New Format
ITALIAN POETRY – Early to 1400	ITALIAN POETRY – To 1400
ROME – History – Aboriginal and early period	ROME – History – To 510 B.C.
UNITED STATES – History – 1849-1877	UNITED STATESE – History – 1849-1877
UNITED STATES – History – Civil War	UNITED STATES – History – Civil War, 1861-1865
UNITED STATES – History – 1865-	UNITED STATES – History – 1865-
UNITED STATES – History – 1865-1898	UNITED STATES – History – 1865-1898
UNITED STATES – History – 1865-1921	UNITED STATES – History – 1865-1921

All subject subdivisions (identified by dashes) file ahead of inverted modifiers, which are punctuated by commas. Inverted modifiers, in turn, file ahead of parenthetical qualifiers. Last of all come phrases which start with the primary term:

Old Format	New Format
CHILDREN	CHILDREN
CHILDREN – Accidents	CHILDREN – Accidents
CHILDREN – Growth	CHILDREN – Growth
CHILDREN – Recreation	CHILDREN – Recreation
CHILDREN (CHRISTIAN THEOLOGY)	CHILDREN, ADOPTED
CHILDREN (INTERNATIONAL LAW)	CHILDREN, FIRST-BORN
CHILDREN (ROMAN LAW)	CHILDREN, VAGRANT
CHILDREN, ADOPTED	CHILDREN (CHRISTIAN THEOLOGY)
CHILDREN, FIRST BORN	CHILDREN (INTERNATIONAL LAW)
CHILDREN, VAGRANT	CHILDREN (ROMAN LAW)
CHILDREN AND ANIMALS	CHILDREN AND ANIMALS
CHILDREN AND STRANGERS	CHILDREN AND STRANGERS
CHILDREN AS WITNESSES	CHILDREN AS WITNESSES
CHILDREN IN AFRICA	CHILDREN IN AFRICA
CHILDREN IN LITERATURE	CHILDREN IN LITERATURE
CHILDREN OF WORKING MOTHERS	CHILDREN OF WORKING MOTHERS

SYNDETIC (CROSS REFERENCE) FEATURES

All primary subject terms appear in boldface roman type. All subdivisions and cross reference tracings, as well as cross references interfiled with the main headings, are in lightface roman type. The directions "sa" (*see also*), "x" (refer from: *see* tracings), and "xx" (refer from: *see also* tracings) are given in lightface italics. They either identify or trace the two kinds of cross references officially associated with main subject terms. The following examples illustrate their usage:

Example 1:

NUCLEAR GEOPHYSICS
  sa Radioactive dating
  x Nuclear geology
  xx Geophysics

These references mean:

Nuclear geophysics. *See also* Radioactive dating
Nuclear geology. *See* Nuclear geophysics
Geophysics. *See also* Nuclear geophysics

The symbol "sa" is read just as it is written, i.e.,

NUCLEAR GEOPHYSICS
   sa   Radioactive dating

is read as:

NUCLEAR GEOPHYSICS
   see also Radioactive dating

The "x" and "xx" symbols are read in inverted order, beginning with the element following the "x" or "xx." Thus,

NUCLEAR GEOPHYSICS
   x   Nuclear geology

is read as:

Nuclear geology
   see   Nuclear geophysics

and

NUCLEAR GEOPHYSICS
   xx   Geophysics

is read as:

GEOPHYSICS
   see also Nuclear geophysics

Example 2:

MAGNETIC PROSPECTING (TN269)
   sa   Magnetic variometer
   x   Prospecting, Magnetic
   xx   Magnetotelluric prospecting
         Prospecting — Geophysical methods

The "*sa* Magnetic variometer" means that if a local catalog has subject entries under both "MAGNETIC PROSPECTING" and "MAGNETIC VARIOMETER," then LC recommends a reference: "MAGNETIC PROSPECTING *see also* MAGNETIC VARIOMETER." If the library has no entries under "MAGNETIC VARIOMETER," then the *see also* reference should not be made.

Suppose next that the local catalog has a different book under "PROSPECTING — Geophysical methods." The "*xx* Prospecting — Geophysical methods" reminds us that we should make a reference: "PROSPECTING—Geophysical methods *see also* MAGNETIC PROSPECTING." If we check the subject list under "PROSPECTING—Geophysical methods," exactly such a reference can be found, among other *sa* listings, as follows:

PROSPECTING—Geophysical methods (TN269)
    sa Electric prospecting
       Geophysical well logging
       Gravity anomalies
       Gravity prospecting
       Magnetic prospecting
       [etc.]

On the other hand, assume that the local catalog has no materials under "MAGNETOTELLURIC PROSPECTING." Strictly speaking, it would be inaccurate to make a reference reading: "MAGNETOTELLURIC PROSPECTING *see also* MAGNETIC PROSPECTING." Some theorists argue that it is nonetheless "administratively justifiable" to make such *see also* references, on the assumption that the term referred from will eventually be activated.[18] Even if it is not, they say, the reference serves to move users from a term not included to one where there may be pertinent materials. Other libraries convert such ambiguous *see also* into *see* references, e.g., "MAGNETOTELLURIC PROSPEC-TING *see* MAGNETIC PROSPECTING." If the term referred from is later activated, they then add the word *"also"* to the *"see"* on the card.

    A recent *Cataloging Service Bulletin* gives interesting insights into LC's cross reference theory.[19] To prevent the occurrence of "orphan headings" (i.e., headings not otherwise integrated into the reference network) the Library of Congress includes at least one *see also* from some broader term to each newly established heading, with few exceptions. At the same time other techniques keep the number of cross references from proliferating unnecessarily.

    As for the *x* tracings, there is never any danger of ambiguity in converting them to the *see* references for which they stand. The "*x* Prospecting, Magnetic" means simply that the subject list includes, in proper alphabetic order, an entry which reads: "PROSPECTING, MAGNETIC *see* MAGNETIC PROSPECTING."

CLASSIFICATION AIDS

    Many primary subject terms, and some subject subdivisions under those terms, are accompanied by LC classification numbers. Sometimes more than one LC class number will be given, with a term from the schedule to show the various facets of classification represented by the subject heading. Frequently a range of numbers is supplied:

CHESTNUT (*Indirect*) (*SD397.C5*)
  Example under NUTS
  —Disease and pest resistance
  —Diseases and pests (*SB608.C45*)
    sa names of pests, e.g. CHESTNUT-BORER

CHESTNUT-BLIGHT (*SB608.C45*)
  Example under PLANT DISEASES—EPIDEMICS

CHESTNUT-BORER (*SB608.C45*)
  Example under CHESTNUT—DISEASES AND PESTS

HOBO SONGS (*M1977.H6; M1978.H6*)

OPERA (*Direct*) (*Aesthetics, ML3858; History and criticism, ML1700-2110*)

SPANISH POETRY (*Direct*) (*Collections, PQ6175-6215; History, PQ6076-6098; Translations, PQ6267-9*)

GEOGRAPHIC SUBJECT HEADINGS

Geographic, jurisdictional, and physiographic names form a large part of any library's subject network. *LCSH*, like most general subject lists, did not until recently include more than a few key examples to illustrate modes of entry and types of subdivision. Since 1976, however, newly established geographic names have been listed in the *LCSH* supplements, to make them readily available to local subject catalogers.[20] One can now find such entries as the examples listed below, although many older headings of similar construction are still missing from the official lists:

ARDINGLY, ENG. WAKEHURST PLACE
BARAČKO LAKE, BOSNIA AND HERZEGOVINA
BYZANTINE EMPIRE
CAPE OF GOOD HOPE—History
CHICAGO—Haymarket Square Riot, 1886
CLINTON, IOWA—Flood, 1965
CLOUD PEAK PRIMITIVE AREA, WYO.
DAW'S HALL WILDFOWL FARM, ENG.
FLINT RIVER WATERSHED, MICH.
FRANCE—History—Wars of the Huguenots, 1562-1598
GENEVA, ILL.—Parks—Good Templar Park
GERMANY. REICHSTAG
LAKE DISTRICT, ENG., IN LITERATURE
LAKE MARACAIBO, BATTLE OF, 1823
LEIPZIGE TIEFLANDSBUCHT, GER.
LEMHI PASS REGION, IDAHO AND MONT.
MISSISSIPPI RIVER

MOUNT KENYA NATIONAL PARK, KENYA
NEWPORT, R.I. WAKEHURST
ORD RIVER DAM, AUSTRALIA
SILL RIVER, AUSTRIA
TAYLOR, MOUNT, REGION, N.M.

Since 1972 the Library of Congress has assigned to all material of local historical or genealogical interest at least one subject heading in which a place name is the first element. Place names reflecting political or jurisdictional changes are incorporated as rapidly as the work-load permits. Such changes usually have greatest impact on descriptive cataloging, but many are also important for establishing subject entries. Special attention has been given to reconstructing headings for Taiwan and the Republic of China, as well as for Czechoslovakia and Poland. Since 1975, LC accepts decisions of the National Library of Canada on forms for Canadian corporate names, including place names. All changes are posted in successive issues of *Cataloging Service Bulletin*. The following lists give examples of recent place name revisions:

Old Format	New Format
AFRICA, SOUTH	SOUTH AFRICA
BRESLAU	WROCLAW, POLAND
BRITISH HONDURAS	BELIZE
BRÜNN	BRNO, CZECHOSLOVAKIA
CEYLON	SRI LANKA
CZECHOSLOVAK REPUBLIC	CZECHOSLOVAKIA
DAHOMEY	BENIN
DANZIG	GDAŃSK, POLAND
EAST (FAR EAST)	EAST ASIA
GERMANY (DEMOCRATIC REPUBLIC, 1949-)	GERMANY, EAST
GERMANY (FEDERAL REPUBLIC, 1949-)	GERMANY, WEST
RUSSIA (1917- R.S.F.S.R.)	RUSSIAN REPUBLIC
STRASSBURG	STRASBOURG

All newly established names of ancient cities, followed by the names of current larger jurisdictions or islands where they are located, have since 1976 been listed in *LCSH*. Examples are "BITHIA, SARDINIA" and "TAANACH, JORDAN." Modern city districts or quarters are also now included in *LCSH* if their names are distinctive. A few examples are:

BEACON HILL, BOSTON
BRONX (BOROUGH)
BROOKLYN
MAGDALENA MIXHUCA, MEXICO (CITY)
MANHATTAN (BOROUGH)
NORTH END, BOSTON
QUEENS (BOROUGH)
RICHMOND CO., N.Y.
TELEGRAPH HILL, SAN FRANCISCO
YAGYŪ SECTION, NARA, JAPAN

GEOGRAPHIC SUBDIVISIONS

The list of revised place names in the previous section includes some jurisdictional name simplifications, such as "GERMANY, EAST" and "RUSSIAN REPUBLIC." The Library of Congress tells us that such a modification "is used only as a subject heading, not as a name heading."[21] In practice, such "unofficial" forms can therefore be used only as geographic subdivisions of topical headings. Any subject reference to the jurisdictional entity in its own right requires that the entry be given in the same form as that prescribed by descriptive cataloging rules of entry. For instance, Rainer Pausch's *Privatisierungsmöglichkeiten bei der Deutschen Bundespost* (LC card 78-365205) is assigned two subject entries by the Library of Congress as follows:

1) GERMANY (FEDERAL REPUBLIC, 1949-   ). DEUTSCHE BUNDESPOST.

2) POSTAL SERVICE—GERMANY, WEST

The examples in the section on Classification Aids show how the LC subject list authorizes local catalogers to supply geographic subdivisions. The code words "Direct" and "Indirect" in parentheses after any entry tell us that place names may be added without having been spelled out in the list. Direct subdivision means that the place name is to be written as spoken, or as used to address a letter, e.g., "OPERA—Thuringia," or "OPERA—Santa Fe, N.M." Indirect subdivision means that the elements of the geographic name are to be arranged hierarchically, with a broader place name preceding the local name, e.g., "CHESTNUT—Australia—Moreton Bay," or"CHESTNUT—Oregon—Portland." In either case, each sequential part of the subdivision is filed in its proper alphabetical order, regardless of its political, administrative, or regional scope.

Users of the local subdivision instructions in the *LCSH8* Introduction (pp. xii-xiii) should be warned that Library of Congress practice has changed since it was published in 1975. That same year the Library announced that it would no longer assign "Direct" subdivision to newly established headings except in rare instances.[22] Headings already established with "Direct" subdivision will be converted to "Indirect" subdivision on a time-available basis. When such conversions are made, they are announced in the *LCSH* supplements. Usually they accompany other changes in the headings, as the following examples illustrate:

Old Heading	New Heading
CANCER RESEARCH—Scholarships, fellowships, etc. (*Direct*)	CANCER—Research—Scholarships, fellowships, etc. (*Indirect*)
CITIZENS RADIO SERVICE (*Direct*)	CITIZENS BAND RADIO (*Indirect*)

Two exceptions were originally identified in the general trend toward indirect subdivision. Legal headings were to be one group where direct division was retained, but a further announcement in 1979 pinpointed legal subdivisions as a project for systematic change.[23] The first two sweeping changes would be to the following subdivisions:

... — Legal status, laws, etc. (*Indirect*) [under headings for groups of people]
... — Law and legislation (*Indirect*) [under all other topical headings]

Few changes are yet being made in phrase headings, or in those using parenthetical qualifiers. Current practice is reflected in the following list:

CHILDREN — Nutrition — Law and legislation (*Indirect*)
DISPLACED HOMEMAKERS — Legal status, laws, etc. (*Indirect*)
DIVORCE (ISLAMIC LAW) (*Direct*)
LAW — Study and teaching (Clinical education) (*Indirect*)
LAW REPORTS, DIGESTS, ETC. (*Direct*)
LEGAL LITERATURE (*Indirect*) [a 1977 change]
RES IPSA LOQUITUR DOCTRINE (*Direct*)
RESCISSION (LAW) (*Direct*)

The second group of headings which *Cataloging Service* exempted in 1975 from change were those with national adjectives, e.g., "JAPANESE POETRY." *LCSH* supplements now show a corresponding shift toward indirect subdivision, as we can see from the following examples:

Old Heading	New Heading
ABKHAZIAN DRAMA (*Direct*)	ABKHAZ DRAMA (*Indirect*)
ABKHAZIAN FICTION (*Direct*)	ABKHAZ FICTION (*Indirect*)
ABKHAZIAN POETRY (*Direct*)	ABKHAZ POETRY (*Indirect*)
CHEREMISSIAN DRAMA (*Direct*)	MARI DRAMA (*Indirect*)
CHEREMISSIAN LITERATURE (*Direct*)	MARI LITERATURE (*Indirect*)

Two reasons are given for the shift to indirect subdivision. First, although general guidelines discriminating "Direct" from "Indirect" usage have been followed for many years, they are hard to interpret consistently. There seem to be capricious jumps from one to the other in closely related subject areas. Another factor is increased use of the MARC format for bibliographic records. In MARC a programmed code imposes a built-in rank-order on all geographic terms used as subdivisions.[24]

A revision of "Indirect" forms was announced in 1976.[25] Existing LC practice interposed national names between topical subject headings and local political, administrative, or geographical divisions, but there were notable exceptions. For most English speaking countries, and major European powers, subordinate jurisdictions (state or provincial rather than national names) were interposed between topical headings and local place names. Now only the major divisions of Canada, Great Britain, the United States, and the Soviet Union displace national names.[26] These changes result in headings such as:

AGRICULTURE — France — Rhone Valley
AGRICULTURE — Italy — Sicily
COMMERCIAL PRODUCTS — Fürstenberg (Principality)
EDUCATION — California — San Diego County
EDUCATION — France — Alsace
EDUCATION — Germany, West — Bavaria
EDUCATION — Germany, West — Munich
FOLK DANCING — Dnieper Valley
GARDENS — Papal States
GEOLOGY — Bermuda Islands
GEOLOGY — Northern Ireland — Ballycastle Region
GEOLOGY — Ukraine — Kiev (Province)
HARBORS — Hansa towns
MUSIC — Australia — Sydney
MUSIC — California — San Joaquin Valley
MUSIC — Quebec (Province) — Quebec (City)
SPORTS — England — London Metropolitan area
SPORTS — Russian Republic — Moscow
STREAM MEASUREMENTS — Austria — Sill River
WATER-SUPPLY — Canary Islands — Teneriffe
ZOOLOGY — Siberia

For geographic subdivisions, even more than for geographic headings, local name changes are observed. For instance, works which formerly would have received the heading "BANKS AND BANKING — Leopoldville, Belgian Congo" are now found under "BANKS AND BANKING — Zaire — Kinshasa." The Library of Congress finds it less disruptive to keep subdivisions updated en masse than to apply the same rigor to primary headings. Its dilemma is aggravated by critics on both sides of the issue. Some feel that all headings should be changed immediately when a name change occurs. Others object to the work involved in making such changes "regardless of the form of the name used in the work cataloged."[27]

If both local and topical, or form, subdivisions are established in the same heading, the first subdivision is customarily the geographic one, e.g., "EDUCATION — Wisconsin — Curricula." However, the trend toward indirect subdivision appears to be accompanied by more cases where the topical subdivision precedes the geographic one. In 1976 the Library of Congress published a list of all (some 75) of its subtopic — place name subdivisions.[28] Typical examples are:

CHEMICAL INDUSTRIES — Safety regulations — Chile — Santiago
FRUIT-TREES — Diseases and pests — North America
MOVING-PICTURES — Collectors and collecting — California —
Los Angeles

Other explanations and illustrations of geographic headings and subdivision practice are issued from time to time. Their best sources are the *Cataloging Service Bulletin* and the introductory pages of the *LCSH* paper supplements.

HEADINGS OMITTED FROM *LCSH*

A troublesome corollary of the principle of specific entry is the inevitable, and seemingly endless, proliferation of subject terms for individual members of certain subject categories. Until recently the Library of Congress omitted from its printed list a wide variety of such terms, which it nonetheless uses for subject headings.[29] To avoid the term "omitted," which is not strictly correct, since those headings are included in the Library's official records, though not, except for a few examples, spelled out in *LCSH8*, they are known technically as "nonprint headings." But this designation confuses unwary local catalogers who associate "nonprint" with audiovisual and other nonbook formats. Most of such headings are proper names, with only a few representative examples incorporated into *LCSH8*. We have seen, though, that all newly established geographic headings are now entered into the list. The Library of Congress says that all examples of most other categories which were traditionally excluded will henceforth be included in the published *List*.[30] These comprise names of:

Sacred books or scriptures
Families, dynasties, and royal houses
Gods and goddesses, legendary and fictitious characters
Archaeological sites, ancient cities, and empires
Structures, buildings, roads, parks, reserves, etc.
Works of art, both movable and permanently located
Biological names
Chemicals

A few examples from recent supplements to *LCSH8* are:

ANU (ASSYRO-BABYLONIAN DEITY)
BERLIN WALL (1961-   ) IN ART
'BRI-GUN-PA (SECT)
BUONARROTI, MICHEL ANGELO, 1475-1564. PIETÀ.
CH'U-CHING T'U (SCROLL)
DARE (INFORMATION RETRIEVAL SYSTEM)
ES 1050 (COMPUTER)
FISTULA, TRACHEOESOPHAGEAL
GOE CLAN, LIBERIA
GREAT WALL OF CHINA
HAYWARD FAMILY
HENRY FRANCIS DU PONT MUSEUM. GARDENS
ILYARACHNIDAE
MAGNESIA AND MAEANDER, TURKEY.   TEMPLE OF
   ARTEMIS. FRIEZE
MODENA. PALAZZO ARCIVESCOVILE
NGADJU (INDONESIAN PEOPLE)
OPERATION HUSKEY, 1943
PĂCALĂ (LEGENDARY CHARACTER)
POLYCHAETA, FOSSIL
POMERANIAN DOGS
PORPHYRINURIA

POTATO MOSAIC VIRUS
SCHULZ, CHARLES M. PEANUTS
SULPHUR HEXAFLOURIDE
TRIAMCINOLINE
TROCHUS SHELL FISHERIES
T͡SARSKOSEL'SKAÍA ÍUBILEĨNAÍA VYSTAVKA, PUSHKIN,
RUSSIA, 1911
URASPIS URASPIS
WATERGATE AFFAIR, 1972-

Personal name inclusions are still largely limited to a few famous people, under whose names "pattern lists" of subdivisions are provided for transfer, when needed by local catalogers, to other names of similar type:

JESUS CHRIST
LINCOLN, ABRAHAM, PRES. U.S., 1809-1865
NAPOLÉON I, EMPEROR OF THE FRENCH, 1769-1821
SHAKESPEARE, WILLIAM, 1564-1616
THOMAS AQUINAS, SAINT, 1225?-1274
WAGNER, RICHARD, 1813-1883
WASHINGTON, GEORGE, PRES. U.S., 1732-1799

FREE-FLOATING SUBDIVISIONS

For many kinds of primary headings (both those dropped from *LCSH8* and those faithfully listed) there are a number of identical, or nearly identical, subdivisions which can be applied as needed, whether or not they are all written into the published *List*. These are collectively designated "free-floating," but they may not be assigned indiscriminately, for they fall into different groups, each with its own rules and examples.

PATTERN HEADINGS

Pattern headings are examples of a particular primary heading type (e.g., the personal names listed above) which have been entered into the published *List* to show all the possible subdivisions which might be used with other specific headings of the same type. A very few may not even apply to the heading under which they are found. For instance, under "SHAKESPEARE, WILLIAM, 1564-1616" a scope note warns us:

> The subdivisions provided under this heading represent for the greater part standard subdivisions useable under all literary author headings and may not necessarily pertain to Shakespeare.

Besides personal names, several other categories of specific subjects have distinctive sets of subdivisions applicable to all examples of their genre. These include place names, universities, monastic and religious orders, languages, musical instruments, industries, and military services. Most are represented by a few examples embedded in the published *List*, but for the uninitiated user they could be hard to find. The Library of Congress therefore includes a schematic array to show where these pattern subdivisions for various kinds of names can be located.[31] The array consists of three parallel columns, as the following excerpt shows:

SUBJECT FIELD	CATEGORY	PATTERN HEADING
Science and technology	Land vehicles	AUTOMOBILES
	Materials	CONCRETE; METALS
	Chemicals	COPPER
	Organs and regions of the body	HEART; FOOT
	Diseases	CANCER; TUBERCULOSIS
	Plants and crops	CORN
	Animals	FISHES
	Livestock	CATTLE

A second group of patterns suggests standard cross references for use with certain other types of omitted ("nonprint") headings.[32] The 1976 decision to print specific headings of types formerly omitted did not extend to all their cross references. While most *see* references are explicitly traced under the entry and written into the *List*, only one *see also* is included. It is usually under the general category to which the specific entry belongs, and is given to help the user of the *List* find all the specific entries scattered through the alphabet.[33] Two examples are:

Category	Example

Archaeological sites
  xx [country] — Antiquities
      [people]
	el HAJJ, TALL, SYRIA
	  x Tall el Hajj, Syria
	      Tell el Hajj, Syria
	  xx Syria — Antiquities

Art works (movable)
  xx [art form or medium — country,
      except paintings]
	RETABLE DE LA PASSION (SCULPTURE)
	  x Huyard altarpiece (Sculpture)
	      Retable de Lirey (Sculpture)
	      Retable of the Passion (Sculpture)
	  xx Altarpieces — France
	      Sculpture, Renaissance — France

Local libraries should supply the full complement of *see also* references in each case from the patterns offered in *LCSH8* (pp. ix-xii). Thus, for the first example above, in addition to "SYRIA — Antiquities *see also* el HAJJ, TALL, SYRIA," we are instructed to make a reference reading: "EXCAVATIONS (ARCHAEOLOGY) — Syria," although the latter is a "nonprint" reference.

PLACE NAME SUBDIVISIONS

To encourage correct expansion of geographic headings without identifying every unique possibility, LC developed two standard lists: one to use with specific names of regions, countries, states, etc., and the other for use under names of cities. The original listings in *LCSH8* are revised and enlarged from time to time through the *Cataloging Service Bulletin* and the *LCSH8* paper supplements.[34]

MOST COMMONLY USED SUBDIVISIONS

Besides its pattern headings and schematized lists of subdivisions for special application, *LCSH* carries an "intentionally incomplete" but regularly updated list of topical and form subdivisions for more general application.[35] These "most commonly used" divisions represent only about one-third of the total LC subdivision file, being selected according to the following criteria:

1) that with few exceptions they apply to more than one major subject area,

2) that they are not already given under a pattern heading (but those used with place names are included),

3) that they apply fairly frequently.

The list includes standard subdivision terms followed by scope notes and suggested cross references, in similar format to the full subject list, except that scope notes play a more prominent role than in the list proper. One example of a commonly used division is:

STATISTICS, VITAL
Use as a form subdivision under names of regions, countries, cities, etc., as well as under names of ethnic groups, for compilations of birth, marriage, and death statistics.
  sa Mortality
      Population
      Statistics, Medical
  x Vital statistics

PHRASE HEADINGS

In patterned phrase headings it is the initial word which changes. This type is still limited to a very few pattern phrases, chiefly:

  . . . IN ART [e.g., "ETHNIC ATTITUDES IN ART"]
  . . . IN DRAMA [e.g., "RELIGION IN DRAMA"]
  . . . IN FICTION [e.g., "CHILDREN IN FICTION"]
  . . . IN POETRY [e.g., "NAMES IN POETRY"]
  . . . IN LITERATURE [e.g., "HORSES IN LITERATURE"]

The local cataloger should not take every " . . . IN . . ." phrase found in *LCSH* as a pattern phrase. For example, the heading "COLOR IN CLOTHING" does not of itself give license to coin other phrases ending with " . . . IN CLOTHING."[36] The Library of Congress formerly used pattern phrases of the form " . . . AS A PROFESSION" (e.g., "MEDICINE AS A PROFESSION"). It now uses the subdivision " — Vocational guidance" instead (e.g., "SOCCER — Vocational guidance").

PATTERNS IN MUSIC HEADINGS

Music is one subject area where fewer, rather than more, specific headings now make their way into *LCSH*. Headings with qualifiers specifying instruments or vocal parts will no longer be listed if no cross references are required, and if a scope note explaining present practice is given under the generic heading. Thus, a heading such as "STRING QUINTETS (VIOLINS (4), VIOLONCELLO)" would not be listed if it were established today, because it involves no cross references, and there is a general scope note given under "STRING QUINTETS." Omission of such specific headings is justified by use of an accepted order for listing instruments, which may be applied as needed to create the appropriate specific form. Careful instructions are available to help subject catalogers formulate needed headings.[37]

SUBJECT HEADINGS FOR CHILDREN'S LITERATURE

Since 1965 the Library of Congress has issued a special service for children's catalogers. Known as the Annotated Card Program, it provides "more appropriate and in-depth subject treatment of juvenile titles."[38] A list of some 400 specially tailored subject headings is accompanied by a review of commonly-used subdivisions, another of subdivisions and qualifiers not used, and general instructions for applying and modifying standard LC subject terms. The Library's printed cards carry the children's heading forms in brackets. In the MARC format they are tagged specifically as subject terms for children. Some comparative examples are:

LCSH8	Annotated Card List
ACROBATS AND ACROBATISM	ACROBATS AND ACROBATICS
ALPINE FAUNA	ALPINE ANIMALS
FIRE-ENGINES	FIRE ENGINES
GEOGRAPHIC DISTRIBUTION OF ANIMALS AND PLANTS	ANIMAL DISTRIBUTION PLANT DISTRIBUTION
IBN BATUTA, 1304-1377 — Juvenile literature	IBN BATUTA, 1304-1377
PICTURE-BOOKS FOR CHILDREN	ALPHABET BOOKS STORIES WITHOUT WORDS

SCOPE NOTES

Scope notes have already been mentioned in connection with LC's list of Most Commonly Used Subdivisions. They are also sometimes inserted into the full list between subject terms and their suggested cross references (see, for example, the scope note under "SHAKESPEARE, WILLIAM, 1564-1616" which is quoted on page 512). Such notes specify the range of application for a term, or draw distinctions between related terms. Some libraries copy these notes on cards and file them in the catalog just ahead of the subject entries under the same heading. Other libraries provide one or more copies of *LCSH* near the catalog for reference use by patrons doing subject searches. A typical example of an entry with a scope note is the following:

SEXISM (*Indirect*)
   Here are entered works on sexism as an attitude as well as works on attitude and overt discriminatory behavior. Works dealing solely with discriminatory behavior directed toward both of the sexes are entered under SEX DISCRIMINATION.
   sa Sex discrimination
      Sex role
   x Sex bias
   xx Attitude (Psychology)
      Prejudices and antipathies
      Sex (Psychology)
      Sex role
      Sex perception
Note under SEX DISCRIMINATION

CONCLUSION

In spite of perennial criticisms on grounds of its outdated terminology, illogical syntax, and general inefficiency for precise subject retrieval, *LCSH* is the most widely accepted controlled vocabulary list in use in English-language libraries today. The Library of Congress, with considerable prompting from interested bystanders, now and again assesses its virtues and disadvantages, in comparison with other, more scientifically constructed systems. The PRECIS (Preserved Context Index System), inaugurated for the *British National Bibliography* in 1971, received perhaps the strongest consideration as an alternative to, if not a replacement for, *LCSH* when LC card catalogs are frozen in 1981. After cost studies, however, the decision went against any such replacement or supplement. Instead, more intensive efforts are under way to modernize and systematize the existing tool. Many of the features discussed in this chapter represent steps in that direction. A ninth edition will be issued as soon as staff and funding permit. For the forseeable future, this venerable subject list gives every sign of retaining its vitality and preeminence for subject access to library collections.

FOOTNOTES

[1]Library of Congress, Subject Cataloging Division, *Library of Congress Subject Headings*, 8th ed. (Washington, The Library, 1975), 2v. and suppls.

[2]*Canadian Subject Headings* (Ottawa, National Library of Canada, 1978).

[3]Minnie Earl Sears, *Sears List of Subject Headings*, 11th ed., edited by Barbara M. Westby (New York, H. W. Wilson, 1977).

[4]Charles A. Cutter, *Rules for a Dictionary Catalog*, 4th ed., rewritten (Washington, GPO, 1904; republished, London, The Library Association, 1953). The original version of this work was: Charles A. Cutter, "Rules for a Printed Dictionary Catalogue," in *Public Libraries in the United States of America: Their History, Condition, and Management*, United States Bureau of Education (Washington, GPO, 1876), Part II.

[5]For fuller information on the origin and development of the *LC Subject List*, see: Lois Mai Chan, *Library of Congress Subject Headings: Principles and Application* (Littleton, CO, Libraries Unlimited, 1978); and Richard S. Angell, "Library of Congress Subject Headings—Review and Forecast," in *Subject Retrieval in the Seventies: New Directions*, edited by Hans (Hanan) Wellisch and Thomas D. Wilson (Westport, CT, Greenwood Publishing Co., 1972), pp. 143-63.

[6]J. C. M. Hanson, "The Subject Catalogs of the Library of Congress," *Bulletin of the American Library Association* 3 (Sept. 1909):385-97. Further citations to this article will be documented only by page number, which will be included parenthetically in the text.

[7]Cutter, *Rules*, 4th ed., pp. 71-72.

[8]Chan, *Library of Congress*, pp. 48-59.

[9]David Judson Haykin, *Subject Headings: A Practical Guide* (Washington, GPO, 1951), pp. 21-22.

[10]The two new headings replacing the older compound heading are BUDDHISM, and GAUTAMA BUDDHA.

[11]*Cataloging Service*, bulletin 125 (Spring 1978):21-22.

[12]*Cataloging Service Bulletin*, no. 1 (Summer 1978):15-16.

[13]Sanford Berman, *Prejudices and Antipathies: A Tract on the LC Subject Heads Concerning People* (Metuchen, NJ, Scarecrow, 1971).

[14]Hennepin County Library, Cataloging Section, *Cataloging Bulletin*, May 1973- .

[15]Doris H. Clack, *Black Literature Resources: Analysis and Organization* (New York, Marcel Dekker, 1975), p. 10.

[16]*Cataloging Service*, bulletin 119 (Fall 1976):22, 24.

[17]Joan K. Marshall, comp., *On Equal Terms: A Thesaurus for Nonsexist Indexing and Cataloging* (Santa Barbara, CA, American Bibliographical Center — Clio Press, 1977).

[18]See, for example, *Anglo-American Cataloging Rules: North American Text* (Chicago, American Library Association, 1967), p. 173, footnote 1.

[19]*Cataloging Service Bulletin*, no. 1 (Summer 1978):16-20.

[20]*Cataloging Service*, bulletin 117 (Spring 1976):10-12.

[21]*Cataloging Service*, bulletin 121 (Spring 1977):19.

[22]*Cataloging Service*, bulletin 114 (Summer 1975):7.

[23]*Cataloging Service Bulletin*, no. 4 (Spring 1979):12.

[24]Chan, *Library of Congress*, p. 66.

[25]*Cataloging Service*, bulletin 118 (Summer 1976):9.

[26]*Cataloging Service*, bulletin 116 (Winter 1976):4-5.

[27]*Cataloging Service*, bulletin 120 (Winter 1977):10.

[28]*Cataloging Service*, bulletin 118 (Summer 1976):9-10.

[29]Library of Congress, Subject Cataloging Division, *Library of Congress Subject Headings*, 8th ed. (Washington, The Library, 1975), p. viii.

[30]*Cataloging Service*, bulletin 117 (Spring 1976):10-11.

[31]Library of Congress, *LCSH8*, pp. xiii-xiv. Revised in the *LCSH 1977 Supplement*, p. vi.

[32]Library of Congress, *LCSH8*, pp. ix-xii.

[33]Library of Congress, Subject Cataloging Division, *1974-1976 Supplement to LC Subject Headings* (Washington, The Library, 1977), p. v.

[34]See, for instance, *LCSH8*, pp. xv-xviii; its *1977 Supplement*, pp. vii-viii; and the *Cataloging Service Bulletin*, no. 3 (Winter 1979), pp. 12-13.

[35]Library of Congress, *LCSH 8*, pp. xix-lxxii.

[36]*Cataloging Service*, bulletin 123 (Fall 1977):11.

[37]Library of Congress, *1974-1976 Supplement to LC Subject Headings*, p. iii.

[38]Library of Congress, *LCSH8*, p. lxxiii.

28 SEARS LIST OF SUBJECT HEADINGS

INTRODUCTION

The *Sears List of Subject Headings*, now in its eleventh edition, is widely used by small public libraries and by school libraries.[1] It is very much smaller in scope and more general in treatment than *Library of Congress Subject Headings* (*LCSH*), which is commonly used in academic and research libraries. Its history of continuous publication is not so long-standing as that of the LC list, but its first edition is now well over fifty years old:

> Minnie Earl Sears prepared the first edition of this work in response to demands for a list of subject headings that was more suitable to the needs of the small library than the A.L.A. and the Library of Congress lists. Published in 1923 the *List of Subject Headings for Small Libraries* was based on the headings used by nine small libraries that were known to be well cataloged. However, Minnie Sears early recognized the need for uniformity, and she followed the form of the Library of Congress subject headings with few exceptions. This decision was important and foresighted because it allowed a library to add Library of Congress headings as needed when not provided by the Sears List and to graduate to the full use of Library of Congress headings when collections grew too large for a limited subject heading list.[2]

The reliance of *Sears* editors and users on *LCSH* as a kind of sturdy big brother has never ceased. The following hypothetical situation should help make this clear. Suppose that a library using *Sears* acquires a book on the chemical effects of high energy radiation on matter. *Sears* offers the following headings:

RADIATION, which seems too broad
RADIATION – PHYSIOLOGICAL EFFECT, which seems too narrow
CHEMISTRY, PHYSICAL AND THEORETICAL, which seems much too broad
RADIOCHEMISTRY, which seems to fit the book's contents most closely.

However, the cataloger checks the library holdings for which the term "RADIOCHEMISTRY" has been used, and finds that the new work has a distinctly different focus. By consulting *LCSH* he or she learns that the difference is important enough to merit another heading "RADIATION CHEMISTRY." A scope note carefully distinguishes it from

"RADIOCHEMISTRY," making its application to the book at hand clear. The local library can incorporate the borrowed term into its subject authority file, using the cross references suggested by *LCSH* to relate it to existing *Sears* terminology.[3]

TERMINOLOGY

New headings for the eleventh edition of *Sears* were suggested by librarians representing various sizes and types of libraries, and by H. W. Wilson catalogers responsible for the Standard Catalog series and the *Book Review Digest*. Wilson also publishes one special interest companion volume for Canadian libraries.[4] A few *Sears* headings were taken from the eighth edition of *LCSH*, including most of its "Subject Headings for Children's Literature." Some also originated in the *Legislative Indexing Vocabulary* of the LC Congressional Research Service, and in the *HCL Cataloging Bulletin*.[5] Aside from its comparative brevity and simplicity, the following *Sears* differences from *LCSH* are worthy of note:

1. **Simpler phrasing.** *Sears* uses "CITY PLANNING"; *LCSH* uses "CITIES AND TOWNS—Planning."

2. **More current terminology and spelling.** *Sears* uses "AIRPLANES," "CRISIS CENTERS," and "MOTION PICTURES"; *LCSH* until quite recently used "AEROPLANES," and continues to use "CRISIS INTERVENTION (PSYCHIATRY)" and "MOVING-PICTURES" as primary headings. Some more recently established derivative headings, such as "SURREALISM IN MOTION PICTURES," bear witness to its efforts to change.

3. **Less emphasis on specificity.** *Sears* uses "SILK SCREEN PRINTING"; *LCSH* uses only two narrower terms: "SCREEN PROCESS PRINTING" and "SERIGRAPHY."

ELIMINATION OF RACIST, SEXIST, AND PEJORATIVE HEADINGS

The tenth edition of *Sears* was published in 1972, in the midst of considerable furor over the obsolescent, prejudicial terminology lingering in both *Sears* and *LCSH*. A suggested list of terms relating to blacks was appended to that edition. It reworded the older terms using "Negro" and related headings which the editors presumably had not had time to expunge from the list proper. The eleventh edition eliminates the appendix and integrates the updated terms. For instance, "NEGRO POETRY" no longer appears anywhere in *Sears*, having fully given way to "BLACK POETRY."

Similar, though less sweeping, changes can be seen in older terminology which to modern ears would sound sexist. Thus, when the heading, "NEGRO ACTORS," was abandoned, it was replaced by "BLACK ACTORS AND

ACTRESSES." "WOMAN – SOCIAL CONDITIONS" from the tenth edition gave way in the eleventh to "WOMEN – SOCIAL CONDITIONS." The earlier "WOMEN IN AERONAUTICS *see also* AIR LINES – HOSTESSES" now reads "WOMEN IN AERONAUTICS *see also* WOMEN AIR PILOTS," while "AIR LINES – HOSTESSES" has become "AIR LINES – FLIGHT ATTENDANTS."

Other headings with prejudicial connotations have disappeared or undergone purification rites. The tenth edition's "JEWISH QUESTION" is entirely missing from the eleventh edition. "UNDERDEVELOPED AREAS" is downgraded into a *see* reference to "DEVELOPING AREAS." "INSANITY" is likewise converted into a *see* reference to "MENTAL ILLNESS – - JURISPRUDENCE." "MAN, PRIMITIVE" has become "MAN, NONLITERATE."

PROBLEMS OF UPDATING TERMINOLOGY

Some linguistic change would have occurred, no doubt, regardless of the social climate. However, formal subject lists are notoriously conservative in their response to new terminology. In attempting to retain the goodwill of their constituents, they are understandably sensitive to the disruptions caused to a library's cataloging routines when an unduly large number of new subject forms are mandated at one time. Still, the argument that an obsolete form (e.g., "MOHAMMEDANISM" instead of the more acceptable "ISLAM") reflects usage in the bulk of the literature indexed is specious. Furthermore, it becomes misleading as new materials with new terminology are added. On the other hand, librarians fear not only the time and effort required to change large numbers of entries, but also the stresses placed on the filing apparatus when revised cards must be moved from one section of the catalog to another.

Various proposals have been advanced for coping with large-scale subject heading revision. Dowell suggests three major options:[6]

1. For card catalogs, interfiling of "over-printed" cards (on which the subject term is printed above the main entry) or "highlighted" cards (on which one subject tracing is underlined for use as the filing element). Interfiling is seldom fully successful unless there is considerable erasing and retyping, although its purpose is to avoid just those problems. An analogous technique bypasses any marking of the subject entries themselves, preceding them instead with a "guide term" which, through typography or other marks of format and design, shows the full group of subject entries ranged behind or under it. The guide term principle works better in book and microform catalogs, or machine-readable data bases, than for the more traditional card catalog.

2. Cross references connecting the old and revised heading forms. The *see also* references might well carry brief explanations, particularly showing the dates of publication, or of cataloging, covered by each form of the altered headings.

3. Changing old headings to the new forms. We have already suggested that the "interfiling" option for card catalogs usually requires some erasing and retyping of subject cards. The "full change" method extends such revisions to every entry affected by the new heading. Some libraries attempt to remove old markings and reword the entry. Others prepare complete new subject

entries. Either mode involves labor that is both intensive and wasteful. As card catalogs gradually give way to automated catalog production, the possibilities of quick, easy, and accurate subject heading change through computer programming looks more and more attractive.

SEARS' USE OF SUBJECT HEADING THEORY

The general philosophy of *Sears List of Subject Headings* is contained in two phrases, both of which the cataloger should remember as he or she makes specific application of the list to the individual materials in the library's collection.[7]

"The theory of specific entry" means that a specific heading is preferred to a general one. For a book about cats alone, "CATS" is preferred to "DOMESTIC ANIMALS." On the other hand, the headings "SIAMESE CATS" OR "SEAL-POINT SIAMESE CATS" would likely be too specific for most libraries, except possibly a veterinary library. The cataloger must know the collection, know its emphases, and know something of the way people use it, to be prepared to assign subject headings to it.

"The theory of unique heading" means that one subject heading, and one alone, is chosen for all books on that subject. The choice of subject headings must be logical and consistent. Cross references should be inserted in the catalog wherever it is anticipated that patrons are likely to approach the topic through different terminology. A few general principles or guidelines are useful for constructing subject headings:

1) Prefer the English word or phrase unless a foreign one best expresses the idea. *Sears*, for example, carries the reference "Laissez faire *see* INDUSTRY AND STATE."

2) Try to use terms that are used in other libraries as well, unless the library in question is highly specialized or otherwise unique.

3) Try to use terms that will cover the field, i.e., terms that will apply to more than one book.

4) Try to use no more than three subject headings per cataloged item. This rule is not tyrannical; some books may require more than three.

CROSS REFERENCES

Sears breaks down cross references into three main categories, and discusses each in some detail. Among them are seven varieties of *see* references, plus two broad classes of *see also* references:[8]

See references are considered essential to the success of the catalog. Yet the cataloger in a local library may not find necessary every *see* reference suggested in the list. For example, *Sears* proposes "Copybooks *see* PENMANSHIP." But if the library's holdings on penmanship contain nothing about copybooks, then it is potentially misleading to put such a reference into the catalog. The most frequent and helpful varieties of *see* references direct the user from:

1) Synonyms or terms so nearly synonymous that they would cover the same kind of material, e.g., "Chemical geology *see* GEOCHEMISTRY" and "Degrees of latitude and longitude *see* GEODESY."

2) The second part of a compound heading, e.g., "Illusions *see* HALLUCINATIONS AND ILLUSIONS" and "Motels *see* HOTELS, MOTELS, ETC."

3) The second part of an inverted heading, e.g., "Popular music *see* MUSIC, POPULAR (SONGS, ETC.)." *Sears* also suggests for this rather awkward subject heading, "Popular songs *see* MUSIC, POPULAR (SONGS, ETC.)" and "Songs, Popular *see* MUSIC, POPULAR (SONGS, ETC.)."

4) Some inverted headings to normal order, e.g., "Libraries, Music *see* MUSIC LIBRARIES."

5) Variant spellings to the accepted spelling, e.g., "Gipsies *see* GYPSIES" and "K.K.K. *see* KU KLUX KLAN."

6) Opposites when they are included without being specifically mentioned, e.g., "Disobedience *see* OBEDIENCE" and "Truth in advertising *see* ADVERTISING, FRAUDULENT."

7) The singular to the plural when the two forms would not file together, e.g., "Goose *see* GEESE."

See also references pose theoretical and practical problems which jeopardize their efficacy. Yet both *Sears* and *LCSH* make heavy use of them. The above warning against making blind references simply because they are suggested in a standard list holds as true for *see also* references as it does for *see* references. There are two broad classes of *see also* references. We shall note that the second or "general" class proves especially resistant to adequate control:

1) Specific *see also* references. We found in chapter 26 that *see also* references normally move downward from a general term to a more specific term or terms, e.g., "CONSERVATION OF NATURAL RESOURCES *see also* ENERGY CONSERVATION; NATURE CONSERVATION." In this example the general term refers to two more specific terms. The user who pursues the reference by looking under "NATURE CONSERVATION" will find a still more specific downward reference to three more headings: "NATURE CONSERVATION *see also* LANDSCAPE PROTECTION; NATURAL MONUMENTS; WILDLIFE – CONSERVATION."

Sears also indulges in a high number of bilateral or duplicate references, where the movement is horizontal, between related subjects of more or less equal specificity. The following examples have been pruned of extraneous terms, to make their reciprocity more visible:

GODS *see also* MYTHOLOGY; RELIGIONS
MYTHOLOGY *see also* GODS
RELIGIONS *see also* GODS

HYGIENE *see also* SANITATION
SANITATION *see also* HYGIENE

KINDERGARTEN *see also* EDUCATION, PRESCHOOL
EDUCATION, PRESCHOOL *see also* KINDERGARTEN

MOLLUSKS *see also* SHELLS
SHELLS *see also* MOLLUSKS

NATURAL HISTORY *see also* BIOLOGY; ZOOLOGY
BIOLOGY *see also* NATURAL HISTORY; ZOOLOGY
ZOOLOGY *see also* NATURAL HISTORY

ORTHOPEDICS *see also* PHYSICALLY HANDICAPPED
PHYSICALLY HANDICAPPED *see also* ORTHOPEDICS

2) General *see also* references. Here the more specific terms being referred to are so diverse or numerous that the standard list cites only one or two noteworthy illustrations, adding an "etc." to launch the cataloger on his or her own list of additional headings of similar format, as needed to describe the local library collection. The problem raised by these general or "blanket" references is one of control. When *Sears* uses "FORAGE PLANTS *see also* GRASSES . . . also names of specific forage plants, e.g. CORN; HAY; SOYBEAN; etc." but the only book in the library on a specific forage crop is on clover, it seems fairly obvious that the cataloger should change the illustration to read "FORAGE PLANTS *see also* GRASSES . . . also names of specific forage plants, e.g. CLOVER." Or perhaps the format could be simply "FORAGE PLANTS *see also* GRASSES; CLOVER."

If, on the other hand, there are books on several specific topics, not all of which serve as examples in the cross reference, should the cataloger add each new term at the time it first becomes a subject heading? That is, when the list gives "Illustrations *see* subjects with the subdivision *Pictorial Works*; e.g. ANIMALS—PICTORIAL WORKS; U.S.—HISTORY—CIVIL WAR, 1861-1865—PICTORIAL WORKS; etc." and the library which has subject entries for both referrals adds a book consisting largely of pictures of children, should the cataloger revise the reference entry by inserting "CHILDREN—PICTORIAL WORKS" as a third illustration?[9] Or can he or she depend on the "etc." to cover all subsequent examples? Most libraries follow the second option, thus throwing the burden of search on the user, who probably either will not understand the instructions, or after a bit of desultory searching, will give up. However well the user copes, valuable materials may be overlooked.[10]

Sears enumerates seven major types of general *see also* references:

1) Common names of different species of a class, e.g., "DOGS *see also* classes of dogs, e.g. GUIDE DOGS; etc.; also names of specific breeds, e.g. COLLIES; etc."

2) Names of individual persons, e.g., "PRESIDENTS – U.S. *see also* names of presidents, e.g. KENNEDY, JOHN FITZGERALD, PRES. U.S.; etc."

3) Names of particular institutions, buildings, societies, etc., e.g., "BRIDGES *see also* names of cities and rivers with the subdivision *Bridges* (e.g. CHICAGO – BRIDGES; HUDSON RIVER – BRIDGES; etc.) also names of bridges, e.g. GOLDEN GATE BRIDGE; etc."

4) Names of particular geographic features, e.g., "NATURAL MONUMENTS *see also* WILDERNESS AREAS; also names of natural monuments, e.g. NATURAL BRIDGE, VA.; etc."

5) Geographic treatment of a general subject, e.g., "IMMIGRATION AND EMIGRATION *see also* ALIENS; . . . also names of countries with the subdivision *Immigration and emigration* (e.g. U.S. – IMMIGRATION AND EMIGRATION; etc.); names of countries, cities, etc. with the subdivision *Foreign population* (e.g. U.S. – FOREIGN POPULATION; etc.); and names of nationality groups, e.g. MEXICAN AMERICANS; MEXICANS IN THE U.S.; etc."

6) Form divisions, e.g., "INDEXES *see also* SUBJECT HEADINGS; also subjects with the subdivision *Indexes*, e.g. NEWSPAPERS – INDEXES; PERIODICALS – INDEXES; SHORT STORIES – INDEXES; etc."

7) National literatures, e.g., "ESSAYS *see also* AMERICAN ESSAYS; ENGLISH ESSAYS; etc.; also general subjects with the subdivision *Addresses and essays*, e.g. AGRICULTURE – ADDRESSES AND ESSAYS; U.S. – HISTORY – ADDRESSES AND ESSAYS; etc."

STRUCTURE OF SUBJECT HEADINGS

Like LC subject headings, *Sears* terms consist of a variety of forms, ranging from a single noun to different kinds of complex descriptive phrases:[11]

1) The single noun is the most desirable form of subject heading if it is specific enough to fit the book at hand and the needs of the library. This point was discussed earlier under "Theory of Specific Entry." In general, if there is a significant difference between the singular and plural forms the plural is preferred (e.g., "MOUSE *see* MICE"). However, there are situations where the singular form is used to cover abstract ideas or general usage (e.g., "SONATA" as a musical form), while the plural designates individual examples of the form, frequently collected into anthologies or the like.

2) The modified noun takes at least three forms: a) normal word order (e.g., "HEALTH MAINTENANCE ORGANIZATIONS"), b) inverted word order (e.g., "ARTIFICIAL SATELLITES, RUSSIAN"), and c) explanatory modifier added in parentheses (e.g., "HOTLINES (TELEPHONE

COUNSELING)"). There is usually no reliable way of predicting which form of modification will be used. Some topics, such as "EDUCATION," exhibit a luxuriant variety of forms (e.g., "ADULT EDUCATION," "EDUCATION, SECONDARY," and "PRISONERS—EDUCATION"). Some theorists try to justify these "inconsistencies," but for the most part they seem to be the result of habit and a reluctance to make extensive unnecessary changes.

3) The compound heading is usually two nouns joined by "and," but the nouns are sometimes also modified (e.g., "COTTON MANUFACTURE AND TRADE"). The terms are conjoined for various reasons:

a) To link related topics. Usually both ideas are covered in a single treatise, e.g., "ANARCHISM AND ANARCHISTS," "BICYCLES AND BICYCLING," "CLOCKS AND WATCHES," and "PUPPETS AND PUPPET PLAYS."

b) To link opposites. Again, the pairs are often discussed together, e.g., "CORROSION AND ANTICORROSIVES," "GOOD AND EVIL," and "JOY AND SORROW."

c) To dispel ambiguity when the primary term is susceptible to more than one interpretation, e.g., "FILES AND FILING." The second term is added to distinguish storage files from the tools used by carpenters and mechanics. *LCSH*, as might be expected, is even more precise with these homonyms. It uses two subject headings: "FILES AND FILING (DOCUMENTS)" and "FILES AND RASPS."

In most cases, usage dictates the order of terms, but when that fails, alphabetical order is preferred. If a library should acquire enough materials under one of two such terms (e.g., "FRATERNITIES AND SORORITIES") to make searching difficult or tiresome, the cataloger might consider splitting the subject heading into its two components, with linking cross references. For example, *LCSH* has broken its former heading "ANTIGENS AND ANTIBODIES" into "ANTIBODIES" and "ANTIGENS."

4) The phrase heading may be prepositional (e.g., "COST OF LIVING"), serial (e.g., "PLOTS (DRAMA, FICTION, ETC.)"), or an intriguing combination of forms (e.g., "GEOGRAPHIC DISTRIBUTION OF ANIMALS AND PLANTS," "INSECTS AS CARRIERS OF DISEASE," or "LIFE SUPPORT SYSTEMS (MEDICAL ENVIRONMENT)").

TYPES OF SUBDIVISIONS

Subject subdivisions indicate a specialized aspect of a broad subject or point of view, e.g., "RADIO—REPAIRING." They are set off from the primary heading by a dash, and are presumably distinguishable from inverted modifiers, which restrict or narrow the topic, e.g., "RADIO, SHORT WAVE." Yet *Sears* no longer separates the two categories, but interfiles them in straight alphabetical order, letter by letter to the end of each word, disregarding punctuation.[12] The only concession it makes to categorical filing is in alphabetizing all punctuated headings together under the primary entry word, following them with all phrase headings in a second alphabet, e.g.:

COOKERY
COOKERY, FRENCH
COOKERY — MAINE
COOKERY, MICROWAVE
COOKERY, OUTDOOR
COOKERY, QUANTITY
COOKERY — SOUTHERN STATES
COOKERY — VEGETABLES
Cookery for institutions, etc. *see* COOKERY, QUANTITY
COOKERY FOR THE SICK

The primary purpose of the subject subdivision is to group related materials in the catalog under one topic if it is quite broad, or if there is much written about it, e.g., "EDUCATION." That is, linguistic random access is partially replaced by a modified classing device. A patron seeking all available materials on "PHOTOGRAPHY," for instance, would have to examine several different trays of cards from one end of the catalog to the other if subdivisions, inverted modifiers, and phrase headings were not clustered under that word in the standard lists.

Subdivisions may be compounded under a given topic. As many as three are used for such a subtopic as "U.S. — HISTORY — CIVIL WAR, 1861-1865 — MEDICAL AND SANITARY AFFAIRS." In it are displayed several of the different types of subdivisions:

1) Form divisions are used, like the Dewey Decimal Classification form divisions, to indicate the physical (e.g., " . . . — BIBLIOGRAPHY") or philosophical (e.g., " . . . — RESEARCH") form of the work. The eleventh edition of *Sears* gives a table of general form subdivisions which may be used by the cataloger to divide practically any subject heading in the list.[13]

2) Special topic divisions cannot so readily be transferred from one subject to another. *Sears* lists a basic group which, although not quite universal, may be applied by the cataloger to appropriate subject entries.[14] Still other subdivisions are specially tailored to bring out important aspects of individual topics, e.g., "CHILDREN — CARE AND HYGIENE" or "AIRPLANES — PILOTING." One could not reasonably use "CHILDREN — PILOTING" or "AIRPLANES — CARE AND HYGIENE." Such divisions are listed in full in the body of the list, being for the most part non-transferrable.

3) Time divisions, which apply most frequently to history, define a specific chronology for the primary topic. Some consist merely of dates (e.g., "EUROPE — HISTORY — 1789-1900"). More often the date or dates follow a descriptive phrase (e.g., "CHURCH HISTORY — EARLY CHURCH, ca. 30-600" or "CIVILIZATION, MODERN, 1950-   "). Occasionally the chronological designation is an inverted qualifier rather than a subdivision. It may be used without dates (e.g., "CIVILIZATION, ANCIENT"), but more often dates are added (e.g., "GETTYSBURG, BATTLE OF, 1863" and "WORLD WAR, 1939-1945").

4) Geographic divisions are of two forms: a) area — subject, e.g., "CHICAGO — FOREIGN POPULATION," and b) subject — area, e.g., "GEOLOGY — BOLIVIA." *Sears* adds parenthetical instructions to those headings in its list which may be divided by place, e.g., "GEOLOGY (May

subdiv. geog.).'' Under some headings the instructions are more detailed, e.g., "PARKS (May subdiv. geog. country or state) *see also* AMUSEMENT PARKS; . . . also names of cities with the subdivision *Parks*, e.g. CHICAGO—PARKS; etc.'' Or the place term might be an inverted modifier, e.g., "ETHICS (May subdiv. geog. adjective form, e.g. ETHICS, JAPANESE; ETHICS, JEWISH; etc.).''

Area—subject situations are less conspicuous in the list, but play an important role in most library catalogs. Instructions may take the form: "ITALY . . . May be subdivided like U.S. except for *History*.'' A similar example is: "NEUTRALITY *see also* names of countries with the subdivision *Neutrality*, e.g. U.S.—NEUTRALITY; etc.''

Subject headings in the fields of science, technology, economics, education, and the arts usually are subdivided by place. Those in history, geography, politics, and the social sciences usually are made subdivisions under place.[15] It is assumed that the real subject of a book about Colorado history, and the one the patron will most likely consult, is "COLORADO,'' not "HISTORY.'' In *Sears*, the subject entry, "HISTORY,'' is used only for general works on history as an intellectual discipline. If the subject is an institution such as a library the real subject might be either the institution or the area, depending on the type of area. *Sears* will specify, e.g., "LIBRARIES (May subdiv. geog. country or state).'' Subdivision by city is thus precluded, and the *see also* note includes the phrase " . . . names of cities with the subdivision *Libraries* (e.g. CHICAGO—LIBRARIES).'' This means that a discussion of the libraries of a state or country will fall under the topical heading, e.g., "LIBRARIES—CANADA'' and "LIBRARIES—QUEBEC (PROVINCE).'' By contrast, a discussion of the libraries of a local jurisdiction will fall under the place heading, e.g., "QUEBEC (CITY)—LIBRARIES.''

Individual works of belles-lettres (e.g., novels, plays, and poetry) are not usually assigned subject headings. It is assumed that patrons are more likely to seek access to these materials through author or title. Reference librarians also find certain published indexes, such as H. W. Wilson's *Fiction Catalog* and F. W. Faxon's series of indexes to full-length plays, sufficient. If not, they make, or request the catalogers to make, special demand files. In the list of form subdivisions supplied by *Sears* " . . .—FICTION'' appears as a suggested option for libraries that prefer to make subject headings for fictionalized history or biography. Thus, a novel about the Six Day War in the Middle East might be given the subject heading, "ISRAEL-ARAB WAR, 1967—FICTION.''

Literary anthologies are far more likely to receive subject headings. As discussed above, plural nouns (e.g., "SONATAS'') are used to differentiate collections of actual works from discussions of the form, for which the singular noun would be used. In situations where plural and singular words are not normally distinguished, the subdivision " . . .—COLLECTIONS'' is available for the cataloger to add as needed (e.g., "POETRY—COLLECTIONS'').[16]

PHYSICAL CHARACTERISTICS
AND FORMAT OF *SEARS*

The eleventh edition of *Sears* opens with a preface which gives its historical setting, and identifies the authoritative sources and the new features incorporated in it. It is followed by an explanatory essay which has become a *Sears* tradition, undergoing considerable expansion in scope and detail over the years. In the eleventh edition this essay is called "Principles of the Sears List of Subject Headings."[17] It treats both the theoretical and practical aspects of subject heading work. It merits the careful reading, not only of those planning to use the *Sears* list, but of anyone wishing to gain knowledge of traditional subject list usage.

In the list proper, the right half of each page is blank. All entries, references, and instructions are confined to the left columns, to leave space for the local cataloger to add any new headings, references, or comments needed to convert the volume into an authority file. Subject entries are printed in boldface type. *See* references appear in lightface type in the same alphabet. Filing in *Sears* has already been discussed under "Types of Subdivisions." The following excerpt shows the various elements which may be included under a subject entry, although not every entry requires all of these elements:

> **Children's Poetry** 808.81; 811; 811.08; etc.
> Use for collections of poetry for children by one or more authors. Materials on poetry written by children are entered under **Children as Authors**
> *See also* **Children's Songs; Lullabies; Nursery Rhymes**
> *x* Poetry for children
> *xx* **Children's Literature; Poetry — Collections**

Dewey Decimal numbers, which had long accompanied subject headings in the list, were dropped from the ninth and tenth editions. Since DDC schedules are edited and printed by an entirely different publisher, various objections had been raised to the gratuitous, unofficial association of certain DDC numbers with the subject entries. It was feared that *Sears* might be used as a substitute index to the DDC schedules, or worse yet, as a substitute for the schedules themselves. However, upon catalogers' insistence, the eleventh edition once again carries them, with admonitions about the differences between classification and subject heading work, as well as strong recommendations that both the DDC index and the schedules be consulted before any classification is done. The above example shows the associated DDC numbers in their customary place, on the same line with the subject entry. Note that three numbers are specifically included, together with an "etc." to remind the user that he or she might profitably seek further in the Dewey Decimal Classification to find the best number for the particular need.

Scope notes are an exception, rather than the rule, but the one in the example above is typical. The reader receives first a positive instruction on appropriate use of the entry. Then comes a negative instruction (albeit stated positively) on the kinds of material which should be placed under a different entry.

The words "See also" in italics normally follow the scope note, or, if there is no scope note, the entry proper. They precede a list in boldface of closely related headings which the user might like to explore. Each boldface entry in this list is a legitimate subject heading. Reference to these *see also* headings might very well lead to further *see also* headings which could help expand or modify the search to reveal the full range of materials available in the particular collection. But a *see also* reference should never be made unless the catalog actually has material under the heading referred to.

The letter *x* before one or more terms means that a *see* reference is recommended from each such term to the heading under which the *x* appears. Terms preceded by an *x* are never used as subject headings. The letters *xx* before one or more terms mean that a *see also* reference should be made from each such term used in the catalog to the heading under which the *xx* appears. Thus, *Sears* suggests the following cross references for the subject entry, "CHILDREN'S POETRY," but the local cataloger is expected to consider each on its merits, in view of the terminology used by the library's clientele and the presence of other subject entries in the catalog:

CHILDREN'S POETRY *see also* CHILDREN'S SONGS
LULLABIES
NURSERY RHYMES

Poetry for children *see* CHILDREN'S POETRY

CHILDREN'S LITERATURE *see also* CHILDREN'S POETRY

POETRY—COLLECTIONS *see also* CHILDREN'S POETRY

The *x* and *xx* are tracings of a sort, to help the cataloger fit the most appropriate specific subject entries to each individual item in the collection and keep track of their interrelationships. The "*x* Poetry for children" under "CHILDREN'S POETRY" is there as a reminder that a user might very well go first to the P's, looking under "Poetry for children." If so, a simple reference could save both time and frustration. "POETRY—COLLECTIONS" is in boldface under the "*xx* CHILDREN'S LITERATURE; POETRY—COLLECTIONS." It might be a subject entry in the catalog, but according to the theory of specific entry it is too broad for a work confined to children's poetry. However, the "*xx* POETRY—COLLECTIONS" serves the dual purpose 1) of reminding the cataloger to make a "POETRY—COLLECTIONS *see also* CHILDREN'S POETRY" reference, and 2) of helping anyone who has access to the printed list to work back to the broader heading, where some entries may lead to poetry anthologies which actually contain some poetry for children. In most libraries the *see also* reference will be filed after all the subject entries bearing the heading "POETRY—COLLECTIONS."

Sears supplies two pages of minute instructions for Checking and Adding Headings.[18] Here the technique of checking all terms in the list which have been transferred to the local catalog, and the uses of the blank right-hand columns to record the headings and cross references added by the local cataloger, are fully explained. Many smaller libraries find this type of subject authority file the simplest and quickest to prepare. There is one serious drawback, however. When a new edition of *Sears* appears, all checks and entries must be laboriously recopied, or the library's subject control will suffer. If the older edition is retained for its authority records, all new headings and changes must be entered, making it increasingly messy and difficult to read. If the new edition is adopted without reviewing and checking former practices, inconsistencies will soon weaken the power of the subject access structure.

Sears includes a three-part list of "Headings to Be Added by the Cataloger."[19] Eight varieties of proper names, and five each of corporate names and common names are identified, for which there is no attempt to include all possibilities in the printed list. One or two obvious names of each variety can be found in the list proper, to serve as examples, or because important or typical subdivisions have been given. The cataloger is also reminded that general *see also* references imply other specific names which the cataloger is to add as needed, using available reference sources to establish correct entry forms.

Closely related are the "Key Headings" or prominent specific names where full displays of possible subdivisions are listed, not just for those names, but for most or all names of the same type.[20] Eight key entries are given, exemplifying four major categories of headings and subdivisions to be added by the cataloger:

Persons

> **PRESIDENTS – U.S.** (to illustrate subdivisions which may be used under the name of any president)
> **SHAKESPEARE, WILLIAM** (to illustrate subdivisions which may be used under any voluminous author)

Places

> **UNITED STATES (or U.S.)**   (to illustrate subdivisions
> **OHIO**   except for historical periods)
> **CHICAGO**

Languages and Literatures

> **ENGLISH LANGUAGE**
> **ENGLISH LITERATURE**

Wars

> **WORLD WAR, 1939-1945**   (to illustrate subdivisions
> which may be used under any war
> or battle)

There are two additional sections in *Sears*. The "List of Subdivisions" really includes two lists of differing generality.[21] Reference was made to it in the discussion of "Types of Subdivision." It is followed by the full printed list, which occupies the bulk of the volume.

Instead of issuing quarterly supplements, as does *LCSH, Sears* updates its usage by successive editions at intervals of five to seven years. A parallel contrast holds between the sporadic revisions of the Dewey Decimal Classification and the quarterly Additions and Changes of the LC classification. The relatively limited scope of *Sears* and DDC, for use in small- and medium-sized libraries, makes comprehensive revision more manageable for both editors and users. The results are possibly more coherently integrated. However, nine, seven, or even five years is a long time to wait for the updated version of a subject access tool in today's rapidly developing bibliographic environment. The Library of Congress's quarterly supplements to both its classification scheme and its subject heading list permit (if they do not always ensure) early professional response on the part of one enormous library to inevitable, but generally unpredictable, shifts in publishing interests and emphases. While they may absorb and distribute better the shocks of linguistic and epistemological change, they quickly clutter one's work space with their numerous partial revisions, at least in their paper formats. Actually neither approach monopolizes all the advantages. What matters is that every viable subject access mode remain under constant surveillance and revision, offering a dynamic compromise between rigid custom and assimilative change.

CONCLUSION

The assigning of subject headings is a discipline which inevitably seems complicated and bewildering to the neophyte cataloger. Unlike other cataloging disciplines, it has no logical progression other than the linguistic development of knowledge itself. Even the assigning of a classification number to a book is less forbidding, for the novice usually has some sort of previous orientation to the Dewey system, and can see, if dimly, the divisions of knowledge and why they should exist. Subject headings are, however, not difficult once the cataloger learns to handle them. Both *Sears* and *LCSH* are quite explicit in their directions; both have comprehensive, intelligible introductions; both contain lists of general subdivisions with specific instructions for their use. If followed consistently, they will provide useful reference guides for the user, including the reference librarian.

A beginning cataloger should study the subject list used in the local library. It would be helpful to choose a subject in which he or she is personally interested, tracing it throughout the list, and observing the interrelation of *see also*, *x*, and *xx* references. There are other aids, such as the reference tools in the library. They amplify subjects and clarify aspects not immediately understood, especially in an age when no one can expect to know everything. The library's shelf list and public catalog are also helpful. The former can suggest subject headings if the cataloger has a classification number in mind, since most shelf lists nowadays consist of full unit records, with tracings for the subject entries of each cataloged item. The public catalog can suggest classification numbers if the would-be cataloger has a subject heading in mind. Neither is a completely reliable crutch. Books are very often written about new subjects and about more than one subject. The vagaries of past and present individual catalogers, however experienced, may mislead. Yet both resources are generally helpful; both serve to characterize the practices of the local library. To become a successful cataloger, one must know what is current local practice, and work within that frame of reference. Major changes should not be put into effect until the reasons for what is done are fully understood, and the reactions of other users and fellow librarians can be anticipated.

FOOTNOTES

¹The eleventh edition of *Sears* is briefly reviewed in *Catholic Library World* 49 (Sept. 1977):87; and by Edith Phillips in *School Media Quarterly* 6 (Winter 1978):143-44.

²Minnie Earl Sears, *Sears List of Subject Headings*, 11th ed., edited by Barbara M. Westby (New York, H. W. Wilson, 1977), p. vii.

³For further discussion of the hazards and techniques of integrating *LCSH* headings into a *Sears* authority file, *see* the introduction to chapter 27, "Library of Congress Subject Headings," especially p. 494.

⁴K. R. Haycock and L. Isberg, comps., *Sears List of Subject Headings: Canadian Companion* (New York, H. W. Wilson, 1978).

⁵Library of Congress, Congressional Research Service, *Legislative Indexing Vocabulary*, 11th ed. (Washington, The Library, 1977); Hennepin County Library, Cataloging Section, *Cataloging Bulletin*, May 1973- .

⁶Arlene Taylor Dowell, *Cataloging with Copy: A Decision-Maker's Handbook* (Littleton, CO, Libraries Unlimited, 1976), pp. 118-24; 128-29.

⁷For more detailed discussion of the theory of subject headings, refer to chapter 26, "Verbal Subject Analysis," especially pp. 485-86. See also *Sears*, pp. xii-xiv.

⁸The list of reference types is copied from *Sears*, pp. xxvi-xxvii, but the examples are changed, to give alternative insights.

⁹Note that the example given is a *see*, rather than a *see also*, reference. The principle involved is the same.

¹⁰*Sears*, pp. xxviii-xxix offers some advice on this problem.

¹¹For a review of the structure of LC headings, and further comment on some of the points mentioned here, *see* "Types of Subject Headings" in chapter 27, and "The Choice of Subject Headings" section in chapter 26.

¹²*See* p. 502 to compare the filing used by *LCSH* with that found in *Sears*. Chapter 31 presents still other filing options.

¹³*Sears*, p. xl.

¹⁴*Sears*, pp. xl-xli.

¹⁵*Sears*, p. xvi.

¹⁶*Sears*, p. xxiv.

¹⁷Much of the foregoing discussion is based on this essay.

[18]*Sears*, pp. xxxvi-xxxvii.

[19]*Sears*, p. xxxviii.

[20]*Sears*, p. xxxix.

[21]*Sears*, pp. xl-xli.

29 OTHER TYPES OF VERBAL ANALYSIS

INTRODUCTION

For well over a century libraries have provided subject retrieval from their holdings through the use of pre-coordinate lists of integrated and cross-referenced topical headings. The preceding chapters have discussed *Sears* and *LCSH*, which remain the most universally recognized linguistic tools for analyzing library collections. But recent developments in information science, with its many similarities to, and differences from, library science, offer new modes of indexing which throw both practical and theoretical light on traditional subject lists. Some of the rival techniques are offered as supplements, or even substitutes, for traditional subject catalogs. This chapter will review those enterprises most pertinent to library subject retrieval, and will explain briefly the applications of the more successful ones.

RECENT DEVELOPMENTS IN DOCUMENT INDEXING

The word "index" still connotes book and periodical indexes more often than it does subject catalogs for library collections. However, library indexes and catalogs are nearly as old as alphabets, being present in some form with almost every organized collection of written records as far back as the early Mesopotamian and Egyptian archives. In the final years of the nineteenth and the early years of the twentieth centuries, catalogers frequently made numerous "analytics" to significant informational works in their libraries. Books were expensive. The high cost of acquisitions and the relative scarcity of printed materials were countered with efforts to exploit collections intensively. Librarians were a captive labor force, often with "disposable time" on the job. And what more profitable "pick-up work" could there be than making analytic indexes to anthologies and treatises? If the cards followed standard cataloging practices they were filed into the official catalog. If they were less carefully constructed, they might be kept in a desk drawer or a shoe box in the reference department. John Rothman points to a continuing reciprocity between library classification and indexing:

> Although indexing is often clearly differentiated from cataloging and classification, there is considerable overlapping in practice, and the development of new cataloging techniques or new classification systems is bound to affect indexing practices. Thus the development of the Dewey and other decimal classification systems for library catalogs was paralleled by the development of decimal, coded, and faceted topical indexing systems.[1]

COORDINATE INDEXING

The post-World War II information explosion dramatized the values of good indexing. Older methods which had gone into eclipse were revived and improved. New theories sprang up to support other techniques. A major departure from the relatively simple hierarchical use of subordinate divisions and inverted modifiers in traditional subject heading lists was the idea of post-coordinate searching, in which the searcher could play a more active role. A coordinate index consists of a list of subject terms in a standard format. Each term is independent of all others, except for cross references, and is designed to retrieve all documents for which it is specifically relevant. A user can stop at the single-term level of search if he or she is satisfied with the results. However, true coordinate searching moves on to a second level. Taking two or more terms which together delimit a still more specific search topic, and comparing the records indexed under each, the searcher retrieves only those items which have been indexed under all the chosen terms.

Suppose the searcher is looking for material on the use of solar energy for drying grain. The index might offer the terms "Solar energy," "Heat engines," and "Grain." Perhaps five document citations emerge because they are all entered under all three terms. The searcher makes the matches and consults those documents. In a traditional subject catalog this type of post-coordinate searching is awkward and difficult. The underlying assumption is that the list itself is pre-coordinate. That is, the assimilation and matching of concepts has already been done by the cataloger, and is implicit in the terminology of the list. Thus, *LCSH* offers the subject heading, "SOLAR ENERGY IN AGRICULTURE," with a *see also* reference from "AGRICULTURE," as the one correct subject identifier for the above items. If *Sears* were used, the subject entry or entries would be broader. Probably both "SOLAR ENERGY" and "GRAIN" would be assigned, but there would be no way of matching the two concepts to specify the available items except by comparing subject entries under each term, or examining full unit entries to find those on which both terms were traced.

In post-coordinate indexing, the coordination of terms is the responsibility of the searcher, rather than of the subject cataloger. The terms are usually single nouns, and the specific document citations frequently take the form of accession numbers (rarely hierarchical class or call numbers). In 1953 Mortimer Taube introduced what he called the Uniterm index, to emphasize its post-coordinate use of single terms as opposed to composite headings.[2] It was primarily a manual system, using cards with headings displayed at the top, and ten columns in which document accession numbers could be entered according to the number's final digit. For example, documents 56A, 306, 96, 1176, and 1006 might all be listed in column 6 of each of the three cards bearing the Uniterms "Solar energy," "Heat engines," and "Grain." The technique, known as terminal digit posting, has been most successful in its computerized applications, where some of the tediousness and error-proneness of manual listing is forestalled. The CROSS (Computer Rearrangement of Subject Specialties) Index of Biosciences Information Service (BIOSIS) is one example. The searcher must still make the visual comparisons and match the reference numbers under the chosen headings. Precision of search and in-depth subject retrieval are the obvious rewards, but any extensive search involves eyestrain, mental fatigue, and an inordinate amount of time.

To overcome the disadvantages of a visual search, other modes of post-coordinate indexing soon developed. Mechanical scanning devices are based on the fact that cards may be precisely gridded for punched holes to replace the columns of written or printed numbers. Two or more of these punched cards (e.g., the three carrying the headings "Solar energy," "Heat engines," and "Grain") may be laid together and held up to the light, or otherwise probed, to extract the reference numbers which they index in common. Various brands of these cards have been marketed. Foskett prefers to call them all optical coincidence cards, but he recognizes other popular names such as "peek-a-boo," "peephole," and "feature" cards.[3]

POPULAR SPECIAL VARIETIES OF INDEXING

Post-coordinate indexing has never been popular with library catalogers. Still obedient to Cutter's "convenience of the user," they prefer to build their index terms on natural language syntax, with only enough formalized vocabulary control to promote uniformity and specificity. Still, nuclear concept indexing has proved quite successful, especially for scientific and technical materials. As their proportion in library collections increases, new indexing patterns appear, sometimes experimentally but often permanently, in periodical indexes and abstracting tools. Their influence on subject cataloging has been profound, even if few of them yet replace the old, familiar subject heading lists. Whatever the application, most subject thesauri or lists show a mixed terminology, using both expressions derived from the literature, and terms assigned for conceptual expressiveness or search convenience. Some of the more common types of word indexing are discussed below.

Catchword indexing. The early German "Schlagwort" index was the parent of this approach. It focuses primarily on the author (or the literature), selecting its terms when possible from those used in the document being indexed. Foskett reminds us that it "has been used for many years in such bibliographical tools as *British books in print* and in the indexes issued by periodicals, for example *Nature*."[4] The Library of Congress formerly used inverted titles to create entries under significant terms. Thus Clifford W. Hague's *Textbook of Printing Occupations* (LC card number 22-6175) was given two added entries: 1) the subject entry, "PRINTING, PRACTICAL" and 2) the inverted title entry "Printing occupations, Textbook of." The Library of Congress no longer uses this type of inversion.

Keyword in Context (KWIC) indexing. Inverted or permuted title indexing owes its popularity to successful computer programming. H. P. Luhn introduced the name, together with the methodology, for KWIC indexing some twenty years ago.[5] Computer recognition of alphabetic character strings makes automated word manipulation more accurate and speedy than manual indexing. Document titles or subjects, once reduced to machine-readable form, are scanned to pick up every significant word. Stop-lists of articles, prepositions, conjunctions, and the like prevent the computer from blindly stuffing the index with entries of little or no search value. Each filing word appears in the display (paper sheet, cathode ray tube, or whatever) in a pre-determined key position which is usually somewhere near the center of the entry line. There the filing words, surrounded by the context of the full entry, are alphabetized for quick retrieval. One recent use of KWIC indexing for subject catalogers is in "Set V—Subject Keyword Index," of the *Combined Indexes to the Library of Congress Classification Schedules.*[6] The entries from the indexed volumes of the LC schedules are permuted and alphabetized, showing also the particular schedule and number span from which each was taken. The following selected list of entries comprises those relating particularly to the topic of abandoned and neglected children:

```
                         ABANDONED CHILDREN
                           HV 873-887   [SUPPLEMENTS]
                         CHARITIES FOR CHILDREN, NEGLECTED
                           HV 873-887   [H (3RD ed)]
             ABANDONED    CHILDREN
                           HV 873-887   [SUPPLEMENTS]
             DESTITUTE    CHILDREN
                           HV 873-87    [H (3RD ED)]
             NEGLECTED    CHILDREN
                           HV 873-887   [H (3RD ED)]
                         CHILDREN, DESTITUTE
                           LC 4051-4100 [L (3RD ED)]
   PAUPER CHILDREN, SEE   CHILDREN, DESTITUTE
                             [L (3RD ED)]
                         CHILDREN, DESTITUTE, STATE
                             FEEDING AND CLOTHING
                           LB 3473-79   [L (3RD ED)]
     STATE FEEDING AND    CLOTHING
                           LB 3473-79   [L (3RD ED)]
                         DESTITUTE CHILDREN
                           HV 873-87    [H (3RD ED)]
              CHILDREN,   DESTITUTE, STATE FEEDING AND
                             CLOTHING
                           LB 3473-79   [L (3RD ED)]
CHARITIES FOR CHILDREN,   NEGLECTED
                           HV 873-887   [H (3RD ED)]
                         NEGLECTED CHILDREN
                           HV 873-887   [H (3RD ED)]
                         PAUPER CHILDREN SEE CHILDREN, DESTITUTE
                             [L (3RD ED)]
   CHILDREN, DESTITUTE,   STATE FEEDING AND CLOTHING
                           LB 3473-79   [L (3RD ED)]
```

Keyword Out of Context (KWOC) indexing. The format used for KWIC indexes, with the filing word in the center of the line, is confusing to some users. KWOC indexes are designed to combine the left-hand entry position of traditional and catchword indexing with the contextual framework of KWIC indexing. Keywords appear first in alphabetical order, each followed by the full document title or entry phrase. In one sense all library subject catalogs which use full unit records (rather than short form or limited data entries) use a variation on the principle of KWOC indexing.

HIERARCHIC OR SUBORDINATION INDEXING

The subsuming of narrower terms or subdivisions under broader terms is familiar to librarians in many contexts. We spoke in previous chapters of its use for library subject catalogs. Book indexes frequently indent secondary words under primary ones, and make use of *see* and *see also* references. *The New York Times Index,* and most of the H. W. Wilson indexes, such as *Readers' Guide to Periodical Literature,* do the same. The rapid growth of machine-readable data bases which analyze periodical articles, books, report literature, patents, and the like for rapid retrieval in nearly all disciplines has led to the publication of search-oriented thesauri to aid users with their search strategies. The term, thesaurus, is endemic to discussions of subject retrieval. Its general meaning is little different from "subject heading list," although it is likely to cover a limited discipline or cross-disciplinary area, whereas *Sears* and the LC list are designed for unrestricted application. These thesauri also tend to hybridize or blend hierarchical classification with syndetic (cross referencing) structures even more than *Sears* and *LCSH* do. In place of *see, see also, x* and *xx,* they usually tag entries and references with names or mnemonic initials.

One very simple example of such a search strategy manual is the *Thesaurus of Psychological Index Terms.*[7] Its users guide explains:

Each *Thesaurus* term is listed alphabetically, cross-referenced, and displaced with its broader, narrower and related terms. An array term, representing an extremely broad conceptual area, is denoted by a slash (/). . . .

The *Use* reference directs the user from a term that cannot be used in indexing or searching to a preferred term. . . .

Scholastic Aptitude
   Use Academic Aptitude

The *Used for* reference is the reciprocal reference for the *Use* reference, as seen with:

AVOIDANCE CONDITIONING
   Used for Conditioning (Avoidance)

The *Broader-Narrower* term designators are reciprocals and are used to indicate the genus-species hierarchical relationships, as in these examples:

PSYCHOMOTOR DEVELOPMENT
   Broader Motor Development
   Physical Development
   Psychogenesis

INTERPERSONAL INTERACTION
Narrower Bargaining
           Conflict
           Conversation
           Cooperation

A *Related* term designator is used to show relationships that are semantic or conceptual but not hierarchical. Related term references serve to broaden the perspective of searchers or indexers by directing them to terms they have not considered but which may have a bearing on their subject matter interest as in this example:

STRESS
Related Anxiety
         Disasters
         Endurance

In the *Thesaurus of ERIC Descriptors* each descriptor (main term) is accompanied by one or more notations: UF — *Used for*; NT — *Narrower term*; BT — *Broader term*; RT — *Related term*.[8] "Use" is the mandatory reciprocal of UF, putting the non-postable terms (*see* references) into place. SN precedes a scope note. Under postable terms two more kinds of information are given. The date is the "add" (first entry) date. Search strategies for materials entered into the data base prior to that time should in most instances use different terminology. Posting counts (the number of citations available when the *Thesaurus* was published) are given for both the *Current Index to Journals in Education* and *Resources in Education*. Examples of *Thesaurus* entries are given below:

Dressmakers
   Use Seamstresses

Drill Presses
   Use Machine tools

```
DRINKING              May 1974
       CIJE: 45      RIE: 42
   SN   Consumption of alcoholic
          or other beverages
   UF   Social Drinking
   BT   Activities
   RT   Alcohol Education
        Alcoholic Beverages
        Alcoholism
        Health
        Health Education
        Recreational Activities
```

A final, more complex example comes from the *INSPEC Thesaurus* of the Institution of Electrical Engineers.[9] It uses the following abbreviations:

UF: *Used for*	indicates the 'lead-in' term from which reference is made
NT: Narrower Term	indicates a more specific term, one level lower in the hierarchy
BT: *Broader Term*	indicates a more general term, one level higher in the hierarchy
TT: *Top Term*	indicates the most general term in the hierarchy
RT: *Related Term*	indicates conceptual relationships between terms, not related hierarchically
CC: *Classification Code*	version of the INSPEC classification code as used in INSPEC Magnetic Tape Services. This indicates the subject area in which the particular term is commonly used.
FC: *Full Classification Code*	full version of the INSPEC classification code as input to the data base. This indicates the subject area in which the particular term is commonly used.

Two examples of *INSPEC Thesaurus* listings follow:

> DIELECTRIC THIN FILMS
> *see also ferroelectric thin films; insulating thin films;*
> *optical films; piezoelectric thin films*
> NT ferroelectric thin films
>   piezoelectric thin films
> BT thin films
> TT films
> RT dielectric materials
>   insulating thin films
>   optical films
>   polymer films
> CC A7755 B2830
> FC a7755 + rb2830-x
>
> dielectric triodes
>   USE space-charged limited devices

The programs written to retrieve information from computer-stored data bases nearly all make use of the Boolean logic operators "and," "or," and "not." With these machine-manipulated instructions, search commands which are highly sophisticated and very powerful examples of post-coordinate searching can be executed. For example, someone using the ERIC data base might want to examine material on the consumption of alcohol in clubs, at social gatherings, and the like, but not have to wade through all those discussing related problems of health. Using the *ERIC Thesaurus*, he or she could construct the search command "(Drinking *or* Alcoholic Beverages) *and* ((Activities *or* Recreational Activities) *not* (Health *or* Health Education))." Since the commands within parentheses are executed first, all documents indexed under the following rubrics would be retrieved:

Drinking *and* Activities *but not* Health
Drinking *and* Activities *but not* Health Education
Drinking *and* Recreational Activities *but not* Health
Drinking *and* Recreational Activities *but not* Health Education
Alcoholic Beverages *and* Activities *but not* Health
Alcoholic Beverages *and* Activities *but not* Health Education
Alcoholic Beverages *and* Recreational Activities *but not* Health
Alcoholic Beverages *and* Recreational Activities *but not* Health
   Education

As library catalogs go online, the allowable number of subject entries may increase, since the old storage and filing difficulties in large card files will likely prove less expensive and troublesome. Search programs built upon Boolean operators could then enhance subject retrieval, giving it a precision, breadth, and depth not possible in manual searching.

THE PRESERVED CONTEXT INDEXING SYSTEM (PRECIS)

In chapter 26 chain indexing was discussed in connection with classified catalog access. Chain indexes, while bearing a format resemblance to keyword indexes, usually are built upon a more selective, indexer-controlled vocabulary. They delete unnecessary context, and all subheadings are superordinate terms. Key entries are as specific as possible. Where they are hierarchically subordinate to broader terms in the search vocabulary, the next broader term is added for context. This type of alphabetical chain index was used for subject access to *The British National Bibliography* (*BNB*) from 1950 to 1970. Since then, a different system, based on a set of working procedures, rather than an established list of terms, has been used. It is called PRECIS, an acronym for Preserved Context Indexing System. Derek Austin states:

> The system is firmly based upon the concept of an open-ended
> vocabulary, which means that terms can be admitted into the index
> at any time, as soon as they have been encountered in literature.
> Once a term has been admitted, its relationships with other terms
> are handled in two different ways, distinguished as the syntactical
> and the semantic sides of the system.[10]

The Library of Congress developed its Machine Readable Cataloging (MARC) tapes in the mid-1960s. *BNB*, which is now part of the Bibliographic Services Division of the British Library, launched its cooperative UK/MARC Project in 1968. But *BNB* was not satisfied with the subject access provided by existing MARC fields, such as the title, DDC, and LC classification and subject heading fields. Drawing on its twenty-year chain indexing experience, it constructed a new system which, since the revisions adopted in 1974, has become a serious rival to traditional subject lists and catalogs.[11] Phyllis Richmond ran a two-year comparison of PRECIS with *Library of Congress*

Subject Headings (*LCSH*) and with KWIC index retrieval from the sample titles. She concluded that PRECIS can make subject material more accessible, both quantitatively and qualitatively, than either of the other two techniques:

> The indexing produced in these operations cannot be duplicated in either LCSH or . . . Keyword-in-Context methodology or even with both used together. . . . Aside from differences in the terminology used to convey concepts, which may be as much a matter of taste as of customary usage, the two greatest problems in all indexing are ambiguity and semantic confusion occasioned by inadequate context accompanying terms of dubious ancestry. These terms include homonyms, homographs, metaphor, allusion, neologisms and, of course, public words with private meanings. Lack of context in subject headings and the general unwillingness to add clarifying terms to titles in the various processes of indexing by title ensure the continuation of both problems. PRECIS stops them dead in their tracks.[12]

Austin often starts his descriptions of PRECIS with a series of negative points, to dispel misconceptions. It is not a fully computer-generated program, but requires human processing for preparation of input. It is not a subject heading list, but is characterized by a set of established procedures rather than a set of accepted terms. Also, it is not a library classification, although its computerized thesaurus, like those of the hierarchical indexing systems examined above, embodies certain principles of classification. PRECIS operates with an open-ended vocabulary, so that terms can be adopted as soon as they appear in the literature. Entries are pre-coordinated, context-dependent strings of terms in which each term is semantically defined and syntactically related by *see* and *see also* references to synonyms and other associated words of different specificity. A Reference Indicator Number (RIN) is the computer address where the particular term, plus all references to it, may be accessed.

From established index strings, with their separate terms and RINs, all of the verbal parts of a PRECIS index can be generated. For reasons of bulk and cost, actual bibliographic citations are not included in such indexes. Instead, citations are usually sequenced and systematically grouped elsewhere by serial number according to a classification scheme. For bibliographic records in the MARC Project, *BNB* provides each index string with a packet of subject data consisting of the string itself, a DDC number, an LC class number, LC subject headings as required, and the pertinent RINs to ensure appropriate cross references. A Subject Indicator Number (SIN) is then assigned as a computer address for each packet. The indexer does not write the chosen subject terms or strings on the worksheet of the item being cataloged. Rather, he or she tags the worksheet with the appropriate SINs and the document retrieval number. If a new topic, with new references, is needed in the thesaurus, the indexer makes the various necessary subject decisions, assigning corresponding RINs and SINs. The computer can perform all subsequent manipulation, such as alphabetizing, responding to subject requests, and generating output, at high speed.

Suppose, for instance, that an item to be cataloged is about the training of personnel in the cotton industries in India. The indexer would start by establishing a context-dependent, hierarchical concept string such as: "India — Cotton industries — Personnel — Training." The terms form a sequence in which, much as in a traditional subject heading, each is directly related to the next one in the string. Standard permutation (e.g., a KWIC index) would generate entries under each term as follows:

> INDIA. Cotton industries. Personnel. Training
> COTTON INDUSTRIES. Personnel. Training. India
> PERSONNEL. Training. India. Cotton industries
> TRAINING. India. Cotton industries. Personnel

Simple permutation indexes are most successful in retrieving natural language forms, such as book and article titles, or loosely controlled terminology such as that used in the indexes to the Library of Congress Classification schedules. For indexing subject materials with a controlled vocabulary and a high degree of entry concentration at given levels of specificity, something more sophisticated is needed. Indeed, simple KWOC transposition of each term to the entry position could raise serious ambiguities, as in the entry below under "Personnel," where directly dependent terms in the original string are no longer adjacent, which raises the question of whether the personnel are doing, or receiving, the training.

> INDIA. Cotton industries. Personnel. Training
> COTTON INDUSTRIES. India. Personnel. Training
> PERSONNEL. India. Cotton industries. Training
> TRAINING. India. Cotton industries. Personnel

To meet this inherent danger as economically and elegantly as possible, PRECIS uses a two-line print-out which can be diagramed:

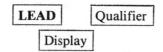

The Lead, as the filing element, is printed in boldface. The Qualifier position carries any broader term which gives the Lead context. Each successive Qualifier term broadens that context. The Display represents hierarchic movement in the opposite direction. Each successive Display term narrows the context. Not all entries must have Qualifier or Display terms attached. If the topic has no broader, or narrower, context, those positions are blank. Setting our example into the print-out matrix gives entries as shown on page 545.

When organizing terms into entries, indexers strive for consistency of lead concepts, and of the input order of qualifiers and displays. They can use either conventional visual code markings (e.g., a check-mark or "tick" marks the lead in such a compound term as "cotton industries"), or they can assign machine-readable manipulation codes for computer handling in automated systems.

INDIA
   Cotton industries. Personnel. Training

COTTON INDUSTRIES. India
   Personnel. Training

PERSONNEL. Cotton industries. India
   Training

TRAINING. Personnel. Cotton industries. India

The dollar sign ($) is a standard UK/MARC convention to distinguish certain instructions from the succeeding concept terms to which they apply. With it, two connective codes ("v" and "w") provide a defense against ambiguity in permuted entries. Thus, for such a topic as "the erosive effects of wind on rock" the indexer would code the lead terms in the string as follows:

rocks

erosion $v by $w of

winds

The three resulting index entries would be:

ROCKS
   Erosion by winds

EROSION. Rocks
   By winds

WINDS
   Erosion of rocks

Three other codes, called theme interlinks, identify the thematic role of each term in a given string. An "x" identifies the first element of any separate theme, while "y" identifies each component of any theme coded by a previous "x," and "z" identifies concepts common to all those themes which occur at the beginning or the end of a given string. Suppose the indexer is coding a document on two themes which share a common component, e.g., "Water as a contaminant of lubricating oils" and "Measuring the viscosity of lubricating oils." The terms would be coded:

(z) lubricating oils   (common term)

(x) contaminants $w of   (theme 1 term)

(y) water   (context dependent term in theme 1)

(x) viscosity   (theme 2 term)

(y) measurement   (context dependent term in theme 2)

The indexer has decided against using the term "measurement" in the lead, and accordingly has not ticked it. Index entries developed from this coding would include:

> LUBRICATING OILS
>   Contaminants. Water
>
> CONTAMINANTS. Lubricating oils
>   Water
>
> WATER. Contaminants of lubricating oils
>
> LUBRICATING OILS
>   Viscosity. Measurement
>
> VISCOSITY. Lubricating oils
>   Measurement

The table of role operators, reproduced on page 547,[13] gives the codes used to organize index strings. All operators except connectives and theme interlinks have syntactic or semantic roles in a string. Syntactic relationships give the overall meaning of the string by determining the order in which its component terms are set down. Semantic relationships exist between a specific concept and the group of interconnected ideas to which it belongs. *See* and *see also* references evolve from these connections. Syntactic and semantic operators provide the precision and consistency which allow permutation without loss or distortion of meaning.

In indexing for computer manipulation, main line operators identify the basic components of a compound subject and regulate the order in which they are written down. Interposed operators can appear between main line operators to increase specificity, but they cannot start a string. Differencing operators, being semantic rather than syntactic, identify the adjectives that fix a given term's connotation. A primary nine-character code precedes each subject element in the string. The function of each of the nine characters may be summarized as shown on page 548.

APPENDIX 1. ROLE OPERATORS

Main line operators

Environment of observed system	0 Location
Observed system (Core operators)	1 Key system: *object of transitive action; agent of intransitive action*
	2 Action/Effect
	3 Agent of transitive action; Aspects; Factors

A

Data relating to observer	4 Viewpoint as-form
Selected instance	5 Sample population/Study region
Presentation of data	6 Target/Form

Interposed operators

Dependent elements	p Part/Property
	q Member of quasi-generic group
	r Aggregate
Concept interlinks	s Role definer
	t Author attributed association
Coordinate concepts	g Coordinate concept

B

Differencing operators	h Non-lead direct difference
(prefixed by $)	i Lead direct difference
	j Salient difference
	k Non-lead indirect difference
	m Lead indirect difference
	n Non-lead parenthetical difference
	o Lead parenthetical difference
	d Date as a difference

Connectives

(Components of linking phrases; prefixed by $)	v Downward reading component
	w Upward reading component

C

Theme interlinks	x First element in coordinate theme
	y Subsequent element in coordinate theme
	z Element of common theme

1st — The primary code tag ($)

2nd — Theme interlink (no syntactical function)

    x — The first concept in a subtheme

    y — An element of a subtheme

    z — An element of the common theme

3rd — The main line role operator. Determines not only format but typography and punctuation. Terms introduced by numerical operators appear in the string in numerical order. Alphabetic operators follow other rules which determine their order in the string.

4th — Focus in lead

    0 — Not a lead term

    1 — A lead term

5th — Substitute phrase (when permutation requires a change of grammar)

    0 — Not a substitute

    1-9 — A substitute, suppressing the designated number of earlier terms when a later term appears as lead

6th — Display and Qualifier indicator

    0 — Do not print under preceding or following concept

    1 — Print under preceding, but not under following concept

    2 — Do not print under preceding concept; print under following concept

    3 — Print under both preceding and following concept

7th — Not yet used (0)

8th — The term code tag ($)

9th — The term code. Identifies type of term:

    a — Common noun: normal term not promoting any special action on the part of the computer

    b — Common noun, salient focus. Not yet used in practice

    c — Proper name: person or institution

    d — Place name[14]

The codes and subject terms used for the topic "training of personnel in the cotton industries in India" would be:

$z 0 103 0$d   India
$z 1 103 0$a   cotton industries
$z p 103 0$a   personnel
$z 2 103 0$a   training

As entered into the computer, the full string would be:

$z01030$dIndia$z11030$acotton industries$zp1030$apersonnel $z21030$atraining

The computer can be programmed to read such a string far easier and quicker than can the human eye. However, the coded strings can be visually analyzed as well. For the initial subject term of the above string, the first and second manipulation characters ($z) identify "India" as an element of the common theme. The third character (0) sets the environment or location as the broadest term in the string. Character 4 (1) ensures its use as a lead term. Character 5 (0) shows that there is no need to suppress earlier terms when they appear as a lead. Character 6 (3) represents a "normal" case in which the subject term is tagged to print under both the preceding and the following concept. The following concept in this string is "cotton industries," but there is no preceding concept. For proper computer manipulation, this position uses a special algorithm involving a double instruction by means of stacked codes.[15] Character 7 (0) is presently meaningless. The eighth and ninth characters ($d) form a "term" code identifying the term as a place name.

PRECIS strings sometimes include secondary codes consisting of only two characters, the $ tag and a differencing operator or connective. A secondary code applies only to the string element immediately following it. One of its functions is to ensure context dependency where one or more permutations requires reformatting in a non-standard way. The example "erosive effects of wind on rock" requires a type of reformatting called "predicate transformation." The fully coded string, using the secondary connective codes "$v" and "$w" to tag the reciprocal prepositions "by" and "of" would appear as follows:

$z11030$arocks$z21030$aerosionvbywof$z31030$awinds

PRECIS indexing has been applied successfully to all sorts of subject disciplines and formats: films, instructional aids, books, periodical articles, abstracts, technical reports, etc. In this brief review, many of its technical requirements and possibilities have been omitted. For instance, little or nothing has been said about the generation of cross-references. While it is a complex tool, developed to perform a complex job, its designers claim that beginners can learn to construct simple strings in a matter of hours. They freely admit that, like any human-based indexing system, it can never ensure that different indexers will arrive systematically at the same entries for the same document. However, it provides a climate of semantic control which fosters adaptability and creativity without degenerating into anarchy. At the same time, its syndetic structure, as represented in its three-part entry print-out, allows full statement of a compound subject under any of its significant terms without loss of either meaning or concepts. More than in any other known system of subject indexing, terminological access is both controlled and presented in a logical context.

There has been strong pressure in both Canada and the United States for libraries to adopt PRECIS as either a replacement for or a supplement to traditional subject headings. Valentina de Bruin reported in 1976, as one reason for the University of Toronto's decision to abandon *LCSH* in favor of PRECIS:

> Growing dissatisfaction among the staff with LC subject access, especially since it is realized that in a machine-readable environment we are tied to subject headings that resist change simply because they were not designed in the first place to be machine-readable and machine-manipulable. (Here I would like to acknowledge our great debt to *LCSH*, which, manifestly, has done a great job through the years. Gratitude, not denigration, is the keyword.)[16]

G. Donald Cook, addressing "The Practical Possibilities of PRECIS in North America," found that PRECIS assigned an average of 5.52, as compared to *LCSH*'s 4.09, distinctive words per bibliographic record. The average PRECIS string, without its manipulation codes, is some 25 percent longer than the average *LCSH* entry for the same record. He warned that in neither system would all such words serve as useful access points, but he affirmed that, with permutation, access through PRECIS is triple that through *LCSH*.[17]

In response to this type of comment, the Library of Congress conducted a feasibility study on the addition of PRECIS to its existing subject heading system when it closes its card catalogs to go online. While the study admittedly could not show the future level of public demand for PRECIS, it indicated that a suitably designed retrieval system using Boolean logic with existing MARC fields (title, subject, fixed fields, and the geographic area code) would usually give access to the same words provided in analogous PRECIS strings. Moreover, the number of subject headings per record would likely increase, once the 3x5-inch card ceased to dominate record formats. For those libraries wishing to continue their card catalogs, PRECIS entries, with their two-line formats, would waste space and PRECIS strings would be hard to read and interpret. But the major drawback was the anticipated cost. Forty-five additional catalogers and editors would be needed. Work space, salaries, and related costs would amount to approximately $1,000,000 per year. In view of the lack of user demand, the Library did not feel justified in asking Congress for the money to support two subject heading/indexing systems.[18] Not everyone is content with the decision,[19] but there is no evidence that it will be reconsidered.

An indexing technique similar to PRECIS is POPSI (Postulate-based Permuted Subject Indexing). This approach was developed at the Documentation Research and Training Centre in Bangalore, India, where Ranganathan was the director until his death. It is often thought to be a particular string index language associated with the Colon Classification. However, it can be applied to different languages, according to the postulates recognized. The postulates comprise the definitions and the rules of grammar or syntax, which control associative as well as hierarchical relationships. Both POPSI and PRECIS are rotated pre-coordinate indexing systems, but whereas PRECIS developed out of a set of linguistic terms and a thesaurus, POPSI indexing developed directly from classification schedules and chain indexing.[20]

SWITCHING LANGUAGES

We have made a cursory examination of a number of subject access systems available for use in modern library cataloging. Most are self-contained, providing their own categories and terminology, with syntactical rules designed to express complex or multi-faceted concepts. Each exhibits both strengths and weaknesses. Not one has yet proved sufficient to meet all needs, nor demonstrably better than all others in every situation. In consequence, a movement toward "switching languages" has emerged. Eric Coates tells us:

> The problem is thus to devise a mechanism for making index information, originally input in a particular indexing language, immediately usable by another institution employing a different indexing language. A possible answer to this problem has for some time been exercising French documentalists of the Groupe d'Etude sur l'Information Scientifique of the CRNS at Marseilles. The Groupe proposes what is variously called a mediating indexing language, an intermediate indexing language, or, by appropriating a term from another discipline (a procedure which in the long run indexers and vocabulary controllers may come to rue) a switching language.[21]

The information explosion, together with rapid developments in automation, made intercommunication among subject disciplines, libraries, and nations both a possibility and a growing necessity. With a multilateral translation program, materials already indexed would be more readily available, while libraries and information centers could avoid future duplication by joining systems of shared cataloging without discarding or revamping their own catalogs and indexes.

Many enthusiasts favored an umbrella classification, a coarse approach recognizing only two to four hierarchical levels, for use by several agencies to construct a cumulative thesaurus or to share indexing on a general level. One example is the Committee on Scientific and Technical Information's *COSATI Subject Category List*, a scheme of 22 broad research-oriented topical areas, each with one or two levels of subdivision. It is used by a number of government agencies and research organizations to order their abstracting and indexing tools, and for similar purposes. But the problems of depending on such an ad hoc system are obvious. Lacking breadth as well as specificity, it does not provide a satisfactory universal switching language.

Another effort, backed by the Fédération Internationale de Documentation (FID) and Unesco, has produced a subject code schedule called the Broad System of Ordering (BSO).[22] It is basically a classification system designed to serve as a switching mechanism between various indexing languages. Its proponents claim:

> A classification, more than any other form of indexing language, is amenable to easy, predictable, yet at the same time fully controlled updating. This is the essential ground upon which it is the preferred form of indexing language for the universal switching application. That existing universal classifications have failed, or are visibly failing, precisely in this respect does not vitiate the argument.[23]

Criteria established for BSO include flexibility, structural simplicity, and easy manipulation in either manual or automated information systems. In its present form it is an umbrella mechanism for shallow indexing and collocation of large blocks of related information, rather than for retrieving specific documents from different in-depth indexing systems.

Several other illuminating experiments have taken place. The interested student will have no trouble finding descriptions of most of them in the literature. Whether a single switching language can perform equally well at all levels of specificity remains to be seen. Meanwhile there are other, less ambitious attacks on the problem. Linda C. Smith reports an effort to "map" a portion of the *Medical Subject Headings* (MeSH), which the National Library of Medicine uses in its preparation of *Index Medicus*, to three other controlled vocabularies, namely *Subject Headings for Engineering* (SHE), used in *Engineering Index*; the *NASA Thesaurus*, used for *Scientific and Technical Aerospace Reports* (STAR); and *Subject Headings Used by the USAEC*. She explains:

> The alternative to a master switching language is to work with the individual vocabularies themselves, identifying terms from the two vocabularies used to index identical concepts and establishing such terms as equivalent for searching. While this device has been variously labelled in the literature as a table of equivalents or concordance, the mechanism to be used in converting from terms in one vocabulary to those in another is more rigorously defined by the mathematical concept of mapping. Since it is possible to mechanize only that which can be explicitly defined, it is useful to view the mapping as an algorithm for translating the terms of one vocabulary into equivalent terms used by another.[24]

This particular effort was only partially successful. Test searches showed that *Index Medicus* alone could retrieve 81 percent of the materials retrieved through mapping all four sources. Where the mapping increased the number of documents retrieved, some loss of precision occurred. The experiment did suggest possible alternative approaches to the clerical conversion of terms from one index language to another. This and other programs for machine translation and automated index transformations are still in the developmental stage.

AUTOMATED CLASSIFICATION

Closely related to the above proposals are efforts to apply computer techniques to the process of classification. These focus primarily on two areas.

Automated methods for devising a classification system. Most traditional classification schemes are based on a logical division of the universe of knowledge. By contrast, computer-based classification systems are empirical and descriptive, attempting to develop thesauri with but one thing in common: a set of descriptors well suited to manipulation (e.g., a title or a synthetic class number). The descriptors are then used to generate additional entries by a set pattern. A number of mathematical techniques are applicable to the subject analysis of a given document. It is possible to evaluate subject content of two documents by characterizing each as a list of shared content work terms (keywords). Subsets may be derived by means of the "theory of CLUMPS," which is based on a Boolean lattice model. Experimentation in this area at the Cambridge Language Research Unit seems promising.[25] Subsets are also derived by factor analysis, which is a form of martrix algebra; Borko and Bernier combined factor analysis to derive a classification system with a factor score technique to classify documents by machine into their proper categories.[26] Initial studies indicate that these automatically produced categories are reasonably descriptive of the document collection.

Automated methods of classifying documents. This research requires specific mathematical procedures for computing the probability of a document's belonging to a designated category. Such methods include Baysian prediction formulas, factor scores, latent class analysis, information theory measures, discriminant analysis, several types of linguistic analysis, and the use of citations.

CONCLUSION

It is encouraging to note that a great deal of effort still goes into improving methods of information retrieval, both through classificatory arrangements and through more random, or at least more arbitrary, linguistic and alphabetical approaches. The purpose of this chapter has been to carry forward an examination of linguistic indexing theory and practice from the traditional library subject heading list, with its controlled and pre-coordinated vocabulary, to various other techniques, most of which are venerable, but many of which exhibit refinements, with ingenious new modes of implementation.

Modern systems such as chain indexes, string indexes, and most abstracting and indexing tools in technology and the sciences, generally incorporate familiar features, such as hierarchical ordering of terms, vocabulary control and cross referencing, or the use of Boolean logic for post-coordinate searching. Controlled vocabulary subject lists have long tolerated various stylized forms of modifier inversion and thematic subordination. Certain theorists charge that classification is thereby surreptitiously introduced into techniques ostensibly based on the principle of specific entry. KWIC and KWOC permutations incorporate the older catchword principle of freely using terminology found in indexed documents or their titles. Computers tend to increase significantly the number of access terms available in such catchword systems, but they also increase the hazards of an uncontrolled vocabulary. Such indexes are more adapted to title or abstract searching than to in-depth subject analysis of full texts. Truncation searching on cognate words with identical first syllables is another device whose power is significantly increased by computerization, although it similarly opens the gate to much useless, or unwanted, drops.

A significant body of theoretical, as well as practical, literature on subject and document retrieval has been produced. Dagobert Soergel argues that the goal of indexing is to develop a thesaurus with a set of descriptors as the essential ingredient of any controlled language, classification scheme, or system vocabulary.[27] In his view, conceptual structure and terminological control are dependent on neither the indexing approach (human or mechanized) nor on the technical devices employed (e.g., alphabetical book or card catalogs, peek-a-boo or key-sort devices, etc.). These uses are secondary to the successful construction and maintenance of the thesaurus.

Borko and Bernier attempt to consolidate indexing theory with a list of measures for evaluating the characteristics and quality of bibliographical retrieval systems.[28] Their criteria include such features as size, arrangement, and accuracy (e.g., the percentage of correctly spelled entries). However, as we saw in Chapter 26, not all students of the problem are convinced that linguistic indexing need be the most rewarding. Coates and his colleagues remind us that an indexing language can influence the indexer to apply rigorous concept analysis to the data, or, alternatively, allow him or her to fall away into mere verbal level analysis.[29]

The egregious diversity and lack of standardization in information retrieval may continue to cost us confusion, time, and money in the foreseeable future. Still, the analytical, competitive atmosphere is, on the whole, encouraging and healthy. Most of this chapter emphasizes techniques which combine machine manipulation with human monitoring and input. However, there are services which rely almost exclusively on automated routines. A detailed discussion of the more promising ones should be an integral part of any advanced course in subject retrieval.

FOOTNOTES

[1]John Rothman, "Index, Indexer, Indexing," in *Encyclopedia of Library and Information Science*, Vol. 11 (New York, Marcel Dekker, 1974), p. 289.

[2]Mortimer Taube and Associates, *Studies in Coordinate Indexing* (Washington, Documentation, Incorporated, 1953).

[3]A. C. Foskett, *The Subject Approach to Information*, 3rd ed. (London, Clive Bingley; Hamden, CT, Linnet Books, 1977), p. 383.

[4]Foskett, *Subject Approach*, p. 43.

[5]Hans Peter Luhn, "Keyword in Context Index for Technical Literature (KWIC Index)," *American Documentation* 11 (1960):288-95.

[6]Nancy B. Olson, *Combined Indexes to the Library of Congress Classification Schedules* (Washington, United States Historical Documents Institute, 1974), "Set V—Subject Keyword Index," 6v.

[7]*Thesaurus of Psychological Index Terms*, 2nd ed. (Washington, American Psychological Association, 1977), p. ii.

[8]*Thesaurus of ERIC Descriptors*, 7th ed. (New York, Macmillan Information; London, Collier Macmillan, 1977), pp. 59-60.

[9]*INSPEC Thesaurus*, 1977 [3rd ed.] (London, Institution of Electrical Engineers, 1976), p. 83.

[10]Derek Austin, "Progress in Documentation: The Development of PRECIS; A Theoretical and Technical History," *Journal of Documentation* 30:47 (March 1974). In addition to this excellent article, the serious student is referred to: Derek Austin, *PRECIS: A Manual of Concept Analysis and Subject Indexing* (London, The Council of the British National Bibliography, 1974); and *The PRECIS Index System: Principles, Applications, and Prospects*, Proceedings of the International PRECIS Workshop, ed. by Hans H. Wellisch (New York, H. W. Wilson, 1977).

[11]Derek Austin and Jeremy A. Digger, "PRECIS: The Preserved Context Index System," *Library Resources & Technical Services* 21 (Winter 1977):13-30.

[12]Phyllis A. Richmond, "PRECIS Compared with Other Indexing Systems," in *The PRECIS Index System*, p. 113.

[13]Austin, *PRECIS*, p. 423.

[14]Adapted from: Derek Austin, "Management Aspects of PRECIS, and Current Research and Development," in *The PRECIS Index System*, p. 63.

[15]*Austin, PRECIS*, pp. 252, 440.

[16]Valentine De Bruin, "PRECIS in a University Library," in *The PRECIS Index System*, p. 143.

[17]C. Donald Cook, "The Practical Possibilities of PRECIS in North America," in *The PRECIS Index System*, p. 189.

[18]*Library of Congress Information Bulletin* 37 (March 3, 1978):154.

[19]*See*, for instance: Mary Dykstra, "The Lion That Squeaked: A Plea to the Library of Congress to Adopt the British PRECIS System, and to Reconsider the Decision to Overhaul the LC Subject Headings," *Library Journal* 103 (Sept. 1, 1978):1570-72.

[20]G. Bhattacharyya and A. Neelameghan, "Postulate-Based Subject Heading for Dictionary Catalogue System," in Documentation Research and Training Centre, *Annual Seminar* 7 (1969):221-54; and G. Bhattacharyya, "Chain Procedure and Structuring of a Subject," *Library Science with a Slant to Documentation* 9:585-635 (1972).

[21]Eric J. Coates, "Switching Languages for Indexing," *Journal of Documentation* 26 (June 1970):103.

[22]Eric J. Coates, et al., *BSO, Broad System of Ordering: Schedule and Index* (The Hague, IFLA; Paris, Unesco, 1978).

[23]Eric J. Coates, et al., *The BSO Manual: The Development, Rationale and Use of the Broad System of Ordering* (The Hague, FID, 1979), p. 35.

[24]Linda A. Smith, "Systematic Searching of Abstracts and Indexes in Interdisciplinary Areas," *Journal of the American Society for Information Science* 25 (Nov.-Dec. 1974):344.

[25]Karen Sparck Jones, "CLUMPS, Theory of," in *Encyclopedia of Library and Information Science*, Vol. 5 (New York, Marcel Dekker, 1971), pp. 208-224.

[26]H. Borko, "Research in Computer Based Classification Systems," in *Classification Research: Proceedings of the Second International Study Conference* (Copenhagen, Munksgaard, 1965), pp. 220-57.

[27]Dagobert Soergel, *Indexing Languages and Thesauri: Construction and Maintenance* (Los Angeles, Melville Publishing Company, c1974), p. 4.

[28]Harold Borko and Charles L. Bernier, *Indexing Concepts and Methods* (New York, Academic Press, 1978), pp. 211-12.

[29]Coates, et al., *The BSO Manual*, p. 55.

Part IV — Organization

30 CENTRALIZED PROCESSING AND NETWORKING

INTRODUCTION

Because of such problems as the growth in volume of published materials, the emphasis on rapid transfer of documents and bibliographic records from producer to consumer, and the resultant need for more and better library service, traditional patterns of cataloging and processing are changing significantly. Most libraries and library systems of any size have either centralized their technical services or entered into cooperative arrangements with other libraries. Smaller institutions usually purchase most of their processing from commercial vendors or non-commercial suppliers such as the Library of Congress. In fact, for nearly all American libraries, LC has long been the primary source of bibliographical data, since most other vendors, as well as cooperative and locally centralized processors, merely repackage or reformat LC products. Generally, original cataloging is undertaken only if the Library of Congress has for some reason not cataloged the work at hand. Major processing offices usually have two production lines operating side-by-side. The bigger one, staffed by well-trained technicians called "copy catalogers," works from LC records in machine-readable form, reproduced on printed cards or proofslips, in the *National Union Catalog*, or elsewhere. Only a handful of professionally trained "original catalogers" prepare the non-LC records.

TYPES OF PROCESSING CENTERS

Historically, each library service unit was responsible for its own ordering, cataloging, and the physical preparation of materials. Administrative efforts to increase efficiency and economy gradually substituted larger, or more coordinated, programs which took various experimental forms. The introduction and rapid growth of automation, while essentially unrelated, soon exercised a powerful influence over the development and success of those programs.

CENTRALIZED PROCESSING

In integrated library systems serving an entire region, county, municipality, university, public school district, commercial enterprise, or government agency, a central processing office normally handles the acquisition and preparation of materials for all public service branches. Subunits may do a final checking of records and file those records in their branch catalogs, but if any significant revision of the work is needed, it usually goes back to the central office. Although this type of organization is by no means new, it received strong emphasis with the rapid growth of library systems after World War II.

The term "centralized processing" may be broadly defined as any consolidated effort to bring under one control the technical operations necessary to prepare library materials for access and use at different service points. In the ensuing discussion several comments will be made which apply equally well — perhaps with some slight modification — to cooperative efforts and even to commercial sources of cataloging. The reader can carry over such observations into those discussions where they have a bearing.

Processing centers take a variety of forms, but can generally be grouped into broad categories according to one or more notable characteristics. Grouping by type of services rendered gives: 1) centers responsible for acquisition and complete technical processing, down to the physical marking and/or jacketing, 2) centers that order, catalog, and classify, and 3) centers that only catalog and classify.

Some of the factors that determine the character of a processing center and the type of services it renders are:

1. Population to be served
2. Standards of previous cataloging practice
3. Types of services desired by the system's branches (e.g., cataloging only versus complete processing)
4. Budget size and allocations
5. Size, competency, and deployment of staff
6. Amount of and restrictions on local, state, and federal monies available for establishing, and possibly continuing, the center
7. Willingness to adopt uniform policies and procedures that are needed to achieve the efficiency and economics of a given operation

Librarians cite many arguments for processing centers. These are often directly related to local needs and practices, or to preliminary descriptive surveys, which tend toward enthusiasm about the administrative and economic advantages. There are a few studies of theoretically desirable models giving optimum requirements for such operations, but reports of "How Our System Succeeded" predominate, showing little or no attempt at generalized conclusions.[1]

There are, of course, advantages to setting up a processing center for a group of libraries or branches. They include:

1. Increased efficiency in handling more material at less cost
2. Higher quality cataloging
3. Centralization and simplification of business routines
4. Better deployment of staff through specialization
5. Use of more sophisticated equipment
6. Opportunities to create union catalogs

But there are problems as well. Local variations in practice have to be identified and coordinated, or, if necessary, eliminated. Economic justification must be carefully determined, both before and after decision-making, to ensure that it is real, not imaginary. Many descriptive reports of individual centers lack critical self-appraisal and follow-up studies, especially in their cost analyses. Efficiency of operation is often the function of size. The "optimum" volume of processing in a given center should be determined. Combining several different types of libraries (e.g., school and public) within one system may lead to problems which even a highly structured organization cannot solve. We often learn as much from our failures as from our more successful attempts at consolidation.

COOPERATIVE SYSTEMS

The chief trait differentiating cooperative from centralized processing is that the cooperative approach involves several independent libraries or systems. Each member usually continues to perform some of its own technical service work, depending on exchange of data to achieve broader coverage, or leaving a sizeable portion of its processing to be performed as a group project. Again, better use of resources, personnel, and equipment, as well as higher discounts on bulk purchases, is anticipated. The need for more standardization in ordering, cataloging, and processing may become either an advantage or a disruptive factor.

COMMERCIAL PROCESSING

Over a century ago, Charles C. Jewett, librarian of the Smithsonian Institution, proposed "A Plan for Stereotyping Catalogues by Separate Titles. . . ." The Smithsonian was at that time a copyright depository. As it produced bibliographic records, they could, he suggested, be preserved on stereotype plates for a variety of applications, including the printing of cards for sale to other libraries on demand. While Jewett's proposal did not itself endure, it presaged the marketing of printed cards undertaken by the Library of Congress in 1901. Neither venture was "commercial" in the strict sense.

However, they were later imitated by a host of business concerns. Barbara Westby defines "commercial cataloging" as "centralized cataloging performed and sold by a non-library agency operating for profit."[2] In most cases it is a by-product of other commercial interests, e.g., the Standard Catalog compilations of H. W. Wilson, the vending emphasis of a book jobber such as Baker & Taylor, or the promotional activities of a corporation like the Society for Visual Education.

The Wilson Printed Catalog Card Service supplied many school and public libraries with simple but adequate card copy at nominal cost for widely-read books from 1938 to 1975. During that period over one hundred other distributors and publishers followed the Wilson example of supplying a packet of cards with each book sold. In 1969 *LRTS* published a directory giving names, addresses, and specifications for the cards available from some 85 commercial processing firms.[3] Many are no longer in the business, or have radically changed their character. An updated list of processing services is in Appendix D of Dowell's *Cataloging with Copy*. Technological advances are responsible for much of the change. Books-With-Cards gave way to Cataloging-in-Publication, which will be discussed later in this chapter. Catalog card vendors began to supplant or supplement their print services with microform or even online data retrieval systems which promised greater speed at reduced cost.[4] Now, changes occur so rapidly that no reliable recommendations of particular systems or services can be made, but the Commercial Processing Services Committee of the Resources and Technical Services Division (RTSD) does offer a set of guidelines that any cataloger interested in making an intelligent choice should apply.[5]

UNION CATALOGS

Union catalog projects are not, strictly speaking, a type of processing arrangement, but they are essential to a successful processing center, and can be the *sine qua non* of a bibliographic research center. For example, the Bibliographical Center for Research (BCR) in Denver started in 1936 with a WPA grant to develop a union catalog based on a depository set of Library of Congress cards marked to show the holdings of member libraries in the Rocky Mountain area. The catalog was designed chiefly to serve BCR as a clearinghouse for regional interlibrary loans. In 1975, after a period of waning membership and reduced revenues, new objectives were announced, including the brokerage of OCLC services, with aid to members in other, related fields of communication, systems study, and network stimulation. The union catalog and interlibrary loan (ILL) services continued, but were de-emphasized in favor of newer forms of cooperation. As at BCR, most union catalog projects in printed card form are now valued primarily for having fostered early efforts at library cooperation which are presently coming to fruition in many kinds of consortia and networks.

BIBLIOGRAPHIC SERVICES
OF THE LIBRARY OF CONGRESS

In 1975 the Card Division of the Library of Congress changed its name to the Cataloging Distribution Service.[6] The change reflected a trend from print to machine-readable format (i.e., MARC tapes) in its distribution of bibliographic records. The print formats are still widely used. We have LC's assurance that they will continue after its own card catalogs are closed on January 1, 1981.[7] This distribution of print formats includes the sale of proof-sheets as well as printed cards, the distribution of a limited number of card depository sets, the Cataloging-in-Publication (CIP) program, the publication of book catalogs and cataloging tools, including the *National Union Catalog* (*NUC*), various bibliographies, the *Library of Congress Classification* schedules, *Library of Congress Subject Headings*, *New Serial Titles*, *Name Headings with References*, etc. The Library also maintains the *NUC* on cards.

LIBRARY OF CONGRESS CARDS

LC printed cards offer complete coverage for materials, both foreign and domestic, cataloged by the Library. It is of course the copyright depository for domestic works. Two federal legislative acts have significantly increased its coverage of foreign materials in the past two decades. First, the 1958 Dingell Amendment to Public Law 83-480 – "The Agricultural Trade Development and Assistance Act" – added Section 104-n to Title I, authorizing the use of foreign "soft" currencies to acquire selected materials and help pay for their cataloging in U.S. libraries and research centers. Since it was funded in 1962 this act has improved LC's bibliographic control over materials from Indonesia, India, Pakistan, the United Arab Republic, Israel, Yugoslavia, etc., where the book trades and national bibliographies are still developing.

Second, "The Higher Education Act" of 1965 (Public Law 89-329), amended to include Title II-C, further authorized LC to acquire, catalog, and distribute bibliographic records for all materials of research value published in foreign countries. The thrust of the legislation was once more to benefit not only the Library of Congress, but all American research libraries. It was called the National Program for Acquisitions and Cataloging (NPAC). To expedite this program several acquisitions and cataloging offices were opened abroad. They accepted ISBD descriptive cataloging from each national bibliography as a standard, with the modifications needed for consistency with LC format. The shared cataloging from this program is identified by initials of the foreign offices (e.g., GB, C, F, GRF, USSR, Aus, It, SW, etc.). They do much to increase the output and international coverage of LC cards.

Most of today's card output is produced on demand from MARC tapes, and packaged by machine through use of automated optical scanning equipment, although orders for non-MARC cards must still be filled manually from inventory stocks. The pamphlet, *Catalog Cards*, available on request, gives information on how to open an account and interpret the various order codes and pricing structures. Standard order slips of the kind reproduced below are furnished free to subscribers; multiple order forms compatible with LC optical character recognition devices are available from all major library supply houses.

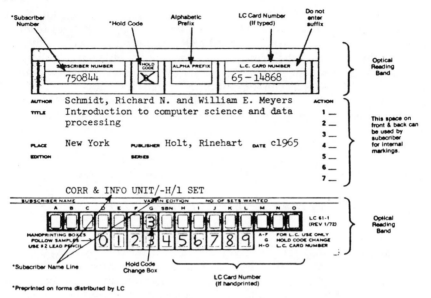

Ordering by LC card number rather than by author or title is more economical, and usually more satisfactory. This number can be found in standard bibliographies and book selection tools, such as the *Cumulative Book Index* (*CBI*), the *Weekly Record* (*WR*), the *American Book Publishing Record* (*BPR*), *Library Journal* (*LJ*), etc. It is also included, along with CIP data, on the title-page verso of most current books.

Proof sheets are copies of new LC cards issued on paper strips, five cards to a sheet. They can be purchased in either galley form or cut and punched to 3x5-inch card size. They are grouped by broad subject categories corresponding in general to the main classes of LC classification. Many libraries use them to select materials, and to become quickly aware of what the Library of Congress is cataloging. They appear sooner than the *NUC*, though not until *after* the cards are printed, thus belying their "proofsheet" designation. While they do not include copy for audiovisual media, maps, revised reprints, history, and information titles, or Chinese, Japanese, and Korean language titles, they may now be selectively ordered for current MARC English titles, MARC non-English titles, or non-MARC titles.

Depository card sets were formerly maintained by many research libraries, but the *NUC* now serves the same purpose at very real economy of both filing time and storage space. Only about fifty ARL libraries cooperating in the NPAC and Shared Cataloging programs still receive and maintain depository files of cards for noting LC omissions and cooperating to achieve increased catalog coverage for foreign publications.

CATALOGING-IN-PUBLICATION

Most current American books carry a partial bibliographic description, namely author, title, series statement, notes, subject and added entries, LC call number, DDC number, and LC card number, on the verso of the title page. Approximately 1,500 publishers now cooperate by sending galley proofs to the Library of Congress for preliminary cataloging prior to publication of their books. CIP records are available on MARC tapes, being later supplanted when the full record becomes machine-readable. The number of titles so handled since the program was initiated in 1971 is well over 100,000. It is useful as a ready source of LC card numbers, for authoritative establishment of name headings, and for libraries doing "fast-cat" preliminary, or full, cataloging prior to, or instead of, acquiring full LC records. The illustration below shows the format and appearance of CIP data. *See also* the verso of the title page of this textbook.

Copyright © 1978, American Library Association,
Canadian Library Association,
and The Library Association

Library of Congress Cataloging in Publication Data

Main entry under title:

Anglo-American cataloguing rules.
    Includes index.
    1. Descriptive cataloging—Rules. I. Gorman,
Michael, 1941–   II. Winkler, Paul Walter.
III. American Library Association.
Z694.A5   1978   025.3'2   78-13789
ISBN 0-8389-3210-X
ISBN 0-8389-3211-8 pbk.

LC BOOK PUBLICATIONS DISPLAYING CATALOGING

A wealth of bibliographic information can be obtained from the printed catalogs of the Library of Congress. The *Catalog of Books Represented by Library of Congress Printed Cards Issued to July 31, 1942* has been continued by cumulative serial publication of the *NUC*. A separate retrospective set, the *National Union Catalog, pre-1956 Imprints*, is nearly completed. Library of Congress book catalogs include *Audiovisual Materials; Music, Books on Music, and Sound Recordings; Monographic Series*; and the *Subject Catalog*.

MACHINE-READABLE CATALOGING (MARC)

The importance of the Library of Congress for setting catalog practice became even more evident with the introduction of the MARC Distribution Service. The initial study began in 1964; since that time, extensive experimentation has proceeded in the MARC I and MARC II, the Retrospective Conversion (RECON), the Cooperative Machine-Readable Cataloging (COMARC), and the British UK/MARC pilot projects.[8] MARC has been instrumental in establishing International Standard Bibliographic Description as the accepted format for the exchange of bibliographic data (e.g., SUPERMARC, UNIMARC, and INTERMARC). It has recently joined the Research Libraries Information Network (RLIN) in building a data base as a tool for describing the elements of, and maintaining specifications for, an integrated U.S. MARC format.[9] In the course of expansion, conflicts in element descriptions or examples have inadvertently shown up in the various formats for books, films, manuscripts, maps, music, and serials. The Library of Congress is editing out these and other discrepancies, adding comments on tag repeatability and current format practice. New editions of the MARC formats will then be published.

At first, records were available only for English-language monographs, but they now go online for all the formats just named plus nearly all monographic works in some 130 roman alphabet languages.[10] The MARC data base now includes approximately one million records.

The MARC Retriever Search Service permits anyone to utilize MARC's bibliographic resources on a fee basis as computer time becomes available. The user may request searches on the contents of any variable field, subfield, or fixed field, as well as on specific tags, indicators, and subfield code values. Searches have been made for books published by a particular firm, for books in translation published after 1969, for records having the word "Early" in any subject added entry, etc. A new program, Janus, provides sequential batch searching in either the internal MARC format or the Multiple Use MARC System (MUMS). A text retrieval facility, the Subject-Context-Oriented Retriever for Processing Information On-Line (SCORPIO) is presently expanding the number of data bases (e.g., *Congressional Record Abstracts*) on which it is operational.[11]

The Conversion of Serials (CONSER) automated data base was sponsored by the Council on Library Resources, using the online facilities of OCLC, and distributed through the MARC Distribution Service—Serials. Starting in mid-1976 with the nearly 30,000 LC/MARC serial records, and accepting input from fourteen North American libraries, it amassed over 200,000 records in its initial two years. Only one-third of them were authenticated by the Library of Congress and the National Library of Canada (the Designated Centers of Responsibility), but the number of verifications increased each year. Original plans were for LC to take over full support at the close of the two-year pilot program, but when it ran into difficulties in expanding its automation capacity, OCLC agreed to retain the data base, assuming managerial responsibility as well. The *MARC Serials Editing Guide: CONSER*

Edition will continue to govern all future input, and the Library of Congress will maintain its current staff and bibliographic support of the work.

The growth and nearly universal acceptance of the MARC formats, and even more, the publication of *AACR 2*, have highlighted the need for machine-readable authority records. Using the format in *Name Headings with References*, the Library of Congress is now converting retrospective manual authority records, for which the only source citation will be the work for which the heading was originally established, plus any biographical or historical information from any cited source.[12] Coding has also begun for *AACR 2* records, as well as for those which are "*AACR 2*-compatible." The authority records are marked accordingly. If the heading does not fit *AACR 2*, a cross reference tracing from the *AACR 2* form is included with the warning: "Do not make until used." During 1978, 78,369 name authority records were verified and 714 more updated. The cumulative total of machine-readable authority records at that time was 87,918.[13]

ONLINE BIBLIOGRAPHIC NETWORKING

Various definitions of networking spell out theoretical criteria or conditions. In practice, however, the term covers any systematic interchange of materials, bibliographic data, services, information, or occasionally, the transfer of such resources from a central office to a number of libraries. "Network" has been used to describe multi-library organizations designed to facilitate inter-library loan, reference, duplicate exchange, processing, and the like. Our concern in this section is with the last named activity.

There are at present three major online bibliographic networks in the United States: OCLC, Inc., the Research Libraries Information Network (RLIN), and the Washington Library Network (WLN). The Network Development Office of the Library of Congress uses the term "bibliographic utility" for these and other online processing systems of individual libraries such as that of the University of Chicago, and Northwestern University's NOTIS (Northwestern On-line Totally Integrated System).[14] This term distinguishes originators of computerized cataloging from bibliographic service centers, e.g., the Southeastern Library Network (SOLINET) and the New England Library Information Network (NELINET), which serve as regional brokers, providing intermediate communication, training, and service for participating libraries. The possibility of such a service center's becoming a utility is not precluded if it later assumes the responsibility of maintaining some component of a national library network data store.[15]

Bibliographic utilities seek to make catalog data widely and conveniently available, to foster processing speed and efficiency, to reduce the staff and cost of technical operations, and to facilitate resource sharing. Emphasis varies with the types of library a utility is designed to serve. RLIN, for example, caters to the needs of major research libraries, while OCLC appeals to a wider spectrum. As most bibliographic utilities evolved, their goals broadened to include support for different library functions. An intriguing recent possibility is providing services direct to the user. OCLC, for example, has participated through interactive cable television in a "Home Book Club" discussion series, which it hopes eventually will lead to an expanded Home Delivery of Library Services Program.[16]

Although the objectives of the three major bibliographic utilities are similar, their services, costs, and operating procedures differ considerably. Each offers unique features that involve advantages and disadvantages for different members. The library that has potential access to more than one network must consider carefully such factors as cost, size of data base, adaptation to its needs, types of service contracts, training and support arrangements, and the membership among neighboring libraries. If and when a national library network data store is completed, it will provide an interface to the data bases of all utilities regardless of an individual library's primary affiliation.

OCLC, Inc.

This oldest and largest of the bibliographic networks was incorporated in 1967 as the Ohio College Library Center, establishing an online, shared cataloging system with an online union catalog to the academic libraries of Ohio. Operations began in 1971 and expanded rapidly. By July 1979 there were 1,923 member libraries throughout the country, cataloging 94 percent of their incoming materials through use of the existing online records, and inputting their original catalog records for cooperative use by other members. In 1978 it changed its name to the present initialism, downplaying the former regional connotation. At the same time, the governing structure was altered to allow libraries outside Ohio equal participation in its governance. A Users' Council of nearly sixty members, elected from participants grouped in the regional service networks, chooses from among its members six of the fifteen who serve on the Board of Trustees. The Users' Council also advises the Board, which is the corporation's governing body.[17]

OCLC serves individual libraries for the most part through broker networks such as AMIGOS, NELINET, SOLINET, SUNY, and BCR. Although there are scattered independent members, only the western states have a regional service center maintained by OCLC itself. Even the original Ohio libraries have now formed OHIONET. The brokers negotiate group contracts on behalf of their affiliates, perform profiling and staff training according to each one's specific needs, handle billing and other business procedures, and offer general assistance in effective utilization of OCLC services. Most regional networks are financed through membership fees plus surcharges on OCLC's first-time use charges.

The primary OCLC service has always been the Online Cataloging Subsystem. Because of its widespread use, it will be described briefly here, but this overview is not intended to be a full introduction to its operation.[18] A library using the subsystem has access to a data base that numbers over five and one-half million bibliographic records, for which there are over forty million locations listed. LC MARC tapes and additional cataloging by affiliates are constantly expanding the data base. An authorized library staff member at any one of the 2,600 CRT (cathode ray tube) terminals in the system may access any record, then edit the data to agree with the book being processed, and add holdings statements, locations, or other in-house data, requesting catalog cards as specified in the library's predetermined profile. Cards are produced offline at OCLC headquarters in Columbus, Ohio, and shipped daily to members. They come arranged in packs according to member specifications, ready for immediate filing in local catalogs. Over two million are produced for the 300,000 new records input and the existing record copies ordered each week. Other products available from the system are magnetic tapes carrying records in the MARC format and local accessions lists. Offline COM (Computer-Output-in-Microform) catalog production, as well as online local catalogs, are planned for future development.

In addition to the 2,600 CRTs, more than 400 authorized institutions use asynchronous print terminals through either direct dial-up telephones or the TYMNET network. The data base may be searched by personal or corporate author (including added as well as main entries), author/title, title, series title, LC card number, OCLC control number, ISBN, ISSN, or CODEN. As yet there is no subject access to the file, chiefly because of the enormous computing power needed to provide it on so large a data base for so many simultaneous users. OCLC continues to study subject access, and intends to make it available as soon as it becomes economically feasible.

All records appear in MARC formats, including books, serials, AV media, kits and special instructional materials, manuscripts, maps, music scores, and sound recordings. OCLC also uses a MARC-type format for realia, for which there is not yet an official Library of Congress format. There are, of course, standard protocols for cataloging at the OCLC terminals. For one, member libraries are obliged to follow the *Anglo-American Cataloguing Rules* (*AACR 2* beginning January 1981). However, the system is highly flexible, allowing members to adapt local records to meet local practices and conventions.

Quality control exists in published standards to which participating libraries are expected to adhere. Participants are encouraged to report any errors they find in the data base. OCLC staff members check and correct the master records from these reports. Eventually certain authorized libraries (e.g., the Library of Congress) will be able to correct errors directly. Unnecessary duplication of records has been a problem. Some 9 percent of the new entries fall into this category, although MARC records, when received, replace some duplicates. OCLC is developing an algorithm with which not only new duplicates, but those already in the system, can be detected.

Consultation of training manuals, and above all, hands-on use, are needed to gain skill in tagging worksheets and operating the terminals. Most people who have been properly trained find the techniques simple to master. Suggested sources for further information include OCLC's *Online Systems. Cataloging: User Manual* and other texts produced by participating networks. SOLINET offers an excellent self-instructional package on audio tape, which a student can use independently. It must be remembered, however, that the

Online Catalog Subsystem is constantly developing and changing. Only recent tools should be used. In fact, it is often necessary to supplement published manuals with the serial, *OCLC Technical Bulletins*, and their accompanying documentation to learn the latest instructions for using the system.

In mid-1979 first-time cataloging charges were set at $1.25 for the use of a record in the data base. A 6 percent discount reduced the charge to $1.17 if paid annually in advance. The 3.6 cents per printed card cost is subject to a similar discount. These fees do not of course cover communications line fees, regional service network surcharges, and the like.

Although the subsystem is designed specifically for cataloging support, online access to a bibliographic data base of nearly six million records is in fact a general service resource. Other subsystems are being introduced which interface with it, or use it as a point of reference. A Serials Check-In Subsystem was activated in 1977, but is still used only by a small portion of the membership. The Inter-Library Loan (ILL) Subsystem was field-tested in 1979, with evidence that it would be widely utilized. The Acquisitions Subsystem was developing well with field tests planned for late 1979. The Board of Trustees voted at its December 1979 meeting to implement a long-anticipated online Circulation Subsystem.

RESEARCH LIBRARIES INFORMATION NETWORK (RLIN)

RLIN resulted from adoption of Stanford University's Bibliographic Automation of Large Library Operations (BALLOTS) by the Research Libraries Group (RLG). RLG, Inc. was originally formed in 1976 by Columbia, Harvard, and Yale universities, and the New York Public Library. Harvard withdrew at the time RLIN was formed, to be replaced by Stanford University. As of June 1979 the membership totalled eleven research libraries, with more being actively recruited.[19] In addition, over 200 other institutions, including several law and art libraries, were purchasing its services.[20]

The corporate objective is to foster inter-institutional support of scholarly communication and instruction in a rapidly changing climate of increasing costs and shrinking resources. Sixteen voting officers are elected annually by the member institutions to a Board of Directors. Together with the President — RLG's executive officer whom the Board elects and who then serves on the Board ex officio — they establish policies, programs, budgets, and fee structures, and appoint committees. Over them is a Board of Governors, to which each member library sends a representative. At its quarterly meetings it reviews the actions of the Board of Directors, as well as those of other officers and committees.

The primary programs of RLG are shared access to materials, collection management and cooperative development, preservation of research materials, and provision of sophisticated bibliographic tools. The fourth, bibliographic component, originally known as BALLOTS but now called RLIN, consists of a computerized set of data files and data manipulation programs. Like OCLC, the RLIN system can transmit data in either a "full-face" (covering an entire CRT screen) or a "line-by-line" mode, depending on the user's hardware. It provides catalog worksheets, printed cards, magnetic tapes in the U.S. MARC communications format, and a variety of other acquisitions and in-process forms.

BALLOTS developed a comprehensive technical processing system except for serials check-in and fiscal control. The RLIN systems presently offer members:

1. The ability to create and search their own online bibliographic and information files for such purposes as cataloging, acquisitions, and information retrieval.

2. The ability to view selected online data of other research libraries for such purposes as collection development decision making and interlibrary loan.

3. The ability to use automated technical processing as a basis for other cooperative programs.[21]

Three currently operational subsystems may be identified by the data base with which each deals:

1) The "Books System" provides the user with online searching on LC MARC records from 1972 to date and on monographic cataloging input by users. All entries are in the MARC books format, including added copy cataloging and record maintenance. One of its strengths is its powerful query potential. Search terms can be used singly or in any sequence. They comprise LC card numbers, all or part of call numbers, and LC subject headings. Truncation searching on main and added entry words includes personal surnames and names of corporate bodies and geographic entities. The Boolean logic operators "and," "or," and "not" help tailor search strategies. All searches are interactive and can be negotiated or changed as searching progresses. Not yet available to all members, but operational online in the Stanford University Libraries, are acquisitions and in-process control, and a cross-reference file to Stanford's cataloging since 1973.

2) The "Non-books System," implemented in the spring of 1979, gives search and cataloging facilities for the U.S. MARC films, maps, manuscripts, music scores, sound recordings, and serials formats. Searching is also available on approximately 100,000 name authority records and 100,000 subject authority records, plus the quarterly updates now provided by MARC tapes. While the non-books system uses command language, screen formats, and combined index searching similar to that in the older books system, it has a greater variety of indexes. Techniques for fine-tuning index searches, input commands, and tagging are introduced, which makes it intermediate between the original Books System and the "Network File System" being developed.

3) The "Archive Books System," newest of the three, provides a data base of records cataloged by RLIN members in other, non-RLIN systems. Constructed from tapes converted to the RLIN format, it uses the indexing and search keys provided in the non-books system.

The RLIN data base is considerably smaller than that of OCLC. In 1979 it still lacked MARC records produced between 1968 and 1972. The cost for first-time use of records for cataloging is comparable to that of OCLC, but fixed costs for telecommunications are substantially higher to some areas of the country. In spite of these drawbacks, RLIN is now a serious competitor in the field of networking. Its programs have a strong appeal to research libraries. One of the most recent, as was mentioned in the section on MARC, is collaboration with the Library of Congress in creating a new data base of U.S. MARC elements. It is an expansion of the BALLOTS *Data Elements Dictionary* and is designed to encourage uniform usage of MARC tags in the various bibliographic formats. RLIN will manage the data base and provide programming support, in anticipation of the upgraded Network File System currently being developed. The work will appear initially in a looseleaf package integrating all present MARC formats.

WASHINGTON LIBRARY NETWORK (WLN)

WLN was initiated by the State Library of Washington to give public and private libraries of the state a comprehensive bibliographic control system. While online operations began only in 1977 with ten pilot libraries, it has developed rapidly to become the most complete, though still the smallest, of the three major U.S. bibliographic utilities. Using equipment at both the Washington State Data Processing Service in Olympia and the Washington State University Computing Center in Pullman, it can be accessed online either by leased telephone lines or by dial-up, although such network services as TYMNET and TELENET are not yet available.[22] Its first out-of-state clients, the Alaska State Library at Juneau and the University of Alaska Library at Fairbanks, joined in the spring of 1978. By mid-1979 WLN extended its coverage to much of the Pacific Northwest, with three state, thirteen public, twelve academic, and eight community college libraries, plus one law library, participating. These 37 institutions held a total of 100 terminals in Alaska, Idaho, Oregon, and the home state. While WLN gives first priority to libraries in its region, it agreed in early 1979 to provide its software on trial to the National Library of Australia (NLA) in Canberra. NLA now accesses the Bibliographic Subsystem via trans-Pacific telephone. If the experiment is successful, a permanent licensing agreement will put NLA on WLN's Acquisitions Subsystem as well.

Like RLIN, WLN is well on its way to becoming a "full service" network. It supports two operational subsystems, with two more in advanced stages of development. Its Bibliographic Subsystem provides catalog support services notable for their quality control. All LC MARC formats are used. WLN will, like the other networks, conform to Library of Congress policy in adopting *AACR 2* headings with indicated notes and *see* references. Headings are linked to a network-wide authority data base that is more sophisticated than those of either OCLC or RLIN. Catalog records can be accessed, edited, or input online. Passwords, which may be changed as a precaution against unauthorized use, give access to specific files. Authorized participants are intensively trained in MARC tagging and input/edit techniques. Modifications in either bibliographic or authority data are automatically reviewed by the central Bibliographic Maintenance staff, who alone carry the right to replace existing records with modified records.

The Inquiry Module uses algorithms that are both powerful and flexible enough to support reference services as well as the Bibliographic Subsystem. They include subject and keyword, as well as author (personal and corporate names), title (including keyword and uniform titles), series, LC card number, ISBN, and ISSN search keys. Boolean operators expand the search capabilities.

Book catalogs, COM catalogs, printed cards, and processing kits are producible offline, to fit the individual client's profile. A COM union catalog in quarterly issues is supplemented with bi-weekly local library accessions lists. Holdings information, keyed to 700 locations, facilitates ILL and other searches.

The Acquisitions Subsystem, like the bibliographic one, adapts to profiled user specifications. It contains order, claiming, receiving, and payment records for all kinds of library materials. It can generate printed order forms and claim notices, monitor purchase requests and subscriptions, provide accounting on encumbered and expended funds, place temporary records in the Bibliographic Subsystem to serve as pre-entries in the main data base, and warn of needed cataloging at the time an item is received. Payment history records are maintained by an Account Status File, a Name and Address File (covering vendors, and library and branch library acquisitions profiles), and a History File for completed acquisitions records.

At present, serials control capabilities include ordering, subscription record maintenance, and fund accounting through the Acquisitions Subsystem, with summary holdings updates in the Bibliographic Subsystem. Check-in and binding facilities are under design.

A Circulation Control Subsystem, now available to libraries within the state, includes a circulation file searchable by author, title, patron ID number and book call number. The subsystem accommodates reserves, recalls, overdue and fine notices, AV booking, collection inventory records on missing and lost items, transfer charges of materials to secondary locations, and statistics. The subsystem will soon be offered through the Bibliographic Subsystem to out-of-state participants if they independently acquire the necessary software from Dataphase Systems, Inc.

At a demonstration to the Library of Congress, WLN representatives showed:

> The redundant storage of data is minimized in the system by interrelating the principal files: holdings, authorities, bibliographic, and local data. Thus, an individual institution may hold data unique to it, while more general data will be stored in the central system to be implemented at the level most appropriate for its operation.[23]

In March 1979 WLN sealed a historic agreement to start exchanging LC MARC, non-MARC, and other data bases with RLIN. Initially, the exchange products will be magnetic tapes, but the eventual goal is to interface online. The two networks will also cooperate on development programs in serials specification, acquisitions, authority control, interlibrary loan, and a combined package for export of their software and data bases to other networks. It should be noted that the program does not imply a "cooperative national library network." Even a possible further linkage to OCLC and the Library of Congress would not achieve that goal in its strict sense. But the WLN/RLIN agreement marks a first functional step in that direction.

Like its two elder brothers, WLN reached a point where its growing constituency called for representation in its administrative decisions. There is no talk of its breaking away from the State Library of Washington as NELINET and SOLINET did from their parent institutional structures; however, it recently expanded the governance of one of its major components, the Washington Library Network Computer Service. Four representatives from in-state, and one each from every other state with five or more participants (currently Idaho and Alaska) will sit on a Computer Service Council, together with Washington Data Processing Authority and Pacific Northwest Bibliographic Center representatives, and the Washington State Librarian, who is also WLN's Executive Director.

CANADIAN NETWORK CATALOGING

Canadian efforts toward computer-based network cataloging were sparked largely by the University of Toronto Library Automation Systems (UTLAS). In 1963 the Ontario New Universities Library Project started work on computer-produced book catalogs representing the initial library collections for five new campuses in the province.[24] The project was to facilitate selection, acquisition, and cataloging, while remaining flexible in its record format, access, and products. Implementation in 1965 led to the University's participation in the Library of Congress MARC project. By 1970 it was producing cards from MARC tapes for sale to clients, including in 1971 the College Bibliocentre, a processing center for nineteen colleges of applied technology. It started supplying computer-based systems and services to libraries in 1973. Its online network now includes 94 institutional and consortia members, with over 500 individual libraries receiving some or all of its products and services. Its equipment can be connected via telephone lines, TYMNET circuits, etc. to any North American or European-United Kingdom location. In 1975 it cut its direct fiscal dependence on the University of Toronto Library to become a self-supporting division of the University.

The UTLAS goal of flexibility to meet the needs of each user led to problems of standardization when it was recognized that a union file, holding a single record of any given work, was needed to keep storage and operating costs under control. An Ontario-and-Quebec union catalog and support service consortium now called UNICAT/TELECAT established input standards incorporating CAN/MARC, to which the one million retrospective machine-readable UTL records did not conform. However, UTLAS agreed to follow the standards in all future cataloging. Six Ontario and two Quebec universities joined the cooperative venture to build an English-French union file. By mid-1978 UNICAT/TELECAT included seven of the fifteen Ontario university libraries, all Quebec universities except the University of Quebec, one federal government library, the Quebec National Library, and one large public library. The National Library of Canada agreed to participate, in exchange for rights to full Canadian distribution of the system.

Meanwhile, UTLAS developed conversion programs to make Canadian, British, and American MARC, as well as the College Bibliocentre machine-readable formats, compatible with its own. Data files (including full cumulative LC and CAN/MARC files) may be searched, and produce functions activated. The UTLAS Catalogue Support System (CATSS) provides original, derived, and shared cataloging of monographs, serials, AV materials, government documents, and other formats. The specific services of CATSS include:

    1) A data base of about six million records, including national source and client files

    2) Separate client files of both copied (derived) and original records which may be shared on request, but not altered in any way by another client

    3) Up-to-date files for each system user

    4) Online interactive editing, with no waiting for records to be updated in batch mode

    5) Online verification of headings for authority control

    6) Generation of printed cards, book catalogs, COM catalogs, acquisitions lists, order lists, selective book lists (e.g., by type of medium, language, or location), and various batch products to support record editing

The data base may be searched in three modes:

    1) Precise Match Mode, by UTLAS, LC card, ISBN, ISSN, local accession, NLM, and OCLC numbers, as well as by title (forty characters)

    2) Browsable Mode, by main and added entries (including personal and corporate authors), titles, series, and subjects. In this mode Boolean combinations can lead online to random access as well as sequential browsing.

    3) Keyword Mode, where Boolean operators assist online searchers to selected terms in titles, series, and corporate entries in bibliographic records, as well as subjects for authority records.[25]

Among its clients at present are the University of Alberta, the University of Regina, and the Tri-University Libraries (TRIUL) network. Several of Ontario's larger public libraries and some regional systems also receive

UTLAS data in machine-readable or hard-copy form.[26] Automated authority and circulation control subsystems are now being developed.

The University of Toronto closed its public card catalogs as of June 30, 1976. Its 1.2 million retrospective holdings records are now available on COM fiche, supplemented every four weeks by cumulations of new cataloging.[27]

GENERAL CONSIDERATIONS

In most libraries, the professional cataloger's role with respect to online cataloging procedures will be supervisory and managerial, although it is not uncommon for professionals to edit machine records, to revise non-professionals' input, and to use the data base in problem solving routines. Even direct supervision of terminal operators is considered para-professional in many libraries. The essentially professional contribution is to organize policies and procedures to make the most efficient use of the system.

Research shows that use of an online cataloging system does not always result in major organizational or procedural change.[28] However, the introduction of such a tool into a traditional catalog department is potentially a powerful change agent. It should at least stimulate revaluation of long-standing policies and procedures. The measures taken by librarians to adapt their operations to the new environment affect their success in reducing per-unit cataloging costs, speeding the flow of materials through the processing department, and achieving related objectives. Some of the factors to be considered when utilizing network services and designing efficient interface procedures are described below.

Cataloging Networks as a General Bibliographic Resource

Library managers should encourage use of the data base for pre-order verification, for location spotting in ILL work, for public service uses such as citation verification, and for bibliographic problem solving. It is unfortunate that many libraries overlook these potential uses of the system, since cataloging networks usually do not charge extra for them.[29] Charges generally occur only when the system is used for cataloging, except for terminals reserved exclusively for public service use. Not only can full use of the system improve such tasks as pre-order searching, but it can foster goodwill and acceptance by introducing more staff to use of the terminals. Staff resistance to online cataloging comes most often from those who do not use the terminals in their jobs. It is generally good policy to introduce the full staff to the fundamentals of terminal operation, encouraging them to use the system as part of their daily routines if possible.

It is true, however, that administrative emphasis on full utilization of the system complicates matters such as terminal placement, scheduling, and decisions to purchase additional ones. These problems are cited most often where use has been restricted to the catalog department. On the other hand, non-cataloging uses seldom require large amounts of terminal time, in comparison to cataloging use. It is usually possible to schedule these functions, either with an "interrupt priority" or with one or more terminals completely unscheduled for catalog production.

Unfortunately, sometimes a perceived encroachment on cataloging time is actually the result of inefficient, wasteful cataloging procedures. Time must be treated as a valuable resource if the system is to provide optimum support to all appropriate technical and public service functions. Cataloging routines should proceed in a manner that conserves terminal time. This point will be further discussed in the section on procedural design.

Also related to maximizing use of some online cataloging systems is the decision to acquire a library's archive tapes, the machine-readable records of all transactions the library makes on the system. While cards are the principal system product for the great majority of libraries, the possibility of owning, very inexpensively, a machine-readable record of a library's holdings is an important by-product. Even though there may be no immediate need for the archive tapes, it is a good idea to place a subscription when a library joins such an online system. Current developments point to a future in which machine-readable bibliographic products such as COM will be common-place.

Cataloging Policy

It is more convenient to edit copy to local standards with online cataloging than when using printed cards from LC or other sources. Still, a high degree of local variation from standard LC practice tends to slow work-flow, due largely to the need to consult local authority files and shelflist records.

To profit most from online cataloging, it is a good idea to review all local variations from standard practice at the time a library enters the system. This is not to suggest that all variations are misguided. Many local prerogatives are necessary because of inconsistent precedents over the years on the part of LC itself. Others may be justified by special local conditions. However, librarians should review all such variations in the light of their costs and their effects on processing efficiency. Any decision will affect online cataloging in areas such as terminal staffing, policies on the use of other libraries' records, and the organization of authority (integration) procedures.

The majority of titles added to a member library's collections will be cataloged in accordance with records existing in the data base. Policies related to accepting and modifying records created by another institution are now among the most critical ones a library makes — even more important than those related to original cataloging. Arlene Dowell's *Cataloging with Copy* is a detailed examination of copy-cataloging which is still timely, although based on the use of non-machine-readable techniques.[30]

Procedural Design

Local cataloging procedures related to online networking fall into five general groups:

    1) The pre-cataloging search for copy, either as an acquisitions or as a cataloging responsibility

2) Cataloging with exact-match LC copy from the data base

3) Cataloging with LC copy which requires editing and/or with non-LC copy from the data base

4) Inputting original cataloging

5) Receiving, routing, and filing cards from the central office.

For best results, these functions must be well coordinated to avoid duplicate effort. They must be assigned to appropriate staff, with proper supervision and revision. They must also be integrated into an organizational structure designed to fit the new conditions resulting from network membership. Many issues arise when catalogers set up interface procedures with an online system. Among them are the following:

1) To what extent should clerical operators be restricted to using exact copy, or be allowed to edit "near copy" at the terminal?

2) To what extent should they be allowed to accept non-LC records?

3) What information should the pre-order search, or a special pre-catalog search, provide them?

4) How should the Acquisitions Department sort and route incoming books in accordance with the availability and type of data base copy?

5) Where should authority work take place for author, series, and subject entries?

6) To what extent must the shelflist be consulted in the course of cataloging?

7) What amount of revision is needed for each type of terminal operation?

8) Who should perform the revision?

Obviously, the above questions are interrelated. For example, appropriate revision of clerical operators' work will depend on the amount of editing and authority determination they may perform, and on the type of copy they are permitted to use. Collectively, the answers to such questions will decide a library's program for interfacing with the network. The system's efficiency helps determine whether the library meets its goals for network participation. To reduce turn-around time, cut the cost spiral, and improve cataloging quality, the interface must be as efficient as possible.

No single combination of procedures and policies would fit the majority of situations, since each interface emerges from the meshing of network capabilities with unique library conditions. A few simple guidelines may be useful, however, when setting up or evaluating such procedures:

1) **Conserve terminal time.** The point has been made that cataloging should be designed to avoid needless waste of time. Techniques can be used such as batching offline activities (particularly authority processing), avoiding unnecessary transcription (such as nonproductive printing of information

from the terminals), and avoiding unnecessary call-ups of records (e.g., using a second or third call-up to produce cards if all the processing information is available the first time).

2) **Coordinate authority procedures.** One task that an online cataloging system does not do for a library is to ensure that the cataloging it initiates is compatible with that already existing at the library. Authority control is still largely manual and, if poorly executed, can nullify the advantages of online operation. Establishing authority records for names, for series, and for subjects should be handled as separate processes. A decision on whether to do any one of them before, during, or after cataloging at the terminal should be carefully weighed.

3) **Take advantage of the special capabilities of the system.** Major differences between online cataloging and the manual techniques it replaces are the speed of copy work and that of card production. It is no longer necessary to backlog bibliographic records while waiting for cards to arrive or for typists to produce them. With appropriate priorities, a library can expedite books for which exact LC copy is available, thus considerably reducing the familiar cataloging gap. Some of these capabilities are:

   1) Priority staffing such that the copy-catalog work remains fully staffed regardless of attrition in the department as a whole
   2) Special staff assignments on a temporary basis to meet peak load conditions in copy-catalog work
   3) Expeditious sorting of recently acquired books according to the types of catalog copy available
   4) Frequent recycling of arrearages for which catalog copy is likely to become available. Some libraries follow a "first in, first out" rule, which mixes all categories of materials regardless of their difficulty, or the availability of catalog copy.

As has been previously said, it is a good idea to revaluate continuously a library's procedures in the light of systems capability within the network. Such changes inevitably include the constant growth of the data base and the evolution of operating procedures and subsystems. In the volatile network environment no cataloging interface can become so immutable as the techniques it replaces long appeared to be.

FUTURE PROSPECTS

It is now reasonable to speculate about a future in which a full range of computer-based bibliographic services is available through a National Bibliographic Network, giving access to the complete store of the nation's (perhaps eventually many nations') machine-readable catalog data files. A great deal of national level planning and coordination must take place before such a goal can be realized. The competitive element in current relationships among bibliographic utilities could become a roadblock to national planning. There is still considerable uncertainty about the proper future roles of the three major bibliographic networks, the Library of Congress, the regional service networks, and organizations such as the Council on Library Resources and the Association of Research Libraries. Responsible speculation about the specific organizational and governance configuration which a national bibliographic network will take is hazardous.

However, trends in computer technology and progress in developing bibliographic standards are encouraging. Recent advances in computer technology indicate that mini-computers will have the capacity to operate local online catalogs and other processing functions, such as acquisitions and serials control, at reasonable cost. Advances in telecommunication make possible distributed networks, consisting of a series of separate individual library catalogs interconnected by telecommunications links. Such a configuration is especially attractive in areas where many libraries engage in extensive resource sharing and coordinated collection development.

If local online catalogs come to be operated by in-house computers, libraries will still find the large network data bases valuable as sources for extended record searching. Cataloging will continue in much the same way as today, except for the transfer of the edited machine-readable record into the local online data base rather than to card stock. Closing of card catalogs, at least in the larger libraries, will be the next major step in the evolution of materials processing toward quality improvement and control in standardized entry, descriptive detail, filing, physical preparation, and economical production of records.

The professional cataloger's contribution to an exclusively online situation is sometimes questioned. It is possible that many libraries that acquire only standard trade books and accept existing cataloging without modifcation will no longer need professional processing staff. On the other hand, there will likely be greater coordination of the national cataloging effort. It is unlikely that the Library of Congress can maintain timely coverage of the world's entire publication output. Other libraries at home and abroad will no doubt take responsibility for cataloging in specific languages or subject categories. Consistently high standards will be kept in relatively few cataloging centers throughout the world. The number of professional catalogers may well be reduced, but the highly skilled bibliographer with special language or subject competency will be in greater demand than ever. Moreover, public service librarians will find that in-depth knowledge of catalog codes and conventions, machine search strategies, and MARC or other machine-readable formats will immeasurably increase their effectiveness in reference work, information exchange, and bibliographic problem solving.

FOOTNOTES

[1]"Guidelines for Centralized Technical Services," prepared by the ALA Resources and Technical Services Division, Regional Processing Committee, can serve as a classic example of a "pragmatic" approach. Cf. *Library Resources & Technical Services* 10 (Spring 1966):233-40.

[2]Barbara M. Westby, "Commercial Services," *Library Trends* 16 (July 1967):46.

[3]Barbara M. Westby, "Commercial Processing Firms: A Directory," *Library Resources & Technical Services* 13 (Spring 1969):209-86.

[4]Nancy Hoyt Knight, "Microform Catalog Data Retrieval Systems: A Survey," *Library Technology Reports*, May 1975.

[5]American Library Association, Resources and Technical Services Division, Commercial Processing Services Committee, "Guidelines for Selecting a Commercial Processing Service," *Library Resources & Technical Services* 21 (Spring 1977):170-73.

[6]*Cataloging Service*, bulletin 113 (Spring 1975):7-8.

[7]*Cataloging Service*, bulletin 119 (Fall 1976):25-26.

[8]Henriette D. Avram, *MARC: Its History and Implications* (Washington, Library of Congress, 1975).

[9]*The Library of Congress Information Bulletin* 38 (April 6, 1979):125.

[10]*Cataloging Service*, bulletin 121 (Spring 1977):3; bulletin 122 (Summer 1977):3; and bulletin 125 (Spring 1978):8.

[11]Library of Congress, *Annual Report of the Librarian of Congress for the Fiscal Year Ending September 30, 1977* (Washington, The Library, 1978), p. 74.

[12]*Library of Congress Information Bulletin* 37 (Dec. 1, 1978):726; *Cataloging Service Bulletin*, no. 6 (Fall 1979):46-54.

[13]Library of Congress, *Annual Report of the Librarian of Congress for the Fiscal Year Ending September 30, 1978* (Washington, The Library, 1979), p. 54.

[14]Library of Congress, Network Development Office, "A Glossary for Library Networking," *Network Planning Paper*, no. 2 (Washington, The Library, 1978), p. 7.

[15]"Glossary for Library Networking," p. 22.

[16]*OCLC Newsletter*, no. 124 (Aug. 13, 1979), p. 1.

[17]Frederick G. Kilgour, "Shared Cataloging at OCLC," *Online Review* 3 (Sept. 1979):275-79

[18]For a general description and comparison of the three major utilities see: Susan K. Martin, *Library Networks, 1978/79* (White Plains, NY, Knowledge Industry Publications, 1978), pp. 35-53.

[19]Research Libraries Group, Inc., *A Plan for the Development of a Research Libraries Information Network* (Branford, CT, RLG, 1979).

[20]Jan Thomson and Jennifer Hartzell, "RLG's Research Libraries Information Network: Bibliographic and Information Services," *Online Review* 3 (Sept. 1979):281-82

[21]Research Libraries Group, Inc., *Progress Report*, June 1979, p. 12.

[22]Richard Woods, "The Washington Library Network Computer System," *Online Review* 3 (Sept. 1979):298.

[23]*Library of Congress Information Bulletin* 36 (Dec. 30, 1977):845.

[24]Gordon H. Wright, "The Canadian Mosaic — Planning for Shared Partnership in a National Network," *ASLIB Proceedings* 30 (Feb. 1978):96-102; and Harriet Velazquez, "University of Toronto Library Automation System," *Online Review* 3 (Sept. 1979):254.

[25]Velazquez, p. 260.

[26]Margaret Beckman, "Automated Cataloguing Systems and Networks in Canada," *Canadian Library Journal* 35 (June 1978):173-74.

[27]Valentine DeBruin, "Sometimes Dirty Things Are Seen on the Screen: A Mini-Evaluation of the COM Microcatalogue at the University of Toronto Library," *Journal of Academic Librarianship* 3 (Nov. 1977):256-66.

[28]Joe A. Hewitt, *OCLC, Impact and Use* (Columbus, Ohio State University Libraries, Office of Educational Services, 1977), pp. 122-24.

[29]Hewitt, pp. 60-61.

[30]Arlene Taylor Dowell, *Cataloging with Copy: A Decision-Maker's Handbook* (Littleton, CO, Libraries Unlimited, 1976).

31 CATALOG AND SHELFLIST FILING

INTRODUCTION

Neophyte catalogers are surprised to discover many alternative filing codes. They learn not only that choice of catalog arrangement (dictionary or divided) affects filing decisions, but that choice of entry is to some extent interactive with filing questions. Arbitrary groupings, exceptions from strict alphabetical order, and other complexities are directly related to the forms of subject headings and other catalog entries. Filing problems resulting from entry conflicts between the old *ALA Cataloging Rules* and *AACR* are a major impetus to the closing of such large catalogs as those of The New York Public Library and the Library of Congress. Some libraries attempt to interfile old and new forms of the same entry, while others file all forms exactly as they appear. In either case, ample use of cross reference is necessary.

Research libraries have long adhered to one or another of various kinds of "categorical filing," particularly in those parts of their catalogs where relatively large numbers of highly formalized entries are concentrated. Categorical filing is based on the assumption that the user knows his discipline well enough to prefer a partially classified arrangement over straight adherence to the alphabet. Less scholarly libraries generally prefer the more simplistic, therefore more readily-grasped alpha-arrangement. Even the big academic and research collections are gradually succumbing to popular demand, and to the requirements of computer filing.[1]

For instance, the Library of Congress used to arrange its entries for individual books and groups of books of the Bible in canonical order, as part of an intricate categorical arrangement.[2] Today, those entries are filed alphabetically:

Former Arrangement		Present Arrangement		
Bible. O.T. Pentateuch		Bible. N.T. Acts		
"	" Genesis	"	"	Colossians ....
"	" Exodus	"	"	1 Corinthians ....
"	" Leviticus	"	"	2 Corinthians ....
"	" Numbers	"	"	Ephesians ....
"	" Deuteronomy	"	"	Epistles ....

(Example continues on page 582)

Former Arrangement (cont'd)	Present Arrangement (cont'd)
Bible O.T. Historical books	Bible. N.T. Epistles and Gospels ....
" " Joshua	" " Epistles of John ....
" " Judges	[etc.]
" " Five scrolls	
" " Ruth	Bible. O.T. Amos ....
[etc.]	" " Apochryphal books ....
	" " 1 Chronicles ....
" N.T. Gospels	" " 2 Chronicles ....
" " Matthew	" " Daniel ....
" " Mark	" " Deuteronomy ....
" " Luke	" " Exodus ....
[etc.]	[etc.]

Some libraries adopt published filing codes, e.g., the *ALA Rules*[3] Others develop sets of rules tailored to their own preferences. In almost every case questions arise which cannot be answered by a simple appeal to the alphabet.

FAMILIAR FILING DILEMMAS

In the first place, there is a significant difference between alphabetizing straight through to the end of a phrase entry, and observing the breaks in the string which occur at the end of each word. Most filers know the admonition "nothing before something," or "blank to Z." It means that library catalogs are generally arranged letter-by-letter to the end of each word. However, not all files in libraries are based on this premise. Reference librarians have to remember that the *American Peoples Encyclopedia*, the *Americana*, and the *World Book* are arranged word-by-word, while *Britannica*, *Collier's*, and *Compton's* prefer uninterrupted letter-by-letter filing to the close of the entry phrase. The differences are in some areas important, e.g.:

Word-by-word	Letter-by-letter
New Hampshire	Newark (N.J.)
New Haven (Conn.)	Newcastle (N.S.W.)
New York (N.Y.)	Newfoundland
New York (U.S. : State)	New Hampshire
New Zealand	New Haven (Conn.)
Newark (N.J.)	Newman, Arthur
Newcastle (N.S.W.)	Newport (Isle of Wight)
Newfoundland	NEWSPAPERS
Newman, Arthur	New York (N.Y.)
Newport (Isle of Wight)	New York (U.S. : State)
NEWSPAPERS	New Zealand

In entries containing dates, early historical periods usually precede later ones. However, codes differ on whether longer periods should precede or follow shorter ones starting with the same year. The *ALA Rules* (*see* Rule 32G1) say to arrange periods of time beginning with the same year so as to bring the longest period first. They give examples from which the following selection was made:

> U.S. – HISTORY – 1783-1865
> U.S. – HISTORY – CONFEDERATION, 1783-1789
> U.S. – HISTORY – CONSTITUTIONAL PERIOD, 1789-1809
> U.S. – HISTORY – 1865-
> U.S. – HISTORY – 1865-1898
> U.S. – HISTORY – 1898-
> U.S. – HISTORY – WAR OF 1898
> U.S. – HISTORY – 20TH CENTURY

In the "ITALY – History" sequence below, from *LCSH 8*, longer periods follow shorter ones starting with the same year.

> Holmes, Oliver Wendell, 1809-1894
> Holmes, Oliver Wendell, 1841-1935
>
> ITALY – History, to 476 A.D.
> ITALY – History – 476-1268
> ITALY – History – 476-1492
> ITALY – History – 13th century
> ITALY – History, 1268-1492
> ITALY – History – 15th century
> ITALY – History – 1492-1559
> ITALY – History – 1492-1870
> ITALY – History – Expedition of Charles VIII, 1494-1496
> ITALY – History – 16th century
> ITALY – History – 1559-1789

If there are two or more editions or impressions of a work, edition dates or numbers may be added to the entry line, solely as filing elements. Again, codes differ on whether the earliest or latest should file first. The *ALA Rules* (*see* Rule 26B9a in the full edition) say to arrange editions in straight chronological order, with earliest date first. The following example is given:

Briscoe, Herman Thompson
General chemistry for colleges. [c1935]
General chemistry for colleges. [c1938]
General chemistry for colleges. 3d ed. [1943]
General chemistry for colleges. 4th ed. [1949]

In the list below, the latest ones come first, on the assumption that they are the ones the user is most likely to want.

Imagism and the imagists. 3rd ed.
Imagism and the imagists. [1st ed.]

Principles of cardiac surgery. 1979 ed.
Principles of cardiac surgery. [1967 ed.]

Numbers or digits in catalog entries give further challenges. They may be roman numerals, as in the names of kings and popes, where most subject entries are accompanied by dates of birth and death. In these cases numerical and chronological order coincide. If numerals appear in the title of an item, however, they are usually filed as if spelled out in the language of the rest of the title, e.g.,

HENRY I, KING OF ENGLAND, 1068-1135   [Henry King of England 1]
HENRY V, KING OF ENGLAND, 1367-1413   [Henry King of England 5]
HENRY VIII, KING OF ENGLAND, 1491-1547 [Henry King of England 8]
Henry the Eighth and his court.
Henry VIII and his wives. [Henry the Eighth]
Henry VIII's fifth wife. [Henry the Eighth's]
Henry the Fifth of England.

Twenty-four dramatic cases of the International Academy of
    Trial Lawyers.
The 24th Congress of the CPSU and its contribution to
    Marxism-Leninism.
XXIVth International Congress of Pure and applied Chemistry,
    main section lectures presented at ....
The twenty-fourth session of the International Labour
    Conference ....

Arabic numerals are far more common. In manual filing numerals are most often filed as spelled, and spelled "as spoken," whatever that may be. Interpretation becomes most critical when the primary filing element of a title is expressed on the chief source of information in numerals. For instance, it is conceivable, though not very likely, that the two delightful books (one by Walter Sellar, the other by Reginald Arkell) entitled *1066 and All That*, will be lost forever to the patron who cannot transcribe "1066" appropriately. More hazardous is the alphabetizing of titles which start with a number in the 100s.

They are collocated together, usually with interspersed entries and a guide card starting with the words "one hundred." Nevertheless, as the file grows, interpretations of rules, even with examples, become increasingly difficult. The following selections were gleaned, in the order shown here, from a research library catalog. To indicate the inconsistencies in this list the words in brackets indicate how the numbers should be "spoken" according to the ALA rules for filing.

An Equivocal File of Entries under Various Forms of "100"

100 American drawings. [one hundred]
One hundred and eleven poems.
One hundred and fifty years of collecting ....
One hundred and forty years of the Tennant companies ....
119 years of the Atlantic. [one hundred and nineteen]
One hundred & one ballades.
101 nudes. [one hundred and one]
One hundred and one ways to make money by writing.
One hundred and sixty cat proverbs & proverbial similes.
One hundred and two H-bombs.
100 classical studies for flute. [one hundred]
108 kritis of Sri Tyagaraja. [one hundred and eight]
One hundred eighty landings of United States Marines ....
111 days in Stanleyville. [one hundred and eleven]
One hundred eleven don'ts for writers.
150th commemorative recital. [one hundred and fiftieth]
One hundred fifty years; a history of publishing ....
150 years of British steam locomotives. [one hundred and fifty]
The 158-pound marriage. [one hundred and fifty-eight]
140 Jewish marshals, generals and admirals. [one hundred and forty]
199 ways to review a book. [one hundred and ninety-nine]
101 American vacations from $25 to $250. [one hundred and one]
One hundred one-act plays.
101 best nature games and projects. [one hundred and one]
176 keys: music for two pianos. [one hundred and seventy-six]
173 drawings and illustrations. [one hundred and seventy-three]
160 edible plants commonly found in the Eastern USA. [one hundred and sixty]
The 103rd ballot. [one hundred and third]
One hundred thousand tractors.
100,000 years of art. [one hundred thousand]

As displayed here the problems are fairly obvious; in a large file of several hundred entries they become more elusive. Compare this faulty list with the examples given on page 593. The Library of Congress programming of all *LCSH 8* numerals in numeric order ahead of alphabetic entries may eventually replace "as spoken" filing in all libraries.[4] It requires, of course, plentiful use of *see also* references to tie together all the dispersed entries.

Extensive use of acronyms and initialisms has in recent years aggravated the familiar problem of how to file abbreviations. As discussed in the "filing" section of chapter 27, "Library of Congress Subject Headings," computerized filing throws new light on the difficulties encountered in traditional approaches. In the past, initials were most often treated as one-letter words, regardless of whether spaces or punctuation intervened. For machine-readable data bases it is easier to file strings of letters, or letters-and-numbers, lacking spacing or punctuation as multi-character words. It is immaterial whether they consist entirely of capitals (e.g., FORTRAN) or of a combination of upper and lower case (e.g., MeSH or Unesco). Nor does pronounceability affect the filing (e.g., *LCSH 8* locates "GTO AUTOMOBILE" after "GROWTH DISORDERS" and before "GUANO," rather than ahead of "GAELIC LANGUAGE," as *LCSH 7* would have done).

Abbreviated titles of respect or position (e.g., Mr., Dr., St.) are generally filed as if spelled out in full. But social pressures, as well as the computer, have effected changes. For example, *Webster's New International Dictionary* (2nd edition) defined "Mrs." as "the form of Mistress when used as a title."[5] The problems ensuing from that edict were impressive. Fortunately, *Webster's* third edition substitutes a more contemporary (and considerably more round-about) explanation which in effect recognizes the abbreviation at its face value. Meanwhile, many libraries had already decided to file "Mrs." and "Ms." as written.

Initial articles are usually suppressed as filing words, especially in titles. The practice extends to all languages using articles, since even in inflected languages the number of articles is relatively limited. They can be tabulated for manual filing, or programmed out of machine filing.[6] But homonyms (e.g., the French article "la," as in "la belle epoque," and the British interjection, as in "La! she was a lady") must be differentiated. Also, articles which initiate proper names (e.g., "La Crosse, Herman Thomas" and "Los Angeles (Calif.)") are always filed for American or English names, and for other languages as well where usage so dictates.

In dictionary catalogs the order of entries with identical wording, which nonetheless are punctuated differently, must be decided. The conventional arrangement is: author, subject, title. In practice, it is highly unusual to find an author entry, a subject entry, and a title entry, all with exactly the same wording; the question bears more often on different kinds of entries which start with the same word. Application of the "authors first" guideline leaves unanswered the ordering of surnames and given name entries which start alike (e.g., "Thomas . . ."). Some libraries file given name entries (e.g., "Francis, of Assisi, Saint" and "Francis Xavier, Saint") ahead of the same word used as a surname (e.g., "Francis, Connie"). The *ALA Rules* (Rule 19A) reverse that preference, filing all surname entries first, subarranged by given names, following them with all other entries under the same word.

Many libraries, particularly large ones with comprehensive collections by and about certain versatile writers, have separated out main and added entries for those persons into at least two categories. However, the original edition of the *ALA Rules* discouraged the practice:

Arrange in one file all the entries, both main and secondary, for a person as author, joint author, compiler, editor, illustrator, translator and general added entry. Subarrange alphabetically by the title of the book. *Note:* An earlier practice, still followed in some libraries, is to arrange the secondary author entries in a separate alphabet after the main author entries. This practice is not recommended because users of the catalog overlook entries so filed.[7]

The practice of using designation of function terms with personal name headings (e.g., comp., ed., ill., and tr.) is slowly decaying, partly because of the added difficulties they cause in machine filing programs. *AACR 1* originally said:

. . . an abbreviated designation is added at the end of the heading to indicate the function performed by the person under whom an added entry is made.[8]

In 1975 the words "may be" were substituted for "is" in the above statement.[9] The Library of Congress announced later that year:

Under this option the Library of Congress will drop all such added entry designations except "joint author," which is required for the filing arrangement in its catalogs.[10]

AACR 2 addresses this option in Rule 21.0D (*see* page 267).

It was observed in chapter 1 that divided catalogs permit a simpler filing scheme than do dictionary catalogs. The simplifications obviously depend on the way in which the division is made. Most commonly, subject entries are alphabetized separately from author and title entries. Persons (e.g., "Shakespeare, William") who are both authors and subjects of books have entries in each catalog, rather than having all the entries about them collocated immediately behind all the entries by them. Titles that happen to be identical with a subject heading (e.g., *Freedom of the Press*) are similarly located in a separate file. There is perhaps less danger of the title entries' being misfiled or overlooked, but closely related titles and subjects are divorced from each other, and many title entries are made and filed which in a dictionary catalog could be omitted in favor of the equivalent subject entry.

Cross-references are likewise automatically multiplied in a divided catalog. In either type of catalog there is seldom any doubt about where to file a *see* reference, but there are definitely two schools of thought on the location of *see also* references. Most catalogers place them immediately after those entries from which they lead, on the theory that the user will have exhausted his search at that point, and be most ready for new suggestions. However, the *ALA Rules* (Rule 35C) say categorically to file *see also* references before the first entry under the same word or words.

THE ALA RULES FOR FILING CATALOG CARDS

The first edition of the *A.L.A. Rules for Filing Catalog Cards* was published in 1942. A Subcommittee of the American Library Association's Editorial Committee was established exactly twenty years later to prepare a revision which would correlate with the 1967 publication of the *Anglo-American Cataloging Rules*. The new edition of filing rules, like the first, was primarily designed for a dictionary catalog.[11] Except for the surname-first groupings in cases of identical entry words, single-alphabet arrangements are preferred over categorical considerations in nearly all cases. Machine filing experiments undoubtedly influenced the trend toward straight alphabetization. Yet the *ALA Rules* were designed for the manually filed catalogs which would continue to predominate for another two decades.

Two formats of the *ALA Rules*, second edition, were published simultaneously: the full edition and a paperback abridged edition. The brief summary which follows is designed to reproduce essential rules and examples which the filer in a modest collection would be most likely to use. Rule numbers are not consecutive, since they are excerpted from those used in the full and the abridged editions. All direct quotations are so punctuated except for the headings, which are consistently borrowed from one or the other of the two formats.

1) **Basic alphabeting rule**

A.   **Alphabet.** "Arrange all entries, both English and foreign, alphabetically according to the order of the English alphabet" (1968, full).

B.   **Word by word.** "Arrange word by word, alphabeting letter by letter within the word. Begin with the first word on the first line, then go to the next word, etc. Apply the principle of 'nothing before something,' considering the space between words as 'nothing' " (1968, full).

2) **Modified letters.** "Disregard the modification of all letters. This includes umlauts and all kinds of accents and diacritical marks in foreign languages" (1968, abridged).

3) **Punctuation marks.** All punctuation including parentheses are generally ignored. "For punctuation in relation to order of entries under the same word, see Rule 19" (1968, full).

4) **Articles.**

A.   **Initial articles.** "Disregard an initial article in all languages and file by the word following it. . . . An exception to this rule is certain foreign proper names beginning with an article (see Rule 14 . . .)" (1968, abridged).

B.   **Articles within the entry.** Every word in the entry, including articles and prepositions, is generally regarded (1968, full).

Examples of the Four Basic ALA Rules

LIFE
Life—a bowl of rice
"Life after death"
LIFE (BIOLOGY)
Life, its true genesis
LIFE—ORIGIN
Life! physical and spiritual
Life, Spiritual. *See* SPIRITUAL LIFE
LIFE STYLES

The man of his time
Man of La Mancha
A man of the age
Les miserables
Muellen, *See also* the spelling Mullen (or Müllen, filed as Mullen)
Muellen, Abraham
Muellenbach, Ernst
Mullen (or Müllen). *See also* the spelling Muellen
Mullen, Allen
Müllen, Gustav
Mullen, Pat

New York
Newark

Rolston, Brown
Rolvaag, Ole Edvart
Rølyat, Jane

5) Initials.

A. "Arrange initials, single or in combination, as one-letter words" (1968, full).

B. "Arrange initials standing for names of organizations as initials, not as abbreviations, i.e. not as if spelled in full" (1968, abridged). The full edition of the rules also prescribes that variations in spacing and punctuation be disregarded.

E. "Arrange acronyms as words, unless written in all capitals with a space or period between the letters" (1968, abridged).

Examples

> A.
> A.A.
> A., A. J. G.
> AAUN news
> A apple pie
> A. B.
> The ABC about collecting
> A. B. C. programs
> ABM. *See* ANTIMISSILE MISSILES
> Aabel, Marie
>
> U.N.E.S.C.O. *See* UNESCO and Unesco.
> Unesco
> UNESCO bibliographical handbooks
> Unesco fellowship handbook

6) **Abbreviations.**

A.   "Arrange abbreviations as if spelled in full in the language of the entry, except 'Mrs.,' which is filed as written" (1968, abridged).

B.   "Arrange initials and other abbreviations for geographical names . . . as if written in full" (1968, full).

C.   "If subject subdivisions are abbreviated in subject headings as they commonly are in the tracing, arrange them as if written in full" (1968, abridged).

Examples

> Concord (Mass.)
> The Concord saunterer
> CONCORD (VT.)
> Concord (Va.)
>
> Dr. Christian's office
> Doctor come quickly
> Doktor Brents Wandlung
> Dr. Mabuse der Spieler   [in German]
>
> The great Brink's holdup
> Gt. Brit. Office of Commonwealth Relations
> Gt. Brit. on trial
> Great Britain or little England?
> Gt. Brit. Entries beginning with this abbreviation are filed as if spelled
>   "Great Britain."

(Examples continue on page 591)

Mr. Adam
Mistress. *See also* entries beginning with "Mrs."
Mr. Entries beginning with this abbreviation are filed as if spelled "Mister."
Mrs. *See also* entries beginning with "Mistress."
Mrs. Miniver

7) **Elisions, possessives, etc.** "Arrange elisions, contractions, and possessives as written" (1968, abridged).

Examples

Bibliothèque d'art
Bibliothèque de la Fondation Thiers
Bibliothèque de l'Usine
Bibliothèque d'histoire
Boys and girls at school
The boys' book of airships
Boys will be boys

East o' the sun and west o' the moon
East of Eden
East of the sun and west of the moon

Whoa, Grandma!
Who'd be a doctor?
Whodunit?

8) **Signs and symbols.**

A.   "Disregard signs, such as . . . or −, at the beginning of or within titles" (1968, abridged).

B.   "Arrange the ampersand (&) as 'and,' 'et,' 'und,' etc., according to the language in which it is used" (1968, abridged).

C.   "Arrange signs and symbols that are ordinarily spoken as words as if they were written out" (1968, abridged).

(Examples are on page 592)

Examples

And another thing
— and beat him when he sneezes
And so . . . accounting
Art and beauty
Art & commonsense
ART AND INDUSTRY
L'art et la beauté
L'art & la guerre
L'art et les artistes

$$$ and sense	[Dollars and sense]
% of gain	[Percent of gain]
3 x 3: Stairway to the sea	[Three by three . . .]
$20 a week	[Twenty dollars a week]
2 x 2 = 5	[Two times two equals five]

9)   **Numerals.**

  A.   "Arrange numerals . . . as if spelled out in the language of the entry. Spell numerals and dates as they are spoken, placing 'and' before the last element in compound numbers in English, except in a decimal fraction" (1968, full).

  B.   "Arrange a numeral following a given name in a title as if spelled out in the language of the rest of the title, as spoken. In English the numeral is read as an ordinal preceded by 'the' " (1968, abridged).

  C.   "Arrange the names of classes of aircraft, boats, etc. in which a numeral is an integral part of the heading alphabetically as spoken" (1968, abridged).

Examples

B. F. V.	
B-58 BOMBER	[fifty-eight]
B-17 BOMBER	[seventeen]
Baab, August	

Dix, Morgan	
10 ans de politique social en Pologne	[dix]
Dix ans d'études historiques	
Europe since 1815	[eighteen fifteen]
Europe since 1500	[fifteen hundred]
Europe since Napoleon	

(Examples continue on page 593)

Nineteen centuries of Christian
    song
1918, the last act   [nineteen eighteen]
Nineteen eighty-four
One hundred. *See also* entries beginning with "Hundred"
150 science experiments step-by-step   [one hundred and fifty]
One hundred and five sonnets
101 best games for teen-agers   [one hundred and one]
130,000 kilowatt power station   [one hundred and thirty thousand]
One hundred best books
1,999 belly laughs   [one thousand nine hundred and ninety-nine]
112 Elm Street   [one twelve]

10) **Words spelled different ways.** "Choose one spelling . . . and file all entries under that spelling" (1968, abridged). However, names spelled in different ways are arranged separately, regardless of how slight the difference (*see* Rule 18).

Examples

Andersen. *See also* the spellings Anderson, Anderssen, Andersson
Andersen, Hans Christian
Anderson. *See also* the spellings Andersen, Anderssen, Andersson
Anderson, Arthur
Anderssen. *See also* the spellings Andersen, Anderson, Andersson
Anderssen, Adolf

Color. Here are filed all entries beginning with the words "Color" and
    "Colour."
Colour harmony in dress
COLOR PHOTOGRAPHY
Colorado
Coloured glasses
Colors: what they can do for you
The colossus again
Colour. For entries beginning with the above word see the spelling
    "Color."
Colowick, Sidney P.

11) **Words written in different ways.**

A. "Arrange hyphened words as separate words when the parts are complete words. . . . The hyphen is treated as a space for filing purposes" (1968, abridged).

B. "In the case of compound words . . . written both as two separate words (or hyphened) and as a single word, interfile all entries . . . under the one-word form" (1968, abridged). For compound proper names *see* Rule 13.

C. "Arrange as one word, words beginning with a prefix or combining form such as anti-, bi-, co-, electro-, ex-, extra-, inter-, trans-, etc." (1968, abridged).

Examples

> Camp fire. For entries beginning with the above words, written with or without a hyphen, see the one-word form "Campfire."
> Campbell, Thomas J.
> Campfire. Here are filed all entries beginning with the words "Campfire," "Camp fire," and "Camp-fire."
> Campfire adventure stories
> Camp-fire and cotton-field
> Camp Fire Girls
>
> An epoch in life insurance
> Epoch-making papers in United States history
> The epoch of reform
>
> Pan- Words beginning with the above combining form are alphabetized as one word.
> Pan in ambush
> Panama
> Pan American Bureau
> Pan-American Congress

13) **Compound proper names.** File as separate words (1968, abridged).

14) **Proper names with a prefix.**

A. Spell as written, but file as one word (1968, abridged).

B. "Arrange names beginning with the prefixes M' and Mc as if written Mac" (1968, full).

Examples

> De senectute
> De Alberti, Amelia
> Defoe, Daniel
> De la Roche, Mazo
> Del Mar, Eugene
> De Marco, Clara

Elagin, Ivan
EL ALAMEIN, BATTLE OF, 1942   [Arabic place name]
Elam, Elizabeth
El Dorado, Ark.   [Spanish place name]
Eldorado, Neb.
El-Wakil, Mohamed Mohamed   [Arabic personal name]
Elwell, Floyd

Hall & Patterson
Hall Co., Tex.
Hall-Edwards, Craig
HALL OF FAME
Hall Williams, Lionel

M'... Celtic names beginning with M' are filed as if spelled "Mac"
          African names beginning with M' are filed as one word.
Mach, Ernst
McHenry, Lawson
MACHINERY
MacHugh, Angus
Maclaren, Ian
MacLaren, J
M'Laren, J   Wilson
McLaren, Jack
MacLaren, James
M'Bengue, Mamadou Seyni
Mc ... Names beginning with Mc are filed as if spelled "Mac."
Mead, Edwin Doak

18) **Proper names spelled differently.** Arrange separately (1968, abridged). *See* example under Rule 10.

19) **Order of entries under same word.**

    A.   Arrange in two main groups:
        1. Single surname entries, followed by
        2. All other entries arranged alphabetically disregarding kind of entry, form of heading, and punctuation (1968, abridged).

    B.   "Arrange subject entries under a person or corporate name immediately after the author entries for the same name" (1968, abridged).

    C.   "Interfile title added entries and subject entries that are identical and subarrange alphabetically by their main entries" (1968, abridged).

20) **Surname entries.**

   B.   Single surnames are arranged:

   1. Surname only,

   2. Surname with dates only,

   3. Surname with designation, forenames or initials (1968, abridged).

25) **Given name entries.** "Arrange . . . after the single surname entries of the same name, interfiling alphabetically in the group of titles, etc." (1968, full).

Examples

Charles, William
Charles   [title]
Charles Ann, Sister
Charles City, Iowa
Charles de Blois
Charles Douglas, freedom fighter   [title]
Charles, Duke of Burgundy
CHARLES FAMILY
Charles III, King of France
Charles I, King of Great Britain

Homer, Winslow
Homer   [author]
HOMER   [subject]
Homer   [title]
Homer and history

Smith,   [surname alone]
Smith,   fl. 1641 [surname followed only by date]
Smith, Adam
Smith, Captain   [surname followed only by title]
Smith, John
Smith, Mrs. John
Smith, John, pseud.
Smith, Sir John
Smith, John, surgeon
Smith, John, 1563-1616
Smith, John, 1798-1888
Smith, John, b. 1823

26) **Author arrangement.**

A. "Under an author heading arrange different kinds of entries in groups in the following order" (1968, abridged):

1. Works *by* the author, main and added entries interfiled. For added entries disregard author main entry, file by title of main entry.

2. Works *about* the author.

a. Without subdivision, arrange alphabetically by main entries.

b. With subdivision, arrange alphabetically by subdivision.

Examples

1st:	Love, Harold G	1878-1926
	The chemical industry ...	

1. "Works *by* the author"

2nd:	Love, Harold G	1911-
	Behaviour of nocturnal primates ...	
3rd:	Love, Harold G	1911- , ill.[12]
	The primates of Africa	
	Love, Harold G	1911-
4th:	Atkins, Francis Harrison	
	Psychological studies of the great apes ...	
5th:	Love, Harold G	1911- , ed.
	Symposium on the social organization of anthropoid apes ...	

2. "Works *about* the author subdivided"

	LOVE, HAROLD G	1911-
6th:	Driscoll, Maynard	
	Cousins, once removed ...	
	LOVE, HAROLD G – BIBLIOGRAPHY	
7th:	Coffin, Lyle Warner	
	Books by and about Harold Love ...	
	LOVE, HAROLD G – COLLECTED WORKS	
8th:	Love, Harold G	1911-
	The writings of Harold Love ...	

	Love	[title]
9th:	James, Samuel	
	LOVE	[subject]
10th:	Adams, Philip	
	Love and beauty	[title]
11th:	Hansen, Sigurd	

B. **Works by the author.** *See* pages 583-84 for part of this rule.

31) **Place arrangement.**

A. "Entries beginning with a geographical name follow the same name used as a single surname" (1968, full).

B. "Arrange all entries beginning with the same geographical name in one straight alphabetical file, word by word, disregarding punctuation" (1968, full).

C. Different kinds of geographical name entries are grouped in this order:

1. Author without subheading, subarranged by titles.

2. Subject without subdivision, and identical titles inter-filed, subarranged by main entries.

3. Heading with subdivisions, subdivisions interfiled alphabetically with each other and with titles, etc. (1968, full).

Examples

Lincoln, William Sever
Lincoln and Ann Ruthledge
LINCOLN BATTLE OF, 1217
LINCOLN CO. (KY.)
LINCOLN (ENGLAND)
Lincoln (Neb.)
LINCOLN (NEB.) – BIOGRAPHY
Lincoln plays

London, Jack
London   [title]
London and Londoners
LONDON (DOG)
LONDON (ENGLAND)
LONDON (ENGLAND) – DESCRIPTION
London (England) National Gallery
London (Ky.)

32. **Subject arrangement.**

A. "Subject entries follow the same word used as a single surname" (1968, full).

B. "Arrange entries with the same subject heading alphabetically by their main entries, then by title (1968, abridged).

C. "Arrange a subject, its subdivisions, etc., in groups in the following order" (1968, full).

1. Subject without subdivision: interfile with identical titles, alphabetically by their main entries.

2. Period divisions: arrange chronologically by the first date in the heading. (*See* Rule 32E below.)

3. All form, subject and geographical subdivisions, inverted subject headings, parenthetical terms, and phrase subject headings: interfile word by word with titles and other headings starting with the same word. Disregard all punctuation.

G. Period divisions. (*See also* page 583)

1. Open dates (e.g., 1865-   ) and periods beginning with the same year are arranged so as to bring the longest period first.

2. Periods expressed in words (e.g., "−COLONIAL PERIOD") or in words and dates (e.g., "−CONFEDERATION, 1783-1789") are arranged chronologically, *not* alphabetically.

3. Subdivisions for language and literature (e.g., "−OLD FRENCH," "−18TH CENTURY," etc.) are arranged chronologically.

4. Inverted chronological modifiers (e.g., "ART, MEDIEVAL") are arranged alphabetically, not chronologically, even when followed by a date (e.g., "HISTORY, MODERN−19TH CENTURY"). When used as further divisions of a subdivision, they are arranged chronologically (e.g., "MUSIC−HISTORY AND CRITICISM−ANCIENT") (1968, full).

Examples

COOKERY
COOKERY, AMERICAN
COOKERY, AMERICAN−ALASKA
COOKERY, AMERICAN−BIBLIOGRAPHY
COOKERY, AMERICAN−CALIFORNIA
COOKERY (APPLES)
COOKERY, CHINESE
COOKERY−DICTIONARIES
COOKERY FOR DIABETICS
Cookery for girls   [title]
COOKERY, INTERNATIONAL
COOKERY−YEARBOOKS

(Examples continue on page 600)

Examples (cont'd)

U.S. Entries beginning with this abbreviation are filed as if spelled
   "United States."
United States   [author]
UNITED STATES   [subject]
U.S. Adjutant-General's Office
U.S. – Agriculture. *See* AGRICULTURE – U.S.
U.S. – FOREIGN POPULATION
U.S. – FOREIGN RELATIONS
U.S. – FOR.REL. – TREATIES
U.S. foreign trade policy   [title]
U.S. – HISTORY
U.S. – HISTORY – COLONIAL PERIOD   [chronological]
U.S. – HISTORY – FRENCH AND INDIAN WAR, 1755-1763
U.S. – HISTORY – REVOLUTION
U.S. – HISTORY – REVOLUTION – CAMPAIGNS AND BATTLES
U.S. – HISTORY – 1783-1865
U.S. – HISTORY – CONFEDERATION, 1783-1789
U.S. – HISTORY – 1865-
U.S. – HISTORY – 1865-1898
U.S. – HISTORY – 1898-
U.S. – HISTORY – WAR OF 1898
U.S. – HISTORY – 20TH CENTURY
U.S. – HISTORY – 1933-1945
U.S. – HISTORY – BIO-BIBLIOGRAPHY   [alphabetical]
U.S. – HISTORY – DICTIONARIES
U.S. – HISTORY – PHILOSOPHY
U.S. – HISTORY – STUDY AND TEACHING

35) **Cross references.**

   A. "A reference or explanatory note precedes all other entries under the same word or words."

   B. "File *see* references in their alphabetical places."

   C. "File a *see also* reference before the first entry under the same word or words. If *see also* references are made for headings under which there are no entries in the catalog, file the reference where the heading itself would be filed"[13] (1968, abridged).

ALTERNATE FILING RULES

The *ALA Rules* summarized above were a response to a feeling that traditional practices embodied in *A.L.A. Rules* (1942 ed.) were too complex, too awkward, and too concerned with fine theoretical distinctions. Not everyone agrees, as is evidenced by the fact that many libraries have not fully implemented the changes. There are two major considerations: 1) it would be prohibitively expensive to re-file a card catalog for a collection of, say, a million volumes or more; and 2) there is a direct relationship between the size of the collection and the need for a fine-tuned filing system. John Rather argues the case for meaningful complexity:

> Filing arrangement is the capstone of the system of bibliographic control that begins with descriptive cataloging and includes subject analysis and classification. The entire effort to achieve bibliographic control necessarily reaches its fulfillment in the means of displaying catalog information to users. If the arrangement of the file violates the form or meaning of the headings, users will be hampered in their efforts to use the catalog successfully.[14]

The primary issue is categorical versus alphabetical filing. Research libraries hold that the 1968 *ALA Rules* to some extent "violate the form or meaning of the headings." The 1968 *ALA Rules* Subcommittee claimed:

> An attempt was made to develop an alternative code of rules based on a consistent regard for punctuation, but that method also proved to be not entirely satisfactory, because of lack of consistency in punctuation.[15]

The Subcommittee's reference was a major 1942 rule requiring that subject entries beginning with the same initial element be arranged by type as signified by differing marks of punctuation, in the following order:

1. The subject alone, unqualified, e.g., LOVE

2. The subject followed by a dash (−), e.g.,
LOVE – QUOTATIONS

3. The subject followed by a comma (,), e.g., LOVE,
MATERIAL

4. The subject followed by a parenthetical gloss, e.g.,
LOVE (THEOLOGY)

The Subcommittee held that many of the disadvantages of alpha arrangements could be overcome by adding state or country designations after all city names, and using parenthetical explanatory terms after all homonyms or homonymous phrases. There is a contemporary movement in favor of at least the first suggestion. (As stated in chapter 23 *AACR 2* optionally recommends additions to all local place and jurisdictional names.) The following examples compare the arrangements achieved by applying first one, then the other, of the 1942 and 1968 versions to the same group of entries:

1942 ALA Rules	1968 ALA Rules
Love, David T.	Love, David T.
LOVE, DAVID T.	LOVE, DAVID T.
Love, Zachary	Love, Zachary
The Love Corp.	LOVE [subject]
Love County (Okla.)	Love [title]
LOVE [subject]	Love and beauty
LOVE – LETTERS	The Love Corp.
LOVE – QUOTATIONS	Love County (Okla.)
LOVE, MATERIAL	LOVE – LETTERS
LOVE (THEOLOGY)	LOVE, MATERIAL
Love [title]	LOVE POETRY
Love and beauty	LOVE – QUOTATIONS
LOVE POETRY	Love songs, old and new
Love songs, old and new	LOVE (THEOLOGY)
Love your neighbor	Love your neighbor

The 1942 *ALA Rules* responded to the wide diversity of filing practices by including alternatives or variants for 60 percent of the rules. The 1968 Sub-committee opted for simplicity in this respect as well, developing a consistent code derived from one basic principle, with as few exceptions as possible. But if there were libraries which found the 1968 *ALA Rules* too simplistic, there were other, smaller libraries for which they were perhaps too complex. A simplified arrangement advocated by some school librarians and others is to interfile all entries, regardless of kind, in a literal alphabetical arrangement, like a telephone book.[16] The above set of terms would then be filed:

Straight alphabetizing

LOVE   [subject]
Love   [title]
Love and beauty
The Love Corp.
Love County (Okla.)
Love, David T.
LOVE, DAVID T.
LOVE – LETTERS
LOVE, MATERIAL
LOVE POETRY
LOVE – QUOTATIONS
Love songs, old and new
LOVE (THEOLOGY)
Love your neighbor

SHELFLIST FILING

The notation of most modern classifications, whether pure or mixed, includes arabic numerals (both integers and decimals) which are filed in normal mathematical sequence. A typical series of class numbers from the DDC schedules, which use a pure decimal notation, could appear as follows:

DDC Class Number Order

001	- Knowledge
010	- Bibliography
016	- Subject bibliographies
070.01	- Theory of journalism
070.1	- News media
070.17	- Printed media
070.172	- Newspapers
070.19	- Radio and television
070.4	- Journalistic activities
070.41	- Editing
070.509	- History of publishing
070.59	- Kinds of publishers
078	- Journalism in Scandinavia
100	- Philosophy
101	- Theory of philosophy
110	- Metaphysics
	[etc.]

Class number notation for the Library of Congress system is mixed. In its simplest form it consists of one to three roman alphabet letters followed by one to four integers. However, decimals in both pure numeric form and in alphanumeric form may be introduced at various points. A typical sequence might be:

LC Class Number Order

DJ288	- Netherlands history under Queen Juliana, 1948-
DJ401	- Local history in the Netherlands
DJ401.G35	- Goeree-en-Overflakke
DJ401.G4	- Groningen
DJK1	- Serials on Eastern European history
DJK24	- Social life and customs in Eastern Europe
DJK46	- Eastern European history by period
DJK46.4	- The Bulgars

(Example continues on page 604)

LC Class Number Order (cont'd)

T20   - History of technology in the 20th century
T26.G3   - History of technology in Germany
T26.G5B5 - History of technology in Berlin
TP572   - Directories of brewing and malting
TP573.A1 - General histories of brewing and malting
TP573.5   - Biography of brewers and malters
TP573.5A1 - Collective biography of brewers and malters
TP574   - Schools of brewing and malting
TP1107   - Exhibitions of plastics and plastics manufacture
TP1130   - Handbooks, manuals, tables, etc. of plastics
TP1135   - Plastics plants and equipment
            [etc.]

Book number notation also varies with the system. Libraries which use DDC may use book numbers assigned through use of the Cutter two- or three-figure alphanumeric tables or the Cutter-Sanborn tables. Two-figure Cutter and Cutter-Sanborn numbers can be filed in straight integer sequence, but those from the three-figure Cutter table must be arranged decimally, as shown:

DDC call numbers with three-figure Cutter book numbers

333 D189   - A work on land economics by an author surnamed Falkinson
333 D19   - A similar work by an author surnamed Fallaby
333 D191   - A similar work by an author surnamed Fallentz
333 D21   - A similar work by an author surnamed Famareus
333 D218   - A similar work by an author surnamed Fantine

Workmarks consisting of lower case letters, and most often corresponding to the first significant word of the item's title, may be added to the Cutter number as follows:

DDC call numbers with workmarks

515.33 R41i - Introduction to Differential Calculus, by an author
               surnamed Richmond
515.33 R41m- Mean Value Theorems, by the same author
515.33 R41t - Total and Directional Derivatives, by the same author

Many smaller libraries using DDC bypass the Cutter tables in favor of adding one to three or more capital letters from the main entry word of the item to the DDC class number. These book symbols are of course arranged alphabetically as follows. In such libraries congested files are rare, so that lower case workmarks are not often needed:

DDC call numbers with alphabetic book numbers

799.1 ROB - A book on fishing by an author surnamed Robb
799.1 ROBE - A similar book by an author surnamed Robertson
799.1 ROBI - A similar book by an author surnamed Robinson

The Library of Congress assigns its own unique book numbers to materials, as discussed in chapter 24 — Library of Congress Classification. Many LC call numbers include two "cutter" numbers, of which only the final one is, or incorporates, the book number. The official shelflist at the Library of Congress will show, with or without intervening entries, the following arrangement:

Library of Congress Shelflist Arrangement

HC59.7.B7	- Broekmeijer, M. W. J. M. *Fiction and truth about the decade of development.* (66-25082)
HC59.7.C28	- Caiden, Naomi. *Planning and budgeting in poor countries.* (73-12312)
HC59.7.C6	- Committee for Economic Development. *How low income countries can advance their growth.* (66-29453)
HN438.C5G2	- Galpern, A. N. *The religions of the people in sixteenth-century Champagne.* (75-35993)
HN438.P3R8	- Rudé, George F. E. *Paris and London in the eighteenth century.* (73-148267)
HN438.P6H52	- Higonnet, Patrice L. R. *Pont-de-Montvert; social structure and politics in a French village, 1700-1914.* (70-133209)

Dates or edition numbers may be added as a third element to either DDC or LC call numbers to distinguish different issues of the same title. These might be filed in either chronological or retrospective order, just as in catalog filing, but the majority of libraries prefer chronological shelflist filing. Location symbols of various kinds may also accompany call numbers of some materials. The shelflist filing of such additions is purely a matter of local preference.

CONCLUSION

The final results of the filing debates are by no means settled. Still, progress has been made. Perhaps universal standardization should not be our goal, given the diverse objectives of different libraries and types of libraries.

Besides, most of the disputes and examples illustrate "worst case" situations, rather than routine arrangements. Yet some theorists feel that not enough research has gone into clear enunciation of basic filing principles. Herbert Hoffman says of the 1968 *ALA Rules*:

> . . . this impressive body of specific rules is, in the end, nothing more than could be expected from a team of librarians trained to solve problems by data collection rather than analysis: a rich collection of traditions supported by only three very brief paragraphs on general principles that occupy less than a full page.[17]

Librarians have long been noted more for their pragmatism than for their theory. Yet significant progress has been made in understanding this feature of our bibliographic access problems, and worthy efforts continue. The Filing Committee of the Resources and Technical Services Division of the Library of Congress is presently working on the rules for its new machine-readable catalog which will be opened in 1981. A recent report says:

> The RTSD filing rules can be summarized as follows. The basic order of characters is (1) spaces, periods, dashes, hyphens, diagonal slashes; (2) numerals, 0-9; (3) letters of the English alphabet, a-z; and (4) letters of nonroman alphabets. Modified letters are treated like their plain equivalent in the English alphabet. All other punctuation marks and all non-alphabetic signs and symbols are ignored in filing except for the ampersand which is filed as its spelled-out language equivalent. If two records have identical access points, the function of the access point is considered as follows: (1) see-also references for main and added entries; (2) main and added entries interfiled; (3) see-also references for subject entries; and (4) subject entries. In general, main and added entries are subarranged by a title field and the imprint date; subject entries are subarranged by main entry, title field, and imprint date. Initial articles that form an integral part of place names and personal names (in personal, corporate, and conference headings) are regarded for filing purposes. All other initial articles in titles and topical subjects are disregarded. Numerals are arranged according to their numerical significance and roman numerals are filed with their arabic equivalent. In access points beginning with a surname, all terms of honor and address (for example, Dame, Lady, Lord, Sir, Mrs.) are disregarded for filing purposes. In all other access points, terms of honor and address are regarded for filing purposes.[18]

FOOTNOTES

[1]Kelley L. Cartwright, "Mechanization and Library Filing Rules," *Advances in Librarianship*, vol. 1 (New York, Academic Press, 1970), p. 59.

[2]*A Catalog of Books Represented by Library of Congress Printed Cards Issued to July 31, 1942* (Ann Arbor, MI, Edwards Brothers, 1943); vol. 14, pp. 3-13 gives full explanation of the arrangement.

[3]*ALA Rules for Filing Catalog Cards*, 2nd ed. (Chicago, American Library Association, 1968). The RTSD Board has approved and recommended for publication in 1980 a third edition of the rules (although a title alteration is possible). The new rules have been formulated within the context of *AACR 2* and the MARC formats.

[4]For a comparison of *LCSH 8* with *LCSH 7* filing practices, *see* pp. 502-503.

[5]*Webster's New International Dictionary of the English Language*, 2nd ed., unabr. (Springfield, MA, G.& C. Merriam, 1959), p. 1605.

[6]*See*, for instance, the Appendix to *ALA Rules*, 2nd ed., pp. 233-39.

[7]*A.L.A. Rules for Filing Catalog Cards* (Chicago, American Library Association, 1942), p. 25.

[8]*Anglo-American Cataloging Rules*, North American Text (Chicago, American Library Association, 1967), p. 10.

[9]*Cataloging Service*, bulletin 112 (Winter 1975):1.

[10]*Cataloging Service*, bulletin 114 (Summer 1975):3.

[11]*See* Pauline Seely, "ALA Filing Rules—New Edition," *Library Resources & Technical Services* 11 (Summer 1967):377-79; and Pauline Seely, "ALA Rules for Filing Catalog Cards: Differences Between 2d and 1st Editions (Arranged by 2d Rule Numbers)," *Library Resources & Technical Services* 13 (Spring 1969):291-94. A modification of these ALA 1968 Rules for a three-way divided catalog is found in Grant W. Morse, *Filing Rules: A Three-Way Divided Catalog* (Hamden, CT, Linnet Books, 1971).

[12]*See* the discussion of function terms on p. 587.

[13]Further discussion of the issues raised in this rule can be found on pp. 530-31 and 587.

[14]John C. Rather, "Filing Arrangement in the Library of Congress Catalogs," *Library Resources & Technical Services* 16 (Spring 1972):240-61.

[15]*ALA Rules*, 2nd ed., p. vi.

[16]Joseph T. Popecki, "A Filing System for the Machine Age," *Library Resources & Technical Services* 9 (Summer 1965):333-37.

[17]Herbert H. Hoffman, *What Happens in Library Filing?* (Hamden, CT, Linnet Books, 1976).

[18]*Library of Congress Information Bulletin* 37 (Aug. 25, 1978):520.

32 CATALOGING RECORDS AND ROUTINES

INTRODUCTION

Efficiency of bibliographic retrieval, and the quality of bibliographic description, are affected not only by the care and standards used to catalog each item, but by several other important factors. One is the recording of local decisions and practices and keeping the department files and records current; another is the organization and routines facilitating each phase of the process; a third is the continuing maintenance and editing of the catalog. Each of these factors should be carefully evaluated and efficiently administered. Here we will consider briefly the major responsibilities, summarizing those features for which patterns of implementation may vary from library to library. Organizational structure, including the specification of staff duties, is not within the scope of this text.[1]

Cataloging, as we know, is usually divided into two kinds of activity: description and subject analysis. These activities are in turn subdivided. Descriptive cataloging records the essential identifying bibliographic and physical details of an item. It also establishes non-topical access points through selection of entries and forms of heading. In the course of selecting access terms, references from terms not selected are frequently helpful or even necessary.

Subject access is generally provided in two complementary modes: by shelf arrangement and by descriptive terms. Both of these modes exhibit categories indicative of topical content, as well as other categories showing literary or publication form. The first mode consists of assigning unique call numbers to each item, using the notation of a systematic classification scheme, plus other identifiers for the specific piece. The other aspect of subject cataloging is choosing linguistic terms to characterize the item's content. These terms are in most libraries selected from a pre-coordinated "subject heading list." Since these, like non-topical access points, use a controlled vocabulary, references again provide bridges from terms not chosen to those chosen.

CATALOGING RECORDS AND FILES

A catalog department maintains files essential for accuracy, efficiency, standardization, and record keeping. Until recently, such files were nearly always formatted on cards or slips. Technology now offers new formats, which have been successfully introduced into several libraries. From the cataloger's, as well as the user's, viewpoint each embodies certain advantages, as well as some less attractive features.

ALTERNATIVE CATALOG FORMATS

The historical development and present uses of various catalog formats were briefly reviewed in chapter 1, "Principles of Cataloging." The dictionary catalog on 3x5-inch cards still predominates in most libraries; the maintenance problems faced in large research collections and multi-branch public library systems will be discussed in a subsequent section on "Closing Card Catalogs." Active vendor merchandizing of proprietary machine-readable data bases now brings alternative catalogs within the reach of smaller public and school libraries or systems. In many cases the existing card catalog remains in use, while another format is adopted to supplement and continue it.

Book catalogs may be produced in two ways, as was noted in chapter 1. In photoreproduction the book pages carry images of catalog cards, filed in order and reduced in size, but still in most cases quite legible. Varied type faces, type sizes, and local characteristics are all preserved. The original card catalog should, of course, be carefully groomed before it is photographed. Many manual operations, such as correcting errors, retyping poor quality cards, and checking the filing, are unavoidable prerequisites. Computer-based book catalogs have also been produced with varying degrees of success. Entries in such works are less likely to reflect a card-type appearance, being amenable to a denser column-and-line presentation.

Book catalogs are frequently limited to author (or main entry) lists, or to subject lists. They are far more compact and easy to scan than are card files, but they cannot be continuously cumulated, as can card lists. Periodically cumulated reprints are possible, but expensive. Most libraries prefer to supplement the latest book edition with a card file, an acquisitions list, or some other means of showing recent additions to the collection. The human tendency to overlook, or neglect to search, more than one file makes multiple access lists an ever-present hazard.

Computer output microform (COM) catalogs, like the other alternatives, are primarily a technological innovation. Still, their impact on cataloging procedures may be significant, and has not yet been fully assessed.[2] While initially expensive, COM per-unit cost is significantly reduced by mass production. Particularly in large libraries, where many service points need ready and full information about the entire collection, extra issues of the catalog at minimum cost are a real benefit. To be sure, other expenses, such as the purchase or lease of reading machines, and the keyboarding of all bibliographic records for the computer's data base, must be met. COM catalogs, like book catalogs, cannot be continuously expanded and updated. New cumulations must be reissued from time to time. Or supplements must provide the records for incoming materials in a separate alphabetical file, and possibly in a different format. Moreover, since microforms cannot be read with the naked eye, some simple form of indexing must accompany them. Microfiche indexing is more precise and easier to use than film indexing, which depends on sequential searching, but both are somewhat awkward. Another drawback is the reluctance of many people to work with microforms, which require different reading skills and attitudes than do print materials. Yet COM catalogs are increasing in number. Many large public systems, such as those in Hennepin County (Minnesota), St. Louis County (Missouri), Chicago, and Los Angeles County (California) now use them.

At the initial conversion stage, the machine-readable records may be stored in a large network data base, in commercial automated service facilities, on archival tapes, or in the in-house computers of individual libraries. Whatever the storage arrangements, COM catalogs, in either fiche or film, at various reduction ratios, can be issued in batch mode—that is, at times when online demands for computer power are minimal. Record and format quality depends on the needs and budget of the library. There are grades of difference, at varying prices. For example, the use of lower as well as upper case type faces, or the inclusion of special characters, will raise the cost of production, but will also result in a more pleasing, and usually a more readable, appearance.

Online machine-readable catalogs are still rare in libraries, although their number is growing. Some administrators now feel that it will be ultimately more satisfactory to wait until they can put their bibliographic records directly online, rather than adopting interim solutions in the forms of book or COM catalogs.

In some institutions computers were installed before their proponents knew precisely what would be their most effective applications. Librarians were thus encouraged to experiment with online catalogs to help absorb the computer potential and the fixed costs. More recently, various commercial services contract their hardware and software to libraries for the development of such products as online circulation systems, acquisitions systems, shelflists, and catalogs. A third source has come in the form of spin-offs from the large multi-institutional data bases that some cataloging networks, such as RLIN, supply. The future may provide further approaches, as well as new production technologies. The online catalog, with its bank of CRTs, retains the continuous expansion features of the card catalog, along with the compactness, speed, and ease of access characteristic of book and COM catalogs. Cost is still prohibitive for many libraries but will probably go down, rather than up, as computer services are expanded and refined.

THE SHELFLIST

The shelflist is a complete record of all titles in a collection, arranged by call number as the books stand on the shelves. Its primary purpose is to provide an official inventory record of the collection. Its classified arrangement shows what titles have been placed in a specific class number. It serves, then, as an important classification aid, for catalogers consult it to verify their library's past use of each number. The shelflist also displays, within certain limitations, related materials more general and more specific on either side of the number referred to. In addition, it furnishes the matrix on which unique book numbers and work marks are assigned, to differentiate titles collocated in the same class.

If the shelflist is in card format, the cataloger inserts a temporary hold slip, or other place marker, for each new item entered, to avoid duplication of call numbers, and to provide some information (not necessarily full cataloging) until the permanent record is made. That permanent record very likely will be a unit card, showing the entire bibliographic description plus tracings. Multiple volumes and copies, including location symbols for duplicates in reference, in children's rooms, branches, and the like, are noted. This information makes it not only easier, but more accurate, to browse the shelflist than to go directly to the shelves, where a number of items may be out in circulation, or otherwise displaced. The shelflist is thus useful not only to catalogers, but to reference staff and knowledgeable patrons. For these reasons many libraries make their shelflists available to the public. Others keep the official shelflist in the catalog office, perhaps placing a less detailed one near the card catalog.

Some libraries keep on their shelf cards brief records of costs, accession numbers, acquisition dates, sources, missing and withdrawn copies, or anything else considered pertinent to the current status of each title. Information of this kind is more likely to be added to a shelflist in card format than to a machine-readable list. With computerized production such information is often available in other subsystems or files. A typical "full information" shelf card is shown on page 613. It indicates that two copies of volume 1 have been purchased, but one is missing. In addition, the purchase source, date, and price of each volume and copy are shown. On an official card, of which this shelf card is a copy, the cataloger has checked the tracings which were actually used. In this particular library, no series card was made.[3]

OFFICIAL CATALOGS

Some libraries maintain an official card catalog, kept in the technical services area. Essentially, it is a tool of convenience, duplicating to some extent the information found in the public catalog or in the shelflist. Frequently, it is limited to one main entry per cataloged title. It often serves as the authority file, including information on the choice of all non-subject and subject added entries, explanatory cards, and cross references. Usually, it identifies materials held in departmental libraries or special collections. Since it is not open to the public, it may show additional non-bibliographic details for the guidance of the staff, such as administrative decisions on the use of analytics, and other notes which might be missed in the department manual.

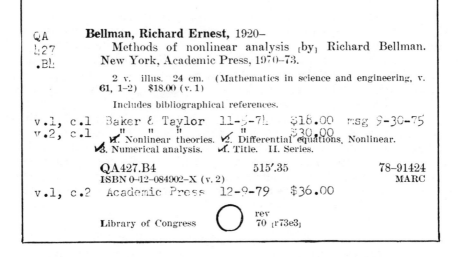

The shelflist approach is classificatory, showing the location of materials as they stand on the shelves. The official catalog, with its alphabetic approach, is complementary, but the high cost of keeping one prevents many libraries from indulging in a dispensable file. Such factors as library size, building layout, a decision to separate technical processes from public service areas, or responsibility for servicing more than one library unit are most likely to precipitate a separate official catalog.

AUTHORITY FILES

The purpose of an authority file, or files, is to standardize and control a library's use of non-subject entries, subject headings, and their respective cross references. In many smaller libraries its upkeep has often been more honored in the breach than in the observance. Such libraries obviously depend on their prime cataloging sources (e.g., the Library of Congress) to suggest cross references and to keep the use of heading forms in standard order. The inconsistencies that inadvertently creep in, through rule changes, error, and the like, are remedied if and when found. In a limited operation there may be some economic justification for this ad hoc approach. However, in larger libraries, where inconsistent and erroneous entries cause mis-filing, and otherwise obscure valuable entries in extensive files, the interest in authority files has recently escalated.[4]

Many libraries use the public catalog, or the official catalog, as their authority list, but some information that should be available to the acquisitions or catalog librarian does not lend itself to inclusion in a public file. Moreover, the introduction of *AACR 1* in 1967, and even more of *AACR 2* in 1978, stimulated a deal of soul searching about authority records among libraries great and small.

Name authority records bring together in an alphabetic list all name headings, personal, corporate, or geographic, which are used in a given catalog as main, added, analytic, or subject entries. Authority records for series, uniform titles, and topical subjects may be added, turning the list into a general authority file. Or they may be handled in other, separate files.

In 1974 the Library of Congress began to publish its quarterly, cumulative *Name Headings with References.* All newly established personal and corporate names, geographical names used for jurisdictions of civil governments, and uniform title headings for anonymous works, are given if references are added to help the searcher find them.[5] In 1976 it began distribution of LC subject authority records in machine-readable form.[6] Soon after, a pilot project for gradual conversion of name authority records to magnetic tape was started. By late 1978 the English Language Section III of LC's Descriptive Cataloging Division was ready to convert all such records that were not in the automated name authorities system, and were needed for materials being cataloged. Additional sections will be phased in successively.

> Machine-readable retrospective authority records will differ from such records for newly established headings insofar as the only source citation will be the work for which the heading was originally established. In addition biographical or historical information found in certain sources cited on the manual authority card will be combined into a single epitome note. Once converted to machine-readable form, however, retrospective records will be handled as any other record; that is, any additions or corrections will be made in full.[7]

Discussions sponsored by the Council on Library Resources indicate that a nationally shared authority file system is both desirable and possible. The files now existing in several libraries could be integrated as a cornerstone of any future national bibliographic network. Procedures for making additions could be placed under quality control at the Library of Congress, which has already converted to magnetic tape the 5,500 names it has used more than 25 times for headings.

> LC name authority records, including a small number prepared by the Government Printing Office and Northwestern University, are the only authorities presently available through the Library's MARC (machine-readable cataloging) tape distribution service.[8]

NAL, NLM, NYPL (a major component of RLIN), WLN, the University of Chicago system, and some commercial suppliers of bibliographic services, such as Blackwell North America, each have their own well-developed authority control programs. None is yet merged with the MARC system, although many of their records are based on LC's authority work. OCLC promises to provide its members with LC's authority file in early 1980, but will give no control over non-MARC name headings in its data base.

The most favored integration plan would merge high quality authority files from other institutions with those of the Library of Congress to build a unified file of names used for headings more than three times. With the help of a CLR grant the basic integrated file should be ready by January 1, 1981, when the Library of Congress adopts *AACR 2*.

Most libraries that maintain name authority records still do so in card form.[9] The steps suggested below demonstrate the essential features of localized authority control. First, it is important to understand the process of verification, which here means determining the existence of an author or other entity, and the accepted form of heading to use. Verification often involves consulting a number of bibliographic sources or reference tools. The name is first recorded as it appears in the work being cataloged. The item's title, date, and the location of the name, if it is not on the title page, are noted. If the name as it appears fulfills the requirements of *AACR 2* for establishing headings (e.g., Rule 22.1 — General Rule for Headings for Persons, or Rule 24.1 — Basic Rule for Headings for Corporate Bodies) the cataloger's decision to that effect is duly recorded. If verification problems emerge, such as the existence of different names or different forms of the same name, further sources of information must be consulted. These might be other works by the same author, NUC, CBI, BPR, *Name Headings with References*, or reliable directories or biographical dictionaries. The one or more sources used as authoritative should be cited on the card, together with any pertinent cross references. Reference cards should then be typed, as well as a revised authority card with the established form of the name at the top in entry position. The following illustration shows one format that the authority card might take:

```
Dowson, Mary Emily, 1948-

LC Name Headings with References, 1977

x Palmer, W. Scott        (LC)
x Palmer, William Scott   (LC)
x Dowson, M. E.           (local)



828      Michael Fairless; her life and writings,
B234Bd      by W. Scott Palmer (M. E. Dowson) and
         A. M.           Haggard. 1913.
```

Subject authority records usually represent the adaptation of one or more generalized subject heading lists to the needs of a particular library. LC and *Sears* lists are frequently marked and annotated to show local practice and are thus used directly as the authority file. *Sears* has consistently, throughout its many editions, supplied a blank one-half page alongside each column of subject terms and references, for the local library to record new decisions on subject usage as they are made. The hindrance to this method is the work entailed in transferring hand-written emendations into the new edition when it is published. Yet the need to transfer is possibly a spur to thorough revision from time to time of the library's subject practice. It has already been noted that the Library of Congress started to issue its subject authority records on magnetic tape in 1976.

An example of a subject authority card, indicating its source, is given below.

LITERATURE AND SCIENCE   (PN55; English literature, PR149.S4)

   sa LITERATURE AND TECHNOLOGY
       SCIENCE FICTION

   x Poetry and science
      Science and literature
      Science and poetry

   xx SCIENCE AND THE HUMANITIES

                                     LC 8th ed.

IN-PROCESS FILES

Certain areas of acquisitions and cataloging overlap. Each library's requirements must be studied to avoid duplication of record keeping, verification, etc. This is a continuous administrative responsibility. Some file, whether maintained by the cataloger or by the order librarian, must show "books in process." Its records continuously trace the status of each item from the time it is received in the library until it goes to the shelf, with its permanent catalog cards filed. Libraries that use multiple order forms can reserve one section for the in-process record. Others use the original requisition slip, once the book has been invoiced. Since the correct main entry may not be established until the book is cataloged, most libraries arrange their in-process files by title rather than by author. If printed cards are ordered separately from the works they describe (e.g., card orders from the Library of Congress) a separate file may be necessary for those card sets that arrive ahead of the books.

CATALOG DEPARTMENT MANUALS

The purpose of a department manual is to codify all pertinent decisions and procedures. A copy should be readily available to every member of the library staff, and it should contribute to the in-service training of every new cataloging employee. Even public service staff should be able and willing to consult it on problems of local catalog interpretation and use. It is most effective in looseleaf format, so the various tagged and indexed sections can be withdrawn and replaced by updated material as needed. Foster recommends that it give complete coverage of responsibilities and practices, and that it be easy to use, to read, and to revise. He gives the following points to remember during its preparation:

1. Arrange material in logical order so that related information is found together.
2. Use precise and concrete words, not abstract words. And illustrate whenever possible.
3. Be alert to details. Write the manual so that there is no question about procedures and so that the newcomer can easily understand and follow each routine.
4. But do not over-detail. Too much detail provides no room for individual variation and will not allow for minor changes without complete rewriting.
5. Anticipate future revisions and additions.
6. Before adding a new procedure into the manual, test it out to discover and correct unforeseen problems.
7. Take advantage of auxiliary sources, particularly publications from the Library of Congress.[10]

CATALOGING ROUTINES

We know that most cataloging performed in the United States today derives from LC copy in either print or machine-readable form.[11] Since the Library of Congress uses ISBD and *AACR 1* (*AACR 2* starting in January 1981), most present-day descriptive cataloging embodies the precepts of these two compatible and internationally recognized paradigms. ISBD is a recommendation from the IFLA Committee on Cataloguing relative to sequencing, punctuation, capitalization, abbreviation, etc. of a bibliographic description. It offers a frame by which significant areas such as the statement of responsibility, the imprint, the series statement, etc. can be recognized whether or not a user is familiar with the language of the record. *AACR 2* is a code providing rules for the choice and presentation of descriptive details and for choosing non-subject entries or access points, with their forms (headings) as they are to appear in a catalog.

As for subject analysis, the Library of Congress provides with most of its records a suggested DDC class number, as well as its own full call number, with possible alternative LC and DDC class numbers for such materials as bibliographies, biographies, and the separate parts of a monographic series. It also shows the subject headings it has chosen for the work. Local catalogers may use LC decisions as they stand, or modify them to reflect variations in edition, impression, or format, to complete the DDC class numbers, to adjust official LC call numbers to their local shelflists, to substitute *Sears* or other subject list terms for the LC subject headings, and to omit, add, or change other tracings. Original cataloging is usually necessary for a work without an available record from the Library of Congress or some other reliable bibliographic agency.

USE OF WORK FORMS

Whether the task is copy cataloging or original cataloging, work forms are useful to routinize procedures and ensure full coverage of essential points. In print format they are sheets, cards, or slips pre-printed to exhibit the standard categories of information that catalogers must consider. Many catalogers use typewriters. For them, some form of the 3x5-inch card (actually 7.5x12.5 cm.) or a larger work slip may be sufficient. Some libraries use one part of the multiple copy order forms available from library supply houses, but these leave little room for corrections and additions. If printed cards are purchased, especially from the Library of Congress or a commercial vendor, necessary changes to fit the local item may be made directly on the card set, or perhaps on one unit card, which can then be reproduced to give added copies for secondary entries, departmental or branch libraries, and shelflists.

Other catalogers prefer to use longhand on work sheets which are forwarded to typists for card production or inputting into machine-readable files. If the cataloging is based primarily on a large union file of machine-readable records, and done at a CRT (see Fig. 32.1), the operator usually can call up prepared work forms. These are filled in in substantive detail directly at the keyboard. Where the MARC format is used, pre-selected fields and tags are changed or expanded as needed. On the other hand, the cataloger may prefer to start in longhand on a printed form (*see* Fig. 32.2), handing the completed sheet to a terminal operator for inputting.

**Fig. 32.1. OCLC work form. [This form is reproduced by permission
from** *Cataloging: User Manual C79-1* **(Columbus, OH, OCLC, 1979), p. 6.]**

```
▶NO HOLDINGS IN XXX -  FOR HOLDINGS ENTER dh DEPRESS  DISPLAY RECD SEND
 OCLC: 3349989        Rec stat: n Entrd: 771108        Used: 781103 ¶
▶Type: a Bib lvl: m Govt pub:  Lang:  eng Source:   Illus: a
 Repr:    Enc lvl:   Conf pub: 0 Ctry:  nyu Dat tp: s M/F/B: 10
 Indx: 1 Mod rec:    Festschr: 0 Cont: b
 Desc: i Int lvl:    Dates: 1977,     ¶
  ▶ 1 010       77-77941 ¶
  ▶ 2 040       DLC ‡c DLC ¶
  ▶ 3 020       0525171940 : ‡c $17.95 ¶
  ▶ 4 050 0     GN31.2 ‡b .L43 1977 ¶
  ▶ 5 082       573.2 ¶
  ▶ 6 090        ‡b ¶
  ▶ 7 049       XXXM ¶
  ▶ 8 100 10    Leakey, Richard E. ¶
  ▶ 9 245 10    Origins : ‡b what new discoveries reveal about the
 emergence of our species and its possible future / ‡c Richard E. Leakey
 and Roger Lewin. ¶
 ▶10 260 0     New York : ‡b Dutton, ‡c c1977. ¶
 ▶11 300       264 p. : ‡b ill. (some col.) ; ‡c 25 cm. ¶
 ▶12 504       Bibliography: p. 257. ¶
 ▶13 500       Includes index. ¶
 ▶14 650  0    Anthropology. ¶
 ▶15 650  0    Human evolution. ¶
 ▶16 700 10    Lewin, Roger, ‡e joint author. ¶
```

Fig. 32.2. An OCLC Participant's Workform as adapted from the above MARC record for producing local catalog cards and archive tapes.

Type: a   Bib lvl: m   ~~Govt pub:~~   Lang: ~~eng~~ Source: ~~Illus:~~ a
Repr: Enc lvl: I   ~~Conf pub:~~ O   ~~Ctry:~~ nyu Dat tp: s   M/F/B: 1 0
~~Indx:~~ l Mod rec: ~~Festschr:~~ O   ~~Cont:~~ b
Desc: i   Int lvl: Dates: 1977

Note: positions crossed out are optional.

010	LCCN	77-77941	050	LC Call No. GN31.2 #b .L43 1977
040	Cat. Source	DLC	082	Dewey Class 573.2
020	ISBN	0525171940	090/092	Local Call No. 573 #b L47o
041	Lang.			

100	1 0 Main Entry	Leakey, Richard E.
245	1 0 Title	Origins : #b what new discoveries reveal about the emergence of our species and its possible future / #c Richard E. Leakey and Roger Lewin.
250	Edition	
260	0_ Imprint	New York : #b Dutton, #c c1977
300 / 350	Collation / Price (non ISBD(M))	264 p. : #b ill. (some col.) ; #c 25 cm.
4_	_Series	
504	Notes	Bibliography : p. 257.
500	Notes	Includes index.
505	_Contents	
650	0 Subject	anthropology
650	0 Subject	Human evolution.
6_	_Subject	
700	1 0 Added entry	Lewin, Roger.
7_	_Added entry	
7_	_Added entry	
8_	_Series traced differently	
910	_User option	

DESCRIPTIVE CATALOGING

Most libraries follow the Library of Congress in conforming to ISBD and *AACR* requirements, or some modification thereof. *AACR 2* outlines three levels of description, with increasing detail included at each of the two higher levels. It also offers options throughout, which frequently have to do with adding further details to the record. Main and added (non-subject) entries are determined in accordance with *AACR 2*, or perhaps with some adjustments for established practice. Any changes from LC practice, or *AACR 2* options exercised, should be described in the catalog department manual. All new headings should be recorded in the local authority list, along with cross references as indicated. Authority control was discussed earlier.

ASSIGNING CALL NUMBERS

After examining the item to be cataloged in the light of the classification schedules used by the library, a cataloger usually consults the shelflist to see if the class number chosen, or its possible alternative, has been previously used for similar or different materials. When the appropriate class number is selected, the distinguishing book number, with any necessary additions, such as work mark, edition date, or location symbol, is added. The full call number is recorded in the shelflist, on the item proper (with volume and copy number if needed), and on the work form. If catalog and shelflist are in card form, a temporary slip should be inserted in the shelflist, with possibly another in the catalog main entry position, pending arrival of permanent cards. Libraries using non-card catalogs frequently maintain card shelflists for recent additions, until a new cumulated non-card issue is available. In machine-readable files new entries are likely to be held or "saved" online until an authorized reviser has approved them, but this routine does not take so long that a temporary substitute is considered necessary.

ASSIGNING SUBJECT HEADINGS

The subject heading list and subject authority file used by the library must be consulted for consistent selection and recording of accepted headings and references. Obsolete terminology may be caught and changed at once, although it is usually better to postpone major overhauls to a designated time, in order to expedite new cataloging in progress. The work form for the particular item can carry instructions for the typist or keyboard operator to use when preparing added entries, tracings, new references, subject analytics, and the like. At this point the item, with its work form, is generally ready for final preparation. In most libraries the work form must be manually translated by a typist into cards, pockets, and labels before the work travels to the preparations department for final processing. Other libraries have this step performed by commercial suppliers, by a network central office, or by in-house automated printers.

CARD CATALOG MAINTENANCE

Like any ongoing function, a catalog is subject to wear and tear, obsolescence, inadvertent clerical and professional errors, inconsistency, and a variety of related ills. It therefore requires continual editing and maintaining, although libraries, being traditionally shorthanded, often neglect or postpone the responsibility, to the detriment of effective service. As collections grow, the efforts needed to keep a card catalog in satisfactory condition tend to increase exponentially. Outdated and disreputable cards, filing backlogs, and blind cross references (from headings once used but incompletely or inaccurately withdrawn) are among the major maintenance problems encountered. Attention to physical elements such as repair of damaged drawers or replacement of worn and soiled cards is important. Tray labels, guide cards, and instructions for use inside and outside the file should be altered whenever improvements are possible. Expansion inevitably requires occasional shifting of cards.

Catalog editing is needed to eliminate unnecessary entries, to suggest improvements, and to plan for future growth and development. Old entries may not have been pulled during cancellation of a title. Inconsistent headings, misleading or blind references, filing errors, missing cards, wrong call numbers, etc. all cause perplexity and ill will. The normal, rapid obsolescence of terminology mandates constant surveillance to modify or expand existing terms and references. The intricacies of connecting references between old and new headings, as established according to changes in rules of entry, must be adjudicated. Changes in filing rules also present problems. Some entries may need to be refiled, to keep pace with shifting needs of the library and its users. Foster describes a number of grooming functions that should be assigned as full- or part-time responsibilities, depending on the size and age of the catalog.[12]

REPRODUCING CATALOG CARDS

Libraries can obtain catalog cards in several ways. Some of the more common ones are:

1. The purchase of sets of unit cards from the Library of Congress, from a centralized or cooperative processor, or from any one of several commercial book jobbers or card suppliers. The purchaser adds call numbers, added entry lines, and other adjustments to tailor each set to its special needs.

2. The purchase of fully prepared card sets from a non-commercial or commercial processor.

3. The purchase of one unit card or proofslip (usually from the Library of Congress), adjusting and reproducing full card sets therefrom.

4. The adaptation of cataloging information from CIP, NUC, BPR, etc., formatting a unit card for reproduction.

5. The use of MARC tapes or some other machine-readable data base to produce cards by computer. This option may be exercised through the library's own computer hard and software, or through network facilities.

6. Subscription to LC generated cataloging data repackaged in a microform format. Cards are reproduced from the microforms in one of several ways, depending on the supplier.

7. Reproduction of cards from the library's original cataloging.[13]

Most libraries combine two or more of the above methods, depending on the type of materials being cataloged and the availability of copy. Small libraries often type all cards they produce from original cataloging, while buying most of their card sets in unit card form or fully processed. Others choose to invest in a small stencil duplicator. Still others prefer xerography.[14] Bibliographic network members can, and usually do, have their card sets fully prepared and pre-filed at the center headquarters.

No single method of card reproduction can meet the needs of all libraries. Appropriate reproduction policy is based on several variable factors, such as:

1. the percentage of available catalog records in printed card form
2. the quality of cataloging information needed
3. the number of cards needed per set
4. delivery time (insertion of temporary records is expensive)
5. card preparation for foreign language materials

RECLASSIFICATION AND RECATALOGING

There is inevitably a certain amount of recataloging to be performed in any library. Recataloging may be either a mass production affair or an individualized, single item performance. During the 1960s and early 1970s many medium-sized and larger libraries, especially academic ones, mounted full conversion projects from DDC to LC classification. Large-scale conversion was sometimes undertaken on special collections or a selected part of a collection. In the course of most such efforts, brief, inaccurate, or obsolete cataloging could be caught and redone. Many collections were at the same time weeded and surveyed for needed new materials.

More commonly, however, recataloging is performed on individual items for which the former records prove unsatisfactory. Class numbers within a given classification scheme (e.g., DDC or LC) may need changing because the schedules have been revised or because of new interpretations and needs within the collection. Recataloging on a greater or lesser scale is also the consequence of adopting a new or revised descriptive cataloging code. For instance, *AACR 2* severely restricts the use of corporate headings for main entries. Catalogers whose libraries are not yet ready to close their card files and start new ones based strictly on the changed rules, must decide what to do about superseded usages, particularly changed headings for already used entries that are likely to be used again. Not all practices have been officially standardized to meet this dilemma. The next few years will see a variety of solutions offered. Some will attempt to solve it with full sets of *see also* references linking old and new forms of headings in unified or split files without actually recataloging the older works. Others will try a combination of refiling old headings under guide-cards carrying the new heading forms, leaving *see* references at the old positions to assist users who still search under those outdated forms. Still other libraries will recatalog under the new forms, particularly if there are only a limited number of entries under the obsolete forms.

CLOSING CARD CATALOGS

In 1965 studies were made at the New York Public Library which confirmed that a staggering number of the cards (actually 29 percent) in the public catalog of the Research Libraries Division were illegible, damaged, dirty, badly worn, or otherwise unfit to remain. The problem was aggravated by the fact that some entries had been there for over one hundred years. It was a dramatic instance of a malaise that was reaching epidemic proportions in many long-established research libraries. Besides the deterioration problem, upkeep and maintenance were expensive and unsatisfactory. Space, lighting, and furniture pose real logistics problems in files of over ten million cards. Labor costs for filing and revising are increasing rapidly.

The NYPL studies led to a decision to photograph the existing catalog prior to discarding it in favor of conversion to book format.[15] All new cataloging would be made available in a combination of card and book formats from a store of machine-readable records.[16]

The NYPL venture, along with other, similar experiments, encouraged the Library of Congress to announce in late 1977 that it would soon implement a similar solution to its card catalog proliferation.[17] LC's original plans were to "freeze" its existing files on January 1, 1980. The particular point in time was intentionally orchestrated to the appearance of *AACR 2*, but other research libraries, fearful of the consequences of so "precipitous" an action, persuaded the Library of Congress to postpone the change until January 1, 1981.

The Library proposed to abandon at the same time its practice of "superimposition," by which it retained most of its established headings regardless of rule changes, following *AACR* dictates only for those headings being established for the first time. Superimposition had been an attempt to avoid the Herculean task of updating all forms rendered obsolete by the new rules. But even with liberal use of cross references, it confounded catalogers and catalog users alike, with its legacy of inconsistent access forms in a single file. Starting in 1981, with all obsolete headings officially frozen in a searchable, but defunct, catalog, headings for new materials can be established according to *AACR 2* regardless of whether a given entry is identified differently in the old catalog. It must be remembered that complete bibliographic access to all the records in *both* catalogs under many personal, corporate, and geographic headings will require that the search be conducted under heading forms that differ from one catalog to the other. The kind and number of cross references to be used in one or both catalogs has occasioned much discussion.

Not all librarians are yet convinced that a step as radical as closing one catalog and starting afresh on another is the best solution to our problems of catalog lag. As yet, only very large research collections have tried it, and the evidence is by no means all in. Smaller collections will probably find no compelling reasons to try at any foreseeable future time such an unproved and disputed alternative to their existing card catalogs.

FOOTNOTES

[1]Other reliable texts are available for this purpose. *See*, for example: Marty Bloomberg and G. Edward Evans, *Introduction to Technical Services for Library Technicians*, 4th ed. (Littleton, CO, Libraries Unlimited, 1980); and Donald L. Foster, *Managing the Catalog Department* (Metuchen, NJ, Scarecrow, 1975).

[2]Ellen Altman, "Reactions to a COM Catalog," *Journal of Academic Librarianship* 3 (Nov. 1977):267-68; Richard W. Meyer and Bonnie Juergens, "Computer Output Microfiche Catalogs: Some Practical Considerations," *Journal of Micrographics* 11 (Nov. 1977):91-96; and William Saffady, *Computer-Output Microfilm: Its Library Applications*. Chicago, American Library Association, 1978.

[3]For additional examples of shelflist cards and explanations, *see* Bloomberg and Evans, *Technical Services*.

[4]*See*, for instance: S. Michael Malinconico, "Bibliographic Data Base Organization and Authority File Control," *Wilson Library Bulletin* 54 (Sept. 1979):36-45.

[5]Library of Congress, *Name Headings with References*, 1974-date.

[6]*Cataloging Service*, bulletin 119 (Fall 1976):4-5.

[7]*Cataloging Service Bulletin*, no. 3 (Winter 1979):7.

[8]*CLR Recent Developments*, vol. 8, no. 1 (Jan. 1980):[1].

[9]For procedures used to establish a name authority card file at the Simmons College Library, *see*: Edith K. Baecker and Dorothy C. Senghas, *A Little Brief Authority: A Manual for Establishing and Maintaining a Name Authority File* (Boston, Dedoss Associates, 1978).

[10]Foster, *Managing the Catalog Department*, p. 189.

[11]For discussion of adapting copy in the cataloging process, *see* Arlene Taylor Dowell, *Cataloging with Copy: A Decision-Maker's Handbook* (Littleton, CO, Libraries Unlimited, 1976).

[12]Foster, *Managing the Catalog Department*, pp. 14-20.

[13]Nancy Hoyt Knight, "Microform Catalog Data Retrieval Systems: A Survey," *Library Technology Reports*, May 1975.

[14]Recent surveys of card reproduction can be found in: Dowell, *Cataloging with Copy*, pp. 17-19; and Bloomberg and Evans, *Technical Services.*

[15]S. Michael Malinconico and James A. Rizzolo, "New York Public Library Automated Book Catalog Subsystem," *Journal of Library Automation* 6 (March 1973):3-36.

[16]James W. Henderson and Joseph A. Rosenthal, *Library Catalogs: Their Preservation and Maintenance by Photographic and Automated Techniques* (Cambridge, MA, The M.I.T. Press, 1968), p. ix.

[17]"LC to Freeze Card Catalog," *Library of Congress Information Bulletin* 36 (Nov. 4, 1977):743-44; "Freezing the Library of Congress Catalog," *Library of Congress Information Bulletin* 37 (March 3, 1978):152-56; and "Information on Freezing the Catalog Updated," *Library of Congress Information Bulletin* 37 (July 21, 1978):415-19.

CATALOGING AND CLASSIFICATION AIDS

Fortunately, many aids are available today to help the cataloger with the various difficult aspects of his or her work. Library interest in bibliography and biography provides important reference tools that help the cataloger verify personal names and corporate bodies. More specific tools are designed for classification and choice of subject headings. Still different tools furnish complete cataloging records, as prepared by the Library of Congress, or perhaps another cataloging source, for individual works.

The beginning cataloger must know the principles and rules underlying the techniques of cataloging and classification before he or she can make intelligent use of these aids. For this reason, introductory cataloging courses emphasize original cataloging, in which the student does both the descriptive and subject cataloging from scratch, even though a shelflist and pre-processed bibliographic records (when available) are generally used in an on-the-job situation. The cataloging aids listed below are by no means the only ones available. They suggest only some of the landmark titles available for consultation, indicating the range of information and specialization within the field.

CODES, SCHEDULES, AND MANUALS

Classification and Shelflisting

Cutter, C. A. *Two-Figure Author Table* (Swanson-Swift Revision), 1969; *Three-Figure Author Table* (Swanson-Swift Revision), 1969; and *Cutter-Sanborn Three-Figure Author Table* (Swanson-Swift Revision), 1969. Distributed by Libraries Unlimited, Inc., Littleton, CO.

Dewey, Melvil. *Dewey Decimal Classification and Relative Index.* ed. 19. Albany, NY, Forest Press, 1979. 3 v.

Library of Congress. *Library of Congress Classification: Classes A-Z.* var. eds. Washington, The Library, 1917-   . 33 v.

Library of Congress. Decimal Classification Division. *Conversion Table of a Substantial Number of Changes from Edition 18 to Edition 19 in Edition 19 Order.* Albany, NY, Forest Press, 1980.

Olson, Nancy B. *Combined Indexes to the Library of Congress Classification Schedules.* Washington, United States Historical Documents Institute, 1974. 15v.

Swanson, Gerald L. *Dewey to LC Conversion Tables.* New York, CCM Information Corp., 1972.

Description, Entry, and Heading

Anglo-American Cataloguing Rules. 2nd ed. Chicago, American Library Association, 1978.

Filing

ALA Rules for Filing Catalog Cards. 2nd ed. Chicago, American Library Association, 1968.

ALA Rules for Filing Catalog Cards. 2nd ed., abridged. Chicago, American Library Association, 1968.

Library of Congress. *Filing Rules for the Dictionary Catalogs of the Library of Congress.* Washington, GPO, 1956.

New York Public Library. "The Research Libraries Proposed Filing Rules for Prospective Catalog (Preliminary Version)," in *Library Catalogs: Their Preservation and Maintenance by Photographic and Automated Techniques* (M.I.T. Report No. 14). Cambridge, MA, The M.I.T. Press, 1968. pp. 247-60.

Rather, John C. "Proposed Filing Rules for the LC Catalogs (Abridged Version)," *Library Resources & Technical Services* 16 (Spring 1972):249-61.

Subject Headings

Haycock, Ken, and Lynne Isberg. *Sears List of Subject Headings: Canadian Companion.* New York, H. W. Wilson, 1978.

Library of Congress. *Library of Congress Subject Headings.* 8th ed. Washington, The Library, 1975.

Marshall, Joan K., comp. *On Equal Terms: A Thesaurus for Nonsexist Indexing and Cataloging.* Santa Barbara, CA, American Bibliographical Center-Clio Press, 1977.

National Library of Canada. *Canadian Subject Headings.* Ottawa, The Library, 1978.

Sears, Minnie Earl. *Sears List of Subject Headings.* 11th ed. Edited by Barbara M. Westby. New York, H. W. Wilson, 1977.

Terminology

A.L.A. Glossary of Library Terms. Chicago, American Library Association, 1943.

Harrod, Leonard Montague. *The Librarians' Glossary.* 4th ed. Boulder, CO, Westview Press, 1977.

These tools to a large extent define the parameters of present-day American/Canadian cataloging. The *A.L.A. Glossary*, while dated, is still useful for traditional terminology. A glossary appended to *AACR 2* supplies more recent contexts and definitions where needed. As for filing codes, both the ALA and the LC rules are designed for manually filed catalogs. The Library of Congress has not yet issued an official update of its 1956 rules.[1] Both the Rather and the NYPL proposals serve primarily to show the direction in which automated filing is headed. More insight can be gained from the introduction to the eighth edition of *Library of Congress Subject Headings.*

GENERAL TEXTBOOKS

Bloomberg, Marty, and G. Edward Evans. *Introduction to Technical Services for Library Technicians.* 4th ed. Littleton, CO, Libraries Unlimited, 1980.

Chan, Lois Mai. *Immroth's Guide to the Library of Congress Classification.* 3rd ed. Littleton, CO, Libraries Unlimited, 1980.

Chan, Lois Mai. *Library of Congress Subject Headings: Principles and Applications.* Littleton, CO, Libraries Unlimited, 1978.

Dowell, Arlene Taylor. *Cataloging with Copy: A Decision-Maker's Handbook.* Littleton, CO, Libraries Unlimited, 1976.

Foster, Donald L. *Managing the Catalog Department.* Metuchen, NJ, Scarecrow Press, 1975.

Haykin, David J. *Subject Headings: A Practical Guide.* Washington, GPO, 1951.

Horner, John. *Special Cataloguing, with Particular Reference to Music, Films, Maps, Serials and the Multi-Media Computerized Catalogue.* Hamden, CT, Linnet Books & Clive Bingley, 1973.

Merrill, William S. *Code for Classifiers.* 2nd ed. Chicago, American Library Association, 1939.

Tillin, Alma M., and William J. Quinly. *Standards for Cataloging Nonprint Materials.* 4th ed. Washington, Association for Educational Communications and Technology, 1976.

Weihs, Jean Riddle, Shirley Lewis, and Janet Macdonald. *Nonbook Materials: The Organization of Integrated Collections.* 2nd ed. Ottawa, Canadian Library Association, 1979.

Wynar, Bohdan S., with the assistance of John Phillip Immroth. *Introduction to Cataloging and Classification.* 5th ed. Littleton, CO, Libraries Unlimited, 1976.

Some of these textbooks may seem outdated because of such recent changes as the revisions of *AACR,* of *LCSH, Sears,* Dewey, the LC Classification schedules, etc. Nevertheless, they will help the beginning cataloger locate materials on basic principles of cataloging and classification. The introductory pages in *LCSH* and the *Sears* list, and the "Editor's Introduction" to the *Dewey Decimal Classification* can also be very helpful.

NATIONAL BIBLIOGRAPHIES AND CATALOGS

Books in Series in the United States. 2nd ed. New York, Bowker, 1979.

Library of Congress. *Catalog of Books Represented by Library of Congress Printed Cards.* Ann Arbor, MI, Edwards Brothers, 1942-1955. 191 v. (Title varies).

Library of Congress. *Library of Congress Catalog, Books: Subjects.* 1950- . (Various publishers).

Library of Congress. *Library of Congress Catalogs: Monographic Series.* Washington, The Library, 1974- .

National Union Catalog: A Cumulative Author List Representing Library of Congress Printed Cards and Titles Reported by Other American Libraries. Washington, Library of Congress, 1956- .

National Union Catalog: Pre-1956 Imprints. London, Mansell, 1968- . (In progress).

New Serial Titles: A Union List of Serials Commencing Publication after December 31, 1949. Washington, Library of Congress, 1953- .

Union List of Serials in Libraries of the United States and Canada. 3rd ed. New York, H. W. Wilson, 1965. 5 v.

These tools are undoubtedly among the most important of all cataloging aids, useful particularly for verifying entries and providing authoritative descriptive cataloging and classification. While they represent a considerable financial investment, even a medium-sized library would find these basic sets, supplements, and current volumes invaluable as both cataloging and reference tools. Several foreign national bibliographies and catalogs published by the British Museum, the Bibliothèque Nationale, etc. might also be useful.

ADDITIONAL AIDS

For verifying entries and suggesting class numbers and subject headings:

BPR: American Book Publishing Record. New York, Bowker, 1960- .

Children's Catalog. 13th ed. New York, H. W. Wilson, 1976. (Supplements).

Elementary School Library Collection: A Guide to Books and Other Media, Phases 1-2-3. 12th ed. New Brunswick, NJ, Bro-Dart Foundation, 1979.

Fiction Catalog. 9th ed. New York, H. W. Wilson, 1975. (Supplements).

Junior High School Library Catalog. 3rd ed. New York, H. W. Wilson, 1975. (Supplements).

Senior High School Library Catalog. 11th ed. New York, H. W. Wilson, 1977. (Supplements).

Standard Catalog for Public Libraries. 6th ed. New York, H. W. Wilson, 1973. (Supplements).

Weekly Record. New York, Bowker, 1974- .

For verifying entries and heading forms:

Book Review Digest. New York, H. W. Wilson, 1905- .

Booklist. Chicago, American Library Association, 1905- .

Cumulative Book Index: A World List of Books in the English Language. New York, H. W. Wilson, 1898- .

Library of Congress. *Library of Congress Name Headings with References.* Washington, The Library, 1974- .

United States. Superintendent of Documents. *Monthly Catalog of United States Government Publications.* Washington, GPO, 1895- .

United States Government Manual, 1979/80. Washington, Office of the Federal Register, National Archives and Records Service, General Services Administration, 1979. (Formerly *United States Government Organization Manual*).

For verifying names, dates, and other biographical data:

Contemporary Authors. Detroit, Gale Research, 1962- .

Current Biography: Who's News and Why. New York, H. W. Wilson, 1940- .

Dictionary of American Biography. New York, Scribner's, 1928-1936. 20 v., index, and 3 supplements.

Dictionary of National Biography. 1885-1936. 63 v. and 6 supplements. Additional supplements to 1960. Reissued in 22 v. by Oxford University Press, 1938.

The New Century Cyclopedia of Names. New York, Appleton-Century-Crofts, 1954. 3 v.

The New York Times Obituaries Index 1858-1968. New York, The New York Times, 1970.

Webster's Biographical Dictionary. Springfield, MA, Merriam, 1972.

Who's Who: An Annual Biographical Dictionary. London, Black, 1849- .

Who's Who in America: A Biographical Dictionary of Notable Living Men and Women. Chicago, Marquis, 1899- .

In addition, catalogers use many specialized biographical directories, such as *American Men and Women of Science, Directory of American Scholars, Twentieth Century Authors, Who's Who in Education*, etc. Many special handbooks, gazetteers and general reference tools, including encyclopedias, are also useful.

For verifying geographical names:

Library of Congress. *Library of Congress Catalogs. A Cumulative List of Works Represented by Library of Congress Printed Cards: Maps and Atlases.* v. 1-3. Washington, The Library, 1953-1955.

United States. Geographic Board. *Sixth Report*, 1890-1932. Washington, GPO, 1933- . (Supplements).

While other sources of geographic name verification, including some titles previously cited, are reliable, the basic sources of standard forms on which American libraries rely are the publications of the U.S. Board on Geographic Names and its predecessors, the Board on Geographic Names (1934-1947) and the Geographic Board (1890-1934). The principal sources for foreign names are the *Gazetteers* of the present Board. Many foreign gazetteers and geographical reference sources will supplement this information.

For current information and updating:

Cataloging and Classification Quarterly. 1979- . (Quarterly).

Cataloging Service Bulletin, no. 1- . Washington, The Library of Congress, 1978- . (Quarterly). Supersedes *Cataloging Service*, bulletins 1-125 (1945-1978).

Hennepin County Library. Cataloging Section. *HCL Cataloging Bulletin*, May 1973- .

Library of Congress Information Bulletin. Washington, The Library, 1942- . (Weekly).

Library of Congress. Decimal Classification Division. *Dewey Decimal Classification: Additions, Notes and Decisions.* Washington, The Library, 1959- . (Irregular).

Library of Congress. Subject Cataloging Division. *L.C. Classification—Additions and Changes.* Washington, 1928- . (Quarterly).

Library of Congress Classification Schedules: A Cumulation of Additions and Changes, 1974-77. Helen Savage, ed. Detroit, Gale, 1978.

Library of Congress Classification Schedules: A Cumulation of Additions and Changes Through 1973. Helen Savage, ed. Detroit, Gale, 1974.

Library of Congress Subject Headings Supplement. Washington, The Library, 1908- . (Quarterly, plus microform quarterly cumulations).

Library Resources & Technical Services. Chicago, American Library Association, 1957- . (Quarterly).

Footnotes

[1]S. C. Biebel, "Filing Committee," *Library of Congress Information Bulletin* 37 (Aug. 25, 1978):519-20.

GLOSSARY OF SELECTED TERMS
AND ABBREVIATIONS

Defined in this glossary are selected basic terms for students of cataloging, including a number of terms and identifiers used in descriptive cataloging, classification, subject heading work, filing, document indexing, networking, and other topics treated in this text. Consult the *AACR 2* Glossary (Appendix D) and Abbreviations (Appendix B) for additional terms used in the rules. Fuller discussion of a few of the terms included here may be found in Phyllis A. Richmond's "AACR 2 – A Review Article," in *Journal of Academic Librarianship*, vol. 6, no. 1 (March 1980), pages 30-37.

Access point. See **Choice of access points.**

Accession number. A number assigned to each book as it is received in the library. Accession numbers may be assigned through continuous numbering (e.g., 30291, 30292) or a coded system (67-201, 67-202, etc.).

Accompanying materials. Dependent materials, such as answer books, teacher's manuals atlases, portfolios of plates, slides, and phonodiscs.

Add instructions. Notes in classification schedules that specify what digits to add to what base number; they replace divide-like notes in DDC.

Added entry. A secondary access point – i.e., any other than the main entry. An added entry record often duplicates the main entry record except that it has an additional heading to represent in the catalog a subject, joint author, illustrator, editor, compiler, translator, collaborator, series, etc. (Subject entry is excluded from this definition in LC usage.)

AMIGOS. A regional bibliographic service center network in Arizona, Arkansas, New Mexico, Oklahoma, and Texas for facilitating the use of OCLC and other cooperative programs.

Analytical entry. An entry for a part of a work or for a whole work contained in a series or a collection for which a comprehensive entry is made. Name-title analytics may be made in the form of added entries.

Anonymous work. One in which the author's name does not appear anywhere in the book; a work of unknown authorship.

Area. A major section of a catalog entry – e.g., edition area or physical description area.

Artifact. See **Realia.**

Author. The person chiefly responsible for the intellectual or artistic content of a work – e.g., writer of a book, compiler of a bibliography, composer of a musical work, artist, photographer, etc.

Author number. See **Book number.**

Authority file. A record of the correct forms of names, series, or subjects used in the catalog. The purpose of the authority file is to keep entries uniform.

Auxiliary table. A generalized subdivision table appended to a classification schedule for use in building specific class numbers where indicated in the schedule proper.

BALLOTS. Bibliographic Automation of Large Library Operations using a Time-sharing System, at Stanford University, now reorganized into RLIN.

BCR. Bibliographical Center for Research, a regional service network headquartered in Denver, Colorado.

Bibliographic record. A catalog entry in card, microtext, machine-readable, or other form carrying full cataloging information for a given item in a library.

Bibliographic service center. A regional broker, providing intermediate communication, training, and service for libraries participating in an online bibliographic network.

Bibliographic utility. An online processing center based on a machine-readable data base of catalog records.

Book number. The symbols, usually a combination of letters and numbers, used to distinguish books with the same classification number in order to maintain the alphabetical order (by author) of books on the shelves; also called an author number. Cutter number is another term used, deriving from the widespread use of Cutter-Sanborn Tables to devise book number symbols.

Books in sets. See **Monographs in collected sets.**

Boolean operators. The terms, "and," "or," and "not," as used to construct search topics through post-coordinate indexing.

Broad classification. A scheme that omits detailed subdivision of its main classes, or that facilitates the use in smaller libraries of only its main classes and subdivisions.

BSO. Broad System of Ordering, a classification developed for a proposed worldwide information network covering the whole field of knowledge.

Call number. The notation used to identify and locate a particular book on the shelves; it consists of the classification number and author number, and it may also include a work number (workmark).

CAN/MARC. A machine-readable bibliographic record format for monographs and serials compatible with LC/MARC, developed by the National Library of Canada.

Catalog. A list of books, maps, recordings, coins, or any other medium that composes a collection. It may be arranged by alphabet, by number, or by subject. It may be in the form of cards, book, computer output microform (COM), or computer online.

Cataloging. The process of describing an item in the collection and assigning a classification number. See also **Descriptive cataloging** and **Subject cataloging.**

Catchword indexing. Use of significant words from a title or a text as index entries.

Categorical filing. The preference in some areas of a filing system of partially classified arrangements over a straight alphabetical sequence.

Centralized processing. Any cooperative effort that results in the centralization of one or more of the technical processes involved in getting material ready for use in a library.

Chain index. A direct and specific index based on the extracted vocabulary of a classification system. It retains all necessary context but deletes unnecessary context; all subheadings are superordinate terms.

Chief source of information. The source in an item that is prescribed by the rules as the major source of data for use in preparing a bibliographic description.

Choice of access points. The process of selecting the main entry or heading and any added entries under which an item is to be listed in the catalog.

CIP. Cataloging in Publication, a program sponsored by the Library of Congress and cooperating publishers; a partial bibliographic description is provided on the verso of the title page of a book.

Classification number. The number assigned to an item of a collection to show the subject area and to indicate its location in the collection.

Classification schedule. The printed scheme of a particular classification system.

Close classification. The use of minute subdivisions for arranging materials by highly specific topics.

Closed stacks. Library collections not open to public access or limited to a small group of users.

CLR. Council on Library Resources, Inc., a private foundation with the principal objective of aiding in the solution of library problems.

CODEN. A system of unique letters assigned for ready identification of periodicals and serials, now administered by Chemical Abstracts Service (CAS).

Collection. Three or more works or parts of works by one author published together, or two or more works or parts of works by more than one author published together. Each work in a collection was originally written independently or as part of an independent publication.

COM. Computer Output on Microform.

COMARC. Cooperative MARC, an experimental program for LC to develop modes of cooperation with outside libraries and network utilities in building high-quality bibliographic data bases and authority records.

Compiler. One who brings together written or printed matter from the works of various authors or the works of a single author.

Composite work. An original work produced by the collaboration of two or more authors in which the contribution of each forms a separate and distinct part.

Computer-produced catalog. A catalog based on machine-readable cataloging records.

CONSER. Conversion of Serials project, a shared national data base of serial records from selected libraries, now maintained by OCLC.

Continuation. 1) A work issued as a supplement to an earlier one. 2) A part issued in continuance of a book, a serial, or a series.

Coordinate indexing. Information retrieval through the use of related terms in a catalog or data base to identify concepts.

Copyright. The exclusive right to publish a work for a specified number of years. The copyright date of a book is printed on the title page or the verso of the title page.

Corporate body. An organization or group of persons who are identified by a name and who act as an entity.

Cross reference. A reference made from one entry in a catalog to another: *see* reference and *see also* reference.

CRT. Cathode Ray Tube, an electronically stimulated screen on which computer-stored data may be visually displayed.

Cutter number. See **Book number.**

Dash. A symbol of punctuation and separation which in printing consists of a single line and in typing is made by striking the hyphen key twice in succession. In descriptive cataloging the dash usually appears with one space on either side; for subject subdivisions no spaces are used.

DDC. Dewey Decimal Classification.

Descriptive cataloging. The phase of the cataloging process concerned with the identification and description of library material and the recording of this information in the form of a catalog entry.

Divide-like note. A place in a classification schedule referring the user to another location where analogous sequencing and notation set a pattern.

Edition. In the case of books, all the impressions of a work printed at any time or times from one setting of type; also, one of the successive forms in which a literary text is issued either by the author or by a subsequent editor. In the case of nonbook materials, all the copies of an item made from one master copy.

Edition area. Includes the following elements: named and/or numbered edition statement, and statement of responsibility relating to a particular edition, if any.

Editor. One who prepares for publication or supervises the publication of a work or collection of works or articles that are not his own. Responsibility may extend to revising, providing commentaries and introductory matter, etc.

Element. A sub-section of an area in the catalog entry; for example, the alternative title is an element of the title and statement of authorship area.

Entry. A representation of a bibliographic record at a particular point in a catalog. There can be one or more entries for any one heading. See also **Heading.**

Entry word. The word by which the entry is arranged in the catalog, usually the first word (other than an article) of the heading. Also called filing word.

Expansive classification. A scheme in which a set of coordinated schedules gives successive development possibilities from very simple (broad) to very detailed (close) subdivision.

Explanatory reference. A reference that gives the detailed guidance necessary for effective use of the headings involved.

FID. Fédération Internationale de Documentation (International Federation for Documentation).

Filing word. See **Entry word.**

Fixed location. The assignment of each item in a collection to a definite position on a certain shelf.

Form division. See **Standard subdivision.**

Form heading. A subject list term that refers to the literary or artistic form, or the publication format of a work rather than to its topical content.

Form of entry. The specific spelling and wording used to record an access point on a catalog record.

Generalia class. That part of a classification system designed to hold materials of a general nature, usually covering many diverse topics.

Geographic name. The place name usually used in reference to a geographic area. It is not necessarily the political name. See also **Political name.**

GMD. General Material Designation, a term that is given in the catalog record to indicate the class of material to which an item belongs (e.g., motion picture).

Guide card. A labeled card with a noticeable projection that distinguishes it from other catalog cards. It is inserted in a card catalog to help the user find a desired place or heading in the catalog.

Hanging indention. This form of indention is used when the main entry is under title; the title begins at first indention and all succeeding lines of the body of the record begin at second indention.

Heading. The "official" uniform mode of representing the name of a person, corporate body, geographic area, title of a work, or subject. Usually provided at the top of the catalog record to provide an access point in the catalog.

Hierarchical notation. In classification, the use of symbol groups of varying combinations and lengths to reflect a hierarchy of topics and subdivisions.

Holdings note. One note in the bibliographic record for a serial that tells which parts of the serial are held by the library. See also **Numeric and/or alphabetic, chronological, or other designation area.**

IFLA. International Federation of Library Associations.

IFLAI. International Federation of Library Associations and Institutions. Formerly IFLA.

ILL. Inter-Library Loan.

Imprint. See **Publication, distribution, etc., area.**

Indentions. Designated spaces or margins at which parts of a catalog record begin; used especially in typing cards.

Index. A tool that exhibits the analyzed contents of a bibliographic entity or a group of such entities, as contrasted with a library catalog, which lists and describes the holdings of a particular collection.

INTERMARC. A French language format for bibliographic exchange for monographs; similar to LC-MARC formats. See also **SUPERMARC.**

ISBD. International Standard Bibliographic Description, an internationally accepted format for the representation of descriptive information in bibliographic records. ISBDs developed so far include: **ISBD(A)**, ISBD for Ancient Books; **ISBD(CM)**, ISBD for Cartographic Materials; **ISBD(G)**, General; **ISBD(M)**, ISBD for Monographic Materials; **ISBD(NBM)**, ISBD for Non-Book Materials; **ISBD(PM)**, ISBD for Printed Music; **ISBD(S)**, ISBD for Serials.

ISBN. International Standard Book Number, a distinctive and unique number assigned to a book. ISBNs are used internationally; the U.S. agency for ISBNs is R. R. Bowker Company.

ISDS. International Serials Data System, a network of national and international centers sponsored by Unesco. The centers develop and maintain registers of serial publications; this includes the assignment of ISSNs and key title.

ISSN. International Standard Serial Number, a distinctive number assigned by ISDS.

Joint author. A person who collaborates with one or more associates to produce a work in which the individual contributions of the authors cannot be distinguished.

Key heading. See **Pattern heading.**

KWIC indexing. Key-Word-In-Context, a format for showing index entries within the context in which they occur.

KWOC indexing. Key-Word-Out-of-Context, the use of significant words from titles or texts for subject index entries.

LC. Library of Congress or Library of Congress Classification.

LC-MARC. See **MARC.**

LCSH. *Library of Congress Subject Headings.*

Leaf. A single thickness of paper; i.e., two pages.

Literary warrant. The development of certain parts of a classification scheme in response to the volume of materials available for classification.

Machine-readable data base. A collection of data on punched tape or cards, magnetic tape or disc, or in another form, which can be identified, deciphered and displayed by machine.

Main class. A principal division of a classification scheme.

Main entry. 1) The major access point chosen; the other access points are added entries. 2) A full catalog entry headed by the access point chosen as main entry (definition 1), which gives all the information necessary for the complete identification of a work. This entry also bears the tracing of all the other headings under which the work is entered.

Manufacturer. The agency that has made the item being cataloged (e.g., printer of a book).

Map series. A group of map sheets having the same scale and cartographic specifications, identified collectively by the producing agency, that, when the series is completed, will cover a given geographic area.

MARC. Machine Readable Cataloging, a program of the Library of Congress, which distributes machine-readable cataloging in LC format.

Material specific details area. Includes elements needed in the bibliographic description of certain special materials. See **Mathematical data area** and **Numeric and/or alphabetic, chronological or other designation area.**

Mathematical data area. Includes the following elements in description of cartographic material: scale, projection, and optionally, coordinates and equinox.

Microfiche. A flat sheet of photographic film designed for storage of complete texts in multiple micro-images, and with an index entry visible to the naked eye displayed at the top.

Microfilm. A length of photographic film containing sequences of micro-images of texts, title-pages, bibliographic records, etc.

Microform. Usually a reproduction photographically reduced to a size difficult or impossible to read with the naked eye; some microforms are not reproductions but original editions. Microforms include microfilm, microfiche, microopaques, and aperture cards.

Mixed notation. A notation that combines two or more kinds of symbols, such as a combination of letters and numbers.

Mnemonic devices. Devices intended to aid or assist the memory.

Monograph. A complete bibliographic unit; it may be issued in successive parts at regular or irregular intervals, but it is *not* intended to continue indefinitely. It may be a single work or a collection that is not a serial.

Monographic series. A series of monographs with a collective title.

Monographs in collected sets. Collections or compilations by one or more authors issued in two or more volumes.

NAL. National Agricultural Library, Washington, D.C.

Name authority file. A file of the name (author) headings used in a given catalog, and the references made to them from other forms.

Name-title added entry. An added entry that includes the name of a person or corporate body and the title of a work.

NELINET. New England Library Information Network, a regional bibliographic service center network with over sixty members in the New England area.

NLA. The National Library of Australia, Canberra.

NLM. The National Library of Medicine, Washington, D.C.

Nonbook materials. Term used to designate collectively maps, globes, motion pictures, filmstrips, videorecordings, sound recordings, etc.

Notation. A system of numbers and/or letters used to represent a classification scheme.

Note area. Reserved for recording catalog data that cannot be incorporated in the preceding parts of the record. Each note is usually recorded in a separate paragraph.

NOTIS. Northwestern Online Totally Integrated System, a computer-based system of circulation control and technical processing developed for the Northwestern University libraries, used also by the Garrett Evangelical and Seabury theological seminary libraries.

NUC. The *National Union Catalog*, a publication in the *Library of Congress Catalogs* series.

Numeric and/or alphabetic, chronological or other designation area. The publication record of a serial. It does not necessarily indicate the volumes or parts of a serial held by a library. See also **Holdings note.**

OCLC. Ohio College Library Center, a regional library network. Among other services, it provides a machine-readable data base for cataloging.

Online retrieval. Direct use of a computer to access stored data.

Open entry. A part of the descriptive cataloging not completed at the time of cataloging. Used for uncompleted works such as serials, series, etc.

Open stacks. A library collection where all users are admitted directly to the shelves.

Other title. A title other than the title proper (and parallel title)—e.g., a subtitle.

Parallel title. The title proper written in another language or in another script.

Pattern heading. A representative heading from a category of terms that would normally be excluded from a subject heading list (e.g., names of individuals), included as an example of normal subdivision practice within that category.

Periodical. A publication with a distinctive title, which appears in successive numbers or parts at stated or regular intervals and which is intended to continue indefinitely. Usually each issue contains articles by several contributors. Newspapers and memoirs, proceedings, journals, etc., of corporate bodies primarily related to their internal affairs are not included in this definition. See also **Serial** and **Monograph.**

Phonograph records. See **Sound recordings.**

Physical description area. The section of a catalog entry that includes extent of an item, dimensions, and other physical details.

Place name. See **Geographic name.**

Plate. An illustrative leaf that is not included in the pagination of the text; it is not an integral part of a text gathering; it is often printed on paper different from that used for the text.

Political name. The proper name of a geographical area according to the law. This name often changes with a change in government.

Post-coordinate indexing. The grouping of a large number of entries under simple concepts in such a way that the user can combine them to locate material on the compound subjects in which he or she is interested.

PRECIS. Preserved Context Indexing System, a British technique for subject retrieval in which an open-ended vocabulary can be organized according to a scheme of role-indicating operators for either manual or computer manipulation.

Pre-coordinate indexing. The combination of subject terms at the time of indexing for use in the retrieval of materials on complex concepts.

Preliminaries. The title page or title pages, the verso of each title page, the cover, and any pages preceding the title page.

Processing center. A central office where the materials of more than one library are processed and distributed. Such a center may also handle the purchasing of materials for its constituents.

Producer. Person or agency responsible for financial and administrative production of a motion picture or machine-readable data file, and for its commercial success.

Proof slips. Individual paper copies of LC catalog cards cut from proofsheets.

Proofsheets. Paper copies of LC catalog cards, issued on long sheets with five cards to a sheet.

Pseudonym. A false name assumed by an author to conceal identity.

Pseudo-serial. A frequently reissued and revised publication which at first publication is usually treated as a monographic work.

Publication, distribution, etc., area. Includes the following elements: place of publication, distribution, etc.; name of publisher, distributor, etc.; date of publication, distribution, etc.; and sometimes place of manufacture, name of manufacturer, and date of manufacture.

Publisher. The person, corporate body, or firm responsible for issuing printed matter.

Pure notation. A notation that consistently uses only one kind of symbol (e.g., either letters *or* numbers, but not both).

Realia. Actual objects (artifacts, specimens, etc.) rather than replicas.

RECON. Retrospective Conversion of Library of Congress records to MARC format, an experimental project on the results of which LC determined that it is not economically feasible to make a complete conversion of its existing card catalogs.

Relative index. An index to a classification scheme that not only provides alphabetical references to the subjects and terms in the classification but also shows some of the relations between subjects and aspects of subjects.

Relative location. A classificatory arrangement of library materials, allowing the insertion of new material in its proper relation to that already on the shelves.

Reprint. A new printing of an item either by photographic methods or by resetting the type for substantially unchanged text.

RLG. Research Libraries Group, a consortium formed originally by Columbia, Harvard, and Yale universities, and the New York Public Library, now consisting of over ten large research libraries, but minus Harvard.

RLIN. Research Libraries Information Network, a regional bibliographic network based at Stanford University, resulting from the reorganization of its BALLOTS system under the aegis of RLG.

Romanization. The representation of the characters of a non-roman alphabet by roman characters.

Roof code. See **Umbrella classification.**

Scope note. A statement delimiting the meaning and associative relations of a subject heading or a classification number.

Score. A notation arranging all of the parts of a piece of music one under another on different staves. A series of staves on which is written music composed originally for one instrument is not considered a score. Thus, "piano score" is used to designate, not music written originally for the piano, but music written originally for instrumental or vocal parts that has been arranged for the piano.

SCORPIO. Subject-Context Oriented Retriever for Processing Information Online, a text retrieval facility in operation at the Library of Congress.

Secondary entry. See **Added entry.**

"See also" reference. A reference indicating related entries or headings.

"See" reference. A direction from a heading not used to a heading that is used.

Serial. A publication issued in successive parts at regular or irregular intervals and intended to continue indefinitely. Included are periodicals, newspapers, proceedings, reports, memoirs, annuals, and numbered monographic series. See also **Periodical** and **Monograph.**

Series. A number of separate works, usually related in subject or form, that are issued successively. They are usually issued by the same publisher, distributor, etc. and in uniform style, with a collective title.

Series area. The area of a catalog record that gives series information.

Series authority file. A file of series entries used in a catalog with the record of references made to them from other forms.

Series title. The collective title given to volumes or parts issued in a series.

Shared authorship. More than one author is responsible for the work.

Shelflist. A record of the items in a library; entries are arranged in the order of the items on the shelves.

s.l. Place of publication, distribution, etc. unknown (*sine loco*).

s.n. Name of publisher, distributor, etc. unknown (*sine nomine*).

SOLINET. Southeastern Library Network, possibly the largest, in both membership and geographic area, of the regional bibliographic service networks in the United States.

Sound recordings. Aural recordings, including discs (i.e., phonograph records), cartridges, cassettes, cylinders, etc.

Specific entry. A principle observed in most library subject lists, by which material is listed under the most specific term available, rather than under some broader heading.

Standard number and terms of availability area. Includes ISBN or ISSN and, optionally, price or other terms on which the item is available.

Standard subdivisions. Divisions used in DDC that apply to the form a work takes. Form may be physical (as in a periodical or a dictionary) or it may be philosophical (such as a philosophy or history of a subject). Formerly called form divisions.

Statement of responsibility. A statement in the item being described that gives persons responsible for intellectual or artistic content, corporate bodies from which the content emanates, or persons or bodies responsible for performance.

Subject authority file. A file of the subject headings used in a given catalog, with the record of the references made to them.

Subject cataloging. The assignment of classification numbers and subject headings to the items of a library collection.

Subject entry. The catalog entry for a work under the subject heading.

Subject heading. A word or group of words indicating a subject.

Subject subdivision. A restrictive word or group of words added to a subject heading to limit it to a more specific meaning.

Subtitle. A secondary title, often used to expand or limit the title proper.

Superimposition. A Library of Congress policy decision that only entries being established for the first time would follow *AACR 1* rules for form of entry, and that only works new to LC would follow *AACR 1* rules for choice of entry. When LC adopts *AACR 2* and freezes its card catalogs on January 1, 1981, superimposition will no longer apply to any entries in the new online catalog.

SUPERMARC. A projected format for international exchange of machine-readable bibliographic data that will not duplicate any of the formats presently in use in the various national systems. See also **INTERMARC.**

Switching language. A mediating or communication indexing language used to establish subject indication equivalencies among various local indexing languages.

Terminal digit posting. The listing of subject indexed documents according to the last digits of their serial numbers to facilitate post-coordinate matching for retrieval of compound-concept materials.

Thesaurus. A specialized authority list of terms used with automated information retrieval systems; very similar to a list of subject headings.

Title and statement of responsibility area. The section of a catalog entry that gives the title of a work and information on its authorship.

Title page. A page that occurs very near the beginning of a book and that contains the most complete bibliographic information about the book, such as the author's name, the fullest form of the book's title, the name and/or number of the book's edition, the name of the publisher, and the place and date of publication.

Title proper. The title that is the chief name of an item; excludes any parallel title or other title information.

Tracing. The record on the main entry record of all the additional entries under which the work is listed in the catalog.

Transliteration. A representation of the characters of one alphabet by those of another. See also **Romanization.**

UDC. Universal Decimal Classification.

UK/MARC. A machine-readable bibliographic record format compatible with LC/MARC, developed by British National Bibliography for use in the United Kingdom.

Umbrella classification. A coarse "switching language" with two to four hierarchical levels, for use by several agencies to construct a cumulative thesaurus or to share indexing on a general level.

UNICAT/TELECAT. An Ontario-Quebec library consortium providing a union catalog and bibliographic support services to its members.

Uniform title. The title chosen for cataloging purposes when a work has appeared under varying titles.

UNIMARC. Universal MARC format, a 1977 development of the Library of Congress to be an international communications format for the exchange of machine-readable cataloging records between national bibliographic agencies.

Union catalog. A catalog that lists, completely or in part, the holdings of more than one library or collection.

Unit record. The basic catalog record, in the form of a main entry, which when duplicated may be used as a unit for all other entries for that work in the catalog by the addition of appropriate headings.

UTLAS. University of Toronto Library Automated Systems, a computer-based bibliographic network offering its data base and services to a variety of Canadian libraries, with authority and circulation control subsystems now under development.

Verification. Determining the existence of an author and the form of name as well as the correct title of a particular work; in short, using bibliographic sources to verify—i.e., prove—the existence of an author and/or work.

Vernacular name. A person's name in the form used in reference sources in his own country.

Verso of the title page. The page immediately following the title page; i.e., the page on the back side of the title page.

Videorecording. A recording originally generated in the form of electronic impulses and designed primarily for television playback. The term includes videocassettes, videodiscs, and videotapes.

Volume. In the bibliographical sense, a major division of a work distinguished from the other major divisions of that work by having its own chief source of information.

WLN. Washington Library Network, a regional bibliographic network based at the State Library of Washington, now servicing nearly forty libraries in Alaska, Idaho, Oregon, Washington, and Australia.

Work slip. A card or other form that accompanies a book throughout the cataloging and preparation processes. The cataloger notes on the work slip any directions and information needed to prepare catalog entries, cross references, etc.

Workmark. A letter (or letters) placed after the cutter number. A workmark may consist of one or two letters, the first of which is the first letter of the title of a work (exclusive of articles). Also called work number.

Worksheet. See **Work slip.**

BIBLIOGRAPHY

Consult "Cataloging and Classification Aids," pages 627-31, for a listing of textbooks and bibliographic tools.

Advances in Librarianship. New York, Academic Press, 1970- . (Annual).

A.L.A. Cataloging Rules for Author and Title Entries. Chicago, American Library Association, 1949.

Anglo-American Cataloging Rules, North American Text. Chicago, American Library Association, 1967.

Austin, Derek. *PRECIS: A Manual of Concept Analysis and Subject Indexing.* London, The Council of the British National Bibliography, 1974.

Avram, Henriette D. *MARC: Its History and Implications.* Washington, Library of Congress, 1975.

Baecker, Edith K., and Dorothy C. Senghas. *A Little Brief Authority: A Manual for Establishing and Maintaining a Name Authority File.* Boston, Dedoss Associates, 1978.

Batty, C. D. *Introduction to Colon Classification.* Hamden, CT, Archon Books, 1966.

Berman, Sanford. *Prejudices and Antipathies: A Tract on the LC Subject Heads Concerning People.* Metuchen, NJ, Scarecrow, 1971.

Bliss, Henry Evelyn. *A Bibliographic Classification: Extended by Systematic Auxiliary Schedules for Composite Specification and Notation.* New York, H. W. Wilson, 1940-1953. 4 v. in 3.

Bliss, Henry Evelyn. *The Organization of Knowledge and the System of the Sciences.* New York, Holt, 1929.

Bliss, Henry Evelyn. *The Organization of Knowledge in Libraries and the Subject Approach to Books.* 2nd ed., rev. and partly rewritten. New York, H. W. Wilson, 1939.

Bliss Bibliographic Classification. 2nd ed. Edited by Jack Mills and Vanda Broughton with the assistance of Valerie Lang. Boston, Butterworths, 1977- .

Borko, Harold, and Charles L. Bernier. *Indexing Concepts and Methods.* New York, Academic Press, 1978.

Brown, James Duff. *Subject Classification: With Tables, Indexes, etc., for the Subdivision of Subjects.* 3rd ed., rev. and enl. by James Douglas Stewart. London, Grafton, 1939.

Cannan, Judith Proctor. *Special Problems in Serials Cataloging.* Washington, Library of Congress, 1979.

Clack, Doris H. *Black Literature Resources: Analysis and Organization.* New York, Marcel Dekker, 1975.

Classification Research: Proceedings of the Second International Study .Conference ... 14-18 Sept. 1964. Copenhagen, Munksgaard, 1965.

"Close the Card Catalog?," *College & Research Libraries News* 41 (Feb. 1980):25-27.

Coates, Eric, Geoffrey Lloyd, and Dusan Simandl. *BSO, Broad System of Ordering: Schedule and Index.* The Hague, IFLA; Paris, Unesco, 1978.

Coates, Eric, Geoffrey Lloyd, and Dusan Simandl. *The BSO Manual: The Development, Rationale and Use of the Broad System of Ordering.* The Hague, Fédération Internationale de Documentation, 1979.

Commercial COM Catalogs: How to Choose, When to Buy. Compiled by the Catalog Use Committee, Reference and Adult Services Division, American Library Association. Chicago, A.L.A., 1978.

Cutter, Charles Ammi. *Expansive Classification, Part 1: The First Six Classifications.* Boston, C. A. Cutter, 1891-93.

Cutter, Charles Ammi. *Expansive Classification, Part 2: Seventh Classification.* Edited by William Parker Cutter. Boston, 1904.

Cutter, Charles Ammi. *Rules for a Dictionary Catalog.* 4th ed., rewritten. Washington, GPO, 1904.

Encyclopedia of Library and Information Science. Edited by Allen Kent and Harold Lancour. New York, Marcel Dekker, 1968- . (In progress).

Fédération Internationale de Documentation. *Classification Décimale Universelle.* 2e ed. Bruxelles, Institute International de Bibliographie, 1927-1953. 4v.

Fédération Internationale de Documentation. *10-Year Supplement to Abridged UDC Editions: 1958-1968.* The Hague, F.I.D./Unesco, 1969.

Fédération Internationale de Documentation. *UDC Revision and Publication Procedures.* The Hague, F.I.D., 1968. (In English, French, and German).

Fédération Internationale de Documentation. *Universal Decimal Classification.* Abridged English Edition. 3rd rev., 1961. London, British Standards Institution, 1963.

Fédération Internationale de Documentation. *Universal Decimal Classification. Complete English Edition.* 4th international ed. London, British Standards Institution, 1943- . (In progress).

Foskett, A. C. *The Subject Approach to Information.* 3rd ed. London, Clive Bingley; Hamden, CT, Linnet Books, 1977.

Freezing Card Catalogs: A Program Sponsored by the Association of Research Libraries, May 5, 1978, Nashville, Tennessee. Washington, Association of Research Libraries, 1979.

The Future of Card Catalogs: Report of a Program Sponsored by the Association of Research Libraries, January 18, 1975. Washington, Association of Research Libraries, 1975.

Gore, Daniel, Joseph Kimbrough, and Peter Spyers-Duran, eds. *Requiem for the Card Catalog: Management Issues in Automated Cataloging.* Westport, CT, Greenwood Press, 1979.

Gorman, Michael. "the Anglo-American Cataloguing Rules, Second Edition," *Library Resources & Technical Services* 22 (Summer 1978):209-226.

Guide to the Universal Decimal Classification. London, British Standards Institution, 1963.

Hagler, Ronald. *Where's That Rule? A Cross-Index of the Two Editions of the Anglo-American Cataloguing Rules.* Ottawa, Canadian Library Association, 1979.

Hunter, Eric J. *AACR 2: An Introduction to the Second Edition of Anglo-American Cataloguing Rules.* Rev. ed. London, C. Bingley; Hamden, CT, Linnet Books, 1979.

Hyman, Richard J. *From Cutter to MARC: Access to the Unit Record.* Flushing, NY, Queens College of the City University of New York, 1977.

International Conference on Cataloguing Principles, Paris, 9th-18th October, 1961. *Report.* London, International Federation of Library Associations, 1963.

International Federation of Library Associations. International Office for UBC. *Examples of ISBD(M) Usage in European Languages.* London, IFLA Committee on Cataloguing, 1976.

International Federation of Library Associations and Institutions.
The following ISBDs have been published by the IFLA International Office for UBC in London:

ISBD(A): International Standard Bibliographic Description for Ancient Books. 1980.

ISBD(CM): International Standard Bibliographic Description for Cartographic Materials. 1977.

ISBD(G): General International Standard Bibliographic Description: Annotated Text. 1977.

ISBD(M): International Standard Bibliographic Description for Monographic Publications. Rev. ed. 1978.

ISBD(NBM): International Standard Bibliographic Description for Non-Book Materials. 1977.

ISBD(PM): International Standard Bibliographic Description for Printed Music. 1979.

ISBD(S): International Standard Bibliographic Description for Serials. 197?.

International Federation of Library Associations and Institutions. *Names of Persons: National Usages for Entry in Catalogues.* 3rd ed. London, IFLA International Office for UBC, 1977.

Kelm, Carol R. "The Historical Development of the Second Edition of the Anglo-American Cataloguing Rules," *Library Resources & Technical Services* 22 (Winter 1978):22-33.

Library of Congress. MARC Development Office. *Books: A MARC Format.* 5th ed. Washington, GPO, 1972.

Library of Congress. MARC Development Office. *Books: A MARC Format. Addenda.* Washington, GPO, 1972- .

Library of Congress. MARC Development Office. *Serials: A MARC Format.* 2nd ed. Washington, GPO, 1974.

Lubetzky, Seymour. *Cataloging Rules and Principles: A Critique of the ALA Rules for Entry and a Proposed Design for Their Revision.* Washington, Processing Dept., Library of Congress, 1953.

Lubetzky, Seymour. *Code of Cataloging Rules, Author, and Title; an Unfinished Draft ... with an Explanatory Commentary by Paul Dunkin.* Washington, American Library Association, 1960.

Malinconico, S. Michael, and Paul J. Fasana. *The Future of the Catalog: The Library's Choices.* White Plains, NY, Knowledge Industry Publications, 1979.

Mann, Margaret. *Introduction to Cataloging and the Classification of Books.* 2nd ed. Chicago, American Library Association, 1943.

Martin, Susan K. *Library Networks, 1978/79.* White Plains, NY, Knowledge Industry Publications, 1978.

Mills, Jack. *A Modern Outline of Library Classification.* London, Chapman & Hall, 1968.

Mills, Jack. *The Universal Decimal Classification.* New Brunswick, NJ, Rutgers, The State University School of Library Science, 1964.

Osborn, Andrew. "The Crisis in Cataloging," *Library Quarterly* 11 (Oct. 1941):393-411.

Osborn, Andrew. *Serial Publications: Their Place and Treatment in Libraries.* 2nd ed., rev. Chicago, American Library Association, 1973.

Painter, Ann F., comp. *Reader in Classification and Descriptive Cataloging.* Washington, NCR Microcard Editions, 1972.

Perreault, Jean. *Towards a Theory for U.D.C.: Essays Aimed at Structural Understanding and Operational Improvement.* Hamden, CT, Archon Books, 1969.

Potter, William Gray. "When Names Collide: Conflict in the Catalog and AACR 2," *Library Resources & Technical Services* 24 (Winter 1980):3-16.

The PRECIS Index System: Principles, Applications, and Prospects. Proceedings of the International PRECIS Workshop. Edited by Hans H. Wellisch. New York, H. W. Wilson, 1977.

Ranganathan, Shiyali Ramamrita. *Colon Classification.* 6th rev. ed. London, Asia Publishing House, 1963.

Richmond, Phyllis A. "AACR 2 — A Review Article," *Journal of Academic Librarianship,* vol. 6, no. 1 (March 1980):30-37.

Sayers, W. C. Berwick. *Sayers' Manual of Classification for Librarians.* 5th ed. Revised by Arthur Maltby. London, Andre Deutsch, 1975.

Shera, Jesse H., and Margaret E. Egan. *The Classified Catalog: Basic Principles and Practices.* Chicago, American Library Association, 1956.

Simonton, Wesley. "An Introduction to AACR 2," *Library Resources & Technical Services* 23 (Summer 1979):321-39.

Smith, Lynn S. *A Practical Approach to Serials Cataloging.* Greenwich, CT, JAI Press, 1978.

Soergel, Dagobert. *Indexing Languages and Thesauri: Construction and Maintenance.* Los Angeles, Melville Publishing Co., c1974.

Thompson, Jim. "News about AACR 2 Implementation Studies," *RTSD Newsletter* 5 (Jan./Feb. 1980):1-2, and following issues.

Vickery, B. C. *Classification and Indexing in Science.* 3rd ed. London, Butterworths, 1975.

Vickery, B. C. *Techniques of Information Retrieval.* Hamden, CT, Archon Books, 1970.

AUTHOR/TITLE/SUBJECT INDEX

National City
Public Library

Library Science Text Series

ISBN 0-87287-221-1